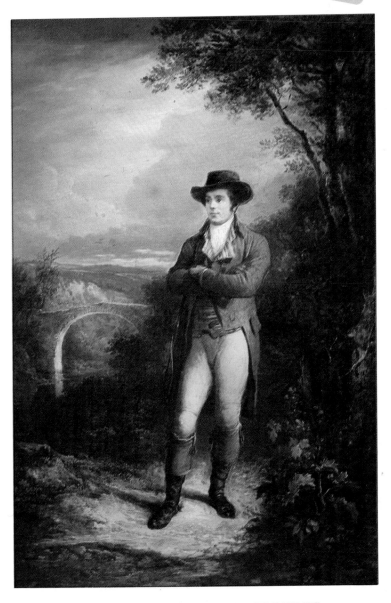

FULL-LENGTH PORTRAIT OF BURNS
by Alexander Nasmyth, painted in 1828
*by courtesy of the National Galleries of Scotland, Edinburgh*

BURNS COTTAGE, ALLOWAY

## EDITORIAL NOTE

This edition of the poetical works of Robert Burns is intended as a tribute to Scotland's national bard, the poet of humanity and all mankind, in commemoration of the bicentenary of his death in July 1796 in his 38th year, at an age when most men have not yet attained their peak. Although much of his reputation still rests on *Poems, Chiefly in the Scottish Dialect* which he had published himself at Kilmarnock ten years earlier, some of his greatest poems, notably 'Tam o Shanter', belonged to the last years of his life. It was in this period, however, that Burns turned his attention increasingly to the folk-song of Scotland, rescuing from oblivion the fragments of many ancient ballads which he mended and for which he wrote new verses. Burns's importance as a pioneer song-collector is now getting its due recognition.

In 1986 I edited *The Complete Works of Robert Burns*, published by the Burns Federation and Alloway Publishing as a tribute to the bicentenary of the Kilmarnock Poems. The text of the present volume is essentially that of the 1986 edition, and the pagination of the songs and poems (pp 43-615) has been retained deliberately, for the very good reason that most writers on Burns since 1986 have used this page numbering for reference purposes.

The opportunity has been taken, however, to revise the text thoroughly, in light of the best manuscript sources. At the same time, the side-notes have been expanded, both as regards the meanings of dialect and archaic words and phrases, and also concerning allusions to persons and places that might otherwise be obscure to the reader. At the same time, the head-notes accompanying each poem or song have been extensively re-written. This has become necessary in light of the vast number of new facts discovered, and old myths exploded, resulting from my research into primary sources for my biography *Burns*, published in 1992. In particular, the names of several of the poet's heroines have been changed: Helen Kilpatrick has now given way to Helen Blair as the heroine of the poet's very first song 'Handsome Nell', Alison Begbie, who rejected Burns in 1781, is now shown to have been Elizabeth Gebbie, the heroine of 'The Lass o Cessnock Banks' and 'Farewell to Eliza', and the Highland Lassie to whom Burns turned in 1786 is now proven to have been Margaret, not Mary, Campbell. Many other names have been altered, and fresh identifications made, as a result of research into parish registers of births and marriages, kirk session minutes and other contemporary records

In *Burns A-Z, the Complete Word-Finder* (1990) I included, as an appendix, the text of all known spurious and dubious works ever ascribed to Burns. Several other poems, either spurious, dubious or previously inedited, have since come to light and these are now published as an appendix to this volume.

# The Complete Poetical Works
## of
# ROBERT BURNS
## 1759 - 1796

### Edited by
### Dr. JAMES A. MACKAY

## BI-CENTENARY EDITION
## COMPLETELY REVISED

Alloway Publishing

Darvel · Ayrshire · Scotland

First Published, December 1993


© Introduction & Notes
James A. Mackay, 1993



ISBN 0-907526-64-0
Standard Edition



Alloway Publishing Ltd.
Darvel, Ayrshire.



Printed and bound in Scotland

Design and Printing
Walker & Connell Ltd., Darvel, Ayrshire.
Bell & Bain Ltd., Thornliebank, Glasgow.

Binding
Hunter & Foulis Ltd., Edinburgh.

# INTRODUCTION

Robert Burns, now regarded as one of the ten greatest world poets of all time, came from the sturdy peasant class of Scotland, but the image of the heaven-taught ploughman-poet is a false one, even if Burns himself played up to it while he was lionised by the Edinburgh literati and high society. He had very little formal education, but he was singularly fortunate in a teacher who perceived his intellectual gifts. He was a voracious reader who knew his Bible, the plays of Shakespeare and Vanbrugh, the poetry of Milton, Dryden and Pope, and the novels of his own time. He was fluent in French and had as much Latin as most educated men of his time. He had studied mathematics (a prerequisite of his Excise calling) and took a keen interest in the social and political questions of the period. His voluminous correspondence with men and women of all degrees in society, reveals a man of high intelligence, candour and independent mind.

By Jean Armour he had nine children, but he fathered bairns on Elizabeth Paton, Jenny Clow, Ann Park and Helen Armstrong. Margaret 'Highland Mary' Campbell *may* have died in childbirth, while Margaret 'May' Cameron took out a paternity suit against him (though this was dropped after she aborted or miscarried). In the context of his time, however, such behaviour (and its consequences) were by no means uncommon. So, too, the old *canard* of Burns the heavy drinker does not stand up to serious examination. Given the volume of poetry and correspondence produced by a man who was running a farm and carrying out the exhausting duties of an Excise officer, Burns was a workaholic, not an alcoholic. Plagued by intermittent ill-health since his teens, he suffered from rheumatic fever, nervous depression, possibly brucellosis and latterly severe toothache. The actual cause of death was sub-acute bacterial endocarditis which was probably induced by streptococcal infection released into the bloodstream following a dental extraction in the winter of 1795.

It is idle to speculate on what other paths Burns's genius might have followed had he lived; he had ambitions to become a playwright, but a handful of prologues, soliloquies and that great cantata of love and liberty, 'The Jolly Beggars' are all that remain of his dramatic work. There is no doubt that he would have progressed far in his chosen career, the Excise. He was on the list for promotion to Supervisor (in 1797) and thereafter might have gone right to the top. He was not only an able and efficient officer, well thought-off by colleagues and superiors alike, but he applied his powerful intellect to ways and means of re-organising the service, and had the ear of the Commissioners of Excise themselves. A superb narrative poet, profound delineator of human emotions, whose soaring powers to convey the full range of feelings have touched a deeply responsive chord in the heart of all mankind, Burns has left us a legacy of outstanding importance to world literature, transcending both the time and place of their creation.

**Truly is Robert Burns a great poet for all time.**

# CONTENTS

1757    William Burnes (1721-84) tenant-farmer of Alloway, marries Agnes Broun (1732-1820) of Craigenton, Maybole.

1759    25th January. Robert Burns born at Alloway.

1760    28th September. Gilbert Burns born. Later children: Agnes (1762-1834), Annabella (1764-1832), William (1767-90), John (1769-85) and Isabella (1771-1858).

1765    Robert and Gilbert taught by John Murdoch (1747-1824), engaged by William Burnes and four neighbours; a three-year period of formal and intensive education.

1766    William Burnes moves to Mount Oliphant, a 70-acre farm (£40 annual rent) near Alloway.

1768    Murdoch leaves Alloway; William Burnes continues his sons' education himself.

1772    Robert and Gilbert attend Dalrymple school, week about, during the summer quarter.

1773    Murdoch now at Ayr. Robert has three weeks' tuition in English grammar, French and some Latin, and is introduced to the poetry of Alexander Pope.

1774    Despite hard times at Mount Oliphant, Burns writes his first song, `Handsome Nell', for Helen Blair.

1775    Burns studies mathematics under Hugh Rodger at Kirkoswald.

1777    Whitsun. The Burnes family move to Lochlie, Tarbolton, 130 acres at an annual rent of £130. Burns now a voracious reader and student of all manner of subjects. Burns attends a dancing class in Tarbolton `to give my manners a brush' – the beginning of a period of antipathy between father and son,' ... one cause of the dissipation which marked my future years'.

1780    The Tarbolton Bachelors' Club formed by Burns and six others.

1781    Burns courts Elizabeth Gebbie. Dispute between Burnes and his landlord, David MacLure, begins.

          4th July. Burns inducted into St David's Lodge, No. 174, Tarbolton; passed and raised in the same lodge on 1st October.

          Mid-July. Burns goes to Irvine to learn the trade of flax-dressing.

1782    1st January. The flax shop in the Glasgow Vennel, Irvine 'burnt to ashes and left me, like a true poet, not worth a sixpence'. Burns returns to Lochlie. *Tristram Shandy* and *The Man of Feeling* his favourite reading matter. Interest in poetic composition developing.

          24th September. Dispute between Burnes and MacLure referred to arbiters.

1783    16th January. Burns awarded £3 premium for linseed growing.

          April, Burns begins his first Commonplace Book (1CPB).

          17th May. Burnes's financial difficulties culminate in a writ of sequestration.

          18th August. The 'Oversman' reports in favour of Burnes.

          25th August. Burnes makes his first appeal to the Court of Session.

          Autumn. Robert and Gilbert secretly arrange to lease Mossgiel, 118 acres at £90 a year, from Gavin Hamilton 'as an asylum for the family in case of the worst.'

1784    27th January. Court of Session upholds William Burnes.

          13th February. William Burnes dies.

          March. Burns and his family move into Mossgiel, about three miles from Lochlie, in Mauchline parish.

          27th July. Burns elected Depute Master of St James's Lodge

Kilwinning, Tarbolton.

1785 April. Race Week. Burns first meets Jean Armour at a dance in Mauchline.

22nd May. Birth of Elizabeth, the poet's daughter by Elizabeth Paton.

September. Burns 'attests' his marriage to Jean Armour.

October. John, the poet's youngest brother, dies. Burns finishes his first Commonplace Book.

1786 March. James Armour, master-mason of Mauchline, faints on learning of his daugher's pregnancy. Burns repudiated by the Armour family and marriage attestation mutilated. Burns contemplates emigration to Jamaica, but plans to publish his poems first.

3rd April. Proposals for the Kilmarnock Edition sent to the printer; published eleven days later.

23rd April. James Armour repudiates Burns as a son-in-law; Jean sent off to relatives in Paisley. Burns takes up with Margaret Campbell, dairymaid at Coilsfield.

14th May. Burns and Margaret meet for the last time at Failford, exchange 'matrimonial vows' and part to make their respective arrangements to emigrate.

June. Copy for the Kilmarnock Edition sent to John Wilson.

10th June. Jean Armour confesses by letter to the Kirk Session, that she is pregnant by Robert Burns.

25th June. Burns appears before the Kirk Session. In July and August he makes the requisite three appearances before the congregation and gets his certificate from 'Daddy' Auld.

22nd July. Robert transfers his share of Mossgiel to Gilbert.

30th July. Burns goes into hiding, after Jean Armour gets a writ 'to throw me in jail till I find security for an enormous sum ... and I am wandering from one friend's house to another.'

31st July. *Poems, Chiefly in the Scottish Dialect* published at Kilmarnock, price 3s.

6th August. Last penitential appearance before the Mauchline congregation.

1st September. Voyage to Jamaica first postponed.

3rd September. Jean Armour gives birth to twins, christened Robert and Jean.

27th September. Voyage to Jamaica again postponed; Burns planning a second edition.

October. Margaret Campbell dies at Greenock, possibly in premature childbirth induced by typhus. Burns now abandons all plans to emigrate, and first considers the Excise as a career.

15th November. Correspondence with Mrs Dunlop of Dunlop begins.

27th November. Burns sets out for Edinburgh, arriving there two days later.

1st December. Elizabeth Paton accepts Burns's settlement of her claim.

9th December. Henry Mackenzie praises the Kilmarnock *Poems*, reviewed in *The Lounger*.

14th December. William Creech issues proposals for the second (first Edinburgh) edition of the *Poems*.

1787 7th January. Burns forms an association 'with a very pretty girl, a Lothian farmer's daughter, whom I have almost persuaded to accompany me to the west country.'

13th January. The Grand Lodge of Scotland toasts Burns as 'Caledonia's Bard'.

14th January. Patrick Miller of Dalswinton discusses with Burns the possible lease of a farm near Dumfries.

6th February. Burns writes to the Bailies of the Canongate seeking permission to erect a memorial to Robert Fergusson 'my elder brother in misfortune'.

22nd March. Burns completes the proof-reading of the first Edinburgh Edition and plans 'to make leisurely pilgrimages through Caledonia'.

9th April. Second Commonplace Book (2 CPB) begun.

17th April. First Edinburgh Edition published.

23rd April. Burns sells his copyright to Creech for 100 guineas.

5th May – 1st June. Burns tours the Borders with Robert Ainslie.

22nd May. First volume of *Scots Musical Museum* (SMM) published by James Johnson.

2nd June. Burns receives May Cameron's letter of 26th May advising him of her pregnancy. Burns writes to Ainslie: 'send for the wench and give her ten or twelve shillings ... and advise her out to some country friends'.

4th June. Burns made an Honorary Burgess of Dumfries.

8th June. Burns returns *éclatant* to Mauchline.

late June. Burns makes a tour of the West Highlands, as far as Inveraray.

2nd August. Autobiographical letter to Dr John Moore.

8th August. Burns returns to Edinburgh.

15th August. Burns freed of writ *in meditatione fugae* brought by May Cameron.

25th August. Burns begins his Highland tour with William Nicol.

16th September. Burns returns to Edinburgh, via Queensferry at the end of his tour.

4th October. Burns begins a tour of Stirlingshire with Dr Adair.

20th October. Burns again in Edinburgh. The poet's infant daughter Jean dies. Burns takes up residence with William Cruickshank in St James's Square. First London edition of the *Poems* published.

November. Burns begins serious collaboration with Johnson in *The Scots Musical Museum.* Burns meets Patrick Miller at Dalswinton to discuss the lease of a farm, before returning to Edinburgh.

4th December. Burns meets Mrs Agnes McLehose ('Clarinda').

7th December. Burns dislocates his knee in a carriage accident.

28th December. Correspondence between Sylvander and Clarinda begins.

1788    4th January. Burns's first visit to Clarinda at home.

7th January. Burns seeks the patronage of Graham of Fintry in the Excise.

14th February. Second volume of *Scots Musical Museum* published. Sylvander-Clarinda correspondence peaks, with four letters in two days.

18th February. Burns leaves Edinburgh for Ayrshire.

23rd February. Burns returns to Mauchline, buys Jean 'a mahogany bed' and sets up house with her. 'Farthing taper' letter to Clarinda.

27th (?) February. Burns visits Ellisland with John Tennant of Glenconner as his adviser.

9th March. Jean Armour gives birth to twin girls who die on 10th and 22nd March. 'Horse litter' letter to Ainslie.

13th March (?). Burns returns to Edinburgh.

18th March. Burns signs the lease of Ellisland.

20th March. Burns leaves Edinburgh, and makes preparations to settle down at Ellisland (annual rent of £50).

March-April. Burns receives a course of Excise instruction at Mauchline and Tarbolton.

28th April. Excise commission issued to Burns.

11th June. Burns settles at Ellisland.

5th August. Authenticity of the marriage between Burns and Jean Armour recognised by the Rev. William Auld and Mauchline Kirk Session.

August. Friendship established between Burns and the Millers of Dalswinton and the Riddells of Friars' Carse.

September. Burns commuting between Nithsdale and Mauchline.

November. Jenny Clow, with whom Burns had had an affair in Edinburgh during his platonic friendship with Clarinda, bears him a son.

December. Jean Armour moves to Nithsdale and joins Burns in rented accommodation at the Isle.

1789    16th February. Burns in Edinburgh to settle accounts with Creech and the writ taken out against him by Jenny Clow.

27th February. Legal process with Jenny Clow settled.

28th February. Burns returns to Ellisland.

April. Burns orders a dictionary and the works of Shakespeare; plans the Monkland Friendly Society with Robert Riddell in Dunscore parish, Nithsdale.

May. Reading Adam Smith's *Wealth of Nations*. Hopes for an Excise appointment promising.

June or July. Burns meets Captin Francis Grose at Friars' Carse.

18th August. Francis Wallace Burns born.

7th September. Burns commences work as an Excise officer at a salary of £50 per annum.

October. Election for the Dumfries Burghs; Burns composes 'The Five Carlins'.

November. Burns ill with 'malignant squinancy and low fever.'

23rd December. Burns, influenced by reading Shakespeare, plans 'some thoughts of the Drama', but dreams of becoming a playwright are never realised.

1790    January. Burns riding up to 200 miles a week on Excise duties and attempting to run a farm at the same time, but complains of 'An incessant headache, depression of spirits, and all the truly miserable consequences of a deranged nervous system..'

February. Third volume of *Scots Musical Museum* published.

18th February. Inaugural meeting of subscribers of the Dumfries Theatre, of which Burns and Robert Riddell were among the chief instigators.

July. Burns tranferred to the Dumfries Third Division of Excise. Burns introduces Francis Grose to Dugald Stewart.

24th July. William Burns (the poet's younger brother) dies in London.

November. Burns composes 'Tam o Shanter'; manuscript sent to Grose on 1st December.

1791 January. Burns crippled by a fall 'not from my horse, but with my horse.'

27th January. Death of the Earl of Glencairn at Falmouth, on return from Portugal.

31st March. Ann Park, barmaid of the Globe Inn, gives birth to a daughter, Elizabeth, fathered by Burns.

9th April. William Nicol Burns born.

April. 'Tam o Shanter' published in the second volume of Grose's *Antiquities of Scotland.*

27th April. Glenriddell Manuscript collection formed.

11th June. Burns intervenes on behalf of James Clark of Moffat.

17th June. The Earl of Buchan invites Burns to the coronation of Thomson's bust.

19th – 22nd June. Burns in Ayrshire, attending Gilbert's wedding.

25th August. Burns's crops auctioned at Ellisland. Over thirty people engaged in a drunken riot for three hours after the roup; 'Such a scene of drunkenness was hardly ever seen in this country.'

August – September. Burns sends an account of the Monkland Friendly Society to Sir John Sinclair for inclusion in the *Statistical Account.*

10th September. Formal renunciation of the Ellisland lease.

11th November. The Burns family moves to Dumfries, and takes up residence in a three-room apartment in the Wee Vennel (now Bank Street), above John Syme's office.

29th November – 11th December. Burns in Edinburgh.

6th December. Burns and Mrs McLehose meet for the last time, at Lamont's Land.

27th December. Burns sends Clarinda 'Ae Fond Kiss' as a parting gift.

1792 February. Burns transferrd to the Dumfries Port Division 'worth twenty pounds a year more than any other Division, besides as much rum and brandy as will easily supply an ordinary family.' His salary was now £70 a year, with £15-£20 extra in perquisites.

29th February. Capture of the brig *Rosamond* at Gretna.

10th April. Burns made an honorary member of the Royal Company of Archers.

16th April. Burns offers Creech 'about fifty pages of new material' for a fresh edition of his *Poems.*

19th April. Sale of the *Rosamond's* carronades, which Burns tried to send to the French revolutionaries.

August. Fourth volume of *Scots Musical Museum,* including 60 songs contributed by Burns.

September. Burns visits Ayrshire.

16th September. Burns undertakes to contribute to George Thomson's *Select Collection of Scottish Airs.*

29th September. The Theatre Royal, Dumfries opens in Shakespeare Street.

October. Burns begins work on contributions to a fifth volume of *Scots Musical Museum*.

13th November. Burns subscribes to the Edinburgh *Gazetteer*.

21st November. Birth of Elizabeth Riddell Burns.

December. Four-day visit to Dunlop House with Dr Adair, Burns's last. First General Convention of the Friends of the People at Edinburgh; much political commotion in Dumfries.

31st December. John Mitchell, Collector of Excise, ordered by his Board to investigate Burns's political conduct 'as a person disaffected to Government'.

1793   5th January. Burns defends himself to Robert Graham of Fintry, Excise Commissioner.

18th February. Second Edinburgh edition of the *Poems* published by Creech.

March. Burns asks for, and receives, burgess privileges in the Dumfries School for his children.

19th May. Burns family move to a house in Millbrae Vennel (now Burns Street).

May. First set of Thomson's *Select Collection* published. Over twenty letters, many with songs enclosed, from Burns to Thomson in the ensuing seven months alone.

27th July – 2nd August. Burns and John Syme tour Galloway.

1st August. Burns meets Pietro Urbani at the home of Lord Selkirk, St Mary's Isle.

October. Meeting between Burns and Nathaniel Gow, the celebrated fiddler and son of Neil Gow.

December. Burns lends his collection of bawdy ballads to John McMurdo of Drumlanrig: 'I have for some years been making ... There is not another copy of the collection in the world.'

9th December. Isabella Burns married at Mossgiel.

Late December. 'Rape of the Sabines' incident at Friars' Carse; rift between Burns and the Riddells.

1794   7th January. Burns proposes the reorganization of the Dumfries excise service.

12th January. Maria Riddell breaks with Burns.

20th April. Robert Riddell dies.

1st May (?) Burns declines a post with the *Morning Chronicle*, London.

June. Friars' Carse put up for sale.

25th – 28th June. Burns and Syme make their second tour of Galoway.

12th August. Birth of James Glencairn Burns.

November. Burns commences his notes on songs for Thomson, and seeks out English ballads for the *Select Collection*.

22nd December. Burns promoted to Acting Supervisor of Excise, Dumfries. Correspondence with Maria Riddell resumed.

1795   January. Burns working harder than ever for the Excise, but income much reduced: 'Therse accursed times, by stopping up Importation, have for this year at least lopt off a full third of my income.'

12th January. Burns writes the letter which estranges Mrs

Dunlop.

31st January. Burns a founder member of the Dumfries Volunteers.

February – March. Burns and Maria Riddell fully reconciled.

March. Patrick Heron declares his candidacy for the Election in the Stewarty.

April. Alexander Reid paints a miniature portrait of Burns. Alexander Findlater resumes his duties as Excise Supervisor at Dumfries.

24th June. Death of Wiliam Smellie, Burns's Edinburgh printer.

September. Death of Elizabeth Riddell Burns.

December – January. Burns ill with 'a most severe Rheumatic fever'.

1796   31st January. Burns 'beginning to crawl across my room'.

January – March. Famine in Dumfries. 'Many days my family, and hundreds of other families, are absolutely without one grain of meal; as money cannot purchase it.'

12th – 14th March. Food riots in Dumfries.

June. Burns's last letter to Johnson.

3rd – 16th July. Burns at the Brow Well.

12th July. Last letter to Thomson, begging for five pounds in order to pay off `A cruel scoundrel of a Haberdasher to whom I owe an account ... '

18th July. Burns writes his last letter: to his father-in-law James Armour.

21st July. Burns dies in Dumfries.

25th July. Funeral of Burns, and birth of his son Maxwell.

December. Fifth volume of *Scots Musical Museum* published.

# INDEX OF TITLES AND FIRST LINES

Titles are given in capitals, alternative names are given in capitals followed by an asterisk, and first lines in lower-case lettering.

## INDEX OF TITLES AND FIRST LINES
Titles are given in capitals, alternative names are given in capitals followed by an asterisk, and first lines in lower-case lettering.

## INDEX OF TITLES AND FIRST LINES

Titles are given in capitals, alternative names are given in capitals followed by an asterisk, and first lines in lower-case lettering.

INDEX OF TITLES AND FIRST LINES
Titles are given in capitals, alternative names are given in capitals followed by an asterisk, and first lines in lower-case lettering.

# INDEX OF TITLES AND FIRST LINES

Titles are given in capitals, alternative names are given in capitals followed by an asterisk, and first lines in lower-case lettering.

Titles are given in capitals, alternative names are given in capitals followed by an asterisk, and first lines in lower-case lettering.

## INDEX OF TITLES AND FIRST LINES

Titles are given in capitals, alternative names are given in capitals followed by an asterisk, and first lines in lower-case lettering.

## INDEX OF TITLES AND FIRST LINES

Titles are given in capitals, alternative names are given in capitals followed by an asterisk, and first lines in lower-case lettering.

## INDEX OF TITLES AND FIRST LINES

Titles are given in capitals, alternative names are given in capitals followed by an asterisk, and first lines in lower-case lettering.

## INDEX OF TITLES AND FIRST LINES

Titles are given in capitals, alternative names are given in capitals followed by an asterisk, and first lines in lower-case lettering.

# INDEX OF TITLES AND FIRST LINES

Titles are given in capitals, alternative names are given in capitals followed by an asterisk, and first lines in lower-case lettering.

Titles are given in capitals, alternative names are given in capitals followed by an asterisk, and first lines in lower-case lettering.

## INDEX OF TITLES AND FIRST LINES

Titles are given in capitals, alternative names are given in capitals followed by an asterisk, and first lines in lower-case lettering.

THE BACHELORS' CLUB, TARBOLTON

PORTRAIT OF BURNS
by Alexander Nasmyth, painted in 1787
*by courtesy of the National Galleries of Scotland, Edinburgh*

# INDEX OF TITLES AND FIRST LINES

Titles are given in capitals, alternative names are given in capitals followed by an asterisk, and first lines in lower-case lettering.

2

# INDEX OF TITLES AND FIRST LINES

Titles are given in capitals, alternative names are given in capitals followed by an asterisk, and first lines in lower-case lettering.

## INDEX OF TITLES AND FIRST LINES

Titles are given in capitals, alternative names are given in capitals followed by an asterisk, and first lines in lower-case lettering.

INDEX OF TITLES AND FIRST LINES

Titles are given in capitals, alternative names are given in capitals followed by an asterisk, and first lines in lower-case lettering.

INDEX OF TITLES AND FIRST LINES

Titles are given in capitals, alternative names are given in capitals followed by an asterisk, and first lines in lower-case lettering.

INDEX OF TITLES AND FIRST LINES

Titles are given in capitals, alternative names are given in capitals followed by an asterisk, and first lines in lower-case lettering.

# INDEX OF TITLES AND FIRST LINES

Titles are given in capitals, alternative names are given in capitals followed by an asterisk, and first lines in lower-case lettering.

# HANDSOME NELL

*TUNE: I am a man unmarried*

In the autumn of 1774 Burns 'first committed the sin of RHYME' as he later wrote to Dr. Moore: 'You know our country custom of coupling a man and woman together as Partners in the labors of Harvest. In my fifteenth autumn my Partner was a bewitching creature who just counted an autumn less... a bonie, sweet sonsie lass.' According to Isobel Begg, the poet's sister (1850), the girl was Helen Kilpatrick of Dalrymple, but as she was born in February 1759 she does not answer the poet's description of someone a year younger. It is more likely that Helen Blair, named in editions of the works of Burns up to 1850, was in fact the heroine. She is also referred to in the third stanza of the poem 'To the Guidwife of Wauchope House' (271-2).

O once I lov'd a bonie lass,
    Ay, and I love her still!
And whilst that virtue warms my breast,
    I'll love my handsome Nell.

As bonie lasses I hae seen,
    And monie full as braw,           *handsome*
But for a modest gracefu mien
    The like I never saw.

A bonie lass, I will confess,
    Is pleasant to the e'e;
But without some better qualities
    She's no a lass for me.

But Nelly's looks are blythe and sweet,
    And what is best of a',
Her reputation is complete,
    And fair without a flaw.

She dresses ay sae clean and neat,
    Both decent and genteel;
And then there's something in her gait
    Gars onie dress look weel.           *makes*

A gaudy dress and gentle air
    May slightly touch the heart;
But it's innocence and modesty
    That polishes the dart.

'Tis this in Nelly pleases me,
    'Tis this enchants my soul;
For absolutely in my breast
    She reigns without controul.

# NOW WESTLIN WINDS

*TUNE: Port Gordon*

Composed in the summer of 1775, while studying mathematics at Hugh Rodger's school in Kirkoswald. Peggy (fourth stanza) was Margaret Thompson, 'a charming Fillette who lived next door to the school overset my Trigonometry, and set me off at a tangent from the sphere of my studies'.

Now westlin winds and slaught'ring guns        western
     Bring Autumn's pleasant weather;
The moorcock springs on whirring wings
     Amang the blooming heather:
Now waving grain, wide o'er the plain,
     Delights the weary farmer;
And the moon shines bright, as I rove by night,
     To muse upon my charmer.

The paitrick lo'es the fruitfu fells,        partridge
     The plover lo'es the mountains;
The woodcock haunts the lonely dells,
     The soaring hern the fountains:        heron
Thro lofty groves the cushat roves,        pigeon
     The path o man to shun it;
The hazel bush o'erhangs the thrush,
     The spreading thorn the linnet.

Thus ev'ry kind their pleasure find,
     The savage and the tender;
Some social join, and leagues combine,
     Some solitary wander:
Avaunt, away, the cruel sway!
     Tyrannic man's dominion!
The sportsman's joy, the murd'ring cry,
     The flutt'ring, gory pinion!

But, Peggy dear, the ev'ning's clear,
     Thick flies the skimming swallow;
The sky is blue, the fields in view,
     All fading-green and yellow:
Come let us stray our gladsome way,
And view the charms of Nature;
The rustling corn, the fruited thorn,
     And ilka happy creature.        every

We'll gently walk, and sweetly talk,
     While the silent moon shines clearly;
I'll clasp thy waist, and, fondly prest,
     Swear how I lo'e thee dearly:
Not vernal show'rs to budding flow'rs,
     Not Autumn to the farmer,
So dear can be as thou to me,
     My fair, my lovely charmer!

# I DREAM'D I LAY

*TUNE: The Young Man's Dream*

'These two stanzas I composed when I was seventeen and are among the eldest of my printed pieces' – Burns.

I dream'd I lay where flowers were springing
   Gaily in the sunny beam,
List'ning to the wild birds singing,
   By a falling crystal stream;
Straight the sky grew black and daring,
   Thro the woods the whirlwinds rave,
Trees with aged arms were warring
   O'er the swelling, drumlie wave.           turbid

Such was my life's deceitful morning,
   Such the pleasures I enjoy'd!
But lang or noon, loud tempests storming,      ere
   A' my flowery bliss destroy'd.
Tho fickle Fortune has deceiv'd me
   (She promis'd fair, and perform'd but ill),
Of monie a joy and hope bereav'd me,      many
   I bear a heart shall support me still.

# MY NANIE, O

The date of composition is unknown but Burns described it as 'done at a very early period of life, and consequently....incorrect'. Nanie, according to Gilbert Burns, was probably Agnes Fleming, daughter of a Tarbolton farmer. In the original version the river in line 1 was the Stinchar, which Burns thought 'horridly prosaic'. Afton, Girvan and Lugar were later alternatives.

Behind yon hills where Lugar flows,
   'Mang moors an mosses many, O,      bogs
The wintry sun the day has clos'd,
   And I'll awa to Nanie, O.

The westlin wind blaws loud an shill;      western, shrill
   The night's baith mirk and rainy, O;     murky
But I'll get my plaid an out I'll steal,
   An owre the hill to Nanie, O.

My Nanie's charming, sweet, an young;
   Nae artfu wiles to win ye, O:
May ill befa' the flattering tongue
   That wad beguile my Nanie, O.

Her face is fair, her heart is true;
   As spotless as she's bonie, O;
The op'ning gowan, wat wi dew,                   *daisy*
   Nae purer is than Nanie, O.

A country lad is my degree,
   An few there be that ken me, O;
But what care I how few they be?
   I'm welcome ay to Nanie, O.

My riches a's my penny-fee,
   An I maun guide it cannie, O;        *manage carefully*
But warl's gear ne'er troubles me,        *wordly goods*
   My thoughts are a' – my Nanie, O.

Our auld guidman delights to view
   His sheep an kye thrive bonie, O;        *cattle*
But I'm as blythe that hauds his pleugh,   *holds, plough*
   An has nae care but Nanie, O.

Come weel, come woe, I care na by;       *do not care*
   I'll tak what Heav'n will send me, O:
Nae ither care in life have I,
   But live, an love my Nanie, O.

# TRAGIC FRAGMENT

These lines are thought to have been written in 1777 at Mount Oliphant and reflect the misery of the Burnes family at this time, before William Burnes was able to throw off the burden of this lease and move to Lochlie at Whitsun that year.

All villain as I am – a damned wretch,
A hardened, stubborn, unrepenting sinner –
Still my heart melts at human wretchedness,
And with sincere, tho unavailing sighs
I view the helpless children of distress.
With tears indignant I behold the oppressor
Rejoicing in the honest man's destruction,
Whose unsubmitting heart was all his crime.
Ev'n you, ye hapless crew! I pity you;
Ye, whom the seeming good think sin to pity:
Ye poor, despised, abandoned vagabonds,
Whom Vice, as usual, has turn'd o'er to ruin.

Oh! but for friends and interposing Heaven,
I had been driven forth, like you forlorn,
The most detested, worthless wretch among you!
O injured God! Thy goodness has endow'd me
With talents passing most of my compeers,
Which I in just proportion have abused,
As far surpassing other common villains
As Thou in natural parts has given me more.

# O TIBBIE, I HAE SEEN THE DAY

*TUNE: Invercauld's Reel*

Composed when Burns was about seventeen years old. Tibbie was Isabella Steven of
Littlehill, near Lochlie which the poet's father farmed from Whitsun 1777.

### CHORUS

*O Tibbie, I hae seen the day,*             
 *Ye wadna been sae shy!*        would not have been
*For laik o gear ye lightly me,*       lack of wealth
 *But, trowth, I care na by.*      I care not in return

Yestreen I met you on the moor,       Last night
Ye spak na, but gaed by like stoure!    went by like dust
Ye geck at me because I'm poor –    toss your head
 But fient a hair care I!         not

When comin hame on Sunday last,
Upon the road as I cam past,
Ye snufft an gae your head a cast –    sniffed
 But, trowth, I care't na by!      cared

I doubt na, lass, but ye may think,
Because ye hae the name o clink,      money
That ye can please me at a wink,
 Whene'er ye like to try.

But sorrow tak him that's sae mean,
Altho his pouch o coin were clean,
Wha follows onie saucy quean,       girl
 That looks sae proud and high!

Altho a lad were e'er sae smart,
If that he want the yellow dirt,
Ye'll cast your head anither airt,                          direction
    And answer him fu dry.

But if he hae the name o gear,
Ye'll fasten to him like a brier,
Tho hardly he for sense or lear,                          learning
    Be better than the kye.                          cows

But, Tibbie, lass, tak my advice:
Your daddie's gear maks you sae nice,
The Deil a ane wad spier your price,                          ask
    Were ye as poor as I.

There lives a lass beside yon park,
I'd rather hae her in her sark                          shift
Than you wi a' your thousand mark,
    That gars you look sae high.                          makes

# ONE NIGHT AS I DID WANDER

### A FRAGMENT

Date unknown, but probably early.

One night as I did wander,
    When corn begins to shoot,
I sat me down to ponder
    Upon an auld tree-root
Auld Ayr ran by before me,
    And bicker'd to the seas;
A cushat crooded o'er me,                          pigeon
    That echoed through the trees.

# THE RIGS O BARLEY

*TUNE: Corn Rigs*

Burns composed this version of a well-known old song about 1782. The girl named in the first stanza was Anne Rankine, youngest daughter of John Rankine of Adamhill. In that year she married John Merry, inn-keeper at New Cumnock, where the poet lodged in August 1786.

## CHORUS

> *Corn rigs, an barley rigs,*
> *An corn rigs are bonie:*
> *I'll ne'er forget that happy night,*
> *Amang the rigs wi Annie.*

It was upon a Lammas night,
　　When corn rigs are bonie,           *ridges*
Beneath the moon's unclouded light,
　　I held awa to Annie;
The time flew by, wi tentless heed;     *careless*
　　Till, 'tween the late and early,
Wi sma' persuasion she agreed
　　To see me thro the barley.

The sky was blue, the wind was still,
　　The moon was shining clearly;
I set her down, wi right good will,
　　Amang the rigs o barley:
I ken't her heart was a' my ain;       *knew*
　　I lov'd her most sincerely;
I kiss'd her owre and owre again,
　　Amang the rigs o barley.

I lock'd her in my fond embrace;
　　Her heart was beating rarely:
My blessings on that happy place,
　　Amang the rigs o barley!
But by the moon and stars so bright,
　　That shone that hour so clearly!
She ay shall bless that happy night
　　Amang the rigs o barley.

I hae been blythe wi comrades dear;
　　I hae been merry drinking;
I hae been joyfu gath'rin gear;     *making money*
　　I hae been happy thinking:
But a' the pleasures e'er I saw,
　　Tho three times doubl'd fairly –
That happy night was worth them a',
　　Amang the rigs o barley.

## FAREWELL TO ELIZA

*TUNE: Gilderoy*

Scholars have previously identified the heroine of this song as Elizabeth Barbour or Elizabeth Miller of Mauchline, ignoring the fact that the song was written by 1782, long before Burns met either girl. It is more probable that Eliza was Elizabeth Gebbie (1762-1823) of Pearsland, Galston, the recipient of the mysterious E letters of 1781 and thus the girl Burns alleged to Moore had jilted him that summer. In November 1781 Elizabeth married Hugh Brown, a stockingmaker who became a prominent Glasgow hosier. She was also the heroine of 'The Lass of Cessnock Banks'.

From thee, Eliza, I must go,
    And from my native shore:
The cruel fates between us throw
    A boundless ocean's roar;
But boundless oceans, roaring wide
    Between my love and me,
They never, never can divide
    My heart and soul from thee.

Farewell, farewell, Eliza dear,
    The maid that I adore!
A boding voice is in mine ear,
    We part to meet no more!
But the latest throb that leaves my heart,
    While Death stands victor by,
That throb, Eliza, is thy part,
    And thine that latest sigh!

## WINTER: A DIRGE

*TUNE: MacPherson's Rant*

Burns (1CPB) mentioned Winter as his favourite season which 'may be partly owing to my misfortunes giving my mind a melancholy cast'. Elsewhere he wrote 'In one of these seasons, just after a tract of misfortunes I composed the following song.'

The wintry west extends his blast,
    And hail and rain does blaw;
Or the stormy north sends driving forth
    The blinding sleet and snaw:
Wild-tumbling brown, the burn comes down,
    And roars frae bank to brae:    slope
And bird and beast in covert rest,
    And pass the heartless day.

'The sweeping blast, the sky o'ercast,'
    The joyless winter day
Let others fear, to me more dear
    Than all the pride of May:
The tempest's howl, it soothes my soul,
    My griefs it seems to join;
The leafless trees my fancy please,
    Their fate resembles mine!

Thou Pow'r Supreme, whose mighty scheme
    These woes of mine fulfil,
Here, firm I rest, they must be best,
    Because they are Thy will!
Then all I want (O do Thou grant
    This one request of mine!):
Since to enjoy Thou dost deny,
    Assist me to resign.

# THE LASS OF CESSNOCK BANKS

*TUNE: The Butcher Boy*

The subject of this song has now been identified as Elizabeth, daughter of Thomas Gebbie of Pearsland, and niece of Alexander Gebbie, miller of Cessnock. Burns himself never published this song of similes and it was first recovered in 1808 by Cromek who heard it from the lips of the lady herself in Glasgow.

On Cessnock banks a lassie dwells,
    Could I describe her shape and mien!
Our lasses a' she far excels –
    An she has twa sparkling, rogueish een!           *eyes*

She's sweeter than the morning dawn,
    When rising Phoebus first is seen,
And dew-drops twinkle o'er the lawn –
    An she has twa sparkling, rogueish een!

She's stately like yon youthful ash,           *yonder*
    That grows the cowslip braes between,     *hillsides*
And drinks the stream with vigour fresh –
    An she has twa sparkling, rogueish een!

She's spotless like the flow'ring thorn,
    With flow'rs so white and leaves so green,
When purest in the dewy morn –
    An she has twa sparkling, rogueish een!

Her looks are like the vernal May,
   When ev'ning Phoebus shines serene,
While birds rejoice on every spray –
   An she has twa sparkling, rogueish een!

Her hair is like the curling mist,
   That climbs the mountain-sides at e'en,
Then flow'r-reviving rains are past –
   An she has twa sparkling, rogueish een!

Her forehead's like the show'ry bow,
   When gleaming sunbeams intervene,
And gild the distant mountain's brow –
   An she has twa sparkling, rogueish een!

Her cheeks are like yon crimson gem,
   The pride of all the flowery scene,
Just opening on its thorny stem –
   An she has twa sparkling, rogueish een!

Her bosom's like the nightly snow,
   When pale the morning rises keen,
While hid the murm'ring streamlets flow –
   An she has twa sparkling, rogueish een!

Her lips are like yon cherries ripe,
   That sunny walls from Boreas screen:
They tempt the taste and charm the sight –
   An she has twa sparkling, rogueish een!

Her teeth are like a flock of sheep,
   With fleeces newly washen clean,
That slowly mount the rising steep –
   An she has twa sparkling, rogueish een!

Her breath is like the fragrant breeze,
   That gently stirs the blossom'd bean,
When Phoebus sinks behind the seas –
   An she has twa sparkling, rogueish een!

Her voice is like the ev'ning thrush,
   That sings on Cessnock banks unseen,
While his mate sits nestling in the bush –
   An she has twa sparkling, rogueish een!

But it's not her air, her form, her face,
   Tho matching Beauty's fabled Queen:
'Tis the mind that shines in ev'ry grace –
   An chiefly in her rogueish een!

# TO RUIN

Written in the winter of 1781-2, a melancholy period when his rejection by Elizabeth Gebbie, his father's misfortunes, and poor health left Burns in a very sombre mood.

All hail, inexorable lord!
At whose destruction-breathing word,
   The mightiest empires fall!
Thy cruel, woe-delighted train,
The ministers of grief and pain,
   A sullen welcome, all!
With stern-resolv'd, despairing eye,
   I see each aimed dart;
For one has cut my dearest tie,
   And quivers in my heart.
      Then low'ring and pouring,
        The storm no more I dread;
      Tho thick'ning, and black'ning,
        Round my devoted head.

And thou grim Pow'r, by Life abhorr'd,
While Life a pleasure can afford,
   Oh! hear a wretch's pray'r!
No more I shrink appall'd, afraid;
I court, I beg thy friendly aid,
   To close this scene of care!
When shall my soul, in silent peace,
   Resign Life's joyless day?
My weary heart its throbbings cease,
   Cold-mould'ring in the clay?
      No fear more, no tear more
        To stain my lifeless face,
      Enclasped and grasped,
        Within thy cold embrace!

# A PRAYER IN THE PROSPECT OF DEATH

Though usually assigned to 1784, this poem was probably composed in December 1781, at a time when Burns was writing from Irvine to his father '....my only pleasurable employment is looking backwards and forwards in a moral and religious way - I am quite transported at the thought that ere long, perhaps very soon, I shall bid an eternal adiew to all the pains, and uneasiness and disquietudes of this weary life.'

O Thou unknown, Almighty Cause
   Of all my hope and fear!
In whose dread presence, ere an hour,
   Perhaps I must appear!

If I have wander'd in those paths
   Of life I ought to shun –
As something, loudly, in my breast,
   Remonstrates I have done –

Thou know'st that Thou hast formed me
   With passions wild and strong;
And list'ning to their witching voice
   Has often led me wrong.

Where human weakness has come short,
   Or frailty stept aside,
Do Thou, All-Good - for such Thou art –
   In shades of darkness hide.

Where with intention I have err'd,
   No other plea I have,
But, Thou art good;  and Goodness still
   Delighteth to forgive.


## STANZAS, ON THE SAME OCCASION

Why am I loth to leave this earthly scene?
   Have I so found it full of pleasing charms?
Some drops of joy with draughts of ill between;
   Some gleams of sunshine 'mid renewing storms?
Is it departing pangs my soul alarms?
   Or death's unlovely, dreary, dark abode?
For guilt, for guilt, my terrors are in arms:
   I tremble to approach an angry God,
And justly smart beneath His sin-avenging rod.

Fain would I say: 'Forgive my foul offence,'
   Fain promise never more to disobey;
But, should my Author health again dispense,
   Again I might desert fair virtue's way;
Again in folly's path might go astray;
   Again exalt the brute and sink the man;
Then how should I for heavenly mercy pray,
   Who act so counter heavenly mercy's plan?
Who sin so oft have mourn'd, yet to temptation ran?

O Thou great Governor of all below!
    If I may dare a lifted eye to Thee –
Thy nod can make the tempest cease to blow,
    Or still the tumult of the raging sea:
With that controlling pow'r assist ev'n me,
    Those headlong furious passions to confine,
For all unfit I feel my pow'rs to be,
    To rule their torrent in th' allowed line;
O, aid me with Thy help, Omnipotence Divine!

## PRAYER UNDER THE PRESSURE
## OF VIOLENT ANGUISH

Burns annotated this poem in 1CPB (March 1784): 'There was a certain period of my life that my spirit was broke by repeated losses and disasters, which threatened, and indeed effected the utter ruin of my fortune. My body too was attacked by that most dreadful distemper, a Hypochondria, or confirmed Melancholy: in this wretched state, the recollection of which makes me yet shudder, I hung my harp on the Willow tree, except in some lucid intervals, in which I composed the following.'

O Thou Great Being! what Thou art,
    Surpasses me to know;
Yet sure I am, that known to Thee
    Are all Thy works below.

Thy creature here before Thee stands,
    All wretched and distrest;
Yet sure those ills that wring my soul
    Obey Thy high behest.

Sure Thou, Almighty, canst not act
    From cruelty or wrath!
O, free my weary eyes from tears,
    Or close them fast in death!

But, if I must afflicted be
    To suit some wise design,
Then man my soul with firm resolves
    To bear and not repine!

# FICKLE FORTUNE

*TUNE: I dream'd I lay*

'An extempore under the pressure of a heavy train of Misfortunes' (1CPB)

Tho fickle Fortune has deceived me,
  (She promis'd fair and perform'd but ill);
Of mistress, friends, and wealth bereav'd me,
  Yet I bear a heart shall support me still.

I'll act with prudence as far as I'm able,
  But if success I must never find,
Then come, Misfortune, I bid thee welcome –
  I'll meet thee with an undaunted mind!

# RAGING FORTUNE

Like the previous poem, written during the sombre winter of 1781-2

O, raging Fortune's withering blast
  Has laid my leaf full low!
O, raging Fortune's withering blast
  Has laid my leaf full low!

My stem was fair, my bud was green,
  My blossom sweet did blow;
The dew fell fresh, the sun rose mild,
  And made my branches grow.

But luckless Fortune's northern storms
  Laid a' my blossoms low!
But luckless Fortune's northern storms
  Laid a' my blossoms low!

# I'LL GO AND BE A SODGER

Allegedly a reference to the sudden collapse of the poet's business as a flax-dresser at Irvine in the winter of 1781. 'My partner was a scoundrel of the first water who made money by the mystery of thieving; and to finish the whole, while we were giving a welcome carousel to the New Year, our shop burnt to ashes and left me, like a true poet, not worth a sixpence.'

O, why the deuce should I repine,
  And be an ill foreboder?
I'm twenty-three, and five feet nine,
  I'll go and be a sodger!                    soldier

I gat some gear wi meikle care,                    wealth, much
   I held it weel thegither;                      together
But now it's gane – and something mair:    gone, more
    I'll go and be a sodger!

## PARAPHRASE OF THE FIRST PSALM

This and the next poem provide interesting evidence of the poet's recourse to religion at a time of deep crisis in his life. Burns clearly felt that the lines of the 1st and 90th Psalms contained much that was relevant to his condition and he derived great comfort from them. These exercises in versification were for him the natural outcome.

The man, in life wherever plac'd,
   Hath happiness in store,
Who walks not in the wicked's way
   Nor learns their guilty lore!

Nor from the seat of scornful pride
   Casts forth his eyes abroad,
But with humility and awe
   Still walks before his God!

That man shall flourish like the trees,
   Which by the streamlets grow:
The fruitful top is spread on high,
   And firm the root below.

But he, whose blossom buds in guilt,
   Shall to the ground be cast,
And, like the rootless stubble, tost
   Before the sweeping blast.

For why? that God the good adore,
   Hath giv'n them peace and rest,
But hath decreed that wicked men
   Shall ne'er be truly blest.

## THE NINETIETH PSALM VERSIFIED

O Thou, the first, the greatest friend
    Of all the human race!
Whose strong right hand has ever been
    Their stay and dwelling place!

Before the mountains heav'd their heads
    Beneath Thy forming hand,
Before this ponderous globe itself
    Arose at Thy command.

That Pow'r, which rais'd and still upholds
    This universal frame,
From countless, unbeginning time
    Was ever still the same.

Those mighty periods of years
    Which seem to us so vast,
Appear no more before Thy sight
    Than yesterday that's past

Thou giv'st the word: Thy creature, man,
    Is to existence brought;
Again Thou say'st: 'Ye sons of men,
    Return ye into nought!'

Thou layest them, with all their cares,
    In everlasting sleep;
As with a flood Thou tak'st them off
    With overwhelming sweep.

They flourish like the morning flower,
    In beauty's pride array'd,
But long ere night, cut down, it lies
    All wither'd and decay'd.

## MY FATHER WAS A FARMER

*TUNE: The Weaver and his Shuttle, O*

Probably composed early in 1782 following his return to Lochlie from Irvine.

My father was a farmer upon the Carrick border, O,
And carefully he bred me in decency and order, O.
He bade me act a manly part, though I had ne'er a farthing, O,
For without an honest manly heart, no man was worth regarding, O.

Then out into the world my course I did determine, O,
Tho to be rich was not my wish, yet to be great was charming, O.
My talents they were not the worst, nor yet my education, O,
Resolv'd was I, at least to try, to mend my situation, O.

In many a way, and vain essay, I courted Fortune's favour, O:
Some cause unseen still stept between, to frustrate each
        endeavour, O.
Sometimes by foes I was o'erpower'd, sometimes by friends
        forsaken, O,
And when my hope was at the top, I still was worst mistaken, O.

Then sore harass'd, and tir'd at last, with Fortune's vain
        delusion, O,
I dropt my schemes, like idle dreams, and came to this
        conclusion, O -
The past was bad, and the future hid, its good or ill untried, O,
But the present hour was in my pow'r, and so I would enjoy it, O.

No help, nor hope, nor view had I, nor person to befriend me, O,
So I must toil, and sweat, and moil, and labour to sustain me, O.
To plough and sow, to reap and mow, my father bred me early, O;
For one, he said, to labour bred, was a match for Fortune fairly, O.

Thus all obscure, unknown, and poor, thro life I'm doom'd to
        wander, O,
Till down my weary bones I lay in everlasting slumber, O.
No view nor care, but shun whate'er might breed me pain or
        sorrow, O,
I live to-day as well's I may, regardless of to-morrow, O.

But cheerful still, I am as well as a monarch in a palace, O,
Tho Fortune's frown still hunts me down, with all her wonted
        malice, O:
I make indeed my daily bread, but ne'er can make it farther, O,
But, as daily bread is all I need, I do not much regard her, O.

When sometimes by my labour, I earn a little money, O,
Some unforeseen misfortune comes gen'rally upon me, O;
Mischance, mistake, or by neglect, or my good-natur'd folly, O:
But, come what will, I've sworn it still, I'll ne'er be melancholy, O.

All you who follow wealth and power with unremitting ardour, O,
The more in this you look for bliss, you leave your view the
        farther, O,
Had you the wealth Potosi boasts, or nations to adore you, O,  Latin
A cheerful honest-hearted clown I will prefer before you, O.  American
                                                              silvermine

# MONTGOMERIE'S PEGGY

*TUNE: Galla Water*

Written in imitation of an old song 'McMillan's Peggy', it immortalises the housekeeper at Coilsfield House. The least-known of the poet's heroines '....Peggy was my Deity for six, or eight months. She had been bred....in a style of life rather elegant....A vanity of showing my parts in Courtship....made me lay siege to her; and when, as I always do in my foolish gallantries, I had battered myself into a very warm affection for her, she told me that her fortress had been for some time before the rightful property of another; but with the greatest friendship and politeness, she offered my every alliance, except actual possession.' Montgomerie's Peggy may, in fact, have been Margaret 'Highland Mary' Campbell, who was for some time the mistress of Captain James Montgomerie of Coilsfield.

Altho my bed were in yon muir,                                         *that*
    Amang the heather, in my plaidie,
Yet happy, happy would I be,
    Had I my dear Montgomerie's Peggy.

When o'er the hill beat surly storms,
    And winter nights were dark and rainy,
I'd seek some dell, and in my arms
    I'd shelter dear Montgomerie's Peggy.

Were I a Baron proud and high,
    And horse and servants waiting ready,
Then a' 'twad gie o joy to me –                               *'twould give*
    The sharin't with Montgomerie's Peggy.             *sharing it*

# JOHN BARLEYCORN: A BALLAD

*TUNE: Lull me beyond thee*

Numerous variants of an ancient folk ballad are extant, dealing with the legend of the corn spirit and allegorising the treatment of barley from the threshing and winnowing of the harvest to the brewing of ale. Burns (1CPB) recalled the first three stanzas and 'some scraps' of one such version and developed this poem out of these fragments.

There was three kings into the east,
    Three kings both great and high,
And they hae sworn a solemn oath
    John Barleycorn should die.

They took a plough and plough'd him down,
    Put clods upon his head,
And they hae sworn a solemn oath
    John Barleycorn was dead.

But the cheerful Spring came kindly on,
    And show'rs began to fall;
John Barleycorn got up again,
    And sore surpris'd them all.

The sultry suns of Summer came,
    And he grew thick and strong;
His head weel arm'd wi pointed spears,
    That no one should him wrong.

The sober Autumn enter'd mild,
    When he grew wan and pale;
His bending joints and drooping head
    Show'd he began to fail.

His colour sicken'd more and more,
    He faded into age;
And then his enemies began
    To show their deadly rage.

They've taen a weapon, long and sharp,
    And cut him by the knee;
They ty'd him fast upon a cart,
    Like a rogue for forgerie.

They laid him down upon his back,
    And cudgell'd him full sore.
They hung him up before the storm,
    And turn'd him o'er and o'er.

They filled up a darksome pit
    With water to the brim,
They heav'd in John Barleycorn –
    There, let him sink or swim!

They laid him out upon the floor,
    To work him farther woe;
And still, as signs of life appear'd,
    They toss'd him to and fro.

They wasted o'er a scorching flame
    The marrow of his bones;
But a miller us'd him worst of all,
    For he crush'd him between two stones.

And they hae taen his very heart's blood,
    And drank it round and round;
And still the more and more they drank,
    Their joy did more abound.

John Barleycorn was a hero bold,
   Of noble enterprise;
For if you do but taste his blood,
   'Twill make your courage rise.

'Twill make a man forget his woe;
   'Twill heighten all his joy:
'Twill make the widow's heart to sing,
   Tho the tear were in her eye.

Then let us toast John Barleycorn,
   Each man a glass in hand;
And may his great posterity
   Ne'er fail in old Scotland!

# THE DEATH AND DYING WORDS
# OF POOR MAILIE     Mollie

### THE AUTHOR'S ONLY PET YOWE:    ewe
### AN UNCO MOURNFU TALE    uncommonly

Gilbert Burns, writing to Dr Currie in April 1798, said that the events were pretty much as described. Robert had 'partly by way of frolic, bought a ewe and two lambs from a neighbour, and she was tethered in a field adjoining the house at Lochlie...Poor Mailie was set to rights, and when we returned from the plough in the evening, he repeated to me her Death and Dying Words pretty much in the way they now stand.'

As Mailie, an her lambs thegither,    together
Was ae day nibblin on the tether,
Upon her cloot she coost a hitch,    hoof, looped
An owre she warsl'd in the ditch:    floundered
There, groanin, dying, she did lie,
When Hughoc he cam doytin by.    staggering

Wi glowrin een, and lifted han's    staring
Poor Hughoc like a statue stan's;
He saw her days were near-hand ended,
But, wae's my heart! he could na mend it!    woe
He gaped wide, but naething spak,
At length poor Mailie silence brak: –

'O thou, whase lamentable face
Appears to mourn my woefu case!
My dying words attentive hear,
An bear them to my Master dear.

'Tell him, if e'er again he keep           *own*
As muckle gear as buy a sheep –      *much money*
O, bid him never tie them mair,
Wi wicked strings o hemp or hair!
But ca' them out to park or hill,         *drive*
An let them wander at their will:
So may his flock increase, an grow
To scores o lambs, and packs o woo'!

'Tell him, he was a Master kin',
An ay was guid to me an mine;
An now my dying charge I gie him,
My helpless lambs, I trust them wi him.

'O bid him save their harmless lives,
Frae dogs, an tods, an butcher's knives!    *foxes*
But gie them guid cow-milk their fill,
Till they be fit to fend themsel;       *look after*
An tent them duly, e'en an morn,     *tend, evening*
Wi taets o hay an ripps o corn.    *morsels, handfuls*

'An may they never learn the gaets,     *ways*
Of ither vile, wanrestfu pets –       *restless*
To slink thro slaps, an reave an steal,   *broken fences*
At stacks o pease, or stocks o kail!
So may they, like their great forbears,
For monie a year come thro the sheers:
So wives will gie them bits o bread,
An bairns greet for them when they're dead.   *children weep*

'My poor toop-lamb, my son an heir,     *tup*
O, bid him breed him up wi care!
An if he live to be a beast,
To pit some havins in his breast!     *conduct*

'An warn him - what I winna name –     *will not*
To stay content wi yowes at hame;     *ewes*
An no to rin an wear his cloots,
Like ither menseless, graceless brutes.   *unmannerly*

'An niest, my yowie, silly thing,                                    next
Gude keep thee frae a tether string!
O, may thou ne'er forgather up,                            make friends
Wi onie blastit, moorland toop;
But ay keep mind to moop an mell,                    nibble and meddle
Wi sheep o credit like thysel!

    'And now, my bairns, wi my last breath,
I lea'e my blessin wi you baith:
An when you think upo your mither,
Mind to be kind to ane anither.

    'Now, honest Hughoc, dinna fail,
To tell my master a' my tale;
An bid him burn this cursed tether,
An for thy pains thou'se get my blether.'              bladder

    This said, poor Mailie turn'd her head,
An clos'd her een amang the dead!                            eyes


# POOR MAILIE'S ELEGY

This sequel to the previous poem was written in 1785-86 to accompany it in the
Kilmarnock Edition.

Lament in rhyme, lament in prose,
Wi saut tears trickling down your nose;                     salt
Our Bardie's fate is at a close,
    Past a' remead!
The last, sad cape-stane of his woes;                    keystone
    Poor Mailie's dead!

It's no the loss of warl's gear,                            world's
That could sae bitter draw the tear
Or mak our bardie, dowie, wear                            gloomy
    The mourning weed:
He's lost a friend and neebor dear,                    neighbour
    In Mailie dead.

Thro a' the town she trotted by him;
A lang half-mile she could descry him;
Wi kindly bleat, when she did spy him,
    She ran wi speed:
A friend mair faithfu ne'er came nigh him,
    Than Mailie dead.

BURNS AT THE HOUSE OF FRANCIS GROSE by Robert Scott Lauder

*courtesy of the Dick Institute, Kilmarnock*

**BURNS MONUMENT AND MUSEUM**
Kay Park, Kilmarnock

I wat she was a sheep o sense,         *wot*
An could behave hersel wi mense:      *grace*
I'll say't, she never brak a fence,
    Thro thievish greed.
Our Bardie, lanely, keeps the spence    *parlour*
    Sin' Mailie's dead.

Or, if he wanders up the howe,      *glen*
Her living image in her yowe,      *ewe*
Comes bleating to him, owre the knowe,  *knoll*
    For bits o bread;
An down the briny pearls rowe      *roll*
    For Mailie dead.

She was nae get o moorlan tips,    *issue, tups*
Wi tawted ket, an hairy hips;    *matted coat*
For her forbears were brought in ships,
    Frae 'yont the Tweed:
A bonier fleesh ne'er cross'd the clips  *fleece, clippers*
    Than Mailie's dead.

Wae worth that man wha first did shape,  *woe betide*
That vile, wanchancie thing – a rape!  *dangerous, rope*
It maks guid fellows girn an gape,    *grin*
    Wi chokin dread;
An Robin's bonnet wave wi crape
    For Mailie dead.

O, a' ye Bards on bonie Doon!
An wha on Ayr your chanters tune!
Come, join the melancholious croon
    O Robin's reed!
His heart will never get aboon!
    His Mailie's dead!

3

## REMORSE

This poem was inspired by Adam Smith's *Theory of Moral Sentiments* (1759). The poet's copy of this philosophical work is now preserved in the library of Glasgow University.

Of all the numerous ills that hurt our peace,
That press the soul, or wring the mind with anguish,
Beyond comparison the worst are those
By our own folly, or our guilt brought on:
In ev'ry other circumstance, the mind
Has this to say: – 'It was no deed of mine.'
But, when to all the evil of misfortune
This sting is added: – 'Blame thy foolish self!'
Or, worser far, the pangs of keen remorse,
The torturing, gnawing consciousness of guilt,
Of guilt, perhaps, where we've involved others,
The young, the innocent, who fondly lov'd us;
Nay, more, that very love their cause of ruin!
O burning Hell! in all thy store of torments
There's not a keener lash!

Lives there a man so firm, who, while his heart
Feels all the bitter horrors of his crime,
Can reason down its agonizing throbs,
And, after proper purpose of amendment,
Can firmly force his jarring thoughts to peace?
O happy, happy, enviable man!
O glorious magnanimity of soul!

## NO CHURCHMAN AM I

*TUNE: Prepare, my dear Brethren*

Earlier editors assigned this work to 1781-2 and associated it with the Bachelors' Club and the Masonic Lodge at Tarbolton, but Kinsley has demonstrated (from a verse cut out in 1787) that it must date from 1783, when the parliamentary enquiry into Warren Hastings's administration of India was under way and Pitt became Chancellor of the Exchequer in December 1783.

No churchman am I for to rail and to write,
No statesman nor soldier to plot or to fight,
No sly man of business contriving a snare,
For a big-belly'd bottle's the whole of my care.

The peer I don't envy, I give him his bow;
I scorn not the peasant, tho ever so low;
But a club of good fellows, like those that are here,
And a bottle like this, are my glory and care.

Here passes the squire on his brother – his horse,
There centum per centum, the cit with his purse,
But see you *The Crown* how it waves in the air?
There a big-belly'd bottle still eases my care.

The wife of my bosom, alas! she did die;
For sweet consolation to church I did fly;
I found that old Solomon proved it fair,
That a big-belly'd bottle's a cure for all care.

I once was persuaded a venture to make;
A letter inform'd me that all was to wreck;
But the pursy old landlord just waddled upstairs,
With a glorious bottle that ended my cares.

'Life's cares they are comforts' – a maxim laid down
By the Bard, what d'ye call him? that wore the black gown;
And faith I agree with th' old prig to a hair:
For a big-belly'd bottle's a heav'n of a care.

A STANZA ADDED IN A MASON LODGE

Then fill up a bumper and make it o'erflow,
And honours Masonic prepare for to throw:
May ev'ry true Brother of the Compass and Square
Have a big-belly'd bottle, when harass'd with care!

## ON AN INNKEEPER IN TARBOLTON

Andrew Manson kept an inn now marked by a plaque on the corner of Burns and Garden Streets.

Here lies 'mang ither useless matters,
A. Manson wi his endless clatters.

## EPITAPH ON JAMES GRIEVE, LAIRD OF BOGHEAD, TARBOLTON

This quatrain lampooned the laird of an estate just to the west of Lochlie, and was probably written in 1783-84.

Here lies Boghead amang the dead
    In hopes to get salvation;
But if such as he in Heav'n may be,
    Then welcome – hail! damnation.

# THE RUINED FARMER

*TUNE: Go from my window, Love, do*

Probably inspired by the tragedy which overtook the poet's father in the winter of 1783-84. William Burnes fell into arrears with the rent of Lochlie and the landlord, David McLure took the luckless Burnes to the Sheriff Court. Though Burnes won his appeal to the Court of Session on 27th January 1784 he died two weeks later of 'a phthisical consumption' aggravated by hardship and worry.

The sun he is sunk in the west,
All creatures retired to rest,
While here I sit, all sore beset,
    With sorrow, grief, and woe:
And it's O, fickle Fortune, O!

The prosperous man is asleep,
Nor hears how the whirlwinds sweep;
But Misery and I must watch
    The surly tempests blow:
And it's O, fickle Fortune, O!

There lies the dear Partner of my breast
Her cares for a moment at rest!
Must I see thee, my youthful pride,
    Thus brought so very low? –
And it's O, fickle Fortune, O!

There lie my sweet babes in her arms;
No anxious fear their little hearts alarms;
But for their sake my heart does ache,
    With many a bitter throe:
And it's O, fickle Fortune, O!

I once was by Fortune carest,
I once could relieve the distrest,
Now life's poor support, hardly earn'd,
    My fate will scarce bestow:
And it's O, fickle Fortune, O!

No comfort, no comfort I have!
How welcome to me were the grave!
But then my wife and children dear –
    O, whither would they go!
And it's O, fickle Fortune, O!

O, whither, O, whither shall I turn,
All friendless, forsaken, forlorn?
For, in this world, Rest or Peace
    I never more shall know:
And it's O, fickle, Fortune, O!

## MARY MORISON

*TUNE: Duncan Davison*

A girl of this name, daughter of the adjutant of the 104th Regiment, died of consumption at the age of 20 in 1791 and her tombstone can still be seen in Mauchline Kirkyard. The story that she was the subject of this song originated with her sister, who communicated it to the Rev. Dr Edgar of Mauchline. But Burns described it as 'one of my juvenile works', written in 1784-5 (when this girl was barely fourteen) and it is significant that he made no mention of the untimely death of the adjutant's daughter when sending this song to George Thomson. Kinsley shrewdly observed that 'Morison is not an uncommon name, and many Morisons are Marys'. More probably the name, like Peggy Alison (319), was merely invented by Burns to fit the metre.

O Mary, at thy window be!
    It is the wish'd the trysted hour.
Those smiles and glances let me see,
    That make the miser's treasure poor.
How blythely wad I bide the stoure,       *bear the struggle*
    A weary slave frae sun to sun,
Could I the rich reward secure –
    The lovely Mary Morison!

Yestreen, when to the trembling string    *Last night*
    The dance gaed thro the lighted ha',    *went*
To thee my fancy took its wing,
    I sat, but neither heard nor saw:
Tho this was fair, and that was braw,    *fine*
    And yon the toast of a' the town,    *the other*
I sigh'd, and said amang them a' –
    'Ye are na Mary Morison!'

O, Mary, canst thou wreck his peace
    Wha for thy sake wad gladly die?
Or canst thou break that heart of his
    Whase only faut is loving thee?    *fault*
If love for love thou wilt na gie,    *give*
    At least be pity to me shown:
A thought ungentle canna be    *cannot*
    The thought o Mary Morison.

# EPITAPH ON MY OWN FRIEND AND MY FATHER'S FRIEND, WM. MUIR IN TARBOLTON MILL

A true friend of the Burnes family, William Muir (1745-93) gave lodging to Jean Armour in March 1788 when she was cast out by her own family 'banished like a martyr - forlorn, destitute, and friendless'. Burns repaid this kindness by helping Muir's widow, through Gavin Hamilton. This mock epitaph was composed in April 1784 (1CPB). With the seven ensuing epitaphs it was chosen by Burns to complete the Kilmarnock Edition of 1786.

An honest man here lies at rest,
As e'er God with his image blest:
The friend of man, the friend of truth,
The friend of age, and guide of youth:
Few hearts like his – with virtue warm'd,
Few heads with knowledge so inform'd:
If there's another world, he lives in bliss;
If there is none, he made the best of this.

# EPITAPH ON A CELEBRATED RULING ELDER

Dated April 1784 in 1 CPB where it is annotated 'Epitaph on Wm. Hood, Senr. In Tarbolton.'

Here Souter Hood in death does sleep;          Cobbler
    To hell if he's gane thither,
Satan, gie him thy gear to keep;          possessions
    He'll haud it weel thegither.          hold together

# EPITAPH ON A NOISY POLEMIC

The subject of this verse was James Humphrey (1755-1844) a Mauchline stone-mason employed at Lochlie and Mossgiel. He had a smattering of book-learning which induced him to engage in arguments with Burns, but the shallowness of his knowledge resulted in him invariably losing the debate. Humphrey was quite flattered to be the butt of the poet's Muse, and recalled these occasions with affection to Allan Cunningham in 1834.

Below thir stanes lie Jamie's banes:          those
    O Death, it's my opinion,
Thou ne'er took such a bleth'rin bitch          garrulous
    Into thy dark dominion.

# EPITAPH ON 'WEE JOHNIE'

*Hic Jacet wee Johnie*

Though commonly believed that the subject was John Wilson (c. 1751-1839), schoolmaster, grocer, pharmacist and session clerk in Tarbolton, the original of 'Dr. Hornbook' Burns himself identified the Rev. John Kennedy of Ochiltree.

Whoe'er thou art, O reader, know
That Death has murder'd Johnie,
An here his *body* lies fu low;
For saul he ne'er had onie.

# EPITAPH ON MY HONOURED FATHER

One of the group of epitaphs which Burns selected to complete the Kilmarnock Edition, William Burnes died at Lochlie on 13th February 1784.

O ye whose cheek the tear of pity stains,
    Draw near with pious rev'rence, and attend!
Here lie the loving husband's dear remains,
    The tender father, and the gen'rous friend.
The pitying heart that felt for human woe,
    The dauntless heart that fear'd no human pride,
The friend of man – to vice alone a foe;
    For 'ev'n his failings lean'd to virtue's side.'

# EPITAPH FOR ROBERT AIKEN, ESQ.

Robert Aiken, 'Orator Bob' (1739-1807), lawyer in Ayr, a close friend of Burns from 1783, and the recipient of many of the poet's most frank and intimate letters. It was Aiken's spirited defence of Gavin Hamilton before the Presbytery of Ayr in 1785 that inspired 'Holy Willie's Prayer'.

Know thou, O stranger to the fame
Of this much lov'd, much honour'd name!
(For none that knew him need be told)
A warmer heart Death ne'er made cold.

# EPITAPH FOR GAVIN HAMILTON ESQ.

Gavin Hamilton (1751-1805), solicitor in Mauchline who sub-let Mossgiel to the Burns brothers in 1784, encouraged Robert to publish his poems and was the dedicatee of the Kilmarnock Edition. This poetic dedication aligned Burns with the liberals in the struggle between the Auld Lichts and the New Lichts.

> The poor man weeps – here Gavin sleeps,
>     Whom canting wretches blam'd;
> But with such as he, where'er he be,
>     May I be sav'd or damn'd!

# BALLAD ON THE AMERICAN WAR

### TUNE: *Killiecrankie*

Probably written in 1784 in the aftermath of the War of Independence but too politically sensitive for inclusion in the Kilmarnock Edition. In December 1786 Burns wrote: 'I showed the enclosed political ballad to my lord Glencairn, to have his opinion whether I should publish it; as I suspect my political tenets, such as they are, may be rather heretical in the opinion of some of my best Friends.'

| | |
|---|---|
| When Guilford good our pilot stood, | Frederick, Lord North |
|    An did our hellim thraw, man; | helm turn |
| Ae night, at tea, began a plea, | Boston Tea Party, 1773 |
|    Within America, man: | |
| Then up they gat the maskin-pat, | teapot |
|    And in the sea did jaw, man; | dash |
| An did nae less, in full Congress, | Continental Congress 1774-6 |
| Than quite refuse our law, man. | |
| | |
| Then thro the lakes Montgomery takes, | The Great Lakes |
|    I wat he was na slaw, man; | Richard Montgomery |
| Down Lowrie's Burn he took a turn, | St. Lawrence river |
|    And Carleton did ca', man: | Guy Carleton |
| But yet, whatreck, he, at Quebec, | what matter |
|    Montgomery-like did fa', man, | |
| Wi sword in hand, before his band, | |
|    Amang his en'mies a', man. | |

Poor Tammy Gage within a cage      *General Gage, governor*
  Was kept at Boston-ha', man;      *of Massachusetts*
Till Willie Howe took o'er the knowe      *hill, Sir William Howe*
  For Philadelphia, man;
Wi sword an gun he thought a sin
  Guid Christian bluid to draw, man;
But at New-York, wi knife an fork,      *A reference to the seizure of*
  Sir-Loin he hacked sma', man.      *the rebels' cattle at Peekskill*
                            *on Hudson, 1776.*

Burgoyne gaed up, like spur an whip,      *Sir John Burgoyne*
  Till Fraser brave did fa', man;      *Brigadier Simon Fraser*
Then lost his way, ae misty day,
  In Saratoga shaw, man.                  *woods*
Cornwallis fought as lang's he dought,      *could, Charles Cornwallis*
  An did the buckskins claw, man;      *American colonists*
But Clinton's glaive frae rust to save,      *Sir Henry Clinton, sword*
  He hung it to the wa', man.

Then Montague, an Guilford too,      *John Montague,*
  Began to fear a fa', man;      *Earl of Sandwich*
And Sackville doure, wha stood the stoure,      *Lord George Sackville*
  The German chief to thraw, man:      *obstinate, fight*
For Paddy Burke, like onie Turk,      *thwart*
  Nae mercy had at a', man;      *Edmund Burke*
An Charlie Fox threw by the box,      *Charles James Fox*
  An lows'd his tinkler jaw, man.      *let loose*

Then Rockingham took up the game,      *Charles Wentworth,*
  Till death did on him ca', man;      *Marquis of Rockingham*
When Shelburne meek held up his cheek,      *Earl of Shelburne*
  Conform to gospel law, man:
Saint Stephen's boys, wi jarring noise,      *members of the House*
  They did his measures thraw, man;      *of Commons*
For North an Fox united stocks,
  An bore him to the wa', man.

Then clubs an hearts were Charlie's cartes,
  He swept the stakes awa, man,
Till the diamond's ace, of Indian race,      *Fox's East India Bill*
  Led him a sair *faux pas*, man:
The Saxon lads, wi loud placads      *cheers*
  On Chatham's boy did ca', man:      *William Pitt the younger*
An Scotland drew her pipe an blew,
  'Up, Willie, waur them a', man!      *worst*

Behind the throne then Granville's gone,
   A secret word or twa, man;
While slee Dundas arous'd the class
   Be-north the Roman wa', man:
An Chatham's wraith, in heav'nly graith,
   (Inspired bardies saw, man),
Wi kindling eyes, cry'd: 'Willie rise!
   Would I hae fear'd them a', man?'

*William Wyndham,*
*Lord Grenville*
*sly, Henry Dundas*
*North of*
*garments*
*the elder Pitt died in 1778*

But, word an blow, North, Fox, and Co.
   Gowff'd Willie like a ba', man,
Till Suthron raise, an coost their claise
   Behind him in a raw, man:
An Caledon threw by the drone,
   An did her whittle draw, man;
An swoor fu rude, thro dirt an bluid,
   To mak it guid in law, man.

*Golfed*
*rose, cast clothes*
*bagpipes*
*blade*

# ADDRESS TO THE UNCO GUID
## OR THE RIGIDLY RIGHTEOUS

*My Son, these maxims make a rule,*
   *An lump them ay thegither:*
*The Rigid Righteous is a fool,*
   *The Rigid Wise anither;*
*The cleanest corn that e'er was dight*
   *May hae some pyles o caff in;*
*So ne'er a fellow-creature slight*
   *For random fits o daffin.*

*sifted*
*chaff*

*larking*

1 CPB (March 1784) contains two observations: 'that every man even the worst, have something good about them' (*sic*) and 'I have yet found among [Blackguards] some of the noblest Virtues, Magnanimity, Generosity, disinterested friendship and even modesty, in the highest perfection.' In this poem he illustrates the idea of natural sympathy as the root of the moral consciousness.

O ye, wha are sae guid yoursel,
   Sae pious and sae holy,
Ye've nought to do but mark and tell
   Your neebours' fauts and folly!
Whase life is like a weel-gaun mill,
   Supplied wi store o water;
The heapet happer's ebbing still,
   An still the clap plays clatter!

*well-going*

*hopper*
*clapper of a mill*

Hear me, ye venerable core,                     crowd
   As counsel for poor mortals
That frequent pass douce Wisdom's door      sober
   For glaikit Folly's portals:             silly
I for their thoughtless, careless sakes,
   Would here propone defences –        restive
Their donsie tricks, their black mistakes,  unlucky in sexual
Their failings and mischances.           adventures

Ye see your state wi theirs compared,
   And shudder at the niffer;          exchange
But cast a moment's fair regard,
   What maks the mighty differ?
Discount what scant occasion gave;
   That purity ye pride in;
And (what's aft mair than a' the lave)      rest
   Your better art o hidin.

Think, when your castigated pulse
   Gies now and then a wallop,
What ragings must his veins convulse,
   That still eternal gallop!
Wi wind and tide fair i your tail,
   Right on ye scud your sea-way;
But in the teeth o baith to sail,
   It maks an unco lee-way           uncommon

See Social Life and Glee sit down,
   All joyous and unthinking,
Till, quite transmugrify'd, they're grown
   Debauchery and Drinking:
O, would they stay to calculate
   Th' eternal consequences,
Or your more dreaded hell to state –
   Damnation of expenses!

Ye high, exalted, virtuous dames,
   Tied up in godly laces,
Before ye gie poor Frailty names,
   Suppose a change o cases:
A dear-lov'd lad, convenience snug,
   A treach'rous inclination –
But, let me whisper i your lug,          ear
   Ye're aiblins nae temptation.       perhaps

Then gently scan your brother man,
   Still gentler sister woman;
Tho they may gang a kennin wrang,
   To step aside is human:
One point must still be greatly dark,
   The moving *Why* they do it;
And just as lamely can ye mark,
   How far perhaps they rue it.

Who made the heart, 'tis He alone
   Decidedly can try us:
He knows each chord, its various tone,
   Each spring, its various bias:
Then at the balance let's be mute,
   We never can adjust it;
What's done we partly may compute,
   But know not what's resisted.

# THE RONALDS OF THE BENNALS

The Bennals was a 200 acre farm near Lochlie, owned by William Ronald. His daughters Jean and Anne were admired by Robert and Gilbert, but these feelings were not reciprocated. This poem pokes mild fun at the Ronalds and their wealth. They were not connected with the Mauchline tobacconist of the same name who went bankrupt in November 1789 and of whom Burns wrote: 'You will easily guess, that from his insolent vanity in his sunshine of life, he will feel a little retaliation from those who thought themselves eclipsed by him...' The Ronalds continued to prosper at the Bennals till they emigrated to Australia where they farm to this day.

In Tarbolton, ye ken, there are proper young men,
   And proper young lasses and a', man:
But ken ye the Ronalds that live in the Bennals?      know
   They carry the gree frae them a', man.      bear the bell

Their father's a laird, and weel he can spare't,
   Braid money to tocher them a', man:      Broad, to dower
To proper young men, he'll clink in the hand
   Gowd guineas a hunder or twa, man.      Gold

There's ane they ca' Jean, I'll warrant ye've seen
   As bonie a lass or as braw, man;      well set up
But for sense and guid taste she'll vie wi the best,
   And a conduct that beautifies a', man.

The charms o the min', the langer they shine
    The mair admiration they draw, man;
While peaches and cherries, and roses and lilies,
    They fade and they wither awa, man.

If ye be for Miss Jean, tak this frae a frien',
    A hint o a rival or twa, man:
The Laird o Blackbyre wad gang through the fire,     *would go*
    If that wad entice her awa, man.

The Laird o Braehead has been on his speed,
    For mair than a towmond or twa, man:     *twelve months*
The Laird o the Ford will straught on a board,     *stretch*
    If he canna get her at a', man.

Then Anna comes in, the pride o her kin,
    The boast of our bachelors a', man:
Sae sonsy and sweet, sae fully complete,     *pleasant*
    She steals our affections awa, man.

If I should detail the pick and the wale     *choice*
    O lasses that live here awa, man,     *around*
The faut wad be mine, if they didna shine     *fault*
    The sweetest and best o them a', man.

I lo'e her mysel, but darena weel tell,
    My poverty keeps me in awe, man;
For making o rhymes, and working at times,
    Does little or naething at a', man.

Yet I wadna choose to let her refuse     *would not*
    Nor hae't in her power to say na, man:     *have it*
For though I be poor, unnoticed, obscure,
    My stomach's as proud as them a', man.

Though I canna ride in weel-booted pride,
    And flee o'er the hills like a craw, man,
I can haud up my head wi the best o the breed,     *hold*
    Though fluttering ever so braw, man.     *fine*

My coat and my vest, they are Scotch o the best;
    O pairs o guid breeks I hae twa, man,     *breeches*
And stockings and pumps to put on my stumps,
    And ne'er a wrang steek in them a', man.     *stitch*

My sarks they are few, but five o them new –        *shirts*
    Twal' hundred, as white as the snaw, man!
A ten-shillings hat, a Holland cravat –     *fine linen necktie*
    There are no monie Poets sae braw, man!    *well dressed*

I never had frien's weel stockit in means,    *well endowed*
    To leave me a hundred or twa, man;
Nae weel-tocher'd aunts, to wait on their drants, *prosings, -dowered*
    And wish them in hell for it a', man.

I never was cannie for hoarding o money,    *careful*
    Or claughtin't together at a', man;    *grasping it*
I've little to spend and naething to lend,
    But devil a shilling I awe, man.    *owe*

# THE TARBOLTON LASSES

Composed in 1784, at the same time as the preceding. Faile is a hamlet in Tarbolton parish.

If ye gae up to yon hill-tap,
    Ye'll there see bonie Peggy:
She kens her father is a laird,
    And she forsooth's a leddy.    *lady*

There's Sophy tight, a lassie bright,    *prepared or dressed*
    Besides a handsome fortune:
Wha canna win her in a night,
    Has little art in courtin.

Gae down by Faile, and taste the ale,
    And tak a look o Mysie:
She's dour and din, a deil within,    *stubborn, swarthy*
    But aiblins she may please ye.    *perhaps*

If she be shy, her sister try,
    Ye'll may be fancy Jenny:
If ye'll dispense wi want o sense
    She kens herself she's bonie.

As ye gae up by yon hillside,                             *that*
    Spier in for bonie Bessy:                        *call*
She'll gie ye a beck, and bid ye light,           *curtsy*
    And handsomely address ye.

There's few sae bonie, nane sae guid
    In a' King George' dominion:
If ye should doubt the truth o this,
    It's Bessy's ain opinion!

# THE BELLES OF MAUCHLINE

*TUNE: Bonie Dundee*

Written about 1784-5 about Helen Miller (b.1762) and her sister Betty (b. 1768), Jean
Markland (b. 1765), Jean Smith (sister of James) (b. 1767), Christina Morton (b. 1768)
and, of course, Jean Armour (1765-1834) herself.

In Mauchline there dwells six proper young belles,
    The pride of the place and its neighbourhood a',
Their carriage and dress, a stranger would guess,
    In Lon'on or Paris, they'd gotten it a'.

Miss Miller is fine, Miss Markland's divine,
    Miss Smith she has wit, and Miss Betty is braw,        *elegant*
There's beauty and fortune to get wi Miss Morton,
    But Armour's the jewel for me o them a'.

# O, LEAVE NOVELS

*TUNE: Donald Blue*

Probably composed in 1784-5, before Burns turned his attention to Jean Armour.

O, leave novéls, ye Mauchline belles –
    Ye're safer at your spinning-wheel!
Such witching books are baited hooks
    For rakish rooks like Rob Mossgiel.

Your fine *Tom Jones and Grandisons*,
  They make your youthful fancies reel!
They heat your brains, and fire your veins,
  And then you're prey for Rob Mossgiel.

Beware a tongue that's smoothly hung,
  A heart that warmly seems to feel!
That feeling heart but acts a part –
  'Tis rakish art in Rob Mossgiel.

The frank address, the soft caress,
  Are worse than poisoned darts of steel:
The frank address, and politesse,
  Are all finesse in Rob Mossgiel.

## THE MAUCHLINE LADY

*TUNE: I had a horse, and I had nae mair*

The lady of this poem is thought to have been Jean Armour herself. 'Stewart Kyle' alludes
to the Burns family's move to Lochlie in 1777. The move to Mossgiel took place in
February 1784.

When first I came to Stewart Kyle,
  My mind it was na steady:
Where'er I gaed, where'er I rade,                          went, rode
  A mistress still I had ay.

But when I cam roun' by Mauchline toun,
  Not dreadin anybody,
My heart was caught, before I thought,
  And by a Mauchline lady.

# GREEN GROW THE RASHES, O

Derived from the ancient ballad 'Cou thou me the raschyes grene' first published in 1549, with other versions set down in 1627 and 1740. Burns's version appears in 1 CPB following a prose musing on categorizing young men into the grave and the merry.

### CHORUS

*Green grow the rashes, O;*
*Green grow the rashes, O;*
*The sweetest hours that e'er I spend,*
*Are spent among the lasses, O.*


There's nought but care on ev'ry han',
    In every hour that passes, O:
What signifies the life o man,
    An 'twere na for the lasses, O.

The war'ly race may riches chase,             *worldly*
    An riches still may fly them, O;
An tho at last they catch them fast,
    Their hearts can ne'er enjoy them, O.

But gie me a cannie hour at e'en,         *quiet, evening*
    My arms about my dearie, O,
An war'ly cares an war'ly men,
    May a' gae tapsalteerie, O!         *topsy-turvy*

For you sae douce, ye sneer at this;       *sober*
    Ye're nought but senseless asses, O:
The wisest man the warl' e'er saw,
    He dearly lov'd the lasses, O.

Auld Nature swears, the lovely dears
    Her noblest work she classes, O:
Her prentice han' she try'd on man,
    An then she made the lasses, O.

# MY GIRL SHE'S AIRY

*TUNE: Black Joke*

Composed in 1784, during the poet's brief affair with Elizabeth Paton of Lairgieside. The affair blossomed after the death of William Burnes. The result of this liaison was 'Dear-bought Bess', the poet's first illegitimate child, born on 22nd May 1785. The Black Joke of the tune title was a bawdy name for the female genitalia.

My girl she's airy, she's buxom and gay;
Her breath is as sweet as the blossoms in May;
   A touch of her lips it ravishes quite.
She's always good natur'd, good humour'd and free;
She dances, she glances, she smiles with a glee;
   Her eyes are the lightenings of joy and delight;
Her slender neck, her handsome waist,
Her hair well buckled, her stays well lac'd,
   Her taper white leg with an et, and a, c,      etcetera (i.e.
For her a, b, e, d, and her c, u, n, t,      other charms)
And oh, for the joys of a long winter night!!!

# EPISTLE TO JOHN RANKINE

## *ENCLOSING SOME POEMS*

The tenant-farmer of Adamhill near Tarbolton, Rankine (died 1810) was a close friend of Burns in the latter part of the Lochlie period. He discovered early on that Elizabeth Paton was pregnant by Burns and twitted the poet about it. Burns retaliated with these verses, using the analogy of the poacher to describe his adulterous activities.

O rough, rude, ready-witted Rankine,
The wale o cocks for fun an drinkin!      pick
There's monie godly folks are thinkin
   Your dreams and tricks
Will send you, Korah-like, a-sinkin      Num. xvi 29-33
   Straught to Auld Nick's.

Ye hae sae monie cracks an cants,      anecdotes
And in your wicked drucken rants,      drunken ravings
Ye mak a devil o the saunts,
   An fill them fou;
And then their failings, flaws, an wants,
   Are a' seen thro.

Hypocrisy, in mercy spare it!
That holy robe, O, dinna tear it!
Spare't for their sakes, wha aften wear it –
    The lads in black;
But your curst wit, when it comes near it,
    Rives't aff their back.                      *rips*

Think, wicked sinner, wha ye're skaithing:    *injuring*
It's just the Blue-gown badge an claithing
O saunts;  tak that, ye lea'e them naething
    To ken them by
Frae onie unregenerate heathen,
    Like you or I.

I've sent you here some rhymin ware,
A' that I bargain'd for, an mair;
Sae, when ye hae an hour to spare,
    I will expect,
Yon sang ye'll sen't, wi cannie care,    *send it*
    And no neglect.

Tho faith, sma' heart hae I to sing:
My muse dow scarcely spread her wing!    *can*
I've play'd mysel a bonie spring,    *melody*
    An danc'd my fill!
I'd better gaen an sair't the King    *have gone, served*
    At Bunker's Hill.    *one of the first battles*
          *in the American War*

'Twas ae night lately, in my fun,
I gaed a rovin wi the gun,    *went*
An brought a paitrick to the grun' –    *partridge*
    A bonie hen;
And, as the twilight was begun,
    Thought nane wad ken.    *know*

The poor, wee thing was little hurt;
I straikit it a wee for sport,    *stroked a little*
Ne'er thinkin they wad fash me for't;    *worry*
    But Deil-ma-care!
Somebody tells the Poacher-Court    *Kirk Session*
    The hale affair.    *whole*

Some auld, us'd hands had taen a note,
That sic a hen had got a shot;
I was suspected for the plot;
 I scorn'd to lie;
So gat the whissle o my groat,     lost my fourpence
 An pay't the fee.

But, by my gun, o guns the wale,     pick
An by my pouther an my hail,     gunpowder
An by my hen, an by her tail,
 I vow an swear!
The game shall pay, owre moor an dale,
 For this, niest year!       next

As soon's the clockin-time is by,    incubation
An the wee pouts begun to cry,     chicks
Lord, I'se hae sportin by an by     I'll
 For my gowd guinea;
Tho I should herd the buckskin kye  American cattle
 For't, in Virginia!

Trowth, they had muckle for to blame!
'Twas neither broken wing nor limb,
But twa-three chaps about the wame,  blows, belly
 Scarce thro the feathers;
An baith a yellow George to claim   a guinea
 An thole their blethers!   tolerate nonsense

It pits me ay as mad's a hare;
So I can rhyme nor write nae mair;
But pennyworths again is fair,    tit-for-tat
 When time's expedient:
Meanwhile, I am, respected Sir,
 Your most obedient.

## EPITAPH ON JOHN RANKINE

Composed in 1785 as a sequel to the preceding Epistle.

| | |
|---|---|
| Ae day, as Death, that gruesome carl, | One, fellow |
| Was driving to the tither warl' | other world |
| A mixtie-maxtie motley squad, | jumbled |
| And monie a guilt-bespotted lad: | |
| Black gowns of each denomination, | preachers |
| And thieves of every rank and station, | lawyers |
| From him that wears the star and garter, | |
| To him that wintles in a halter: | dangles on a noose |
| Asham'd himself to see the wretches, | |
| He mutters, glowrin at the bitches: – | |
| 'By God I'll not be seen behint them, | |
| Nor 'mang the sp'ritual core present them, | crowd |
| Without at least ae honest man, | |
| To grace this damn'd infernal clan!' | |
| By Adamhill a glance he threw, | |
| 'Lord God!' quoth he, 'I have it now, | |
| There's just the man I want, i faith!' | |
| And quickly stoppit Rankine's breath. | |

## REPLY TO AN ANNOUNCEMENT BY JOHN RANKINE

Allegedly the poet's answer to Rankine's reactions on learning that Elizabeth Paton was expecting his child.

| | |
|---|---|
| I am a keeper of the law | |
| In some sma' points, altho not a'; | |
| Some people tell me, gin I fa' | if I fall |
| Ae way or ither | one, other |
| The breaking of ae point, tho sma' | |
| Breaks a' thegither. | together |
| | |
| I hae been in for't ance or twice, | |
| And winna say o'er far for thrice, | will not, too certainly |
| Yet never met wi that surprise | |
| That broke my rest. | |
| But now a rumour's like to rise – | |
| A whaup's i the nest! | curlew |

# EPITAPH ON THE AUTHOR

This mock epitaph probably belongs to the Mossgiel period.

He who of Rankine sang, lies stiff and deid,
And a green grassy hillock hides his heid:
Alas! alas! a devilish change indeed!

# EPISTLE TO DAVIE, A BROTHER POET

### JANUARY

David Sillar (1760-1830) was the third of the four sons of Patrick Sillar of Spittalside near Lochlie. Though self-educated he ran his own school. He was a member of the Tarbolton Bachelors' Club. His own inferior verses were published at Kilmarnock in 1789.

| | |
|---|---|
| While winds frae aff Ben-Lomond blaw, | |
| And bar the doors wi drivin snaw, | |
| And hing us owre the ingle, | hang over fire |
| I set me down to pass the time, | |
| And spin a verse or twa o rhyme, | |
| In hamely, westlin jingle: | western |
| While frosty winds blaw in the drift, | |
| Ben to the chimla lug, | Right to the chimney corner |
| I grudge a wee the great-folk's gift, | a little |
| That live sae bien an snug: | prosperous |
| I tent less, and want less | value |
| Their roomy fire-side; | |
| But hanker, and canker, | |
| To see their cursed pride. | |

| | |
|---|---|
| It's hardly in a body's pow'r, | |
| To keep, at times, frae being sour, | |
| To see how things are shar'd; | |
| How best o chiels are whyles in want, | chaps, sometimes |
| While coofs on countless thousands rant, | fools, roister |
| And ken na how to ware't; | spend |
| But, Davie, lad, ne'er fash your head | trouble |
| Tho we hae little gear; | wealth |
| We're fit to win our daily bread, | |
| As lang's we're hale and fier: | sound |
| 'Mair spier na, nor fear na,' | |
| Auld age ne'er mind a feg; | fig |
| The last o't, the warst o't, | |
| Is only but to beg. | |

To lie in kilns and barns at e'en,
When banes are craz'd, and bluid is thin,
   Is, doubtless, great distress!
Yet then content could make us blest;
Ev'n then, sometimes, we'd snatch a taste
   Of truest happiness.
The honest heart that's free frae a'
   Intended fraud or guile,
However Fortune kick the ba',
   Has ay some cause to smile;
      And mind still, you'll find still,
     A comfort this nae sma';
   Nae mair then, we'll care then,
    Nae farther we can fa'.

What tho, like commoners of air,
We wander out, we know not where,
   But either house or hal'?              *without (small) holding*
Yet Nature's charms, the hills and woods,
The sweeping vales, and foaming floods,
   Are free alike to all.
In days when daisies deck the ground,
   And blackbirds whistle clear,
With honest joy our hearts will bound,
   To see the coming year:
      On braes when we please then,          *slopes*
       We'll sit an sowth a tune;           *hum*
      Syne rhyme till't, we'll time till't,      *Then*
       An sing't when we hae done.

It's no in titles nor in rank:
It's no in wealth like Lon'on Bank,
   To purchase peace and rest,
It's no in makin muckle, mair;                  *much, more*
It's no in books, it's no in lear,              *learning*
   To make us truly blest:
If happiness hae not her seat
   An centre in the breast,
We may be wise, or rich, or great,
   But never can be blest!
   Nae treasures nor pleasures
     Could make us happy lang;
   The heart ay's the part ay
    That makes us right or wrang.

Think ye, that sic as you and I,
Wha drudge and drive thro wet and dry,
   Wi never ceasing toil;
Think ye, are we less blest than they,
Wha scarcely tent us in their way,
   As hardly worth their while?
Alas! how oft in haughty mood,
   God's creatures they oppress!
Or else, neglecting a' that's guid,
   They riot in excess!
      Baith careless and fearless
        Of either Heaven or Hell;
      Esteeming and deeming
        It's a' an idle tale!

Then let us cheerfu acquiesce,
Nor make our scanty pleasures less
   By pining at our state:
And, even should misfortunes come
I here wha sit, hae met wi some,
   An's thankfu for them yet,               And am
They gie the wit of age to youth;
   They let us ken oursel;
They make us see the naked truth –
   The real guid and ill:
      Tho losses and crosses
        Be lessons right severe,
      There's wit there, ye'll get there,
        Ye'll find nae other where.

But tent me, Davie, ace o hearts!           listen to
(To say aught less wad wrang the cartes,    anything, cards
   And flatt'ry I detest)
This life has joys for you and I;
And joys that riches ne'er could buy,
   And joys the very best.
There's a' the pleasures o the heart,
   The lover an the frien:
Ye hae your Meg, your dearest part,
   And I my darling Jean!
      It warms me, it charms me
        To mention but her name:
      It heats me, it beets me,             kindles
        An sets me a' on flame!

O all ye Pow'rs who rule above!
O Thou whose very self art love!
   Thou know'st my words sincere!
The life-blood streaming thro my heart,
Or my more dear immortal part,
   Is not more fondly dear!
When heart-corroding care and grief
   Deprive my soul of rest,
Her dear idea brings relief,
   And solace to my breast.
     Thou Being, All-seeing,
       O, hear my fervent pray'r!
     Still take her, and make her
       Thy most peculiar care!

All hail! ye tender feelings dear!
The smile of love, the friendly tear,
   The sympathetic glow!
Long since, this world's thorny ways
Had number'd out my weary days,
   Had it not been for you!
Fate still has blest me with a friend
   In every care and ill;
And oft a more endearing band,
   A tie more tender still.
     It lightens, it brightens
       The tenebrific scene,
     To meet with, and greet with
       My Davie, or my Jean!

O, how that Name inspires my style!
The words come skelpin rank an file,       *spanking*
   Amaist before I ken!       *Almost, know*
The ready measure rins as fine,
As Phoebus an the famous Nine,
   Were glowrin owre my pen.       *watching over*
My spaviet Pegasus will limp,       *spavined*
   Till ance he's fairly het;       *hot*
And then he'll hilch, an stilt, and jimp,       *hobble, limp, jump*
   And rin an unco fit;       *uncommon burst*
But least then the beast then
   Should rue this hasty ride,
I'll light now, and dight now       *wipe*
   His sweaty, wizen'd hide.

# THE TWA HERDS: OR, THE HOLY TULZIE

Squabble

### AN UNCO MOURNFU TALE

unduly

*Blockheads with reason, wicked wits abhor,*
*But fool with fool is barbarous civil war.*—POPE

This satirical lamentation was based on the unseemly quarrel over parish boundaries, between two Auld Licht ministers, Alexander Moodie of Riccarton and John Russell of Kilmarnock. Matters came to a head at the Presbytery of Irvine 'where the reverend divines..lost all command of temper and abused each other, with a fiery virulence of invective.' Scottish liberals were abused as Arminians, named after Arminius of Leyden (1609) who opposed Calvinism.

O a' ye pious godly flocks,
Weel fed on pastures orthodox,
Wha now will keep you frae the fox,
    Or worrying tykes?     *dogs*
Or wha will tent the waifs an crocks,     *tend, stragglers*
    About the dykes?     *and old ewes,*
        *stone fences*

The twa best herds in a' the wast,     *shepherds, west*
That e'er gae gospel horn a blast     *gave*
These five an twenty simmers past –
    O, dool to tell! –     *sad*
Hae had a bitter, black out-cast     *quarrel*
    Atween themsel.     *Between*

O Moodie, man, an wordy Russell,
How could you raise so vile a bustle?
Ye'll see how New-Light herds will whistle,
    An think it fine!
The Lord's cause gat na sic a twistle     *such a twist*
    Sin I hae min'.     *can recall*

O Sirs! whae'er wad hae expeckit
Your duty ye wad sae negleckit?     *would have so*
Ye wha were no by lairds respeckit
    To wear the plaid,
But by the brutes themselves eleckit,
    To be their guide!

What flock wi Moodie's flock could rank
Sae hale an hearty every shank?
Nae poison'd, soor Arminian stank     *leg*
    He let them taste;     *stagnant pool*
Frae Calvin's fountain-head they drank,'
    O, sic a feast!

The thummart, wilcat, brock, an tod             polecat, wildcat,
Weel kend his voice thro a' the wood;           badger and fox
He smell'd their ilka hole an road,                  every
     Baith out an in;
An weel he lik'd to shed their bluid,
     An sell their skin.

What herd like Russell tell'd his tale?
His voice was heard thro muir and dale;
He ken'd the Lord's sheep, ilka tail,
     O'er a' the height;
An tell'd gin they were sick or hale,                   if
     At the first sight.

He fine a mangy sheep could scrub;
Or nobly fling the gospel club;
Or New-Light herds could nicely drub
     And pay their skin;
Or hing them o'er the burning dub,           hang, puddle
     Or heave them in.

Sic twa – O! do I live to see't? –
Sic famous twa sud disagree't,               should have
An names like villain, hypocrite,
     Ilk ither gi'en                        each other
While New-Light herds, wi laughin spite,
     Say neither's liein!                 lying

A' ye wha tent the gospel fauld,           pay heed to
Thee Duncan deep, an Peebles shaul',       shallow
But chiefly great apostle Auld,        Robert Duncan
     We trust in thee,            (1753-1815)
That thou wilt work them, hot an cauld,    William Peebles
     Till they agree!            (1753-1826)

Consider, sirs, how we're beset:
There's scarce a new herd that we get
But comes frae 'mang that cursed set,
     I winna name:                 will not
I hope frae heav'n to see them yet
     In fiery flame!           William Dalrymple
                                (1723-1814); William
                                McGill (1732-1807);
Dalrymple had been lang our fae,       William McQuhae
M'Gill has wrought us meikle wae,    (1737-1823); David (1719
An that curs'd rascal ca'd M'Quhae,   -1810) and Andrew (1741-
     An baith the Shaws,           1805)
That aft hae made us black an blae,
     Wi vengeful paws.

Auld Wodrow lang has hatch'd mischief:                Patrick Wodrow
We thought ay death wad bring relief,                         (1713-93)
But he has gotten to our grief,
    Ane to succeed him,
A chield wha'll soundly buff our beef –            chap, strike our flesh
    I meikle dread him.                                            greatly

And monie mae that I could tell,
Wha fain would openly rebel,
Forby turn-coats amang oursel:                                Besides
    There's Smith for ane –              George Smith (d. 1823)
I doubt he's but a greyneck still,                             gambler
    An that ye'll fin'!

O! a' ye flocks o'er a' the hills,
By mosses, meadows, moors, an fells,              bogs, hillsides
Come, join your counsel and your skills
    To cowe the lairds,                                        frighten
An get the brutes the power themsels
    To chuse their herds!

Then Orthodoxy yet may prance,
An Learning in a woody dance,                        hangman's noose
An that fell cur ca'd Common-sense,                     formidable
    That bites sae sair
Be banished o'er the sea to France –
    Let him bark there!

Then Shaw's an D'rymple's eloquence,
M'Gill's close, nervous excellence,
M'Quhae's pathetic, manly sense,
    An guid M'Math,                     John McMath (1755-1825)
Wha thro the heart can brawly glance,
    May a' pack aff!

## HOLY WILLIE'S PRAYER

*And send the godly in a pet to pray* - POPE

The prototype of this burlesque prayer was William Fisher (1737-1809) of Montgarswood, an elder of Mauchline parish at whose instigation the Kirk Session took action against Gavin Hamilton for failure to observe the Sabbath in the proper manner. Burns described Fisher as 'a rather oldish bachelor, much and justly famed for that polemical chattering which ends in tippling orthodoxy, and for that spiritualised bawdry which refines to liquorish devotion.'

O Thou that in the Heavens does dwell,
Wha, as it pleases best Thysel,
Sends ane to Heaven, an ten to Hell,
   A' for Thy glory,
And no for onie guid or ill
   They've done before Thee!

I bless and praise Thy matchless might,
When thousands Thou hast left in night,
That I am here before They sight,
   For gifts an grace
A burning and a shining light
   To a' this place.

What was I, or my generation,
That I should get sic exaltation?          such
I, wha deserv'd most just damnation
   For broken laws,
Sax thousand years ere my creation,      Six
   Thro Adam's cause!

When from my mither's womb I fell,
Thou might hae plung'd me deep in Hell,
To gnash my gooms, and weep and wail,   gums
   In burning lakes,
Whare damned devils roar and yell,
   Chain'd to their stakes.

Yet I am here a chosen sample,
To show Thy grace is great and ample:
I'm here a pillar o Thy temple,
   Strong as a rock,
A guide, a buckler, and example,     shield
   To a' Thy flock!

But yet, O Lord! confess I must,
At times I'm fash'd wi fleshly lust;     irked
An sometimes, too, in warldly trust,
   Vile self gets in;
But Thou remembers we are dust,
   Defil'd wi sin.

O Lord! yestreen, Thou kens, wi Meg –        *last night*
Thy pardon I sincerely beg –
O, may't ne'er be a livin plague
    To my dishonour!
An I'll ne'er lift a lawless leg
    Again upon her.

Besides, I farther maun avow,        *must*
Wi Leezie's lass, three times I trow –
But, Lord, that Friday I was fou,        *drunk*
    When I cam near her,
Or else, Thou kens, Thy servant true
    Wad never steer her.        *would, meddle with*

Maybe Thou lets this fleshly thorn
Buffet Thy servant e'en and morn,
Lest he owre proud and high should turn,
    That he's sae gifted:
If sae, Thy han' maun e'en be borne,
    Until Thou lift it.

Lord, bless Thy chosen in this place,
For here Thou has a chosen race!
But God confound their stubborn face,
    An blast their name,
Wha bring Thy elders to disgrace
    An open shame.

Lord, mind Gau'n Hamilton's deserts:
He drinks, an swears, an plays at cartes,        *cards*
Yet has sae monie takin arts,        *many*
    Wi great and sma',
Frae God's ain Priest the people's hearts
    He steals awa.

And when we chasten'd him therefore,
Thou kens how he bred sic a splore,        *row*
And set the warld in a roar
    O laughin at us;
Curse Thou his basket and his store,
    Kail an potatoes!

Lord, hear my earnest cry and pray'r,
Against that Presbyt'ry o Ayr!
Thy strong right hand, Lord, mak it bare
    Upo' their heads!
Lord, visit them, an dinna spare,        *do not*
    For their misdeeds!

O Lord, my God! that glib-tongu'd Aiken,    Robert Aiken
My vera heart and flesh are quakin,
To think how we stood sweatin, shakin,
    An pish'd wi dread,
While he, wi hingin lip, an snakin,    sneering
    Held up his head.

Lord, in Thy day o vengeance try him!
Lord, visit them wha did employ him!
And pass not in Thy mercy by them,
    Nor hear their pray'r,
But for Thy people's sake destroy them,
    An dinna spare.

But, Lord, remember me and mine
Wi mercies temporal and divine,
That I for grace an gear may shine,    wealth
    Excell'd by nane,
And a' the glory shall be Thine –
    Amen, Amen!

## EPITAPH ON HOLY WILLIE

Here Holy Willie's sair worn clay    very
    Taks up its last abode;
His saul has ta'en some other way –    soul
    I fear, the left-hand road.

Stop! there he is as sure's a gun!
    Poor, silly body, see him!
Nae wonder he's as black's the grun –    ground
    Observe wha's standing wi him!

Your brunstane Devilship, I see    brimstone
    Has got him there before ye!
But haud your nine-tail cat a wee,    hold back a little
    Till ance you've heard my story.    once

Your pity I will not implore,
    For pity ye have nane.
Justice, alas! has gi'en him o'er,
    And mercy's day is gane.

But hear me, Sir, Deil as ye are,
    Look something to your credit:
A cuif like him wad stain your name,    blockhead
    If it were kent ye did it!

# DEATH AND DOCTOR HORNBOOK

## A TRUE STORY

The prototype was John Wilson (c.1751-1839), appointed schoolmaster at Tarbolton in 1781. A hornbook consisted of a sheet of paper bearing the alphabet, numbers, Lord's Prayer and rules of spelling, mounted on a wooden board and protected by a thin plate of transparent horn. This primitive teaching aid was in widespread use till about 1800. 'Hornbook' thus became a popular nickname for schoolmasters. Burns was inspired to write this satire in 1785 after hearing Wilson airing this medical knowledge at a meeting of Tarbolton Masonic Lodge.

Some books are lies frae end to end,
And some great lies were never penn'd:
Ev'n ministers, they hae been kend,
 In holy rapture,
A rousing whid at times to vend,          lie
 And nail't wi Scripture.

But this that I am gaun to tell,            going
Which lately on a night befel,
Is just as true's the Deil's in Hell
 Or Dublin city:
That e'er he nearer comes oursel
 'S a muckle pity!

The clachan yill had made me canty,      village ale, jolly
I was na fou, but just had plenty:         drunk
I stacher'd whyles, but yet took tent ay   staggered sometimes
 To free the ditches;         took care to avoid
An hillocks, stanes, an bushes, kend ay      always
 Frae ghaists an witches.

The rising moon began to glowr         stare
The distant Cumnock Hills out-owre:       above
To count her horns, wi a' my pow'r,
 I set mysel;
But whether she had three or four,
 I cou'd na tell.

I was come round about the hill,
An todlin down on Willie's mill,
Setting my staff wi a' my skill,
 To keep me sicker;           steady
Tho leeward whyles, against my will,
 I took a bicker.            run

I there wi *Something* does forgather,
That pat me in an eerie swither;     put, ghostly panic
An awfu scythe, out-owre ae shouther,   across one shoulder
 Clear-dangling, hang;
A three-tae'd leister on the ither       trident
 Lay, large an lang.

BURNS STATUE SQUARE, AYR

BURNS IN EDINBURGH by C.M. Hardie

Its stature seem'd lang Scotch ells twa,                    metres
The queerest shape that e'er I saw,
For fient a wame it had ava;                    not a belly at all
    And then its shanks,                    legs
They were as thin, as sharp an sma'
    As cheeks o branks.                    horse-bridle bits

'Guid-e'en', quo I; 'Friend! hae ye been mawin,    Good evening, said
When ither folk are busy sawin?'
It seem'd to mak a kind o stan,                    halt
    But naething spak.
At length, says I, 'Friend! whare ye gaun?
    Will ye go back?'

It spak right howe, – 'My name is *Death*,                    hollow
But be na fley'd' – Quoth I, 'Guid faith,                    frightened
Ye're may be come to stap my breath;
    But tent me, billie:                    heed, comrade
I red ye weel, tak care o skaith,                    counsel, injury
    See, there's a gully!'                    large knife

'Gudeman,' quo he, 'put up your whittle,    Tenant farmer, blade
I'm no design'd to try its mettle;
But if I did, I wad be kittle                    ticklish
    To be mislear'd:                    mischievous
I wad na mind it, no that spittle
    Out-owre my beard.'

'Weel, weel!' says I, 'a bargain be't;
Come, gie's your hand, an sae we're gree't;                    agreed
We'll ease our shanks, an tak a seat:
    Come, gie's your news:
This while ye hae been monie a gate,                    road
    At monie a house.'

'Ay, ay!' quo he, an shook his head,
'It's e'en a lang, lang time indeed
Sin' I began to nick the thread,                    cut
    An choke the breath:
Folk maun do something for their bread,
    An sae maun *Death*.'

'Sax thousand years are near-hand fled                    well-nigh
Sin' I was to the butching bred,                    butchery
An monie a scheme in vain's been laid,
    To stap or scar me;                    scare
Till ane Hornbook's ta'en up the trade,
    An faith! he'll waur me.'                    get the better of

'Ye ken Jock Hornbook i the clachan?
Deil mak his king's-hood in a spleuchan! –    *scrotum, tobacco-pouch*
He's grown sae weel acquaint wi *Buchan*    *Dr. William Buchan*
   And ither chaps,    *(1729-1805) author*
The weans haud out their fingers laughin,    *of Domestic Medicine*
   An pouk my hips.'    *children, poke*

'See, here's a scythe, an there's a dart,
They hae pierc'd monie a gallant heart;
But Doctor Hornbook wi his art
   An cursed skill,
Has made them baith no worth a fart,
   Damn'd haet they'll kill!'    *The devil a one*

'Twas but yestreen, nae farther gane,    *gone*
I threw a noble throw at ane;
Wi less, I'm sure, I've hundreds slain;
   But Deil-ma' care!
It just play'd dirl on the bane,    *tinkle*
   But did nae mair.'

'Hornbook was by wi ready art,
An had sae fortify'd the part,
That when I looked to my dart,
   It was sae blunt,
Fient haet o't wad hae pierc'd the heart
   Of a kail-runt.'    *cabbage-stalk*

'I drew my scythe in sic a fury,
I near-hand cowpit wi my hurry,    *tumbled*
But yet the bauld Apothecary
   Withstood the shock;
I might as weel hae try'd a quarry
   O hard whin-rock.'    *granite*

'Ev'n them he canna get attended,
Altho their face he ne'er had kend it,    *known*
Just shite in a kail-blade, an send it,    *cabbage-leaf*
   As soon's he smells 't,
Baith their disease, and what will mend it,
   At once he tells 't.'

'And then a' doctor's saws and whittles,    *scalpels*
Of a' dimensions, shapes and mettles,
A' kinds o boxes, mugs, and bottles,
   He's sure to hae;
Their Latin names as fast he rattles
   As A B C.'

'Calces o fossils, earths, and trees;
True *sal-marinum* o the seas:
The *farina* of beans an pease,
   He has't in plenty;
*Aqua-fontis*, what you please,
   He can content ye.'

'Forbye some new, uncommon weapons,
*Urinus spiritus* of capons;
Or mite-horn shavings, filings, scrapings,
   Distill'd *per se*;
*Sal-alkali* o midge-tail-clippings,
   And monie mae.'                 *many more*

'Waes me for Johnie Ged's Hole now,'
Quoth I, 'if that thae news be true!          *these*
His braw calf-ward whare gowans grew,   *pasture, daisies*
   Sae white and bonie,
Nae doubt they'll rive it wi the plew:     *split, plough*
   They'll ruin Johnie!'

The creature grain'd an eldritch laugh,   *groaned, unearthly*
And says: 'Ye needna yoke the pleugh,
Kirkyards will soon be till'd eneugh,
   Tak ye nae fear:
They'll a' be trench'd wi monie a sheugh,     *ditch*
   In twa-three year.'

'Whare I kill'd ane, a fair strae death     *straw [bed]*
By loss o blood or want o breath,
This night I'm free to tak my aith,
   That Hornbook's skill
Has clad a score i their last claith,      *cloth*
   By drap an pill.'                 *drop*

'An honest wabster to his trade,      *weaver*
Whase wife's twa nieves were scarce weel-bred   *fists*
Gat tippence-worth to mend her head,
   When it was sair;
The wife slade cannie to her bed,      *aching*
   But ne'er spak mair.'      *crept quietly*

'A countra laird had ta'en the batts,      *colic*
Or some curmurring in his guts,      *commotion*
His only son for Hornbook sets,
   An pays him well:
The lad, for twa guid gimmer-pets      *pet ewes*
   Was laird himsel.'

'A bonie lass – ye kend her name –
Some ill-brewn drink had hov'd her wame;    upset, stomach
She trusts hersel, to hide the shame,
 In Hornbook's care;
Horn set her aff to her lang hame
 To hide it there.

'That's just a swatch o Hornbook's way;     sample
Thus goes he on from day to day,
Thus does he poison, kill, an slay,
 An's weel paid for't;
Yet stop me o my lawfu prey,
 Wi his damn'd dirt.'

'But hark! I'll tell you of a plot,
Tho dinna ye be speakin o't!
I'll nail the self-conceited sot,
 As dead's a herrin;
Niest time we meet, I'll wad a groat,   Next, wager fourpence
 He gets his fairin!'         reward

But just as he began to tell,
The auld kirk-hammer strak the bell
Some wee short hour ayont the twal,    beyond twelve
 Which rais'd us baith:      got us on our feet
I took the way that pleas'd mysel,
 And sae did *Death*.


# ON TAM THE CHAPMAN

Written about Thomas Kennedy of Ayr who died in Homor, Courtland County, New York
in 1846.

As Tam the chapman on a day        pedlar
Wi death forgather'd by the way,
Weel pleas'd, he greets a wight so famous,   sturdy person
And Death was nae less pleas'd wi Thomas,
Wha cheerfully lays down his pack,
And there blaws up a hearty crack:    conversation
His social, friendly, honest heart
Sae tickled Death, they could na part;
Sae, after viewing knives and garters,
Death taks him hame to gie him quarters.

# EPISTLE TO J. LAPRAIK

## AN OLD SCOTTISH BARD – APRIL 1, 1785

John Lapraik (1727-1807), farmer of Dalfram, Muirkirk, nine miles from Mauchline. The failure of the Ayr Bank (1773) forced him to sell his farm, and in 1785 he was gaoled for debt at Ayr. While in prison he turned to poetry and, encouraged by the success of Burns, he published his own poems at Kilmarnock in 1788. His friendship stimulated Burns to write two of his best verse-epistles.

While briers an woodbines budding green,
An paitricks scraichin loud at e'en,     partridges
An morning poussie whiddin seen,      hare scudding
  Inspire my Muse,
This freedom, in an unknown frien'
  I pray excuse.

On Fasten-e'en we had a rockin,       meeting
To ca' the crack and weave our stockin;    have a chat
And there was muckle fun and jokin,
  Ye need na doubt;
At length we had a hearty yokin,       set-to
  At 'sang about.'

There was ae sang, amang the rest,
Aboon them a' it pleas'd me best,       Above
That some kind husband had addrest
  To some sweet wife:
It thirl'd the heart-strings thro the breast,   thrilled
  A' to the life.

I've scarce heard ought describ'd sae weel,   Dr. James Beattie (1735-
What gen'rous, manly bosoms feel;     1803) professor of Moral
Thought I, 'Can this be Pope, or Steele,    Philosophy, Aberdeen
  Or Beattie's wark?'            work
They tald me 'twas an odd kind chiel      chap
  About Muirkirk.

It pat me fidgin-fain to hear't,     tingle with excitement
An sae about him there I spier't;      enquired
Then a' that kent him round declar'd
  He had ingine;              genius
That nane excell'd it, few cam near't,
  It was sae fine:

That, set him to a pint of ale,
An either douce or merry tale,         sober
Or rhymes an sangs he'd made himsel,
  Or witty catches,
'Tween Inverness and Teviotdale,
  He had few matches.

Then up I gat, an swoor an aith,     *swore, oath*
Tho I should pawn my pleugh an graith,     *equipment*
Or die a cadger pownie's death,     *hawker, pony*
   At some dyke-back,     *behind a fence*
A pint an gill I'd gie them baith,
   To hear your crack.     *chat*

But, first an foremost, I should tell,
Amaist as soon as I could spell,
I to the crambo-jingle fell;     *rhyming*
   Tho rude an rough –
Yet crooning to a body's sel,
   Does weel eneugh.

I am nae poet, in a sense;
But just a rhymer like by chance,
An hae to learning nae pretence;
   Yet, what the matter?
Whene'er my Muse does on me glance,
   I jingle at her.

Your critic-folk may cock their nose,
And say, 'How can you e'er propose,
You wha ken hardly verse frae prose,
   To mak a sang?'
But, by your leaves, my learned foes,
   Ye're maybe wrang.

What's a' your jargon o your schools,
Your Latin names for horns an stools?
If honest Nature made you fools,
   What sairs your grammars?     *serves*
Ye'd better taen up spades and shools,     *shovels*
   Or knappin-hammers.     *stone-breaking*

A set o dull, conceited hashes     *fools*
Confuse their brains in college-classes,
They gang in stirks, and come out asses,     *bullocks*
   Plain truth to speak;
An syne they think to climb Parnassus     *then*
   By dint o Greek!

Gie me ae spark o Nature's fire,
That's a' the learning I desire;
Then, tho I drudge thro dub an mire     *puddle*
   At pleugh or cart,
My Muse, tho hamely in attire,
   May touch the heart.

O for a spunk o Allan's glee        *spark, Allan Ramsay*
Or Fergusson's, the bauld an slee,      *sly, Robert Fergusson*
Or bright Lapraik's, my friend to be,
     If I can hit it!
That would be lear eneugh for me,        *learning*
     If I could get it.

Now, sir, if ye hae friends enow,
Tho real friends I b'lieve are few;
Yet, if your catalogue be fow,         *full*
     I'se no insist:
But, gif ye want ae friend that's true,
     I'm on your list.

I winna blaw about mysel,         *brag*
As ill I like my fauts to tell;
But friends, an folk that wish me well,
     They sometime roose me;        *praise*
Tho I maun own, as monie still
     As far abuse me.

There's ae wee faut they whyles lay to me,     *sometimes*
I like the lasses – Gude forgie me!       *God*
For monie a plack they wheedle frae me      *farthing*
     At dance or fair;
Maybe some ither thing they gie me,
     They weel can spare.

But Mauchline Race or Mauchline Fair,
I should be proud to meet you there:
We'se gie ae night's discharge to care,
     If we forgather;
And hae a swap o rhymin-ware
     Wi ane anither.

The four-gill chap, we'se gar him clatter,      *cup*
An kirsen him wi reekin water;     *christen, steaming*
Syne we'll sit down an take our whitter,      *draught*
     To cheer our heart;
An faith, we'se be acquainted better
     Before we part.

Awa ye selfish, warly race,         *wordly*
Wha think that havins, sense, an grace,      *manners*
Ev'n love an friendship should give place
     To Catch-the-Plack!        *Hunt-the-Coin*
I dinna like to see your face,
     Nor hear your crack.

But ye whom social pleasure charms,
Whose hearts the tide of kindness warms,
Who hold your being on the terms,
   'Each aid the others.'
Come to my bowl, come to my arms,
   My friends, my brothers!

But, to conclude my lang epistle,
As my auld pen's worn to the grissle,
Twa lines frae you would gar me fissle,       *make tingle*
   Who am most fervent,
While I can either sing or whistle,
   Your friend and servant.

# SECOND EPISTLE TO J. LAPRAIK

## APRIL 21, 1785

Lapraik replied to the first epistle in similar vein, sending his son to deliver his verses while Burns was sowing in a field at Mossgiel. This, in turn, provoked the second epistle, dwelling on the bad luck which both poets had experienced and leading up to a declaration on the value of humility and contentment.

While new-ca'd kye rowte at the stake       *new-driven, low*
An pownies reek in pleugh or braik,       *steam, harrow*
This hour on e'enin's edge I take,
   To own I'm debtor
To honest-hearted, auld Lapraik,
   For his kind letter.

Forjesket sair, with weary legs,       *very tired*
Rattlin the corn out-owre the rigs,
Or dealing thro amang the naigs       *distributing*
   Their ten-hours' bite;
My awkwart Muse sair pleads and begs,
   I would na write.

The tapetless, ramfeezl'd hizzie,       *feckless, tired girl*
She's saft at best an something lazy:
Quo she, 'Ye ken we've been sae busy
   This month an mair,
That trowth, my head is grown right dizzie,
   An something sair.'

Her dowff excuses pat me mad:      dull
'Conscience,' says I, 'ye thowless jad!    lazy
I'll write, an that a hearty blaud,     screed
  This vera night;
So dinna ye affront your trade,
  But rhyme it right.

'Shall bauld Lapraik, the king o hearts,
Tho mankind were a pack of cartes,
Roose ye sae weel for your deserts,    Praise
  In terms sae friendly;
Yet ye'll neglect to shaw your parts
  An thank him kindly?'

Sae I gat paper in a blink,
An down gaed stumpie in the ink:    quill-pen
Quoth I, 'Before I sleep a wink,
  I vow I'll close it;
An if ye winna mak it clink,      rhyme
  By Jove, I'll prose it!'

Sae I've begun to scrawl, but whether
In rhyme, or prose, or baith thegither,
Or some hotch-potch that's rightly neither,
  Let time mak proof;
But I shall scribble down some blether   nonsense
  Just clean aff-loof.       off the cuff

My worthy friend, ne'er grudge an carp,
Tho Fortune use you hard an sharp;
Come, kittle up your moorland harp   tickle
  Wi gleesome touch!
Ne'er mind how Fortune waft an warp;  weft
  She's but a bitch.

She's gien me monie a jirt an fleg,   jerk, scare
Sin' I could striddle owre a rig;    straddle
But, by the Lord, tho I should beg
  Wi lyart pow,        grey head
I'll laugh an sing, an shake my leg,
  As lang's I dow!       can

Now comes the sax-and-twentieth simmer
I've seen the bud upo' the timmer,   woods
Still persecuted by the limmer    jade
  Frae year to year;
But yet, despite the kittle kimmer,   idle gossip
  I, Rob, am here.

Do ye envy the city gent,
Behind a kist to lie an sklent;                     counter, cheat
Or purse-proud, big wi cent. per cent.
   An muckle wame,                                 belly
In some bit brugh to represent                      borough
   A bailie's name?                              magistrate

Or is't the paughty feudal thane,                   haughty
Wi ruffl'd sark an glancing cane,                   shirt
Wha thinks himself nae sheep-shank bane,
   But lordly stalks;
While caps an bonnets aff are taen,
   As by he walks?

'O Thou wha gies us each guid gift!
Gie me o wit an sense a lift,                        load
Then turn me, if Thou please adrift,
   Thro Scotland wide;
Wi cits nor lairds I wadna shift,                   city people
   In a' their pride!'

Were this the charter of our state,
'On pain o hell the rich an great,'
Damnation then would be our fate,
   Beyond remead;                               remedy
But, thanks to heaven, that's no the gate          way
   We learn our creed.

For thus the Royal mandate ran,
When first the human race began:
'The social, friendly, honest man,
   Whate'er he be,
'Tis he fulfils great Nature's plan,
   And none but he.'

O mandate glorious and divine!
The followers o the ragged Nine –                   the Muses
Poor, thoughtless devils! – yet may shine
   In glorious light;
While sordid sons o Mammon's line
   Are dark as night!

Tho here they scrape, an squeeze, an growl,
Their worthless nievefu of a soul                   fistful
May in some future carcase howl,
   The forest's fright;
Or in some day-detesting owl
   May shun the light.

Then may Lapraik and Burns arise,
To reach their native, kindred skies,
And sing their pleasures, hopes an joys
    In some mild sphere;
Still closer knit in friendship's ties,
      Each passing year!


## EPISTLE TO WILLIAM SIMPSON

### SCHOOLMASTER, OCHILTREE – MAY 1785

William Simpson (1758-1815) studied at Glasgow University and was originally intended for the Church, but became a schoolmaster instead. Like Lapraik he was something of a poetaster, whose verse-epistle to Burns provoked this response, describing the psychology of poetic composition.

I gat your letter, winsome Willie;
Wi gratefu heart I thank you brawlie,           *handsomely*
Tho I maun say't, I wad be silly
    And unco vain,                           *mighty*
Should I believe, my coaxin billie,          *fellow*
    Your flatterin strain.

But I'se believe ye kindly meant it:
I sud be laith to think ye hinted
Ironic satire, sidelins sklented       *squinted sideways*
    On my poor Musie;
Tho in sic phraisin terms ye've penn'd it,     *wheedling*
    I scarce excuse ye.

My senses wad be in a creel,
Should I but dare a hope to speel,
Wi Allan, or wi Gilbertfield,          *Allan Ramsay*
    The braes of fame;       *William Hamilton of*
Or Fergusson, the writer-chiel,     *Gilbertfield (1665-1751)*
    A deathless name.       *lawyer, Robert Fergusson*

(O Fergusson! thy glorious parts
Ill suited law's dry, musty arts!
My curse upon your whunstane hearts,     *whinstone*
    Ye E'nbrugh gentry!
The tythe o what ye waste at cartes     *tenth*
    Wad stow'd his pantry!)     *stored*

Yet when a tale comes i my head,
Or lassies gie my heart a screed –                          ache
As whiles they're like to be my dead,                       death
    (O sad disease!)
I kittle up my rustic reed;                                 tickle
    It gies me ease.

Auld Coila, now, may fidge fu fain,              tingle with delight
She's gotten bardies o her ain;
Chiels wha their chanters winna hain,                       spare
    But tune their lays,
Till echoes a' resound again
    Her weel-sung praise.

Nae poet thought her worth his while,
To set her name in measur'd style;
She lay like some unkend-of-isle
    Beside New Holland,                         Australia
Or whare wild-meeting oceans boil
    Besouth Magellan.                            south of

Ramsay an famous Fergusson
Gied Forth an Tay a lift aboon;                             lift-up
Yarrow an Tweed, to monie a tune,
    Owre Scotland rings;
While Irwin, Lugar, Ayr an Doon
    Naebody sings.

Th' Illissus, Tiber, Thames, an Seine,
Glide sweet in monie a tunefu line:
But, Willie, set your fit to mine,                  strain of music
    And cock your crest!
We'll gar our streams an burnies shine              make, brooks
    Up wi the best!

We'll sing auld Coila's plains an fells
Her moors red-brown wi heather bells,
Her banks an braes, her dens and dells,             slopes, dingles
    Whare glorious Wallace
Aft bure the gree, as story tells,                  bore off the prize
    Frae Suthron billies.

At Wallace' name, what Scottish blood
But boils up in a spring-tide flood?
Oft have our fearless fathers strode
    By Wallace' side
Still pressing onward, red-wat-shod,             shoes wet with blood
    Or glorious dy'd!

O, sweet are Coila's haughs an woods,               *hollows*
Where lintwhites chant amang the buds,           *linnets*
And jinkin hares, in amorous whids,      *darting, gambols*
    Their loves enjoy;
While thro the braes the cushat croods    *wood-pigeon coos*
    With wailfu cry!

Ev'n winter bleak has charms to me,
When winds rave thro the naked tree;
Or frosts on hills of Ochiltree
    Are hoary gray;
Or blinding drifts wild-furious flee,
    Dark'ning the day!

O Nature! a' thy shews an forms
To feeling, pensive hearts hae charms!
Whether the summer kindly warms,
    Wi life an light;
Or winter howls, in gusty storms,
    The lang, dark night!

The Muse, nae poet ever fand her,               *found*
Till by himsel he learn'd to wander,
Adown some trottin burn's meander,         *brook's*
    An no think lang:
O sweet to stray, an pensive ponder
    A heart-felt sang!

The warly race may drudge an drive,          *wordly*
Hog-shouther, jundie, stretch, an strive,  *push with the shoulder,*
Let me fair Nature's face descrive,          *jostle*
    And I, wi pleasure,
Shall let the busy, grumbling hive
    Bum owre their treasure.                 *Hum*

Fareweel, my rhyme-composing brither!
We've been owre lang unkend to ither:      *unknown*
Now let us lay our heads thegither,
    In love fraternal:
May envy wallop in a tether,      *dangle at a rope's end*
    Black fiend, infernal!

While Highlandmen hate tolls an taxes;
While moorlan herds like guid, fat braxies;  *sheep carcases*
While Terra Firma, on her axis,
    Diurnal turns;
Count on a friend, in faith an practice,
    In Robert Burns.

POSTSCRIPT

| | |
|---|---|
| My memory's no worth a preen: | pin |
| I had amaist forgotten clean, | almost |
| Ye bade me write you what they mean | |
|     By this New-Light, | |
| 'Bout which our herds sae aft hae been | shepherds |
|     Maist like to fight. | |

| | |
|---|---|
| In days when mankind were but callans | striplings |
| At grammar, logic, an sic talents, | |
| They took nae pains their speech to balance, | |
|     Or rules to gie; | |
| But spak their thoughts in plain, braid Lallans, | Lowland Scots |
|     Like you or me. | |

| | |
|---|---|
| In thae auld times, they thought the moon, | those |
| Just like a sark, or pair o shoon, | shirt, shoes |
| Wore by degrees, till her last roon | round |
|     Gaed past their viewin; | went |
| An shortly after she was done | |
|     They gat a new ane. | |

| | |
|---|---|
| This past for certain, undisputed; | |
| It ne'er cam i their heads to doubt it, | |
| Till chiels gat up an wad confute it, | fellows |
|     An ca'd it wrang; | |
| An muckle din there was about it, | |
|     Baith loud an lang. | |

| | |
|---|---|
| Some herds, weel learn'd upo' the Beuk, | |
| Wad threap auld folk the thing misteuk; | maintain |
| For 'twas the auld moon turn'd a neuk | corner |
|     An out o sight, | |
| An backlins-comin to the leuk, | backward looking |
|     She grew mair bright. | |

| | |
|---|---|
| This was deny'd, it was affirm'd; | |
| The herds and hissels were alarm'd; | flocks |
| The rev'rend gray-beards rav'd an storm'd, | |
|     That beardless laddies | |
| Should think they better were inform'd, | |
|     Than their auld daddies. | |

| | |
|---|---|
| Frae less to mair, it gaed to sticks; | |
| Frae words an aiths, to clours an nicks; | oaths, blows, cuts |
| An monie a fallow gat his licks, | punishment |
|     Wi hearty crunt; | whack |
| An some, to learn them for their tricks, | |
|     Were hang'd an brunt. | burned |

This game was play'd in monie lands,
An Auld-Light caddies bure sic hands,                    lackeys
That faith, the youngsters took the sands    fled into the wilderness
    Wi nimble shanks;
Till lairds forbade, by strict commands,
    Sic bluidy pranks.

But New-Light herds gat sic a cowe,              got such a trouncing
Folk thought them ruin'd stick-an-stowe;                 entirely
Till now, amaist on ev'ry knowe                            knoll
    Ye'll find ane placed;
An some, their New-Light fair avow,
    Just quite barefac'd.

Nae doubt the Auld-Light flocks are bleatin;
Their zealous herds are vex'd and sweatin;
Mysel, I've even seen them greetin                       weeping
    Wi girnin spite,                                     snarling
To hear the moon sae sadly lie'd on
    By word an write.

But shortly they will cowe the louns!                    rascals
Some Auld-Light herds in neebor touns             neighbouring
Are mind't, in things they ca balloons,              determined
    To tak a flight;
An stay ae month amang the moons
    An see them right.

Guid observation they will gie them;
An when the auld moon's gaun to lea'e them,
The hindmost shaird, they'll fetch it wi them,            shard
    Just i their pouch;
An when the New-Light billies see them,
    I think they'll crouch!

Sae, ye observe that a' this clatter
Is naething but a 'moonshine-matter';
But tho dull prose-folk Latin splatter
    In logic tulzie,                                     quarrel
I hope we, Bardies, ken some better
    Than mind sic brulzie.                                brawl

# A POET'S WELCOME TO HIS LOVE-BEGOTTEN DAUGHTER

Compared with the sexual boastfulness over this episode, expressed in 'Epistle to John Rankine', this poem following the birth of Elizabeth Burns expresses only warm tenderness. The child was raised at Mossgiel under the care of the poet's mother. She married John Bishop and died in January 1817, allegedly in childbirth.

Thou's welcome, wean! Mishanter fa' me,     *child, mishap, befall*
If thoughts of thee, or yet thy mammie,
Shall ever daunton me or awe me
    My sweet, wee lady,
Or if I blush when thou shalt ca' me
    Tyta or daddie!

What tho they ca' me fornicator,
An tease my name in kintra clatter,     *country gossip*
The mair they talk, I'm kend the better,
    E'en let them clash!     *tattle*
An auld wife's tongue's a feckless matter     *feeble*
    To gie ane fash.     *give annoyance*

Welcome my bonie, sweet, wee dochter!
Tho ye come here a wee unsought for,
And tho your comin I hae fought for,
    Baith kirk and queir;     *church, court*
Yet, by my faith, ye're no unwrought for –
    That I shall swear!

Sweet fruit o monie a merry dint,     *occasion*
My funny toil is no a' tint,     *not all lost*
Tho thou cam to the warl' asklent,     *askew*
    Which fools may scoff at,
In my last plack thy part's be in't     *farthing*
    The better half o't.

Tho I should be the waur bestead,     *worse provided*
Thou's be as braw and bienly clad,     *well, finely*
And thy young years as nicely bred     *comfortably*
    Wi education,
As onie brat o wedlock's bed,
    In a' thy station.

Wee image o my bonie Betty,     *Elizabeth Paton*
As fatherly I kiss and daut thee,     *caress*
As dear, and near my heart I set thee
    Wi as guid will,
As a' the priests had seen me get thee
    That's out o Hell.

Gude grant that thou may ay inherit         *God*
Thy mither's looks an gracefu merit,
An thy poor, worthless daddie's spirit,
   Without his failins!
'Twill please me mair to see thee heir it,
   Than stocket mailins.         *well-stocked farms*

And if thou be what I wad hae thee,
An tak the counsel I shall gie thee,
I'll never rue my trouble wi thee –
   The cost nor shame o't –
But be a loving father to thee,
   And brag the name o't.

## THE FORNICATOR

*TUNE: Clout the Cauldron*

Believed to have been written in celebration of the poet's affair with Elizabeth Paton.

Ye jovial boys who love the joys,
   The blissful joys of Lovers;
Yet dare avow with dauntless brow,
   When th' bony lass discovers;         *reveals pregnancy*
I pray draw near and lend an ear,
   And welcome in a Frater,         *brother (Latin)*
For I've lately been on quarantine,
   A proven Fornicator.

Before the Congregation wide
   I pass'd the muster fairly,
My handsome Betsey by my side,
   We gat our ditty rarely;         *sermon*
But my downcast eye by chance did spy
   What made my lips to water,
Those limbs so clean where I, between,
   Commenc'd a Fornicator.

With rueful face and signs of grace
   I pay'd the buttock-hire,
The night was dark and thro the park
   I could not but convoy her;         *accompany*
A parting kiss, what could I less,
   My vows began to scatter,
My Betsey fell – lal de dal lal lal,
   I am a Fornicator.

But for her sake this vow I make,
   And solemnly I swear it,
That while I own a single crown,
   She's welcome for to share it;
And my roguish boy his Mother's joy,
   And the darling of his Pater,
For him I boast my pains and cost,
   Although a Fornicator.

Ye wenching blades whose hireling jades
   Have tipt you off blue-boram,      *passed on a social disease*
I tell ye plain, I do disdain
   To rank you in the Quorum;
But a bony lass upon the grass
   To teach her esse Mater,      *to be a mother (Latin)*
And no reward but for regard,
   O that's a Fornicator.

Your warlike Kings and Heros bold,
   Great Captains and Commanders;
Your mighty Cesars fam'd of old,
   And Conquering Alexanders;
In fields they fought and laurels bought
   And bulwarks strong did batter,
But still they grac'd our noble list
   And ranked Fornicator!!!

# THE VISION

## DUAN FIRST

Opinion is divided concerning the date of composition. Dewar considered a time prior
to the move to Mossgiel early in 1784, but Kinsley argued for a date in late 1785, and
Burns substituted or added several stanzas in 1786-7. The division of this poem into
Duan was influenced by Macpherson's 'Ossian' (from Gaelic *dán*, poetry).

The sun had clos'd the winter day,
The curlers quat their roaring play,
And hunger'd maukin taen her way,      *finished*
   To kail-yards green,      *hungry hare*
While faithless snaws ilk step betray
   Whare she has been.      *each*

The thresher's weary flingin-tree,     flail-swingle
The lee-lang day had tired me;      live-long
And when the day had clos'd his e'e,
 Far i the west,
Ben i the spence, right pensivelie,    Back, parlour
 I gaed to rest.           went

There, lanely by the ingle-cheek      -side
I sat an ey'd the spewing reek,      eddying
That fill'd, wi hoast-provoking smeek,  cough, smoke
 The auld clay biggin;       building
An heard the restless rattons squeak    rats
 About the riggin.         roof

All in this mottie, misty clime,      spotty
I backward mus'd on wasted time:
How I had spent my youthfu prime,
 An done naething,
But stringing blethers up in rhyme,   nonsense
 For fools to sing.

Had I to guid advice but harkit,     listened
I might, by this, hae led a market,
Or strutted in a bank and clarkit
 My cash-account:
While here, half-mad, half-fed, half-sarkit, half-clothed
 Is a' th' amount.

I started, mutt'ring 'Blockhead! coof!'
An heav'd on high my waukit loof,   calloused palm
To swear by a' yon starry roof,
 Or some rash aith,        oath
That henceforth would be rhyme-proof
 Till my last breath –

When click! the string the snick did draw;  latch
And jee! the door gaed to the wa;
And by my ingle-lowe I saw,     -flame
 Now bleezin bright,
A tight, outlandish hizzie, braw,    hussy
 Come full in sight.

Ye need na doubt, I held my whisht;   peace
The infant aith, half-form'd, was crusht;
I glowr'd, as eerie's I'd been dusht,  stared, touched
 In some wild glen;
When sweet, like modest Worth, she blusht,
 An stepped ben.         inside

Green, slender, leaf-clad holly-boughs
Were twisted, gracefu round her brows;
I took her for some Scottish Muse,
    By that same token;
And come to stop those reckless vows,
    Would soon been broken.

A 'hair-brain'd, sentimental trace'
Was strongly marked in her face;
A wildly-witty, rustic grace
    Shone full upon her;
Her eye, ev'n turn'd on empty space,
    Beam'd keen with honor.

Down flow'd her robe, a tartan sheen,          *bright*
Till half a leg was scrimply seen;          *barely*
And such a leg! my bonie Jean
    Could only peer it;          *equal*
Sae straught, sae taper, tight an clean –    *straight, slim*
    Nane else came near it.

Her mantle large, of greenish hue,
My gazing wonder chiefly drew;
Deep lights and shades, bold-mingling, threw
    A lustre grand;
And seem'd, to my astonish'd view,
    A well-known land.

Here, rivers in the sea were lost;
There, mountains to the skies were toss't;
Here, tumbling billows mark'd the coast,
    With surging foam;
There, distant shone Art's lofty boast,
    The lordly dome.

Here, Doon pour'd down his far-fetch'd floods;
There, well-fed Irwine stately thuds:          *beats*
Auld hermit Ayr staw thro his woods,          *stole*
    On to the shore;
And many a lesser torrent scuds,
    With seeming roar.

Low, in a sandy valley spread,
An ancient borough rear'd her head;
Still, as in Scottish story read,
    She boasts a race
To ev'ry nobler virtue bred,
    And polish'd grace.

By stately tow'r, or palace fair,
Or ruins pendent in the air,
Bold stems of heroes, here and there,
   I could discern;
Some seem'd to muse, some seem'd to dare,
    With feature stern.

My heart did glowing transport feel,
To see a race heroic wheel,
And brandish round the deep-dyed steel,
   In sturdy blows;
While, back-recoiling, seem'd to reel
    Their suthron foes.

His Country's Saviour, mark him well!    William Wallace (d. 1305)
Bold Richardton's heroic swell;    Adam Wallace of Riccarton
The chief, on Sark who glorious fell    John Wallace of Craigie
   In high command;    (d. 1449)
And he whom ruthless fates expel    Sir William Wallace Dunlop,
    His native land.    forced to sell Craigie, 1783.

There, where a sceptr'd Pictish shade
Stalk'd round his ashes lowly laid,
I mark'd a martial race, pourtray'd    the Montgomeries of Coilsfield
   In colours strong:
Bold, soldier-featur'd, undismay'd,
    They strode along.

Thro many a wild, romantic grove,    Barskimming
Near many a hermit-fancied cove
(Fit haunts for friendship or for love,
   In musing mood),
An aged Judge, I saw him rove,    Alexander Boswell (1707-82)
    Dispensing good.

With deep-struck, reverential awe,    Matthew Stewart (1717-85)
The learned Sire and Son I saw:    Dugald Stewart (1753-1828)
To Nature's God, and Nature's law,  professors of moral philosophy
   They gave their lore;    Edinburgh University
This, all its source and end to draw,
    That, to adore.

Brydon's brave ward I well could spy,    William Fullarton (1754-
Beneath old Scotia's smiling eye;    1808) ward of
Who call'd on Fame, low standing by,    Patrick Brydone
   To hand him on,
Where many a patriot-name on high,
    And hero shone.

DUAN SECOND

With musing-deep, astonish'd stare,
I view'd the heavenly-seeming Fair;
A whisp'ring throb did witness bear
 Of kindred sweet,
When with an elder sister's air
 She did me greet.

'All hail! my own inspired Bard!
In me thy native Muse regard!
Nor longer mourn thy fate is hard,
 Thus poorly low!
I come to give thee such reward,
 As we bestow!

'Know, the great Genius of this land
Has many a light aerial band,
Who, all beneath his high command
 Harmoniously,
As arts or arms they understand,
 Their labours ply.

'They Scotia's race among them share:
Some fire the soldier on to dare;
Some rouse the patriot up to bare
 Corruption's heart;
Some teach the bard – a darling care –
 The tuneful art.

''Mong swelling floods of reeking gore,
They, ardent, kindling spirits pour;
Or, 'mid the venal Senate's roar,
 They, sightless, stand,
To mend the honest patriot-lore,
 And grace the hand.

'And when the bard, or hoary sage,
Charm or instruct the future age,
They bind the wild poetic rage
 In energy,
Or point the inconclusive page
 Full on the eye.

'Hence, Fullarton, the brave and young;
Hence, Dempster's zeal-inspired tongue;
Hence, sweet, harmonious Beattie sung
 His *Minstrel* lays;
Or tore, with noble ardour stung,
 The sceptic's bays.

William Fullarton
George Dempster, M.P.
(1732-1818), Dr. James
Beattie (1735-1803)
published 1771

'To lower orders are assign'd
The humbler ranks of human-kind,
The rustic bard, the laboring hind,
    The artisan;
All chuse, as various they're inclin'd,
    The various man.

'When yellow waves the heavy grain,
The threat'ning storm some strongly rein
Some teach to meliorate the plain,
    With tillage-skill;
And some instruct the shepherd-train,
    Blythe o'er the hill.

'Some hint the lover's harmless wile;
Some grace the maiden's artless smile;
Some soothe the laborer's weary toil
    For humble gains,
And make his cottage-scenes beguile
    His cares and pains.

'Some, bounded to a district-space,
Explore at large man's infant race,
To mark the embryotic trace
    Of rustic bard;
And careful note each opening grace,
    A guide and guard.

'Of these am I – Coila my name:
And this district as mine I claim,
Where once the Campbells, chiefs of fame,     Loudoun, a Campbell
    Held ruling pow'r:     earldom since 1633
I mark'd thy embryo-tuneful flame,
    Thy natal hour.

'With future hope I oft would gaze
Fond, on thy little early ways:
Thy rudely caroll'd, chiming phrase,
    In uncouth rhymes;
Fir'd at the simple, artless lays
    Of other times.

'I saw thee seek the sounding shore,
Delighted with the dashing roar;
Or when the North his fleecy store
    Drove thro the sky,
I saw grim Nature's visage hoar
    Struck thy young eye.

'Or when the deep green-mantled earth
Warm cherish'd ev'ry flow'ret's birth,
And joy and music pouring forth
    In ev'ry grove;
I saw thee eye the gen'ral mirth
    With boundless love.

'When ripen'd fields and azure skies
Call'd forth the reapers' rustling noise,
I saw thee leave their ev'ning joys,
    And lonely stalk,
To vent thy bosom's swelling rise,
    In pensive walk.

'When youthful Love, warm-blushing, strong,
Keen-shivering, shot thy nerves along,
Those accents grateful to thy tongue,
    Th' adorèd *Name*,
I taught thee how to pour in song,
    To soothe thy flame.

'I saw thy pulse's maddening play,
Wild-send thee Pleasure's devious way,
Misled by Fancy's meteor-ray,
    By passion driven;
But yet the light that led astray
    Was light from Heaven.

'I taught thy manners-painting strains,
The loves, the ways of simple swains,
Till now, o'er all my wide domains
    Thy fame extends;
And some, the pride of Coila's plains,
    Become thy friends.

'Thou canst not learn, nor can I show,
To paint with Thomson's landscape glow;      James Thomson
Or wake the bosom-melting throe,                  (1700-48)
    With Shenstone's art;          William Shenstone (1714-63)
Or pour, with Gray, the moving flow      Thomas Gray (1716-71)
    Warm on the heart.

'Yet, all beneath th' unrivall'd rose,
The lowly daisy sweetly blows;
Tho large the forest's monarch throws
    His army-shade,
Yet green the juicy hawthorn grows,
    Adown the glade.

'Then never murmur nor repine;
Strive in thy humble sphere to shine;
And trust me, not Potosi's mine,                        in S. W. Bolivia
    Nor king's regard,
Can give a bliss o'ermatching thine,
    A rustic Bard.

'To give my counsels all in one,
Thy tuneful flame still careful fan;
Preserve the dignity of Man,
    With soul erect:
And trust the Universal Plan
    Will all protect.

'And wear thou *this*' – She solemn said,
And bound the holly round my head:
The polish'd leaves and berries red
    Did rustling play;
And, like a passing thought, she fled
    In light away.

# EPISTLE TO JOHN GOLDIE, IN KILMARNOCK

## AUGUST 1785

John Goldie (1717-1809), son of the miller of Craigmill, Galston – cabinet-maker, inventor, wine-merchant, methematician, astronomer, theologian, speculator in coalmines and canals, and one of the guarantors for the Kilmarnock Edition - a prime example of the Augustan virtuoso.

O Goudie, terror o the Whigs,
Dread o blackcoats and rev'rend wigs!
Sour Bigotry on his last legs
    Girns an looks back,                                snarls
Wishing the ten Egyptian plagues
    May seize you quick.

Poor gapin, glowerin Superstition!                      staring
Wae's me, she's in a sad condition!
Fye! bring Black Jock, her state physician,   Rev. John Russell
    To see her water!
Alas! there's ground for great suspicion
    She'll ne'er get better.

Enthusiasm's past redemption
Gane in a gallopin consumption:
Not a' her quacks, wi a' their gumption,                    initiative
    Can ever mend her;
Her feeble pulse gies strong presumption,
    She'll soon surrender.

Auld Orthodoxy lang did grapple,
For every hole to get a stapple;                           stopper
But now she fetches at the thrapple,             gags, gullet
    An fights for breath:
Haste, gie her name up in the chapel,
    Near unto death!

'Tis you an Taylor are the chief             Rev. Dr. Taylor of Norwich,
To blame for a' this black mischief;     apostle of New Light doctrine
But gin the Lord's ain folk gat leave,                            if
    A toom tar barrel                                        empty
An twa red peats wad bring relief,
    And end the quarrel.

For me, my skill's but very sma',
An skill in prose I've nane ava;                             at all
But, quietlenswise, between us twa,                  confidentially
    Weel may ye speed!
And, tho they sud you sair misca',
    Ne'er fash your head!                                   bother

E'en swinge the dogs, and thresh them sicker!     flog, thoroughly
The mair they squeel ay chap the thicker,                  strike
An still 'mang hands a hearty bicker                       beaker
    O something stout!
It gars an owthor's pulse beat quicker,          makes, author's
    And helps his wit.

There's naething like the honest nappy:                   liquor
Whare'll ye e'er see men sae happy,
Or women sonsie, saft and sappy         pleasant, soft succulent
    'Tween morn and morn,
As them wha like to taste the drappie,                     drop
    In glass or horn?

I've seen me daez't upon a time,                          dazed
I scarce could wink or see a styme;            faintest outline
Just ae half-mutchkin does me prime,           half-measure
    (Ought less is little,)
Then back I rattle on the rhyme,
    As gleg's a whittle.                              sharp, knife

## MAN WAS MADE TO MOURN - A DIRGE

*TUNE: Peggy Bawn*

Gilbert, writing to Dr. Currie about his brother: 'He used to remark to me that he could not well conceive a more mortifying picture of human life than a man seeking work. In casting about in his mind how this sentiment might be brought forward the elegy Man was made to mourn was composed.'

When chill November's surly blast
    Made fields and forests bare,
One ev'ning, as I wander'd forth
    Along the banks of Ayr,
I spied a man, whose aged step
    Seem'd weary, worn with care,
His face was furrow'd o'er with years,
    And hoary was his hair.

'Young stranger, whither wand'rest thou?'
    Began the rev'rend Sage;
'Does thirst of wealth thy step constrain,
    Or youthful pleasure's rage?
Or haply, prest with cares and woes,
    Too soon thou has began
To wander forth, with me to mourn
    The miseries of Man.

'The sun that overhangs yon moors,
    Out-spreading far and wide,
Where hundreds labour to support
    A haughty lordling's pride;
I've seen yon weary winter-sun
    Twice forty times return;
And ev'ry time has added proofs,
    That Man was made to mourn.

'O Man! while in thy early years,
    How prodigal of time!
Mis-spending all thy precious hours,
    Thy glorious, youthful prime!
Alternate follies take the sway,
    Licentious passions burn:
Which tenfold force gives Nature's law,
    That Man was made to mourn.

'Look not alone on youthful prime,
　　Or manhood's active might;
Man then is useful to his kind,
　　Supported is his right:
But see him on the edge of life,
　　With cares and sorrows worn,
Then Age and Want – oh! ill-matched pair! –
　　Shew man was made to mourn.

'A few seem favourites of Fate,
　　In pleasure's lap carest;
Yet think not all the rich and great
　　Are likewise truly blest:
But oh! what crowds in ev'ry land,
　　All wretched and forlorn,
Thro weary life this lesson learn,
　　That Man was made to mourn.

'Many and sharp the num'rous ills
　　Inwoven with our frame!
More pointed still we make ourselves,
　　Regret, remorse, and shame!
And Man, whose heav'n-erected face
　　The smiles of love adorn, –
Man's inhumanity to man
　　Makes countless thousands mourn!

'See yonder poor, o'erlabour'd wight,
　　So abject, mean, and vile,
Who begs a brother of the earth
　　To give him leave to toil;
And see his lordly fellow-worm
　　The poor petition spurn,
Unmindful, tho a weeping wife
　　And helpless offspring mourn.

'If I'm design'd yon lordling's slave –
　　By Nature's law design'd –
Why was an independent wish
　　E'er planted in my mind?
If not, why am I subject to
　　His cruelty, or scorn?
Or why has Man the will and pow'r
　　To make his fellow mourn?

'Yet let not this too much, my son,
    Disturb thy youthful breast:
This partial view of human-kind
    Is surely not the last!
The poor, oppressed, honest man
    Had never, sure, been born,
Had there not been some recompense
    To comfort those that mourn!

'O Death! the poor man's dearest friend,
    The kindest and the best!
Welcome the hour my aged limbs
    Are laid with thee at rest!
The great, the wealthy fear thy blow,
    From pomp and pleasure torn;
But, oh! a blest relief for those
    That weary-laden mourn!'


# YOUNG PEGGY

*TUNE: The last time I came o'er the Moor*

The subject of this poem was Margaret Kennedy (1766-95), daughter of Robert Kennedy
of Daljarrock, factor to the Earl of Cassilis and brother-in-law of Gavin Hamilton. Burns
met her at the latter's house and sent her this poem in the autumn of 1785 as 'a small
tho' grateful tribute...I have, in these verses, attempted some faint sketches of your
PORTRAIT in the unimbellished simple manner of descriptive TRUTH. Flattery I leave
to your LOVERS.' She was subsequently seduced by Captain Andrew McDoual, by
whom she had a daughter in 1794. The gallant Captain denied paternity but in 1798
the Consistorial Court declared in favour of a secret marriage and the child's legitimacy.
Tragically, Peggy died before the action was concluded. The Court of Session overturned
this judgement but awarded £3,000 to the dead woman, and alimentary provision for
the child.


Young Peggy blooms our boniest lass,
    Her blush is like the morning,
The rosy dawn the springing grass
    With early gems adorning.
Her eyes outshine the radiant beams
    That gild the passing shower,
And glitter o'er the crystal streams,
    And cheer each fresh'ning flower.

Her lips, more than the cherries bright –
　　A richer dye has graced them –
They charm the admiring gazer's sight,
　　And sweetly tempt to taste them.
Her smile is as the evening mild,
　　When feather'd pairs are courting,
And little lambkins wanton wild,
　　In playful bands disporting.

Were Fortune lovely Peggy's foe,
　　Such sweetness would relent her;
As blooming Spring unbends the brow
　　Of surly, savage Winter.
Detraction's eye no aim can gain,
　　Her winning powers to lessen,
And fretful Envy grins in vain
　　The poison'd tooth to fasten.

Ye Pow'rs of Honour, Love and Truth
　　From ev'ry ill defend her!
Inspire the highly-favour'd youth
　　The destinies intend her!
Still fan the sweet connubial flame
　　Responsive in each bosom,
And bless the dear parental name
　　With many a filial blossom!

# THE BRAES O BALLOCHMYLE

Written in 1785 when Sir John Whitefoord (1734-1803) was forced to sell his estate to the Alexander family, in the aftermath of the collapse of the Ayr Bank of Douglas, Heron and Company. 'Maria' was Mary Anne Whitefoord, eldest of Sir John's four daughters. Her sister-in-law, Helen D'Arcy, married Professor Dugald Stewart who owned the Catrine woods mentioned in the song. The music for this song was composed by Allan Masterton, for the *Scots Musical Museum*.

The Catrine woods were yellow seen,
　　The flowers decay'd on Catrine lea,
Nae lav'rock sang on hillock green,　　　　　　　　　　lark
　　But nature sicken'd on the e'e.
Thro faded groves Maria sang,
　　Hersel in beauty's bloom the while,
And aye the wild-wood echoes rang:-
　　Fareweel the braes o Ballochmyle!

Low in your wintry beds, ye flowers,
 Again ye'll flourish fresh and fair;
Ye birdies, dumb in with'ring bowers,
 Again ye'll charm the vocal air;
But here, alas! for me nae mair
 Shall birdie charm, or floweret smile;
Fareweel the bonie banks of Ayr!
 Fareweel! fareweel! sweet Ballochmyle!

## THIRD EPISTLE TO J. LAPRAIK

### SEPTEMBER 13, 1785

Composed at harvest-time, hence the reference to 'the staff o bread.'

Guid speed and furder to you, Johnie,
Guid health, hale han's, an weather bonie! — whole hands
Now, when ye're nickin down fu cannie — cutting, skilfully
 The staff o bread, — corn
May ye ne'er want a stoup o bran'y — cup
 To clear your head!

May Boreas never thresh your rigs, — north wind
Nor kick your rickles aff their legs, — corn-rigs
Sendin the stuff o'er muirs an haggs — bogs
 Like drivin wrack! — storm-tossed seaweed
But may the tapmost grain that wags
 Come to the sack!

I'm bizzie, too, an skelpin at it, — busy, driving
But, bitter, daudin showers hae wat it; — pelting, wet
Sae my auld stumpie-pen, I gat it, — quill
 Wi muckle wark,
An took my jocteleg an whatt it, — clasp-knife, whittled
 Like onie clark.

It's now twa month that I'm your debtor,
For your braw, nameless, dateless letter, — fine
Abusin me for harsh ill-nature
 On holy men,
While deil a hair yoursel ye're better,
 But mair profane!

But let the kirk-folk ring their bells!
Let's sing about our noble sel's:
We'll cry nae jads frae heathen hills     *call*
    To help or roose us,     *rouse*
But browster wives an whisky stills –     *brewer*
    They are the Muses!

Your friendship, sir, I winna quat it,     *will not yield*
An if ye mak objections at it,
Then hand in nieve some day we'll knot it,     *fist*
    An witness take,
An, when wi usquabae we've wat it,     *whisky*
    It winna break.

But if the beast and branks be spar'd     *horse and bridle*
Till kye be gaun without the herd,     *cattle, going, keeper*
And a' the vittel in the yard,     *grain*
    An theckit right,     *thatched*
I mean your ingle-side to guard     *fire-*
    Ae winter night.

Then Muse-inspirin aqua-vitae
Shall mak us baith sae blythe an witty,
Till ye forget ye're auld an gatty,     *enervated*
    And be as canty     *jolly*
As ye were nine years less than thretty –     *thirty*
    Sweet ane an twenty!

But stooks are cowpet wi the blast,     *rigs upset*
And now the sinn keeks in the wast;     *sun peeps*
Then I maun rin amang the rest,     *must*
    An quat my chanter;     *leave my song*
Sae I subscribe mysel in haste,
    Yours, Rab the Ranter.

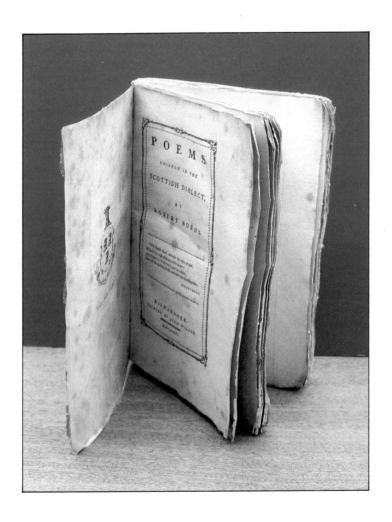

THE KILMARNOCK EDITION OF BURNS'S POEMS
IN ITS ORIGINAL BINDING

*courtesy of the Trustees of the Burns Monument, Burns Cottage, Alloway.*

BURNS MONUMENT, ALLOWAY

# EPISTLE TO THE REV. JOHN McMATH

### INCLOSING A COPY OF "HOLY WILLIE'S PRAYER" WHICH HE HAD REQUESTED, SEPT. 17, 1785

John McMath (1755-1825) was born in Galston, educated at Glasgow University, and ordained assistant to Patrick Wodrow, minister of Tarbolton. He was a New Licht liberal who championed Gavin Hamilton. He took to drink, resigned in 1791, enlisted as a private soldier and ended his days on the island of Mull.

| | |
|---|---:|
| While at the stook the shearers cow'r | corn-sheaf, stoop |
| To shun the bitter blaudin show'r, | pelting |
| Or, in gulravage rinnin, scowr: | horseplay, scour |
|     To pass the time, | |
| To you I dedicate the hour | |
|     In idle rhyme. | |
| | |
| My Musie, tir'd wi monie a sonnet | |
| On gown an ban', an douse black-bonnet, | sober |
| Is grown right eerie now she's done it, | fearful |
|     Lest they should blame her, | |
| An rouse their holy thunder on it | |
|     And anathem her. | |
| | |
| I own 'twas rash, an rather hardy, | |
| That I, a simple, countra Bardie, | |
| Should meddle wi a pack sae sturdy, | |
|     Wha, if they ken me, | |
| Can easy wi a single wordie, | |
|     Louse Hell upon me. | |
| | |
| But I gae mad at their grimaces, | |
| Their sighin, cantin, grace-proud faces, | furious |
| Their three-mile prayers, an hauf-mile graces, | |
|     Their raxin conscience, | elastic |
| Whase greed, revenge, an pride disgraces | |
|     Waur nor their nonsense. | worse than |
| | |
| There's Gau'n, misca'd waur than a beast, | Gavin Hamilton |
| Wha has mair honor in his breast | |
| Than monie scores as guid's the priest | |
|     Wha sae abus't him: | |
| And may a Bard no crack his jest | |
|     What way they've use't him? | |

5

See him, the poor man's friend in need,
The gentleman in word an deed –
An shall his fame an honor bleed
    By worthless skellums,                   scoundrels
An not a Muse erect her head
    To cowe the blellums?                  blusterers

O Pope, had I thy satire's darts            Alexander Pope
To gie the rascals their deserts,
I'd rip their rotten, hollow hearts,
    An tell aloud
Their jugglin, hocus-pocus arts
    To cheat the crowd!

God knows, I'm no the thing I should be,
Nor am I even the thing I could be,
But twenty times I rather would be
    An atheist clean,
Than under gospel colors hid be
    Just for a screen.

An honest man may like a glass,
An honest man may like a lass;
But mean revenge, an malice fause          false
    He'll still disdain,
An then cry zeal for gospel laws,
    Like some we ken.

They take Religion in their mouth,
They talk o Mercy, Grace an Truth:
For what? to gie their malice skouth       play
    On some puir wight;
An hunt him down, o'er right an ruth,      pity
    To ruin streight.                 straight

All hail, Religion! Maid divine!
Pardon a Muse sae mean as mine,
Who in her rough imperfect line
    Thus daurs to name thee;
To stigmatise false friends of thine
    Can ne'er defame thee.

Tho blotch't and foul wi monie a stain,
An far unworthy of thy train,
With trembling voice I tune my strain,
    To join with those
Who boldly dare thy cause maintain
    In spite of foes:

In spite o crowds, in spite o mobs,
In spite o undermining jobs,
In spite o dark banditti stabs
     At worth an merit,
By scoundrels, even wi holy robes,
     But hellish spirit!

O Ayr! my dear, my native ground,
Within thy presbyterial bound
A candid lib'ral band is found
     Of public teachers,
As men, as Christians too, renown'd,
     An manly preachers.

Sir, in that circle you are nam'd;
Sir, in that circle you are fam'd;
An some, by whom your doctrine's blam'd
     (Which gies ye honor),
Even, Sir, by them your heart's esteem'd,
     An winning manner.

Pardon this freedom I have ta'en,
An if impertinent I've been,
Impute it not, good Sir, in ane
     Whase heart ne'er wrang'd ye,
But to his utmost would befriend
     Ought that belang'd ye.

# TO A MOUSE

## ON TURNING HER UP IN HER NEST WITH THE PLOUGH, NOVEMBER 1785

Wee sleekit, cow'rin, tim'rous beastie,       glossy-coated
O, what a panic's in thy breastie!
Thou need na start awa sae hasty,
     Wi bickering brattle!          rushing, scurry
I wad be laith to rin an chase thee,      loth
     Wi murdering pattle!       plough-scraper

I'm truly sorry man's dominion
Has broken Nature's social union,
An justifies that ill opinion,
     Which makes thee startle
At me, thy poor, earth-born companion,
     An fellow mortal!

I doubt na, whyles, but thou may thieve;     *sometimes*
What then? poor beastie, thou maun live!
A daimen icker in a thrave     *odd ear in 24 sheaves*
   'S a sma request;
I'll get a blessin wi the lave,     *remainder*
   An never miss't!

Thy wee-bit housie, too, in ruin!
Its silly wa's the win's are strewin!     *feeble*
An naething, now, to big a new ane,
   O foggage green!     *coarse grass*
An bleak December's win's ensuin,
   Baith snell an keen!     *bitter*

Thou saw the fields laid bare an waste,
An weary winter comin fast,
An cozie here, beneath the blast,
   Thou thought to dwell,
Till crash! the cruel coulter past     *ploughshare*
   Out thro thy cell.

That wee bit heap o leaves an stibble,     *stubble*
Has cost thee monie a weary nibble!
Now thou's turn'd out, for a' thy trouble,
   But house or hald,     *without, holding*
To thole the winter's sleety dribble,     *endure*
   An cranreuch cauld!     *hoar-frost*

But Mousie, thou art no thy lane,     *alone*
In proving foresight may be vain:
The best-laid schemes o mice an men
   Gang aft agley,     *often go awry*
An lea'e us nought but grief an pain,
   For promis'd joy!

Still thou art blest, compar'd wi me!
The present only toucheth thee:
But och! I backward cast my e'e,
   On prospects drear!
An forward, tho I canna see,
   I guess an fear!

# THE HOLY FAIR

*A robe of seeming truth and trust*
  *Hid crafty observation;*
*And secret hung, with poison'd crust,*
  *The dirk of defamation:*
*A mask that like the gorget show'd,*
  *Dye-varying on the pigeon;*
*And for a mantle large and broad,*
  *He wrapt him in Religion* – HYPOCRISY À-LA-MODE

Written in 1785, probably following the annual Communion, held at Mauchline on the second Sunday in August. Burns completely revised the text early in 1786 prior to publication. Several parishes would join forces for the annual sacrament, attracting large numbers of communicants from the surrounding countryside for a 'holy fair' of preachings and prayer meetings extending over several days prior to the Communion itself (cf. the *Orduighean beaga* of the Free Church in the Highlands and Islands to this day). In Burns's day, however, the holy fair had deteriorated into a curious mixture of solemnity and carnival, symbolic of the double standards of the Church at the time.

Upon a simmer Sunday morn,
  When Nature's face is fair,
I walked forth to view the corn,
  An snuff the caller air.      *fresh*
The rising sun, owre Galston Muirs
  Wi glorious light was glintin;      *glancing*
The hares were hirplin down the furs,      *hopping, furrows*
  The lav'rocks they were chantin      *larks*
    Fu sweet that day.

As lightsomely I glowr'd abroad,      *gazed*
  To see a scene sae gay,
Three hizzies, early at the road,      *girls*
  Cam skelpin up the way.      *spanking along*
Twa had manteeles o dolefu black,
  But ane wi lyart lining;      *grey*
The third, that gaed a wee a-back,      *walked a bit behind*
  Was in the fashion shining,
    Fu gay that day.

The twa appear'd like sisters twin,
  In feature, form, an claes;      *clothing*
Their visage wither'd, lang an thin,
  An sour as onie slaes;      *blackthorn (sloes)*
The third cam up, hap-step-an-lowp      *hop, step and jump*
  As light as onie lambie,
An wi a curchie low did stoop,      *curtsey*
  As soon as e'er she saw me,
    Fu kind that day.

Wi bonnet aff, quoth I, 'Sweet lass,
   I think ye seem to ken me;
I'm sure I've seen that bonie face,
   But yet I canna name ye.'
Quo she, an laughin as she spak,
   An taks me by the han's,
'Ye, for my sake, hae gien the feck                             bulk
   Of a' the Ten Comman's
      A screed some day.'                               rip

'My name is Fun – your cronie dear,
   The nearest friend ye hae;
An this is Superstition here,
   An that's Hypocrisy.
I'm gaun to Mauchline Holy Fair,                         going
   To spend an hour in daffin:                   larking
Gin ye'll go there, yon runkl'd pair,               wrinkled
   We will get famous laughin
      At them this day.'

Quoth I, 'Wi a' my heart, I'll do't;
   I'll get my Sunday's sark on,                    shirt
An meet you on the holy spot;
   Faith, we'se hae fine remarkin!'            we'll have
Then I gaed hame at crowdie-time,            porridge-time
   An soon I made me ready;
For roads were clad, frae side to side,
   Wi monie a weary body,
      In droves that day.

Here farmers gash, in ridin graith,      self-satisfied, kit
   Gaed hoddin by their cotters;               jogging
There swankies young, in braw braid-claith,  strapping youngsters
   Are springin owre the gutters.
The lasses, skelpin barefit, thrang,     padding, thronging
   In silks an scarlets glitter;
Wi sweet-milk cheese, in monie a whang,     thick slice
   An farls, bak'd wi butter,                cookies
      Fu crump that day.                   crisp

When by the plate we set our nose,
    Weel heaped up wi ha'pence,
A greedy glowr black-bonnet throws,       *church elder*
    An we maun draw our tippence.
Then in we go to see the show:
    On ev'ry side they're gath'rin,
Some carrying dails, some chairs an stools,     *planks*
    An some are busy bleth'rin       *gossiping*
      Right loud that day.

Here stands a shed to fend the show'rs,     *keep off*
    An screen our countra gentry;
There Racer Jess, an twa-three whores,    *Janet Gibson, half-witted*
    Are blinkin at the entry.     *daughter of Poosie Nansie*
Here sits a raw o tittlin jads,     *whispering jades*
    Wi heavin breasts an bare neck;
An there a batch o wabster lads,     *weaver*
    Blackguardin frae Kilmarnock,     *Roistering*
      For fun this day.

Here some are thinkin on their sins,
    An some upo their claes;
Ane curses feet that fyl'd his shins,     *defiled*
    Anither sighs an prays:
On this hand sits a chosen swatch,     *sample*
    Wi screw'd-up, grace-proud faces;
On that a set o chaps, at watch,
    Thrang winkin on the lasses     *busy*
      To chairs that day.

O happy is that man, an blest!
    Nae wonder that it pride him!
Whase ain dear lass, that he likes best,
    Comes clinkin down beside him!
Wi arm repos'd on the chair back,
    He sweetly does compose him;
Which, by degrees, slips round her neck,
    An's loof upon her bosom,     *and his palm*
      Unkend that day.     *unknown*

Now a' the congregation o'er
  Is silent expectation;
For Moodie speels the holy door,          Rev. Alexander Moodie,
  Wi tidings o damnation:                    (1728-99); climbs
Should Hornie, as in ancient days,                 the Devil
  'Mang sons o God present him,
The vera sight o Moodie's face,
  To 's ain het hame had sent him                hot home
    Wi fright that day.

Hear how he clears the points o Faith
  Wi rattlin an thumpin!
Now meekly calm, now wild in wrath,
  He's stampin, an he's jumpin!
His lengthen'd chin, his turn'd-up snout,
  His eldritch squeel an gestures,             unearthly
O how they fire the heart devout,
  Like cantharidian plaisters               aphrodisiacs
    On sic a day!

But hark! the tent has chang'd its voice;
  There's peace an rest nae langer;
For a' the real judges rise,
  They canna sit for anger,
Smith opens out his cauld harangues,      Rev. George Smith (d. 1823)
  On practice and on morals;               A New Light moderate
An aff the godly pour in thrangs,                  crowds
  To gie the jars an barrels
    A lift that day.

What signifies his barren shine,
  Of moral powers an reason?
His English style, an gesture fine
  Are a' clean out o season.
Like Socrates or Antonine,
  Or some auld pagan heathen,
The moral man he does define,
  But ne'er a word o faith in
    That's right that day.

In guid time comes an antidote
    Against sic poison'd nostrum;
For Peebles, frae the water-fit,         *William Peebles of Newton-*
    Ascends the holy rostrum:             *on-Ayr*
See, up he's got the word o God,
    An meek an mim has view'd it,             *demure*
While Common-sense has taen the road     *Dr. John MacKenzie of*
    An aff, an up the Cowgate            *Mauchline*
        Fast, fast that day.

Wee Miller niest, the guard relieves,      *Rev. Alexander Miller*
    An Orthodoxy raibles,            *(d. 1804) of Kilmaurs*
Tho in his heart he weel believes,            *recites*
    An thinks it auld wives' fables:
But faith! the birkie wants a manse,            *fellow*
    So, cannilie he hums them;            *humbugs*
Altho his carnal wit an sense
    Like hafflins-wise o'ercomes him         *nearly half*
        At times that day.

Now butt an ben the change-house fills,   *tavern, backwards and forwards*
    Wi yill-caup commentators;           *ale-cup*
Here's cryin out for bakes and gills,          *biscuits*
    An there the pint-stowp clatters;
While thick an thrang, an loud an lang,
    Wi logic an wi Scripture,
They raise a din, that in the end
    Is like to breed a rupture
        O wrath that day.

Leeze me on drink! it gies us mair         *Blessings*
    Than either school or college;
It kindles wit, it waukens lear,            *learning*
    It pangs us fou o knowledge:         *crams full*
Be't whisky-gill or penny wheep,      *beer sold for a penny*
    Or onie stronger potion,           *a bottle*
It never fails, on drinkin deep,
    To kittle up our notion,            *tickle*
        By night or day.

The lads an lasses, blythely bent
  To mind baith saul an body,
Sit round the table, weel content,
  An steer about the toddy:               stir
On this ane's dress, an that ane's leuk,
  They're makin observations;
While some are cozie i the neuk,          corner
  An forming assignations
    To meet some day.

But now the Lord's ain trumpet touts,    sounds
  Till a' the hills are rairin,          roaring
And echoes back return the shouts;
  Black Russell is na spairin:     Rev. John Russell of
His piercin words, like Highlan swords,   Cromarty (1740-1817)
  Divide the joints an marrow;
His talk o Hell, whare devils dwell,
  Our vera 'sauls does harrow'
    Wi fright that day!

A vast, unbottom'd, boundless pit,
  Fill'd fou o lowin brunstane,      flaming brimstone
Whase ragin flame, an scorchin heat,
  Wad melt the hardest whun-stane!    whinstone
The half-asleep start up wi fear,
  An think they hear it roarin;
When presently it does appear,
  'Twas but some neebor snorin      neighbour
    Asleep that day.

'Twad be owre lang a tale to tell,
  How monie stories past;
An how they crouded to the yill,
  When they were a' dismist;
How drink gaed round, in cogs an caups,   beakers, cups
  Amang the furms an benches;       forms
An cheese an bread, frae women's laps,
  Was dealt about in lunches,     full portions
    An dawds that day.          lumps

In comes a gawsie, gash guidwife,          *showy, smart*
   An sits down by the fire,
Syne draws her kebbuck an her knife;       *Then, cheese*
   The lasses they are shyer:
The auld guidmen, about the grace,
   Frae side to side they bother;
Till some ane by his bonnet lays,
   An gies them't, like a tether,            *rope*
      Fu lang that day.

Waesucks! for him that gets nae lass,      *Alas*
   Or lasses that hae naething!
Sma need has he to say a grace,
   Or melvie his braw claithing!           *meal-dust*
O wives, be mindfu ance yoursel
   How bonie lads ye wanted;
An dinna, for a kebbuck-heel,              *cheese-rind*
   Let lasses be affronted
      On sic a day!

Now Clinkumbell, wi rattlin tow,          *the bell-ringer, rope*
   Begins to jow an croon;                 *swing, toll*
Some swagger hame the best they dow,      *can*
   Some wait the afternoon.
At slaps the billies halt a blink,        *fence-gaps, chaps*
   Till lasses strip their shoon:
Wi faith an hope, an love an drink,
   They're a' in famous tune
      For crack that day.          *chat*

How monie hearts this day converts
   O sinners and o lasses!
Their hearts o stane, gin night, are gane   *by nightfall*
   As saft as onie flesh is:                *any*
There's some are fou o love divine;
   There's some are fou o brandy;
An monie jobs that day begin,
   May end in houghmagandie                 *fornication*
      Some ither day.

# THE TWA DOGS

## A TALE

According to Gilbert Burns this poem 'was composed after the resolution of publishing was nearly taken. Robert had had a dog, which he called Luath, that was a great favourite. The dog had been killed by the wanton cruelty of some person the night before my father's death. Robert said to me, that he should like to confer such immortality as he could bestow upon his old friend...Caesar was merely the creature of the poet's imagination.'

| | |
|---|---:|
| 'Twas in that place o Scotland's Isle, | Kyle |
| That bears the name of auld King Coil, | |
| Upon a bonie day in June, | |
| When wearin thro the afternoon, | |
| Twa dogs, that were na thrang at hame, | busy |
| Forgathered ance upon a time. | encountered |
|     The first I'll name, they ca'd him Caesar, | |
| Was keepit for 'his Honor's' pleasure: | |
| His hair, his size, his mouth, his lugs, | ears |
| Shew'd he was nane o Scotland's dogs; | |
| But whalpit some place far abroad, | pupped |
| Whare sailors gang to fish for cod. | Newfoundland |
|     His locked, letter'd, braw brass collar | |
| Shew'd him the gentleman an scholar; | |
| But tho he was o high degree, | |
| The fient a pride, nae pride had he; | devil |
| But wad hae spent an hour caressin, | |
| Ev'n wi a tinkler-gipsy's messin: | cur |
| At kirk or market, mill or smiddie, | smithy |
| Nae tawted tyke, tho e'er sae duddie, | matted mongrel, ragged |
| But he wad stan't, as glad to see him, | |
| An stroan't on stanes an hillocks wi him. | pissed |
|     The tither was a ploughman's collie, | other |
| A rhyming, ranting, raving billie, | fellow |
| Wha for his friend an comrade had him, | |
| And in his freaks had Luath ca'd him, | |
| After some dog in Highland sang, | MacPherson's Ossian |
| Was made lang syne – Lord knows how lang. | |
|     He was a gash an faithfu tyke, | respectable |
| As ever lap a sheugh or dyke. | ditch, stone wall |
| His honest, sonsie, baws'nt face | pleasant, white-streaked |
| Ay gat him friends in ilka place; | Always, every |
| His breast was white, his tousie back | shaggy |
| Weel clad wi coat o glossy black; | |
| His gawsie tail, wi upward curl, | jolly |
| Hung owre his hurdies wi a swirl. | buttocks |

Nae doubt but they were fain o ither,     *happy in each other*
And unco pack an thick thegither;     *confidential*
Wi social nose whyles snuff'd an snowkit;     *now, poke with nose*
Whyles mice an moudieworts they howkit;     *moles, dug up*
Whyles scour'd awa in lang excursion,
An worry'd ither in diversion;
Till tir'd at last wi monie a farce,
They set them down upon their arse,
An there began a lang digression
About the 'lords o the creation.'


CAESAR

I've aften wonder'd, honest Luath,
What sort o life poor dogs like you have;
An when the gentry's life I saw,
What way poor bodies liv'd ava.     *at all*
  Our laird gets in his racked rents,     *paid in kind*
His coals, his kain, an a' his stents:     *dues*
He rises when he likes himsel;
His flunkies answer at the bell;
He ca's his coach; he ca's his horse;
He draws a bonie silken purse,
As lang's my tail, whare, thro the steeks,     *stitches*
The yellow letter'd Geordie keeks.     *guinea, peeps*
  Frae morn to e'en it's nought but toiling,
At baking, roasting, frying, boiling;
An tho the gentry first are stechin,     *cramming*
Yet ev'n the ha' folk fill their pechan     *servants, stomach*
Wi sauce, ragouts, an sic like trashtrie     *rubbish*
That's little short o downright wastrie.     *wasteful*
Our whipper-in, wee, blastit wonner,     *Hugh Andrew, huntsman*
Poor, worthless elf, it eats a dinner,     *at Coilsfield*
Better than onie tenant-man
His Honor has in a' the lan;
An what poor cot-folk pit their painch in,     *put, paunch*
I own it's past my comprehension.

LUATH

Trowth, Caesar, whyles they're fash't eneugh: bothered
A cotter howkin in a sheugh, digging
Wi dirty stanes biggin a dyke, building
Baring a quarry, an sic like; clearing
Himsel, a wife, he thus sustains,
A smytrie o wee duddie weans, litter, brats
An nought but his han-darg to keep manual labour
Them right an tight in thack an rape. thatch, rope
An when they meet wi sair disasters,
Like loss o health or want o masters,
Ye maist wad think, a wee touch langer,
An they maun starve o cauld and hunger:
But how it comes, I never kend yet, knew
They're maistly wonderfu contented;
An buirdly chiels, an clever hizzies, stout lads, girls
Are bred in sic a way as this is.


CAESAR

But then to see how ye're negleckit,
How huff'd, an cuff'd, an disrespeckit!
Lord man, our gentry care as little
For delvers, ditchers, an sic cattle;
They gang as saucy by poor folk, go
As I wad by a stinking brock. badger
I've notic'd, on our laird's court-day,
(An monie a time my heart's been wae),
Poor tenant bodies, scant o cash,
How they maun thole a factor's snash: an allusion to the harsh
He'll stamp an threaten, curse an swear treatment of William
He'll apprehend them, poind their gear; Burnes
While they maun stan, wi aspect humble,
An hear it a', an fear an tremble!
I see how folk live that hae riches;
But surely poor-folk maun be wretches!

LUATH

They're no sae wretched's ane wad think:
Tho constantly on poortith's brink,              *poverty*
They're sae accustom'd wi the sight,
The view o't gies them little fright.
    Then chance and fortune are sae guided,
They're ay in less or mair provided;
An tho fatigu'd wi close employment,
A blink o rest's a sweet enjoyment.
    The dearest comfort o their lives,
Their grushie weans an faithfu wives;         *growing*
The prattling things are just their pride,
That sweetens a' their fireside.
    An whyles twalpennie worth o nappy
Can mak the bodies unco happy:
They lay aside their private cares,
To mind the Kirk and State affairs;
They'll talk o patronage an priests,
Wi kindling fury i' their breasts,
Or tell what new taxation's comin,
An ferlie at the folk in Lon'on.           *wonder*
    As bleak-fac'd Hallowmass returns,
They get the jovial, ranting kirns,      *harvest-homes*
When rural life, of ev'ry station,
Unite in common recreation;
Love blinks, Wit slaps, an social Mirth    *glances*
Forgets there's Care upo the earth.
    That merry day the year begins,
They bar the door on frosty win's;
The nappy reeks wi mantling kirns,         *froth*
An sheds a heart-inspiring steam;
The luntin pipe, an sneeshin mill,    *smoking, snuff-mull*
Are handed round wi right guid will;
The cantie auld folks crackin crouse,  *jolly, conversing cheerfully*
The young anes ranting thro the house –    *romping*
My heart has been sae fain to see them,    *sore*
That I for joy hae barkit wi them.

Still it's owre true that ye hae said,
Sic game is now owre aften play'd;                    too often
There's monie a creditable stock
O decent, honest, fawsont folk,                       well-doing
Are riven out baith root an branch,
Some rascal's pridefu greed to quench,
Wha thinks to knit himsel the faster
In favor wi some gentle master,
Wha, aiblins thrang a parliamentin,                   perhaps
For Britain's guid his saul indentin –                indenturing

## CAESAR

Haith, lad, ye little ken about it:                   know
For Britain's guid! guid faith! I doubt it.
Say rather, gaun as Premiers lead him:                going
An saying aye or no's they bid him:
At operas an plays parading,
Mortgaging, gambling, masquerading:
Or maybe, in a frolic daft,
To Hague or Calais taks a waft,
To mak a tour an tak a whirl,          go on the Grand Tour of Europe
To learn *bon ton*, an see the worl.
   There, at Vienna or Versailles,
He rives his father's auld entails;                   splits
Or by Madrid he takes the rout,                       road
To thrum guitars an fecht wi nowt;                    fight bulls
Or down Italian vista startles,                       courses
Whore-hunting amang groves o myrtles;
Then bowses drumlie German-water,            muddy spa water
To mak himsel look fair an fatter,
An clear the consequential sorrows,
Love-gifts of Carnival signoras.
   For Britain's guid! for her destruction!
Wi dissipation, feud an faction.

## LUATH

Hech man! dear sirs! is that the gate         way
They waste sae monie a braw estate!         fine
Are we sae foughten an harass'd         troubled
For gear to gang that gate at last?         wealth
   O would they stay aback frae courts,
An please themsels wi countra sports
It wad for ev'ry ane be better,
The laird, the tenant, an the cotter!
For thae frank, rantin, ramblin billies,     those roistering
Fient haet o them's ill-hearted fellows:     not one of
Except for breakin o their timmer,     timber
Or speakin lightly o their limmer,     whore
Or shootin of a hare or moor-cock
The ne'er-a-bit they're ill to poor folk.
   But will ye tell me, master Caesar,
Sure great folk's life's a life o pleasure?
Nae cauld nor hunger e'er can steer them,
The vera thought o't need na fear them.

## CAESAR

   Lord, man, were ye but whyles whare I am,
The gentles, ye wad ne'er envy 'em!
   It's true, they need na starve or sweat,
Thro winter's cauld, or simmer's heat;
They've nae sair wark to craze their banes,     hard
An fill auld age wi grips an granes;     gripes, groans
But human bodies are sic fools,
For a' their colleges an schools,
That when nae real ills perplex them,
They mak enow themsels to vex them;
An aye the less they hae to sturt them,     fret
In like proportion, less will hurt them.
   A countra fellow at the pleugh,
His acre's till'd, he's right eneugh;
A countra girl at her wheel,
Her dizzen's dune, she's unco weel;     dozen
But gentlemen, an ladies warst,     worst
Wi ev'n down want o wark are curst.     downright
They loiter, lounging, lank an lazy;
Tho deil-haet ails them, yet uneasy:     nothing
Their days insipid, dull an tasteless;
Their nights unquiet, lang an restless.

An ev'n their sports, their balls an races,
Their galloping through public places,
There's sic parade, sic pomp an art,
The joy can scarcely reach the heart.
　The men cast out in party-matches,
Then sowther a' in deep debauches;　　　　　　　　　patch up
Ae night they're mad wi drink an whoring,
Niest day their life is past enduring.　　　　　　　　next
　The ladies arm-in-arm in clusters,
As great an gracious a' as sisters;
But hear their absent thoughts o ither,
They're a' run deils and jads thegither.　　　　　　positively
Whyles, owre the wee bit cup and platie,
They sip the scandal-potion pretty;
Or lee-lang nights, wi crabbit leuks　　　　　　　　live-long
Pore owre the devil's pictur'd beuks;　　　　　　playing cards
Stake on a chance a farmer's stackyard,
An cheat like onie unhang'd blackguard.
　There's some exceptions, man an woman;
But this is Gentry's life in common.

　By this, the sun was out o sight,
An darker gloamin brought the night;　　　　　　　twilight
The bum-clock humm'd wi lazy drone;　　　　　　　beetle
The kye stood rowtin i' the loan;　　cattle, lowing, driving-road
When up they gat an shook their lugs,　　　　　　　ears
Rejoic'd they were na men but dogs;
An each took aff his several way,
Resolv'd to meet some ither day.

# THE COTTER'S SATURDAY NIGHT

## INSCRIBED TO R. AIKEN, ESQ.

*Let not Ambition mock their useful toil,*
  *Their homely joys, and destiny obscure;*
*Nor Grandeur bear, with a disdainful smile,*
  *The short and simple annals of the poor* – GRAY

Composed over the winter of 1785-6, using the Spenserian stanza popular in the
eighteenth century, for sentimental poetry extolling the merits of rustic simplicity. It
was dedicated to Robert Aiken (1739-1807), addressed in the opening stanza.

My lov'd, my honour'd, much respected friend!
  No mercenary bard his homage pays;
With honest pride, I scorn each selfish end,
  My dearest meed, a friend's esteem and praise:
  To you I sing, in simple Scottish lays,
The lowly train in life's sequester'd scene;
  The native feelings strong, the guileless ways;
What Aiken in a cottage would have been;
Ah! tho his worth unknown, far happier there I ween!

November chill blaws loud wi angry sugh;                    wail
  The short'ning winter-day is near a close;
The miry beasts retreating frae the pleugh;
  The black'ning trains o craws to their repose:
  The toil-worn Cotter frae his labor goes, –
This night his weekly moil is at an end,
  Collects his spades, his mattocks, and his hoes,
Hoping the morn in ease and rest to spend,
And weary, o'er the moor, his course does hameward bend.

At length his lonely cot appears in view,
  Beneath the shelter of an aged tree;
Th' expectant wee-things, toddlin, stacher through          stagger
  To meet their dad, wi flichterin noise and glee.          fluttering
  His wee bit ingle, blinkin bonilie,
His clean hearth-stane, his thrifty wifie's smile,
  The lisping infant, prattling on his knee,
Does a' his weary kiaugh and care beguile,                  anxiety
An makes him quite forget his labor and his toil.

Belyve, the elder bairns come drapping in,                  By and by
  At service out, amang the farmers roun;
Some ca' the pleugh, some herd, some tentie rin             heedful run
  A cannie errand to a neebor town:                         neighbouring
  Their eldest hope, their Jenny, woman grown,
In youthfu bloom, love sparkling in her e'e,
  Comes hame; perhaps, to show a braw new gown,
Or deposits her sair-won penny-fee,                         hard-earned
To help her parents dear, if they in hardship be.          wages

With joy unfeign'd, brothers and sisters meet,
   And each for other's welfare kindly spiers:           enquires
The social hours, swift-wing'd, unnotic'd fleet;
   Each tells the uncos that he sees or hears.         marvels
   The parents partial eye their hopeful years;
Anticipation forward points the view;
   The mother, wi her needle and her sheers        scissors
Gars auld claes look amaist as weel's the new;    makes clothes
The father mixes a' wi admonition due.

Their master's and their mistress's command,
   The younkers a' are warned to obey;          youngsters
And mind their labors wi an eydent hand,         diligent
And ne'er tho out o sight, to jauk or play;      fool about
   'And O! be sure to fear the Lord alway,
And mind your duty, duly, morn and night;
   Lest in temptation's path ye gang astray,
Implore His counsel and assisting might:
They never sought in vain that sought the Lord aright.'

But hark! a rap comes gently to the door;
   Jenny, wha kens the meaning o the same,
Tells how a neebor lad came o'er the moor,
   To do some errands, and convoy her hame.      accompany
   The wily mother sees the conscious flame
Sparkle in Jenny's e'e, and flush her cheek;
   With heart-struck anxious care, inquires his name,
While Jenny hafflins is afraid to speak;          half
Weel-pleas'd the mother hears, it's nae wild, worthless rake.

Wi kindly welcome, Jenny brings him ben;         inside
   A strappin youth, he takes the mother's eye;
Blythe Jenny sees the visit's no ill taen;
   The father cracks of horses, pleughs, and kye.   chats, cattle
   The youngster's artless heart o'erflows wi joy,
But blate an laithfu, scarce can weel behave;    shy, sheepish
   The mother, wi a woman's wiles, can spy
What makes the youth sae bashfu and sae grave;
Weel-pleas'd to think her bairn's respected like the lave.   child, rest

O happy love! where love like this is found:
   O heart-felt raptures! bliss beyond compare!
I've paced much this weary, mortal round,
   And sage experience bids me this declare, –
'If Heaven a draught of heavenly pleasure spare,
One cordial in this melancholy vale,
   'Tis when a youthful, loving, modest pair
In other's arms, breathe out the tender tale,
Beneath the milk-white thorn that scents the ev'ning gale.'

Is there, in human form, that bears a heart,
    A wretch! a villain! lost to love and truth!
That can, with studied, sly, ensnaring art,
    Betray sweet Jenny's unsuspecting youth?
    Curse on his perjur'd arts! dissembling, smooth!
Are honor, virtue, conscience, all exil'd?
    Is there no pity, no relenting ruth,
Points to the parents fondling o'er their child?
Then paints the ruin'd maid, and their distraction wild?

But now the supper crowns their simple board,
    The halesome parritch, chief o Scotia's food;    *wholesome porridge*
The soupe their only hawkie does afford,    *milk, cow*
    That, 'yont the hallan snugly chows her cood:    *beyond partition*
    The dame brings forth, in complimental mood,
To grace the lad, her weel-hain'd kebbuck, fell;    *-saved, cheese,*
    And aft he's prest, and aft he ca's it guid:    *pungent*
The frugal wifie, garrulous, will tell,
How 'twas a towmond auld, sin lint was i' the bell.    *twelve month,*
    *flax, flower*

The chearfu supper done, wi serious face,
    They, round the ingle, form a circle wide;
The sire turns o'er, wi patriarchal grace,
    The big ha'-Bible, ance his father's pride.
    His bonnet rev'rently is laid aside,
His lyart haffets wearing thin and bare;    *grey side-locks*
    Those strains that once did sweet in Zion glide,
He wales a portion with judicious care;    *chooses*
And 'Let us worship God!' he says with solemn air.

They chant their artless notes in simple guise,
    They tune their hearts, by far the noblest aim;
Perhaps *Dundee's* wild-warbling measures rise,    *three popular*
    Or plaintive *Martyrs*, worthy of the name;    *Psalm tunes*
    Or noble *Elgin* beets the heavenward flame,    *fans*
The sweetest far of Scotia's holy lays:
    Compar'd with these, Italian trills are tame;
The tickl'd ears no heart-felt raptures raise;
Nae unison hae they, with our Creator's praise.

The priest-like father reads the sacred page,
    How Abram was the friend of God on high;
Or, Moses bade eternal warfare wage
    With Amalek's ungracious progeny;
    Or, how the royal Bard did groaning lie
Beneath the stroke of Heaven's avenging ire;
    Or Job's pathetic plaint, and wailing cry;
Or rapt Isaiah's wild, seraphic fire;
Or other holy Seers that tune the sacred lyre.

Perhaps the Christian volume is the theme:
 How guiltless blood for guilty man was shed;
How He, who bore in Heaven the second name,
 Had not on earth whereon to lay His head;
 How His first followers and servants sped;
The precepts sage they wrote to many a land:
 How he, who lone in Patmos banishèd,     St. John AD 95
Saw in the sun a mighty angel stand,
And heard great Bab'lon's doom pronounc'd by Heaven's command.

Then kneeling down to Heaven's Eternal King,
 The saint, the father, and the husband prays:
Hope 'springs exulting on triumphant wing.'
 That thus they all shall meet in future days,
 There, ever bask in uncreated rays,
No more to sigh or shed the bitter tear,
 Together hymning their Creator's praise,
In such society, yet still more dear;
While circling Time moves round in an eternal sphere.

Compar'd with this, how poor Religion's pride,
 In all the pomp of method, and of art;
When men display to congregations wide
 Devotion's ev'ry grace, except the heart,
 The Power, incens'd, the pageant will desert,
The pompous strain, the sacerdotal stole;
 But haply, in some cottage far apart,
May hear, well-pleas'd, the language of the soul;
And in His Book of Life the inmates poor enroll.

Then homeward all take off their sev'ral way,
 The youngling cottagers retire to rest:
The parent-pair their secret homage pay,
 And proffer up to Heaven the warm request,
 That he who stills the raven's clam'rous nest,
And decks the lily fair in flow'ry pride,
 Would, in the way His wisdom sees the best,
For them and for their little ones provide;
But, chiefly, in their hearts with Grace Divine preside.

From scenes like these, old Scotia's grandeur springs
 That makes her lov'd at home, rever'd abroad:
Princes and lords are but the breath of kings,
 'An honest man's the noblest work of God';
 And certes, in fair Virtue's heavenly road,
The cottage leaves the palace far behind;
 What is a lordling's pomp? a cumbrous load,
Disguising oft the wretch of human kind,
Studied in arts of Hell, in wickedness refin'd!

O Scotia! my dear, my native soil!
    For whom my warmest wish to Heaven is sent!
Long may thy hardy sons of rustic toil
    Be blest with health, and peace, and sweet content!
    And O! may Heaven their simple lives prevent
From Luxury's contagion, weak and vile!
    Then, howe'er crowns and coronets be rent,
A virtuous populace may rise the while,
And stand a wall of fire around their much-lov'd Isle.

O Thou! who pour'd the patriotic tide,
    That stream'd thro Wallace's undaunted heart,
Who dar'd to, nobly, stem tyrannic pride,
    Or nobly die, the second glorious part:
    (The patriot's God, peculiarly Thou art,
His friend, inspirer, guardian, and reward!)
    O never, never Scotia's realm desert;
But still the patriot, and the patriot-bard
In bright succession raise, her ornament and guard!

# HALLOWEEN

*Yes! let the rich deride, the proud disdain,*
*The simple pleasures of the lowly train:*
*To me more dear, congenial to my heart,*
*One native charm, than all the gloss of art* – GOLDSMITH

The fourth in the group of ambitious essays in 'manners-painting', this poem deals with ancient customs surrounding Halloween, allegedly obsolete even by Burns's time. This poetic record derives much of its material from the stories and legends told to him by his mother and Betty Davidson. The Feast of All Saints (1st November) coincided with the ancient Celtic pagan festival of Samhuinn, hence the blend of Christian ritual and superstition surviving till modern times.

| | |
|---|---|
| Upon that night, when fairies light | |
|     On Cassilis Downans dance, | hillocks of Cassilis, |
| Or owre the lays, in splendid blaze, | Kirkmichael |
|     On sprightly coursers prance; | |
| Or for Colean the rout is taen, | Culzean Castle, road |
|     Beneath the moon's pale beams; | |
| There, up the Cove, to stray and rove, | Culzean Bay |
|     Amang the rocks and streams | |
|         To sport that night: | |

Amang the bonie winding banks,         
 Where Doon rins, wimplin, clear:      winding
Where Bruce ance ruled the martial ranks,  Robert de Brus,
 An shook his Carrick spear;   father of King Robert I
Some merry, friendly, country-folks   southern Ayrshire
 Together did convene.
To burn their nits, an pou their stocks,   nuts, pull, plants
 An haud their Halloween       keep
  Fu blythe that night.

The lasses feat an cleanly neat,       spruce
 Mair braw than when they're fine;     fair
Their faces blythe fu sweetly kythe,     show
 Hearts leal, an warm, an kin':     loyal
The lads sae trig, wi wooer-babs   smart, love-knots
 Weel-knotted on their garten;     garters
Some unco blate, an some wi gabs    shy, talk
 Gar lasses' hearts gang startin     make
  Whyles fast at night.       sometimes

Then, first an foremost, thro the kail,
 Their stocks maun a' be sought ance;
They steek their een, an grape an wale  shut, grope, chose
 For muckle anes, an straught anes.   big, straight
Poor hav'rel Will fell aff the drift,    foolish
 An wandered thro the bow-kail,    cabbage
An pow't, for want o better shift,    pulled
 A runt, was like a sow-tail     stalk
  Sae bow't that night.      bent

Then, straught or crooked, yird or nane,   earth
 They roar an cry a' throu'ther;    pell-mell
The vera wee-things, toddlin, rin,
 Wi stocks out-owre their shouther:  upon, shoulder
An gif the custock's sweet or sour,    if, pith
 Wi joctelegs they taste them;   clasp-knives
Syne coziely, aboon the door,    then, above
 Wi cannie care, they've plac'd them   prudent
  To lie that night.

The lasses staw frae 'mang them a',     stole
 To pou their stalks o corn;
But Rab slips out, an jinks about,     larks
 Behint the muckle thorn:
He grippet Nelly hard an fast;
 Loud skirl'd a' the lasses;
But her tap-pickle maist was lost,  grain at the end of the stalk
 Whan kiutlin in the fause-house  cuddling, conical frame of
  Wi him that night.       haystack

The auld guid-wife's weel-hoordet nits       *well-hoarded*
    Are round an round divided,
An monie lads' an lasses' fates
    Are there that night decided:
Some kindle couthie, side by side,       *comfortably*
    An burn thegither trimly;
Some start awa wi saucy pride,
    An jump out-owre the chimlie       *fireplace*
        Fu high that night.

Jean slips in twa, wi tentie e'e;       *watchful*
    Wha 'twas, she wadna tell;
But this is Jock, and this is me,
    She says in to hersel:       *whispers*
He bleez'd owre her, an she owre him,
    As they wad never mair part;
Till fuff! he started up the lum,       *chimney*
    And Jean had e'en a sair heart
        To see't that night.

Poor Willie, wi his bow-kail runt,
    Was burnt wi primsie Mallie;       *precise*
An Mary, nae doubt, took the drunt,       *huff*
    To be compar'd to Willie:
Mall's nit lap out, wi pridefu fling,
    An her ain fit, it burnt it;       *foot*
While Willie lap, an swoor by jing,       *leaped*
    'Twas just the way he wanted
        To be that night.

Nell had the fause-house in her min',
    She pits herself an Rob in;
In loving bleeze they sweetly join,
    Till white in ase they're sobbin:       *ashes*
Nell's heart was dancin at the view;
    She whisper'd Rob to leuk for't:
Rob, stownlins, prie'd her bonie mou,       *stealthily, mouth*
    Fu cozie in the neuk for't,       *corner*
        Unseen that night.

But Merran sat behint their backs,
    Her thoughts on Andrew Bell;
She lea'es them gashing at their cracks,       *chattering*
    An slips out by hersel:
She thro the yard the nearest taks,
    An to the kiln she goes then,
An darklins grapit for the bauks,       *in the dark, baulks*
    And in the blue-clue throws then,       *ball of blue yarn used for*
        Right fear't that night.       *divining*

An ay she win't, an ay she swat –                                    wound, sweated
   I wat she made nae jaukin;                                     bet, trifling
Till something held within the pat,                                  pot
   Guid Lord! but she was quakin!
But whether 'twas the Deil himsel,
   Or whether 'twas a bauk-en,                                     beam-end
Or whether it was Andrew Bell,
   She did na wait on talkin
      To spier that night.                                        ask

Wee Jenny to her graunie says,              Jenny Brown, the poet's cousin
   'Will ye go wi me, graunie?
I'll eat the apple at the glass,
   I gat frae uncle Johnie':
She fuff't her pipe wi sic a lunt,                                   puffed, smoke
   In wrath she was sae vap'rin,
She notic't na an aizle brunt                                        burning ember
   Her braw, new, worset apron                                     worsted
      Out thro that night.

'Ye little skelpie-limmer's-face!                                    hussy
   I daur you try sic sportin,
As seek the Foul Thief onie place,                                   Devil
   For him to spae your fortune:                                   tell
Nae doubt but ye may get a sight!
   Great cause ye hae to fear it;
For monie a ane has gotten a fright,
   An liv'd an died deleeret,                                      delirious
      On sic a night.

'Ae hairst afore the Sherra-moor,      harvest, Battle of Sheriffmuir,
   I mind't as weel's yestreen –                   1715: remember
I was a gilpey then, I'm sure                                        young girl
   I was na past fyfteen:
The simmer had been cauld an wat,
   An stuff was unco green;                                        grain
An ay a rantin kirn we gat,                  rollicking, harvest-home
   An just on Halloween
      It fell that night.

'Our stibble-rig was Rab M'Graen,                                   chief harvester
   A clever, sturdy fallow
His sin gat Eppie Sim wi wean,                                       son, child
   That liv'd in Achmachalla:                      a fictitious placename
He gat hemp-seed, I mind it weel,
   An he made unco light o't;
But monie a day was by himsel,                                      out of his mind
   He was sae sairly frighted
      That vera night.'

Then up gat fechtin Jamie Fleck,         *fighting*
  An he swoor by his conscience,
That he could saw hemp-seed a peck;         *sow*
  For it was a' but nonsense:         *all merely*
The auld guidman raught down the pock,     *reached, bag*
  An out a handfu gied him;
Syne bad him slip frae 'mang the folk,
  Sometime when nae ane see'd him,
    An try't that night.

He marches thro amang the stacks,
  Tho he was something sturtin;       *staggered*
The graip he for a harrow taks,       *pitchfork*
  An haurls at his curpin:       *trails, crupper*
And ev'ry now and then, he says,
  'Hemp-seed I saw thee,
An her that is to be my lass
  Come after me, an draw thee
    As fast this night.'

He whistl'd up *Lord Lenox' March*,
  To keep his courage cheery;
Altho his hair began to arch,
  He was sae fley'd an eerie;     *scared, awe-stricken*
Till presently he hears a squeak,
  An then a grane an gruntle;     *groan*
He by his shouther gae a keek,   *glances over his shoulder*
  An tumbled wi a wintle     *somersault*
    Out-owre that night.

He roar'd a horrid murder-shout,
  In dreadfu desperation!
An young an auld come rinnin out,
  An hear the sad narration:
He swoor 'twas hilchin Jean M'Craw,     *crippled*
  Or crouchie Merran Humphie –   *hump-backed, Marion*
Till stop! she trotted thro them a';
  And wha was it but grumphie     *the pig*
    Asteer that night?     *Astir*

Meg fain wad to the barn gaen,   *would gladly have gone*
  To winn three wechts o naething,     *sievefuls*
But for to meet the Deil her lane,     *on her own*
  She pat but little faith in:
She gies the herd a pickle nits,     *shepherd, few*
  An twa red-cheekit apples,
To watch, while for the barn she sets,
  In hopes to see Tam Kipples
    That vera night.

She turns the key wi cannie thraw,     careful twist
 An owre the threshold ventures;
But first on Sawnie gies a ca',
 Syne bauldly in she enters:
A ratton rattl'd up the wa',       rat
 An she cry'd Lord preserve her!
An ran thro midden-hole an a',
 An pray'd wi zeal and fervour,
  Fu fast that night.

They hoy't out Will, wi sair advice;    urged
 They hecht him some fine braw ane;  promised
It chanc'd the stack he faddom't thrice,  fathomed
 Was timmer-propt for thrawin;   shored up
He taks a swirlie, auld moss-oak    gnarled
 For some black, gruesome carlin;   beldam
An loot a winze, an drew a stroke, uttered a curse, aimed a blow
 Till skin in blypes cam haurlin  shreds, flying off his fists
  Aff's nieves that night.

A wanton widow Leezie was,
 As cantie as a kittlin;      lively, kitten
But och! that night, amang the shaws,   woods
 She gat a fearful settlin!
She thro the whins, an by the cairn,
 An owre the hill gaed scrievin;    careering
Whare three lairds' lands met at a burn,  brook
 To dip her left sark-sleeve in,    shirt-
  Was bent that night.

Whyles owre a linn the burnie plays,  Now, waterfall
 As thro the glen it wimpl't;
Whyles round a rocky scaur it strays,   cliff
 Whyles in a wiel it dimpl't;     eddy
Whyles glitter'd to the nightly rays,
 Wi bickerin, dancin dazzle;
Whyles cookit underneath the braes,   hid
 Below the spreading hazel
  Unseen that night.

Amang the brachens, on the brae,  bracken, hillside
 Between her an the moon,
The Deil, or else an outler quey,  keifer, outdoors
 Gat up an gae a croon:
Poor Leezie's heart maist lap the hool;  sheath
 Near lav'rock-height she jumpit,   lark-high
But mist a fit, an in the pool  missed her footing
 Out-owre the lugs she plumpit,   ears
  Wi a plunge that night.

In order, on the clean hearth-stane,
   The luggies three are ranged;                  *wooden dishes*
An ev'ry time great care is taen
   To see them duly changed;
Auld uncle John, wha wedlock's joys
   Sin' Mar's-year did desire,     *1715, the year of the Rebellion*
Because he gat the toom dish thrice,    *led by the Earl of Mar*
   He heav'd them on the fire,                 *empty*
      In wrath that night.

Wi merry sangs, an friendly cracks,
   I wat they did na weary;
And unco tales, an funnie jokes –
   Their sports were cheap an cheery:
Till butter'd sow'ns, wi fragrant lunt,    *sour pudding, steam*
   Set a' their gabs a-steerin;        *tongues wagging*
Syne, wi a social glass o strunt,           *liquor*
   They parted aff careerin
      Fu blythe that night.

## THE MAUCHLINE WEDDING

Written in the late autumn of 1785, but not sent to Mrs. Dunlop till 21st August 1788, with a note explaining that it was written in retaliation for the poet's rejection by Elizabeth Miller. Her brother William married Nansie Bell for the £500 left to her by her brother, Alexander Bell who had died in Jamaica. Her sister Helen married Burns's friend, Dr John Mackenzie.

When Eighty-five was seven month auld,
   And wearing thro the aught,
When rotting rains and Boreas bauld
   Gied farmer-folks a faught;
Ae morning quondam Mason Will,
   Now Merchant Master Miller,
Gaed down to meet wi Nansie Bell
   And her Jamaica siller,
      To wed, that day.

The rising sun o'er Blacksideen
   Was just appearing fairly,
When Nell and Bess got up to dress    *Elizabeth and*
   Seven lang half-hours o'er early!   *Helen Miller*
Now presses clink and drawers jink,
   For linnens and for laces;
But modest Muses only think
   What ladies' underdress is,
      On sic a day.

But we'll suppose the stays are lac'd,
 And bony bosoms steekit;        held in place
Tho, thro the lawn – but guess the rest –      linen
 An Angel scarce durst keek it:        dare peep
Then stockins fine, o silken twine,
 Wi cannie care are drawn up;        prudent
And gartened tight, whare mortal wight
 ...............
  ...............

But now the gown wi rustling sound,
 Its silken pomp displays;
Sure there's no sin in being vain
 O siccan bony claes!         such clothes
Sae jimp the waist, the tail sae vast –    narrow, rump
 Trouth, they were bony Birdies!
O Mither Eve, ye wad been grave
 To see their ample hurdies        buttocks
  Sae large that day!!!

Then Sandy wi's red jacket braw        fine
 Comes, whip-jee-whoa! about,
And in he gets the bony twa –
 Lord send them safely out!
And auld John Trot wi sober phiz      countenance
 As braid and braw's a Bailie,        broad
His shouthers and his Sunday's giz     shoulders, wig
 Wi powther and wi ulzie      powder, unguent
  Weel smear'd that day.

## THE AULD FARMER'S NEW-YEAR MORNING SALUTATION TO HIS AULD MARE, MAGGIE

### ON GIVING HER THE ACCUSTOMED RIPP OF CORN TO HANSEL IN THE NEW-YEAR

be a first gift

Mentioned by Burns in his letter to John Richmond (17th February 1786) and probably composed shortly before.

A Guid New-Year I wish thee, Maggie!
Hae, there's a ripp to thy auld baggie:   handful from sheaf, belly
Tho thou's howe-backit now, an knaggie,   hollow-backed, knobbly
 I've seen the day
Thou could hae gaen like onie staggie,      gone, colt
 Out-owre the lay.           lea

Tho now thou's dowie, stiff an crazy,    drooping
An thy auld hide as white's a daisie,
I've seen thee dappl't, sleek an glaizie,   glossy
 A bonie gray:
He should been tight that daur't to raize thee, ready, excite
 Ance in a day.

Thou ance was i' the foremost rank,
A filly buirdly, steeve an swank:  elegant, trim, limber
An set weel down a shapely shank,
 As e'er tread yird;       earth
An could hae flown out-owre a stank,   pool
 Like onie bird.

It's now some nine-an-twenty year
Sin' thou was my guid-father's meere; father-in-law's mare
He gied me thee, o tocher clear,    dowry
 An fifty mark;
Tho it was sma', 'twas weel-won gear,
 An thou was stark.       strong

When first I gaed to woo my Jenny,    went
Ye then was trottin wi your minnie:   mother
Tho ye was trickie, slee, an funnie,    sly
 Ye ne'er was donsie;     mischievous
But hamely, tawie, quiet, an cannie,   docile
 An unco sonsie.     good-tempered

That day, ye pranc'd wi muckle pride,
When ye bure hame my bonie bride:
An sweet an gracefu, she did ride,
 Wi maiden air!
Kyle-Stewart I could bragged wide,  central Ayrshire
 For sic a pair.

Tho now ye dow but hoyte and hobble,  can, stumble
An wintle like a saumont-coble,  stagger, salmon-boat
That day, ye was a jinker noble,    goer
 For heels an win'!
An ran them till they a' did wauble,   wobble
 Far, far, behin'!

When thou an I were young an skiegh,  skittish
An stable-meals at fairs were driegh,   tedious
How thou wad prance, an snore, an skriegh. snort, whinny
 An tak the road!
Town's-bodies ran, an stood abiegh,   aback
 An ca't thee mad.

When thou was corn't, an I was mellow,          *fed*
We took the road ay like a swallow:
At brooses thou had ne'er a fellow,       *wedding-races*
   For pith an speed;              *stamina*
But ev'ry tail thou pay't them hollow,
   Where'er thou gaed.

The sma', droop-rumpl't, hunter cattle     *short-rumped*
Might aiblins waur't thee for a brattle;  *perhaps have beaten*
But sax Scotch miles thou try't their mettle,   *sprint*
   An gar't them whaizle:       *made wheeze*
Nae whip nor spur, but just a wattle      *wand*
   O saugh or hazle.           *willow*

Thou was a noble fittie-lan',    *rear left-hand plough-horse*
As e'er in tug or tow was drawn!
Aft thee an I, in aught hours' gaun,
   On guid March-weather,
Hae turn'd sax rood beside our han',    *to our own cheek*
   For days thegither.

Thou never braing't, an fetch't, an fliskit;  *pulled rashly, stopped*
But thy auld tail thou wad hae whiskit,   *suddenly: capered*
An spread abreed thy well-fill'd brisket,
   Wi pith an pow'r;
Till sprittie knowes wad rair't an riskit   *rooty knolls would have*
   An slypet owre.    *roared: cracked, slipped over*

When frosts lay lang, an snaws were deep,
An threaten'd labour back to keep,
I gied thy cog a wee bit heap          *dish*
   Aboon the timmer:          *edge*
I ken'd my Maggie wad na sleep,       *knew*
   For that, or simmer.         *ere*

In cart or car thou never reestit;
The steyest brae thou wad hae fac't it;   *steepest slope*
Thou never lap, an sten't, an breastit,   *leaped, sprang*
   Then stood to blaw;
But just thy step a wee thing hastit,
   Thou snoov't awa.         *jogged along*

My pleugh is now thy bairntime a',   *ploughing-team, issue*
Four gallant brutes as e'er did draw;
Forbye sax mae I've sell't awa,       *more*
   That thou hast nurst:
They drew me thretteen pund an twa,
   The vera warst.

THE ARCHIBALD SKIRVING PORTRAIT OF BURNS
*courtesy of the National Galleries of Scotland*

| | |
|---|---|
| Monie a sair darg we twa hae wrought, | hard day's work |
| An wi the weary warl' fought! | |
| An monie an anxious day, I thought | |
|     We wad be beat! | |
| Yet here to crazy age we're brought, | |
|     Wi something yet. | |

| | |
|---|---|
| An think na, my auld trusty servan', | |
| That now perhaps thou's less deservin, | |
| An my auld days may end in starvin; | |
|     For my last fow, | bushel |
| A heapet stimpart, I'll reserve ane | quarter of a peck |
|     Laid by for you. | |

| | |
|---|---|
| We've worn to crazy years thegither; | |
| We'll toyte about wi ane anither; | totter |
| Wi tentie care I'll flit thy tether | prudent, change |
|     To some hain'd rig, | reserved space |
| Whare ye may nobly rax your leather, | stretch your stomach |
|     Wi sma' fatigue. | |

## ADDRESS TO THE DEIL

*O Prince! O chief of many throned pow'rs!*
*That led th' embattl'd seraphim to war*—MILTON

Composed in the winter of 1785-6, in three parts - a mock invocation, a recital of the Devil's occupations and satirical farewell. The middle part owes much to Burns's recollection of 'an old Maid of my Mother's (Betty Davidson), remarkable for her ignorance, credulity and superstition. She had, I suppose, the largest collection in the county of tales and songs concerning devils, ghosts, fairies, brownies, witches, warlocks, spunkies, kelpies, elf-candles, dead-lights, wraiths, apparitions, cantraips, giants, enchanted towers, dragons and other trumpery.'

| | |
|---|---|
| O Thou! whatever title suit thee – | |
| Auld Hornie, Satan, Nick, or Clootie – | cloven-hoofed |
| Wha in yon cavern grim an sootie, | |
|     Clos'd under hatches, | |
| Spairges about the brunstane cootie, | splashes, brimstone dish |
|     To scaud poor wretches! | scald |

Hear me, Auld Hangie, for a wee,             Old Hangman
An let poor damned bodies be;
I'm sure sma' pleasure it can gie,
    Ev'n to a deil,
To skelp an scaud poor dogs like me,         spank
    An hear us squeel.

Great is thy pow'r an great thy fame;
Far kend an noted is thy name;
An tho yon lowin heugh's thy hame,      flaming, hollow
    Thou travels far;
An faith! thou's neither lag, nor lame,      backward
    Nor blate, nor scaur.           bashful, afraid

Whyles, ranging like a roarin lion,           Now
For prey, a' holes an corners trying;
Whyles, on the strong-wing'd tempest flyin
    Tirlin the kirks;            stripping
Whyles, in the human bosom pryin,
    Unseen thou lurks.

I've heard my rev'rend graunie say,
In lanely glens ye like to stray;
Or, where auld ruin'd castles grey
    Nod to the moon,
Ye fright the nightly wand'rer's way,
    Wi eldritch croon.           unearthly

When twilight did my graunie summon,
To say her pray'rs, douce, honest woman!      sober
Aft yont the dyke she's heard you bummin,   beyond, humming
    Wi eerie drone;
Or, rustlin, thro the boortrees comin,       alders
    Wi heavy groan.

Ae dreary, windy, winter night,
The stars shot down wi sklentin light,      slanting
Wi you mysel, I gat a fright:
    Ayont the lough;            pond
Ye, like a rash-buss, stood in sight,    clump of rushes
    Wi waving sugh.            moan

The cudgel in my nieve did shake,        fist
Each bristl'd hair stood like a stake;
When wi an eldritch, stoor 'quaick, quaick.'      harsh
    Amang the springs,
Awa ye squatter'd like a drake,
    On whistling wings.

Let warlocks grim, an wither'd hags,
Tell how wi you, on ragweed nags,                    ragwort
They skim the muirs an dizzy crags,
    Wi wicked speed;
And in kirkyards renew their leagues,
    Owre howkit dead.                         exhumed

Thence, countra wives, wi toil an pain,
May plunge an plunge the kirn in vain;               churn
For O! the yellow treasure's taen
    By witching skill;
An dawtit, twal-pint hawkie's gaen        petted, twelve-pint, cow
    As yell's the bill.                          dry, bull

Thence, mystic knots mak great abuse
On young guidmen, fond, keen an croose;      husbands, cocksure
When the best wark-lume i' the house,      working tool (penis)
    By cantraip wit,                             magic
Is instant made no worth a louse,
    Just at the bit.                          nick of time

When thowes dissolve the snawy hoord,        thaws, hoard
An float the jinglin icy boord,                     surface
Then, water-kelpies haunt the foord,
    By your direction,
An 'nighted trav'llers are allur'd               benighted
    To their destruction.

And aft your moss-traversing spunkies        bog-, demons
Decoy the wight that late an drunk is:
The bleezin, curst, mischievous monkies
    Delude his eyes,
Till in some miry slough he sunk is,
    Ne'er mair to rise.

When Mason's mystic word an grip
In storms an tempests raise you up,
Some cock or cat your rage maun stop,                must
    Or, strange to tell!
The youngest brother ye wad whip
    Aff straught to Hell.                        straight

Lang syne in Eden's bonie yard,                      garden
When youthfu lovers first were pair'd,
An all the soul of love they shar'd
    The raptur'd hour,
Sweet on the fragrant flow'ry swaird,
    In shady bow'r:

| | |
|---|---|
| Then you, ye auld, snick-drawing dog! | scheming |
| Ye came to Paradise incog, | |
| An play'd on man a cursed brogue, | trick |
| (Black be your fa'!) | |
| An gied the infant warld a shog, | shake |
| 'Maist ruin'd a'. | Almost |
| | |
| D'ye mind that day when in a bizz | flurry |
| Wi reekit duds, an reestit gizz, | smoky, scorched wig |
| Ye did present your smoutie phiz | smutty face |
| 'Mang better folk, | |
| An sklented on the man of Uzz | squinted, Job |
| Your spitefu joke? | |
| | |
| An how ye gat him i' your thrall, | |
| An brak him out o house an hal', | |
| While scabs an botches did him gall. | blotches |
| Wi bitter claw; | |
| An lows'd his ill-tongu'd wicked scaul – | scold |
| Was warst ava? | |
| | |
| But a' your doings to rehearse, | |
| Your wily snares an fechtin fierce, | fighting |
| Sin' that day Michael did you pierce, | the Archangel |
| Down to this time, | |
| Wad ding a Lallan tongue, or Erse, | beat, Lowland, Irish |
| In prose or rhyme. | |
| | |
| An now, Auld Cloots, I ken ye're thinkin, | |
| A certain Bardie's rantin, drinkin, | roistering |
| Some luckless hour will send him linkin | hurrying |
| To your black Pit; | |
| But, faith! he'll turn a corner jinkin, | dodging |
| An cheat you yet. | |
| | |
| But fare-you-weel, Auld Nickie-ben! | |
| O, wad ye tak a thought an men'! | |
| Ye aiblins might – I dinna ken – | perhaps, know |
| Still hae a stake: | |
| I'm wae to think upo' yon den, | sad |
| Ev'n for your sake! | |

# SCOTCH DRINK

*Gie him strong drink until he wink,*
*That's sinking in despair;*
*An liquor guid to fire his bluid,*
*That's prest wi grief and care:*
*There let him bowse, and deep carouse,*
*Wi bumpers flowing o'er,*
*Till he forgets his loves or debts,*
*An minds his griefs no more.*
– SOLOMON'S PROVERBS, xxxi. 6,7.

Kinsley considered that this poem was probably suggested by Fergusson's 'Caller Water', and it uses the same metre. It was composed in the winter of 1785-6, a copy being sent to Robert Muir of Kilmarnock on 20th March 1786. In 1785 an Act was passed, abolishing the privilege which, since 1690, had allowed the Forbes family of Culloden to distil whisky at Ferintosh, free of duty.

Let other poets raise a fracas
Bout vines, and wines, an drucken Bacchus,
An crabbit names an stories wrack us,     *torment*
    An grate our lug:     *vex, ear*
I sing the juice Scotch bear can mak us,     *barley*
    In glass or jug.

O thou, my Muse! guid auld Scotch drink!
Whether thro wimplin worms thou jink,     *spiral, coils, frisk*
Or, richly brown, ream owre the brink,     *froth*
    In glorious faem,     *foam*
Inspire me, till I lisp an wink,
    To sing thy name!

Let husky wheat the haughs adorn,     *hollows*
An aits set up their awnie horn,     *oats, bearded*
An pease and beans, at e'en or morn,
    Perfume the plain:
Leeze me on thee, John Barleycorn,     *Blessings on thee*
    Thou king o grain!

On thee aft Scotland chows her cood,     *chews, cud*
In souple scones, the wale o food!     *choice*
Or tumbling in the boiling flood
    Wi kail an beef;
But when thou pours thy strong heart's blood
    There thou shines chief.

Food fills the wame, an keeps us livin;     *belly*
Tho life's a gift no worth receivin,
When heavy-dragg'd wi pine an grievin;
    But oil'd by thee,
The wheels o life gae down-hill, scrievin,     *careering*
    Wi rattlin glee.

Thou clears the head o doited Lear,          *muddled*
Thou cheers the heart o drooping Care;
Thou strings the nerves o Labour sair,
   At's weary toil;
Thou ev'n brightens dark Despair
   Wi gloomy smile.

Aft, clad in massy siller weed,          *raiment*
Wi gentles thou erects thy head;
Yet humbly kind in time o need,
   The poor man's wine:
His wee drap parritch, or his bread,    *porridge*
   Thou kitchens fine.

Thou art the life o public haunts;
But thee, what were our fairs and rants?  *without, festivals*
Ev'n godly meetings o the saunts,       *saints*
   By thee inspir'd,
When, gaping, they besiege the tents,
   Are doubly fir'd.

That merry night we get the corn in,
O sweetly, then, thou reams the horn in!
Or reekin on a New-Year mornin       *steaming*
   In cog or bicker,          *bowl, beaker*
An just a wee drap sp'ritual burn in,
   An gusty sucker!         *tasty sugar*

When Vulcan gies his bellows breath,
An ploughmen gather wi their graith,    *gear*
O rare! to see thee fizz an freath      *froth*
   I' th' lugget caup!      *two-eared cup*
Then Burnewin comes on like death    *Blacksmith*
   At every chaup.         *stroke*

Nae mercy, then, for airn or steel:    *iron*
The brawnie, bainie, ploughman chiel,  *bony, chap*
Brings hard owrehip, wi sturdy wheel,
   The strong forehammer,
Till block an studdie ring an reel,    *anvil*
   Wi dinsome clamour.

When skirlin weanies see the light,  *squalling babies*
Thou maks the gossips clatter bright,    *babble*
How fumblin cuifs their dearies slight;   *fools*
   Wae worth the name!     *woe betide*
Nae howdie gets a social night,     *midwife*
   Or plack frae them.     *farthing*

When neebors anger at a plea,　　　　　　　　　　neighbours
An just as wud as wud can be,　　　　　　　　　　　wild
How easy can the barley-brie　　　　　　　　　　　-brew
　　Cement the quarrel!
It's aye the cheapest lawyer's fee,
　　To taste the barrel.

Alake! that e'er my Muse has reason,
To wyte her countrymen wi treason!　　　　　　　charge
But monie daily weet their weason　　　　　　　　throat
　　Wi liquors nice,
An hardly, in a winter season,
　　E'er spier her price.　　　　　　　　　　　　　ask

Wae worth that brandy, burnin trash!
Fell source o monie a pain an brash!　　　　　　　illness
Twins monie a poor, doylt, drucken hash　　　Robs, stupid
　　O half his days;　　　　　　　　　　　　drunken oaf
An sends, beside, auld Scotland's cash
　　To her warst faes.　　　　　　　　　　　　　foes

Ye Scots, wha wish auld Scotland well!
Ye chief, to you my tale I tell,
Poor, plackless devils like mysel!　　　　　　　penniless
　　It sets you ill,　　　　　　　　　　　　　becomes
Wi bitter, dearthfu wines to mell,　　　　　　　meddle
　　Or foreign gill.

May gravels round his blather wrench,　　　　　　bladder
An gouts torment him, inch by inch,
Wha twists his gruntle wi a glunch　　　　　　face, sneer
　　O sour disdain,
Out owre a glass o whisky-punch
　　Wi honest men!

O Whisky! soul o plays an pranks!
Accept a Bardie's gratefu thanks!
When wanting thee, what tuneless cranks　　　　creakings
　　Are my poor verses!
Thou comes – they rattle i' their ranks,
　　At ither's arses!

Thee, Ferintosh! O sadly lost!
Scotland lament frae coast to coast!
Now colic grips, an barkin hoast
　　May kill us a';
For loyal Forbes' charter'd boast
　　Is taen awa!

| | |
|---|---|
| Thae curst horse-leeches o th' Excise, | Those |
| Wha mak the whisky stells their prize! | stills |
| Haud up thy han', Deil! ance, twice, thrice! | |
| There, seize the blinkers! | spies |
| An bake them up in brunstane pies | |
| For poor damn'd drinkers. | |

| | |
|---|---|
| Fortune! if thou'll but gie me still | |
| Hale breeks, a scone, an whisky gill, | Whole breeches |
| An rowth o rhyme to rave at will, | store |
| Tak a' the rest, | |
| An deal't about as thy blind skill | |
| Directs thee best. | |

# BROSE AND BUTTER

According to DeLancey Ferguson, this was Burns's earliest surviving example of his work as a collector of folk songs. He extensively reworked this old Ayrshire ballad, full of sexual innuendo and double entendres: 'brose and butter' (seminal ejaculation), 'grass', 'stibble' (pubic hair), 'dibble' (penis) 'leather' (vagina), 'Mouse', 'Moudiewart' (penis)

CHORUS

*O gie my love brose, lasses;*
   *O gie my love brose and butter;*
*For nane in Carrick wi him*
   *Can gie a cunt its supper.*

| | |
|---|---|
| Jenny sits up i' the laft, | loft |
| Jockie wad fain a been at her; | |
| But there cam a wind out o the west | |
| Made a' the winnocks to clatter. | windows |

| | |
|---|---|
| The laverock lo'es the grass, | lark |
| The paetrick lo'es the stibble: | partridge |
| And hey, for the gardiner lad, | |
| To gully awa wi his dibble! | |

| | |
|---|---|
| My daddie sent me to the hill | |
| To pu my minnie some heather; | cow |
| An drive it in your fill, | |
| Ye're welcome to the leather. | |

The Mouse is a merry wee beast,
  The Moudiewart wants the een;                 mole
And O, for a touch o the thing
  I had in my nieve yestreen.                    fist

We a' were fou yestreen,                    drunk
  The night shall be its brither;
And hey, for a roaring pin           erect penis
  To nail twa wames thegither!         bellies

# EPISTLE TO JAMES SMITH

*Friendship, mysterious cement of the soul!*
*Sweet'ner of Life, and solder of Society!*
*I owe thee much —*            BLAIR

James Smith (1765-1823), brother of one of the 'Mauchline Belles', and a draper in Mauchline, who later emigrated to Jamaica. He shared Burns's propensity for amatory pursuits, with similar results, and he was the recipient of some of the poet's letters on the subject of love and marriage couched in the frankest terms. In this verse-epistle Burns develops his rip-roaring denunciation of the censorious, hypocritical bigots of the period. It also contains (ll.37ff.) his intention to publish his poems.

Dear Smith, the slee'st, pawkie thief,      artful
That e'er attempted stealth or rief!      plunder
Ye surely hae some warlock-breef    wizard-spell
  Owre human hearts;
For ne'er a bosom yet was prief       proof
  Against your arts.

For me, I swear by sun an moon,
An ev'ry star that blinks aboon,       above
Ye've cost me twenty pair o shoon,
  Just gaun to see you;
And ev'ry ither pair that's done,
  Mair taen I'm wi you.           taken

That auld, capricious carlin, Nature,    beldam
To mak amends for scrimpit stature,   stunted
She's turn'd you off, a human-creature
  On her first plan;
And in her freaks, on ev'ry feature
  She's wrote the Man.

Just now I've taen the fit o rhyme,
My barmie noddle's working prime,            seething brain
My fancy yerkit up sublime,                stirred
   Wi hasty summon:
Hae ye a leisure-moment's time
   To hear what's comin?

Some rhyme a neebor's name to lash;
Some rhyme (vain thought!) for needfu cash;
Some rhyme to court the countra clash,         talk
   An raise a din;
For me, an aim I never fash;              heed
   I rhyme for fun.

The star that rules my luckless lot,
Has fated me the russet coat,
And damn'd my fortune to the groat;
   But, in requit,
Has blest me with a random-shot
   O countra wit.

This while my notion's taen a sklent,        turn
To try my fate in guid, black prent;
But still the mair I'm that way bent,
   Something cries 'Hoolie!           Softly
I red you, honest man, tak tent!     counsel, heed
   Ye'll shaw your folly;

'There's ither poets, much your betters,
Far seen in Greek, deep men o letters,
Hae thought they had ensur'd their debtors,
   A' future ages;
Now moths deform, in shapeless tatters,
   Their unknown pages.'

Then farewell hopes o laurel-boughs,
To garland my poetic brows!
Henceforth I'll rove where busy ploughs
   Are whistling thrang;           at work
An teach the lanely heights an howes
   My rustic sang.

I'll wander on, wi tentless heed         careless
How never-halting moments speed,
Till Fate shall snap the brittle thread;
   Then, all unknown,
I'll lay me with th' inglorious dead,
   Forgot and gone!

But why o death begin a tale?
Just now we're living sound an hale;
Then top and maintop crowd the sail,
    Heave Care o'er-side!
And large, before Enjoyment's gale,
    Let's tak the tide.

This life sae far's I understand,
Is a' enchanted fairy-land,
Where Pleasure is the magic-wand,
    That, wielded right,
Maks hours like minutes, hand in hand,
    Dance by fu light.

The magic-wand then let us wield;
For, ance that five-and-forty's speel'd,         climbed
See, crazy, weary, joyless Eild,         Old age
    Wi wrinkl'd face,
Comes hostin, hirplin owre the field,    coughing, limping
    Wi creepin pace.

When ance life's day draws near the gloamin,    twilight
Then fareweel vacant, careless roamin;
An fareweel cheerfu tankards foamin,
    An social noise:
An fareweel dear, deluding Woman,
    The joy of joys!

O Life! how pleasant, in thy morning,
Young Fancy's rays the hills adorning!
Cold-pausing Caution's lesson scorning,
    We frisk away,
Like school-boys, at th' expected warning,
    To joy an play.

We wander there, we wander here,
We eye the rose upon the brier,
Unmindful that the thorn is near,
    Among the leaves;
And tho the puny wound appear,
    Short while it grieves.

Some, lucky, find a flow'ry spot,
For which they never toil'd nor swat;        sweated
They drink the sweet and eat the fat,
    But care or pain;        without
And haply eye the barren hut
    With high disdain.

With steady aim, some Fortune chase;
Keen Hope does ev'ry sinew brace;
Thro fair, thro foul, they urge the race,
    And seize the prey:
Then cannie, in some cozie place,
    They close the day.

And others, like your humble servan',
Poor wights! nae rules nor roads observin,
To right or left eternal swervin,
    They zig-zag on;
Till, curst with age, obscure an starvin,
    They aften groan.

Alas! what bitter toil an straining –
But truce with peevish, poor complaining!
Is Fortune's fickle *Luna* waning?
    E'en let her gang!
Beneath what light she has remaining,
    Let's sing our sang.

My pen I here fling to the door,
And kneel, ye Pow'rs! and warm implore,
'Tho I should wander *Terra* o'er,
    In all her climes,
Grant me but this, I ask no more,
    Ay rowth o rhymes.                          plenty

'Gie dreeping roasts to countra lairds,        dripping
Till icicles hing frae their beards;
Gie fine braw claes to fine life-guards,       clothes
    And maids of honor;
And yill an whisky gie to cairds,              ale, tinkers
    Until they sconner.                        sicken

'A title, Dempster merits it;         George Dempster, M.P.
A garter gie to Willie Pitt;
Gie wealth to some be-ledger'd cit,            city-dweller
    In cent, per cent.;
But give me real, sterling wit,
    And I'm content.

'While ye are pleas'd to keep me hale
I'll sit down o'er my scanty meal,
Be't water brose or muslin-kail,          gruel, beefless broth
    Wi cheerfu face,
As lang's the Muses dinna fail
    To say the grace.'

An anxious e'e I never throws
Behint my lug, or by my nose;          *ear*
I jouk beneath Misfortune's blows        *dodge*
    As weel's I may;
Sworn foe to sorrow, care, and prose,
    I rhyme away.

O ye douce folk that live by rule,
Grave, tideless-blooded, calm an cool,    *sober*
Compar'd wi you – O fool! fool! fool!
    How much unlike!
Your hearts are just a standing pool,
    Your lives, a dyke!           *wall*

Nae hair-brain'd, sentimental traces
In your unletter'd, nameless faces!
In *arioso* trills and graces
    Ye never stray;
But *gravissimo*, solemn basses
    Ye hum away.

Ye are sae grave, nae doubt ye're wise,
Nae ferly tho ye do despise         *marvel*
The hairum-scairum, ram-stam boys,  *headlong*
    The rattling squad:
I see ye upward cast your eyes –
    Ye ken the road!

Whilst I – but I shall haud me there,   *hold*
Wi you I'll scarce gang onie where –
Then, Jamie, I shall say nae mair,
    But quat my sang,
Content wi you to mak a pair,
    Whare'er I gang.

## THE RANTIN DOG, THE DADDIE O'T

*TUNE: Whare'll our gudeman lie*

Burns commented that he wrote this song 'pretty early in life and sent it to a young girl, a very particular acquaintance of mine, who was at that time under a cloud.' But whether Elizabeth Paton or Jean Armour is meant has long been a matter for conjecture. Kinsley draws attention to 'the cheerful impenitence' and the expectation of renewed pleasure, characteristic of Burns.

| | |
|---|---|
| O, wha my babie-clouts will buy? | -linen |
| O, wha will tent me when I cry? | attend to |
| Wha will kiss me where I lie? – | |
| The rantin dog, the daddie o't! | rollicking |
| | |
| O, wha will own he did the faut? | fault |
| O, wha will buy the groanin maut? | midwife's ale |
| O, wha will tell me how to ca't? | name it |
| The rantin  dog, the daddie o't! | |
| | |
| When I mount the creepie-chair, | stool of repentance |
| Wha will sit beside me there? | |
| Gie me Rob, I'll seek nae mair – | |
| The rantin dog, the daddie o't! | |
| | |
| Wha will crack to me my lane? | talk, alone |
| Wha will mak me fidgin fain? | desirous |
| Wha will kiss me o'er again? – | |
| The rantin dog, the daddie o't! | |

## THE AUTHOR'S EARNEST CRY AND PRAYER

### TO THE SCOTCH REPRESENTATIVES IN
### THE HOUSE OF COMMONS

*Dearest of distillation! last and best—*
*How art thou lost!—*PARODY ON MILTON

Written as a reaction to the passing of the Wash Act of 1784 which aimed at terminating the privileged treatment enjoyed by Scottish distillers under the excise laws. The rigorous application of this Act, together with the growth of illicit distilling, had a serious effect on the legitimate whisky industry. London gin distillers, however, continued to object to whisky imports in England and this led to the Scotch Distillery Act of 1786 which imposed even more swingeing taxes on the whisky trade, but actually provoked the Scots into devising more efficient methods of production which paradoxically resulted in a significant expansion of the industry.

| | |
|---|---|
| Ye Irish lords, ye knights an squires, | |
| Wha represent our brughs an shires, | boroughs |
| An doucely manage our affairs | sedately |
| In Parliament, | |
| To you a simple Bardie's prayers | |
| Are humbly sent. | |

Alas! my roupet Muse is haerse!      *husky, hoarse*
Your Honors' hearts wi grief 'twad pierce,
To see her sittin on her arse
    Low i' the dust,
And scriechin out prosaic verse,
    An like to brust!      *burst*

Tell them wha hae the chief direction,
Scotland an me's in great affliction,
E'er sin' they laid that curst restriction
    On aqua-vitae;      *water of life (Latin)*
An rouse them up to strong conviction,   *(cf. uisge beatha in Gaelic)*
    An move their pity.

Stand forth, an tell yon Premier youth   *William Pitt the Younger,*
The honest, open, naked truth:   *Prime Minister at the age of 24*
Tell him o mine an Scotland's drouth,   *thirst*
    His servants humble:
The muckle deevil blaw you south,
    If ye dissemble!

Does onie great man glunch an gloom?   *growl*
Speak out, an never fash your thumb!   *care a lot*
Let posts an pensions sink or soom   *swim*
    Wi them wha grant 'em:
If honestly they canna come,
    Far better want 'em.

In gath'rin votes you were na slack;
Now stand as tightly by your tack:
Ne'er claw your lug, an fidge your back,   *scratch, wriggle*
    An hum an haw;
But raise your arm, an tell your crack
    Before them a'.

Paint Scotland greetin owre her thrissle;   *weeping, thistle*
Her mutchkin stowp as toom's a whissle;   *pint-pot, empty*
An damn'd excisemen in a bustle,
    Seizin a stell,      *still*
Triumphant, crushin't like a mussel,
    Or lampit shell!      *limpet*

Then, on the tither hand, present her –
A blackguard smuggler right behint her,
An cheek-for-chow, a chuffie vintner   *cheek-by-jowl, fat-faced*
    Colleaguing join,
Pickin her pouch as bare as winter   *pocket*
    Of a' kind coin.

Is there, that bears the name o Scot,
But feels his heart's bluid rising hot,
To see his poor auld mither's pot
    Thus dung in staves,                          *broken in bits*
An plunder'd o her hindmost groat,
    By gallows knaves?

Alas! I'm but a nameless wight,
Trode i' the mire out o sight!
But could I like Montgomeries fight,           *Earls of Eglinton*
    Or gab like Boswell,           *James Boswell (1740-95)*
There's some sark-necks I wad draw tight,          *shirt-*
    An tie some hose well.

God bless your Honors! can ye see't,
The kind, auld, cantie carlin greet,        *jolly matron weep*
An no get warmly to your feet,
    An gar them hear it,                   *make*
An tell them wi a patriot-heat,
    Ye winna bear it?

Some o you nicely ken the laws,
To round the period an pause,
An with the rhetoric clause on clause
    To mak harangues:
Then echo thro Saint Stephen's wa's      *House of Commons*
    Auld Scotland's wrangs.

Dempster, a true blue Scot I'se warran;    *George Dempster, M.P.*
Thee, aith-detesting, chaste Kilkerran;    *Sir Adam Ferguson of*
An that glib-gabbet Highland baron,    *Kilkerran; glib-tongued*
    The Laird o Graham;      *James Graham, 3rd Duke*
An ane, a chap that's damn'd auldfarran,    *of Montrose (1755-1836);*
    Dundas his name:            *shrewd, Henry Dundas,*
                          *Viscount Melville (1742-18-11)*
Erskine, a spunkie Norland billie;    *Thomas Erskine, M.P. (1750-1823)*
True Campbells, Frederick and Ilay;    *Lord Frederick Campbell (1736-1816)*
An Livistone, the bauld Sir Willie;    *Sir Ilay Campbell (1734-1823)*
    An monie ithers,        *Sir William Cunninghame of*
Whom auld Demosthenes or Tully    *Livingston, Cicero*
    Might own for brithers.

Thee sodger Hugh, my watchman stented,    *Hugh Montgomerie,*
If Bardies e'er are represented;    *12th Earl of Eglinton*
I ken if that your sword were wanted,
    Ye'd lend your hand;
But when there's ought to say anent it,
    Ye're at a stand.

Arouse, my boys! exert your mettle,
To get auld Scotland back her kettle;      *whisky still*
Or faith! I'll wad my new pleugh-pettle,     *plough-scraper*
 Ye'll see't or lang,
She'll teach you, wi a reekin whittle,     *smoking knife*
 Anither sang.

This while she's been in crankous mood,      *fretful*
Her lost Militia fir'd her bluid;   *alluding to the Militia Bill, 1782*
(Deil na they never mair do guid,    *opposed by Dempster*
 Play'd her that pliskie!)          *trick*
An now she's like to rin red-wud       *berserk*
 About her whisky.

An Lord! if ance they pit her till't,        *to it*
Her tartan petticoat she'll kilt,
An durk an pistol at her belt,
 She'll tak the streets,
An rin her whittle to the hilt,        *knife*
 I' the first she meets!

For God-sake, sirs! then speak her fair,
An straik her cannie wi the hair,      *stroke; gently*
An to the Muckle House repair,     *House of Commons*
 Wi instant speed,
An strive, wi a' your wit an lear,       *learning*
 To get remead.            **redress**

Yon ill-tongu'd tinkler, Charlie Fox,     *Charles James Fox*
May taunt you wi his jeers and mocks;
But gie him't het, my hearty cocks!       *hot*
 E'en cowe the cadie!      *frighten the lackey*
An send him to his dicing box
 An sportin lady.

Tell yon guid bluid of auld Boconnock's,   *Robert Pitt of Boconnoc,*
I'll be his debt twa mashlum bonnocks,   *grandfather of the P. M.*
An drink his health in auld Nanse Tinnock's *hostess of the Sorn Inn,*
 Nine times a-week,      *Castle St., Mauchline*
If he some scheme, like tea an winnocks,   *a reference to the*
 Wad kindly seek.   *Commutation Act, 1784 reducing*
      *the import duty on tea and windows*

Could he some commutation broach,
I'll pledge my aith in guid braid Scotch,      *oath*
He needna fear their foul reproach
 Nor erudition,
Yon mixtie-maxtie, queer hotch-potch,     *mixed-up*
 The 'Coalition.'      *Fox-North administration*
              *of 1783*

Auld Scotland has a raucle tongue;                    bitter
She's just a devil wi a rung;                          cudgel
An if she promise auld or young
    To tak their part,
Tho by the neck she would be strung.
    She'll no desert.

And now, ye chosen Five-and-Forty,          the 45 Scottish MPs
May still your mither's heart support ye;
Then, tho a minister grow dorty,                      pettish
    An kick your place,
Ye'll snap your fingers, poor an hearty,
    Before his face.

God bless your Honors, a' your days
Wi sowps o kail and brats o claes,           sups, broth, scraps
In spite o a' the thievish kaes,                      jackdaws
    That haunt St. Jamie's!         Palace of St James's
Your humble Bardie sings an prays,              (ie the Court)
    While Rab his name is.

POSTSCRIPT

Let half-starved slaves in warmer skies
See future wines, rich-clust'ring, rise;
Their lot auld Scotland ne'er envies,
    But, blythe and frisky,
She eyes her freeborn, martial boys
    Tak aff their whisky.

What tho their Phoebus kinder warms,                    sun
While fragrance blooms and Beauty charms,
When wretches range, in famish'd swarms,
    The scented groves;
Or, hounded forth, dishonour arms
    In hungry droves!

Their gun's a burden on their shouther;             shoulder
They downa bide the stink o powther;               gunpowder
Their bauldest thought's a hank'ring swither          doubt
    To stan' or rin,
Till skelp – a shot – they're aff, a' throw'ther   crack, pell-mell
    To save their skin.

But bring a Scotsman frae his hill,
Clap in his cheek a Highland gill,
Say, such is royal George's will,
    An there's the foe!
He has nae thought but how to kill
    Twa at a blow.

Nae cauld, faint-hearted doubtings tease him;
Death comes, wi fearless eye he sees him;
Wi bluidy han' a welcome gies him;
    An when he fa's,
His latest draught o breathin lea'es him
    In faint huzzas.

Sages their solemn een may steek,             eyes; close
An raise a philosophic reek,                 smoke
An physically causes seek,
    In clime an season;
But tell me whisky's name in Greek;
    I'll tell the reason.

Scotland, my auld, respected mither!
Tho whiles ye moistify your leather,        sometimes
Till whare ye sit on craps o heather,    heather tops
    Ye tine your dam;            lose; water
Freedom an whisky gang thegither
    Tak aff your dram!

# SKETCH

First published by Currie from Burns's holograph, but later rejected on doubt being expressed by Gilbert Burns, and subsequent editors wrongly attributed it to Fergusson but Kinsley demonstrated conclusively that Burns was, in fact, its author. Dewar placed it in the poet's Mossgiel period.

Hail, Poesie! thou nymph reserv'd!
In chase o thee, what crowds hae swerv'd
Frae Common Sense, or sunk ennerv'd
    'Mang heaps o clavers;         idle talk
An Och! o'er aft thy joes hae starv'd
    'Mid a' thy favors!

Say, Lassie, why thy train amang,
While loud the trumps heroic clang,
And Sock and buskin skelp alang      symbols of
    To death or marriage;      Greek drama
Scarce ane has tried the Shepherd-sang
    But wi miscarriage?

In Homer's craft Jock Milton thrives;
Eschylus' pen Will Shakespeare drives;
Wee Pope, the knurlin, 'till him rives       Alexander Pope; dwarf
   Horatian fame;
In thy sweet sang, Barbauld, survives      Mrs Anna Barbauld
   E'en Sappho's flame.                (1743-1825)

But thee, Theocritus, wha matches?
They're no Herd's ballats, Maro's catches;     David Herd
Squire Pope but busks his skinklin patches   (c.1731-1810)
   O Heathen tatters:               glittering
I pass by hunders, nameless wretches,
   That ape their betters.

In this braw age o wit and lear,           learning
Will nane the Shepherd's whistle mair
Blaw sweetly in his native air
   And rural grace;
And wi the far-fam'd Grecian share
   A rival place?

Yes! there is ane; a Scottish callan!         lad
There's ane: come forrit, honest Allan!    Allan Ramsay
Thou need na jouk behint the hallan,      partition
   A chiel sae clever;              fellow
The teeth o Time may gnaw Tamtallan,   Tantallon Castle
   But thou's for ever.

Thou paints auld Nature to the nines,
In thy sweet Caledonian lines;
Nae gowden stream thro myrtles twines      golden
   Where Philomel,
While nightly breezes sweep the vines,
   Her griefs will tell!

Thy rural loves are Nature's sel;
Nae bombast spates o nonsense swell;
Nae snap conceits, but that sweet spell
   O witchin love,
That charm that can the strongest quell,
   The sternest move.

In gowany glens thy burnie strays,        flowery;
Where bonie lasses bleach their claes;      brooklet
Or trots by hazelly shaws and braes    woods, slopes
   Wi hawthorns gray,
Where blackbirds join the shepherd's lays
   At close o day.

# TO A LOUSE

## ON SEEING ONE ON A LADY'S BONNET AT CHURCH

Probably written late in 1785; the use of Lunardi to denote a type of bonnet then the very height of fashion is an allusion to Vincenzo Lunardi who made several balloon flights in Scotland that year. Ironically, the first manned flights in the British Isles were made in September 1784 by James Tytler, Editor of the *Encyclopaedia Britannica* and a collaborator with Burns in the *Scots Musical Museum*.

| | |
|---|---|
| Ha! whare ye gaun, ye crowlin ferlie? | crawling marvel |
| Your impudence protects you sairly; | marvel |
| I canna say but ye strunt rarely | strut |
| Owre gauze and lace, | |
| Tho faith! I fear ye dine but sparely | |
| On sic a place. | |

| | |
|---|---|
| Ye ugly, creepin, blastit wonner, | |
| Detested, shunn'd by saunt an sinner, | |
| How daur ye set your fit upon her – | foot |
| Sae fine a lady! | |
| Gae somewhere else and seek your dinner | |
| On some poor body. | |

| | |
|---|---|
| Swith! in some beggar's hauffet squattle; | Off!, temples squat; |
| There ye may creep, and sprawl, and sprattle, | scramble |
| Wi ither kindred, jumping cattle; | |
| In shoals and nations; | |
| Whare horn nor bane ne'er daur unsettle | |
| Your thick plantations. | |

| | |
|---|---|
| Now haud you there! ye're out o sight, | keep |
| Below the fatt'rils, snug an tight, | falderols |
| Na, faith ye yet! ye'll no be right, | |
| Till ye've got on it – | |
| The vera tapmost, tow'rin height | |
| O Miss's bonnet. | |

| | |
|---|---|
| My sooth! right bauld ye set your nose out, | |
| As plump an grey as onie grozet: | gooseberry |
| O for some rank, mercurial rozet, | resin |
| Or fell, red smeddum, | deadly powder |
| I'd gie you sic a hearty dose o't, | |
| Wad dress your droddum! | backside |

| | |
|---|---|
| I wad na been surpris'd to spy | |
| You on an auld wife's flainen toy; | flannel cap |
| Or aiblins some bit duddie boy, | perhaps, small |
| On's wyliecoat; | ragged vest |
| But Miss's fine Lunardi! fye! | balloon bonnet |
| How daur ye do't? | |

RECITATIVO

| | |
|---|---|
| He ended; and the kebars sheuk | rafters shook |
| Aboon the chorus roar; | Above |
| While frighted rattons backward leuk. | rats |
| An seek the benmost bore: | inmost hole |
| A fairy fiddler frae the neuk, | corner |
| He skirl'd out, *Encore!* | |
| But up arose the martial chuck, | camp whore |
| An laid the loud uproar: – | |

AIR

*TUNE: Sodger Laddie*

I once was a maid, tho I cannot tell when,
And still my delight is in proper young men:
Some one of a troop of dragoons was my daddie,
No wonder I'm fond of a sodger laddie!
    Sing, lal de dal, etc.

The first of my loves was a swaggering blade,
To rattle the thundering drum was his trade;
His leg was so tight, and his cheek was so ruddy,
Transported I was with my sodger laddie.

But the godly old chaplain left him in the lurch
The sword I forsook for the sake of the church;
He risked the soul, and I ventur'd the body,
'Twas then I prov'd false to my sodger laddie.

Full soon I grew sick of my sanctified sot,
The regiment at large for a husband I got;
From the gilded spontoon to the fife I was ready,
I asked no more but a sodger laddie.

| | |
|---|---|
| But the Peace it reduc'd me to beg in despair, | |
| Till I met my old boy in a Cunningham Fair: | northern Ayrshire |
| His rags regimental they flutter'd so gaudy, | |
| My heart it rejoic'd at a sodger laddie. | |

And now I have liv'd – I know not how long!
And still I can join in a cup and a song,
But whilst with both hands I can hold the glass steady,
Here's to thee, my hero, my sodger laddie.

RECITATIVO

| | |
|---|---|
| Poor Merry-Andrew in the neuk | |
| Sat guzzling wi a tinkler-hizzie; | tinker hussy |
| They mind't na wha the chorus teuk, | cared not |
| Between themselves they were sae busy. | |
| At length, wi drink an courting dizzy, | |
| He stoiter'd up an made a face; | struggled |
| Then turn'd an laid a smack on Grizzie, | |
| Syne tun'd his pipes wi grave grimace: – | Then |

AIR

*TUNE: Auld Sir Symon*

| | |
|---|---|
| Sir Wisdom's a fool when he's fou: | drunk |
| Sir Knave is a fool in a session: | session |
| He's there but a prentice I trow, | trust |
| But I am a fool by profession. | |

| | |
|---|---|
| My grannie she bought me a beuk, | book |
| An I held awa to the school: | went off |
| I fear I my talent misteuk, | |
| But what will ye hae of a fool? | |

| | |
|---|---|
| For drink I would venture my neck; | |
| A hizzie's the half of my craft: | |
| But what could ye other expect, | |
| Of ane that's avowedly daft? | mentally deficient |

| | |
|---|---|
| I ance was tyed up like a stirk | once, bullock |
| For civilly swearing and quaffing; | |
| I ance was abus'd i' the kirk, | rebuked |
| For towsing a lass i' my daffin. | indecent handling, fun |

Poor Andrew that tumbles for sport
  Let naebody name wi a jeer:
There's even, I'm tauld, i' the Court
  A tumbler ca'd the Premier.

Observ'd ye yon reverend lad
  Mak faces to tickle the mob?
He rails at our mountebank squad –
  It's rivalship just i' the job!

| | |
|---|---|
| And now my conclusion I'll tell, | |
| For faith! I'm confoundedly dry: | |
| The chiel that's a fool for himsel, | fellow |
| Guid Lord! he's far dafter than I. | |

RECITATIVO

| | |
|---|---|
| Then niest outspak a raucle carlin, | sturdy beldam |
| Wha kent fu weel to cleek the sterlin; | steal money |
| For monie a pursie she had hooked, | |
| An had in monie a well been douked: | ducked |
| Her love had been a Highland laddie, | |
| But weary fa' the waefu woodie! | |
| Wi sighs an sobs she thus began | |
| To wail her braw John Highlandman: – | |

AIR

*TUNE: O, an ye were dead, Guidman*

*CHORUS*

*Sing hey my braw John Highlandman!*
*Sing ho my braw John Highlandman!*
*There's not a lad in a' the lan'*
*Was match for my John Highlandman!*

| | |
|---|---|
| A Highland lad my love was born, | |
| The lalland laws he held in scorn | lowland |
| But he still was faithfu to his clan, | |
| My gallant, braw John Highlandman. | |

| | |
|---|---|
| With his philibeg an tartan plaid, | little kilt |
| An guid claymore down by his side, | broadsword |
| The ladies' hearts he did trepan, | ensnare |
| My gallant, braw John Highlandman. | |

We ranged a' from Tweed to Spey,
An liv'd like lords an ladies gay,
For a lalland face he feared none,
My gallant, braw John Highlandman.

They banished him beyond the sea,
But ere the bud was on the tree,
Adown my cheeks the pearls ran,
Embracing my John Highlandman.

But, och! they catch'd him at the last,
And bound him in a dungeon fast:
My curse upon them every one –
They've hang'd my braw John Highlandman!

And now a widow I must mourn
The pleasures that will ne'er return;
No comfort but a hearty can,
When I think on John Highlandman.

RECITATIVO

| | |
|---|---|
| A pigmy scraper on a fiddle, | |
| Wha us'd to trystes an fairs to driddle, | cattle round-ups, dawdle |
| Her strappin limb an gawsie middle | buxom |
|     (He reach'd nae higher) | |
| Had hol'd his heartie like a riddle, | |
|     An blawn't on fire. | blown it |

| | |
|---|---|
| Wi hand on hainch and upward e'e, | haunch |
| He croon'd his gamut, one, two, three | |
| Then in an *arioso* key, | |
|     The wee Apollo | |
| Set off wi *allegretto* glee | |
|     His *giga* solo:- | |

AIR

*TUNE: Whistle owre the lave o't*

CHORUS

*I am a fiddler to my trade,*
*An a' the tunes that e'er I play'd*
*The sweetest still to wife or maid,*
    *Was 'Whistle owre the lave o't.'*

| | |
|---|---|
| Let me ryke up to dight that tear, | reach, wipe |
| An go wi me an be my dear; | |
| An then your every care an fear | |
|     May whistle owre the lave o't. | |

| | |
|---|---|
| At kirns an weddins we'se be there, | harvest-homes |
| An O, sae nicely's we will fare! | |
| We'll bowse about till Daddie Care | |
|     Sing Whistle owre the lave o't. | |

| | |
|---|---|
| Sae merrily the banes we'll pyke, | bones, pick |
| An sun oursels about the dyke; | fence |
| An at our leisure, when ye like, | |
|     We'll – whistle owre the lave o't! | |

| | |
|---|---|
| But bless me wi your heav'n o charms, | |
| An while I kittle hair on thairms, | tickle, catguts |
| Hunger, cauld, an a' sick harms, | |
|     May whistle owre the lave o't. | |

RECITATIVO

Her charms had struck a sturdy caird,                                      tinker
    As weel as poor gut-scraper;
He taks the fiddler by the beard,
    An draws a roosty rapier;
He swoor by a' was swearing worth,
    To speet him like a pliver,                                      skewer, plover
Unless he would from that time forth
    Relinquish her for ever.

Wi ghastly e'e, poor Tweedle-Dee
    Upon his hunkers bended,                                      haunches
An pray'd for grace wi ruefu face,
    An sae the quarrel ended.
But tho his little heart did grieve
    When round the tinkler prest her,
He feign'd to snirtle in his sleeve,                                      snigger
    When thus the caird address'd her: –

AIR

              *TUNE: Clout the Cauldron*                                      patch

My bonie lass, I work in brass,
    A tinkler is my station:
I've travell'd round all Christian ground
    In this my occupation;
I've taen the gold, an been enrolled
    In many a noble squadron;
But vain they search'd when off I march'd
    To go an clout the cauldron.

Despise that shrimp, that wither'd imp,
    With a' his noise an cap'rin;
An take a share wi those that bear
    The budget and the apron!
An by that stowp! my faith an houpe!                                      cup
    And by that dear Kilbaigie!                                      a Clackmannanshire
If e'er ye want, or meet wi scant,                                      whisky distillery
    May I ne'er weet my craigie.                                      wet, throat

RECITATIVO

The caird prevail'd: th' unblushing fair
   In his embraces sunk;
Partly wi love o'ercome sae sair,
   An partly she was drunk.
Sir Violino, with an air
That show'd a man o spunk,                              spirit
Wish'd unison between the pair,
   An made the bottle clunk
      To their health that night.

But hurchin Cupid shot a shaft,               urchin
   That play'd a dame a shavie:               trick
The fiddler rak'd her fore and aft,
   Behint the chicken cavie.              hen-coop
Her lord, a wight o Homer's craft,
   Tho limpin wi the spavie,              spavin
He hirpl'd up, an lap like daft,       limped, leaped
   An shor'd them Dainty Davie    Rev. David Williamson,
      O boot that night.   a celebrated Covenanter; gratis

He was a care-defying blade
   As ever Bacchus listed!
Tho Fortune sair upon him laid,
   His heart, she ever miss'd it.
He had no wish but – to be glad,
   Nor want but – when he thirsted;
He hated nought but – to be sad,
   An thus the Muse suggested
      His sang that night.

AIR

*TUNE: For a' that, an a' that*

*CHORUS*

*For a' that, an a' that,*
   *An twice as muckle's a' that,*
*I've lost but ane, I've twa behin',*
   *I've wife eneugh for a' that*

I am a Bard of no regard,
   Wi' gentle folks an a' that,
But Homer-like the glowrin byke,        staring crowd
   Frae town to town I draw that.

I never drank the Muses' stank,      *pool*
   Castalia's burn, an a' that;      *brook*
But there it streams, an richly reams –      *froths*
   My Helicon I ca' that.

Great love I bear to a' the fair,
   Their humble slave an a' that;
But lordly will, I hold it still
   A mortal sin to thraw that.      *thwart*

In raptures sweet this hour we meet,
   Wi mutual love an a' that;
But for how lang the flie may stang,      *fly, sting*
   Let inclination law that!

Their tricks an craft hae put me daft,
   They've taen me in, an a' that;
But clear your decks, an here's the Sex!
   I like the jads for a' that.      *jades*

CHORUS

*For a' that an a' that,*
   *An twice as muckle's a' that,*
*My dearest bluid, to do them guid,*
   *They're welcome till't for a' that!*

RECITATIVO

So sung the Bard, and Nansie's wa's      *walls*
Shook with a thunder of applause,
   Re-echo'd from each mouth!
They toom'd their pocks, they pawn'd their duds,      *emptied pockets*
They scarcely left to coor their fuds,      *cover tails*
   To quench their lowin drouth.      *burning thirst*
Then owre again the jovial thrang      *throng*
   The Poet did request
To lowse his pack, an wale a sang      *untie, choose*
   A ballad o the best:
   He rising, rejoicing,
     Between his twa Deborahs,      *Judges v. 12*
   Looks round him, an found them
     Impatient for the chorus: –

AIR

*TUNE: Jolly Mortals, fill your Glasses*

*CHORUS*

*A fig for those by law protected!*
    *Liberty's a glorious feast!*
*Courts for cowards were erected,*
    *Churches built to please the priest!*

See the smoking bowl before us,
    Mark our jovial, ragged ring!
Round and round take up the chorus,
    And in raptures let us sing:

What is title, what is treasure,
    What is reputation's care?
If we lead a life of pleasure,
    'Tis no matter how or where!

With the ready trick and fable,
    Round we wander all the day;
And at night, in barn or stable,
    Hug our doxies on the hay.

Does the train-attended carriage
    Thro the country lighter rove?
Does the sober bed of marriage
    Witness brighter scenes of love?

Life is all a variorum,
    We regard not how it goes;
Let them prate about decorum,
    Who have character to lose.

Here's to budgets, bags and wallets!
    Here's to all the wandering train!
Here's our ragged brats and callets!                    wenches
    One and all, cry out, Amen!

# THE ORDINATION

*For sense, they little owe to frugal Heav'n:*
*To please the mob they hide the little giv'n.*

Probably written in early January 1786, it was mentioned by Burns in his letter of 17th February to John Richmond. It deals with the ordination of the Rev. James Mackinlay (1756-1841) at Kilmarnock's Laigh Kirk. Mackinlay's presentation to the charge (August 1785) was violently opposed by the Moderates, and it was not until 6th April 1786 that he could actually be inducted. This poem was composed as 'an anticipatory view of the approaching ceremony.'

| | |
|---|---|
| Kilmarnock wabsters, fidge an claw, | weavers, shrug, scratch |
| An pour your creeshie nations; | greasy |
| An ye wha leather rax an draw, | stretch |
| Of a' denominations; | |
| Swith! to the Laigh Kirk, ane an a', | Haste! |
| An there tak up your stations; | |
| Then aff to Begbie's in a raw, | later the Angel tavern |
| An pour divine libations | |
| For joy this day. | |

| | |
|---|---|
| Curst Common-sense, the imp o Hell, | |
| Cam in wi Maggie Lauder: | wife of the Rev. Wm. Lindsay |
| But Oliphant aft made her yell, | Rev. James Oliphant, High Kirk |
| An Russel sair misca'd her: | Rev. John Russell, his successor |
| This day Mackinlay taks the flail, | Rev. James Mackinlay |
| An he's the boy will blaud her! | slap |
| He'll clap a shangan on her tail, | cleft stick |
| An set the bairns to daud her | pelt |
| Wi dirt this day. | |

| | |
|---|---|
| Mak haste an turn King David owre, | give out a metrical psalm |
| An lilt wi holy clangor; | |
| O double verse come gie us four, | |
| An skirl up the *Bangor:* | a famous psalm tune |
| This day the Kirk kicks up a stoure, | dust |
| Nae mair the knaves shall wrang her, | |
| For Heresy is in her pow'r, | |
| And gloriously she'll whang her, | flog |
| Wi pith this day. | |

| | |
|---|---|
| Come, let a proper text be read, | |
| An touch it aff wi vigour, | |
| How graceless Ham leugh at his dad, | laughed |
| Which made Canaan a nigger; | |
| Or Phineas drove the murdering blade, | |
| Wi whore-abhorring rigour; | |
| Or Zipporah, the scauldin jade, | jade |
| Was like a bluidy tiger, | |
| I' th' inn that day. | |

**BURNS AND THE VISION**
by James Christie
*by courtesy of Irvine Burns Club*

BURNS HOUSE IN THE MILL VENNEL, DUMFRIES
(now Burns Street)

There, try his mettle on the Creed,
　And bind him down wi caution,
That stipend is a carnal weed　　　　　　　a luxury like tobacco
　He taks but for the fashion –
And gie him o'er the flock to feed,
　And punish each transgression;
Especial, rams that cross the breed　　　　　　fornicators
　Gie them sufficient threshin;
　　Spare them nae day.

Now auld Kilmarnock, cock thy tail,
　An toss thy horns fu canty;　　　　　　　　joyfully
Nae mair thou'lt rowte out-owre the dale,　　　low
　Because thy pasture's scanty;
For lapfu's large o gospel kail
　Shall fill thy crib in plenty,
An runts o grace the pick an wale,　　　　stalks, choice
　No gi'en by way o dainty,
　　But ilka day.　　　　　　　　　　　　　every

Nae mair by Babel's streams we'll weep,　　　Babylon
　To think upon our Zion;
And hing our fiddles up to sleep,
　Like baby-clouts a-drying!
Come, screw the pegs wi tunefu cheep,
　And o'er the thairms be tryin;　　　　　　strings
Oh, rare! to see our elbucks wheep,　　　　elbows
　And a' like lamb-tails flyin,
　　Fu fast this day!

Lang, Patronage, wi rod o airn,　　　a reference to the opposition to
　Has shor'd the Kirk's undoin;　　　　the induction of the Rev.
As lately Fenwick, sair forfairn,　　William Boyd at Fenwick, 1782
　Has proven to its ruin:
Our patron, honest man! Glencairn,
　He saw mischief was brewin;
An like a godly, elect bairn,
　He waled us out a true ane,　　　　　　　　chose
　　And sound this day.

　　　　　　　　　　　　　　　　Rev. John Robertson
Now Robertson, harangue nae mair　　　　　　(1733-99)
　But steek your gab for ever;　　　　　　　shut, mouth
Or try the wicked town of Ayr,
　For there they'll think you clever;
Or, nae reflection on your lear,　　　　　　learning
　Ye may commence a shaver;　　　　　　set up as a barber
Or to the Netherton repair,　　　　　carpet-making district
　An turn a carpet weaver,　　　　　　　of Kilmarnock
　　Aff-hand this day.

7

Mutrie and you were just a match,     Rev. John Mutrie (d. 1785)
  We never had sic twa drones:     Mackinlay's predecessor
Auld Hornie did the Laigh Kirk watch,     The Devil
  Just like a winkin baudrons,     cat
And ay he catch'd the tither wretch,
  To fry them in his caudrons;     cauldrons
But now his Honor maun detach,
  Wi a' his brimstone squadrons,
    Fast, fast this day.

See, see auld Orthodoxy's faes     foes
  She's swingein thro the city!     fogging
Hark, how the nine-tailed cat she plays!
  I vow it's unco pretty:     mighty
There, Learning, with his Greekish face,
  Grunts out some Latin ditty;
And Common-sense is gaun, she says,
  To mak to Jamie Beattie     James Beattie
    Her plaint this day.

But there's Morality himsel,
  Embracing all opinions;
Hear how he gies the tither yell,
  Between his twa companions!
See, how she peels the skin an fell     subcutaneous tissue
  As ane was peelin onions!
Now there, they're packed aff to Hell,
  An banish'd our dominions,
    Henceforth this day.

O happy day! rejoice, rejoice!
  Come bouse about the porter!
Morality's demure decoys
  Shall here nae mair find quarter:
Mackinlay, Russel, are the boys
  That Heresy can torture;
They'll gie her on a rape a hoyse,     rope, hoist
  And cowe her measure shorter     crop
    By th' head some day.

Come, bring the tither mutchkin in,     pint-pot
  And here's – for a conclusion –
To ev'ry New-Light mother's son,
  From this time forth, confusion!
If mair they deave us wi their din     deafen
  Or patronage intrusion,
We'll light a spunk, and ev'ry skin, match
  We'll rin them aff in fusion,
    Like oil some day.

# THE INVENTORY

## IN ANSWER TO A MANDATE BY THE SURVEYOR OF TAXES

MOSSGIEL, *February 22, 1786*

A poetic reaction to the various taxes introduced by William Pitt in 1784-86, to restore the country's fortunes depleted by the recent American War. These fiscal measures taxed carriages, carriage-horses and personal servants (at a higher rate for bachelors than for married men).

| | |
|---|---|
| Sir, as your mandate did request, | |
| I send you here a faithfu list | |
| O guids an gear, an a' my graith, | chattels |
| To which I'm clear to gi'e my aith. | oath |
| | |
| Imprimis, then, for carriage cattle: | cart-horses |
| I hae four brutes o gallant mettle, | |
| As ever drew before a pettle: | plough-scraper |
| My Lan'-afore's a guid auld 'has been' | front left-hand horse |
| An wight an wilfu a' his days been: | strong |
| My Lan'-ahin's a weel gaun fillie, | rear left-hand horse |
| That aft has borne me hame frae Killie, | Kilmarnock |
| An your auld borough monie a time, | Ayr |
| In days when riding was nae crime. | |
| But ance, when in my wooing pride | |
| I, like a blockhead, boost to ride, | |
| The wilfu creature sae I pat to, – | must, needs |
| Lord pardon a' my sins, an that too! | |
| I play'd my fillie sic a shavie, | trick |
| She's a' bedevil'd wi the spavie. | spavin |
| My Fur-ahin's a wordy beast | rear furrow (right hand) worthy |
| As e'er in tug or tow was traced. | |
| The fourth's a Highland Donald hastie, | |
| A damn'd red-wud Kilburnie blastie! | stark mad, Kilbirnie pest |
| Foreby, a cowte, o cowtes the wale, | Besides, colt, pick |
| As ever ran afore a tail: | |
| If he be spar'd to be a beast, | |
| He'll draw me fifteen pund at least. | fetch £15 |
| | |
| Wheel-carriages I ha'e but few, | |
| Three carts, an twa are feckly new | partly |
| An auld wheelbarrow – mair for token, | |
| Ae leg an baith the trams are broken; | shafts |
| I made a poker o the spin'le, | |
| An my auld mither brunt the trin'le. | wheel |

For men, I've three mischievous boys,
Run-deils for fechtin an for noise:    *Right devils, fighting*
A gaudsman ane, a thrasher t'other,    *cattle-drover*
Wee Davoc hauds the nowte in fother.    *David Hutcheson*
I rule them, as I ought, discreetly,    *cattle, fodder*
An aften labour them completely;
An ay on Sundays duly, nightly,
I on the Questions tairge them tightly;    *catechism, discipline*
Till, faith! wee Davoc's grown sae gleg    *sharp*
Tho scarcely langer than your leg,
He'll screed you aff 'Effectual Calling',    *rattle*
As fast as onie in the dwalling.
I've nane in female servan' station,
(Lord keep me ay frae a' temptation!):
I hae nae wife – and that my bliss is –
An ye hae laid nae tax on misses;    *mistresses*
An then, if kirk folks dinna clutch me,
I ken the deevils darena touch me.
Wi weans I'm mair than weel contented:    *brats*
Heav'n sent me ane mair than I wanted!
My sonsie, smirking, dear-bought Bess,    *Elizabeth Burns*
She stares the daddie in her face,
Enough of ought ye like but grace:
But her, my bonie, sweet wee lady,
I've paid enough for her already;
An gin ye tax her or her mither,    *if*
By the Lord, ye'se get them a' thegither!    *altogether*

But pray, remember, Mr. Aiken,    *Robert Aiken*
Nae kind o licence out I'm takin:
Frae this time forth, I do declare
I'se ne'er ride horse nor hizzie mair;    *hussy, more*
Thro dirt and dub for life I'll paidle,    *mire and slush, wade*
Ere I sae dear pay for a saddle;
I've sturdy stumps, the Lord be thankit!
And a' my gates on foot I'll shank it.    *ways*

The Kirk and you may tak you that,
It puts but little in your pat:    *pot*
Sae dinna put me in your beuk,    *do not, book*
Nor for my ten white shillings leuk.

This list wi my ain hand I've wrote it,
The day and date as under notit;
Then know all ye whom it concerns,
*Subscripsi huic,*    ROBERT BURNS    *I have endorsed this (Latin)*

## TO JOHN KENNEDY, DUMFRIES HOUSE

MOSSGIEL, *March 3, 1786*

John Kennedy (1757-1812), a kinsman of Mrs. Gavin Hamilton, was factor to the Earl of Dumfries at Dumfries House near Cumnock, when Burns met him in 1786. These lines accompanied copies of 'To a Mountain Daisy' and 'The Cotter's Saturday Night' which Burns sent to him at his request.

| | |
|---|---|
| Now, Kennedy, if foot or horse | |
| E'er bring you in by Mauchlin Corss | Cross |
| (Lord, man, there's lasses there wad force | would |
| A hermit's fancy; | |
| And down the gate in faith! they're worse, | way |
| An mair unchancy): | dangerous |
| | |
| But as I'm sayin, please step to Dow's, | the Whitefoord Arms, |
| An taste sic gear as Johnie brews, | Mauchline; stuff |
| Till some bit callan bring me news | stripling |
| That ye are there; | |
| An if we dinna hae a bowse, | |
| I'se ne'er drink mair. | I'll |
| | |
| It's no I like to sit an swallow, | not that |
| Then like a swine to puke an wallow; | |
| But gie me just a true good fallow, | |
| Wi right ingine, | wit |
| And spunkie ance to mak us mellow, | liquor, enough |
| An then we'll shine! | |
| | |
| Now if ye're ane o warl's folk, | world's |
| Wha rate the wearer by the cloak, | |
| An sklent on poverty their joke, | look askance |
| Wi bitter sneer, | |
| Wi you nae friendship I will troke, | barter |
| Nor cheap nor dear. | |
| | |
| But if, as I'm informed weel, | |
| Ye hate as ill's the vera Deil | |
| The flinty heart that canna feel – | |
| Come, sir, here's tae you! | |
| Hae, there's my haun, I wiss ye weel, | |
| An Gude be wi you. | |

## ADAM ARMOUR'S PRAYER

Jean Armour's brother (b. 1771) was one of a group of boys in Mauchline who punished a local whore by making her 'ride the stang'. According to Dr. A. Edgar the 'jurr' referred to here was Agnes Wilson, mentioned in a Kirk Session minute of 6th Match 1786 'as being of lewd and immoral practices...the occasion of a late disturbance in this place.' 'Geordie' was George Gibson landlord of Poosie Nansie's, while 'Hav'rel Jean' was his half-wit daughter, otherwise known as Racer Jess.

| | |
|---|---|
| Gude pity me, because I'm little! | God |
| For though I am an elf o mettle, | |
| An can like onie wabster's shuttle | waver's |
| Jink there or here, | Dodge |
| Yet, scarce as lang's a guid kail-whittle, | cabbage-knife |
| I'm unco queer. | quite worth |
| | |
| An now Thou kens our woefu case: | knowest |
| For Geordie's jurr we're in disgrace, | maid |
| Because we stang'd her through the place, | ridden on a rail |
| An hurt her spleuchan; | genitalia |
| For whilk we daurna show our face | dare not |
| Within the clachan. | |
| | |
| An now we're dern'd in dens and hollows, | hidden, ravines |
| And hunted, as was William Wallace, | |
| Wi constables – thae blackguard fallows – | those |
| An sodgers baith; | |
| But Gude preserve us frae the gallows, | |
| That shamefu death! | |
| | |
| Auld, grim, black-bearded Geordie's sel' – | |
| O, shake him owre the mouth o Hell! | |
| There let him hing, an roar, an yell | |
| Wi hideous din, | |
| And if he offers to rebel, | |
| Then heave him in! | |
| | |
| When Death comes in wi glimmerin blink, | glance |
| An tips auld drucken Nanse the wink, | drunken |
| May Sautan gie her doup a clink | bottom, smack |
| Within his yett, | gate |
| An fill her up wi brimstone drink, | |
| Red-reekin het. | hot |
| | |
| Though Jock an hav'rel Jean are merry, | half-witted |
| Some devil seize them in a hurry, | |
| An waft them in th' infernal wherry | |
| Straught through the lake, | straight |
| An gie their hides a noble curry | |
| Wi oil of aik! | oak |

As for the jurr – puir worthless body! –
She's got mischief enough already;
Wi stanget hips and buttocks bluidy    ie. from being ridden out of
   She suffer'd sair;                        town on a rail
But may she wintle in a woody,           dangle in a noose
   If she whore mair!

# THE LASS O BALLOCHMYLE

*TUNE: Ettrick Banks*

The subject of this song was Wilhelmina Alexander (1753-1843), sister of Claud
Alexander of Ballochmyle. Burns saw her while out walking one evening and was
inspired by her beauty to compose this song which he sent to her with an effusively
complimentary letter. Miss Alexander ignored the letter. Ironically she lived out her long
life an old maid, and the poet's letter and this song were the most treasured possessions
of her declining years.

'Twas even: the dewy fields were green,
   On every blade the pearls hang,
The zephyr wanton'd round the bean,
   And bore its fragrant sweets alang,
In ev'ry glen the mavis sang,                   thrush
   All Nature list'ning seem'd the while,
Except where greenwood echoes rang,
   Amang the braes o Ballochmyle.          heights

With careless step I onward stray'd,
   My heart rejoic'd in Nature's joy,
When, musing in a lonely glade,
   A maiden fair I chanc'd to spy.
Her look was like the morning's eye,
   Her air like Nature's vernal smile.
Perfection whisper'd, passing by: –
   'Behold the lass o Ballochmyle!'

Fair is the morn in flowery May,
   And sweet is night in autumn mild,
When roving thro the garden gay,
   Or wand'ring in the lonely wild;
But woman, Nature's darling child –
   There all her charms she does compile;
Even there her other works are foil'd
   By the bonie lass o Ballochmyle.

O, had she been a country maid,
   And I the happy country swain,
Tho shelter'd in the lowest shed
That ever rose on Scotia's plain!
Thro weary winter's wind and rain
   With joy, with rapture, I would toil,
And nightly to my bosom strain
   The bonie lass o Ballochmyle!

Then Pride might climb the slipp'ry steep,
   Where fame and honours lofty shine;
And thirst of gold might tempt the deep,
   Or downward seek the Indian mine!
Give me the cot below the pine,
   To tend the flocks or till the soil;
And ev'ry day have joys divine
   With the bonie lass o Ballochmyle.

# EPISTLE TO JAMES TENNANT
# OF GLENCONNER

James Tennant (1755-1835) was the eldest son of John Tennant of Glenconner whose large family prospered in many different fields. A younger brother Charles (1786-1838) - the 'wabster Charlie' of 1.45 - founded the St. Rollox chemical works, Glasgow and amassed the fortune which henceforward placed the Tennant family in the forefront of national affairs. James himself was a miller in Ochiltree.

| | |
|---|---|
| Auld comrade dear, and brither sinner, | |
| How's a' the folk about Glenconner? | |
| How do you this blae eastlin wind, | livid, easterly |
| That's like to blaw a body blind? | |
| For me, my faculties are frozen, | |
| My dearest member nearly dozen'd. | torpid |
| I've sent you here, by Johnie Simson, | dancing-master, Ochiltree |
| Twa sage philosophers to glimpse on: | |
| Smith, wi his sympathetic feeling, | Adam Smith (1723-90) |
| An Reid, to common sense appealing. | Dr. Thomas Reid (1710-96) |
| Philosophers have fought and wrangled, | |
| An meikle Greek an Latin mangled, | much |
| Till, wi their logic-jargon tir'd | |
| And in the depth of science mir'd, | |
| To common sense they now appeal – | |
| What wives and wabsters see and feel! | weavers |

But, hark ye, friend! I charge you strictly,
Peruse them, an return them quickly:
For now I'm grown sae cursed douse      *serious*
I pray and ponder butt the house;      *at the back*
My shins, my lane, I there sit roastin,      *alone*
Perusing Bunyan, Brown an Boston,      *John Brown (1722-87)*
Till, by and by, if I haud on,      *Thomas Boston (1676-1732)*
I'll grunt a real gospel groan.
Already I begin to try it,
To cast my een up like a pyet      *eyes, magpie*
When by the gun she tumbles o'er,
Flutt'ring an gasping in her gore:
Sae shortly you shall see me bright,
A burning an a shining light.

My heart-warm love to guid auld Glen,      *John Tennant (1725-1810)*
The ace an wale of honest men:      *pick*
When bending down wi auld grey hairs
Beneath the load of years and cares,
May He who made him still support him,
An views beyond the grave comfort him!
His worthy fam'ly far and near,
God bless them a' wi grace and gear!      *wealth*

My auld schoolfellow, preacher Willie,      *Rev. Wm. Tennant (d. 1813)*
The manly tar, my Mason-billie,      *David Tennant (d. 1839)*
And Auchenbay, I wish him joy;      *John Tennant Jr. (1760-1853)*
If he's a parent, lass or boy,
May he be dad, and Meg the mither,      *Margaret Colville*
Just five-and-forty years thegither!
And no forgetting wabster Charlie,
I'm tauld he offers very fairly.
An, Lord, remember singing Sannock,      *Robert Tennant (1774-1841)*
Wi hale breeks, saxpence, an a bannock!      *whole, breeches*
And next, my auld acquaintance, Nancy,      *Agnes Tennant (d. 1787)*
Since she is fitted to her fancy,
An her kind stars hae airted till her      *directed to*
A guid chiel wi a pickle siller!      *chap, little*
My kindest, best respects, I sen' it,
To cousin Kate, an sister Janet:
Tell them, frae me, wi chiels be cautious,
For, faith! they'll aiblins fin' them fashious;      *perhaps, troublesome*
To grant a heart is fairly civil,
But to grant a maidenhead's the devil!

An lastly, Jamie, for yoursel,
May guardian angels tak a spell
An steer you seven miles south o Hell!
But first, before you see Heaven's glory,
May ye get monie a merry story,
Monie a laugh, and monie a drink,
And ay eneugh o needfu clink!                    coin

   Now fare ye weel, an joy be wi you!
For my sake, this I beg it o you:
Assist poor Simson a' ye can;
Ye'll fin' him just an honest man,
Sae I conclude, and quat my chanter,           leave, song
Yours, saint or sinner,
     ROB THE RANTER

# INSCRIBED ON A WORK
# OF HANNAH MORE'S

## PRESENTED TO THE AUTHOR BY A LADY

These lines were included in a letter to Robert Aiken, of 3rd April 1786. The identity of
the lady mentioned in the title is not known, but possibilities include Mrs. William
Campbell of Fairfield, Mrs. Cuninghame of Lainshaw and Mrs. Maxwell Campbell of
Skerrington – all fitting the 'Mrs. C' – mentioned in the letter.

Thou flatt'ring mark of friendship kind,
Still may thy pages call to mind
   The dear, the beauteous donor!
Tho sweetly female ev'ry part,
Yet such a head, and more - the heart
   Does both the sexes honor:
She show'd her taste refin'd and just,
   When she selected thee,
Yet deviating, own I must,
   For sae approving me:
     But, kind still, I'll mind still
      The giver in the gift;
     I'll bless her, an wiss her           regard
      A Friend aboon the lift.           above, rest

## TO A MOUNTAIN DAISY

### ON TURNING ONE DOWN WITH THE PLOUGH, IN APRIL, 1786

Originally entitled 'The Gowan', it was written at a time when Burns was experiencing a great deal of trouble with the Armour family. He sent it to John Kennedy on 20th April 1786 with a letter describing these verses as 'just the native querulous feelings of a heart which, as the elegantly melting Gray says, "Melancholy has marked for her own".'

Wee, modest, crimson-tippèd flow'r,
Thou's met me in an evil hour;
For I maun crush amang the stoure      dust
    Thy slender stem:
To spare thee now is past my pow'r,
    Thou bonie gem.

Alas! it's no thy neebor sweet,
The bonie lark companion meet,
Bending thee 'mang the dewy weet,      wet
    Wi spreckl'd breast!
When upward-springing, blythe, to greet
    The purpling east.

Cauld blew the bitter-biting north
Upon thy early, humble birth;
Yet cheerfully thou glinted forth      shone
    Amid the storm,
Scarce rear'd above the parent-earth
    Thy tender form.

The flaunting flow'rs our gardens yield,
High shelt'ring woods and wa's maun shield;      must
But thou, beneath the random bield      shelter
    O clod or stane,
Adorns the histie stibble-field,      bare
    Unseen, alane.

There, in thy scanty mantle clad,
Thy snawie bosom sun-ward spread,
Thou lifts thy unassuming head
    In humble guise;
But now the share uptears thy bed,
    And low thou lies!

Such is the fate of artless maid,
Sweet flow'ret of the rural shade!
By love's simplicity betray'd,
    And guileless trust;
Till she, like thee, all soil'd, is laid
    Low i' the dust.

Such is the fate of simple Bard,
On Life's rough ocean luckless starr'd!
Unskilful he to note the card
    Of prudent lore,
Till billows rage, and gales blow hard,
    And whelm him o'er!

Such fate to suffering Worth is giv'n,
Who long with wants and woes has striv'n,
By human pride or cunning driv'n
    To mis'ry's brink;
Till, wrench'd of ev'ry stay but Heav'n,
    He, ruin'd, sink!

Ev'n thou who mourn'st the Daisy's fate,
That fate is thine – no distant date;
Stern Ruin's plough-share drives elate,
    Full on thy bloom,
Till crush'd beneath the furrow's weight,
    Shall be thy doom!

# THE LAMENT

## OCCASIONED BY THE UNFORTUNATE ISSUE OF A FRIEND'S AMOUR

### TUNE: *Scots Queen*

*Alas! how oft does Goodness wound itself,*
*And Sweet Affection prove the spring of Woe!* – HOME

The 'friend's amour' of the sub-title was his own illstarred affair early in 1786 with Jean Armour. In his Autobiographical Letter to Dr. Moore he wrote: '... a shocking affair ...and had very nearly given [me] one or two of the principal qualifications for a place among those who have lost the chart of Rationality.'

O thou pale Orb that silent shines
    While care-untroubled mortals sleep!
Thou seest a wretch who inly pines,
    And wanders here to wail and weep!
With Woe I nightly vigils keep,
    Beneath thy wan, unwarming beam;
And mourn, in lamentation deep,
    How life and love are all a dream!

I joyless view thy rays adorn
  The faintly-markèd, distant hill;
I joyless view thy trembling horn,
  Reflected in the gurgling rill:
My fondly-fluttering heart, be still!
  Thou busy pow'r, Remembrance, cease!
Ah! must the agonizing thrill
  For ever bar returning Peace!

No idly-feign'd, poetic pains
  My sad, love-lorn lamentings claim:
No shepherd's pipe – Arcadian strains;
  No fabled tortures quaint and tame.
The plighted faith, the mutual flame,
  The oft-attested Pow'rs above,
The promis'd father's tender name;
  These were the pledges of my love!

Encircled in her clasping arms,
  How have the raptur'd moments flown!
How have I wish'd for Fortune's charms,
  For her dear sake, and her's alone!
And, must I think it! is she gone,
  My secret heart's exulting boast?
And does she heedless hear my groan?
  And is she ever, ever lost?

O! can she bear so base a heart,
  So lost to honour, lost to truth,
As from the fondest lover part,
  The plighted husband of her youth?
Alas! Life's path may be unsmooth!
  Her way may lie thro rough distress!
Then, who her pangs and pains will soothe,
  Her sorrows share, and make them less?

Ye wingèd Hours that o'er us pass'd,
  Enraptur'd more the more enjoy'd,
Your dear remembrance in my breast
  My fondly-treasur'd thoughts employ'd –
That breast, how dreary now, and void,
  For her too scanty once of room!
Ev'n ev'ry ray of Hope destroy'd,
  And not a wish to gild the gloom!

The morn, that warns th' approaching day,
　　Awakes me up to toil and woe;
I see the hours in long array,
　　That I must suffer, lingering slow:
Full many a pang, and many a throe,
　　Keen Recollection's direful train,
Must wring my soul, ere Phoebus, low,
　　Shall kiss the distant western main.

And when my nightly couch I try,
　　Sore-harass'd out with care and grief,
My toil-beat nerves, and tear-worn eye
　　Keep watchings with the nightly thief:
Or, if I slumber, Fancy, chief,
　　Reigns, haggard-wild, in sore affright:
Ev'n day, all-bitter, brings relief
　　From such a horror-breathing night.

O thou bright Queen, who, o'er th' expanse
　　Now highest reign'st, with boundless sway!
Oft has thy silent-marking glance
　　Observ'd us, fondly-wand'ring, stray!
The time, unheeded, sped away,
　　While Love's luxurious pulse beat high,
Beneath thy silver-gleaming ray,
　　To mark the mutual-kindling eye.

O! scenes in strong remembrance set!
　　Scenes, never, never to return!
Scenes if in stupor I forget,
　　Again I feel, again I burn!
From ev'ry joy and pleasure torn,
　　Life's weary vale I'll wander thro;
And hopeless, comfortless, I'll mourn
　　A faithless woman's broken vow!

# DESPONDENCY - AN ODE

Another piece inspired by the melancholy induced by the dramatic events of March-April 1786, when Jean and Robert were compeared before the Kirk Session for fornication, and she was subsequently packed off to Paisley by her father who tried to nullify their irregular (though legal in Scots law) marriage by mutilating the document promising or declaring marriage - the 'unlucky paper' whose destruction 'cut my very veins'.

Oppress'd with grief, oppress'd with care,
A burden more than I can bear,
   I set me down and sigh;
O Life! thou art a galling load,
Along a rough, a weary road,
   To wretches such as I!
Dim-backward, as I cast my view,
   What sick'ning scenes appear!
What sorrows yet may pierce me thro
   Too justly I may fear!
     Still caring, despairing,
      Must be my bitter doom;
     My woes here shall close ne'er
      But with the closing tomb!

Happy! ye sons of busy life,
Who, equal to the bustling strife,
   No other view regard!
Ev'n when the wished end's denied,
Yet while the busy means are plied,
   They bring their own reward:
Whilst I, a hope-abandon'd wight,
   Unfitted with an aim,
Meet ev'ry sad returning night,
   And joyless morn the same.
     You, bustling and justling,
      Forget each grief an pain;
     I, listless yet restless,
      Find ev'ry prospect vain.

How blest the Solitary's lot,
Who, all-forgetting, all-forgot,
  Within his humble cell –
The cavern, wild with tangling roots –
Sits o'er his newly gather'd fruits,
  Beside his crystal well!
Or haply to his ev'ning thought,
  By unfrequented stream,
The ways of men are distant brought,
    A faint-collected dream;
      While praising, and raising
        His thoughts to Heav'n on high,
      As wand'ring, meand'ring,
        He views the solemn sky.

Than I, no lonely hermit plac'd
Where never human footstep trac'd,
  Less fit to play the part;
The lucky moment to improve,
And just to stop, and just to move,
With self-respecting art:
But ah! those pleasures, loves, and joys,
  Which I too keenly taste,
The Solitary can despise –
    Can want, and yet be blest!
      He needs not, he heeds not,
        Or human love or hate;
      Whilst I here must cry here
        At perfidy ingrate!

O enviable early days,
When dancing thoughtless pleasure's maze
  To care, to guilt unknown!
How ill exchang'd for riper times,
To feel the follies, or the crimes,
  Of others, or my own!
Ye tiny elves that guiltless sport,
  Like linnets in the bush,
Ye little know the ills ye court,
  When manhood is your wish!
      The losses, the crosses,
        That active man enrage;
      The fears all, the tears all,
        Of dim declining Age!

## AH, WOE IS ME, MY MOTHER DEAR

*Paraphrase of Jeremiah, 15th chap., 10th verse*

The closing lines of this poem give the clue to the occasion which inspired it: the Armour affair of early 1786.

Ah, woe is me, my Mother dear!
    A man of strife ye've born me:
For sair contention I maun bear;                    *must*
    They hate, revile, and scorn me.

I ne'er could lend on bill or band,
    That five per cent. might blest me;      *might have*
And borrowing, on the tither hand,         *other*
    The deil a ane wad trust me.          *would*

Yet I, a coin-denyed wight,        *sturdy person*
    By Fortune quite discarded,
Ye see how I am, day and night,
    By lad and lass blackguarded!      *miscalled*

## EPITAPH ON A HENPECKED SQUIRE

This epitaph, and the following epigrams, commemorate William Campbell of Netherplace near Mauchline. His domineering wife was Lilias Neilson (d. 1826), daughter of a Glasgow merchant.

As father Adam first was fool'd,
    A case that's still too common,
Here lies a man a woman ruled –
    The Devil ruled the woman.

## EPIGRAM ON SAID OCCASION

O Death, had'st thou but spar'd his life,
    Whom we this day lament!
We freely wad exchanged the wife,
    And a' been weel content.
Ev'n as he is, cauld in his graff,         *grave*
    The swap we yet will do't;
Tak thou the carlin's carcase aff,      *old fellow*
    Thou'se get the saul o boot.    *soul into the bargain*

## ANOTHER

Artemisa, Queen of Halicarnassus, married her brother Mausolus. She was so devoted to him that, following his death c. 353 B.C., she not only erected the Mausoleum, one of the ancient wonders of the world, but ingested his ashes in liquor.

One Queen Artemisa, as old stories tell,
When depriv'd of her husband she loved so well,
In respect for the love and affection he'd show'd her,
She reduc'd him to dust and she drank up the powder.
But Queen Netherplace, of a diff'rent complexion,
When call'd on to order the fun'ral direction,
Would have eat her dead lord, on a slender pretence,
Not to show her respect, but – to save the expense!

## STANZAS ON NAETHING

### EXTEMPORE EPISTLE TO GAVIN HAMILTON, ESQ.

Though undated, this poem must have been composed in the spring of 1786, as it deals with matters then topical: Hamilton's troubles with Daddy Auld and Mauchline Kirk Session, recently resolved, the poet's own moral transgressions which were to lead him to make three penitential appearances in church in July 1786, and his plans to emigrate to Jamaica.

To you, Sir, this summons I've sent
   (Pray, whip till the pownie is fraething!)       pony, frothing
But if you demand what I want,
   I honestly answer you – naething.

Ne'er scorn a poor Poet like me
   For idly just living and breathing,
While people of every degree
   Are busy employed about – naething.

Poor Centum-per-Centum may fast,
   And grumble his hurdies their claithing;      grudge, buttocks
He'll find, when the balance is cast,
   He's gane to the Devil for – naething.

The courtier cringes and bows;
   Ambition has likewise its plaything –
A coronet beams on his brows;
   And what is a coronet? – naething.

Some quarrel the Presbyter gown,          complain of
   Some quarrel Episcopal graithing;        vestments
But every good fellow will own
   The quarrel is a' about – naething.

The lover may sparkle and glow,
   Approaching his bonie bit gay thing;          little
But marriage will soon let him know
   He's gotten – a buskit-up naething.          tricked-out

The Poet may jingle and rhyme
   In hopes of a laureate wreathing,
And when he has wasted his time,
   He's kindly rewarded with – naething.

The thundering bully may rage,
   And swagger and swear like a heathen;
But collar him fast, I'll engage,
   You'll find that his courage is – naething.

Last night with a feminine Whig –
   A poet she couldna put faith in!
But soon we grew lovingly big,
   I taught her, her terrors were – naething.

Her Whigship was wonderful pleased,
   But charmingly tickled wi ae thing;
Her fingers I lovingly squeezed,
   And kissed her, and promised her – naething.

The priest anathemas may threat –
   Predicament, sir, that we're baith in;
But when Honor's reveille is beat,
   The holy artillery's – naething.

And now I must mount on the wave:
   My voyage perhaps there is death in;
But what is a watery grave?
   The drowning a Poet is – naething.

And now, as grim Death's in my thought,
   To you, Sir, I make this bequeathing:
My service as long as ye've ought,
   And my friendship, by God, when ye've – naething.

## ON A SCOTCH BARD

### GONE TO THE WEST INDIES

Written in the summer of 1786, by which time Burns had fixed to go to Jamaica in October. When that time came, however, his fortunes had improved and the course of his life was changing in a literary direction, and plans to emigrate to the West Indies were dropped. The mood of this poem contrasts with the verses immediately preceding it, evidence of Burns's cyclothymic nature.

A' ye wha live by sowps o drink,      sups
A' ye wha live by crambo-clink,      shyme
A' ye wha live and never think
 Come, mourn wi me!
Our billie's gien us a' a jink,    comrade, given the slip
 An owre the sea!

Lament him a' ye rantin core,    roistering crowd
Wha dearly like a random-splore;     frolic
Nae mair he'll join the merry roar,
 In social key;
For now he's taen anither shore,
 An owre the sea!

The bonie lasses weel may wiss him,     wish
And in their dear petitions place him:
The widows, wives, an a' may bless him
 Wi tearfu e'e,
For weel I wat they'll sairly miss him    wot
 That's owre the sea!

O Fortune, they hae room to grumble!
Hadst thou taen aff some drowsy bummle,   drone
Wha can do nought but fyke an fumble,    fuss
 'Twad been nae plea;
But he was gleg as onie wumble,   sharp, wimble
 That's owre the sea!

Auld, cantie Kyle may weepers wear,    cheerful
An stain them wi the saut, saut tear:     salt
'Twill mak her poor auld heart, I fear,
 In flinders flee:         splinters
He was her Laureat monie a year,
 That's owre the sea!

He saw Misfortune's cauld nor-west
Lang-mustering up a bitter blast;
A jillet brak his heart at last,      jilt
 Ill may she be!
So, took a berth afore the mast,
 An owre the sea.

To tremble under Fortune's cummock,        *rod*
On scarce a bellyfu o drummock,        *gruel*
Wi his proud, independent stomach,
  Could ill agree;
So, row't his hurdies in a hammock,    *rolled, buttocks*
  An owre the sea.

He ne'er was gien to great misguiding,
Yet coin his pouches wad na bide in;     *pockets*
Wi him it ne'er was under hiding;
  He dealt it free;
The Muse was a' that he took pride in,
  That's owre the sea.

Jamaica bodies, use him weel,
An hap him in a cozie biel:        *shelter, place*
Ye'll find him ay a dainty chiel,       *fellow*
  An fou o glee:
He wad na wrang'd the vera Deil,
  That's owre the sea.

Fareweel, my rhyme-composing billie!    *friend*
Your native soil was right ill-willie;    *unkind*
But may ye flourish like a lily,
  Now bonilie!
I'll toast you in my hindmost gillie,    *last gill*
  Tho owre the sea!

# SECOND EPISTLE TO DAVIE

## A BROTHER POET

Addressed to David Sillar (1760-1830), see page 86. This epistle was evidently written some time before the publication of Burns's poems at the end of July 1786.

Auld Neebor,
I'm three times doubly o'er your debtor
For your auld-farrant, frien'ly letter;    *old-fashioned*
Tho I maun say't, I doubt ye flatter,    *must*
  Ye speak sae fair;
For my puir, silly, rhymin clatter      *babble*
  Some less maun sair.           *serve*

Hale be your heart, hale be your fiddle!
Lang may your elbuck jink an diddle,       elbow, dance, shake
To cheer you thro the weary widdle       wriggle
   O war'ly cares,
Till bairns' bairns kindly cuddle       grandchildren
   Your auld grey hairs!

But Davie, lad, I'm red ye're glaikit;       afraid, foolish
I'm tauld the Muse ye hae negleckit;
An gif it's sae, ye sud be lickit       if, whipped
   Until ye fyke;       fidget
Sic han's as you sud ne'er be faiket,       spared
   Be hain't wha like.       except

For me, I'm on Parnassus' brink,
Rivin the words to gar them clink;       Tearing, make rhyme
Whyles daez't wi love, whyles daez't wi drink,       now dazed
   Wi jads or Masons;       jades, Freemasons
An whyles, but ay owre late, I think
   Braw sober lessons.       Fine

Of a' the thoughtless sons o man,
Commen' me to the Bardie clan;
Except it be some idle plan
   O rhymin clink –
The devil-haet that I sud ban! –       Heaven forbid
   They never think.

Nae thought, nae view, nae scheme o livin,
Nae cares to gie us joy or grievin,
But just the pouchie put the nieve in,       pocket, fist
   An while ought's there,
Then, hiltie-skiltie, we gae scrievin,       Helter-skelter, careering
   An fash nae mair.       trouble

Leeze me on rhyme! it's ay a treasure,       Blessings
My chief, amaist my only pleasure;       almost
At hame, a-fiel', at wark or leisure,
   The Muse, poor hizzie!       hussy
Tho rough an raploch be her measure,       homespun
   She's seldom lazy.

Haud to the Muse, my dainty Davie:       stick
The warl' may play you monie a shavie,       trick
But for the Muse, she'll never leave ye,
   Tho e'er sae puir;
Na, even tho limpin wi the spavie       spavin
   Frae door to door.

# TO GAVIN HAMILTON, ESQ., MAUCHLINE

## RECOMMENDING A BOY

### MOSSGAVILLE, *May 3, 1786*

According to Cromek 'Master Tootie' (1.2) was a rascally Mauchline cattle-dealer who filed and polished off the rings on his cows' horns ('auld Crummie's nicks) to conceal their true age. 'Mossgaville' is the posh rendering of Mossgiel.

I hold it, Sir, my bounden duty  
To warn you how that Master Tootie,  
   *Alias* Laird M'Gaun,  
Was here to hire yon lad away  
'Bout whom ye spak the tither day,  
   An wad hae done't aff han';           out of hand  
But lest he learn the callan tricks –        teach, lad  
   As faith! I muckle doubt him –       much  
Like scrapin out auld Crummie's nicks,  
   An tellin lies about them,  
   As lieve then, I'd have then         Rather  
      Your clerkship he should sair,    serve  
     If sae be ye may be  
     Not fitted otherwhere.

Altho I say't, he's gleg enough,         bright  
An 'bout a house that's rude an rough,  
   The boy might learn to swear;  
But when wi you he'll be sae taught,  
An get sic fair example straught,     straight  
   I hae na onie fear.              any  
Ye'll catechise him, every quirk,  
   An shore him weel wi 'Hell';     threaten  
An gar him follow to the kirk –      make  
   Ay when ye gang yoursel!        go  
     If ye, then, maun be then     must  
      Frae hame this comin Friday,  
    Then please, Sir, to lea'e, Sir,  
    The orders wi your lady.

My word of honour I hae gi'en,
In Paisley John's that night at e'en,
To meet the 'warld's worm';               John Dow, landlord of the
To try to get the twa to gree,               Whitefoord Arms
An name the airles an the fee,               miserable, reptile
   In legal mode an form:                    contractual payment
I ken he weel a snick can draw,               latch
When simple bodies let him;
An if a devil be at a'.
   In faith he's sure to get him.
   To phrase you an praise you,
   Ye ken, your Laureat scorns:
   The pray'r still you share still,
   Of grateful MINSTREL BURNS.

# A DEDICATION

## TO GAVIN HAMILTON, ESQ.

This poem was intended originally to appear at the end of the Kilmarnock Edition. Its curious position within that volume is explained by the fact that Burns added several poems while the book was going through the press.

   Expect na, Sir, in this narration,
A fleechin, fleth'rin Dedication,            wheedling, flattering
To roose you up, an ca' you guid,             praise
An sprung o great an noble bluid,
Because ye're surnam'd like His Grace –   ie the Duke of Hamilton
Perhaps related to the race;
Then, when I'm tir'd – and sae are ye,
Wi monie a fulsome, sinfu lie, –
Set up a face how I stop short,
For fear your modesty be hurt.

   This may do – maun do, Sir, wi them wha
Maun please the great-folk for wamefou;      bellyful
For me! sae laigh I need na bow,              low
For, Lord be thankit, I can plough;
And when I downa yoke a naig,             cannot
Then, Lord be thankit, I can beg;
Sae I shall say an that's nae flatt'rin,
It's just sic poet an sic patron.

The Poet, some guid angel help him,
Or else, I fear, some ill ane skelp him!          *beat*
He may do weel for a' he's done yet,
But only he's no just begun yet.

The Patron (sir, ye maun forgie me;
I winna lie, come what will o me),
On ev'ry hand it will allow'd be,
He's just – nae better than he should be.

I readily and freely grant,
He downa see a poor man want;
What's no his ain he winna tak it;          *will not*
What ance he says, he winna break it;
Ought he can lend he'll no refus't,
Till aft his guidness is abus'd;
And rascals whyles that do him wrang,          *sometimes*
Ev'n that, he does na mind it lang,
As master, landlord, husband, father,
He does na fail his part in either.

But then, nae thanks to him for a' that;
Nae godly symptom ye can ca' that;
It's naething but a milder feature
Of our poor, sinfu, corrupt nature:
Ye'll get the best o moral works,
'Mang black Gentoos, and pagan Turks,          *Hindus*
Or hunters wild on Ponotaxi,          *Cotopaxi, Ecuador*
Wha never heard of orthodoxy.
That he's the poor man's friend in need,
The gentleman in word and deed,
It's no thro terror of damnation;
It's just a carnal inclination,
An och! that's nae regeneration.

Morality, thou deadly bane,
Thy tens o thousands thou hast slain!
Vain is his hope, whase stay an trust is
In moral mercy, truth, and justice!

No – stretch a point to catch a plack;          *farthing*
Abuse a brother to his back;
Steal thro the winnock frae a whore,          *window*
But point the rake that taks the door;
Be to the poor like onie whunstane,          *whinstone*
And haud their noses to the grunstane;          *grindstone*
Ply ev'ry art o legal thieving;
No matter – stick to sound believing.

Learn three-mile pray'rs, an half-mile graces,
Wi weel-spread looves, an lang, wry faces;         *palms*
Grunt up a solemn, lengthen'd groan,
And damn a' parties but your own;
I'll warrant then, ye're nae deceiver,
A steady, sturdy, staunch believer.

O ye wha leave the springs o Calvin,
For gumlie dubs of your ain delvin!       *muddy puddles*
Ye sons of Heresy and Error,
Ye'll some day squeel in quaking terror,
When Vengeance draws the sword in wrath,
And in the fire throws the sheath;
When Ruin with his sweeping besom,
Just frets till Heav'n commission gies him;
While o'er the harp pale Misery moans,
And strikes the ever-deep'ning tones,
Still louder shrieks, and heavier groans!

Your pardon, sir, for this digression:
I maist forgat my Dedication;       *almost*
But when divinity comes 'cross me,
My readers still are sure to lose me.

So, Sir, you see 'twas nae daft vapour;      *mad*
But I maturely thought it proper,
When a' my works I did review,
To dedicate them, Sir, to you:
Because (ye need na tak it ill),
I thought them something like yoursel.

Then patronize them wi your favor,
And your petitioner shall ever –
I had amaist said, ever pray,
But that's a word I need na say;
For prayin, I hae little skill o't;
I'm baith dead-sweer, an wretched ill o't;  *very loath, bad at it*
But I'se repeat each poor man's pray'r,
That kens or hears about you, Sir –      *knows*

'May ne'er Misfortune's growling bark,
Howl thro the dwelling o the clerk!
May ne'er his gen'rous, honest heart,
For that same gen'rous spirit smart!
May Kennedy's far-honor'd name
Lang beet his hymeneal flame,
Till Hamiltons, at least a dizzen,
Are frae their nuptial labors risen:
Five bonie lasses round their table,
And sev'n braw fellows, stout an able,
To serve their king an country weel,
By word, or pen, or pointed steel!
May Health and Peace, with mutual rays,
Shine on the ev'ning o his days;
Till his wee, curlie John's ier-oe,
When ebbing life nae mair shall flow,
The last, sad, mournful rites bestow!'

*a reference to Hamilton's position as Clerk of the Court*

*Helen Kennedy of Daljarrock, Hamilton's wife*

*dozen*

*poetic exaggeration: Hamilton had two sons & two daughters*

*great-grandchild*

I will not wind a lang conclusion,
With complimentary effusion;
But, whilst your wishes and endeavours
Are blest with Fortune's smiles and favours,
I am, dear sir, with zeal most fervent,
Your much indebted, humble servant.

But if (which Pow'rs above prevent)
That iron-hearted carl, Want,
Attended, in his grim advances,
By sad mistakes, and black mischances,
While hopes, and joys, and pleasures fly him,
Make you as poor a dog as I am,
Your 'humble servant' then no more;
For who would humbly serve the poor?
But, by a poor man's hopes in Heav'n!
While recollection's pow'r is giv'n.
If, in the vale of humble life,
The victim sad of Fortune's strife,
I thro the tender-gushing tear,
Should recognise my master dear;
If friendless, low, we meet together,
Then, Sir, your hand – my Friend and Brother!

# A BARD'S EPITAPH

This was the last poem printed in the Kilmarnock Edition.

Is there a whim-inspired fool,
Owre fast for thought, owre hot for rule,                    too
Owre blate to seek, owre proud to snool?        modest, cringe
 Let him draw near;
And owre this grassy heap sing dool,                        woe
  And drap a tear.

Is there a Bard of rustic song,
Who, noteless, steals the crowds among,
That weekly this area throng?
 O, pass not by!
But, with a frater-feeling strong,                        brother-
  Here, heave a sigh.

Is there a man, whose judgment clear
Can others teach the course to steer,
Yet runs, himself, life's mad career,
 Wild as the wave? –
Here pause – and, thro the starting tear,
  Survey this grave.

The poor inhabitant below
Was quick to learn and wise to know,
And keenly felt the friendly glow,
 And softer flame;
But thoughtless follies laid him low,
  And stain'd his name!

Reader, attend! whether thy soul
Soars Fancy's flights beyond the pole,
Or darkling grubs in this earthly hole,
 In low pursuit;
Know, prudent, cautious, self-control
  Is wisdom's root.

# EPISTLE TO A YOUNG FRIEND

*15 May, 1786*

This was addressed to Andrew Hunter Aiken, son of Robert Aiken, later merchant in Liverpool and British consul in Riga where he died in 1831.

I lang hae thought, my youthfu friend,
    A something to have sent you,
Tho it should serve nae ither end
    Than just a kind memento:
But how the subject-theme may gang,
    Let time and chance determine:
Perhaps it may turn out a sang;
    Perhaps, turn out a sermon.

Ye'll try the world soon, my lad;
    And, Andrew dear, believe me,
Ye'll find mankind an unco squad,           *strange*
    And muckle they may grieve ye:
For care and trouble set your thought,
    Ev'n when your end's attained;
And a' your views may come to nought,
    Where ev'ry nerve is strained.

I'll no say, men are villains a':
    The real, harden'd wicked,
Wha hae nae check but human law,
    Are to a few restricked;
But, och! mankind are unco weak,          *mighty*
    An little to be trusted;
If self the wavering balance shake,
    It's rarely right adjusted!

Yet they wha fa' in Fortune's strife,
    Their fate we should na censure;
For still, th' important end of life
    They equally may answer:
A man may hae an honest heart,
    Tho poortith hourly stare him;         *poverty*
A man may tak a neebor's part,
    Yet hae nae cash to spare him.

Ay free, aff han', your story tell,
    When wi a bosom cronie;
But still keep something to yoursel
    Ye scarcely tell to onie:
Conceal yoursel as weel's ye can
    Frae critical dissection:
But keek thro ev'ry other man,          *look*
    Wi sharpen'd, sly inspection.

The sacred lowe o weel-plac'd love,               flame
   Luxuriantly indulge it;
But never tempt th' illicit rove,
   Tho naething should divulge it:
I waive the quantum o the sin,
   The hazard of concealing;
But, och! it hardens a' within,
   And petrifies the feeling!

To catch Dame Fortune's golden smile,
   Assiduous wait upon her;
And gather gear by ev'ry wile
   That's justify'd by honor:
Not for to hide it in a hedge,
   Nor for a train-attendant;
But for the glorious privilege
   Of being independent.

The fear o Hell's a hangman's whip
   To haud the wretch in order;
But where ye feel your honour grip,
   Let that ay be your border:
Its slightest touches, instant pause –
   Debar a' side-pretences;
And resolutely keep its laws,
   Uncaring consequences.

The great Creator to revere,
   Must sure become the creature;
But still the preaching cant forbear,
   An ev'n the rigid feature:
Yet ne'er with wits profane to range
   Be complaisance extended;
An atheist-laugh's a poor exchange
   For Deity offended!

When ranting round in Pleasure's ring,            frolicking
   Religion may be blinded;
Or if she gie a random sting,
   It may be little minded;
But when on Life we're tempest-driv'n –
   A conscience but a canker –
A correspondence fix'd wi' Heav'n,
   Is sure a noble anchor!

Adieu, dear, amiable youth!
  Your heart can ne'er be wanting!
May prudence, fortitude, and truth,
  Erect your brow undaunting!
In ploughman phrase, 'God send you speed,'
  Still daily to grow wiser;
And may ye better reck the rede,             heed, advice
  Than ever did th' adviser!

## LINES WRITTEN ON A BANK-NOTE

Composed in the summer of 1786 when Burns was seriously considering emigration
as the solution to his moral and financial problems. Notaphilists may care to learn that
this poem was written on a one-guinea note of the Bank of Scotland issued 1st March
1780.

Wae worth thy power, thou cursed leaf!         woe betide
Fell source o a' my woe and grief,             Deadly
For lack o thee I've lost my lass,
For lack o thee I scrimp my glass!
I see the children of affliction
Unaided, through thy curs'd restriction.
I've seen the oppressor's cruel smile
Amid his hapless victims' spoil;
And for thy potence vainly wish'd,
To crush the villain in the dust.
For lack o thee, I leave this much-lov'd shore,
Never, perhaps, to greet old Scotland more.

                      R.B.

KYLE

# MY HIGHLAND LASSIE, O

*TUNE: MacLauchlin's Scots-Measure*

In his annotation of Robert Riddell's interleaved copy of *The Scots Musical Museum*, Burns sentimentalised his relationship with Margaret 'Highland Mary' Campbell (1766-86), to whom he turned after James Armour had broken up his affair with Jean. Joseph Train presented a different picture of her in his note to Lockhart, based on the recollections of John Richmond: 'Her character was loose in the extreme. She was kept for some time by a brother of Lord Eglinton's, and even while a servant with Gavin Hamilton, and during the period of Burns' attachment, it was well known that her meetings with Montgomery were open and frequent.' She died at Greenock in the autumn of 1786: whether from a fever or from premature childbirth is a matter of controversy to this day.

CHORUS

*Within the glen sae bushy, O,*
  *Aboon the plain sae rashy, O,*          Above, rushy
*I set me down wi right guid will,*
  *To sing my Highland lassie, O!*

Nae gentle dames, tho ne'er sae fair,          highborn ladies
Shall ever be my Muse's care:
Their titles a' are empty show;
Gie me my Highland lassie, O!

O, were yon hills and vallies mine,
Yon palace and yon gardens fine,
The world then the love should know
I bear my Highland lassie, O!

But fickle Fortune frowns on me,
And I maun cross the raging sea;          must
But while my crimson currents flow,
I'll love my Highland lassie, O!

Altho thro foreign climes I range,
I know her heart will never change;
For her bosom burns with honour's glow,
My faithful Highland lassie, O!

For her I'll dare the billows' roar,
For her I'll trace a distant shore,
That Indian wealth may lustre throw
Around my Highland lassie, O!

She has my heart, she has my hand,
By secret troth and honor's band!
'Till the mortal stroke shall lay me low,
I'm thine, my Highland lassie, O!

Farewell the glen sae bushy, O!
Farewell the plain sae rashy, O!
To other lands I now must go
To sing my Highland lassie, O!

KIRK ALLOWAY

## ADDRESS OF BEELZEBUB

HELL, June 1st, Anno Mundi 5790

To the Right Honorable the Earl of Breadalbane, President of the Right Honorable the Highland Society, which met on the 23rd of May last, at the Shakespeare, Covent Garden, to concert ways and means to frustrate the designs of five hundred Highlanders who, as the Society were informed by Mr. M'Kenzie of Applecross, were so audacious as to attempt an escape from their lawful lords and masters whose property they were, by emigrating from the lands of Mr. Macdonald of Glengary to the wilds of Canada, in search of that fantastic thing – LIBERTY.

This Address was provoked by the controversy over whether Highlanders should be encouraged to remain at home or emigrate. Burns took the view that the reaction of Lord Breadalbane and the Highland Society was autocratic. Furthermore, in view of his own decision not to emigrate, he did not credit Highlanders with similar attitudes - that no one left their native soil unless economic necessity dictated. It is ironic that the very gentlemen then trying to prevent emigration should, within a few years, take up the cause with a vengeanace and perpetrate the forced exodus known as the Highland Clearances.

| | |
|---|---|
| Long life, my lord, an health be yours, | |
| Unskaith'd by hunger'd Highland boors! | |
| Lord grant nae duddie, desperate beggar, | ragged |
| Wi dirk, claymore, or rusty trigger, | |
| May twin auld Scotland o a life | rob |
| She likes - as lambkins like a knife! | |
| Faith! you and Applecross were right | Thomas MacKenzie of |
| To keep the Highland hounds in sight! | Applecross |
| I doubt na! they wad bid nae better | offer |
| Than let them ance out owre the water! | once |
| Then up amang thae lakes and seas, | these |
| They'll mak what rules and laws they please: | |
| Some daring Hancock, or a Franklin, | John Hancock (1737-93) |
| May set their Highland bluid a-ranklin; | Benjamin Franklin (1706-90) |
| Some Washington again may head them, | George Washington (1732-99) |
| Or some Montgomery, fearless, lead them; | Richard Montgomery (d. 1775) |
| Till (God knows what may be effected | |
| When by such heads and hearts directed) | |
| Poor dunghill sons of dirt an mire | |
| May to Patrician rights aspire! | Frederick, Lord North (1732-92) |
| Nae sage North now, nor sager Sackville, | Lord George Sackville (1716-85) |
| To watch and premier o'er the pack vile! | |
| An whare will ye get Howes and Clintons, | Sir Henry Clinton (1738-95) |
| To bring them to a right repentence? | William, Viscount Howe |
| To cowe the rebel generation, | (1729-1814) |
| An save the honor o the nation? | |

8

*They*, an be damn'd! what right hae they
To meat or sleep, or light o day?
Far less to riches, pow'r, or freedom,
But what your lordship likes to gie them?
But hear, my lord! Glengary, hear!     *Macdonell of Glengarry*
Your hand's owre light on them, I fear:
Your factors, grieves, trustees, and bailies,
I canna say but they do gaylies:     *gaily*
They lay aside a' tender mercies,
An tirl the hullions to the birses;     *strip, sluts, bristles*
Yet while they're only poind and herriet,     *distrained, harried*
They'll keep their stubborn Highland spirit.
But smash them! crush them a' to spails,     *splinters*
An rot the dyvors i' the jails!     *debtors, rogues*
The young dogs swinge them to the labour:
Let wark an hunger mak them sober!
The hizzies, if they're aughtlins fawsont,     *hussies, at all good-looking*
Let them in Drury-lane be lesson'd!     *the 'red light' district of*
An if the wives an dirty brats     *London at that time*
Come thiggin at your doors an yetts,     *begging; gates*
Flaffin wi duds, an grey wi beas',     *flogging, rags, vermin*
Frightin awa your ducks an geese;
Get out a horsewhip or a jowler,     *bulldog*
The langest thong, the fiercest growler,
An gar the tatter'd gypsies pack     *make*
Wi a' their bastards on their back!

Go on, my Lord! I lang to meet you,
An in my 'house at hame' to greet you;
Wi common lords ye shanna mingle,     *shall not*
The benmost neuk beside the ingle,     *innermost corner, fireside*
At my right han' assigned your seat,
'Tween Herod's hip an Polycrate;     *Polycrates, tyrant of Samos*
Or (if you on your station tarrow),     *6th century B.C.*
Between Almagro and Pizarro,     *Diego d'Almagro (1475-1538)*
A seat, I'm sure ye're well deservin't;     *Francisco Pizarro (1478-1541)*
An till ye come – your humble servant,     *the Conquistadores of Peru*
              BEELZEBUB

## LIBEL SUMMONS

This mock summons to a fictional Court of Equity parodies both the Bachelors' Club,
Tarbolton (a serious debating society) and the Kirk Session tribunals on fornication. The
text is based on the Hastie MS, with additions from the Egerton MS.

In Truth and Honour's name – Amen
Know all men by these Presents plain:

This fourth o June, at Mauchline given,
The year 'tween eighty five and seven,
We, Fornicators by profession,
As per extractum from each Session,
In way and manner here narrated,
Pro bono Amor congregated;    for the sake of Love
And by our brethren constituted,     (Latin)
A Court of Equity deputed.
With special authoris'd direction
To take beneath our strict protection,
The stays-out-bursting, quondam maiden,
With Growing Life and anguish laden;
Who by the rascal is deny'd,
That led her thoughtless steps aside.
He who disowns the ruin'd Fair-one,
And for her wants and woes does care none;
The wretch that can refuse subsistence
To those whom he has given existence;
He who when at a lass's by-job,     fornication
Defrauds her wi a frig or dry bob;    masturbation
The coof that stands on clishmaclavers  fool; nonsense
When women haflins offer favors: –     partly
All who in any way or manner
Disdain the Fornicator's honor,
We take cognisance thereanent,
The proper Judges competent.

First, Poet Burns he takes the chair,
Allow'd by a', his title's fair;
And pass'd nem. con. without dissension,
He has a duplicate pretension. –
Next, Merchant Smith, our worthy Fiscal,  James Smith
To cow each pertinaceous rascal;    (1765-1823)
In this, as every other state,
His merit is conspicuous great:
Richmond the third, our trusty Clerk,  John Richmond
The minutes regular to mark,     (1765-1846)
And sit dispenser of the law,
In absence of the former twa;

The fourth our Messenger At Arms,
When failing all the milder terms,
Hunter, a hearty, willing brother,　　　　　William Hunter,
Weel skill'd in dead and living leather.　　　a Mauchline
Without Preamble less or more said,　　　　shoemaker
We, body politic aforesaid,
With legal, due Whereas, and Wherefore,
We are appointed here to care for
The interests of our constituents,
And punish contravening truants,
Keeping a proper regulation
Within the lists of Fornication.

Whereas, our Fiscal, by petition,
Informs us there is strong suspicion,
You, Coachman Dow, and Clockie Brown,　　Alex Dow, John
Baith residenters in this town;　　　　　　Brown a clockmaker
In other words, you, Jock, and Sandy,
Hae been at wark at Houghmagandie;　　　　fornication
And now when facts are come to light
The matter ye deny outright.

First, You, John Brown, there's witness borne,
And affidavit made and sworn,
That ye hae bred a hurly-burly
'Bout Jeany Mitchel's tirlie-whirlie,　　　　genitalia
And blooster'd at her regulator,
Till a' her wheels gang clitter-clatter.
And farther still, ye cruel Vandal,
A tale might even in hell be scandal!
That ye hae made repeated trials
Wi drugs and draps in doctor's phials,
Mixt, as ye thought, wi fell infusion,
Your ain begotten wean to poosion.　　　　child
And yet ye are sae scant o grace,
Ye daur to lift your brazen face,
And offer for to take your aith,
Ye never lifted Jeany's claith. –　　　　　clothing
But tho ye should yoursel manswear,
Laird Wilson's sclates can witness bear,　　slates
Ae e'ening of a Mauchline fair,
That Jeany's masts they saw them bare;
For ye had furl'd up her sails,
And was at play – at heads and tails.

Next, Sandy Dow, you're here indicted
To have, as publickly you're wyted,                    accused
Been clandestinely upward whirlin
The petticoats o Maggy Borelan,
And giein her canister a rattle,
That months to come it winna settle.
And yet, ye offer your protest,
Ye never herried Maggy's nest;                         harried
Tho, it's weel ken'd that at her gyvel                 vagina
Ye hae gien mony a kytch and kyvel.                    thrust, bang
Then Brown and Dow, before design'd,
For clags and clauses there subjoin'd,                 claims
We, Court aforesaid cite and summon,
That on the fifth o July comin,
The hour o cause, in our Court-ha',
At Whitefoord's arms, ye answer Law!

But, as reluctantly we Punish,
An rather, mildly would admonish:
Since Better Punishment prevented,
Than Obstinacy sair repented.

Then, for that ancient Secret's sake,
You have the honor to partake;
An for that noble Badge you wear,
You, Sandie Dow, our Brother dear,
We give you as a Man an Mason,
This private, sober, friendly lesson.

Your Crime, a manly deed we view it,
As Man alone, can only do it;
But, in denial persevering,
Is to a Scoundrel's name adhering.
The best o men, hae been surpris'd;
The best o women been advis'd:
Nay, cleverest Lads hae haen a trick o't,
An, bonniest Lasses taen a lick o't.

Then Brother Dow, if you're asham'd
In such a Quorum to be nam'd,
Your conduct much is to be blam'd.
See, ev'n himsel – there's godly Bryan,                a notorious reprobate
That auld whatreck he has been tryin;                  fornication
When such as he put to their han',
What man on character need stan'?
Then Brother dear, lift up your brow,
And, like yoursel, the truth avow;

Erect a dauntless face upon it,
An say, 'I am the man has done it;
'I Sandie Dow gat Meg wi wean,
'An 's fit to do as much again.'
Ne'er mind their solemn rev'rend faces,
Had they – in proper times an places,
But seen an fun' – I mukle dread it,          *much*
They just would done as you an we did.
To tell the truth 's a manly lesson,
An doubly proper in a Mason.

You Monsieur Brown, as it is proven,
Jean Mitchel's wame by you was hoven;     *belly, distended*
Without you by a quick repentance
Acknowledge Jean's an your acquaintance,
Depend on't, this shall be your sentence.
Our beadles to the Cross shall take you,
And there shall mither naked make you;
Some canie grip near by your middle,
They shall it bind as tight 's a fiddle;
The raep they round the pump shall tak     *rope*
An tye your han's behint your back;
Wi just an ell o string allow'd
To jink an hide you frae the croud:     *dodge*
There ye shall stan', a legal seizure,
In during Jeanie Mitchel's pleasure;
So be, her pleasure dinna pass
Seven turnings of a half-hour glass:
Nor shall it in her pleasure be
To louse you out in less than three.     *release*

This, our futurum esse Decreet,
We mean it not to keep a secret;
But in our summons here insert it,
And whoso dares, may controvert it.
This, mark'd before the date and place is,
Sigillum est, per,     *'The Seal is by...' (Latin)*
   Burns the Preses.     *Chairman*
This Summons and the signet mark,
Extractum est, per,     *'Is extracted by' (Latin)*
   Richmond, Clerk,
At Mauchline, idem date of June,
'Tween six and seven, the afternoon,
You twa, in propria personae,
Within design'd, Sandy and Johny,
This Summons legally have got,
As vide witness underwrote:
Within the house of John Dow, vinter,
Nunc facio hoc,     *'I now make this' (Latin)*
   Gullelmus Hunter.

## EPITAPH ON JOHN DOVE, INNKEEPER

John Dove or Dow, a native of Paisley, kept the Whitefoord Arms where the Mauchline Bachelors' Club met in 1785.

Here lies Johnie Pigeon:
What was his religion
   Whae'er desires to ken                     know
To some other warl'
Maun follow the carl,                      old chap
   For here Johnie Pigeon had nane!

Strong ale was ablution;
Small beer, persecution;
   A dram was *memento mori;*
But a full flowing bowl
Was the saving his soul,
   And port was celestial glory!

## EPITAPH FOR A WAG IN MAUCHLINE

Cunningham and other early editors identified the subject as James Smith (1765-1823), but Kinsley considers 'Clockie' Brown as more likely - see 'Libel Summons.'

Lament him, Mauchline husbands a',
   He aften did assist ye;
For had ye staid hale weeks awa',            whole
   Your wives they ne'er had missed ye!

Ye Mauchline bairns, as on ye pass        children
   To school in bands thegither,
O, tread ye lightly on his grass –
   Perhaps he was your father!

## WILLIE CHALMERS

William Chalmers, writer and notary-public in Ayr, drew up the assignation of the poet's property in favour of his brother Gilbert in 1786 when he was thinking of emigrating. Chalmers asked Burns to write a poem for him to give to his sweetheart. The result was this humorous piece of advice to the young lady.

Wi braw new branks in mickle pride,      fine bridle
   And eke a braw new brechan,       also, collar
My Pegasus I'm got astride,
   And up Parnassus pechin:          panting
Whyles owre a bush wi downward crush   sometimes
   The doited beastie stammers,         stupid
Then up he gets, and off he sets
   For sake o Willie Chalmers.

I doubt na, lass, that weel kend name         well-known
    May cost a pair o blushes:
I am nae stranger to your fame,
    Nor his warm-urged wishes.
Your bonie face, sae mild and sweet,
    His honest heart enamours;
And faith! ye'll no be lost a whit,
    Tho wair'd on Willie Chalmers.         bestowed

Auld Truth hersel might swear ye're fair,
    And Honor safely back her:
And Modesty assume your air,
    And ne'er a ane mistak her;
And sic twa love-inspiring een         eyes
    Might fire even holy palmers:
Nae wonder then they've fatal been
    To honest Willie Chalmers!

I doubt na Fortune may you shore
    Some mim-mou'd pouther'd priestie,     prim-lipped powdered
Fu lifted up wi Hebrew lore
    And band upon his breastie;
But O! what signifies to you
    His lexicons and grammars?
The feeling heart's the royal blue,
    And that's wi Willie Chalmers.

Some gapin, glowrin countra laird     staring
    May warsle for your favour:     struggle
May claw his lug, and straik his beard,     scratch, ear, stroke
    And hoast up some palaver.     cough
My bonie maid, before ye wed
    Sic clumsy-witted hammers,     dunces
Seek Heaven for help, and barefit skelp     spank
    Awa wi Willie Chalmers.

Forgive the Bard! my fond regard
    For ane that shares my bosom
Inspires my Muse to gie 'm his dues,
    For deil a hair I roose him.     not, flatter
May powers aboon unite you soon,
    And fructify your amours,
And every year come in mair dear,
    To you and Willie Chalmers!

# A DREAM

Thoughts, words, and deeds, the Statute blames with reason;
But surely *Dreams* were ne'er indicted Treason.

On reading in the public papers, the Laureate's Ode, with the other
parade of June 4, 1786, the Author was no sooner dropt asleep,
than he imagined himself transported to the Birthday Levee; and,
in his dreaming fancy made the following Address: –

The 'parade' referred to was the national celebration of the 48th birthday of King George
III, and the Ode was composed by Thomas Warton (1728-90), Professor of Poetry at
Oxford (1757-67) and Poet Laureate (1785-90). According to Christopher North 'the
gods had made him poetical, but not a poet' and he is remembered today only indirectly,
from having been the cause of this poem. Mrs Dunlop of Dunlop urged Burns to omit
it from his second edition as it gave offence to 'numbers at London.' But Burns was
urepentant.

| | |
|---|---|
| Guid-mornin to your Majesty! | |
| May heaven augment your blisses, | |
| On ev'ry new birthday ye see, | |
| A humble Poet wishes! | |
| My Bardship here, at your Levee, | |
| On sic a day as this is, | |
| Is sure an uncouth sight to see, | |
| Amang thae birthday dresses | those |
| Sae fine this day. | |

| | |
|---|---|
| I see ye're complimented thrang, | effusively |
| By monie a lord an lady; | |
| 'God save the King' 's a cuckoo sang | |
| That's unco easy said ay: | very |
| The poets, too a venal gang, | |
| Wi rhymes weel-turn'd an ready, | |
| Wad gar you trow ye ne'er do wrang, | make, think |
| But ay unerring steady, | |
| On sic a day. | |

| | |
|---|---|
| For me! before a Monarch's face, | |
| Ev'n there I winna flatter; | |
| For neither pension, post, nor place, | |
| Am I your humble debtor: | |
| So, nae reflection on your Grace, | |
| Your Kingship to bespatter; | |
| There's monie waur been o the race, | worse |
| And aiblins ane been better | a reference to the |
| Than you this day. | Young Pretender |

'Tis very true, my sovereign King,
   My skill may weel be doubted;
But facts are chiels that winna ding,         *fellows, upset*
   An downa be disputed:                  *cannot*
Your royal nest, beneath your wing,
   Is e'en right reft and clouted,      *torn and patched*
And now the third part o the string,
   An less, will gang about it              *go*
      Than did ae day.

Far be't frae me that I aspire
   To blame your legislation,
Or say, ye wisdom want, or fire
   To rule this mighty nation:
But faith! I muckle doubt, my sire,       *greatly*
   Ye've trusted ministration
To chaps wha in a barn or byre        *cowshed*
   Wad better fill'd their station,
      Than courts yon day.

And now ye've gien auld Britain peace,    *given*
   Her broken shins to plaister;
Your sair taxation does her fleece,
   Till she has scarce a tester:       *sixpence*
For me, thank God, my life's a lease,
   Nae bargain wearin faster,
Or faith! I fear, that, wi the geese,
   I shortly boost to pasture          *behove*
      I' the craft some day.           *croft*

I'm no mistrusting Willie Pitt,
   When taxes he enlarges,
(An Will's a true guid fallow's get,      *offspring*
   A name not envy spairges)        *spatters*
That he intends to pay your debt,
   An lessen a' your charges;
But, God sake! let nae saving fit
   Abridge your bonie barges
      An boats this day.

Adieu, my Liege! may Freedom geck         toss the head
    Beneath your high protection;
An may ye rax Corruption's neck,             stretch
    And gie her for dissection!
But since I'm here, I'll no neglect,
    In loyal, true affection,
To pay your Queen, wi due respect,
    My fealty an subjection
       This great birthday.

Hail, Majesty most Excellent!
    While nobles strive to please ye,
Will ye accept a compliment,
    A simple Bardie gies ye?
Thae bonie bairntime Heav'n has lent,         brood
    Still higher may they heeze ye          hoist
In bliss, till Fate some day is sent,
    For ever to release ye
       Frae care that day.

For you, young Potentate o Wales,     George, Prince of Wales,
    I tell your Highness fairly,       later Prince Regent and
Down Pleasure's stream, wi swelling sails,    King George IV
    I'm tauld ye're driving rarely;        (1762-1830)
But some day ye may gnaw your nails,    a reference to 'Prinny's'
    An curse your folly sairly,          affair with
That e'er ye brak Diana's pales,       Mrs Fitzherbert
    Or rattl'd dice wi Charlie       Charles James Fox
       By night or day.

Yet aft a ragged cowte's been known,       colt
    To mak a noble aiver;          old horse
So, ye may doucely fill a throne,        soberly
    For a' their clish-ma-claver:       gossip
There, him at Agincourt wha shone,     Prince Hal (later
    Few better were or braver;        Henry V)
And yet, wi funny, queer Sir John,      Falstaff
    He was an unco shaver
       For monie a day.

For you, right rev'rend Osnaburg,  *Frederick Augustus,*
　　Nane sets the lawn-sleeve sweeter,  *Duke of York, younger*
Altho a ribban at your lug  *son of George III and*
　　Wad been a dress completer:  *Bishop of Osnabruck (1764)*
As ye disown yon paughty dog,  *the Pope*
　　That bears the keys of Peter,
Then swith! an get a wife to hug,  *haste!*
　　Or trowth, ye'll stain the mitre  *a reference to the Duke-Bishop's*
　　　　Some luckless day!  *affair with the former mistress*
　　　　　　　　　　　　　　　　　　*of Rann the notorious highwayman*

Young, royal Tarry-breeks, I learn,  *Prince William, later Duke of*
　　Ye've lately come athwart her –  *Clarence and King William IV*
A glorious galley, stem an stern,  *(1830-7)*
　　Well rigg'd for Venus' barter;  *his affair with Sarah Martin*
But first hang out that she'll discern  *of Portsmouth*
　　Your hymeneal charter;
Then heave aboard your grapple-airn,  *grappling-iron*
　　An, large upon her quarter,
　　　　Come full that day.

Ye, lastly, bonie blossoms a',  *the daughters of George III:*
　　Ye royal lasses dainty,  *Charlotte, Augusta, Elizabeth*
Heav'n mak ye guid as weel as braw,  *Mary, Sophia and Amelia*
　　An gie you lads-a-plenty!
But sneer na British boys awa!
　　For kings are unco scant ay,
An German gentles are but sma',  *noblemen*
　　They're better just than want ay
　　　　On onie day.

God bless you a'! consider now,
　　Ye're unco muckle dautet;  *extremely pampered*
But ere the course o life be through,
　　It may be bitter sautet:  *salted*
An I hae seen their coggie fou,  *dish full*
　　That yet hae tarrow't at it.  *tarried*
But or the day was done, I trow,  *trust*
　　The laggen they hae clautet  *bottom, scraped*
　　　　Fu clean that day.

## TO DR. MACKENZIE, MAUCHLINE

### MOSSGIEL, An. M. 5790

John Mackenzie (d. 1837) practised medicine in Mauchline, and became a close friend of Burns through the Masonic lodge St. James, Tarbolton. Dr. Mackenzie gave the poet valuable introductions and recommendations prior to his first visit to Edinburgh.

Friday first's the day appointed
By the Right Worshipful Anointed,
  To hold our grand procession;
To get a blaud o Johnie's morals,             *screed*
An taste a swatch o Manson's barrels   *Manson's Inn, where the*
  I' the way of our profession.       *Tarbolton masonic lodge met*

Our Master and the Brotherhood
  Wad a' be glad to see you.
For me, I wad be mair than proud
  To share the mercies wi you.
    If Death, then, wi skaith, then,       *harm*
      Some mortal heart is hechtin,    *menacing*
    Inform him, an storm him,
      That Saturday you'll fecht him.     *fight*

ROBERT BURNS

## THE FAREWELL

### TO THE BRETHREN OF ST. JAMES'S LODGE, TARBOLTON

*TUNE: Good-night, and joy be wi you a'*

Burns became an apprentice freemason in July 1781, and was 'passed and raised' on 1st October that year. He became Depute-Master on 27th July 1784. It is thought that this song was written for the meeting on 24th June 1786, well before the publication of the Kilmarnock Edition, when Burns was still set on emigrating to Jamaica.

Adieu! a heart-warm, fond adieu;
  Dear Brothers of the *Mystic Tie*!
Ye favoured, ye *enlighten'd* few,
  Companions of my social joy!
Tho I to foreign lands must hie,
  Pursuing Fortune's slidd'ry ba';       *slippery*
With melting heart and brimful eye,
  I'll mind you still, tho far awa.

Oft have I met your social band,
 And spent the cheerful, festive night:
Oft, honour'd with supreme command,
 Presided o'er the *Sons of Light;*
And by that *Hieroglyphic* bright,
 Which none but *Craftsmen* ever saw!
Strong Mem'ry on my heart shall write
 Those happy scenes, when far awa.

May Freedom, Harmony, and Love,
 Unite you in the *Grand Design,*
Beneath th' Omniscient Eye above –
 The glorious *Architect Divine,*
That you may keep th' *Unerring Line,*
 Still rising by the *Plummet's Law,*
Till *Order* bright completely shine,
 Shall be my pray'r when far awa.

And *you,* farewell! whose merits claim
 Justly that *Highest Badge* to wear:
Heav'n bless your honour'd, noble name,
 To *Masonry* and *Scotia* dear!
A last request permit me here
 When yearly ye assemble a',
One *round,* I ask it with a *tear,*
 To him, *the Bard that's far awa.*

## THE FAREWELL

*The valiant, in himself, what can he suffer?*
*Or what does he regard his single woes?*
*But when, alas! he multiplies himself,*
*To dearer selves, to the lov'd tender fair,*
*To those whose bliss, whose beings hang upon him,*
*To helpless children, – then, Oh then he feels*
*The point of misery festering in his heart,*
*And weakly weeps his fortunes like a coward:*
*Such, such am I! – undone! – THOMSON'S Edward and Eleanora*

Written in the summer of 1786, while Burns was still intent on going abroad.

Farewell, old Scotia's bleak domains,
Far dearer than the torrid plains,
 Where rich ananas blow!       pineapples
Farewell, a mother's blessing dear
A brother's sigh, a sister's tear,
 My Jean's heart-rending throe!
Farewell, my Bess! Tho thou'rt bereft     Elizabeth Burns

Of my paternal care,
A faithful brother I have left,                             Gilbert Burns
    My part in him thou'lt share!
    Adieu too, to you too,
        My Smith, my bosom frien';                         James Smith
    When kindly you mind me,
        O, then befriend my Jean!

What bursting anguish tears my heart?
From thee, my Jeany, must I part?
Thou, weeping, answ'rest – 'No!'
Alas! misfortune stares my face,
And points to ruin and disgrace –
    I for thy sake must go!
Thee, Hamilton, and Aiken dear,                            Gavin Hamilton
    A grateful, warm adieu:                                Robert Aiken
I with a much-indebted tear
    Shall still remember you!
        All-hail then, the gale then
        Wafts me from thee, dear shore!
    It rustles, and whistles –
        I'll never see thee more!


## TAM SAMSON'S ELEGY

*An honest man's the noblest work of God* - POPE

Thomas Samson (1722-95) of Kilmarnock, 'a seedsman of good credit, a zealous sportsman, and a good fellow.' On one occasion when they had been out wildfowling, Tam had a foreboding that this would be his last such outing and expressed a wish to be buried on the moors. This inspired Burns to write this epitaph.

Has auld Kilmarnock seen the Deil?
Or great Mackinlay thrawn his heel?                         Rev. James Mackinlay
Or Robertson again grown weel,                             Rev. John Robertson
    To preach an read?
'Na, waur than a'!' cries ilka chiel,                       worse, every chap
    'Tam Samson's dead!'

Kilmarnock lang may grunt an grane,                         groan
An sigh, an sab, an greet her lane,                         sob, cry, alone
An cleed her bairns – man, wife, an wean –                 clothe, child
    In mourning weed;
To Death she's dearly pay'd the kain:                      rent in kind
    Tam Samson's dead!

The Brethren o the mystic level      Masons of St. John, Kilwinning
May hing their head in woefu bevel,         Lodge, Kilmarnock
While by their nose the tears will revel,
    Like onie bead;
Death's gien the Lodge an unco devel:         violent blow
    Tam Samson's dead!

When winter muffles up his cloak,
And binds the mire like a rock;
When to the loughs the curlers flock,
    Wi gleesome speed,
Wha will they station at the cock –            mark
    Tam Samson's dead!

He was the king of a' the core,             crowd
To guard, or draw, or wick a bore,
Or up the rink like Jehu roar
    In time o need;
But now he lags on Death's hog-score:
    Tam Samson's dead!

Now safe the stately sawmont sail,          salmon
And trouts bedropp'd wi crimson hail,
And eels, weel-kend for souple tail,     well-known, supple
    And geds for greed,                 pike
Since, dark in Death's fish-creel, we wail
    Tam Samson's dead!

Rejoice, ye birring paitricks a';          partridges
Ye cootie moorcocks, crousely craw;    leg-plumed, cockily
Ye maukins, cock your fud fu braw,     hares, behind, fine
    Withouten dread;
Your mortal fae is now awa:              foe
    Tam Samson's dead!

That woefu morn be ever mourn'd,
Saw him in shootin graith adorn'd,         gear
While pointers round impatient burn'd,
    Frae couples free'd;              leashes
But, och! he gaed and ne'er return'd:      went
    Tam Samson's dead!

In vain auld age his body batters,
In vain the gout his ancles fetters,
In vain the burns cam down like waters,
    An acre braid!
Now ev'ry auld wife, greetin, clatters:    crying, babbles
    'Tam Samson's dead!'

Owre monie a weary hag he limpit,                    bog
An ay the tither shot he thumpit,
Till coward Death behint him jumpit,
    Wi deadly feide;                               enmity
Now he proclaims wi tout o trumpet:                  blast
    'Tam Samson's dead!'

When at his heart he felt the dagger,
He reel'd his wonted bottle-swagger,
But yet he drew the mortal trigger,
    Wi weel-aim'd heed;
'Lord, five!' he cry'd, an owre did stagger –
    Tam Samson's dead!

Ilk hoary hunter mourn'd a brither;                  Each
Ilk sportsman-youth bemoan'd a father;
Yon auld gray stane, amang the heather,
    Marks out his head;
Whare Burns has wrote, in rhyming blether,           nonsense
    'Tam Samson's dead!'

There, low he lies in lasting rest;
Perhaps upon his mould'ring breast
Some spitefu moorfowl bigs her nest,                 builds
    To hatch and breed:
Alas! nae mair he'll them molest:
    Tam Samson's dead!

When August winds the heather wave,
And sportsmen wander by yon grave,
Three volleys let his memory crave,
    O pouther an lead,                             gunpowder
Till Echo answer frae her cave,
    'Tam Samson's dead!'

'Heav'n rest his saul whare'er he be!'
Is th' wish o' monie mae than me:                    many more
He had twa fauts, or maybe three,
    Yet what remead?                               remedy
Ae social, honest man want we:                       One
    Tam Samson's dead!

THE EPITAPH
Tam Samson's weel-worn clay here lies:
    Ye canting zealots, spare him!
If honest worth in Heaven rise,
    Ye'll mend or ye win near him.

PER CONTRA
Go, Fame, an canter like a filly
Thro a' the streets an neuks o Killie;               corners, Kilmarnock
Tell ev'ry social honest billie                      person
    To cease his grievin;
For, yet unskaith'd by Death's gleg gullie,          unharmed, sharp knife
Tam Samson's leevin!

## TO MR. JOHN KENNEDY

These lines brought to a close a letter from Burns written at Kilmarnock in August 1786, following publication of his poems. Even at this date he was still set on emigration.

Farewell, dear friend! may guid luck hit you,
And 'mong her favourites admit you!
If e'er Detraction shore to smit you,           threaten, smite
   May nane believe him!
And onie Deil that thinks to get you,           any
   Good Lord, deceive him!

## REPLY TO A TRIMMING EPISTLE
## RECEIVED FROM A TAILOR

The subject of this reply was Thomas Walker (d. about 1812) of Pool near Ochiltree, a friend of the schoolmaster William Simson. Walker sent a verse-epistle to Burns, in the hope of a similar reply. Burns apparently ignored it, and this provoked Walker to write, after the appearance of the Kilmarnock Edition, criticising the poet's morals. Clearly Simson had a hand in this, a fact not lost on Burns when he responded with these verses.

What ails ye now, ye lousie bitch
To thresh my back at sic a pitch?               thrash
Losh, man, hae mercy wi your natch!             Lord, notching-blade
   Your bodkin's bauld:                      needle
I didna suffer half sae much
   Frae Daddie Auld.                         Rev. William Auld

What tho at times, when I grow crouse,          set
I gie their wames a random pouse,               bellies, thrust
Is that enough for you to souse                 strike
   Your servant sae?
Gae mind your seam, ye prick-the-louse,         nit-picking
   An jag-the-flae!                          flea

King David o poetic brief                       writ
Wrocht 'mang the lasses sic mischief
As fill'd his after-life wi grief,
   An bluidy rants;                          rows
An yet he's rank'd amang the chief
   O lang-syne saunts.                       old-time saints

And maybe, Tam, for a' my cants,                canters
My wicked rhymes, an drucken rants,             drunken sprees
I'll gie auld Cloven Clootie's haunts           the Devil
   An unco slip yet,
An snugly sit amang the saunts,
   At Davie's hip yet!

But, fegs! the Session says I maun            faith!, must
Gae fa' upo' anither plan
Than garrin lasses coup the cran,       making, upset the cart
    Clean heels owre body,
An sairly thole their mother's ban           endure
    Afore the howdy. midwife

This leads me on to tell for sport
How I did wi the Session sort:
Auld Clinkum at the inner port,          The Bell-ringer
    Cried three times, 'Robin!
Come hither lad, and answer for't,
    Ye're blam'd for jobbin!'            fornication

Wi pinch I put a Sunday's face on,
An snoov'd awa before the Session       toddled off
I made an open, fair confession –
    I scorned to lie –
An syne Mess John, beyond expression,    Master (of Arts)
    Fell foul o me.

A fornicator-loun he call'd me,
An said my faut frae bliss expell'd me.
I own'd the tale was true he tell'd me,
    'But, what the matter?'
(Quo' I) 'I fear unless ye geld me,        castrate
    I'll ne'er be better!'

'Geld you!' (quo' he) 'an what for no?      why not
If that your right hand, leg, or toe
Should ever prove your sp'ritual foe,
    You should remember
To cut it aff – an what for no
    Your dearest member!'

'Na, na,' (quo' I) 'I'm no for that,
Gelding's nae better than 'tis ca't;
I'd rather suffer for my faut,
    A hearty flewit,               flogging
As sair owre hip as ye can draw't,
    Tho I should rue it.'

'Or, gin ye like to end the bother,
To please us a' - I've just ae ither:      one another
When next wi yon lass I forgather,     have intercourse
    Whate'er betide it,
I'll frankly gie her 't a' thegither,
    An let her guide it.'

But, Sir, this pleas'd them warst of a',
An therefore, Tam, when that I saw,
I said 'Guid night', an came awa,
    An left the Session:
I saw they were resolved a'
    On my oppression.

# THE BRIGS OF AYR

### INSCRIBED TO JOHN BALLANTINE, ESQ., AYR

Written in the autumn of 1786, when work on the new bridge was under way. The old bridge dates from c. 1232 and was in dangerous condition by 1786. The new bridge, completed in 1788, was constructed by Alexander Steven, master mason, and John Ballantine, Dean of Guild and a patron of Burns. Ballantine (1743-1812) was a merchant and banker, later (1787) Provost of Ayr.

The simple Bard, rough at the rustic plough,
Learning his tuneful trade from ev'ry bough
(The chanting linnet, or the mellow thrush,
Hailing the setting sun, sweet, in the green thorn bush;
The soaring lark, the perching red-breast shrill,
Or deep-ton'd plovers grey, wild-whistling o'er the hill):
Shall he – nurst in the peasant's lowly shed,
To hardy independence bravely bred,
By early poverty to hardship steel'd,
And train'd to arms in stern Misfortune's field –
Shall he be guilty of their hireling crimes,
The servile, mercenary Swiss of rhymes?
Or labour hard the panegyric close,
With all the venal soul of dedicating prose?
No! though his artless strains he rudely sings,
And throws his hand uncouthly o'er the strings,
He glows with all the spirit of the Bard,
Fame, honest fame, his great, his dear reward.
Still, if some patron's gen'rous care he trace,
Skill'd in the secret to bestow with grace;
When Ballantine befriends his humble name,    a reference to his
And hands the rustic stranger up to fame,    financial support over
With heartfelt throes his grateful bosom swells:    the publication of
The godlike bliss, to give, alone excels.    Burns's poems

'Twas when the stacks get on their winter hap,      *wrapping*
And thack and rape secure the toil-won crap;    *thatch, rope, crop*
Potatoe-bings are snuggèd up frae skaith     *heaps, harm*
O coming Winter's biting, frosty breath;
The bees, rejoicing o'er their summer toils –
Unnumber'd buds' an flowers' delicious spoils,
Sealed up with frugal care in massive waxen piles –    *honeycombs*
Are doom'd by Man, that tyrant o'er the weak,
The death o devils smoor'd wi brimstone reek:    *smothered*
The thundering guns are heard on ev'ry side,
The wounded coveys, reeling, scatter wide;
The feather'd field-mates, bound by Nature's tie,
Sires, mothers, children, in one carnage lie:
(What warm, poetic heart but inly bleeds,
And execrates man's savage, ruthless deeds!)
Nae mair the flower in field or meadow springs;
Nae mair the grove with airy concert rings,
Except perhaps the robin's whistling glee,
Proud o the height o some bit half-lang tree;    *half grown*
The hoary morns precede the sunny days,
Mild, calm, serene, widespreads the noontide blaze,
While thick the gossamour waves wanton in the rays.

'Twas in that season, when a simple Bard,
Unknown and poor – simplicity's reward! –
Ae night, within the ancient brugh of Ayr    *one, burgh*
By whim inspir'd, or haply prest wi care,
He left his bed, and took his wayward route,
And down by *Simpson's* wheel'd the left about:
(Whether, impell'd by all-directing Fate,
To witness what I after shall narrate;
Or whether, rapt in meditation high,
He wander'd forth, he knew not where nor why):
The drowsy Dungeon-Clock had number'd two,    *Tolbooth, Sandgate*
And Wallace Tower had sworn the fact was true;
The tide-swoln Firth, with sullen-sounding roar,
Through the still night dash'd hoarse along the shore;
All else was hush'd as Nature's closed e'e;
The silent moon shone high o'er tower and tree;
The chilly frost, beneath the silver beam,
Crept, gently-crusting, o'er the glittering stream.

When, lo! on either hand the list'ning Bard,
The clanging sugh of whistling wings is heard;        swish
Two dusky forms dart thro the midnight air,
Swift as the gos drives on the wheeling hare;
Ane on th' Auld Brig his airy shape uprears,
The ither flutters o'er the rising piers:
Our warlock rhymer instantly decried        wizard
The Sprites that owre the Brigs of Ayr preside.
(That Bards are second-sighted is nae joke,
And ken the lingo of the sp'ritual folk;        know
Fays, spunkies, kelpies, a', they can explain them,    fairies, jack-o'-
An ev'n the vera deils they brawly ken them).    lanthorns, water demons
Auld Brig appear'd of ancient Pictish race,
The vera wrinkles Gothic in his face:
He seem'd as he wi Time had warstl'd lang,        wrestled
Yet, teughly doure, he bade an unco bang.        toughly, stubborn
New Brig was buskit in a braw new coat,        dressed, fine
That he at Lon'on, frae ane Adams got;        Robert Adam (1728-92)
In's hand five taper staves as smooth's a bead,    architect of the new bridge
Wi virls an whirlygigums at the head.        whorls, flourishes
The Goth was stalking round with anxious search,
Spying the time-worn flaws in ev'ry arch;
It chanc'd his new-come neebor took his e'e,
And e'en a vex'd and angry heart had he!
Wi thieveless sneer to see his modish mien,        forbidding
He, down the water, gies him this guid-een: –        down-river

## AULD BRIG

'I doubt na, frien, ye'll think ye're nae sheep shank,
Ance ye were streekit owre frae bank to bank!        stretched
But gin ye be a brig as auld as me –        if
Tho faith, that date, I doubt, ye'll never see –
There'll be, if that day come, I'll wad a boddle,    wager a farthing
Some fewer whigmeleeries in your noddle.'        crotchets, brain

## NEW BRIG

'Auld Vandal! ye but show your little mense,
Just much about it wi your scanty sense:
Will your poor, narrow foot-path of a street,
Where twa wheel-barrows tremble when they meet,
Your ruin'd, formless bulk o stane an lime,
Compare wi bonie brigs o modern time?
There's men of taste would tak the Ducat stream,    a ford across the Ayr
Tho they should cast the vera sark and swim,        shirt
E'er they would grate their feelings wi the view
O sic an ugly, Gothic hulk as you.'

## AULD BRIG

'Conceited gowk! puffed up wi windy pride!   cuckoo
This monie a year I've stood the flood an tide;
And tho wi crazy eild I'm sair forfairn,   antiquity, worn out
I'll be a brig when ye're a shapeless cairn!
As yet ye little ken about the matter,
But twa-three winters will inform ye better.
When heavy, dark, continued, a'-day rains   day-long
Wi deepening deluges o'erflow the plains;
When from the hills where springs the brawling Coil, four tributaries
Or stately Lugar's mossy fountains boil,   of the River Ayr
Or where the Greenock winds his moorland course,
Or haunted Garpal draws his feeble source,
Arous'd by blustering winds an spotting thowes,  thaws
In monie a torrent down the snaw-broo rowes;  snow-brew rolls
While crashing ice, borne on the roaring speat,  flood
Sweeps dams, an mills, an brigs, a' to the gate;
And from Glenbuck down to the Ratton-Key, village in Muirkirk parish
Auld Ayr is just one lengthen'd tumbling sea –
Then down ye'll hurl (deil nor ye never rise!),  crash
And dash the gumlie jaups up to the pouring skies! muddy splashes
A lesson sadly teaching, to your cost,
That Architecture's noble art is lost!'

## NEW BRIG

'Fine architecture, trowth, I needs must say't o't,
The Lord be thankit that we've tint the gate o't! lost the knack of it
Gaunt, ghastly, ghaist-alluring edifices,
Hanging with threat'ning jut, like precipices;
O'er-arching, mouldy, gloom-inspiring coves,
Supporting roofs fantastic – stony groves;
Windows and doors in nameless sculptures drest,
With order, symmetry, or taste unblest;
Forms like some bedlam statuary's dream,
The craz'd creations of misguided whim;
Forms might be worshipp'd on the bended knee,
And still the second dread Command be free:
Their likeness is not found on earth, in air, or sea!
Mansions that would disgrace the building taste
Of any mason reptile, bird or beast:
Fit only for a doited monkish race,   befuddled
Or frosty maids forsworn the dear embrace,
Or cuifs of later times, wha held the notion,  fools
That sullen gloom was sterling true devotion:
Fancies that our guid brugh denies protection,
And soon may they expire, unblest with resurrection!'

## AULD BRIG

'O ye, my dear-remember'd, ancient yealings,    co-evals
Were ye but here to share my wounded feelings!
Ye worthy proveses, an monie a bailie,    provosts
Wha in the paths o righteousness did toil ay;
Ye dainty deacons, an ye douce conveeners,    sober
To whom our moderns are but causey-cleaners;    street-sweepers
Ye godly councils, wha hae blest this town;
Ye godly brethren o the sacred gown,
Wha meekly gie your hurdies to the smiters;    buttocks
And (what would now be strange), ye godly Writers;    lawyers (Writers
A' ye douce folk I've borne aboon the broo,    to the Signet);
Were ye but here, what would ye say or do?    sedate, above, water
How would your spirits groan in deep vexation,
To see each melancholy alteration;
And, agonising, curse the time and place
When ye begat the base degen'rate race!
Nae langer rev'rend men, their country's glory,
In plain braid Scots hold forth a plain, braid story;
Nae langer thrifty citizens, an douce,
Meet owre a pint, or in the council-house;
But staumrel, corky-headed, graceless gentry,    half-witted
The herryment and ruin of the country;
Men three-parts made by tailors and by barbers,
Wha waste your weel-hain'd gear on damn'd New Brigs
        and harbours!'

## NEW BRIG

'Now haud you there! for faith ye've said enough,
And muckle mair then ye can mak to through.    make good
As for your priesthood, I shall say but little,
Corbies and clergy are a shot right kittle:    Ravens, sort, ticklish
But, under favour o your langer beard,
Abuse o magistrates might weel be spar'd;
To liken them to your auld-warld squad,
I must needs say, comparisons are odd.
In Ayr, wag-wits nae mair can hae a handle
To mouth 'a Citizen' a term o scandal;
Nae mair the council waddles down the street,
In all the pomp of ignorant conceit;
Men wha grew wise priggin owre hops an raisins,    haggling
Or gather'd lib'ral views in bonds and seisins;
If haply Knowledge, on a random tramp,
Had shor'd them with a glimmer of his lamp,    threatened
And would to common-sense for once betray'd them,
Plain, dull stupidity stept kindly in to aid them,'

What farther clish-ma-claver might been said,  nonsense
What bloody wars, if Sprites had blood to shed,
No man can tell; but, all before their sight,
A fairy train appear'd in order bright:
Adown the glittering stream they featly danc'd;
Bright to the moon their various dresses glanc'd;
They footed o'er the wat'ry glass so neat,
The infant ice scarce bent beneath their feet;
While arts of minstrelsy among them rung,
And soul-ennobling Bards heroic ditties sung.

O, had M'Lauchlan, thairm-inspiring sage,  James McLauchlan
Been there to hear this heavenly band engage,  of Inverary
When thro his dear strathspeys they bore with Highland rage;
Or when they struck old Scotia's melting airs,
The lover's raptured joys or bleeding cares;
How would his Highland lug been nobler fir'd,
And ev'n his matchless hand with finer touch inspir'd!
No guess could tell what instrument appear'd,
But all the soul of Music's self was heard;
Harmonious concert rung in every part,
While simple melody pour'd moving on the heart.

The Genius of the Stream in front appears,
A venerable chief advanc'd in years;
His hoary head with water-lilies crown'd,
His manly leg with garter-tangle bound.
Next came the loveliest pair in all the ring,
Sweet female Beauty hand in hand with Spring;
Then, crown'd with flow'ry hay, came Rural Joy,
And Summer, with his fervid-beaming eye;
All-cheering Plenty, with her flowing horn,
Led yellow Autumn wreath'd with nodding corn;
Then Winter's time-bleach'd locks did hoary show,
By Hospitality with cloudless brow;
Next followed Courage, with his martial stride,
From where the Feal wild-woody coverts hide;
Benevolence, with mild, benignant air,
A female form, came from the towers of Stair;
Learning and Worth in equal measures trode,
From simple Catrine, their long-lov'd abode;
Last, white-rob'd Peace, crown'd with a hazel wreath,
To rustic Agriculture did bequeath
The broken, iron instruments of death:
At sight of whom our Sprites forgat their kindling wrath.

## TO AN OLD SWEETHEART

Addressed to Miss Peggy Thomson of Kirkoswald when emigration was still uppermost in the poet's mind.

Once fondly loved and still remember'd dear,
    Sweet early object of my youthful vows,
Accept this mark of friendship, warm, sincere –
    (Friendship! 'tis all cold duty now allows.)

And when you read the simple artless rhymes,
    One friendly sigh for him – he asks no more –
Who, distant, burns in flaming torrid climes,
    Or haply lies beneath th' Atlantic roar.

## THE GLOOMY NIGHT
## IS GATH'RING FAST

*TUNE: Roslin Castle*

Burns is said to have written this song after a solitary walk home from Dr Lawrie's, following what he felt would be his last visit. By now he was all packed and ready to take ship from Greenock and doubtless the thought of leaving Scotland for the uncertainties of the West Indies filled him with foreboding and melancholy.

The gloomy night is gath'ring fast,
Loud roars the wild inconstant blast;
Yon murky cloud is filled with rain,
I see it driving o'er the plain;
The hunter now has left the moor,
The scatt'red coveys meet secure;
While here I wander, prest with care,
Along the lonely banks of Ayr.

The Autumn mourns her rip'ning corn
By early Winter's ravage torn;
Across her placid, azure sky,
She sees the scowling tempest fly;
Chill runs my blood to hear it rave,
I think upon the stormy wave,
Where many a danger I must dare,
Far from the bonie banks of Ayr.

'Tis not the surging billows' roar,
'Tis not that fatal, deadly shore;
Tho death in ev'ry shape appear,
The wretched have no more to fear:
But round my heart the ties are bound,
That heart transpierc'd with many a wound;
These bleed afresh, those ties I tear,
To leave the bonie banks of Ayr.

Farewell, old Coila's hills and dales,
Her heathy moors and winding vales;
The scenes where wretched Fancy roves,
Pursuing past unhappy loves!
Farewell my friends! farewell my foes!
My peace with these, my love with those –
The bursting tears my heart declare,
Farewell, my bonie banks of Ayr!

## THO CRUEL FATE

*TUNE: The Northern Lass*

The last of the valedictory songs written in the autumn of 1786 before Burns abandoned his plan for emigrating.

Tho cruel fate should bid us part
    Far as the pole and line,
Her dear idea round my heart
    Should tenderly entwine.

Tho mountains rise, and deserts howl,
    And oceans roar between,
Yet dearer than my deathless soul,
    I still would love my Jean.

## A FRAGMENT

Sent to John Richmond on 3rd September 1786, with the note announcing 'Armour has just brought me a fine boy and a girl at one throw. God bless the little dears!'

CHORUS

*Green grow the rashes O,*
*Green grow the rashes O,*
*The lasses they hae wimble bores,*
*The widows they hae gashes O.*

In sober hours i am a priest;
    A hero when I'm tipsey, O;
But I'm a king and ev'ry thing,
    When wi a wanton Gipsey, O.

'Twas late yestreen I met wi ane,
    An wow, but she was gentle, O!
Ae han she pat roun my cravat,
    The tither to my pintle O.                    penis

I dought na speak – yet was na fley'd          dared, scared
    My heart play'd duntie, duntie, O;
An ceremony laid aside,
    I fairly fun' her cuntie, O.                  'More follows'
        Multa desunt                          (Latin)

## THE CALF

To the Rev. James Steven, on his text, MALACHI, iv., 2:-
'And ye shall go forth, and grow up as calves of the stall.'

On 8th September 1786 Burns wrote to his close friend Robert Muir (1758-88), a wine merchant of Kilmarnock: 'You will have heard that poor Armour has repaid my amorous mortgages double. A very fine boy and girl have awakened a thousand feelings that thrill, some with tender pleasure, and some with foreboding anguish thro' my soul.' The letter was accompanied by this poem, 'an extemporaneous production, on a wager with Mr. Hamilton that I would not produce a poem on the subject in given time.' Gavin Hamilton asked him to compose a poem based on the text of the sermon that Sunday (3rd September). The Rev. James Steven (d. 1824) was assistant at Ardrossan and was probably preaching at Mauchline on exchange.

Right, sir! your text I'll prove it true,
 Tho heretics may laugh;
For instance, there's yoursel just now,
 God knows, an unco *calf.*

And should some patron be so kind
 As bless you wi a kirk,
I doubt na sir, but then we'll find
 Ye're still as great a *stirk,*        steer

But, if the lover's raptur'd hour
 Shall ever be your lot,
Forbid it, every heavenly Power,
 You e'er should be a *stot!*      young bullock

Tho, when some kind connubial dear
 Your but-an-ben adorns,        cottage
The like has been that you may wear
 A noble head of *horns.*       be a cuckold

And, in your lug, most reverend James,   ear
 To hear you roar and rowte,      rant
Few men o sense will doubt your claims
 To rank among the *nowte.*     cattle

And when ye're number'd wi the dead,
 Below a grassy hillock,
With justice they may mark your head –
 'Here lies a famous *bullock!'*

## NATURE'S LAW

HUMBLY INSCRIBED TO GAVIN HAMILTON, ESQ.

Composed after Jean Armour gave birth to twins on 3rd September 1786.

Great Nature spoke, observant man obey'd – POPE

Let other heroes boast their scars,
 The marks o sturt and strife,       turmoil
And other poets sing of wars,
 The plagues o human life!
Shame fa' the fun: wi sword and gun
 To slap mankind like lumber!
I sing his name and nobler fame
 Wha multiplies our number.

Great nature spoke, with air benign: –
 'Go on, ye human race;
This lower world I you resign;
 Be fruitful and increase.
The liquid fire of strong desire,
 I've poured it in each bosom;
Here on this hand does Mankind stand,
 And there, is Beauty's blossom!'

The Hero of these artless strains,
 A lowly Bard was he,
Who sung his rhymes in Coila's plains
 With meikle mirth an glee:
Kind Nature's care had given his share
 Large of the flaming current;
And, all devout, he never sought
 To stem the sacred torrent.

He felt the powerful, high behest
 Thrill vital thro and thro;
And sought a correspondent breast
 To give obedience due.
Propitious Powers screen'd the young flow'rs
 From mildews of abortion;
And lo! the Bard – a great reward –
 Has got a double portion!

Auld cantie Coil may count the day,      cheerful
 As annual it returns,
The third of Libra's equal sway,
 That gave another Burns,
With future rhymes, an other times
 To emulate his sire,
To sing auld Coil in nobler style
 With more poetic fire!

Ye Powers of peace and peaceful song,
  Look down with gracious eyes,
And bless auld Coila large and long,
  With multiplying joys;
Lang may she stand to prop the land,
  The flow'r of ancient nations,
And Burnses spring her fame to sing
  To endless generations!


# ON MEETING WITH LORD DAER

Basil William Douglas-Hamilton, Lord Daer (1763-94) was the second son of the Earl
of Selkirk. Lord Daer, then a student at Edinburgh University, was staying at the
country home of Professor Dugald Stewart at Catrine when he met Burns on 23rd
October, 1786. This was the poet's first encounter with an aristocrat, though Lord Daer,
admirer of the French Revolution and staunch advocate of Parliamentary reform, was
hardly typical of his class at that time.

This wot ye all whom it concerns:
I, Rhymer Rab, *alias* Burns,
  October twenty-third,
A ne'er-to-be-forgotten day,
Sae far I sprackl'd up the brae,            clambered, hillside
  I dinner'd wi a Lord.

I've been at drucken Writers' feasts,       drunken, lawyers
Nay, been bitch-fou' 'mang godly Priests –            drunk
  Wi rev'rence be it spoken! –
I've even join'd the honor'd jorum,
When mighty Squireships o the Quorum
  Their hydra drouth did sloken.                 thirst, slake

But wi a Lord – stand out my shin!
A Lord, a Peer, an Earl's son! –
  Up higher yet, my bonnet!
An sic a Lord! – lang Scotch ell twa,           over six feet
Our Peerage he looks o'er them a',
  As I look o'er my sonnet.

But O, for Hogarth's magic pow'r,     William Hogarth (1697-1764)
To show Sir Bardie's willyart glow'r,          awkward stare
  An how he star'd an stammer'd,
When, goavin's he'd been led wi branks,   looking dazedly, bridle
An stumpin on his ploughman shanks,
  He in the parlour hammer'd!

254

To meet good Stewart little pain is,      *Prof. Dugald Stewart*
Or Scotia's sacred Demosthenes:      *Dr Hugh Blair*
   Thinks I: 'They are but men!'      *(1718-1800)*
But 'Burns'! - 'My Lord!' - Good God! I doited      *doddered*
My knees on ane anither knoited      *knocked*
   As faltering I gaed ben.      *went inside*

I sidling shelter'd in a neuk,      *corner*
An at his Lordship staw a leuk,      *stole a glance*
   Like some portentous omen:
Except good sense and social glee
An (what surpris'd me) modesty
   I marked naught uncommon.

I watch'd the symptoms o the Great –
The gentle pride, the lordly state,
   The arrogant assuming:
The fient a pride, nae pride had he,      *not*
Nor sauce, nor state, that I could see,
   Mair than an honest ploughman!

Then from his Lordship I shall learn,
Henceforth to meet with unconcern
   One rank as weel's another;
Nae honest, worthy man need care
To meet with noble, youthfu Daer,
   For he but meets a brother.

## MASONIC SONG

*TUNE: Shawn-boy; or Over the water to Charlie*

Written to celebrate the poet's admission as an honorary member of Lodge St. John Kilwinning, Kilmarnock on 26th October 1786.

Ye sons of old Killie, assembled by Willie      *Major William Parker of*
   To follow the noble vocation,      *Assloss, Right Worshipful*
Your thrifty old mother has scarce such another      *Master*
To sit in that honoured station!
I've little to say, but only to pray,
   (As praying's the *ton* of your fashion);
A prayer from the Muse you well may excuse,
   ('Tis seldom her favourite passion) –

'Ye Powers who preside o'er the wind and the tide,
   Who marked each element's border,
Who formed this frame with beneficent aim,
   Whose sovereign statute is order,
Within this dear mansion, may wayward Contention
   Or withered Envy ne'er enter!
May secrecy round be the mystical bound,
   And brotherly Love be the centre!'

# EPIGRAM ON ROUGH ROADS

Attributed by Scott Douglas to Burns and dated October 1786. The roads in question are said to have been those between Kilmarnock and Stewarton. Kinsley, however, considers it more likely to date from the Highland tour; the reference to 'this people' implies residents of a district outside Burns's native Ayrshire.

I'm now arrived – thanks to the gods!
   Thro pathways rough and muddy,
A certain sign that makin roads
   Is no this people's study:
Altho I'm not wi Scripture cram'd,
   I'm sure the Bible says
That heedless sinners shall be damn'd,
   Unless they mend their ways.

# EPISTLE TO MAJOR LOGAN

## Mossgiel, 30th October, 1786

Major William Logan lived in retirement with his sister Susan at Park, Ayr. At the time this poem was written he was, in fact, merely a lieutenant on half-pay; his majority came with service in the West Lowland Fencibles (1794-99).

| | |
|---|---:|
| Hail, thairm-inspirin, rattlin Willie! | fiddle-string |
| Tho Fortune's road be rough an hilly | |
| To every fiddling, rhyming billie, | fellow |
|    We never heed, | |
| But take it like the unbrack'd filly, | unbroken |
|    Proud o her speed. | |
| | |
| When, idly goavin, whyles we saunter | gazing dreamily, |
| Yirr! Fancy barks, awa we canter, | sometimes |
| Up hill, down brae, till some mishanter, | mishap |
|    Some black bog-hole, | |
| Arrests us;  then the scathe an banter | |
|    We're forced to thole. | tolerate |
| | |
| Hale be your heart! hale be your fiddle! | Whole |
| Lang may your elbuck jink an diddle, | elbow dance, shake |
| To cheer you through the weary widdle | wriggle |
|    O this vile warl, | |
| Until you on a cummock driddle, | curved stick, saunter |
|    A grey-hair'd carl. | old man |
| | |
| Come wealth, come poortith, late or soon, | poverty |
| Heaven send your heart-strings ay in tune, | |
| And screw your temper-pins aboon | fiddle-pegs, above |
|    (A fifth or mair), | |
| The melancholious sairie croon | sorrowful note |
|    O cankrie Care. | crabbed |

May still your life from day to day
Nae *lente largo* in the play,
But *allegretto forte* gay,
   Harmonious flow,
A sweeping, kindling, bauld strathspey –         bold
   *Encore! Bravo!*

A' blessings on the cheery gang
Wha dearly like a jig or sang,
An never think o right an wrang
   By square an rule,
But as the clegs o feeling stang,        horseflies, sting
   Are wise or fool.

My hand-wal'd curse keep hard in chase      -picked
The harpy, hoodock, purse-proud race,      grasping
Wha count on poortith as disgrace!
   Their tuneless hearts,
May fireside discords jar a bass
   To a' their parts!

But come, your hand, my careless brither!
I' th' ither warl, if there's anither –
An that there is, I've little swither      doubt
   About the matter –
We, cheek for chow, shall jog thegither –    jowl
   I'se ne'er bid better!

We've faults and failins – granted clearly!
We're frail, backsliding mortals merely;
Eve's bonie squad, priests wyte them sheerly   castigate, wholly
   For our grand fa';
But still, but still, I like them dearly –
   God bless them a'!

Ochon for poor Castalian drinkers,       (ie poets)
When they fa' foul o earthly jinkers!     sportsmen
The witching, curs'd, delicious blinkers    oglers
   Hae put me hyte,            furious
An gart me weet my waukrife winkers,   made wet wakeful eyes
   Wi girnin spite.          snarling

But by yon moon – and that's high swearin!
An every star within my hearin,
An by her een wha was a dear ane      eyes
   I'll ne'er forget,
I hope to gie the jads a clearin,      jades
   In fair play yet!

9

My loss I mourn, but not repent it;
I'll seek my pursie whare I tint it;      lost
Ance to the Indies I were wonted,      Once
    Some cantraip hour      witching
By some sweet elf I'll yet be dinted;      enchanted
    Then *vive l'amour!*

*Faites mes baissemains respectueusè,*      Make my respectful
To sentimental sister Susie,      greeting;
An honest Lucky: no to roose you,      Logan's mother
    Ye may be proud,      flatter
That sic a couple Fate allows ye,      such
    To grace your blood.

Nae mair at present can I measure,
An trowth! my rhymin ware's nae treasure;
But when in Ayr, some half-hour's leisure,
    Be't light, be't dark,
Sir Bard will do himself the pleasure
    To call at Park.
           ROBERT BURNS

# A WINTER NIGHT

*Poor naked wretches, wheresoe'er you are,*
*That bide the pelting of this pityless storm!*
*How shall your houseless heads and unfed sides,*
*Your loop'd and window'd raggedness, defend you*
*From seasons such as these?* – SHAKESPEARE

Sent to John Ballantine on 20th November 1786 as his 'first attempt in that irregular kind of measure in which many of our finest Odes are wrote.'

When biting Boreas, fell and doure,      the north wind, hard
Sharp shivers thro the leafless bow'r;
When Phoebus gies a short-liv'd glow'r,      sun, stare
    Far south the lift,      horizon
Dim-dark'ning thro the flaky show'r,
    Or whirling drift:

Ae night the storm the steeples rocked;      One
Poor Labour sweet in sleep was locked;
While burns, wi snawy wreaths up-choked,      brooks
    Wild-eddying swirl;
Or thro the mining outlet bocked,      vomited
    Down headlong hurl:

List'ning the doors an winnocks rattle,    *windows*
I thought me on the ourie cattle,    *shivering*
Or silly sheep, wha bide this brattle    *endure, clatter*
   O winter war,
And thro the drift, deep-lairing, sprattle    *scramble*
   Beneath a scaur.    *rocky outcrop*

Ilk happing bird – wee, helpless thing! –    *Each hopping*
That in the merry months o spring,
Delighted me to hear thee sing,
   What comes o thee?
Whare wilt thou cow'r thy chittering wing,
   An close thy e'e?

Ev'n you, on murdering errands toil'd,
Lone from your savage homes exil'd,
The blood-stain'd roost, and sheep-cote spoil'd
   My heart forgets,
While pityless the tempest wild
   Sore on you beats!

Now Phoebe, in her midnight reign,    *the moon*
Dark-muffl'd, view'd the dreary plain;
Still crowding thoughts, a pensive train,
   Rose in my soul,
When on my ear this plaintive strain,
   Slow, solemn, stole: –

'Blow, blow, ye winds, with heavier gust!
And freeze, thou bitter-biting frost!
Descend, ye chilly, smothering snows!
Not all your rage, as now united, shows
   More hard unkindness, unrelenting,
   Vengeful malice, unrepenting,
Than heaven-illumin'd Man on brother Man bestows!

'See stern Oppression's iron grip,
   Or mad Ambition's gory hand,
Sending, like blood-hounds from the slip,
   Woe, Want, and Murder o'er the land!
Ev'n in the peaceful rural vale,
   Truth, weeping, tells the mournful tale,
How pamper'd Luxury, Flatt'ry by her side,
   The parasite empoisoning her ear,
   With all the servile wretches in the rear,
Looks o'er proud Property, extended wide;
   And eyes the simple, rustic hind,
Whose toil upholds the glitt'ring show –
   A creature of another kind,
   Some coarser substance, unrefin'd –
Plac'd for her lordly use, thus far, thus vile, below!

'Where, where is Love's fond, tender throe,
With lordly Honor's lofty brow,
   The pow'rs you proudly own?
Is there, beneath Love's noble name,
Can harbour, dark, the selfish aim,
   To bless himself alone?
   Mark Maiden-Innocence a prey
     To love-pretending snares:
This boasted Honor turns away,
Shunning soft Pity's rising sway,
Regardless of the tears and unavailing pray'rs!
   Perhaps this hour, in Misery's squalid nest,
   She strains your infant to her joyless breast,
And with a mother's fears shrinks at the rocking blast!'

     'Oh ye! who, sunk in beds of down,
     Feel not a want but what yourselves create,
     Think, for a moment, on his wretched fate,
   Whom friends and fortune quite disown!
Ill-satisfy'd keen nature's clam'rous call,
   Stretch'd on his straw, he lays himself to sleep;
While through the ragged roof and chinky wall,
   Chill, o'er his slumbers, piles the drifty heap!
   Think on the dungeon's grim confine,
   Where Guilt and poor Misfortune pine!
   Guilt, erring man, relenting view!
   But shall thy legal rage pursue
   The wretch, already crushed low
   By cruel Fortune's undeserved blow?
Affliction's sons are brothers in distress;
A brother to relieve, how exquisite the bliss!'

I heard nae mair, for Chanticleer
   Shook off the pouthery snaw,           powdery
And hail'd the morning with a cheer,
   A cottage-rousing craw.

But deep this truth impress'd my mind:
   Thro all His works abroad,
The heart benevolent and kind
   The most resembles God.

## REPLY TO AN INVITATION

The date and circumstances of composition are unknown. Kinsley places it 'probably in 1785 or 1786.' Bartie is a poetic name, apparently peculiar to Burns, for the Devil.

Sir,
    Yours this moment I unseal,
        And faith! I'm gay and hearty.
    To tell the truth and shame the Deil,
        I am as fou as Bartie.            *drunk as the Devil*
    But Foorsday, Sir, my promise leal,      *Thursday, true*
        Expect me o your partie,
    If on a beastie I can speel             *climb*
        Or hurl in a cartie.              *trundle*
        Yours, – ROBERT BURNS

MAUCHLIN, Monday night, 10 o'clock

## PRAYER - O THOU DREAD POWER

Written about November 1786, following the poet's visit to the home of the Rev. Dr George Lawrie (1727-99) in Edinburgh that autumn. Burns was introduced to the blind Dr Blacklock through Lawrie. Subsequently he attended a soiree given by Lawrie, where Burns first heard the spinet, played by the minister's daughter Christina (b. 1766). This was one of several poems given by Burns to the Lawrie family.

O thou dread Power, who reign'st above,
    I know thou wilt me hear,
When for this scene of peace and love
    I make my prayer sincere.

The hoary Sire – the mortal stroke,
    Long, long be pleas'd to spare:
To bless his little filial flock,
    And show what good men are.

She, who her lovely offspring eyes
    With tender hopes and fears –
O, bless her with a mother's joys,
    But spare a mother's tears!

Their hope, their stay, their darling youth,
    In manhood's dawning blush,
Bless him, Thou God of love and truth,
    Up to a parent's wish.

The beauteous, seraph sister-band –
    With earnest tears I pray –
Thou know'st the snares on every hand,
    Guide Thou their steps alway.

When, soon or late, they reach that coast,
    O'er Life's rough ocean driven,
May they rejoice, no wand'rer lost,
    A family in Heaven!

## THE NIGHT WAS STILL

Another poem presented by Burns to the daughters of Dr Lawrie in the late autumn of 1786.

The night was still, and o'er the hill
    The moon shone on the castle wa',
The mavis sang, while dew-drops hang
    Around her on the castle wa':

Sae merrily they danc'd the ring
    Frae eenin till the cock did craw,                evening
And ay the o'erword o the spring
    Was: – 'Irvine's bairns are bonie a'!'          children

## RUSTICITY'S UNGAINLY FORM

Enclosed in a song-book sent to Archibald Lawrie (1768-1837) on 13th November 1786.

Rusticity's ungainly form
    May cloud the highest mind;
But when the heart is nobly warm,
    The good excuse will find.

Propriety's cold, cautious rules
    Warm Fervour may o'erlook;
But spare poor Sensibility
    Th' ungentle, harsh rebuke.

## ADDRESS TO EDINBURGH

An uncomfortable ode, composed in the stiff Augustan English favoured by poets of the late eighteenth century, it was written shortly after Burns arrived in Edinburgh. The opening line of this Address was seized by a well-known firm of bathroom manufacturers who applied the name 'Edina' to one of their necessary though unpoetic products – according to Maurice Lindsay!

Edina! Scotia's darling seat!
    All hail thy palaces and tow'rs,
Where once, beneath a Monarch's feet,
    Sat Legislation's sov'reign pow'rs:
From marking wildly-scatt'red flow'rs,
    As on the banks of Ayr I stray'd,
And singing, lone, the ling'ring hours,
    I shelter in thy honor'd shade.

Here Wealth still swells the golden tide,
    As busy Trade his labours plies;
There Architecture's noble pride
    Bids elegance and splendour rise:
Here Justice, from her native skies,
    High wields her balance and her rod;
There Learning, with his eagle eyes,
    Seeks Science in her coy abode.

Thy sons, Edina, social, kind,
  With open arms the stranger hail;
Their views enlarg'd, their lib'ral mind,
  Above the narrow, rural vale;
Attentive still to Sorrow's wail,
  Or modest Merit's silent claim:
And never may their sources fail!
  And never Envy blot their name!

Thy daughters bright thy walks adorn,
  Gay as the gilded summer sky,
Sweet as the dewy, milk-white thorn,
  Dear as the raptur'd thrill of joy!
Fair Burnet strikes th' adoring eye,
  Heav'n's beauties on my fancy shine:
I see the Sire of Love on high,
  And own His work indeed divine!

Eliza Burnett, Lord
Monboddo's youngest
daughter (1766-90)

There, watching high the least alarms,
  Thy rough, rude fortress gleams afar;
Like some bold vet'ran, grey in arms,
  And mark'd with many a seamy scar:
The pond'rous wall and massy bar,
  Grim-rising o'er the rugged rock,
Have oft withstood assailing war,
  And oft repell'd th' invader's shock.

With awe-struck thought and pitying tears,
  I view that noble, stately dome,
Where Scotia's kings of other years,
  Fam'd heroes! had their royal home:
Alas, how chang'd the times to come!
  Their royal name low in the dust!
Their hapless race wild-wand'ring roam!
  Tho rigid Law cries out, 'Twas just!'

Wild beats my heart to trace your steps,
  Whose ancestors, in days of yore,
Thro hostile ranks and ruin'd gaps
  Old Scotia's bloody lion bore:
Ev'n I, who sing in rustic lore,
  Haply my sires have left their shed,
And fac'd grim Danger's loudest roar
  Bold-following where your fathers led!

Edina! Scotia's darling seat!
  All hail thy palaces and tow'rs;
Where once, beneath a Monarch's feet,
  Sat Legislation's sov'reign pow'rs,
From marking wildly-scatt'red flow'rs,
  As on the banks of Ayr I stray'd,
And singing, lone, the ling'ring hours,
  I shelter in thy honor'd shade.

## ADDRESS TO A HAGGIS

The closing stanza is said to have been composed extempore during a dinner at the home
of John Morrison, a Mauchline cabinet-maker. The complete poem was written soon
after Burns arrived in Edinburgh, and appeared in the *Caledonian Mercury* – the first
of Burns's poems to be published in any periodical. Oddly enough, the earliest recipe
for Haggis appeared the same year, in *Cookery and Pastry* by Susanna Maciver.

| | |
|---|---|
| Fair fa' your honest, sonsie face, | cheerful |
| Great chieftain o the puddin'-race! | |
| Aboon them a' ye tak your place, | Above |
|   Painch, tripe, or thairm: | paunch, guts |
| Weel are ye wordy of a grace | worthy |
|   As lang's my arm. | |

| | |
|---|---|
| The groaning trencher there ye fill, | |
| Your hurdies like a distant hill, | buttocks |
| Your pin wad help to mend a mill | skewer |
|   In time o need, | |
| While thro your pores the dews distil | |
|   Like amber bead. | |

| | |
|---|---|
| His knife see rustic Labour dight, | wipe |
| An cut you up wi ready slight, | skill |
| Trenching your gushing entrails bright, | Digging |
|   Like onie ditch; | |
| And then, O what a glorious sight, | |
|   Warm-reekin, rich! | -steaming |

| | |
|---|---|
| Then, horn for horn, they stretch an strive: | |
| Deil tak the hindmost, on they drive, | |
| Till a' their weel-swall'd kytes belyve | well-swollen bellies, soon |
|   Are bent like drums; | |
| The auld Guidman, maist like to rive, | burst |
|   'Bethankit' hums. | |

Is there that owre his French *ragout*,
Or *olio* that wad staw a sow,                                    sicken
Or *fricassee* wad mak her spew
    Wi perfect sconner,                                           disgust
Looks down wi sneering, scornfu view
    On sic a dinner?

Poor devil! see him owre his trash,
As feckless as a wither'd rash,                                  weak, rush
His spindle shank a guid whip-lash,
    His nieve a nit;                                              fist, nut
Thro bloody flood or field to dash,
    O how unfit!

But mark the Rustic, haggis-fed,
The trembling earth resounds his tread,
Clap in his walie nieve a blade,                                 choice
    He'll make it whissle;
An legs an arms, an heads will sned,                             trim
    Like taps o thrissle.                                        tops, thistle

Ye Pow'rs, wha mak mankind your care,
And dish them out their bill o fare,
Auld Scotland wants nae skinking ware                           watery
    That jaups in luggies;                            splashes, porringers
But, if ye wish her gratefu prayer,
    Gie her a Haggis!

## VERSES INTENDED TO BE WRITTEN
## BELOW A NOBLE EARL'S PICTURE

On 13th January 1787 Burns sent these verses to the Earl of Glencairn with a letter
seeking permission to publish them in an Edinburgh newspaper. Lord Glencairn (1749-
91) declined, Burns later admitting that he 'does me the honor of giving me his
strictures: his hints, with respect to impropriety or indelicacy, I follow implicity.' It was
not until 1851 that this poem was actually printed.

Whose is that noble, dauntless brow?
    And whose that eye of fire?
And whose that generous princely mien,
    E'en rooted foes admire?

Stranger! to justly show that brow
    And mark that eye of fire,
Would take His hand, whose vernal tints
    His other works inspire.

Bright as a cloudless summer sun,
  With stately port he moves;
His guardian Seraph eyes with awe
  The noble Ward he loves.

Among the illustrious Scottish sons,
  That Chief thou may'st discern:
Mark Scotia's fond-returning eye –
  It dwells upon Glencairn.


# AND MAUN I STILL ON
# MENIE DOAT

*TUNE: Johnny's Grey Breeks*

Early editors assigned this song to 1785-6, but Kinsley considered, from internal evidence, that it was written, wholly or in part during his Edinburgh period.

CHORUS

*And maun I still on Menie doat,*       must, dote
  *And bear the scorn that's in her e'e?*
*For it's jet, jet-black, an it's like a hawk,*
  *An it winna let a body be.*        will not

Again rejoicing nature sees
  Her robe assume its vernal hues:
Her leafy locks wave in the breeze,
  All freshly steep'd in morning dews.

In vain to me the cowslips blaw,
  In vain to me the vi'lets spring;
In vain to me in glen or shaw,       wood
  The mavis and the lint-white sing.     linnet

The merry ploughboy cheers his team
  Wi joy the tentie seedsman stalks;    careful
But life's to me a weary dream,
  A dream of ane that never wauks.     wakes

The wanton coot the water skims,
  Amang the reeds the ducklings cry,
The stately swan majestic swims,
  And ev'ry thing is blest but I.

The sheep-herd steeks his faulding slap,  shuts, fold-gate
  And o'er the moorlands whistles shrill;
Wi wild, unequal, wand'ring step,
  I meet him on the dewy hill.

And when the lark, 'tween light and dark,
  Blythe waukens by the daisy's side,
And mounts and sings on flittering wings,
  A woe-worn ghaist I hameward glide.                    ghost

Come winter, with thine angry howl,
  And raging, bend the naked tree;
Thy gloom will soothe my cheerless soul,
  When nature all is sad like me!

## TO MISS LOGAN

### WITH BEATTIE'S POEMS FOR A NEW-YEAR'S GIFT, JAN. 1, 1787

Dedicated to Susan Logan, sister of Willian Logan of Park, and accompanying a copy
of *The Minstrel* by Dr James Beattie.

Again the silent wheels of time
  Their annual round have driv'n,
And you, tho scarce in maiden prime,
  Are so much nearer Heav'n.

No gifts have I from Indian coasts
  The infant year to hail;
I send you more than India boasts,
  In Edwin's simple tale.

Our sex with guile, and faithless love,
  Is charg'd – perhaps too true;
But may, dear maid, each lover prove
  An Edwin still to you.

## RANTIN, ROVIN ROBIN

### TUNE: *Dainty Davie*

Possibly written in flippant celebration of his 28th birthday, Burns noted down this
autobiographical song in 2CPB about 9th April 1787. Evidently there was some
difference of opinion between Burns and George Thomson concerning the chorus, which
the poet averred should be sung 'to the low part of the tune; and nothing, since a
Highland wench in the Cowgate once bore me three bastards at a birth, has surprised
me so much as your opinion on this subject.'

CHORUS

  *Robin was a rovin boy,*
    *Rantin, rovin, rantin, rovin,*
  *Robin was a rovin boy,*
    *Rantin, rovin Robin!*

There was a lad was born in Kyle,                    at Alloway
  But whatna day o whatna style,
I doubt it's hardly worth the while
  To be sae nice wi Robin.

Our monarch's hindmost year but ane 1759
Was five-and-twenty days begun,
'Twas then a blast of Janwar win'
    Blew hansel in on Robin.

The gossip keekit in his loof,           peered, face
Quo scho: – 'Wha lives will see the proof,
This waly boy will be nae coof:           sturdy, fool
    I think we'll ca' him Robin.'

'He'll hae misfortunes great an sma
But ay a heart aboon them a'.
He'll be a credit till us a':
    We'll a' be proud o Robin!'

'But sure as three times three mak nine,
I see by ilka score and line,           every
This chap will dearly like our kin',
    So leeze me on thee, Robin!'           commend

'Guid faith', quo she, 'I doubt you gar
The bonie lasses lie aspar;           legs apart
But twenty fauts ye may hae waur –     faults, worse
    So blessins on thee, Robin!'

## ELEGY ON THE DEATH OF
## ROBERT RUISSEAUX

This mock-elegy dates form 1787, the subject being the poet himself. Ruisseaux (French – 'brooks, streams') is a play on Robert's surname.

Now Robin lies in his last lair,
He'll gabble rhyme, nor sing nae mair;     more
Cauld poverty wi hungry stare,
    Nae mair shall fear him;           frighten
Nor anxious fear, nor cankert care,     crabbed
    E'er mair come near him.

To tell the truth, they seldom fash'd him,   bothered
Except the moment that they crush'd him;
For sune as chance or fate had hush'd 'em,   soon
    Tho e'er sae short,
Then wi a rhyme or sang he lash'd 'em,
    And thought it sport.

Tho he was bred to kintra-wark,     country-labour
And counted was baith wight and stark   both stout, strong
Yet that was never Robin's mark
    To mak a man;
But tell him, he was learn'd and clark,     scholarly
    Ye roos'd him then!           flattered

# INSCRIPTION FOR THE HEADSTONE OF FERGUSSON THE POET

Robert Fergusson (1750-74), a young poet of immense promise, died insane in the Edinburgh mad-house. His Poems were published a year before his tragic death and had a considerable influence on Burns who was appalled to discover that Fergusson's grave was unmarked. On 6th February 1787 he applied to the Canongate Bailies for permission to erect a headstone. The architect, Robert Burn was commissioned to erect the stone for which Burns composed the following quatrain. The additional stanzas were written in 2CPB. Burns did not settle the bill till 1792. Commenting on the delay he wrote of Mr Burn: 'He was two years in erecting it, after I commissioned him for it; and I have been two years paying him, after he sent me his account; so he and I are quits. He had the *hardiesse* to ask me interest on the sum; but considering that the money was due by one Poet, for putting a tombstone over another, he may, with grateful surprise, thank Heaven that he ever saw a farthing of it.'

No sculptured Marble here, nor pompous lay,
    No storied Urn nor animated Bust:
This simple stone directs pale Scotia's way,
    To pour her sorrows o'er the Poet's dust.

ADDITIONAL STANZAS

She mourns, sweet tuneful youth, thy hapless fate;
    Tho all the powers of song thy fancy fir'd,
Yet Luxury and Wealth lay by in State,
    And, thankless, starv'd what they so much admir'd.

This humble tribute, with a tear, he gives,
    A brother Bard - he can no more bestow:
But dear to fame thy Song immortal lives,
    A nobler monument than Art can show.

# APOSTROPHE TO FERGUSSON

Written in a copy of Fergusson's Poems given to the poetess Rebeccah Carmichael on 19th March 1787.

Curse on ungrateful man, that can be pleas'd,
And yet can starve the author of the pleasure!
O thou, my elder brother in misfortune,
By far my elder brother in the Muse,
With tears I pity thy unhappy fate!
Why is the Bard unfitted for the world,
Yet has so keen a relish of its pleasures?

## LINES ON FERGUSSON, THE POET

Inscribed in a copy of the *World*, a periodical to which Burns subscribed for five years (1785-90). This poem was first published in the *Scots Magazine* in November 1803.

Ill-fated genius! Heaven-taught Fergusson!
    What heart that feels, and will not yield a tear
To think Life's sun did set e'er well begun
    To shed its influence on thy bright career!

O, why should truest Worth and Genius pine
    Beneath the iron grasp of Want and Woe,
While titled knaves and idiot-greatness shine
    In all the splendour Fortune can bestow?

## EPIGRAM ADDRESSED TO AN ARTIST

Allegedly written by Burns on the back of a small sketch, during a visit to an artist's studio in Edinburgh. The unnamed painter was working on a picture of Jacob's dream.

Dear___, I'll gie ye some advice,
    You'll tak it no uncivil:
You shouldna paint at angels, man,
    But try and paint the Devil.

To paint an angel's kittle wark,           ticklish work
    Wi Nick there's little danger:
You'll easy draw a lang-kent face,         long-known
    But no sae weel a stranger. – R.B.

## ON ELPHINSTONE'S TRANSLATION
## OF MARTIAL

James Elphinstone (1721-1809), born in Edinburgh but resident in Kensington where he ran a boarding school. In 1782 he published a translation of Martial's Epigrams. In a letter of 14th January 1788 Burns mentions 'I was sitting in a merchant's shop...waiting somebody; he put Elphinstone into my hand, and asked my opinion of it. I begged leave to write it on a blank leaf.'

O thou whom Poesy abhors,
Whom Prose has turnèd out of doors
Heard'st thou yon groan? – Proceed no further:
'Twas laurel'd Martial calling 'Murther!'

## TO THE GUIDWIFE OF
## WAUCHOPE HOUSE

### (MRS. SCOTT)

### March, 1787

Elizabeth Scott (1729-89), née Rutherford, was a niece of the poetess Alison Cockburn and wife of Walter Scott of Wauchope House near Jedburgh. She had been lent a copy of the Kilmarnock Edition in December 1786 and this started a correspondence between her and the poet who visited Wauchope on 10th May 1787 during his Border tour. Earlier, Mrs Scott had sent Burns a long verse-epistle and this was his reply.

Guid Wife,

| | |
|---|---|
| I mind it weel, in early date, | remember |
| When I was beardless, young, and blate, | bashful |
|    An first could thresh the barn, | |
| Or haud a yokin at the pleugh, | hold, a day's work |
| An tho forfoughten sair eneugh, | exhausted |
|    Yet unco proud to learn; | mighty |
| When first amang the yellow corn | |
| A man I reckon'd was, | |
| An wi the lave ilk merry morn | others, each |
|    Could rank my rig an lass: | ridge |
|      Still shearing, and clearing | reaping |
|      The tither stookèd raw, | row of sheaves |
|      Wi clavers an havers, | gossip, nonsense |
|      Wearing the day awa. | away |

| | |
|---|---|
| E'en then, a wish (I mind its pow'r), | |
| A wish that to my latest hour | |
|    Shall strongly heave my breast, | |
| That I for poor auld Scotland's sake | |
| Some usefu plan or book could make, | |
|    Or sing a sang at least. | |
| The rough burr-thistle spreading wide | |
|    Amang the bearded bear, | barley |
| I turn'd the weeder-clips aside, | -shears |
|    An spar'd the symbol dear. | |
|      No nation, no station, | |
|      My envy e'er could raise; | |
|      A Scot still, but blot still, | without |
|      I knew nae higher praise. | |

| | |
|---|---|
| But still the elements o sang | |
| In formless jumble, right an wrang, | |
|    Wild floated in my brain; | |
| 'Till on that hairst I said before, | harvest |
| My partner in the merry core, | crowd |
|    She rous'd the forming strain. | |

I see her yet, the sonsie quean            pleasant lass
   That lighted up my jingle,
Her witching smile, her pauky een           shrewd
   That gart my heart-strings tingle!        made
     I firèd, inspirèd,
       At ev'ry kindling keek,            glance
     But, bashing and dashing,
       I feared ay to speak.

Hale to the sex! (ilk guid chiel says):     Health, each, chap
Wi merry dance on winter days,
   An we to share in common!
The gust o joy, the balm of woe,
The saul o life, the heav'n below,           soul
   Is rapture-giving Woman.
Ye surly sumphs, who hate the name,       boors
   Be mindfu o your mither;
She, honest woman, may think shame
   That ye're connected with her!
     Ye're wae men, ye're nae men        sad
       That slight the lovely dears;
     To shame ye, disclaim ye,
       Ilk honest birkie swears.           fellow

For you, no bred to barn and byre,        cow-shed
Wha sweetly tune the Scottish lyre,
   Thanks to you for your line!
The marl'd plaid ye kindly spare,       parti-coloured
By me should gratefully be ware;         worn
'Twad please me to the nine.          perfection
I'd be mair vauntie o my hap,       proud, covering
  Douce hingin owre my curple,    soberly, crupper
Than onie ermine ever lap,            folded
Or proud imperial purple.
     Farewell then! lang hale, then,     long health
       An plenty be your fa'!            lot
     May losses and crosses
       Ne'er at your hallan ca'!           porch

R. BURNS

## TO MISS ISABELLA MACLEOD
### EDINBURGH, March 16, 1787

Isabella MacLeod of Raasay was the daughter of that laird who entertained Boswell and Johnson during their Hebridean tour. Burns may have been introduced to the MacLeods by Gavin Hamilton. We do not know what the 'tuneful gift' of line 3 was.

The crimson blossom charms the bee,
   The summer sun the swallow:
So dear this tuneful gift to me
   From lovely Isabella.

Her portrait fair upon my mind
   Revolving time shall mellow,
And mem'ry's latest effort find
   The lovely Isabella.

No Bard nor lover's rapture this
   In fancies vain and shallow!
She is, so come my soul to bliss,
   The lovely Isabella.

## EPIGRAMS
### EXTEMPORE IN THE COURT OF SESSION

Composed in Edinburgh in 1787 during a visit to the Court of Session to hear the case of Campbell v. Campbell. Montgomerie, Captain James Montgomerie and Mrs Maxwell Campbell became lovers, and Mrs. Campbell bore a child in 1784. Maxwell Campbell sued for damages without divorcing his wife and Montgomerie fled to the West Indies. The Lord Advocate was Ilay Campbell (1734-1823), also referred to in 'the Author's Ernest Cry and Prayer'. Henry Erskine (1746-1817), Dean of the Faculty (1786) was noted for his wit and forensic skill. Both men were friends and patrons of Burns.

### LORD ADVOCATE

He clench'd his pamphlets in his fist,
   He quoted and he hinted,
Till in a declamation-mist,
   His argument, he tint it:               lost
He gapèd for't, he grapèd for't,        groped
   He fand it was awa, man;         found
But what his common sense came short,
   He eked out wi law, man.

### MR ERSKINE

Collected, Harry stood awee,       a moment
   Then open'd out his arm, man;
His Lordship sat wi ruefu e'e,         eye
   And ey'd the gathering storm, man;
Like wind-driv'n hail it did assail,
   Or torrents owre a linn, man;
The Bench sae wise lift up their eyes,
   Hauf-wauken'd wi the din, man.

# TO MR. McADAM,
# OF CRAIGEN-GILLAN

### IN ANSWER TO AN OBLIGING LETTER HE SENT IN THE
### COMMENCEMENT OF MY POETIC CAREER

John McAdam (d. 1790) attained celebrity as a leading agricultural improver. It has been assumed, from the sub-title, that this verse-epistle was written in 1786; but McAdam and his family appear only in the addenda and not the main subscription list in the Edinburgh Edition. This would date composition to about March 1787, rather than late 1786 as implied in Burns's annotation in the Glenriddell MS which, long after the event, may have been due to faulty memory.

| | |
|---|---|
| Sir, o'er a gill I gat your card, | drink |
| I trow it made me proud; | trust |
| 'See wha taks notice o the Bard!' | |
| I lap, and cry'd fu loud. | danced |
| | |
| Now deil-ma-care about their jaw, | |
| The senseless, gawky million! | clumsy |
| I'll cock my nose aboon them a', | |
| I'm roos'd by Craigen-Gillan! | praised |
| | |
| 'Twas noble, sir; 'twas like yoursel, | |
| To grant your high protection: | |
| A great man's smile, ye ken fu well, | |
| Is ay a blest infection. | |
| | |
| Tho, by his banes wha in a tub | Diogenes |
| Match'd Macedonian Sandy! | Alexander the Great |
| On my ain legs thro dirt and dub, | puddle |
| I independent stand ay; | |
| | |
| And when those legs to guid warm kail, | broth |
| Wi welcome canna bear me, | |
| A lee dyke-side, a sybow-tail, | stone fence, onion- |
| An barley-scone shall cheer me. | |
| | |
| Heaven spare you lang to kiss the breath | |
| O monie flow'ry simmers, | |
| An bless your bonnie lasses baith, | |
| (I'm tauld they're loosome kimmers!) | lovable wenches |
| | |
| An God bless young Dunaskin's laird, | Col. Quinton McAdam |
| The blossom of our gentry, | (d. 1805) |
| An may he wear an auld man's beard, | |
| A credit to his country! | |

# PROLOGUE

### SPOKEN BY MR WOODS ON HIS BENEFIT NIGHT, MONDAY, 16TH APRIL, 1787

William Woods (1751-1802) began his dramatic career in Southampton, but moved to Edinburgh in the early 1770s where he became a close friend of Robert Fergusson, and it was this that drew Burns to him. John Home's tragedy *Douglas* (1. 21) roused considerable patriotic pride at the time of its debut in 1756, memorable from the cry from the audience 'Whaur's your Wullie Shakespeare noo?' Harley was the hero of Henry Mackenzie's *The Man of Feeling* (1771), one of the poet's favourite novels. Sarah Siddons (1755-1831) played Isabella in *The Fatal Marriage* by Thomas Southerne (1660-1746), one of the most popular dramatic roles of the period.

When by a generous Public's kind acclaim
That dearest need is granted – honest fame;
Where here your favour is the actor's lot,
Nor even the man in private life forgot;
What breast so dead to heavenly Virtue's glow
But heaves impassion'd with the grateful throe?

Poor is the task to please a barb'rous throng:
It needs no Siddons's powers in Southern's song.
But here an ancient nation, fam'd afar
For genius, learning high, as great in war.
Hail, Caledonia! name for ever dear!
Before whose sons I'm honor'd to appear!
Where every science, every nobler art,
That can inform the mind or mend the heart,
Is known (as grateful nations oft have found),
Far as the rude barbarian marks the bound!
Philosophy, no idle pedant dream,
Here holds her search by heaven-taught Reason's beam:
Here History paints with elegance and force
The tide of Empire's fluctuating course;
Here *Douglas* forms wild Shakespeare into plan,
And Harley rouses all the God in man.
When well-form'd taste and sparkling wit unite
With manly lore, or female beauty bright
(Beauty, where faultless symmetry and grace
Can only charm us in the second place),
Witness my heart, how oft with panting fear,
As on this night, I've met these judges here!
But still the hope Experience taught to live:
Equal to judge, you're candid to forgive.
No hundred-headed Riot here we meet,
With Decency and Law beneath his feet;
Nor insolence assumes fair Freedom's name:
Like Caledonians you applaud or blame!

O Thou, dread Power, whose empire-giving hand
Has oft been stretch'd to shield the honor'd land!
Strong may she glow with all her ancient fire;
May every son be worthy of his sire;
Firm may she rise, with generous disdain
At Tyranny's, or direr Pleasure's chain;
Still self-dependent in her native shore,
Bold may she brave grim Danger's loudest roar,
Till Fate the curtain drops on worlds to be no more!

## ADDRESS TO WM. TYTLER, ESQ., OF WOODHOUSELEE

### WITH AN IMPRESSION OF THE AUTHOR'S PORTRAIT

William Tytler (1711-92) was a Writer to the Signet who collaborated with Johnson in the SMM project and helped Burns collect material for the later volumes. The 'impression' accompanying this Address was allegedly the silhouette by John Miers, though Kinsley suggests that it may have been the engraving by John Beugo, from the protrait by Alexander Nasmyth.

Revered defender of beauteous Stuart,
Of Stuart! – a name once respected,
A name which to love was once mark of a true heart,
But now 'tis despis'd and neglected!

Tho something like moisture conglobes in my eye,
Let no one misdeem me disloyal!
A poor friendless wand'rer may well claim a sigh –  Bonnie Prince
Still more, if that wand'rer were royal.     Charlie

My Fathers that name have rever'd on a throne;
My Fathers have fallen right to it:
Those Fathers would spurn their degenerate son,
That name, should he scoffingly slight it.

Still in prayers for King George I most heartily join
The Queen, and the rest of the gentry;
Be they wise, be they foolish, is nothing of mine:
Their title's avow'd by my country.

But why of that epocha make such a fuss
That gave us the Hanover stem?
If bringing them over was lucky for us,
I'm sure 'twas as lucky for them.

But loyalty – truce! we're on dangerous ground:
Who knows how the fashions may alter?
The doctrine, to-day, that is loyalty sound,
To-morrow may bring us a halter!

I send you a trifle, a head of a Bard,
  A trifle scarce worthy your care;
But accept it, good Sir, as a mark of regard,
  Sincere as a saint's dying prayer.

Now Life's chilling evening dim-shades on your eye,
  And ushers the long dreary night;
But you, like the star that athwart gilds the sky,
  Your course to the latest is bright.

## EPIGRAM TO MISS AINSLIE
## IN CHURCH

Burns met Rachel Ainslie (b. 1768) while on his Border tour with her brother Robert.
At Duns parish church early in May 1787 Burns sat next to Miss Ainslie listening to
the 'hell-fire and damnation' sermon of Dr Bowmaker. The lady seemed attentive but
agitated, and Burns was moved to inscribe these extempore lines on the fly-leaf of her
Bible.

Fair maid, you need not take the hint,
  Nor idle texts pursue;
'Twas guilty sinners that he meant,
  Not angels such as you.

## LAMENT FOR THE ABSENCE
## OF WILLIAM CREECH, PUBLISHER

William Creech (1745-1815) publisher and bookseller of the High Street, Edinburgh,
immortalised by Burns on account of his vanity and meanness. Creech was incredibly
slow in settling accounts with the poet for the Edinburgh Edition of 1787 and forced
Burns to visit Edinburgh that winter to obtain satisfaction. This lament, written during
the Border tour, reflects their relationship before the quarrel over the delay in payment.

| | |
|---|---|
| Auld chuckie Reekie's sair distrest, | mother-hen |
| Down droops her ance weel burnish'd crest, | Edinburgh |
| Nae joy her bonie buskit nest | trimmed |
|    Can yield ava: | at all |
| Her darling bird that she lo'es best, | |
|    Willie's awa. | |

| | |
|---|---|
| O, Willie was a witty wight, | |
| And had o things an unco sleight! | uncommon skill |
| Auld Reekie ay he keepit tight, | in order |
|    And trig an braw; | trim, handsome |
| And now they'll busk her like a fright, – | clothe, freak |
|    Willie's awa! | |

The stiffest o them a' he bow'd;
The bauldest o them a' he cow'd;                                      daunted
They durst nae mair than he allow'd –                                 dared
   That was a law:
We've lost a birkie weel worth gowd –                            blade, gold
   Willie's awa!

Now gawkies, tawpies, gowks and fools,           boobies, silly girls, dolts
Frae colleges and boarding schools
May sprout like simmer puddock-stools                            toadstools
   In glen or shaw:                                          wood
He wha could brush them down to mools,                                dust
   Willie's awa!

The brethren o the Commerce-Chaumer
May mourn their loss wi doolfu clamour:                             woeful
He was a dictionar and grammar
   Among them a'.
I fear they'll now mak monie a stammer:
   Willie's awa!

Nae mair we see his levee door
Philosophers and Poets pour,
And toothy Critics by the score,
   In bloody raw:                                               row
The adjutant o a' the core,                                          band
   Willie's awa!

Now worthy Greg'ry's Latin face,              Dr James Gregory (1753-1821);
Tytler's and Greenfield's modest grace,          Alexander Fraser Tytler
M'Kenzie, Stewart, such a brace                  (1747-1813); Rev. William
   As Rome ne'er saw,                        Greenfield (d.1827); Henry
They a' maun meet some ither place –             Mackenzie (1745-1831);
   Willie's awa!                          Dugald Stewart (1753-1828)
                                                                     must

Poor Burns ev'n 'Scotch Drink' canna quicken,
He cheeps like some bewilder'd chicken                             chirps
Scar'd frae its minnie and the cleckin,                    mother, brood
   By hoodie-craw.                                      carrion-crow
Grief's gien his heart an unco kickin,
   Willie's awa!

Now ev'ry sour-mou'd, girnin blellum,          ill-tongued, snarling, nag
And Calvin's folk, are fit to fell him;                               kill
Ilk self-conceited critic-skellum                                 scullion
   His quill may draw:
He wha could brawlie ward their bellum,             finely repel, assault
   Willie's awa!

Up wimpling, stately Tweed I've sped,                    meandering
And Eden scenes on crystal Jed,
And Ettrick banks, now roaring red
    While tempests blaw;
But every joy and pleasure's fled,
    Willie's awa!

May I be Slander's common speech,
A text for Infamy to preach,
And lastly, streekit out to bleach
    In winter snaw,
When I forget thee, Willie Creech,
    Tho far awa!

May never wicked Fortune touzle him,                     ruffle
May never wicked men bamboozle him,
Until a pow as auld's Methusalem                         pate
    He canty claw!                                       cheerfully
Then to the blessed new Jerusalem,
    Fleet-wing awa!

## TO SYMON GRAY

Written in May 1787, during Burns's Border tour. Gray met the poet at church in Duns on 6th May. Gray was a retired businessman and amateur versifier who made many charitable bequests and is commemorated in the local literary society. Gray kept pestering Burns with his poems and these lines were the Bard's successive answers.

Symon Gray,
You're dull to-day.

Dulness, with redoubted sway,
Has seized the wits of Symon Gray.

Dear Cimon Gray,
    The other day,
    When you sent me some rhyme,
I could not then just ascertain
    Its worth, for want of time.

But now today, good Mr. Gray,
    I've read it o'er and o'er,
Tried all my skill, but find I'm still
    Just where I was before.

We auld wives' minions gie our opinions,
    Solicited or no;
Then of its fau'ts my honest thoughts
    I'll give – and here they go.

279

Such damn'd bombast no time that's past
  Will show, or time to come,
So, Cimon dear, your song I'll tear,
  And with it wipe my bum.

## NOTE TO MR. RENTON
## OF LAMERTON

Written about 18th May 1787, during the Border tour. John Renton had invited Burns
to visit him at Mordington House near Berwick, though there is no record of the visit
having taken place.

| | |
|---|---:|
| Your billet, Sir, I grant receipt; | letter |
| Wi you I'll canter onie gate, | any road |
| Tho 'twere a trip to yon blue warl, | |
| Whare birkies march on burning marl: | fellows, hell |
| Then, Sir, God willing, I'll attend ye, | |
| And to His goodness I commend ye. | |

ROBERT BURNS

## BONIE DUNDEE

*TUNE: Adew Dundee*

This is an early example of Burns's collecting fragments of old folk ballads. The opening
stanza was noted down by Burns on the back of a letter dated 1st February 1787, the
remaining lines being composed subsequently. The 'haver-meal bannock' was an
ancient Scots euphemism for the foetus (cf. modern slang 'bun in the oven').

| | |
|---|---:|
| 'O, whar gat ye that hauver-meal bannock?' | oatmeal |
|   'O silly blin' body, O dinna ye see? | |
| I gat it frae a young brisk sodger laddie | soldier |
|   Between Saint Johnston and bonie Dundee. | Perth |

| | |
|---|---:|
| 'O, gin I saw the laddie that gae me't! | would, that |
|   Aft has he doudl'd me upon his knee; | dandled |
| May Heaven protect my bonie Scots laddie, | |
|   And send him safe hame to his babie and me! | |

| | |
|---|---:|
| 'My blessin's upon thy sweet, wee lippie! | |
|   My blessin's upon thy bonie e'e-brie! | eyebrow |
| Thy smiles are sae like my blythe sodger laddie, | |
|   Thou's ay the dearer and dearer to me! | |

| | |
|---|---:|
| 'But I'll big a bow'r on yon bonie banks, | build |
|   Whare Tay rins wimplin by sae clear; | winding |
| An I'll cleed thee in the tartan sae fine, | clothe |
|   And mak thee a man like thy daddie dear.' | |

## EPIGRAM AT ROSLIN INN

Composed early in 1787, after breakfast at Roslin to which Burns and the painter
Nasmyth had walked after a night's carousing in Edinburgh. Nasmyth states that this
epigram, addressed to Mrs. Willson the landlady, was written on the back of the bill.

My blessings on ye, honest wife!
I ne'er was here before;
Ye've wealth o gear for spoon and knife:
Heart could not wish for more.
Heav'n keep you clear o sturt and strife,     trouble
Till far ayont fourscore,        beyond
And by the Lord o death and life,
I'll ne'er gae by your door!

## THE BARD AT INVERARAY

Written on 24th June 1787 when Burns was visiting Dumbarton and the Clyde coast
of Argyll. These terse lines were allegedly inscribed on the window of the inn at
Inveraray, whose landlord was too busy attending to a large house-party of the Duke
of Argyll to serve Burns and other travellers.

Whoe'er he be that sojourns here,
I pity much his case,
Unless he come to wait upon
The lord *their* god, 'His Grace.'

There's naething here but Highland pride,
And Highland scab and hunger:
If Providence has sent me here,
'Twas surely in an anger.

## ELEGY ON THE DEATH OF
## SIR JAMES HUNTER BLAIR

Sir James Hunter Blair (1741-87) was Lord Provost of Edinburgh in 1784 and created
baronet in 1786. This elegy was written shortly after Blair's death on 1st July 1787.

The lamp of day with ill-presaging glare,
Dim, cloudy, sank beneath the western wave;
Th' inconstant blast howl'd thro the darkening air,
And hollow whistled in the rocky cave.

Lone as I wander'd by each cliff and dell,
Once the lov'd haunts of Scotia's royal train;
Or mus'd where limpid streams, once hallow'd, well,
Or mould'ring ruins mark the sacred Fane.

Th' increasing blast roared round the beetling rocks,
　　The clouds, swift-wing'd, flew o'er the starry sky,
The groaning trees untimely shed their locks,
　　And shooting meteors caught the startled eye.

The paly moon rose in the livid east,
　　And 'mong the cliffs disclos'd a stately form
In weeds of woe, that frantic beat her breast,
　　And mix'd her wailings with the raving storm.

Wild to my heart the filial pulses glow:
　　'Twas Caledonia's trophied shield I view'd,
Her form majestic droop'd in pensive woe,
　　The lightning of her eye in tears imbued.

Revers'd that spear redoubtable in war,
　　Reclined that banner, erst in fields unfurl'd,
That like a deathful meteor gleam'd afar,
　　And brav'd the mighty monarchs of the world.

'My patriot son fills an untimely grave!'
　　With accents wild and lifted arms she cried:
'Low lies the hand that oft was stretch'd to save,
　　Low lies the heart that swell'd with honor's pride.

'A weeping country joins a widow's tear;
　　The helpless poor mix with the orphan's cry;
The drooping Arts surround their patron's bier;
　　And grateful Science heaves the heart-felt sigh.

'I saw my sons resume their ancient fire;
　　I saw fair Freedom's blossoms richly blow.
But ah! how hope is born but to expire!
　　Relentless fate has laid their guardian low.

'My patriot falls, but shall he lie unsung,
　　While empty greatness saves a worthless name?
No: every Muse shall join her tuneful tongue,
　　And future ages hear his growing fame.

'And I will join a mother's tender cares
　　Thro future times to make his virtues last
That distant years may boast of other Blairs!'
　　She said, and vanish'd with the sweeping blast.

## TO MISS FERRIER
### ENCLOSING THE ELEGY ON SIR J. H. BLAIR

Jane Ferrier (1767-1846) was the eldest daughter of James Ferrier, W.S. and sister of the novelist Susan Edmondstone Ferrier. She married General Graham, Depute-Governor of Stirling Castle, and published a volume of engravings of its ancient carvings in 1817. She was a famous society beauty when Burns met her in the summer of 1787 and she requested one of his poems.

Nae heathen name shall I prefix,
   Frae Pindus or Parnassus;
Auld Reekie dings them a' to sticks,            *Edinburgh, knocks down*
   For rhyme-inspiring lasses.

Jove's tunefu dochters three times three        *the nine Muses*
   Made Homer deep their debtor;
But gien the body half an e'e,
   Nine Ferriers wad done better!

Last day my mind was in a bog;
   Down George's Street I stoited;        *George St, Edinburgh*
A creeping, cauld, prosaic fog               *New Town*
   My very senses doited.                  *dulled*

Do what I dought to set her free,           *dared*
   My saul lay in the mire:                *soul*
Ye turned a neuk, I saw your e'e,         *corner*
   She took the wing like fire!

The mournfu sang I here enclose,           *song*
   In gratitude I send you,
And pray, in rhyme as weel as prose,
   A' guid things may attend you!

## ON THE DEATH OF JOHN McLEOD, ESQ.
### BROTHER TO A YOUNG LADY, A PARTICULAR FRIEND OF THE AUTHOR

Son of the laird of Rassay who had died in 1786, young John McLeod himself died on 20th July 1787. Burns, who was friendly with John's sister Isabella, sent these lines from Mossgiel on reading of John's death in a newspaper. In the Glenriddell MS Burns added the comment: 'this poetic compliment, what few poetic compliments are, was from the heart.'

Sad thy tale, thou idle page,
   And rueful thy alarms:
Death tears the brother of her love
   From Isabella's arms.

Sweetly deckt with pearly dew
   The morning rose may blow;
But cold successive noontide blasts
   May lay its beauties low.

Fair on Isabella's morn
    The sun propitious smil'd;
But, long ere noon, succeeding clouds
    Succeeding hopes beguil'd.

Fate oft tears the bosom chords
    That Nature finest strung:
So Isabella's heart was form'd,
    And so that heart was wrung.

Dread Omnipotence alone
    Can heal the wound he gave –
Can point the brimful, grief-worn eyes
    To scenes beyond the grave.

Virtue's blossoms there shall blow,
    And fear no withering blast;
There Isabella's spotless worth
    Shall happy be at last.


# YON WILD MOSSY MOUNTAINS

*TUNE: Phebe*

Burns noted cryptically 'The song alludes to a part of my private history, which it is of
no consequence to the world to know.' From this it has been conjectured that the lassie
referred to was a Lanarkshire girl whom the poet encountered on his way to or from
Edinburgh in 1787.

Yon wild mossy mountains sae lofty and wide,
That nurse in their bosom the youth o the Clyde,
Where the grouse lead their coveys thro the heather to feed,
And the shepherd tents his flock as he pipes on his reed.

Not Gowrie's rich valley nor Forth's sunny shores
To me hae the charms o yon wild, mossy moors;
For there, by a lanely, sequestered stream,
Resides a sweet lassie, my thought and my dream.

Amang thae wild mountains shall still be my path,
Ilk stream foaming down its ain green, narrow strath;
For there wi my lassie the day-lang I rove,
While o'er us unheeded flie the swift hours o love.

She is not the fairest, altho she is fair;
O nice education but sma' is her share;
Her parentage humble as humble can be;
But I lo'e the dear lassie because she lo'es me.

To Beauty what man but maun yield him a prize,        must
In her armour of glances, and blushes, and sighs?
And when Wit and Refinement hae polish'd her darts,
They dazzle our een, as they flie to our hearts.

But kindness, sweet kindness, in the fond-sparkling e'e
Has lustre outshining the diamond to me,
And the heart beating love as I'm clasp'd in her arms,
O these are my lassie's all-conquering charms!


## HIGHLAND HARRY BACK AGAIN

*TUNE: The Highland Watch's Farewell to Ireland*

Written some time after August 1787. Burns noted in his personal copy of SMM 'the chorus I pickt up from an old woman in Dunblane; the rest of the song is mine', but 'Knockhaspie's land' was the name of a field at Mossgiel.

### CHORUS

*O, for him back again!*
*O, for him back again!*
*I wad gie a' Knockhaspie's land*
*For Highland Harry back again.*

My Harry was a gallant gay,
   Fu stately strade he on the plain,        strode
But now he's banish'd far away:
   I'll never see him back again.

When a' the lave gae to their bed,        rest
   I wander dowie up the glen,        sadly
I set me down and greet my fill,        cry
   And ay I wish him back again.

O, were some villains hangit high,
   And ilka body had their ain,        every
Then I might see the joyfu sight,
   My Highland Harry back again!

## IMPROMPTU ON CARRON
## IRON WORKS

Written on 26th August 1787 during the Highland tour. The Carron Iron Works, founded in 1759 and world famous for the cannon known as carronades, was forced into liquidation in 1983.

| | |
|---|---|
| We cam na here to view your warks | works |
|     In hopes to be mair wise, | |
| But only, lest we gang to Hell, | |
|     It may be nae surprise. | |
| But when we tirl'd at your door | rattled |
|     Your porter dought na bear us: | could not permit |
| Sae may, should we to Hell's yetts come, | gates |
|     Your billy Satan sair us. | comrade |

## WRITTEN BY SOMEBODY
## ON THE WINDOW

### OF AN INN AT STIRLING, ON SEEING THE ROYAL
### PALACE IN RUIN

Written on or about 27th August 1787 when Burns and William Nicol supped with 'Messrs Doig the Schoolmaster, Bell and Captn. Forrester of the Castle. D a queerish fellow and a pedant, B a joyous, vacant fellow who sings a good song, Forrester a merry swearing kind of man with a dash of the Sodger.'

| | |
|---|---|
| Here Stewarts once in glory reign'd, | |
| And laws for Scotland's weal ordain'd; | |
| But now unroof'd their palace stands, | |
| Their sceptre fallen to other hands; | |
| Fallen indeed, and to the earth, | |
| Whence grovelling reptiles take their birth. | |
| The injured Stewart line is gone, | |
| A race outlandish fills their throne: | i.e. the House of Hanover |
| An idiot race, to honour lost – | |
| Who know them best despise them most. | |

## EPITAPH FOR WILLIAM MICHIE

### SCHOOLMASTER OF CLEISH PARISH, FIFESHIRE

Ebenezer Michie (1766-1812) was introduced to Burns by William Nicol and they spent a convivial evening together. This mock epitaph was composed when Michie collapsed in a stupor. The Wallace-Chambers edition gives his name as Ebenezer, and reads 'Eben Michie' in the first line, but this version is preferred by other editors.

| | |
|---|---|
| Here lie Willie Michie's banes: | bones |
|     O Satan, when ye tak him, | |
| Gie him the schulin o your weans, | schooling, brats |
|     For clever deils he'll mak them! | devils |

## STRATHALLAN'S LAMENT

James Drummond, 5th Viscount Strathallan (d. 1765), is allegedly the speaker of this lament for his father, William, killed at Culloden in 1746-a vehicle used by Burns to air his Jacobite sentiments. The tune to which Burns set these words was specially composed for the occasion by Allan Masterton, an Edinburgh schoolmaster, who shared his Jacobite sympathies. Burns passed through Strathallan on 28th August 1787 and wrote this song on his return to Edinburgh.

Thickest night, surround my dwelling!
    Howling tempests, o'er me rave!
Turbid torrents wintry-swelling,
    Roaring by my lonely cave!
Crystal streamlets gently flowing,
    Busy haunts of base mankind,
Western breezes softly blowing,
    Suit not my distracted mind.

In the cause of Right engaged,
    Wrongs injurious to redress,
Honour's war we strongly waged,
    But the heavens deny'd success.
Ruin's wheel has driven o'er us:
    Not a hope that dare attend,
The wide world is all before us,
    But a world without a friend.

## VERSES WRITTEN WITH A PENCIL

### OVER THE CHIMNEY-PIECE, IN THE PARLOUR
### OF THE INN AT KENMORE, TAYMOUTH

These lines were first published in the *Edinburgh Evening Courant* of 6th September 1787, allegedly communicated by 'O.B. of Kenmore who, a few days ago, being on a visit to Taymouth,... found the following verses (by the celebrated Ayrshire bard) written on the walls of the Hermitage there.' It is more likely that Burns himself contributed the poem to the newspaper. His journal of the Highland tour (29th August 1787) laconically states 'Taymouth-described in rhyme.'

Admiring Nature in her wildest grace,
These northern scenes with weary feet I trace;
O'er many a winding dale and painful steep,
Th' abodes of covey'd grouse and timid sheep,
My savage journey, curious, I pursue,
Till fam'd Breadalbane opens to my view.
The meeting cliffs each deep-sunk glen divides:
The woods, wild-scatter'd, clothe their ample sides;
Th' outstretching lake, imbosomed 'mong the hills,
The eye with wonder and amazement fills:
The Tay meand'ring sweet in infant pride,
The palace rising on his verdant side,

The lawns wood-fring'd in Nature's native taste,
The hillocks dropt in Nature's careless haste,
The arches striding o'er the new-born stream,
The village glittering in the noontide beam –
.   .   .   .   .   .   .   .

Poetic ardors in my bosom swell,
Lone wand'ring by the hermit's mossy cell;
The sweeping theatre of hanging woods,
Th' incessant roar of headlong tumbling floods –
.   .   .   .   .   .   .   .

Here Poesy might wake her heav'n-taught lyre,
And look through Nature with creative fire;
Here, to the wrongs of Fate half reconcil'd,
Misfortune's lighten'd steps might wander wild;
And Disappointment, in these lonely bounds,
Fine balm to soothe her bitter rankling wounds;
Here heart-struck Grief might heav'nward stretch her scan,
And injur'd Worth forget and pardon man.
.   .   .   .   .   .   .   .

## THE BIRKS OF ABERFELDIE

On 30th August 1787 'I composed these stanzas standing under the falls of Aberfeldy,
at, or near, Moness.' The chorus comes from the traditional Aberdeenshire ballad 'Birks
of Abergeldie.'

### CHORUS

*Bonie lassie, will ye go,*
*Will ye go, will ye go?*
*Bonie lassie, will ye go*
    *To the birks of Aberfeldie?*              birches

Now simmer blinks on flow'ry braes,
And o'er the crystal streamlets plays,
Come, let us spend the lightsome days
    In the birks of Aberfeldie!

The little birdies blythely sing,
While o'er their heads the hazels hing,
Or lightly flit on wanton wing
    In the birks of Aberfeldie!

The braes ascend like lofty wa's,                hillsides
The foaming stream, deep-roaring, fa's
O'erhung wi fragrant-spreading shaws,       woods
    The birks of Aberfeldie.

The hoary cliffs are crown'd wi flowers,
White o'er the linns the burnie pours,    cascades, brooks
And, rising, weets wi misty showers        wets
    The birks of Aberfeldie.

Let Fortune's gifts at random flee,
They ne'er shall draw a wish frae me,
Supremely blest wi love and thee
    In the birks of Aberfeldie.

# AMANG THE TREES

*TUNE: The King o France he rade a race*

On 31st August, at Dunkeld, Burns met Neil Gow (1727-1807), the famous fiddler whom he described as 'a short, stout-built Highland figure, with his greyish hair shed on his honest social brow-an interesting face, marking strong common sense, kind openheartedness mixed with unmistrusting simplicity.' This song was intended as a compliment to him.

Amang the trees, where humming bees
    At buds and flowers were hinging, O,    hanging
Auld Caledon drew out her drone,
    And to her pipe was singing, O.
'Twas Pibroch, Sang, Strathspeys and Reels –
    She dirl'd them aff fu clearly, O,       rang
When there cam a yell o foreign squeels,
    That dang her tapsalteerie, O!    knocked upside down

Their capon craws an queer 'ha, ha's,'
    They made our lugs grow eerie, O.       ears
The hungry bike did scrape and fyke,    swarm, make a fuss
    Till we were wae and weary, O.          sad
But a royal ghaist, wha ance was cas'd    King James I
    A prisoner, aughteen year awa,      (1394-1437)
He fir'd a Fiddler in the North,    imprisoned in England,
    That dang them tapsalteerie, O!       1406-24

# THE HUMBLE PETITION OF BRUAR WATER

## TO THE NOBLE DUKE OF ATHOLE

This poem was sent by Burns to Josiah Walker, tutor of the Marquis of Tullibardine, son of the Duke of Atholl, from Inverness on 5th September 1787. It had been composed two or three days earlier: 'at least part of it, the effusion of the half hour that I spent at Bruar. I don't mean it was extempore, for I have endeavoured, to brush it up as well as Mr Nicol's chat and the jogging of the chaise would allow.' Burns met Walker at the home of Dr Blacklock in Edinburgh, and renewed the acquaintance at Blair Atholl on his way north during the Highland tour.

My lord, I know, your noble ear
    Woe ne'er assails in vain;
Embolden'd thus, I beg you'll hear
    Your humble slave complain,
How saucy Phoebus' scorching beams,
    In flaming summer-pride,
Dry-withering, waste my foamy streams,
    And drink my crystal tide.

The lightly-jumping, glowrin trouts,        *staring*
    That thro my waters play,
If, in their random, wanton spouts,
    They near the margin stray;
If, hapless chance! they linger lang,
    I'm scorching up so shallow,
They're left the whitening stanes amang
    In gasping death to wallow.

Last day I grat wi spite and teen,        *wept, vexation*
    As poet Burns came by,
That, to a Bard, I should be seen
    Wi half my channel dry;
A panegyric rhyme, I ween,
    Ev'n as I was, he shor'd me;        *offered*
But had I in my glory been,
    He, kneeling, wad ador'd me.

Here, foaming down the skelvy rocks,        *shelving*
    In twisting strength I rin;
There high my boiling torrent smokes,
    Wild-roaring o'er a linn:        *fall*
Enjoying large each spring and well,
    As Nature gave them me,
I am, altho I say't mysel,
    Worth gaun a mile to see.        *going*

Would, then, my noble master please
    To grant my highest wishes,
He'll shade my banks wi tow'ring trees
    And bonie spreading bushes.
Delighted doubly then, my lord,
    You'll wander on my banks,
And listen monie a grateful bird
    Return you tuneful thanks.

The sober laverock, warbling wild,              lark
    Shall to the skies aspire;
The gowdspink, Music's gayest child,        goldfinch
    Shall sweetly join the choir;
The blackbird strong, the lintwhite clear,    linnet
    The mavis mild and mellow,           thrush
The robin, pensive Autumn cheer
    In all her locks of yellow.

This, too, a covert shall ensure,
    To shield them from the storm;
And coward maukin sleep secure,         hare
    Low in her grassy form:
Here shall the shepherd make his seat
    To weave his crown of flow'rs;
Or find a shelt'ring, safe retreat,
    From prone-descending show'rs.

And here, by sweet, endearing stealth,
    Shall meet the loving pair,
Despising worlds with all their wealth,
    As empty idle care:
The flow'rs shall vie, in all their charms,
    The hour of heav'n to grace;
And birks extend their fragrant arms    birches
    To screen the dear embrace.

Here haply, too, at vernal dawn,
    Some musing Bard may stray,
And eye the smoking, dewy lawn
    And misty mountain grey;
Or, by the reaper's nightly beam,
    Mild-chequering thro the trees,
Rave to my darkly dashing stream,
    Hoarse-swelling on the breeze.

Let lofty firs and ashes cool,
　My lowly banks o'erspread,
And view, deep-bending in the pool,
　Their shadows' wat'ry-bed:
Let fragrant birks, in woodbines drest,
　My craggy cliffs adorn,
And, for the little songster's nest,
　The close embow'ring thorn!

So may, old Scotia's darling hope,
　Your little angel band
Spring, like their fathers, up to prop
　Their honour'd native land!
So may, thro Albion's farthest ken,
　To social-flowing glasses,
The grace be – 'Athole's honest men
And Athole's bonie lasses!'

# A HIGHLAND WELCOME

Written on Sunday 2nd September 1787 when Burns and Nicol went up the Garry to Dalnacardoch and Dalwhinnie.

When Death's dark stream I ferry o'er
　(A time that surely shall come),
In Heaven itself I'll ask no more,
　Than just a Highland welcome.

# LINES ON THE FALLS OF FYERS

## NEAR LOCH-NESS
## WRITTEN WITH A PENCIL ON THE SPOT

Written on Wednesday 5th September, when Burns and Nicol came down the east shore of Loch Ness from Inverness to Foyers.

Among the heathy hills and ragged woods
The roaring Fyers pours his mossy floods;
Till full he dashes on the rocky mounds,
Where, thro a shapeless breach, his steam resounds,
As high in air the bursting torrents flow,
As deep recoiling surges foam below,
Prone down the rock the whitening sheet descends,
And viewless Echo's ear, astonish'd, rends.
Dim-seen through rising mists and ceaseless show'rs
The hoary cavern, wide-surrounding, lours:
Still thro the gap the struggling river toils,
And still, below, the horrid caldron boils –

# CASTLE GORDON

Written after visiting the seat of Alexander, 4th Duke of Gordon, and his beautiful and witty Duchess, Jane Maxwell, near Fochabers on 7th September 1787. Burns, who had met the Duchess in Edinburgh and been invited to call, left Nicol at the inn. After taking wine with his hosts Burns rose to leave, and on being pressed to stay, explained about Nicol. The Duke suggested sending a servant to fetch Nicol, but Burns insisted on accompanying the servant. Nicol, furious at being left behind, was all packed ready to depart. He gave Burns the option of accompanying him there and then, or remaining on his own. Burns had little choice but go on with his angry companion.

Streams that glide in Orient plains,
　Never bound by Winter's chains,
　　Glowing here on golden sands,
There immixed with foulest stains
　　From tyranny's empurpled hands;
These, their richly gleaming waves,
I leave to tyrants and their slaves:
Give me the stream that sweetly laves
　　The banks by Castle Gordon.

Spicy forests ever gay,
Shading from the burning ray
　　Hapless wretches sold to toil;
Or, the ruthless native's way,
　　Bent on slaughter, blood, and spoil;
Woods that ever verdant wave,
I leave the tyrant and the slave:
Give me the groves that lofty brave
　　The storms of Castle Gordon.

Wildly here without control
Nature reigns, and rules the whole;
　　In that sober pensive mood,
Dearest to the feeling soul,
　　She plants the forest, pours the flood.
Life's poor day I'll, musing, rave,
And find at night a sheltering cave,
Where waters flow and wild woods wave
　　By bonie Castle Gordon.

## THE YOUNG HIGHLAND ROVER

*TUNE: Morag*

Composed about the same time as the preceding. The Highland rover of this poem was Prince Charles Edward Stuart.

Loud blaw the frosty breezes,
　The snaws the mountains cover.
Like winter on me seizes,
　　Since my young Highland rover
　　Far wanders nations over.

Where'er he go, where'er he stray,
    May Heaven be his warden!
Return him safe to fair Strathspey
    And bonie Castle Gordon!

The trees, now naked groaning,
    Shall soon wi leaves be hinging,
The birdies, dowie moaning,
    Shall a' be blythely singing,
    And every flower be springing:
Sae I'll rejoice the lee-lang day,
    When (by his mighty Warden)
My youth's return'd to fair Strathspey,
    And bonie Castle Gordon.

# THENIEL MENZIES' BONIE MARY

*AIR: The Ruffian's Rant or Roy's Wife*

The characters of this song appear to be entirely fictitious and not identifiable although the brig o Dye and Darlet are places in Kincardineshire. Burns and Nicol stayed at Stonehaven on 10th September 1787 to meet some of the bard's Burness relatives.

### CHORUS

*Theniel Menzies' bonie Mary,*
    *Theniel Menzies' bonie Mary,*
*Charlie Grigor tint his plaidie,*                                  lost
    *Kissin Theniel's bonie Mary.*

In comin by the brig o Dye,
    At Darlet we a blink did tarry;
As day was dawin in the sky,
    We drank a health to bonie Mary.

Her een sae bright, her brow sae white,
    Her haffet locks as brown's a berry,                            temple
And ay they dimpl't wi a smile,
    The rosy cheeks o' bonie Mary.

We lap an danc'd the lee-lang day,                          leaped, live-long
    Till pipe-lads were wae and weary;                             exhausted
But Charlie gat the spring to pay,
    For kissin Theniel's bonie Mary.

# LADY ONLIE, HONEST LUCKY
### TUNE: *The Ruffian's Rant*

The 'Bucky' of this song is the Banffshire fishing village of Buckie, which Burns visited on 7th September 1787. Thorniebank is a farm about a mile south of the village. This is an early example of a traditional song collected by Burns, on his Highland tour, and subsequently reworked by him.

### CHORUS

*Lady Onlie, honest lucky,*
  *Brews guid ale at shore o Bucky:*
*I wish her sale for her guid ale,*
  *The best on a' the shore o Bucky!*

A' the lads o Thorniebank,
  When they gae to the shore o Bucky,
They'll step in an tak a pint,
  Wi Lady Onlie, honest lucky.

Her house sae bien, her curch sae clean –          snug, kerchief
  I wat she is a dainty chuckie,                          old dear
And cheery blinks the ingle-gleede              glances, -blaze
  O Lady Onlie, honest lucky.

# BLYTHE WAS SHE
### TUNE: *Andro and his Cutty Gun*

Burns records that he composed these verses while staying at Ochtertyre with Sir William Murray in October 1787. The 'Phemie' of 1.3 was Miss Euphemia Murray of Lentrose (b. 1769), nicknamed the Flower of Strathmore on account of her dazzling beauty. Miss Murray is said not to have appreciated the honour done to her by Burns. Perhaps she objected to the tune to which the poem was set: 'cutty gun' is a phallic metaphor.

### CHORUS

*Blythe, blythe and merry was she,*
  *Blythe was she butt and ben,*
*Blythe by the banks of Earn,*
  *And blythe in Glenturit glen!*

By Oughtertyre grows the aik,                                oak
  On Yarrow banks the birken shaw;                    birch, wood
But Phemie was a bonier lass
  Than braes o Yarrow ever saw.                            slopes

Her looks were like a flow'r in May,
  Her smile was like a simmer morn:
She tripped by the banks o Earn,
  As light's a bird upon a thorn.

Her bonie face it was as meek
  As onie lamb upon a lea.
The evening sun was ne'er sae sweet
  As was the blink o Phemie's e'e.                         glance

The Highland hills I've wander'd wide,
  As o'er the Lawlands I hae been,
But Phemie was the blythest lass
  That ever trod the dewy green.


## ON SCARING SOME WATER-FOWL IN LOCH TURIT

Burns visited Sir William Murray and his family when he was touring Clackmannanshire with Dr Adair in 1787, and this poem refers to one of the sporting outings he enjoyed during his stay at Ochtertyre. Euphemia Murray later recalled how Burns recited these lines after supper one evening.


Why, ye tenants of the lake,
For me your wat'ry haunt forsake?
Tell me, fellow-creatures, why
At my presence thus you fly?
Why disturb your social joys,
Parent, filial, kindred ties? –
Common friend to you and me,
Nature's gifts to all are free:
Peaceful keep your dimpling wave,
Busy feed, or wanton lave;
Or, beneath the sheltering rock,
Bide the surging billow's shock.

Conscious, blushing for our race,
Soon, too soon, your fears I trace.
Man, your proud, usurping foe,
Would be lord of all below:
Plumes himself in freedom's pride,
Tyrant stern to all beside.

The eagle, from the cliffy brow,
Marking you his prey below,
In his breast no pity dwells,
Strong necessity compels:
But Man, to whom alone is giv'n
A ray direct from pitying Heav'n,
Glories in his heart humane –
And creatures for his pleasure slain!

In these savage, liquid plains,
Only known to wand'ring swains,
Where the mossy riv'let strays
Far from human haunts and ways,
All on Nature you depend,
And life's poor season peaceful spend.

Or, if Man's superior might
Dare invade your native right,
On the lofty ether borne,
Man with all his powers you scorn;
Swiftly seek, on clanging wings,
Other lakes, and other springs;
And the foe you cannot brave,
Scorn at least to be his slave.

## MY PEGGY'S CHARMS

*TUNE: My Peggy's Charms*

The subject of this song was Margaret Chalmers (1763-1843), a cousin of Gavin
Hamilton, whom Burns may have known from his Mauchline days. He sent her these
verses in October 1787 and when she raised objections to publication he pointed out
that 'The poetic compliments I pay cannot be misunderstood.' She later told Thomas
Campbell the poet that Burns had proposed to her but she gently turned him down and
they remained good, but platonic, friends.

My Peggy's face, my Peggy's form
The frost of hermit Age might warm.
My Peggy's worth, my Peggy's mind
Might charm the first of human kind.

I love my Peggy's angel air,
Her face so truly heavenly fair,
Her native grace so void of art:
But I adore my Peggy's heart.

The lily's hue, the rose's dye,
The kindling lustre of an eye –
Who but owns their magic sway?
Who but knows they all decay?

The tender thrill, the pitying tear,
The generous purpose, nobly dear,
The gentle look that rage disarms –
These are all immortal charms.

## WHERE, BRAVING ANGRY WINTER'S STORMS

*TUNE: Neil Gow's Lament for Abercairny*

This song was also written for Margaret Chalmers soon after Burns had visited her at Harvieston in October 1787. '...when I think I have met with you, and have lived more of real life with you in eight days than I can do with almost anybody I meet with in eight years – when I think on the improbability of meeting you in this world again – I could sit down and cry like a child', he wrote to her a year later, when her marriage to the banker Lewis Hay was imminent.

Where, braving angry winter's storms,
   The lofty Ochils rise,
Far in their shade my Peggy's charms
   First blest my wondering eyes:
As one who by some savage stream
   A lonely gem surveys,
Astonish'd doubly, marks its beam
   With art's most polish'd blaze.

Blest be the wild, sequester'd glade,
   And blest the day and hour,
Where Peggy's charms I first survey'd,
   When first I felt their pow'r!
The tyrant Death, with grim control
   May seize my fleeting breath,
But tearing Peggy from my soul
   Must be a stronger death.

## THE BANKS OF THE DEVON

*TUNE: Bhannerach dhon na chri*

'These verses were composed on a charming girl, a Miss Charlotte Hamilton, who is now married to Jas. McKitrick Adair, Esquire, Physician. She is sister of my worthy friend Gavin Hamilton.' Miss Hamilton (1763-1806) was living at Harvieston when Burns met her in 1787, the 'clear winding Devon' being the river bordering the estate. The song was set to a Gaelic melody which Burns noted down during his visit to Inverness.

How pleasant the banks of the clear winding Devon,
   With green spreading bushes and flow'rs blooming fair!
But the boniest flow'r on the banks of the Devon
   Was once a sweet bud on the braes of the Ayr.

Mild be the sun on this sweet blushing flower,
   In the gay rosy morn, as it bathes in the dew!
And gentle the fall of the soft vernal shower,
   That steals on the evening each leaf to renew!

O, spare the dear blossom, ye orient breezes,
   With chill, hoary wing as ye usher the dawn!
And far be thou distant, thou reptile that seizes
   The verdure and pride of the garden or lawn!

Let Bourbon exult in his gay gilded lilies,
  And England triumphant display her proud rose!
A fairer than either adorns the green vallies,
  Where Devon, sweet Devon, meandering flows.

## EPITAPH FOR WILLIAM NICOL, OF THE HIGH SCHOOL, EDINBURGH

William Nicol (1744-97) was born in Annan and studied theology and medicine in Edinburgh before becoming classical master at Edinburgh High School in 1774. He accompanied Burns on his Highland tour and despite the incident at Blair Atholl remained a close friend of the poet who named one of his sons in 1791 after him.

Ye maggots, feed on Nicol's brain,
  For few sic feasts you've gotten;
And fix your claws in Nicol's heart,
  For deil a bit o't's rotten.

## CA' THE YOWES TO THE KNOWES

In September 1794 Burns wrote to George Thomson: '...it was owing to me that ever it [this song] saw the light. About seven years ago, I was well acquainted with a worthy little fellow of a Clergyman, a Mr Clunzie, who sung it charmingly...when I gave it to Johnson, I added some stanzas to the song and mended others.' This vividly illustrates Burns's role as a preserver and mender of traditional ballads. 'Mr Clunzie' was John Clunie (1757-1819), schoolmaster and precentor at Markinch.

### CHORUS

*Ca' the yowes to the knowes,*                   ewes, hillocks
*Ca' them where the heather grows,*
*Ca' them where the burnie rowes,*                 stream runs
  *My bonie dearie!*

As I gaed down the water-side,                     went
There I met my shepherd lad:
He row'd me sweetly in his plaid,                  wrapped
  An he ca'd me his dearie.

'Will ye gang down the water-side,
And see the waves sae sweetly glide
Beneath the hazels spreading wide?
  The moon it shines fu clearly.'

'Ye sall get gowns and ribbons meet,
Cauf-leather shoon upon your feet,
And in my arms thou'lt lie and sleep,
  An ye sall be my dearie.'

'If ye'll but stand to what ye've said,
I'se gang wi thee, my shepherd lad,
And ye may row me in your plaid,
    And I sall be your dearie.'

'While waters wimple to the sea,                     meander
While day blinks in the lift sae hie,                 sky
Till clay-cauld death sall blin' my e'e,
    Ye sall be my dearie.'

# ON THE DEATH OF
# LORD PRESIDENT DUNDAS

Robert Dundas, Lord Arniston (1713-87) was Lord Advocate (1754) and Lord President of the Court of Session (1760-87). On the death of Dundas on 13th December, Alexander Wood suggested to Burns that he write an elegy, a task which the poet tackled with less than his customary enthusiasm, later admitting that some verses were 'rather commonplace, and others rather hide-bound.' Burns sent the poem with a covering letter to Robert Dundas, jnr. 'His Solicitorship never took the smallest notice of the Letter, the Poem, or the Poet.'

Lone on the bleaky hills, the straying flocks
Shun the fierce storms among the sheltering rocks;
Down foam the rivulets, red with dashing rains;
The gathering floods burst o'er the distant plains;
Beneath the blast the leafless forests groan
The hollow caves return a hollow moan.

Ye hills, ye plains, ye forests, and ye caves,
Ye howling winds, and wintry swelling waves,
Unheard, unseen, by human ear or eye,
Sad to your sympathetic glooms I fly,
Where, to the whistling blast and water's roar
Pale Scotia's recent wound I may deplore!

O heavy loss, thy country ill could bear!
A loss these evil days can ne'er repair!
Justice, the high vicegerent of her God,
Her doubtful balance eyed, and sway'd her rod;
Hearing the tidings of the fatal blow,
She sank, abandon'd to the wildest woe.

Wrongs, injuries, from many a darksome den,
Now gay in hope, explore the paths of men.
See from his cavern grim Oppression rise,
And throw on Poverty his cruel eyes!
Keen on the helpless victim see him fly,
And stifle, dark, the feebly-bursting cry!

Mark ruffian Violence, distained with crimes,
Rousing elate in these degenerate times!
View unsuspecting Innocence a prey,
As guileful Fraud points out the erring way;
While subtile Litigation's pliant tongue
The life-blood equal sucks of Right and Wrong!
Hark, injur'd Want recounts th' unlisten'd tale,
And much-wrong'd Mis'ry pours th' unpitied wail!

Ye dark, waste hills, ye brown, unsightly plains
Congenial scenes, ye soothe my mournful strains.
Ye tempests, rage! ye turbid torrents, roll!
Ye suit the joyless tenor of my soul.
Life's social haunts and pleasures I resign;
Be nameless wilds and lonely wanderings mine,
To mourn the woes my country must endure:
That wound degenerate ages cannot cure.


# SYLVANDER TO CLARINDA

Clarinda was Agnes Craig McLehose (1758-1841), estranged wife of a Glasgow lawyer.
Burns met her at Edinburgh on 4th December 1787 and a sentimental affair developed
between them. Much of this platonic courtship was conducted by letter, using classical
*noms de plume* in the fashion of the time. Frustrated in the physical side of his affair,
Burns returned to Ayrshire and renewed his relationship with Jean Armour – a move
for which Agnes accused him of 'perfidious treachery.' This was the first of ten poems
and songs which Burns wrote in her honour. Sylvander ('man of the woods') was the
hero of a romance published at Edinburgh in 1768, while Clarinda had been a popular
name with romantic poets since the time of Edmund Spenser.

When dear Clarinda, matchless fair,
    First struck Sylvander's raptur'd view,
He gaz'd, he listened to despair –
    Alas! 'twas all he dared to do.

Love from Clarinda's heavenly eyes
    Transfix'd his bosom thro and thro,
But still in Friendship's guarded guise –
    For more the demon fear'd to do.

That heart, already more than lost,
    The imp beleaguer'd all *perdu*;        lost (French)
For frowning Honor kept his post –
    To meet that frown he shrunk to do.

His pangs the Bard refus'd to own,
    Tho half he wish'd Clarinda knew;
But Anguish wrung the unweeting groan –
    Who blames what frantic Pain must do?

That heart, where motley follies blend,
   Was sternly still to Honor true:
To prove Clarinda's fondest friend
   Was what a lover, sure, might do.

The Muse his ready quill employ'd,
   No nearer bliss he could pursue;
This bliss Clarinda cold deny'd –
   'Send word by Charles how you do!'

The chill behest disarm'd his Muse,
   Till Passion, all impatient grew:
He wrote, and hinted for excuse,
   'Twas, 'cause 'he'd nothing else to do.'

But by those hopes I have above!
   And by those faults I dearly rue!
The deed, the boldest mark of love,
   For thee, that deed I dare to do!

O, could the Fates but name the price
   Would bless me with your charms and you,
With frantic joy I'd pay it thrice,
   If human art and power could do!

Then take, Clarinda, friendship's hand
   (Friendship, at least, I may avow),
And lay no more your chill command, –
   I'll write, whatever I've to do.

                        SYLVANDER

## THE BONIE LASS OF ALBANIE

### TUNE: *Mary's Dream*

Charlotte Stuart (1753-89) was the daughter of Bonnie Prince Charlie by his mistress Clementina Walkinshaw who had followed him to the Continent. The affair lasted about eight years before the long-suffering Clementina left the Prince. As his marriage to Princess Louise of Stolberg was childless, Charles sought to have his daughter legitimated, under the title of Duchess of Albany, at Paris on 6th December 1787 – the occasion for the composition of this song.

My heart is wae, and unco wae,                   mighty sad
   To think upon the raging sea,
That roars between her gardens green
   An the bonie lass of Albanie.

This lovely maid's of royal blood
   That ruled Albion's kingdoms three;     England, Scotland
But Oh, alas for her bonie face!            and Ireland
   They hae wrang'd the lass of Albanie.

In the rolling tide of spreading Clyde
   There sits an isle of high degree,          the isle of Bute
And a town of fame, whose princely name     Rothesay
   Should grace the lass of Albanie.

But there is a youth, a witless youth,      Prince George,
   That fills the place where she should be;  later Prince
We'll send him o'er to his native shore,    Regent and
   And bring our ain sweet Albanie!      King George IV

Alas the day, and woe the day!
   A false usurper wan the gree,         highest honours
Who now commands the towers and lands,
   The royal right of Albanie.

We'll daily pray, we'll nightly pray,
   On bended knees most fervently,
The time may come, with pipe and drum
   We'll welcome hame fair Albanie.

# BIRTHDAY ODE
# FOR 31st DECEMBER, 1787

Burns attended a dinner in Edinburgh to celebrate the birthday of 'the King o'er the water.' Those present did not seriously entertain 'any hope of...the restoration of the house of Stewart; but over their sparkling wine, they indulged the generous feelings which the recollection of fallen greatness is calculated to inspire...[Burns] took upon himself the office of poet-laureate.' (Currie vol. 1 181-2). It is perhaps worth noting that the sentimental attachment to the House of Stuart, which was the extent of Burns's Jacobitism, was shared ironically by none other than 'the witless youth', Prince George himself. Prince Charles died at Rome a few weeks later, on 31st January 1788.

Afar the illustrious Exile roams,
   Whom kingdoms on this day should hail,
An inmate in the casual shed,
   On transient pity's bounty fed,
   Haunted by busy Memory's bitter tale!
Beasts of the forest have their savage homes,
   But He, who should imperial purple wear,
Owns not the lap of earth where rests his royal head:
   His wretched refuge, dark despair,
While ravening wrongs and woes pursue,
   And distant far the faithful few
   Who would his sorrows share!

False flatterer, Hope, away,
    Nor think to lure us as in days of yore!
We solemnize this sorrowing natal day,
    To prove our loyal truth - we can no more -
And, owning Heaven's mysterious sway,
    Submissive, low, adore.
Ye honored, mighty Dead,
    Who nobly perish'd in the glorious cause,
    Your King, your Country, and her laws,
From great Dundee, who smiling victory led,      John Graham of
    And fell a Martyr in her arms      Claverhouse, Viscount
    (What breast of northern ice but warms!)      Dundee (1649-89)

To bold Balmerino's undying name,      Arthur Elphinstone,
    Whose soul of fire, lighted at Heaven's high flame,      Lord Balmerino
Deserves the proudest wreath departed heroes claim!      (1688-1746)
    Not unrevenged your fate shall lie,
        It only lags, the fatal hour,
    Your blood shall with incessant cry,
        Awake at last th' unsparing Power;
As from the cliff, with thundering course,
    The snowy ruin smokes along
With doubling speed and gathering force,
Till deep it, crushing, whelms the cottage in the vale,
        So Vengeance' arm, ensanguin'd, strong,
    Shall with resistless might assail,      i.e. the Elector of Hanover
    Usurping Brunswick's pride shall lay,      and Duke of Brunswick-
And Stewart's wrongs and yours, with tenfold weight repay.      Lüneburg

Perdition, baleful child of night,
    Rise and revenge the injured right
        Of Stewart's royal race!
Lead on the unmuzzled hounds of Hell,
Till all the frighted echoes tell
        The blood-notes of the chase!
Full on the quarry point their view,
Full on the base, usurping crew,
The tools of faction and the nation's curse!
    Hark how the cry grows on the wind;
    They leave the lagging gale behind;
    Their savage fury, pityless, they pour;
With murdering eyes already they devour!
See Brunswick spent, a wretched prey,
    His life one poor despairing day,
Where each avenging hour still ushers in a worse!
    Such Havoc howling all abroad,
        Their utter ruin bring,
    The base apostates to their God,
        Or rebels to their King!

My mither sent me to the town,
   To warp a plaiden wab;             weave, web
But the weary, weary warpin o't
   Has gart me sigh and sab.               sob

A bonie, westlin weaver lad           western
   Sat working at his loom;
He took my heart, as wi a net,
   In every knot and thrum.

I sat beside my warpin-wheel,
   And ay I ca'd it roun.             drove
But every shot and every knock,
   My heart it gae a stoun.           ache

The moon was sinking in the west,
   Wi visage pale and wan,
As my bonie, westlin weaver lad
   Convoy'd me thro the glen.

But what was said, or what was done,
   Shame fa' me gin I tell;         befall, if
But Oh! I fear the kintra soon       country
   Will ken as weel's mysel!          know

## I'M O'ER YOUNG TO MARRY YET

Another example of an old chorus, with original verses supplied by Burns.

### CHORUS

*I'm o'er young, I'm o'er young,*      far too
   *I'm o'er young to marry yet!*
*I'm o'er young, "wad be a sin*
   *To tak me frae my mammie yet.*

I am my mammie's ae bairn,        only child
   Wi unco folk I weary, Sir;      strangers
And lying in a strange bed,
   I'm fley'd it make me eerie, Sir.  afraid, apprehensive

Hallowmass is come and gane,
   The nights are lang in winter, Sir,
And you and I in ae bed,           one
   In trowth, I dare na venture, Sir!    truth

Fu loud an shrill the frosty wind
   Blaws thro the leafless timmer, Sir;   woods
But if ye come this gate again,      way
   I'll aulder be gin simmer, Sir.  older be by

## McPHERSON'S FAREWELL

*TUNE: McPherson's Rant*

James McPherson was the illegitimate son of McPherson of Invershie by a gipsy mother, and was renowned as much for his skill as a fiddler as he was feared as a freebooter. He and his gang terrorised the counties of Aberdeen, Banff and Moray until he was captured by Duff of Braco and tried at Banff. Shortly before his execution in the market place of Banff in November 1700 he played this tune on his fiddle and then smashed the instrument before the assembled crowd.

### CHORUS

*Sae rantingly, sae wantonly,*
*Sae dauntingly gaed he,*                                   went
*He play'd a spring, and danc'd it round*
*Below the gallows-tree.*

Farewell, ye dungeons dark and strong,
    The wretch's destinie!
M'Pherson's time will not be long
    On yonder gallows-tree.

O what is death but parting breath?
    On many a bloody plain
I've dared his face, and in this place
    I scorn him yet again!

Untie these bands from off my hands,
    And bring to me my sword,
And there's no man in all Scotland
    But I'll brave him at a word.

I've liv'd a life of sturt and strife;                      trouble
    I die by treacherie:
It burns my heart I must depart,
    And not avenged be.

Now farewell light, thou sunshine bright,
    And all beneath the sky!
May coward shame distain his name,
    The wretch that dare not die!

## STAY, MY CHARMER

*TUNE: An Gille dubh*

Possibly based on an old ballad collected during the Highland tour.

Stay, my charmer, can you leave me?
Cruel, cruel to deceive me!
Well you know how much you grieve me!
    Cruel charmer, can you go?
    Cruel charmer, can you go?

By my love so ill-requited,
By the faith you fondly plighted,
By the pangs of lovers slighted,
   Do not, do not leave me so!
   Do not, do not leave me so!

# MY HOGGIE

*TUNE: Moss Platt*

Based on a traditional ballad, sung by an old lady in the clachan of Moss Platt in Liddesdale.

| | |
|---|---|
| What will I do gin my hoggie die? | should, lamb |
|    My joy, my pride, my hoggie! | |
| My only beast, I had nae mae, | no more |
|    And vow but I was vogie! | vain |
| The lee-lang night we watched the fauld, | live-long, fold |
|    Me and my faithfu doggie; | |
| We heard nocht but the roaring linn, | waterfall |
|    Amang the braes sae scroggie. | slopes, scrubby |
| | |
| But the houlet cry'd frae the castle wa', | owl |
|    The blitter frae the boggie, | snipe |
| The tod reply'd upon the hill: | fox |
|    I trembled for my hoggie. | |
| When day did daw, and cocks did craw, | |
|    The morning it was foggie, | |
| An unco tyke lap o'er the dyke, | strange dog, fence |
|    And maist has kill'd my hoggie! | almost |

# JUMPIN JOHN

Stenhouse says that this is 'a fragment of the old humorous ballad, with some verbal corrections,' but the ballad has not been identified.

## CHORUS

*The lang lad they ca' Jumpin John*
   *Beguil'd the bonie lassie!*
*The lang lad they ca' Jumpin John*
   *Beguil'd the bonie lassie!*

| | |
|---|---|
| Her daddie forbad, her minnie forbad; | mother |
|    Forbidden she wadna be: | would not |
| She wadna trow't, the browst she brew'd | believe, liquor |
|    Wad taste sae bitterlie! | |
| | |
| A cow and a cauf, a yowe and a hauf, | ewe, half |
|    And thretty guid shillins and three: | thirty |
| A vera guid tocher, a cotter-man's dochter, | dowry, daughter |
|    The lass with the bonie black e'e. | |

# UP IN THE MORNING EARLY

'The chorus of this is old,' noted Burns 'the two stanzas are mine.'

### CHORUS

*Up in the morning's no for me,*
  *Up in the morning early!*
*When a' the hills are cover'd wi snaw*
  *I'm sure it's winter fairly!*

Cauld blaws the wind frae east to west,
  The drift is driving sairly,                                    sorely
Sae loud and shrill's I hear the blast –
  I'm sure it's winter fairly!

The birds sit chittering in the thorn,
  A day they fare but sparely;
And lang's the night frae e'en to morn –                      evening
  I'm sure it's winter fairly!


# THE DUSTY MILLER

An expansion of a traditional fragment.

Hey, the dusty miller,
  And his dusty coat!
He will win a shilling,
  Or he spend a groat.                                         Before
Dusty was the coat,
  Dusty was the colour,
Dusty was the kiss
  That I gat frae the miller!

Hey the dusty miller,
  And his dusty sack!
Leeze me on the calling                                      Blessings
  Fills the dusty peck!
Fills the dusty peck,
  Brings the dusty siller!
I wad gae my coatie
  For the dusty miller!

## DUNCAN DAVISON

Based on a snatch of a bawdy ballad which Burns collected on his Border tour. He cleaned up the first four lines and added the rest.

There was a lass, they ca'd her Meg,
    And she held o'er the moors to spin;
There was a lad that follow'd her,
    They ca'd him Duncan Davison.
The moon was driegh, and Meg was skeigh,         *dull, skittish*
    Her favour Duncan could na win;
For wi the rock she wad him knock,                *distaff*
    And ay she shook the temper-pin.        *tuning-screw*

As o'er the moor they lightly foor,             *fared*
    A burn was clear, a glen was green;
Upon the banks they eas'd their shanks,
    And ay she set the wheel between:
But Duncan swoor a haly aith,             *holy oath*
    That Meg should be a bride the morn;     *tomorrow*
Then Meg took up her spinnin-graith,       *-implements*
    And flang them a' out o'er the burn.    *across the brook*

We will big a wee, wee house,              *build*
    And we will live like king and queen,
Sae blythe and merry's we will be,
    When ye set by the wheel at e'en!       *sit beside*
A man may drink, and no be drunk;
    A man may fight, and no be slain;
A man may kiss a bonie lass,
    And ay be welcome back again!

## WHERE HELEN LIES

This well-known old ballad tells the story of Helen Irvine of Kirkconnel near Springkell. She had two suitors one of whom shot at his rival; but Helen, thrusting herself in front of her lover, Adam Fleming, received the fatal wound instead. Fleming killed his assailant on the spot, but fled the country to avoid the legal process and enlisted in the Spanish army. Years later, he returned to Kirkconnel and died by Helen's grave. He was interred alongside her. This tragic event took place in the 16th century. Burns extensively reworked the ballad for both Johnson and Thomson, writing to the latter in 1793 that the original 'is silly, to contemptibility.'

O that I were where Helen lies,
Night and day on me she cries;
O that I were where Helen lies,
    In fair Kirkconnel lee.
O Helen fair beyond compare,
A ringlet of thy flowing hair,
I'll wear it still for ever mair
    Until the day I die.

Curs'd be the hand that shot the shot,
And curs'd the gun that gave the crack!
Into my arms bird Helen lap,                              fell
   And died for sake o me!
O think na ye but my heart was sair;
My Love fell down and spake nae mair;
There did she swoon wi meikle care                  much
   On fair Kirkconnel lee.

I lighted down, my sword did draw,
I cutted him in pieces sma';
I cutted him in pieces sma'
   On fair Kirkconnel lee.
O Helen chaste, thou wert modest,
If I were with thee I were blest
Where thou lies low and takes thy rest
   On fair Kirkconnel lee.

I wish my grave was growing green,
A winding sheet put o'er my een,
And I in Helen's arms lying
   In fair Kirkconnel lee!
I wish I were where Helen lies!
Night and day on me she cries:
O that I were where Helen lies
   On fair Kirkconnel lee.

## WEARY FA' YOU, DUNCAN GRAY

*TUNE: Duncan Gray*

Based on a traditional song in the Herd MSS.

Weary fa' you, Duncan Gray!                Woe betide
   (Ha, ha, the girdin o't!)
Wae gae by you, Duncan Gray!
   (Ha, ha, the girdin o't!)
When a' the lave gae to their play,         rest
Then I maun sit the lee-lang day,     must, live-long
And jeeg the cradle wi my tae,       rock, toe
   And a' for the girdin o't!

Bonie was the Lammas moon,
   (Ha, ha, the girdin o't!)
Glow'rin a' the hills, aboon,           staring
   (Ha, ha, the girdin o't!)
The girdin brak, the beast cam down,   broke
I tint my curch and baith my shoon, lost, kerchief, both shoes
And, Duncan, ye're an unco loun –   awful fool
   Wae on the bad girdin o't!

But, Duncan, gin ye'll keep your aith,
   (Ha, ha, the girdin o't!)
I'se bless you wi my hindmost breath,
   (Ha, ha, the girdin o't!)
Duncan, gin ye'll keep your aith,
The beast again can bear us baith,                        *both*
And auld Mess John will mend the skaith,    *Master, damage*
   And clout the bad girdin o't.                  *patch*

# THE PLOUGHMAN

A typical example of Burns's reworking of a traditional song, known in both polite and bawdy versions.

## CHORUS

*Then up wi't a', my Ploughman lad,*        *with it all*
   *And hey, my merry Ploughman;*
*Of a' the trades that I do ken,*
   *Commend me to the Ploughman.*

The Ploughman he's a bony lad,
   His mind is ever true, jo,                 *darling*
His garters knit below his knee,
   His bonnet it is blue, jo.

My Ploughman he comes hame at e'en,
   He's aften wat and weary,            *often wet*
Cast off the wat, put on the dry,
   And gae to bed, my Dearie.

I will wash my Ploughman's hose,
   And I will dress his o'erlay;        *cravat*
I will mak my Ploughman's bed,
   And cheer him late and early.

I hae been east, I hae been west,
   I hae been at Saint Johnston,       *Perth*
The boniest sight that e'er I saw
   Was th' Ploughman laddie dancin.

Snaw-white stockins on his legs,
   And siller buckles glancin;
A gude blue bonnet on his head,
   And O but he was handsome!

Commend me to the Barn yard,
   And the Corn-mou, man;         *stack of corn*
I never gat my Coggie fou        *corn measure (slang:*
   Till I met wi the Ploughman.         *womb)*

# HEY TUTI TATEY

Composed from some traditional fragments, set to an old air.

### CHORUS

*Hey tuti tatey, How tuti taiti,*
*Hey tuti taiti, wha's fou now.*          drunk

Landlady count the lawin,       reckoning
The day is near the dawin,      dawning
Ye're a' blind drunk, boys,
   And I'm jolly fou.

Cog an ye were ay fou,         cup, full
Cog an ye were ay fou,
I wad sit and sing to you,
   If ye were ay fou.

Weel may we a' be,
Ill may we never see!
God bless the king
   And the Companie!

# RAVING WINDS AROUND HER BLOWING
### TUNE: M'Grigor of Roro's Lament

'I composed these verses', says Burns, 'on Miss Isabella McLeod of Raza, alluding to her feelings on the death of her sister, and the still more melancholy death of her sister's husband, the late Earl of Loudon, who shot himself out of sheer heart-break at some mortifications he suffered, owing to the deranged state of his finances.' The sister was Miss Flora McLeod of Raasay.

Raving winds around her blowing,
Yellow leaves the woodlands strowing,
By a river hoarsely roaring,
Isabella stray'd deploring –

'Farewell hours that late did measure
Sunshine days of joy and pleasure!
Hail, thou gloomy night of sorrow –
Cheerless night that knows no morrow!

'O'er the Past too fondly wandering,
On the hopeless Future pondering,
Chilly Grief my life-blood freezes,
Fell Despair my fancy seizes.

'Life, thou soul of every blessing,
Load to Misery most distressing,
Gladly how would I resign thee,
And to dark Oblivion join thee!'

## MUSING ON THE ROARING OCEAN

*TUNE: Druimionn dubh*

Composed 'out of compliment to a Mrs McLachlan, whose husband is an officer in the
East Indies,' and first published in the second volume of Johnson's *Museum.*

Musing on the roaring ocean,
   Which divides my love and me,
Wearying heav'n in warm devotion
   For his weal where'er he be.

Hope and Fear's alternate billow
   Yielding late to Nature's law,
Whispering spirits round my pillow,
   Talk of him that's far awa.

Ye whom sorrow never wounded,
   Ye who never shed a tear,
Care-untroubled, joy-surrounded,
   Gaudy day to you is dear!

Gentle night, do thou befriend me!
   Downy sleep, the curtain draw!
Spirits kind, again attend me,
   Talk of him that's far awa!

## TO DAUNTON ME

Derived from an old Jacobite ballad, dating from the Rebellion of 1715, the singer being
forced to part from her Highland lad and marry an old man – a variation on the age-old
theme of the elderly lover and his young bride.

### REFRAIN

*To daunton me, to daunton me,*
*An auld man shall never daunton me!*

The blude-red rose at Yule may blaw,
The simmer lilies bloom in snaw,
The frost may freeze the deepest sea,
But an auld man shall never daunton me.

To daunton me, and me sae young,
Wi his fause heart and flatt'ring tongue
That is the thing you ne'er shall see,
For an auld man shall never daunton me.

For a' his meal and a' his maut,          malt
For a' his fresh beef and his saut,         salt
For a' his gold and white monie,         silver
An auld man shall never daunton me.

His gear may buy him kye and yowes,  wealth, cattle, sheep
His gear may buy him glens and knowes;   knolls
But me he shall not buy nor fee,     hire
For an auld man shall never daunton me.

He hirples twa-fauld as he dow,    limps, can
Wi his teethless gab and his auld beld pow, mouth, bald pate
And the rain rains down frae his red blear'd e'e –  eye
That auld man shall never daunton me!

## INTERPOLATION

*TUNE: The Banks of Spey*

Mrs McLehose sent two stanzas to Burns entitled 'Talk not of Love'. Burns replied on 4th January 1788 adding these two verses.

Your friendship much can make me blest,
 Oh, why that bliss destroy!
Why urge the only, one request
 You know I will deny!

Your thought, if love must harbour there,
 Conceal it in that thought;
Nor cause me from my bosom tear
 The very friend I sought.

## O'ER THE WATER TO CHARLIE

Based on a traditional Jacobite song.

### CHORUS

*We'll o'er the water, we'll o'er the sea,*
 *We'll o'er the water to Charlie;*
*Come weal, come woe, we'll gather and go* good fortune
 *And live or die wi Charlie.*

Come boat me o'er, come row me o'er,
 Come boat me o'er to Charlie;
I'll gie John Ross anither bawbee   halfpenny
 To boat me o'er to Charlie.

I lo'e weel my Charlie's name,
 Tho some there be abhor him:
But O, to see auld Nick gaun hame,  the Devil
 And Charlie's faes before him!    foes

I swear and vow by moon and stars,
 And sun that shines so early!
If I had twenty thousand lives,
 I'd die as aft for Charlie. –    often

# UP AND WARN A' WILLIE

A satirical ballad on the Battle of Sherriffmuir (November 1715) between the Hanoverians under Argyll and the Jacobites under the Earl of Mar. Burns extensively revised it for SMM. Burns got the song from Tom Neil of Edinburgh. The title was the cryptic slogan used by the clansmen as a call to arms. Both sides claimed victory. The Jacobites routed the Hanoverian left wing commanded by General Whetham, while Argyll drove the Jacobite left-wing back 2 miles. Argyll was nearly encircled by the Highlanders, but both sides tired and withdrew without forcing the decision. There are other stanzas and alternative endings, not by Burns, the best of which summed up the inconsequential result: 'And we ran, and they ran, and they ran, and we ran, and we ran, and they ran awa, man.'

Up and warn a' Willie,
   Warn, warn a';
To hear my cantie Highland sang,                 joyful, song
   Relate the thing I saw, Willie.

When we gaed to the braes o Mar,                went
   And to the wapon-shaw, Willie,     review of arms
Wi true design to serve the king
   And banish whigs awa, Willie.
Up and warn a', Willie,
   Warn, warn a';
For Lords and lairds came there bedeen      early
   And wow but they were braw, Willie.   handsome

But when the standard was set up
   Right fierce the wind did blaw, Willie;
The royal nit upon the tap                 nut, top
   Down to the ground did fa', Willie.
Up and warn a', Willie,
   Warn, warn a';
Then second-sighted Sandie said
   We'd do nae gude at a', Willie.

But when the army join'd at Perth,
   The bravest ere ye saw, Willie,
We didna doubt the rogues to rout,
   Restore our king and a', Willie.
Up and warn a', Willie,
   Warn, warn a';
The pipers play'd frae right to left
   O whirry whigs awa, Willie.            hurry

But when we march'd to Sherramuir     Sheriffmuir
   And there the rebels saw, Willie;
Brave Argyle attack'd our right,
   Our flank and front and a', Willie.
Up and warn a', Willie,
   Warn, warn a',
Traitor Huntly soon gave way        Earl of Huntly
   Seaforth, St. Clair and a' Willie.   Earl of Seaforth

But brave Glengary on our right,      *MacDonnell of Glengarry*
    The rebel's left did claw, Willie,
He there the greatest slaughter made
    That ever Donald saw, Willie.
Up and warn a', Willie,
    Warn, warn a',
And Whittam shat his breeks for fear    *General Whetham, breeches*
And fast did rin awa, Willie.        *run*

For he ca'd us a Highland mob
    And soon he'd slay us a', Willie;
But we chas'd him back to Stirling brig    *bridge*
    Dragoons and foot and a', Willie.
Up and warn a', Willie,
    Warn, warn a',
At length we rallied on a hill
    And briskly up did draw, Willie.

## A ROSE-BUD BY MY EARLY WALK

*TUNE: A Rose-bud*

Composed on Miss Jean Cruikshank, daughter of William Cruikshank (d. 1795), Latin master at the High School of Edinburgh. Jean was only twelve years old at the time of composition, but even at that tender age she was an accomplished musician, able to sing Burns's songs to her own accompaniment. The air was composed by David Sillar (see p. 86).

A rose-bud, by my early walk
Adown a corn-inclosèd bawk,    *footpath*
Sae gently bent its thorny stalk,
    All on a dewy morning.
Ere twice the shades o dawn are fled,
In a' its crimson glory spread,
And drooping rich the dewy head,
    It scents the early morning.

Within the bush her covert nest
A little linnet fondly prest,
The dew sat chilly on her breast,
    Sae early in the morning.
She soon shall see her tender brood,
The pride, the pleasure o the wood,
Amang the fresh green leaves bedew'd,
    Awauk the early morning.    *awake*

So thou, dear bird, young Jeany fair,
On trembling string or vocal air,
Shall sweetly pay the tender care
    That tents thy early morning!    *guards*
So thou, sweet rose-bud, young and gay,
Shall beauteous blaze upon the day,
And bless the parent's evening ray
    That watch'd thy early morning!

# REVISION FOR CLARINDA

This was Burns's revision of a poem by Mrs. Agnes McLehose entitled 'To a Blackbird singing on a Tree', composed at Morningside in 1784 and which she sent to him on 19th January 1788. He sent his revision to her accompanied by a letter two days later. It later appeared in SMM 1788 entitled 'To a Blackbird, by a Lady'.

Go on, sweet bird, and soothe my care,
Thy tuneful notes will hush Despair;
Thy plaintive warblings void of art
Thrill sweetly thro my aching heart.
Now chuse thy mate and fondly love,
And all the charming transport prove;
While I a lovelorn exile live,
Nor transport or receive or give.

For thee is laughing Nature gay;
For thee she pours the vernal day;
For me in vain is Nature drest,
While joy's a stranger to my breast!
These sweet emotions all enjoy;
Let love and song thy hours employ!
Go on, sweet bird, and soothe my care;
Thy tuneful note will hush Despair.

# AND I'LL KISS THEE YET BONIE PEGGY ALISON
## TUNE: The Braes o Balquhidder

According to Gilbert Burns the heroine of this song was the same as the person who inspired 'Mary Morison' (69), while his sister Isobel suggested Ellison Begbie, now identified as Elizabeth Gebbie (1762-1823); but both Peggy Alison and Mary Morison may merely have been fictitious names invented to fit the metre.

## CHORUS

*And I'll kiss thee yet, yet,*
*And I'll kiss thee o'er again,*
*And I'll kiss thee yet, yet,*
*My bonie Peggy Alison.*

| | |
|---|---|
| Ilk care and fear, when thou art near | each |
| I ever mair defy them, O! | more |
| Young kings upon their hansel throne | good-luck |
| Are no sae blest as I am, O! | |

When in my arms, wi a' thy charms,
I clasp my countless treasure, O!

| | |
|---|---|
| I seek nae mair o Heav'n to share | no more |
| Than sic a moment's pleasure, O! | such |

| | |
|---|---|
| And by thy een sae bonie blue | eyes |
| I swear I'm thine for ever, O! | |
| And on thy lips I seal my vow, | |
| And break it shall I never, O! | |

## RATTLIN, ROARIN WILLIE

William Dunbar (d. 1807) was a Writer to the Signet and 'colonel' of the Crochallan Fencibles, the Edinburgh drinking club with which Burns was associated and for which many of the bawdy ballads in the *Merry Muses* were produced. This song, based on the traditional Border ballad 'Rattling, Rovin Willie,' conveys something of Dunbar's rumbustious good humour. The Crochallan Fencibles, named jokingly after the militia regiments raised at the time of the American War, met in the tavern kept by Dawnie Douglas, a habitual singer of *Crodh Chailein* (Colin's Cattle).

O, rattlin, roarin Willie,       *roistering*
    O, he held to the fair,
An for to sell his fiddle
    An buy some other ware;
But parting wi his fiddle,
    The saut tear blin't his e'e –       *salt*
And rattlin, roarin Willie,
    Ye're welcome hame to me.

O Willie, come sell your fiddle,
    O, sell your fiddle sae fine!
O Willie, come sell your fiddle,
    And buy a pint o wine!
If I should sell my fiddle,
    The warld would think I was mad;
For monie a rantin day       *rollicking*
    My fiddle an I hae had.

As I cam by Crochallan,
    I cannilie keekit ben;       *cautiously peeped inside*
Rattlin, roarin Willie,
    Was sittin at yon boord-en';       *table-end*
Sitting at yon boord-en',
    And amang guid companie;
Rattlin, roarin Willie,
    You're welcome hame to me.

## CLARINDA, MISTRESS OF MY SOUL

In a letter to Agnes McLehose, Burns wrote: 'My song was a real affair. It was *un petit egaremen du coeur*...but circumstances are too romantic to be credited.' The melody to which this is sung was specially composed by Johan Georg Schetky of Darmstadt (1740-1824), who came to Edinburgh in 1772.

Clarinda, mistress of my soul,
    The measur'd time is run!
The wretch beneath the dreary pole
    So marks his latest sun.

To what dark cave of frozen night
  Shall poor Sylvander hie,
Depriv'd of thee, his life and light,
  The sun of all his joy?

We part – but, by these precious drops
  That fill thy lovely eyes,
No other light shall guide my steps
  Till thy bright beams arise!

She, the fair sun of all her sex,
  Has blest my glorious day;
And shall a glimmering planet fix
  My worship to its ray?

## THE WINTER IT IS PAST

Based on a ballad about the notorious Irish highwayman Johnson, hanged in 1750 for armed robbery at the Curragh, Kildare. Burns omitted two stanzas referring to this incident and subjected the rest to considerable variation.

The winter it is past, and the simmer comes at last,
  And the small birds sing on ev'ry tree:
The hearts of these are glad, but mine is very sad,
  For my true love is parted from me.

The rose upon the brier, by the waters running clear
  May have charms for the linnet or the bee:
Their little loves are blest, and their little hearts at rest,
  But my lover is parted from me.

## VERSES TO CLARINDA

### SENT WITH A PAIR OF WINE-GLASSES

Composed shortly before leaving Edinburgh in March 1788, these verses accompanied a present of wineglasses on 17th March.

Fair Empress of the Poet's soul
  And Queen of Poetesses,
Clarinda, take this little boon,
  This humble pair of glasses:

And fill them up with generous juice,
  As generous as your mind;
And pledge me in the generous toast,
  'The whole of human kind!'

'To those who love us!' second fill:
  But not to those whom we love,
Lest we love those who love not us!
  A third – 'To thee and me, love!'

## THE CHEVALIER'S LAMENT

*AIR: Captain O'Kean*

This lament Burns puts into the mouth of Prince Charles Edward Stuart after the battle of Culloden. A draft of the opening lines was sent to Robert Cleghorn on 31st March 1788, as 'Captain O'Kean' was a favourite tune of his. Cleghorn thought that the verses 'fit the tune to a hair.'

The small birds rejoice in the green leaves returning,
The murmuring streamlet winds clear thro the vale,
The primroses blow in the dews of the morning,
And wild scatter'd cowslips bedeck the green dale:
But what can give pleasure, or what can seem fair,
When the lingering moments are number'd by care?
No flow'rs gaily springing, nor birds sweetly singing,
Can soothe the sad bosom of joyless despair!

The deed that dar'd, could it merit their malice,
A king and a father to place on his throne?
His right are these hills, and his right are those valleys,
Where the wild beasts find shelter, tho I can find none!
But 'tis not my suff'rings thus wretched, forlorn –
My brave gallant friends, 'Tis your ruin I mourn!
Your faith prov'd so loyal in hot bloody trial,
Alas! can I make it no better return?

## EPITAPH ON ROBERT MUIR

Robert Muir (1758-88), a Kilmarnock wine merchant whom Burns first met in 1786, became a close friend. He was one of the first to be apprised of the birth of Jean Armour's first pair of twins. He subscribed for 72 copies of the Kilmarnock Edition and 40 of the first Edinburgh Edition. He died of tuberculosis on 22nd April 1788.

What man could esteem, or what woman could love,
    Was he who lies under this sod:
If such Thou refusest admission above,
    Then whom wilt Thou favour, Good God?

## EPISTLE TO HUGH PARKER

Hugh Parker, brother of Major William Parker, was a Kilmarnock banker to whom Burns wrote this verse epistle complaining of the smoke in the hut near the tower of Isle, where he lived while the farmhouse at Ellisland was being erected. Jenny Geddes was Burns's horse, named after the woman who, on 23rd August 1637, threw her foot-stool at the Bishop of Edinburgh in St. Giles Cathedral while trying to introduce *The Book of Common Prayer*.

In this strange land, this uncouth clime,
A land unknown to prose or rhyme;
Where words ne'er cros't the Muses's heckles,                    hackles
Nor limpit in poetic shackles:

A land that Prose did never view it,
Except when drunk he stacher't thro it:                     staggered
Here, ambush'd by the chimla cheek                          chimney
Hid in an atmosphere of reek,                               smoke
I hear a wheel thrum i' the neuk,                           spin, corner
I hear it – for in vain I leuk:                             look
The red peat gleams, a fiery kernel
Enhuskèd by a fog infernal.
Here, for my wonted rhyming raptures,
I sit and count my sins by chapters:
For life and spunk like ither Christians,                  spirit
I'm dwindled down to mere existence:
Wi nae converse but Gallowa' bodies,
Wi nae kend face but Jenny Geddes.                          known
Jenny, my Pegasean pride,
Dowie she saunters down Nithside,                           gloomily
And ay a westlin leuk she throws,                           westering
While tears hap o'er her auld brown nose!                   cover
Was it for this, wi cannie care,                            cautious
Thou bure the Bard through many a shire?                    bore
At howes or hillocks never stumbled,                        hollows
And late or early never grumbled?
O, had I power like inclination,
I'd heeze thee up a constellation!                          elevate
To canter with the Sagitarre,
Or loup the Ecliptic like a bar,                            leap
Or turn the Pole like any arrow;
Or, when auld Phoebus bids good-morrow,
Down the Zodiac urge the race,
And cast dirt on his godship's face:
For I could lay my bread and kail                           wager, broth
He'd ne'er cast saut upo' thy tail! –                       salt
Wi a' this care and a' this grief,
And sma', sma' prospect of relief,
And nought but peat reek i' my head,
How can I write what ye can read? –
Tarbolton, twenty-fourth o June,
Ye'll find me in a better tune;
But till we meet and weet our whistle,                      wet
Tak this excuse for nae epistle.

ROBERT BURNS

## VERSES IN FRIARS'
## CARSE HERMITAGE

Burns took up residence at Ellisland on 13th June 1788 and may have been introduced to Robert Riddell of Glenriddell (1755-94) by his landlord, Patrick Miller of Dalswinton at that time. Within two weeks he was composing these verses in the summer-house on Riddell's estate, to which he had been given a key. This poem was but the first of several inspired by the friendship between Burns and Captain Riddell.

Thou whom chance may hither lead,
Be thou clad in russet weed,
Be thou deckt in silken stole,
Grave these maxims on thy soul.
Life is but a day at most,
Sprung from night in darkness lost;
Hope not sunshine every hour,
Fear not clouds will always lour.

Happiness is but a name,
Make content and ease thy aim.
Ambition is a meteor-gleam;
Fame a restless idle dream;
Pleasures, insects on the wing
Peace, th' tend'rest flow'r of spring,
Those that sip the dew alone –
Make the butterflies thy own;
Those that would the bloom devour –
Crush the locusts, save the flower.

For the future be prepar'd:
Guard wherever thou can'st guard;
But, thy utmost duly done,
Welcome what thou can'st not shun.
Follies past, give thou to air,
Make their consequence thy care.
Keep the name of Man in mind,
And dishonour not thy kind.
Reverence with lowly heart
Him, whose wondrous work thou art;
Keep His Goodness still in view –
Thy trust, and thy example, too.

Stranger, go! Heaven be thy guide!
Quod the Beadsman on Nidside.

## WRITTEN IN FRIARS' CARSE
## HERMITAGE, ON NITHSIDE

*Later Version*

This version was composed some months later, and was sent to Mrs Dunlop on 7th December 1788. Both versions were subsequently put into the Glenriddell MS.

Thou whom chance may hither lead,
Be thou clad in russet weed,
Be thou deckt in silken stole,
Grave these counsels on thy soul.

Life is but a day at most,
Sprung from night, – in darkness lost:
Hope not sunshine ev'ry hour,
Fear not clouds will always lour.

As Youth and Love, with sprightly dance
Beneath thy morning star advance,
Pleasure with her siren air
May delude the thoughtless pair:
Let Prudence bless Enjoyment's cup,
Then raptur'd sip, and sip it up.

As thy day grows warm and high,
Life's meridian flaming nigh,
Dost thou spurn the humble vale?
Life's proud summits would'st thou scale?
Check thy climbing step, elate,
Evils lurk in felon wait:
Dangers, eagle-pinioned, bold,
Soar around each cliffy hold;
While cheerful Peace, with linnet song,
Chants the lowly dells among.

As the shades of ev'ning close,
Beck'ning thee to long repose;
As life itself becomes disease,
Seek the chimney-nook of ease:
There ruminate with sober thought,
On all thou'st seen, and heard, and wrought;
And teach the sportive younkers round,
Saws of experience, sage and sound:
Say, man's true, genuine estimate,
The grand criterion of his fate,
Is not, Art thou high or low?
Did thy fortune ebb or flow?
Did many talents gild thy span?
Or frugal Nature grudge thee one?
Tell them, and press it on their mind,
As thou thyself must shortly find,

The smile or frown of awful Heav'n,
To Virtue or to Vice is giv'n;
Say, to be just, and kind, and wise –
There solid self-enjoyment lies;
That foolish, selfish, faithless ways
Lead to be wretched, vile, and base.

Thus resign'd and quiet, creep
To the bed of lasting sleep:
Sleep, whence thou shalt ne'er awake,
Night, where dawn shall never break;
Till future life, future no more,
To light and joy the good restore,
To light and joy unknown before.
Stranger, go! Heav'n be thy guide!
Quod the Beadsman of Nithside.

## THE FÊTE CHAMPETRE

*TUNE: Killiecrankie*

William Cunnninghame (b. 1757) gave a supper and ball to celebrate his majority and inheritance of his grandfather's estates of Annbank and Enterkin. Most of the respectable families of Ayrshire were invited and the event attracted widespread attention. The dissolution of Parliament was imminent and it was suspected that Cunninghame was using the 'fête' to canvas votes. In the event, however, he stood down. The other would-be candidates were Sir John Whitefoord ('Glencaird') and James Boswell, Johnson's biographer.

O, wha will to Saint Stephen's House,      House of Commons
  To do our errands there, man?
O, wha will to Saint Stephen's House
O, th' merry lads of Ayr, man?
Or will ye send a man o law?
  Or will ye send a sodger?
Or him wha led o'er Scotland a'      James Boswell
  The meikle Ursa-Major?      Great Bear (i.e.
                                   Samuel Johnson)

Come, will ye court a noble lord,
  Or buy a score o lairds, man?
For Worth and Honour pawn their word.
  Their vote shall be Glencaird's, man.
Ane gies them coin, ane gies them wine,
  Anither gies them clatter;      talk
Annbank, wha guess'd the ladies' taste,
  He gies a Fête Champetre.

326

When Love and Beauty heard the news
   The gay green-woods amang, man,
Where, gathering flowers, and busking bowers,      dressing
   They heard the blackbird's sang, man:
A vow, they seal'd it with a kiss,
   Sir Politics to fetter:
As their alone, the patent bliss,
   To hold a Fête Champetre.

Then mounted Mirth on gleesome wing,
   O'er hill and dale she flew, man;
Ilk wimpling burn, ilk crystal sprint,      each winding
   Ilk glen and shaw she knew, man      wood
She summon'd every social sprite,
   That sports by wood or water,
On th' bonie banks of Ayr to meet,
   And keep this Fête Champetre.

Cauld Boreas, wi his boisterous crew
   Were bound to stakes like kye, man;      cattle
And Cynthia's car, o silver fu,
   Clamb up the starry sky, man:      climbed
Reflected beams dwell in the streams,
   Or down the current shatter;
The western breeze steals through the trees
   To view this Fête Champetre.

How many a robe sae gaily floats,
   What sparkling jewels glance, man,
To harmony's enchanting notes,
   As moves the mazy dance, man!
The echoing wood, the winding flood,
   Like Paradise did glitter,
When angels met at Adam's yett      gate
   To hold their Fête Champetre.

When Politics came there, to mix
   And make his ether-stane, man,      adder-
He circled round the magic ground,
   But entrance found he nane, man:
He blush'd for shame, he quat his name,      left
   Forswore it, every letter,
Wi humble prayer to join and share
   This festive Fête Champetre.

## TO ALEX. CUNNINGHAM
### ELLISLAND, NITHSDALE, JULY 27, 1788

Cunningham (d. 1812) was a law student whom Burns met in Edinburgh. 'Anna' was
Anne Stewart (see 'Anna, Thy Charms')

My godlike friend – nay, do not stare:
    You think the phrase is odd-like?
But 'God is Love,' the saints declare,
    Then surely thou art god-like!

And is thy ardour still the same?
    And kindled still in Anna?
Others may boast a partial flame,
    But thou art a volcano!

Even Wedlock asks not love beyond
    Death's tie-dissolving portal;
But thou, omnipotently fond,
    May'st promise love immortal!

Thy wounds such healing powers defy,
    Such symptoms dire attend them,
That last great antihectic try –
    Marriage perhaps may mend them.

Sweet Anna has an air – a grace,
    Divine, magnetic, touching!
She takes, she charms – but who can trace
    The process of bewitching?

## MALLY'S MEEK, MALLY'S SWEET
### TUNE: Deil flee o'er the water
This song formed part of the Law MS, sent to James Johnson from Mauchline in August
1788.

*Mally's meek, Mally's sweet,*
    *Mally's modest and discreet,*
*Mally's rare, Mally's fair*
    *Mally's ev'ry way complete.*

As I was walking up the street,
    A barefit maid I chanc'd to meet;
But O, the road was very hard
    For that fair maiden's tender feet!

It were mair meet that those fine feet
    Were weel laced up in silken shoon!
And 'twere more fit that she should sit
    Within yon chariot gilt aboon!

Her yellow hair, beyond compare,
    Comes tumbling down her swan-like neck,
And her twa eyes, like stars in skies,
    Would keep a sinking ship frae wreck!

# OF A' THE AIRTS
# THE WIND CAN BLAW

TUNE: *Miss Admiral Gordon's Strathspey*

Burns's notes in SMM say 'This air is by Marshall; the song I composed out of
compliment to Mrs. Burns. N.B. It was during the honeymoon.' William Marshall, who
wrote the music, was butler to the Duke of Gordon.

Of a' the airts the wind can blaw
   I dearly like the west,
For there the bonie lassie lives,
   The lassie I lo'e best.
There wild woods grow, and rivers row
   And monie a hill between,
But day and night my fancy's flight
   Is ever wi my Jean.

I see her in the dewy flowers –
   I see her sweet and fair.
I hear her in the tunefu birds –
   I hear her charm the air.
There's not a bonie flower that springs
   By fountain, shaw, or green,
There's not a bonie bird that sings,
   But minds me o my Jean.

# O, WERE I ON PARNASSUS HILL

Included in the Law MS of August 1788, it too was 'made out of compliment to Mrs.
Burns (Jean Armour). Corsincon is a hill in the parish of New Cumnock which Burns
could see from Ellisland.

O, were I on Parnassus hill,
Or had o Helicon my fill,
That I might catch poetic skill
   To sing how dear I love thee!
But Nith maun by my Muse's well,
My Muse maun be thy bonie sel,
On Corsincon I'll glowr and spell,
   And write how dear I love thee.

Then come, sweet Muse, inspire my lay!
For a' the lee-lang simmer's day         live-long
I couldna sing, I couldna say,
   How much, how dear I love thee.
I see thee dancing o'er the green,
   Thy waist sae jimp, thy limbs sae clean,     tiny
Thy tempting lips, thy roguish een –
   By Heav'n and Earth I love thee!

By night, by day, a-field, at hame,
The thoughts o thee my breast inflame,
And ay I muse and sing thy name –
    I only live to love thee.
Tho I were doom'd to wander on,
Beyond the sea, beyond the sun,
Till my last weary sand was run,
    Till then – and then – I'd love thee!

## THE BANKS OF NITH

Described in the Law MS as 'Mr Burns's words', this song was composed on 20th August 1788. In a letter to Mrs. Dunlop the following day Burns wrote: 'The following is the first Compliment I have paid the Nith and was the work of an hour as I jogged up his banks yesterday morning...'

The Thames flows proudly to the sea,
    Where royal cities stately stand;
But sweeter flows the Nith to me,
    Where Cummins ance had high command.          the Red Comyn
When shall I see that honor'd land,
    That winding stream, I love so dear?
Must wayward Fortune's adverse hand
    For ever – ever keep me here?

How lovely, Nith, thy fruitful vales,
    Where bounding hawthorns gayly bloom,
And sweetly spread thy sloping dales,
    Where lambkins wanton thro the broom!
Tho wandering now must be my doom,
    Far from thy bonie banks and braes,
May there my latest hours consume,
    Amang my friends of early days!

## EPISTLE TO ROBERT GRAHAM, ESQ.,
## OF FINTRY

### REQUESTING A FAVOUR

Rough drafts of this verse-epistle were sent to Mrs. Dunlop on 2nd August and 5th September 1788; the finished poem was sent to Robert Graham on 10th September. Although Mrs. Dunlop gave it a good appraisal, it must be admitted that the flattery of a patron he scarcely knew and owed little as yet, with an equally insecure posture of independence, is absurd.

When Nature her great masterpiece design'd,
And fram'd her last, best work, the human mind,
Her eye intent on all the wondrous plan,
She form'd of various parts the various Man.

The useful many first, she calls them forth –
Plain plodding Industry and sober Worth:
Thence peasants, farmers, native sons of earth,
And merchandise' whole genus take their birth:
Each prudent cit a warm existence finds,        city-dweller
And all mechanics' many-apron'd kinds.
Some other rarer sorts are wanted yet –
The lead and buoy are needful to the net:
The caput mortuum of gross desires        dregs in a chemistry
Makes a material for mere knights and squires;   experiment
The martial phosphorus is taught to flow;
She kneads the lumpish philosophic dough,
Then marks th' unyielding mass with grave designs –
Law, physic, politics, and deep divines;
Last, she sublimes th' Aurora of the poles,
The flashing elements of female souls.

The order'd system fair before her stood;
Nature, well pleas'd, pronounc'd it very good;
Yet ere she gave creating labour o'er,
Half-jest, she tried one curious labour more.
Some spumy, fiery, *ignis fatuus* matter,    wandering fire due to
Such as the slightest breath of air might scatter; spontaneous combustion
With arch-alacrity and conscious glee      of gas from decaying
(Nature may have her whim as well as we:     vegetation
Her Hogarth-art, perhaps she meant to show it),  William Hogarth
She forms the thing and christens it – a Poet:  (1697-1764)
Creature, tho oft the prey of care and sorrow,
When blest to-day, unmindful of to-morrow;
A being form'd t' amuse his graver friends,
Admir'd and prais'd – and there the wages ends;
A mortal quite unfit for Fortune's strife,
Yet oft the sport of all the ills of life;
Prone to enjoy each pleasure riches give,
Yet haply wanting wherewithal to live;
Longing to wipe each tear, to heal each groan,
Yet frequent all unheeded in his own.
But honest Nature is not quite a Turk:
She laugh'd at first, then felt for her poor work:
Viewing the propless climber of mankind,
She cast about a standard tree to find;
In pity for his helpless woodbine state,
She clasp'd his tendrils round the truly great:
A title, and the only one I claim,
To lay strong hold for help on bounteous Graham.

Pity the hapless Muses' tuneful train!
Weak, timid landsmen on life's stormy main,
There hearts no selfish, stern, absorbent stuff,
That never gives – tho humbly takes – enough:
The little Fate allows, they share as soon,
Unlike sage, proverb'd Wisdom's hard-wrung boon.
The world were blest did bliss on them depend –
Ah, that 'the friendly e'er should want a friend!'
Let Prudence number o'er each sturdy son,
Who life and wisdom at one race begun,
Who feel by reason and who give by rule,
(Instinct's a brute, and Sentiment a fool!)
Who make poor 'will do' wait upon 'I should' –
We own they're prudent, but who owns they're good?
Ye wise ones, hence! ye hurt the social eye,
God's image rudely etch'd on base alloy!
But come ye who the godlike pleasure know,
Heaven's attribute distinguish'd – to bestow!
Whose arms of love would grasp the human race:
Come thou who giv'st with all a courtier's grace –
Friend of my life, true patron of my rhymes,
Prop of my dearest hopes for future times!
Why shrinks my soul, half blushing, half afraid,
Backward, abash'd to ask thy friendly aid?
I know my need, I know thy giving hand,
I tax thy friendship at thy kind command.
But there are such who court the tuneful Nine –       the Muses
(Heavens! should the branded character be mine!)
Whose verse in manhood's pride sublimely flows,
Yet vilest reptiles in their begging prose.

Mark, how their lofty independent spirit
Soars on the spurning wing of injur'd merit!
Seek you the proofs in private life to find?
Pity the best of words should be but wind!
So, to heaven's gates the lark's shrill song ascends,
But grovelling on the earth the carol ends.
In all the clam'rous cry of starving want,
They dun Benevolence with shameless front;
Oblige them, patronise their tinsel lays –
They persecute you all your future days!
Ere my poor soul such deep damnation stain,
My horny fist assume the plough again!

The pie-bald jacket let me patch once more!
On eighteenpence a week I've liv'd before.          an exaggeration: 18d
Tho, thanks to Heaven, I dare even that last shift,       represented half
I trust, meantime, my boon is in thy gift:          a week's wages of an
That, plac'd by thee upon the wish'd-for height,          Ayrshire farm
With man and nature fairer in her sight,              labourer
My Muse may imp her wing for some sublimer flight.

## THE DAY RETURNS

*TUNE: Seventh of November*

Composed, wrote Burns 'out of compliment to one of the happiest and worthiest married couples in the world, Robert Riddel, Esq. of Glenriddel, and his lady. At their fire-side I have enjoyed more pleasant evenings than at all the houses of fashionable people in this country put together; and to their kindness and hospitality I am indebted for many of the happiest hours of my life.'

The day returns, my bosom burns,
    The blissful day we twa did meet:
Tho winter wild in tempest toil'd,
    Ne'er summer-sun was half sae sweet.
Than a' the pride that loads the tide,
    And crosses o'er the sultry line,
Than kingly robes, than crowns and globes,
    Heav'n gave me more – it made thee mine!

While day and night can bring delight,
    Or Nature aught of pleasure give,
While joys above my mind can move,
    For thee, and thee alone, I live!
When that grim foe of Life below
    Comes in between to make us part,
The iron hand that breaks our band,
    It breaks my bliss, it breaks my heart!

## THE BLUE-EYED LASSIE

The subject of this song was Jean Jaffray (1773-1850) daughter of the Rev. Andrew Jaffray of Ruthwell and later Lochmaben. She was about fifteen years old when this was written.

I gaed a waefu gate yestreen,          went, doleful, way
    A gate I fear I'll dearly rue:
I gat my death frae twa sweet een,             eyes
    Twa lovely een o bonie blue!
'Twas not her golden ringlets bright,
    Her lips like roses wat wi dew,
Her heaving bosom, lily-white:
    It was her een sae bonie blue.

She talk'd, she smil'd, my heart she wyl'd;  beguiled
 She charm'd my soul I wist na how;
And ay the stound, the deadly wound,  pleasurable thrill
 Cam frae her een sae bonie blue.
But 'spare to speak, and spare to speed';
 She'll aiblins listen to my vow:  perhaps
Should she refuse, I'll lay my dead
 To her twa een sae bonie blue.

## A MOTHER'S LAMENT

Sent to Mrs. Dunlop on 27th September 1788 with a letter: 'I was on horseback this morning, for between my wife and my farm is just 46 miles, by three o'clock. As I jogged on in the dark, I was taken with a Poetic-fit, as follows.' It was composed for Mrs Fergusson of Craigdarroch, whose son died on 5th November 1787, but Burns transcribed it in 1791 for the Afton Lodge collection, wherein it was annotated as commemorating Alexander Gordon Stewart of Afton, who died at Strasbourg military academy on 5th December 1787, aged sixteen.

Fate gave the word – the arrow sped,
 And pierc'd my darling's heart,
And with him all the joys are fled
 Life can to me impart.

By cruel hands the sapling drops,
 In dust dishonor'd laid:
So fell the pride of all my hopes,
 My age's future shade.

The mother linnet in the brake
 Bewails her ravish'd young;
So I, for my lost darling's sake,
 Lament the live-day long.

Death, oft I've fear'd thy fatal blow!
 Now fond I bare my breast;
O, do thou kindly lay me low
 With him I love, at rest!

## THE LAZY MIST

Burns sent a copy of this to Dr Blacklock on 15th November 1788.

The lazy mist hangs from the brow of the hill,
Concealing the course of the dark winding rill.
How languid the scenes, late so sprightly, appear;
As Autumn to Winter resigns the pale year!

The forests are leafless, the meadows are brown,
And all the gay foppery of summer is flown.
Apart let me wander, apart let me muse,
How quick Time is flying, how keen Fate pursues!

How long I have liv'd, but how much liv'd in vain!
How little of life's scanty span may remain!
What aspects old Time in his progress has worn!
What ties cruel Fate in my bosom has torn!

How foolish, or worse, till our summit is gain'd!
And downward, how weaken'd, how darken'd how pain'd!
Life is not worth having with all it can give:
For something beyond it poor man, sure, must live.

## WHISTLE O'ER THE LAVE O'T

The air was traditional, but Burns set it to entirely new words, and it is regarded as one
of his finest restorations of an old lyrical motif.

First when Maggie was my care,
Heav'n, I thought, was in her air;
Now we're married, spier nae mair,     ask no more
 But – whistle o'er the lave o't!      rest

Meg was meek, and Meg was mild,
Sweet and harmless as a child:
Wiser men than me's beguil'd –
 Whistle o'er the lave o't!

How we live, my Meg and me,
How we love, and how we gree,
I care na by how few may see –
 Whistle o'er the lave o't!

Wha I wish were maggot's meat,
Dish'd up in her winding-sheet,
I could write (but Meg may see't)
 Whistle o'er the lave o't!

## TAM GLEN

TUNE: *The Merry Beggars*

Sent to Johnson for SMM on 15th November 1788. The 'Valentine's dealing' (line 21)
refers to the old custom of drawing lots for sweethearts on St Valentine's day.

My heart is a-breaking, dear tittie,     sister
 Some counsel unto me come len',
To anger them a' is a pity,
 But what will I do wi Tam Glen?

I'm thinking, wi sic a braw fellow       fine
 In poortith I might make a fen';     poverty, shift
What care I in riches to wallow,
 If I mauna marry Tam Glen?      must not

There's Lowrie the laird o Dumeller:
 'Guid day to you' – brute! he comes ben,
He brags and he blaws o his siller,
 But when will he dance like Tam Glen?

My minnie does constantly deave me,   mother, deafen
 And bids me beware o young men.
They flatter, she says, to deceive me –
 But wha can think sae o Tam Glen?

My daddie says, gin I'll forsake him,      if
 He'd gie me guid hunder marks ten.   £55 sterling
But if it's ordain'd I maun take him,
 O, wha will I get but Tam Glen?

Yestreen at the Valentines' dealing,
 My heart to my mou gied a sten,    mouth, start
For thrice I drew ane without failing,
 And thrice it was written 'Tam Glen!'

The last Hallowe'en I was waukin
 My droukit sark-sleeve, as ye ken –  drenched, shirt-sleeve
His likeness came up the house staukin,     stalking
 And the very grey breeks o Tam Glen!     breeches

Come, counsel, dear tittie, don't tarry!
 I'll gie ye my bonie black hen,
Gif ye will advise me to marry
 The lad I lo'e dearly, Tam Glen.


## TO THE BEAUTIFUL
## MISS ELIZA J---N

### ON HER PRINCIPLES OF LIBERTY AND EQUALITY

The identity of the dedicatee is not known, though Kinsley considered Elizabeth
Johnston, a friend of Dr Blacklock, a possibility.

How, 'Liberty!' Girl, can it be by thee nam'd?
'Equality,' too! Hussey, are not asham'd?
Free and Equal indeed, while mankind thou enchainest,
And over their hearts a proud Despot so reignest.

## SKETCH FOR AN ELEGY

Regarded by most editors as 'the fragment' of an Elegy which Burns originally composed for Matthew Henderson in 1788, and revised and completed in 1790 (see next poem). Craigdarroch was Alexander Fergusson (see 'The Whistle'). 'Black James' may have been Boswell, but more probably Dr Gregory or Sibbald the Edinburgh book-seller.

Craigdarroch, fam'd for speaking art
And every virtue of the heart,
Stops short, nor can a word impart
    To end his sentence,
When mem'ry strikes him like a dart
    With auld acquaintance.

Black James – whase wit was never laith,
But, like a sword had tint the sheath,
Ay ready for the work o death –
    He turns aside,
And strains wi suffocating breath
    His grief to hide.

Even Philosophic Smellie tries                    William Smellie
To choak the stream that floods his eyes:            (1740-95)
So Moses wi a hazel-rice                         Burns's printer
    Came o'er the stane;
But, tho it cost him speaking twice,
    It gush'd amain.

Go to your marble graffs, ye great,                     graves
In a' the tinkler-trash of state!
But by thy honest turf I'll wait,
    Thou man of worth,
And weep the ae best fallow's fate
    E'er lay in earth!

## ELEGY ON CAPTAIN MATTHEW HENDERSON

### A GENTLEMAN WHO HELD THE PATENT FOR HIS HONOURS IMMEDIATELY FROM ALMIGHTY GOD

*Should the poor be flattered* – SHAKESPEARE

Captain Henderson (1737-88) was the son of David Henderson of Tannoch (Ayrshire) and Tannochside (Lanarkshire) and was connected by marriage with James Boswell. Henderson dissipated his family wealth and estates in high living in Edinburgh and died in reduced circumstances in November 1788. He and Burns were fellow-lodgers for a time in a house in St James Square, Edinburgh.

O Death! thou tyrant fell and bloody!
The meikle Devil wi a woodie                      great, noose
Haurl thee hame to his black smiddie,             Trail, smithy
    O'er hurcheon hides,                               hedgehog
And like stock-fish come o'er his studdie         beaten, anvil
    Wi thy auld sides!

He's gane, he's gane! he's frae us torn,        gone
The ae best fellow e'er was born!        one
Thee, Matthew, Nature's sel' shall mourn,
    By wood and wild,
Where, haply, Pity strays forlorn,
    Frae man exil'd.

Ye hills, near neebors o the starns,    neighbours, stars
That proudly cock your cresting cairns!    mould
Ye cliffs, the haunts of sailing yearns,    eagles
    Where Echo slumbers!
Come join ye, Nature's sturdiest bairns,    children
    My wailing numbers!

Mourn, ilka grove the cushat kens!    every, wood-pigeon
Ye hazly shaws and briery dens!    woods, hollows
Ye burnies, wimplin down your glens,    brooks, meandering
    Wi toddlin din,    pattering
Or foaming, strang, wi hasty stens,    strong, bursts
    Frae lin to lin!    cascade

Mourn, little harebells o'er the lea;
Ye stately foxgloves, fair to see;
Ye woodbines, hanging bonilie,
    In scented bowers;
Ye roses on your thorny tree,
    The first o flowers!

At dawn, when every grassy blade
Droops with a diamond at his head;
At ev'n, when beans their fragrance shed,
    I' th' rustling gale;
Ye maukins, whidden thro the glade,    hares, scudding
    Come join my wail!

Mourn, ye wee songsters o the wood;
Ye grouse that crap the heather bud;    crop
Ye curlews, calling thro a clud;    cloud
    Ye whistling plover;
And mourn, ye whirring paitrick brood;    partridge
    He's gane for ever!

Mourn, sooty coots, and speckled teals;
Ye fisher herons, watching eels;
Ye duck and drake, wi airy wheels
    Circling the lake;
Ye bitterns, till the quagmire reels,
    Rair for his sake!    Roar

Mourn, clam'ring craiks, at close o day,        corncrakes
'Mang fields o flow'ring clover gay!
And when you wing your annual way
    Frae our cauld shore,
Tell thae far warlds wha lies in clay,        those
    Wham we deplore.

Ye houlets, frae your ivy bower        owls
In some auld tree, or eldritch tower,        haunted
What time the moon, wi silent glowr        glare
    Sets up her horn,
Wail thro the dreary midnight hour,
    Till waukrife morn!        sleepless

O rivers, forests, hills, and plains!
Oft have ye heard my canty strains:        joyful
But now, what else for me remains
    But tales of woe?
And frae my een the drapping rains
    Maun ever flow.        Must

Mourn, Spring, thou darling of the year!
Ilk cowslip cup shall kep a tear:        catch
Thou, Simmer, while each corny spear
    Shoots up its head,
Thy gay, green, flowery tresses shear,
    For him that's dead!

Thou, Autumn, wi thy yellow hair,
In grief thy sallow mantle tear!
Thou, Winter, hurling thro the air
    The roaring blast,
Wide o'er the naked world declare
    The worth we've lost!

Mourn him, thou Sun, great source of light!
Mourn, Empress of the silent night!
And you, ye twinkling starnies bright,        starlets
    My Matthew mourn!
For through your orbs he's ta'en his flight,
    Ne'er to return.

O Henderson! the man! the brother!
And art thou gone, and gone for ever?
And hast thou crost that unknown river,
    Life's dreary bound?
Like thee, where shall I find another,
    The world around?

Go to your sculptur'd tombs, ye Great,
In a' the tinsel trash o state!
But by thy honest turf I'll wait,
   Thou man of worth!
And weep the ae best fellow's fate
   E'er lay in earth!

### THE EPITAPH

Stop, passenger! my story's brief,
   And truth I shall relate, man:
I tell nae common tale o grief,
   For Matthew was a great man.

If thou uncommon merit hast,
   Yet spurn'd at Fortune's door, man;
A look of pity hither cast,
   For Matthew was a poor man.

If thou a noble sodger art,
   That passest by this grave, man;
There moulders here a gallant heart,
   For Matthew was a brave man.

If thou on men, their works and ways,
   Canst throw uncommon light, man;
Here lies wha weel had won thy praise,
   For Matthew was a bright man.

If thou, at Friendship's sacred ca',
   Wad life itself resign, man;
Thy sympathetic tear maun fa',
   For Matthew was a kind man.

If thou art staunch, without a stain,
   Like the unchanging blue, man;
This was a kinsman o thy ain,
   For Matthew was a true man.

If thou hast wit, and fun, and fire,
   And ne'er guid wine did fear, man;
This was thy billie, dam, and sire,          comrade
   For Matthew was a queer man.

If onie whiggish, whingin sot,              whining
   To blame poor Matthew dare, man;
May dool and sorrow be his lot!          sadness
   For Matthew was a rare man.

## AULD LANG SYNE

'Light be the turf on the breast of the heaven-inspired Poet who composed this glorious Fragment' wrote Burns to Mrs. Dunlop on 7th December 1788. In a note to George Thomson (1793) he describes it as 'the old song of the olden times, and which has never been in print, nor even in manuscript, until I took it down from an old man's singing.' To what extent Burns reworked this traditional ballad has been the subject of speculation for many years. The tune itself has been known in print since 1700.

### CHORUS

For auld lang syne, my dear,        old long ago
 For auld lang syne,
We'll tak a cup o kindness yet,
 For auld lang syne!

Should auld acquaintance be forgot,
 And never brought to mind?
Should auld acquaintance be forgot,
 And auld lang syne?

And surely ye'll be your pint-stowp,      pay for
 And surely I'll be mine,
And we'll tak a cup o kindness yet,
 For auld lang syne!

We twa hae run about the braes,       hillsides
 And pou'd the gowans fine,      pulled, daisies
But we've wander'd monie a weary fit,
 Sin auld lang syne.

We twa hae paidl'd in the burn      waded, stream
 Frae morning sun till dine,     noon, dinner-time
But seas between us braid hae roar'd     broad
 Sin auld lang syne.

And there's a hand my trusty fiere,     companion
 And gie's a hand o thine,
And we'll tak a right guid-willie waught,   goodwill drink
 For auld lang syne.

## EPITAPH FOR JOHN HUNTER, WRITER IN AYR

John Hunter, W.S. of Doonholm was famed for his stature. Burns enclosed this epitaph in a letter to Mrs. Dunlop on 7th December 1788.

Here lies a Scots mile of a chiel,      fellow
If he's in heaven, Lord, fill him weel!

# THE SILVER TASSIE

*TUNE: The Secret Kiss*

'Two other old Stanzas which please me mightily' was Burns's description of this old Jacobite ballad, and it was originally published in SMM as an anonymous traditional song. By September 1793, however, he was claiming it as his own, adding 'the first half stanza of the song is old, the rest is mine.'

Go fetch to me a pint o wine,
    And fill it in a silver tassie;           *goblet*
That I may drink, before I go,
    A service to my bonie lassie:
The boat rocks at the Pier o Leith,
    Fu loud the wind blaws frae the Ferry,    *Queensferry*
The ship rides by the Berwick-law,
    And I maun leave my bony Mary.          *must*

The trumpets sound, the banners fly,
    The glittering spears are ranked ready,
The shouts o war are heard afar,
    The battle closes deep and bloody.
It's not the roar o sea or shore,
    Wad make me langer wish to tarry;
Nor shouts o war that's heard afar –
    It's leaving thee, my bony Mary!

# ODE, SACRED TO THE MEMORY OF MRS. OSWALD OF AUCHENCRUIVE

The daughter of a wealthy plantation owner in Jamaica, Mary Ramsay married Richard Oswald who made his money by speculation during the Seven Years' War (1756-63). In 1764 he bought the estate of Auchencruive, but after her husband's death Mrs Oswald preferred to live in London. Following her own death in 1788, her funeral cortege passed through Dumfriesshire on its way to St Quivox. Burns was lodging at Bailie Whigham's Inn, Sanquhar but was forced to give up his room to the funeral party and ride on a further twelve miles on a wild January night to the next inn, at New Cumnock. As soon as he had thawed out he sat down and composed this savage satire in the white heat of anger.

Dweller in yon dungeon dark,
Hangman of creation, mark!
Who in widow-weeds appears,
Laden with unhonoured years.
Noosing with care a bursting purse,
Baited with many a deadly curse?

## STROPHE

View the wither'd beldam's face:
Can thy keen inspection trace
Aught of Humanity's sweet, melting grace?
Note that eye, 'tis rheum o'erflows –
Pity's flood there never rose.
See those hands, ne'er stretch'd to save,
Hands that took, but never gave.
Keeper of Mammon's iron chest,
Lo, there she goes, unpitied and unblest,
She goes, but not to realms of everlasting rest!

## ANTISTROPHE

Plunderer of Armies! lift thine eyes          a reference to Richard
   (A while forbear, ye torturing fiends),     Oswald's war-profiteering
Seest thou whose step, unwilling, hither bends?
No fallen angel, hurl'd from upper skies!
   'Tis thy trusty, quondam Mate,
   Doom'd to share thy fiery fate:
   She, tardy, hell-ward plies.

## EPODE

And are they of no more avail,
Ten thousand glittering pounds a-year?
In other worlds can Mammon fail,
   Omnipotent as he is here?
O, bitter mockery of the pompous bier!
   While down the wretched vital part is driven,
The cave-lodg'd beggar, with a conscience clear,
   Expires in rags, unknown, and goes to Heaven.

# VERSICLES ON SIGN-POSTS

These random jottings were written in 2CPB at the end of December 1788. The second versicle was later incorporated in his ode to Robert Graham of Fintry in 1791, but the others were apparently never utilised.

He looked just as your sign-post Lions do,
With aspect fierce, and quite as harmless too.

So heavy, passive to the tempest's shocks,
Dull on the sign-post stands the stupid ox.

His face with smile eternal drest
Just like the landlord to his guest,
High as they hang with creaking din,
To index out the Country Inn.

A head, pure, sinless quite of brain and soul,
The very image of a barber's poll:
Just shows a human face, and wears a wig,
And looks, when well friseur'd, amazing big.       coiffeured

## PEGASUS AT WANLOCKHEAD

When Burns, mounted on his new horse Pegasus, called at the smithy in Wanlockhead one frosty day in the winter of 1788-9 the smith was too busy to frost the horse's shoes. Burns composed these lines extempore and addressed them to John Taylor, a man of standing in the community who immediately spoke to the smith and rectified the matter.

With Pegasus upon a day
  Apollo, weary flying,
(Through frosty hills the journey lay),
  On foot the way was plying.

Poor slipshod, giddy Pegasus
  Was but a sorry walker;
To Vulcan then Apollo goes
  To get a frosty caulker.

Obliging Vulcan fell to work,
  Threw by his coat and bonnet,
And did Sol's business in a crack –
  Sol paid him with a sonnet.

Ye Vulcan's sons of Wanlockhead,
  Pity my sad disaster!
My Pegasus is poorly shod –
  I'll pay you like my master.

TO JOHN TAYLOR, Ramage's, 3 o'clock

## A SONNET UPON SONNETS

This appears to have been Burns's first attempt at writing a sonnet, a fourteen-line poem popularised by Shakespeare, and appropriately takes this verse form itself as the subject.

Fourteen, a sonneteer thy praises sings;
What magic myst'ries in that number lie!
Your hen hath fourteen eggs beneath her wings
That fourteen chickens to the roost may fly.
Fourteen full pounds the jockey's stone must be;
His age fourteen – a horse's prime is past.
Fourteen long hours too oft the Bard must fast;
Fourteen bright bumpers – bliss he ne'er must see!
Before fourteen, a dozen yields the strife;
Before fourteen – e'en thirteen's strength is vain.
Fourteen good years – a woman gives us life;
Fourteen good men – we lose that life again.
What lucubrations can be more upon it?
Fourteen good measur'd verses make a sonnet.

## THE CARES O LOVE

HE

The cares o Love are sweeter far
    Than onie other pleasure;             *any*
And if sae dear its sorrows are,
    Enjoyment, what a treasure!

SHE

I fear to try, I dare na try
    A passion sae ensnaring;
For light's her heart and blythe's her sang
    That for nae man is caring.

## LOUIS, WHAT RECK I BY THEE

Probably written in December 1788, when Jean Armour joined Burns in Dumfriesshire.
Louis and Geordie were Louis XVI of France and George III respectively. There is an
unconscious element of irony about these lines penned only months before the dramatic
outbreak of the French Revolution.

Louis, what reck I by thee,
    Or Geordie on his ocean?
Dyvor beggar louns to me!          *bankrupt, chaps*
    I reign in Jeanie's bosom.

Let her crown my love her law,
    And in her breast enthrone me,
Kings and nations – swith awa!         *haste away*
Reif randies, I disown ye!        *Thieving rascals*

## NEW YEAR'S DAY

### TO MRS. DUNLOP

Written on 1st January 1789 and sent to Mrs. Dunlop who commented on this poem
on 22nd January.

    This day Time winds th' exhausted chain,
To run the twelvemonth's length again:
I see the old, bald-pated fellow,
With ardent eyes, complexion sallow,
Adjust the unimpair'd machine
To wheel the equal, dull routine.

    The absent lover, minor heir,
In vain assail him with their prayer:
Deaf as my friend, he sees them press,    *a reference to Mrs. Dunlop's*
Nor makes the hour one moment less.    *deafness*
Will you (the Major's with the hounds;    *Andrew Dunlop (d. 1804)*
The happy tenants share his rounds;

Coila's fair Rachel's care to-day,
And blooming Keith's engaged with Gray)
From housewife cares a minute borrow
(That grandchild's cap will do to-morrow),
And join with me a-moralising;
This day's propitious to be wise in!

First, what did yesternight deliver?
'Another year has gone for ever.'
And what is this day's strong suggestion?
'The passing moment's all we rest on!'
Rest on for what? what do we here?
Or why regard the passing year?
Will Time, amus'd with proverb'd lore,
Add to our date one minute more?
A few days may – a few years must –
Repose us in the silent dust:
Then, is it wise to damp our bliss?
Yes – all such reasonings are amiss!
The voice of Nature loudly cries,
And many a message from the skies,
That something in us never dies
That on this frail uncertain state
Hang matters of eternal weight;
That future life in worlds unknown
Must take its hue from this alone,
Whether as heavenly glory bright
Or dark as Misery's woeful night.

Since, then, my honor'd first of friends,
On this poor being all depends,
Let us th' important Now employ,
And live as those who never die.
Tho' you, with days and honours crown'd,
Witness that filial circle round
(A sight life's sorrows to repulse,
A sight pale Envy to convulse),
Others now claim your chief regard:
Yourself, you wait your bright reward.

Mrs Dunlop's 5th daughter
the youngest daughter.
reading Gray's Elegy

# ELEGY ON THE YEAR 1788
## January 1, 1789

Written on 1st January 1789 and sent to the *Edinburgh Courant*, it provides an interesting reflection on the previous twelve months. The Regency crisis, which arose in November 1788 as a result of the King's insanity centred on the desire of Fox to give Prince George full powers, whereas Pitt argued for a regency with severely limited powers. See also 'Ode on the Departed Regency Bill.'

| | |
|---|---|
| For lords or kings I dinna mourn; | do not |
| E'en let them die – for that they're born; | |
| But O, prodigious to reflect, | |
| A Towmont, sirs, is gane to wreck! | Twelvemonth |
| O Eighty-eight, in thy sma' space | |
| What dire events hae taken place! | |
| Of what enjoyments thou hast reft us! | |
| In what a pickle thou has left us! | |

| | |
|---|---|
| The Spanish empire's tint a head, | Charles III of Spain died |
| An my auld teethles Bawtie's dead; | 13th December 1788 |
| The tulyie's teugh 'tween Pitt and Fox, | tough struggle |
| An our guidwife's wee birdie cocks; | |
| The tane is game, a bluidie devil, | one |
| But to the hen-birds unco civil; | a reference to Fox's |
| The tither's dour – has nae sic breedin, | womanising; stubborn |
| But better stuff ne'er claw'd a midden. | |

| | |
|---|---|
| Ye ministers, come mount the poupit, | pulpit |
| An cry till ye be hoarse an roupet, | husky |
| For Eighty-eight, he wished you weel, | |
| An gaed ye a' baith gear an meal: | gave, both, wealth |
| E'en monie a plack, and monie a peck, | coin |
| Ye ken yoursels, for little feck! | know, return |

| | |
|---|---|
| Ye bonie lasses, dight your een, | wipe |
| For some o you hae tint a frien': | lost |
| In Eighty-eight, ye ken, was taen, | |
| What ye'll ne'er hae to gie again. | virginity |

| | |
|---|---|
| Observe the vera nowte an sheep, | cattle |
| How dowff an dowilie they creep! | dull, languid |
| Nay, even the yirth itsel does cry, | earth |
| For Embro wells are grutten dry! | Edinburgh, wept |

| | |
|---|---|
| O Eighty-nine, thou's but a bairn, | |
| An no owre auld, I hope, to learn! | not very old |
| Thou beardless boy, I pray tak care, | Prince George |
| Thou now has got thy Daddie's chair: | |
| Nae handcuff'd, mizzl'd, half-shackl'd Regent, | |
| But, like himsel, a full free agent, | |
| Be sure ye follow out the plan | |
| Nae waur than he did, honest man! | worse |
| As muckle better as ye can. | much |

## ROBIN SHURE IN HAIRST
### TUNE: *Rob shear'd in hairst*

The subject is not Burns himself, as the name Robin might suggest, but his friend Robert Ainslie (1766-1838), born at Berrywell, near Duns. The last line refers to the quills and pen-knife, traditional tools of the law which was Ainslie's profession.

### CHORUS

*Robin shure in hairst,*     reaped, harvest
   *I shure wi him:*
*Fient a heuk had I,*     not a sickle
   *Yet I stack by him.*     stuck

I gaed up to Dunse,     went
   To warp a wab o plaiden,     weave, web, tweed
At his daddie's yett,     gate
   Wha met me but Robin!

Was na Robin bauld,     bold
   Tho I was a cotter?
Play'd me sick a trick,
   An me the Eller's dochter!     Elder's daughter

Robin promis'd me
   A' my winter vittle:     food
Fient haet he had but three     Devil have it (i.e. nothing)
   Guse-feathers and a whittle!     goose-quills, knife

## COME REDE ME, DAME
### TUNE: *The Quaker's Wife*

The opening lines are traditional, but the rest is Burns's own work and dates from January 1789.

Come rede me, dame, come tell me dame,
   'My dame come tell me truly,
'What length of graith, when weel ca'd hame,     tool, hammered home
   'Will sair a woman duly?'
The carlin clew her wanton tail,     wench, clutched, vulva
   Her wanton tail sae ready –
I learn'd a sang in Annandale,
   Nine inch will please a lady –

But for a koontrie cunt like mine,     country
   In sooth, we're nae sae gentle;
We'll tak tway thumb-bread to the nine,     thumb-breadth
   And that's a sonsy pintle:     plump penis
O Leeze me on my Charlie lad,     Blessings
   I'll ne'er forget my Charlie!
Tway roarin handfu's and a daud,     testicles and penis
   He nidge't it in fu rarely.     press forcibly

But weary fa' the laithron doup,                    lazy buttocks
  And may it ne'er be thrivin!
It's no the length that maks me loup,                leap
  But it's the double drivin.
Come nidge me, Tam, come nudge me, Tam,
  Come nidge me o'er the nyvel!                      navel
Come lowse and lug your battering ram,              loose and pull
  And thrash him at my gyvel!                        vagina

## CALEDONIA

*TUNE: Caledonian Hunt's Delight of Mr. Gow*

Sent to Johnson for SMM on 23rd January 1789. The 'Cameleon-Savage' (1.25) has been
taken to mean the Picts in war-paint, but it is more likely that Burns meant 'Camelon',
near Falkirk, legendary captial of Pictland.

There was on a time, but old Time was then young,
  That brave Caledonia, the chief of her line,
From some of your northern deities sprung
  (Who knows not that brave Caledonia's divine?)
From Tweed to the Orcades was her domain,            Orkney
  To hunt, or to pasture, or do what she would.
Her heav'nly relations there fixed her reign,
  And pledg'd her their godheads to warrant it good.

A lambkin in peace but a lion in war,
  The pride of her kindred the heroine grew.
Her grandsire, old Odin, triumphantly swore: –       an allusion to the old
  'Whoe'er shall provoke thee, th' encounter shall rue!   belief that the
With tillage or pasture at times she would sport,    Picts came from
  To feed her fair flocks by her green rustling corn;    Scandinavia
But chiefly the woods were her fav'rite resort,
  Her darling amusement the hounds and the horn.

Long quiet she reign'd, till thitherward steers
  A flight of bold eagles from Adria's strand.        Roman legions
Repeated, successive, for many long years,
  They darken'd the air, and they plunder'd the land.
Their pounces were murder, and horror their cry;
  They'd conquer'd and ravag'd a world beside.
She took to her hills, and her arrows let fly –
  The daring invaders, they fled or they died!

The Cameleon-Savage disturb'd her repose,           painted Picts
  With tumult, disquiet, rebellion, and strife.
Provok'd beyond bearing, at last she arose,
  And robb'd him at once of his hopes and his life.
The Anglian lion, the terror of France,
  Oft, prowling, ensanguin'd the Tweed's silver flood,   Pictish victory
But, taught by the bright Caledonian lance,          over Ecgfrith at
  He learned to fear in his own native wood.        Nechtansmere, 685 AD

| | |
|---|---|
| The fell Harpy-Raven took wing from the north, | Danes |
| The scourge of the seas, and the dread of the shore; | |
| The wild Scandinavian Boar issued forth | Norwegians |
| To wanton in carnage and wallow in gore; | |
| O'er countries and kingdoms their fury prevail'd, | |
| No arts could appease them, no arms could repel; | Scots |
| But brave Caledonia in vain they assail'd, | victories in |
| As Largs well can witness, and Loncartie tell. | 1263 and 990 |

Thus bold, independent, unconquer'd, and free,
   Her bright course of glory for ever shall run,
For brave Caledonia immortal must be,
   I'll prove it from Euclid as clear as the sun: –
Rectangle-triangle, the figure we'll chuse:
   The upright is Chance, and old Time is the base,
But brave Caledonia's the hypothenuse;
   Then, ergo, she'll match them, and match them always!

## AT WHIGHAM'S INN, SANQUHAR

Edward Whigham (1750-1823) was landlord of the Queensberry Arms at Sanquhar and these lines were inscribed on a window-pane. Burns often called there while travelling between Mauchline and Ellisland.

Envy, if thy jaundiced eye
Through this window chance to spy,
To thy sorrow thou shalt find,
All that's generous, all that's kind
Friendship, virtue, every grace,
Dwelling in this happy place.

## TO WILLIAM STEWART

Written in Brownhill Inn, probably early in 1789. William Stewart was the son of the publican at Closeburn, and became factor of Closeburn Castle, not far from Ellisland. His brother-in-law, Mr John Bacon, was landlord of Brownhill Inn.

Brownhill Monday even:
Dear Sir,

| | |
|---|---|
| In honest Bacon's ingle-neuk, | fireside corner |
| Here maun I sit and think; | must |
| Sick o the warld and warld's fock, | folk |
| And sick, damn'd sick o drink! | |

| | |
|---|---|
| I see, I see there is nae help, | |
| But still down I maun sink; | |
| Till some day, laigh enough, I yelp, | low |
| 'Wae worth that cursed drink!' | |

Yestreen, alas! I was sae fu,       drunk
 I could but yisk and wink;       belch
And now, this day, sair, sair I rue,
 The weary, weary drink.

Satan, I fear thy sooty claws,
 I hate thy brunstane stink,      brimstone
And ay curse the luckless cause,
 The wicked soup o drink.

In vain I would forget my woes
 In idle rhyming clink,
For past redemption damm'd in Prose
 I can do nought but drink.

For you, my trusty, well-try'd friend,
 May Heaven still on you blink,
And may your life flow to the end,
 Sweet as a dry man's drink!

         ROBT. BURNS

## IN THE KIRK OF LAMINGTON

An example of poetic graffiti which, on this occasion roused the anger of the beadle who discovered that the window had been thus defaced, after Burns had sat nearby, possibly in late February 1789. The minister was the Rev. Thomas Mitchell (d. 1811).

As cauld a wind as ever blew,
A cauld kirk, and in't but few,
As cauld a minister's ever spak –
Ye'se a' be het or I come back!   You'll all be hot ere

## SWEET AFTON

Composed before 5th February 1789 when Burns sent these lines to Mrs Dunlop with the comment: 'There is a small river, Afton, that falls into Nith, near New Cumnock; which has some charming wild, romantic scenery on its banks...'

Flow gently, sweet Afton, among thy green braes!  slopes
Flow gently, I'll sing thee a song in thy praise!
My Mary's asleep by thy murmuring stream –
Flow gently, sweet Afton, disturb not her dream!

Thou stock dove whose echo resounds thro the glen,
Ye wild whistling blackbirds in yon thorny den,
Thou green-crested lapwing, thy screaming forbear –
I charge you, disturb not my slumbering Fair.

351

How lofty, sweet Afton, thy neighbouring hills,
Far mark'd with the courses of clear, winding rills!
There daily I wander, as noon rises high,
My flocks and my Mary's sweet cot in my eye.

How pleasant thy banks and green vallies below,
Where wild in the woodlands the primroses blow
There oft, as mild Ev'ning weeps over the lea,
The sweet-scented birk shades my Mary and me.         birch

Thy crystal stream, Afton, how lovely it glides,
And winds by the cot where my Mary resides!          cottage
How wanton thy waters her snowy feet lave,           wash
As, gathering sweet flowerets, she stems thy clear wave!

Flow gently, sweet Afton, among thy green braes!
Flow gently, sweet river, the theme of my lays!
My Mary's asleep by thy murmuring stream –
Flow gently, sweet Afton, disturb not her dream!

## ODE ON THE DEPARTED
## REGENCY BILL

King George III's first bout of insanity occurred between November 1788 and February 1789 and gave rise to a dangerous political crisis in which the supporters of William Pitt and Charles James Fox were polarized for and against restriction of the powers of regency to be given to Prince George and conducted a campaign of passionate ferocity. The King's recovery resolved the crisis and the Regency Bill was abandoned. Burns wrote these lines in March 1789.

Daughter of Chaos' doting years,
Nurse of ten thousand hopes and fears!
Whether thy airy, unsubstantial shade
(The rights of sepulture now duly paid)
Spread abroad its hideous form
On the roaring civil storm,
Deafening din and warring rage
Factions wild with factions wage;
Or under-ground, deep-sunk, profound,
Among the demons of the earth,
With groans that make the mountains shake,
Thou mourn thy ill-starr'd, blighted birth,
Or in the uncreated Void,
Where seeds of future being fight,
With lighten'd step thou wander wide
To greet thy mother – Ancient Night,
And as each jarring, monster-mass is past,
Fond recollect what once thou wast:
In manner due, beneath this sacred oak,
Hear, Spirit, hear! thy presence I invoke!

By a Monarch's heaven-struck fate;
By a disunited State;
By a generous Prince's wrongs;
By a Senate's war of tongues;
By a Premier's sullen pride
Louring on the changing tide;
By dread Thurlow's powers to awe –    Edward, Lord Thurlow
Rhetoric, blasphemy and law;    (1731-1806)
By the turbulent ocean,
At Nation's commotion;
By the harlot-caresses
Of Borough addresses;
By days few and evil;
(Thy portion, poor devil!)
By Power, Wealth, and Show,
    (The Gods by men adored),
By nameless Poverty,
    (Their Hell abhorred),
By all they hope, by all they fear,
Hear! and Appear!
Stare not on me, thou ghostly Power,
Nor, grim with chain'd defiance, lour!
No Babel-structure would I build
    Where, Order exil'd from his native sway,
Confusion might the REGENT-sceptre wield,
    While all would rule and none obey:
Go, to the world of Man relate
    The story of thy sad, eventful fate;
And call presumptuous Hope to hear
And bid him check his blind career;
And tell the sore-prest sons of Care,
    Never, never to despair!
Paint Charles's speed on wings of fire,    Fox
The object of his fond desire,
Beyond his boldest hopes, at hand.
Paint all the triumph of the Portland Band;    followers of the
(Hark! how they lift the joy-exulting voice,    Duke of Portland
And how their num'rous creditors rejoice!)
But just as hopes to warm enjoyment rise,
Cry 'Convalescence!' and the vision flies.

Then next pourtray a dark'ning twilight gloom
    Eclipsing sad a gay, rejoicing morn,
While proud Ambition to th' untimely tomb
    By gnashing, grim, despairing fiends is borne!
Paint Ruin, in the shape of high Dundas    Henry Dundas,
    Gaping with giddy terror o'er the brow:    Viscount Melville
In vain he struggles, the Fates behind him press,    (1742-1811)
    And clam'rous Hell yawns for her prey below!

How fallen That, whose pride late scaled the skies!
And This, like Lucifer, no more to rise!
Again pronouce the powerful word:
See Day, triumphant from the Night, restored!

Then know this truth, ye Sons of Men!
  (Thus ends thy moral tale):
Your darkest terrors may be vain,
  Your brightest hopes may fail!

## THE WOUNDED HARE

On 21st April 1789 Burns wrote to Mrs. Dunlop: 'Two mornings ago as I was at a very early hour, sowing in the fields, I heard a shot, and presently a poor little hare limped by me, apparently very much hurt. You will easily guess, this set my humanity in tears and my indignation in arms. The following was the result.'

Inhuman man! curse on thy barb'rous art,
  And blasted by thy murder-aiming eye;
  May never pity soothe thee with a sigh,
Nor never pleasure glad thy cruel heart!

Go live, poor wanderer of the wood and field,
  The bitter little that of life remains!
  No more the thickening brakes and verdant plains
To thee shall home, or food, or pastime yield.

Seek, mangled wretch, some place of wonted rest,
  No more of rest, but now thy dying bed!
  The sheltering rushes whistling o'er thy head,
The cold earth with thy bloody bosom prest.

Oft as by winding Nith I, musing, wait
  The sober eve, or hail the cheerful dawn,
  I'll miss thee sporting o'er the dewy lawn,
And curse the ruffian's aim, and mourn thy hapless fate.

## A NEW PSALM FOR THE CHAPEL OF KILMARNOCK

### ON THE THANKSGIVING-DAY FOR HIS MAJESTY'S RECOVERY

Thursday 23rd April (St George's Day) was declared a day of public thanksgiving for the King's recent recovery from insanity. Burns looked on 'the whole business as a solemn farce or pageant mummery.' This 'psalm', signed Duncan McLeerie, was sent to the *Edinburgh Star*.

O, sing a new song to the Lord!
  Make, all and every one,
A joyful noise, ev'n for the King
  His restoration!

The sons of Belial in the land
 Did set their heads together.
'Come, let us sweep them off,' said they,
 'Like an o'erflowing river!'

They set their heads together, I say,
 They set their heads together:
On right, on left and every hand,
 We saw none to deliver.

Thou madest strong two chosen ones,
 To quell the Wicked's pride:
That Young Man, great in Issachar,      William Pitt
 The burden-bearing tribe.       Genesis xlix. 14-15

And him, among the Princes, chief       Lord Thurlow
 In our Jerusalem,
The Judge that's mighty in Thy law,
 The man that fears Thy name.

Yet they, even they, with all their strength,
 Began to faint and fail;
Even as two howling, rav'ning wolves
 To dogs do turn their tail.

Th' ungodly o'er the just prevail'd;
 For so Thou hadst appointed,
That Thou might'st greater glory give
 Unto Thine own anointed!

And now Thou hast restored our State,
 Pity our Kirk also;
For she by tribulations
 Is now brought very low!

Consume that high-place, Patronage,
 From off Thy holy hill;
And in Thy fury burn the book
 Even of that man M'Gill!      Rev. Dr William McGill
             (1732-1807)

Now hear our prayer, accept our song,
 And fight Thy chosen's battle!
We seek but little, Lord, from Thee;
 Thou kens we get as little!

## ON JOHN McMURDO, ESQ.

Said to have been inscribed on a window-pane in John McMurdo's house at Drumlanrig.

Blest be M'Murdo to his latest day!
No envious cloud o'ercast his evening ray!
No wrinkle furrow'd by the hand of care,
Nor ever sorrow, add one silver hair!
O may no son the father's honor stain,
Nor ever daughter give the mother pain!

## TO JOHN McMURDO, ESQ.,
## OF DRUMLANRIG

### SENT WITH SOME OF THE AUTHOR'S POEMS

John McMurdo (1743-1803) was chamberlain to the Duke of Queensberry at Drumlanrig Castle. Burns lent him his collection of bawdry, later known as the *Merry Muses*.

O, could I give thee India's wealth,
    As I this trifle send!
Because thy Joy in both would be
    To share them with a friend!

But golden sands did never grace
    The Heliconian stream;
Then take what gold could never buy –
    An honest Bard's esteem.

## INSCRIBED TO THE RIGHT HON.
## C. J. FOX

Charles James Fox (1749-1806) ws the *enfant terrible* of late-18th century politics, best remembered as the champion of the American colonists and the French revolutionaries and the ardent advocate of the liberty of the people against Tory autocracy.

How Wisdom and Folly meet, mix, and unite,
How Virtue and Vice blend their black and their white,
How Genius, th' illustrious father of fiction,
Confounds rule and law, reconciles contradiction,
I sing: If these mortals, the critics should bustle,
I care not, not I: let the critics go whistle!

    But now for a Patron, whose name and whose glory,
At once may illustrate and honor my story: –

Thou first of our orators, first of our wits,
Yet whose parts and acquirements seem mere lucky hits;
With knowledge so vast, and with judgment so strong,
No man, with the half of 'em e'er could go wrong;
With passions so potent, and fancies so bright,
No man with the half of 'em e'er could go right;
A sorry, poor, misbegot son of the Muses,
For using thy name, offers fifty excuses.

Good Lord, what is Man! For as simple he looks,
Do but try to develop his hooks and his crooks!
With his depths and his shallows, his good and his evil,
All in all, he's a problem must puzzle the Devil.

On his one ruling passion Sir Pope hugely labors,       Alexander Pope
That, like th' old Hebrew walking-switch eats up its   neighbours,
Human Nature his show-box - your friend, would you know him? peep-
Pull the string, Ruling Passion - the picture will show him.    show
What pity, in rearing so beauteous a system,
One trifling particular, Truth, should have miss'd him!
For, spite of his fine theoretic positions,
Mankind is a science defies definitions.

Some sort all our qualities each to its tribe,
And think Human Nature they truly describe;
Have you found this, or t'other? There's more in the wind,
As by one drunken fellow his comrades you'll find.
But such is the flaw, of the depth of the plan
In the make of that wonderful creature called Man,
No two virtues, whatever relation they claim,
Nor even two different shades of the same,
Though like as was ever twin brother to brother,
Possessing the one shall imply you've the other.

But truce with abstraction, and truce with a Muse
Whose rhymes you'll perhaps, Sir, ne'er deign to peruse!
Will you leave your justings, your jars, and your quarrels
Contending with Billy for proud-nodding laurels?      William Pitt
My much-honor'd Patron, believe your poor Poet,
Your courage, much more than your prudence, you show it.
In vain with Squire Billy for laurels you struggle:
He'll have them by fair trade – if not, he will smuggle:
Nor cabinets even of kings would conceal 'em,
He'd up the back-stairs, and by God he would steal 'em!
Then feats like Squire Billy's you ne'er can achieve 'em;
It is not, out-do him – the task is, out-thieve him!

## TO PETER STUART

Peter Stuart (d. 1805) founded the *London Star* in 1788, the first regular evening paper in the Metropolis. Soon after he fell out with his partners and formed the *Morning Star*. Burns's connection with him dates from this period.

Dear Peter, Dear Peter,
We poor sons of metre
Are often negleckit, ye ken;                                   know
For instance, your sheet, man,
(Tho glad I'm to see't, man),
I get it no ae day in ten.                                     not one

R. B.

## ON THE DUCHESS OF GORDON'S REEL DANCING

Though written in Burns's style, this poem was certainly not by him. It was published under his name in the *London Star* on 31st March 1789, but Burns wrote to the paper on 13th April disclaiming the 'silly verses on the Duchess of Gordon.' The Duchess was one of his patrons and he was at considerable pains not to risk giving her offence. It later transpired that the verses were written by Henry Dundas – a revelation that was particularly upsetting to Burns.

She kiltit up her kirtle weel                                 petticoat
To show her bonie cutes sae sma',                             ankles
And walloped about the reel,
The lightest louper o them a'!                                dancer

While some, like slav'ring, doited stots          salivating, senile bullocks
Stoit'ring out thro the midden dub,                     Lurching, mud
Fankit their heels amang their coats                         Tangled
And gart the floor their backsides rub;                      made

Gordon, the great, the gay, the gallant,
Skip't like a maukin owre a dyke:                          hare, fence
Deil take me, since I was a callant,                        stripling
Gif e'er my een beheld the like!                             If, eyes

## DELIA

Submitted by Burns to the *London Star*, 18th May 1789: 'your insertion of the inclosed trifle will be succeeded by future communications.'

Fair the face of orient day,
Fair the tints of op'ning rose;
But fairer still my Delia dawns,
More lovely far her beauty blows.

Sweet the Lark's wild-warbled lay,
Sweet the tinkling rill to hear;
But, Delia, more delightful still,
Steal thine accents on mine ear.

The flower-enamour'd busy Bee
The rosy banquet loves to sip;
Sweet the streamlet's limpid lapse
To the sun-brown'd Arab's lip;

But, Delia, on thy balmy lips
Let me, no vagrant insect, rove!
O let me steal one liquid kiss!
For Oh! my soul is parch'd with love!

# THE KIRK'S ALARM

*TUNE: Come rouse, Brother Sportsmen*

The Rev. William McGill (1732-1807), one of the New Licht ministers in Ayr and a friend of Burns and his father, incurred the wrath of the Auld Lichts on the publication of his treatise *The Death of Jesus Christ* (1786). The General Assembly ordered an enquiry at Ayr in July 1789. McGill hastily recanted and the case was dropped after he made a grovelling apology to the Presbytery. The wretched affair provoked this satire, written in the autumn of 1789.

Orthodox! orthodox! wha believe in John Knox –
    Let me sound an alarm to your conscience:
A heretic blast has been blown i' the Wast,
    That what is not sense must be nonsense –
Orthodox! That what is not sense must be nonsense.

Doctor Mac! Doctor Mac, you should stretch on a rack,     Dr McGill
    To strike wicked Writers wi terror:
To join Faith and Sense, upon onie pretence,
    Was heretic, damnable error –
Doctor Mac! 'Twas heretic, damnable error.

Town of Ayr! Town of Ayr! it was rash, I declare,
    To meddle wi mischief a-brewing:
Provost John is still deaf to the Church's relief,     John Ballantine
    And Orator Bob is its ruin –     Robert Aiken
Town of Ayr! and Orator Bob is its ruin.

D'rymple mild! D'rynple mild! tho your heart's like a child!     William
    An your life like the new-driven snaw,     Dalrymple
Yet that winna save ye, auld Satan must have ye,
    For preaching that three's ane an twa –
D'rymple mild! For preaching that three's ane an twa.

Calvin's sons! Calvin's sons! seize your sp'ritual guns,
  Ammunition you never can need;
Your hearts are the stuff will be powther enough,
  And your skulls are storehouses o lead         *powder*
Calvin's sons! Your skulls are storehouses o lead.

Rumble John! Rumble John! mount the steps with a groan,   *Rev. John Russell*
  Cry, 'The Book is wi heresy cramm'd;'
Then lug out your ladle, deal brimstone like adle,   *pull, cow's urine*
  And roar ev'ry note of the damn'd –
Rumble John! And roar ev'ry note of the damn'd.

Simper James! Simper James, leave the fair Killie dames –  *Rev. James MacKinlay*
  There's a holier chase in your view:
I'll lay on your head, that the pack you'll soon lead,
  For puppies like you there's but few –
Simper James! For puppies like you there's but few.

Singet Sawnie! Singet Sawnie, are ye herdin the penny,  *Rev. Alexander Moodie*
  Unconscious what evils await?
Wi a jump, yell, and howl, alarm ev'ry soul,
  For the Foul Fiend is just at your gate,
Singet Sawnie! The Foul Fiend is just at your gate.   *Shrivelled*

Daddie Auld! Daddie Auld, there's a tod in the fauld,  *Rev. William Auld*
  A tod meikle waur than the clerk;   *fox, much worse*
Tho ye do little skaith, ye'll be in at the death,   *damage*
  And gif ye canna bite, ye may bark,   *if*
Daddie Auld! For gif ye canna bite, ye may bark.

Jamie Goose! Jamie Goose! ye hae made but toom roose,  *Rev. James Young*
  In hunting the wicked Lieutenant;   *empty, flattery*
But the Doctor's your mark, for the Lord's haly ark,
  He has cooper'd an ca'd a wrang pin in't,   *knocked*
Jamie Goose! He has cooper'd an ca'd a wrang pin in't.

Davie Rant! Davie Rant, wi a face like a saunt,  *Rev. David Grant*
  And a heart that wad poison a hog,
Raise an impudent roar, like a breaker lee-shore,
  Or the kirk will be tint in a bog.   *lost*
Davie Rant! Or the kirk will be tint in a bog.

Poet Willie! Poet Willie, gie the Doctor a volley,  *Rev. William Peebles*
  Wi your 'Liberty's Chain' and your wit;
O'er Pegasus' side ye ne'er laid a stride,
  Ye but smelt, man, the place where he shit,
Poet Willie! Ye but smelt, man, the place where he shit.

Andro Gowk! Andro Gowk! ye may slander the Book,  *Andrew Mitchell,*
  An the Book no the waur, let me tell ye;   *cuckoo*
Ye are rich, an look big, but lay by hat an' wig,
  An ye'll hae a calf's head o sma' value,
Andro Gowk! Ye'll hae a calf's head o sma' value.

Barr Steenie! Barr Steenie! what mean ye? what mean ye?     Rev.
    If ye meddle nae mair wi the matter,     Stephen Young
Ye may hae some pretence, to havins and sense,
    Wi people wha ken ye nae better,
Barr Steenie! Wi people wha ken ye nae better.

Irvine-side! Irvine-side, wi your turkey-cock pride     Rev. George Smith
    Of manhood but sma' is your share:
Ye've the figure, 'tis true, ev'n your faes maun allow,     foes
    An your friends daurna say ye hae mair,     dare not
Irvine-side! Your friends daurna say ye hae mair.

    John
Muirland Jock! Muirland Jock, whom the Lord gave a stock Sheppard
    Wad act up a tinkler in brass;
If ill-manners were wit, there's no mortal so fit
    To prove the poor Doctor an ass,
Muirland Jock! To prove the poor Doctor an ass.

Holy Will! Holy Will, there was wit i' your skull,     William Fisher
    When ye pilfer'd the alms o the poor;
The timmer is scant when ye're taen for a saunt,     material, taken
    Wha should swing in a rape for an hour,     rope
Holy Will! Ye should swing in a rape for an hour.

Poet Burns! Poet Burns, wi your priest-skelpin turns,     bashing
    Why desert ye your auld native shire?
Your Muse is a gipsy, yet were she e'en tipsy,
    She could ca' us nae waur than we are –     worse
Poet Burns! ye could ca' us nae waur than we are.

### PRESENTATION STANZAS TO CORRESPONDENTS

    John
Afton's Laird! Afton's Laird, when your pen can be spared,     Logan
    A copy of this I bequeath,
On the same sicker score as I mention'd before,
    To that trusty auld worthy, Clackleith –     James Johnson
Afton's Laird! To that trusty auld worthy, Clackleith.

Factor John! Factor John, whom the Lord made alone,     John McMurdo
    And ne'er made anither thy peer,     or John Kennedy
Thy poor servant, the Bard, in respectful regard,
    He presents thee this token sincere.
Factor John! He presents thee this token sincere.

## SONNET TO ROBERT GRAHAM, ESQ., OF FINTRY

### ON RECEIVING A FAVOUR, AUG. 10, 1789

The poet's repeated importuning of the Commissioner of the Board of Excise eventually paid off. Mr Graham's 'warmest exertions' obtained for Burns an appointment to the Dumfries division of the Excise. The favour referred to in the sub-title was Burns's appointment, intimated about this time, though not implemented till 7th September 1789.

I call no Goddess to inspire my strains:
A fabled Muse may suit a Bard that feigns.
Friend of my life! my ardent spirit burns,
And all the tribute of my heart returns,
For boons accorded, goodness ever new,
The gift still dearer, as the giver you.
Thou orb of day! thou other paler light!
And all ye many sparkling stars of night!
If aught that giver from my mind efface,
If I that giver's bounty e'er disgrace,
Then roll to me along your wand'ring spheres
Only to number out a villain's years!
I lay my hand upon my swelling breast,
And grateful would, but cannot, speak the rest.

## THE KEEKIN GLASS

Said to have been written on the back of a letter at Dalswinton, about 1789, on hearing that a drunken judge on the Dumfries bench had pointed to one of Patrick Miller's beautiful daughters and – his vision 'much affected' – asked 'Wha's yon howlet-faced thing in the corner?'

How daur ye ca' me 'Howlet-face'      owl-face
   Ye blear-e'ed, withered spectre?
Ye only spied the keekin glass,       mirror
   An there ye saw your picture.

## INSCRIPTION ON A GOBLET

Said by Cunningham to have been written on a goblet belonging to John Syme, on the second book of Kings, iv. 40.

There's Death in the cup, so beware!
   Nay, more – there is danger in touching;
But who can avoid the fell snare?
   The man and his wine's so bewitching!

## ON ANDREW TURNER

'A vain coxcomb of an English commercial traveller' who tried to patronise Burns over a bottle of wine in the King's Arms, Dumfries. Burns was asked by his friends, whose party had been interrupted by Turner, to give an example of his impromptu versifying. On hearing the Englishman's age and name he produced the following.

In Se'enteen Hunder'n Forty-Nine,
The Deil gat stuff to make a swine,
    An coost it in a corner;                cast
But wiliIy he chang'd his plan,
An shap'd it something like a man,
    An ca'd it Andrew Turner.

## KIRK AND STATE EXCISEMEN

Probably composed in 1789, following his appointment to the Excise, and putting the principle of taxation into proper perspective.

Ye men of wit and wealth, why all this sneering
'Gainst poor Excisemen? Give the cause a hearing.
What are your Landlord's rent-rolls? Taxing ledgers!
What Premiers? What ev'n Monarchs? Mighty Gaugers!
Nay, what are Priests (those seeming godly wise-men)?
What are they, pray, but Spiritual Excisemen!

## A GRACE BEFORE DINNER

O Thou who kindly dost provide
    For ev'ry creature's want!
We bless the God of Nature wide,
    For all Thy goodness lent.

And if it please Thee, heavenly Guide,
    May never worse be sent;
But, whether granted or denied,
    Lord, bless us with content.

## A GRACE AFTER DINNER

O Thou, in whom we live and move,
    Who made the sea and shore,
Thy goodness constantly we prove,
    And, grateful, would adore.

And, if it please Thee, Power above!
    Still grant us with such store
The friend we trust, the fair we love,
    And we desire no more.

## WILLIE BREW'D A PECK O MAUT

In the autumn of 1789 Burns and Allan Masterton (d. 1799), writing master in Edinburgh High School, visited William Nicol, then on holiday at Moffat. 'We had such a joyous evening', wrote Burns, 'that Mr. Masterton and I each in our own way should celebrate the business.' The result was this Bacchanal - words by Burns and music by Masterton. The Willie, Rob and Allan of the first verse are Nicol, Burns and Masterton respectively.

### CHORUS

| | |
|---|---|
| *We are na fou, we're nae that fou,* | drunk |
| *But just a drappie in our e'e!* | droplet |
| *The cock may craw, the day may daw,* | dawn |
| *And ay we'll taste the barley bree!* | brew |

| | |
|---|---|
| O, Willie brew'd a peck o maut, | |
| And Rob and Allan cam to see. | |
| Three blyther hearts, that lee-lang night, | live-long |
| Ye wad na found in Christendie. | |

Here are we met, three merry boys,
Three merry boys I trow are we;
And monie a night we've merry been,
And monie mae we hope to be!

| | |
|---|---|
| It is the moon, I ken her horn, | know |
| That's blinkin in the lift sae hie: | glinting, sky |
| She shines sae bright to wyle us hame, | lure |
| But, by my sooth, she'll wait a wee! | bit |

| | |
|---|---|
| Wha first shall rise to gang awa, | |
| A cuckold, coward loun is he! | fool |
| Wha first beside his chair shall fa', | |
| He is the King amang us three! | |

## THE FIVE CARLINS

*TUNE: Chevy Chase*

In the Parliamentary election of September 1789 the candidates for the Dumfriesshire burghs (Dumfries, Lochmaben, Annan, Kirkcudbright and Sanquhar) were Sir James Johnstone of Westerhall, and Captain Patrick Miller of Dalswinton (son of the poet's landlord), representing the Tory and Whig interests respectively. Though Whig by nature, Burns disliked young Miller and heartily detested the Duke of Queensberry his patron and gradually swung to the Tory side during the election campaign.

| | |
|---|---|
| There was five carlins in the South: | matrons |
| They fell upon a scheme, | |
| To send a lad to London town, | |
| To bring them tidings hame. | |

Nor only bring them tidings hame,
  But do their errands there:
And aiblins gowd and honor baith                    perhaps, gold, both
  Might be that laddie's share.

There was Maggie by the banks o Nith,                      Dumfries
  A dame wi pride eneugh;
And Marjorie o the Monie Lochs,                          Lochmaben
  A carlin auld and teugh.                                  tough

And Blinkin Bess of Annandale,                              Annan
  That dwelt near Solway-side;
And Brandy Jean, that took her gill,              Kirkcudbright
  In Galloway sae wide.

And Black Joan, frae Crichton Peel,                      Sanquhar
O gipsy kith an kin:
Five wighter carlins were na found              more powerful
The South countrie within.

To send a lad to London town,
  They met upon a day;
And monie a knight, and monie a laird,
  This errand fain wad gae.                               would go

O, monie a knight, and monie a laird,
  This errand fain wad gae;
But nae ane could their fancy please,
  O, ne'er a ane but tway!

The first ane was a belted Knight,         Sir James Johnstone
  Bred of a Border band;
And he wad gae to London Town,
  Might nae man him withstand.

And he wad do their errands weel,
  And meikle he wad say;                             much, would
And ilka ane at London court                          everyone
  Wad bid to him guid-day.

The neist cam in a Soger youth,               Captain Miller
  Wha spak wi modest grace;
And he wad gae to London Town,
  If sae their pleasure was.

He wad na hecht them courtly gifts,                      promise
  Nor meikle speech pretend;
But he wad hecht an honest heart,
  Wad ne'er desert his friend.

Now, wham to chuse, and wham refuse,
  At strife thae carlins fell;
For some had gentlefolk to please,
  And some wad please themsel.

Then out spak mim-mou'd Meg o Nith,   prim-mouthed
 And she spak up wi pride,
And she wad send the Soger lad,
 Whatever might betide.

For the auld Guidman o London court  King George III
 She didna care a pin;
But she wad send the Soger lad,
 To greet his eldest son.

Then up sprang Bess o Annandale,
 And swore a deadly aith,     oath
Says: 'I will send the belted Knight,
 Spite of you carlins baith!

'For far-off fowls hae feathers fair,
 And fools o change are fain:
But I hae tried this Border Knight,
 And I'll try him yet again.'

Then Brandy Jean spak owre her drink,
 'Ye weel ken, kimmers a',    gossips
The auld Guidman o London court,
 His back's been at the wa';

And monie a friend that kiss'd his caup  cup
 Is now a fremit wight;     hostile
But it's ne'er be sae wi Brandy Jean, –
 I'll send the Border Knight.

Says Black Joan frae Crichton Peel,
 A carlin stoor and grim: –    stern
'The auld Guidman, and the young Guidman, Prince of Wales
 For me may sink or swim!

'For fools will prate o right or wrang,
 While knaves laugh in their slieve;
But whae blaws best the horn shall win –
 I'll spier nae courtier's leave!'   ask

Then slow raise Marjorie o the Lochs,
 And wrinkled was her brow,
Her ancient weed was russet gray,
 Her auld Scots heart was true: –

'There's some great folk set light by me,
 I set as light by them;
But I will send to London town
 Wham I lo'e best at hame.'

Sae how this sturt and strife may end,  turmoil
 There's naebody can tell;
God grant the King and ilka man
 May look weel to himsel!

## ELECTION BALLAD FOR WESTERHA'

*TUNE: Up on waur them a' Willie*

Composed in late 1789 about Sir James Johnstone (1726-94) but really attacking the Duke of Queensberry. Despite (or because of) this poetic 'support', Johnstone, who had represented the Dumfriesshire burghs since 1784, lost to Captain Miller, son of Burns's landlord, Patrick Miller of Dalswinton. Johnstone sat in Parliament for Weymouth (1791-94).

### CHORUS

*Up and waur them a', Jamie,*
*Up and waur them a'!*
*The Johnstones hae the guidin o't:*
*Ye turncoat Whigs, awa!*

| | |
|---|---|
| The Laddies by the banks o Nith | |
| Wad trust his Grace wi a', Jamie; | |
| But he'll sair them, as he sair'd the King – | serve |
| Turn tail and rin awa, Jamie. | |

| | |
|---|---|
| The day he stude his country's friend, | stood |
| Or gied her faes a claw, Jamie, | foes, scratch |
| Or frae puir man a blessin wan – | won |
| That day the Duke ne'er saw, Jamie. | |

| | |
|---|---|
| But wha is he, his country's boast? | |
| Like him there is na twa, Jamie! | |
| There's no a callant tents the kye, | youth, tends, cattle |
| But kens o Westerha', Jamie. | knows |

| | |
|---|---|
| To end the wark, here's Whistlebirk – | Alex Birtwhistle, |
| Lang may his whistle blaw, Jamie! | Provost of Kirkcudbright |
| And Maxwell true, o sterling blue; | Robert Maxwell, |
| And we'll be Johnstones a', Jamie. | Provost of Lochmaben |

## TO MISS CRUIKSHANK
### A VERY YOUNG LADY

### WRITTEN ON THE BLANK LEAF OF A BOOK, PRESENTED TO HER BY THE AUTHOR

Addressed to Jean Cruikshank, daughter of William Cruikshank of the High School, Edinburgh. The melody was composed by David Sillar.

Beauteous Rosebud, young and gay,
Blooming on thy early May,
Never may'st thou, lovely flower,
Chilly shrink in sleety shower!
Never Boreas' hoary path,
Never Eurus' pois'nous breath,

Never baleful stellar lights,
Taint thee with untimely blights!
Never, never reptile thief
Riot on thy virgin leaf!
Nor even Sol too fiercely view
Thy bosom blushing still with dew!

May'st thou long, sweet crimson gem,
Richly deck thy native stem;
Till some ev'ning, sober, calm,
Dropping dews and breathing balm,
While all around the woodland rings,
And ev'ry bird thy requiem sings,
Thou, amid the dirgeful sound,
Shed thy dying honours round,
And resign to parent Earth
The loveliest form she e'er gave birth.

# THE WHISTLE – A BALLAD

The contest here described took place at Friars' Carse on 16th October 1789. The prize
was a little ebony whistle brought to Scotland by a Dane in the service of Prince George
of Denmark who married Princess (later Queen) Anne in 1683. He lost it in a drinking
contest to Sir Robert Lawrie, first baronet of Maxwelton, one of whose daughters married
Walter Riddell of Glenriddell. The whistle thus passed into the Riddell family. Sir Robert
Lawrie, 3rd baronet, attempted to emulate his grandfather in this drinking coantest
with Robert Riddell and Alexander Fergusson of Craigdarroch. The latter consumed
upwards of 5 bottles of claret before blowing the victory blast. John McMurdo was the
judge and Burns a witness and recorder of the event. The 'good Scottish King' (1.3) was
James VI, whose daughter Anne also married a Prince George of Denmark, but that took
place almost a century earlier.

I sing of a Whistle, a Whistle of worth,
I sing of a Whistle, the pride of the North,
Was brought to the court of our good Scottish King,
And long with this Whistle all Scotland shall ring.

Old Loda, still rueing the arm of Fingal,                    Odin (Scandinavia)
The God of the Bottle sends down from his hall:
'This Whistle's your challenge to Scotland get o'er,
And drink them to Hell, Sir! or ne'er see me more!'

Old poets have sung, and old chronicles tell,
What champions ventur'd, what champions fell:
The son of great Loda was conqueror still,          the Danish contestant
And blew on the Whistle their requiem shrill.

Till Robert, the lord of the Cairn and the Scaur,    Sir Robert Lawrie
Unmatch'd at the bottle, unconquer'd in war,
He drank his poor god-ship as deep as the sea;
No tide of the Baltic e'er drunker than he.

Thus Robert, victorious, the trophy has gain'd;
Which now in his house has for ages remain'd;
Till three noble chieftains, and all of his blood,
The jovial contest again have renew'd.

Three joyous good fellows, with hearts clear of flaw;
Craigdarroch, so famous for wit, worth, and law;
And trusty Glenriddel, so skill'd in old coins;
And gallant Sir Robert, deep-read in old wines.

Craigdarroch began, with a tongue smooth as oil,
Desiring Glenriddel to yield up the spoil;
Or else he would muster the heads of the clan,
And once more, in claret, try which was the man.

'By the gods of the ancients!' Glenriddel replies,
'Before I surrender so glorious a prize,
I'll conjure the ghost of the great Rorie More,    Ruairidh Mór MacLeod
And bumper his horn with him twenty times o'er.'    of MacLeod whose
    drinking horn at Dunvegan
Sir Robert, a soldier, no speech would pretend,    holds 2 litres.
But he ne'er turn'd his back on his foe, or his friend;
Said, 'Toss down the Whistle, the prize of the field,'
And, knee-deep in claret, he'd die ere he'd yield.

To the board of Glenriddel our heroes repair,
So noted for drowning of sorrow and care;
But for wine and for welcome, not more known to fame,
Than the sense, wit, and taste, of a sweet lovely dame. Elizabeth Kennedy.
    who married Riddell,
A Bard was selected to witness the fray,    1784
And tell future ages the feats of the day;
A Bard who detested all sadness and spleen,
And wish'd that Parnassus a vineyard had been.

The dinner being over, the claret they ply,
And ev'ry new cork is a new spring of joy;
In the bands of old friendship and kindred so set,
And the bands grew the tighter the more they were wet.

Gay Pleasure ran riot as bumpers ran o'er;
Bright Phoebus ne'er witness'd so joyous a core,
And vow'd that to leave them he was quite forlorn,
Till Cynthia hinted he'd seen them next morn.

Six bottles a-piece had well wore out the night,
When gallant Sir Robert, to finish the fight,
Turn'd o'er in one bumper a bottle of red,
And swore 'twas the way that their ancestor did.

Then worthy Glenriddel, so cautious and sage,
No longer the warfare ungodly would wage:
A high Ruling Elder to wallow in wine!
He left the foul business to folks less divine.

The gallant Sir Robert fought hard to the end;
But who can with Fate and quart bumpers contend?
Though Fate said, a hero should perish in light;
So uprose bright Phoebus – and down fell the knight.

Next uprose our Bard, like a prophet in drink: –
'Craigdarroch, thou'lt soar when creation shall sink!
But if thou would flourish immortal in rhyme,
Come – one bottle more – and have at the sublime!

'Thy line, that have struggled for freedom with Bruce,
Shall heroes and patriots ever produce:
So thine be the laurel, and mine be the bay;
The field thou hast won, by yon bright God of Day!'

## ANSWER TO AN INVITATION

Allegedly lines written extempore on a page torn from Burns's Excise-book, and preserved at Craigdarroch, according to Cromek, but long suspect as Burns had not yet begun his Excise career. The invitation was to the contest over the whistle, subject of the previous poem.

The King's most humble servant, I
   Can scarcely spare a minute;
But I'll be wi you by an bye,
   Or else the deil's be in it.

## EPISTLE TO DR BLACKLOCK

### ELLISLAND, 21st October, 1789

Thomas Blacklock (1721-91), blinded by smallpox as a baby, was the son of an Annan bricklayer. Largely self-educated, he studied divinity in Edinburgh and was ordained minister of Kirkcudbright in 1762. He retired to Edinburgh in 1765 and devoted the rest of his life to running a boarding school. The friend of Samuel Johnson, David Hume and Benjamin Franklin, Dr Blacklock was a man of broad culture and one of Edinburgh's arbiters of taste. A minor poet, his chief contribution to Scottish literature was to encourage Burns and deflect him from emigration. Robert Heron (1764-1807), assistant to Hugh Blair, was the drunken hack whose memoir of Burns was a subtle exercise in character assassination.

| | |
|---|---|
| Wow, but your letter made me vauntie! | proud |
| And are ye hale, and weel, and cantie? | cheerful |
| I kend it still, your wee bit jauntie | knew, little excursion |
|    Wad bring ye to: | set you up |
| Lord send you ay as weel's I want ye, | |
|    And then ye'll do! | |

The Ill-Thief blaw the Heron south,            *Devil*
And never drink be near his drouth!        *thirst*
He tauld mysel by word o mouth,         *told*
   He'd tak my letter:
I lippen'd to the chiel in trowth,      *trusted, chap*
   And bade nae better.

But aiblins, honest Master Heron        *perhaps*
Had, at the time, some dainty fair one
To ware his theologic care on,
   And holy study,
And, tired o sauls to waste his lear on,  *souls, learning*
   E'en tried the body.

But what d'ye think, my trusty fier?      *friend*
I'm turn'd a gauger – Peace be here!
Parnassian queires, I fear, I fear,      *choirs*
   Ye'll now disdain me,
And then my fifty pounds a year
   Will little gain me!

Ye glaikit, gleesome, dainty damies,     *giddy*
Wha, by Castalia's wimplin streamies,  *meandering*
Lowp, sing, and lave your pretty limbies,   *leap*
   Ye ken, ye ken,
That strang necessity supreme is
   'Mang sons o men.

I hae a wife and twa wee laddies;
They maun hae brose and brats o duddies:  *must have, scraps of*
Ye ken yoursels my heart right proud is –   *clothing*
   I need na vaunt –
But I'll sned besoms, thraw saugh woodies,   *prune brooms*
   Before they want.         *weave, willow twigs*

Lord help me thro this warld o care!
I'm weary-sick o't late and air!       *early*
Not but I hae a richer share
   Than monie ithers;
But why should ae man better fare,
   And a' men brithers?

Come, firm Resolve, take thou the van,
Thou stalk o carl-hemp in man!      *male-hemp*
And let us mind, faint heart ne'er wan   *remember*
   A lady fair:
Wha does the utmost that he can,
   Will whyles do mair.         *sometimes*

But to conclude my silly rhyme
(I'm scant o verse and scant o time):
To make a happy fireside clime
 To weans and wife,        children
That's the true pathos and sublime
 Of human life.

My compliments to sister Beckie,
And eke the same to honest Lucky:
I wat she is a daintie chuckie,       hen
 As e'er tread clay:
And gratefully, my guid auld cockie,
 I'm yours for ay.

       ROBERT BURNS

## THOU LINGERING STAR

*Tune: Mary weep no more for me*

This melancholy song was composed around the third anniversary of the death of
Margaret 'Highland Mary' Campbell. Burns sent it on 8th November 1789 to Mrs Dunlop
as 'a Song I made the other day, of which your opinion (*sic*), as I am too much interested
in the subject of it, to be a Critic.'

Thou ling'ring star, with less'ning ray,
 That lov'st to greet the early morn,
Again thou usher'st in the day
 My Mary from my soul was torn.
O Mary dear departed shade!
 Where is thy place of blissful rest?
See'st thou thy lover lowly laid?
 Hear'st thou the groans that rend his breast?

That sacred hour can I forget?
 Can I forget the hallow'd grove,
Where, by the winding Ayr, we met,
 To live one day of parting love?
Eternity cannot efface
 Those records dear of transports past,
Thy image at our last embrace –
 Ah! little thought we 'twas our last!

Ayr, gurgling, kiss'd his pebbled shore,
 O'erhung with wild-woods, thickening green;
The fragrant birch and hawthorn hoar,
 'Twin'd amorous round the raptur'd scene;
The flowers sprang wanton to be prest,
 The birds sang love on every spray,
Till too, too soon, the glowing west,
 Proclaim'd the speed of winged day.

Still o'er these scenes my mem'ry wakes,
    And fondly broods with miser-care;
Time but th' impression stronger makes,
    As streams their channels deeper wear.
O Mary! dear departed shade!
    Where is thy place of blissful rest?
See'st thou thy lover lowly laid?
    Hear'st thou the groans that rend his breast?


# ON THE LATE CAPTAIN GROSE'S PEREGRINATIONS THRO SCOTLAND

## COLLECTING THE ANTIQUITIES OF THAT KINGDOM

Captain Francis Grose (1731-91), son of a Swiss jeweller in London, was successively an Army officer, Richmond Herald in the College of Arms and paymaster of the Surrey Militia – a position that almost bankrupted him. He is best remembered for his *Antiquities of England and Wales* (1773-87) and the two-volume sequel on Scotland. Burns met him while he was gathering Scottish material in Annandale and Nithsdale, at Friars' Carse in July 1789.

| | |
|---|---|
| Hear, Land o Cakes, and brither Scots | i.e. oatcakes |
| Frae Maidenkirk to Johnie Groat's, | Wigtownshire to Caithness |
| If there's a hole in a' your coats, | |
|     I rede you tent it: | advise, look after |
| A chield's amang you takin notes, | chap |
|     And faith he'll prent it: | |

| | |
|---|---|
| If in your bounds ye chance to light | |
| Upon a fine, fat, fodgel wight, | dumpy |
| O stature short but genius bright, | |
|     That's he, mark weel: | |
| And wow! he has an unco sleight | uncommon skill |
|     O cauk and keel. | chalk, pencil |

| | |
|---|---|
| By some auld, houlet-haunted biggin, | owl, building |
| Or kirk deserted by its riggin, | roof |
| It's ten to ane ye'll find him snug in | |
|     Some eldritch part, | haunted |
| Wi deils, they say, Lord safe's! colleaguin | save us |
|     At some black art. | |

| | |
|---|---|
| Ilk ghaist that haunts auld ha' or chamer, | each, chamber |
| Ye gipsy-gang that deal in glamour, | magic |
| And you, deep-read in hell's black grammar, | |
|     Warlocks and witches: | |
| Ye'll quake at his conjuring hammer, | |
|     Ye midnight bitches! | |

373

It's tauld he was a sodger bred,
And ane wad rather fa'n than fled;    would have
But now he's quat the spurtle-blade,   given up. sword
 And dog-skin wallet,
And taen the – Antiquarian trade,
 I think they call it.

He has a fouth o auld nick-nackets:   fund. nick-nacks
Rusty airn caps and jinglin jackets     iron
Wad haud the Lothians three in tackets,  shoenails
 A towmont guid;       twelvemonth
And parritch-pats and auld saut-backets, porridge-pots, salt-boxes
 Before the Flood.

Of Eve's first fire he has a cinder;
Auld Tubalcain's fire-shool and fender;  Genesis iv. 22
That which distinguished the gender
 Of Balaam's ass;      Numbers xxii. 21
A broomstick o the witch of Endor,  I Samuel xxviii. 7
 Weel shod wi brass.

Forbye, he'll shape you aff fu gleg  Besides, smartly
The cut of Adam's philibeg;      kilt
The knife that nicket Abel's craig   slit, throat
 He'll prove you fully,
It was a faulding jocteleg,     clasp-knife
 Or lang-kail gullie.      cabbage knife

But wad ye see him in his glee –
For meikle glee and fun has he –    much
Then set him down, and twa or three
 Guid fellows wi him;
And port, O port! shine thou a wee,   little
 And then ye'll see him!

Now, by the Pow'rs o verse and prose!
Thou art a dainty chield, O Grose! –
Whae'er o thee shall ill suppose,
 They sair misca' thee;     miscall
I'd take the rascal by the nose,
 Wad say, 'Shame fa' thee.'    befall

## LINES WRITTEN UNDER THE PICTURE
## OF THE CELEBRATED MISS BURNS

Margaret Burns (d. 1792), the poet's 'poor namesake', was a celebrated Edinburgh prostitute, originally from Durham. She and a Sally Anderson kept a brothel in Rose Street which caused great annoyance to their neighbours. The ladies were prosecuted and 'banished forth of the city and liberties for ever.' Miss Burns appealed to the Court of Session which overturned the sentence on 22nd December 1789, but she died at Rosslyn soon afterwards.

> Cease ye prudes, your envious railing!
> Lovely Burns has charms – confess!
> True it is, she had one failing;
> Had ae woman ever less?

## I'LL TELL YOU A TALE OF A WIFE

*TUNE: Auld Sir Symon*

Sent to Provost Maxwell of Lochmaben on 20th December 1789, a satire on puritanical hypocrisy

> I'll tell you a tale of a Wife,
> And she was a Whig and a Saunt;               saint
> She liv'd a most sanctify'd life,
> But whyles she was fash'd wi her —            troubled
> Fal lal &c.

> Poor woman! she gaed to the Priest,
> And till him she made her complaint;
> 'There's naething that troubles my breast
> 'Sae sair as the sins o my —.

> 'Sin that I was herdin at hame,               tending cattle
> Till now I'm three score and ayont,           beyond
> 'I own it wi sin and wi shame
> 'I've led a sad life wi my —.'

> He bade her to clear up her brow,
> And no be discourag'd upon 't;
> For holy gude women enow
> Were mony times waur't wi their —.

> It's naught but Beelzebub's art,
> But that's the mair sign of a saunt,
> He kens that ye're pure at the heart,
> Sae levels his darts at your —.

> What signifies Morals and Works,
> Our works are no wordy a runt!                worthy
> It's Faith that is sound, orthodox,
> That covers the fauts o your —.               faults

Were ye o the Reprobate race
  Created to sin and be brunt,             burned
O then it would alter the case
  If ye should gae wrang wi your —.

But you that is Called and Free
  Elekit and chosen a saunt,            elected
Will 't break the Eternal Decree
  Whatever ye do wi your —?

And now with a sanctify'd kiss
  Let's kneel and renew covenant:
It 's this – and it 's this – and it 's this –
  That settles the pride o your —.

Devotion blew up to a flame;
  No words can do justice upon 't;
The honest auld woman gaed hame
  Rejoicing and clawin her —.

Then high to her memory charge;
  And may he who takes it affront,
Still ride in Love's channel at large,
  And never make port in a — !!!

These lines quoted casually in a letter to Ainslie, 29th July 1787, are apparently an alterntive to the last stanza.

Then ho, for a merry good fellow,
  And hey, for a glass of good strunt;
May never We Sons of Apollo
  E'er want a good friend and a —.

## PROLOGUE SPOKEN AT THE
## THEATRE OF DUMFRIES

### ON NEW YEAR'S DAY EVENING, 1790

George S. Sutherland, manager of the Dumfries theatre company, was the recipient of these lines on 31st December 1789, with a note: 'Jogging home yester night it occured to me that as your next night is the first night of the New Year, a few lines allusive to the Season, by way of Prologue, Interlude or what you please, might take very well...' Burns sent a copy to his brother on 11th January 1790 reporting that Sutherland had 'spouted to his Audience with great applause.'

No song nor dance I bring from yon great city
That queens it o'er our taste – the more's the pity!
Tho, by-the-bye, abroad why will you roam?
Good sense and taste are natives here at home.
But not for panegyric I appear:
I come to wish you all a good New Year!

Old Father Time deputes me here before ye,
Not for to preach, but tell his simple story.
The sage grave Ancient cough'd, and bade me say:
'You're one year older this important day,'
If wiser too – he hinted some suggestion,
But 'twould be rude, you know, to ask the question;
And with a would-be-roguish leer and wink,
He bade me on you press this one word – think!

Ye sprightly youths, quite flush with hope and spirit,
Who think to storm the world by dint of merit,
To you the dotard has a deal to say,
In his sly, dry, sententious, proverb way!
He bids you mind, amid your thoughtless rattle,
That the first blow is ever half the battle;
That, tho some by the skirt may try to snatch him,
Yet by the forelock is the hold to catch him;
That, whether doing, suffering, or forbearing,
You may do miracles by persevering.

Last, tho not least in love, ye youthful fair,
Angelic forms, high Heaven's peculiar care!
To you old Bald-pate smoothes his wrinkled brow,
And humbly begs you'll mind the important – now!
To crown your happiness he asks you leave,
And offers, bliss to give and to receive.

For our sincere, tho haply weak endeavours,
With grateful pride we own your many favours;
And howsoe'er our tongues may ill reveal it,
Believe our glowing bosoms truly feel it.

## NITHSDALE'S WELCOME HAME

William Maxwell, 5th Earl of Nithsdale was sentenced to death after the 1715 Rebellion, but escaped from the Tower of London and died in Rome in 1744. His titles and estates were forfeited, but they were restored to his son, and his grand-daughter Winifred Constable-Maxwell began rebuilding Terregles mansion in 1789. Burns met her that year and identified with her as 'Common Sufferers in a Cause where even to be unfortuante is glorious, the Cause of Heroic Loyalty.' Lady Winifred, touched by this poem, gave Burns a snuff-box in 1791.

The noble Maxwells and their powers
   Are coming o'er the border;
And they'll gae big Terreagles' towers,            build
   And set them a' in order;
And they declare Terreagles fair,
   For their abode they choose it:
There's no a heart in a' the land
   But's lighter at the news o't!

Tho stars in skies may disappear,
   And angry tempests gather,
The happy hour may soon be near
   That brings us pleasant weather;
The weary night o care and grief
   May hae a joyfu morrow;
So dawning day has brought relief —
   Fareweel our night o sorrow!


# GREEN SLEEVES

A reworking of the famous ballad of Tudor times. The air itself was still widely popular in Burns's day.

| | |
|---|---|
| Green sleeves and tartan ties | ribbons |
| Mark my true love where she lies; | |
| I'll be at her or she rise, | before |
|    My fiddle and I thegither. — | |

Be it by the chrystal burn,
Be it by the milk-white thorn,
I shall rouse her in the morn,
   My fiddle and I thegither. —


# TO ALEXANDER FINDLATER

Alexander Findlater (1754-1839) was a native of Burntisland, the son of an exciseman and himself Excise Supervisor at Dumfries (1787-97), 'a gentleman of great information and the first worth.' Although it is undated, this verse-epistle may date around February 1790.

*Ellisland Saturday morning*

| | |
|---|---|
| Dear Sir, | |
|    our Lucky humbly begs | |
| Ye'll prie her caller, new-laid eggs: | taste, fresh |
| Lord grant the Cock may keep his legs, | |
|    Aboon the Chuckies; | |
| And wi his kittle, forket clegs, | tickle, gad-flies |
|    Claw weel their dockies! | backsides |

| | |
|---|---|
| Had Fate that curst me in her ledger, | |
| A Poet poor, and poorer Gager, | Exciseman |
| Created me that feather'd Sodger, | Soldier |
|    A generous Cock, | |
| How I wad craw and strut and roger | |
|    My kecklin Flock! | cackling |

| | |
|---|---|
| Buskit wi mony a bien, braw feather, | clad, snug |
| I wad defied the warst o weather: | |
| When corn or bear I could na gather | barley |
|    To gie my burdies; | |
| I'd treated them wi caller heather, | |
|    And weel-knooz'd hurdies | well-rounded buttocks |

Nae cursed Clerical Excise
On honest Nature's laws and ties;
Free as the vernal breeze that flies
   At early day,
We'd tasted Nature's richest joys,
   But stint or stay.

| | |
|---|---|
| But as this subject's something kittle, | ticklish |
| Our wisest way 's to say but little; | |
| And while my Muse is at her mettle, | |
|    I am, most fervent, | |
| Or may I die upon a whittle! | knife |
|    Your Friend and Servant — | |
|    Robt. Burns. | |

## TO A GENTLEMAN

### WHO HAD SENT A NEWSPAPER, AND
### OFFERED TO CONTINUE IT FREE OF EXPENSE

Kinsley casts doubt on the assumption, by previous editors, that the gentleman in question was Peter Stuart, editor of the Edinburgh Star and Evening Advertiser, although there seems no reason to doubt this. Stuart wrote to Burns in May 1789 seeking a regular contribution and offering him 'a small salary quite as large as his Excise emoluments.' Burns declined to become too firmly committed to any one paper, but he agreed to send occasional poems. In return Stuart put him on the free list. This poem, written early in 1790, takes this gesture as its pretext even though Stuart's decision was taken six or seven months earlier. Burns uses it as a vehicle for reviewing recent events.

| | |
|---|---|
| Kind Sir, I've read your paper through, | |
| And faith, to me, 'twas really new! | |
| How guessed ye, Sir, what maist I wanted? | |
| This monie a day I've grain'd and gaunted, | groaned, gaped |
| To ken what French mischief was brewin; | know |
| Or what the drumlie Dutch were doin; | muddy |
| That vile doup-skelper, Emperor Joseph, | bottom-smacker |
| If Venus yet had got his nose off; | succumbed to V.D. |
| Or how the collieshangie works | war of attrition |
| Atween the Russians and the Turks; | |
| Or if the Swede, before he halt, | Gustavus III (1746-92) |
| Would play anither Charles the Twalt, | Charles XII (1697-1718) |

If Denmark, any body spak o't;
Or Poland, wha had now the tack o't;  lease of it
How cut-throat Prussian blades were hingin,  hanging
How libbet Italy was singin;  Italian castrati
If Spaniard, Portuguese, or Swiss,
Were saying or takin aught amiss;
Or how our merry lads at hame
In Britain's court kept up the game:
How royal George – the Lord leuk o'er him! –
Was managing St. Stephen's quorum;  House of Commons
If sleekit Chatham Will was livin,  William Pitt
Or glaikit Charlie got his nieve in;  Charles James Fox
How Daddie Burke the plea was cookin;  Edmund Burke
If Warren Hastings' neck was yeukin,  the long drawn-out
How cesses, stents, and fees were rax'd,  impeachment of
Or if bare arses yet were tax'd;  Hastings (1788-95)
The news o princes, dukes, and earls,
Pimps, sharpers, bawds, and opera-girls;
If that daft buckie, Geordie Wales,  the Prince of Wales
Was threshin still at hizzies' tails;  hussies'
Or if he was grown oughtlins douser,  any more sedate
And no a perfect kintra cooser:  country stallion
A' this and mair I never heard of,
And, but for you, I might despair'd of.
So, gratefu, back your news I send you,
And pray a' guid things may attend you!

ELLISLAND, *Monday Morning*, 1790


## ELEGY ON WILLIE NICOL'S MARE

Sent to William Nicol on 9th February 1790 with a covering letter: 'That d-mned mare of yours is dead. I would freely have given her price to have saved her: she has vexed me beyond description... I refused fifty-five shillings for her... I fed her up and had her in first order for Dumfries fair; when four or five days before she was seized with an unaccountable disorder in the sinews...'

Peg Nicholson was a good bay mare
    As ever trod on airn;  iron
But now she's floating down the Nith,
    And past the mouth o Cairn.  Cairn Water 4 miles
    south of Ellisland

Peg Nicholson was a good bay mare,
    An rode thro thick and thin;
But now she's floating down the Nith,
    And wanting even the skin.

Peg Nicholson was a good bay mare,
    And ance she bore a priest;
But now she's floating down the Nith,
    For Solway fish a feast.

Peg Nicholson was a good bay mare,
    An the priest he rode her sair;
And much oppress'd, and bruis'd she was,
    As priest-rid cattle are.

## I LOVE MY LOVE IN SECRET

A revision of a fragment of verse and chorus, with new lines added by Burns.

### CHORUS

*My Sandy O, my Sandy O,*
*My bonie, bonie Sandy O!*
*Tho the love that I owe*
*To thee I dare na show,*
*Yet I love my love in secret, my Sandy, O!*

My Sandy gied to me a ring            gave
Was a' beset wi diamonds fine;
But I gied him a far better thing,
I gied my heart in pledge o his ring.

My Sandy brak a piece o gowd,          gold
While down his cheeks the saut tears row'd,   salt, rolled
He took a hauf, and gied it to me,       half
And I'll keep it till the hour I die.

## SWEET TIBBIE DUNBAR

*TUNE: Johny McGill*

Another ancient fragment reworked by Burns.

O, wilt thou go wi me, sweet Tibbie Dunbar?
O, wilt thou go wi me, sweet Tibbie Dunbar?
Wilt thou ride on a horse, or be drawn in a car,
Or walk by my side, O sweet Tibbie Dunbar?

I care na thy daddie, his lands and his money;
I care na thy kin, sae high and sae lordly;
But sae that thou'lt hae me for better or waur,   worse
And come in thy coatie, sweet Tibbie Dunbar.

## THE TAYLOR FELL THRO THE BED

An old song to which Burns added the second and fourth stanzas to transform it and
give it new life and meaning.

The Taylor fell thro the bed, thimble an a',
The Taylor fell thro the bed, thimble an a';
The blankets were thin and the sheets they were sma',
The Taylor fell thro the bed, thimble an a'.

The sleepy bit lassie she dreaded nae ill,
The sleepy bit lassie she dreaded nae ill;
The weather was cauld and the lassie lay still,
She thought that a Taylor could do her nae ill.

Gie me the groat again, cany young man,        fourpence
Gie me the groat again, cany young man;
The day it is short and the night it is lang,
The dearest siller that ever I wan.

There's somebody weary wi lying her lane,        alone
There's somebody weary wi lying her lane,
There's some that are dowie, I trow wad be fain        sad
To see the bit Taylor come skippin again.

## AY WAUKIN, O

Listed as 'Mr. Burns's old words' in Law MS no. 20, and based on a fragment in Herd's
MSS.

### CHORUS

*Ay waukin, O,*        awake
   *Waukin still and weary:*
*Sleep I can get nane*
   *For thinking on my dearie.*

Simmer's a pleasant time:
   Flowers of every colour,
The water rins owre the heugh,        crag
   And I long for my true lover.

When I sleep I dream,
   When I wauk I'm eerie,        apprehensive
Sleep I can get nane,
   For thinkin on my dearie.

Lanely night comes on,
   A' the lave are sleepin,        rest
I think on my bonie lad,
   And I bleer my een wi greetin.        blur, crying

## BEWARE O BONIE ANN

The subject was Ann Masterton, daughter of Burns's friend and composer, Allan Masterton.

Ye gallants bright, I rede you right,          counsel
    Beware o bonie Ann!
Her comely face sae fu o grace,
    Your heart she will trepan:          ensnare
Her een sae bright, like stars by night,        eyes
    Her skin is like the swan.
Sae jimply lac'd, her genty waist,        tightly, neat
    That sweetly ye might span.

Youth, Grace, and Love attendant move,
    And Pleasure leads the van:
In a' their charms, and conquering arms,
    They wait on bonie Ann.
The captive bands may chain the hands
But Love enslaves the man:
Ye gallants braw, I rede you a',          advise
    Beware o bonie Ann!

## MY WIFE'S A WANTON, WEE THING

The first half is traditional, but Burns added the last eight lines.

My wife's a wanton, wee thing,
My wife's a wanton, wee thing,
My wife's a wanton, wee thing,
    She winna be guided by me.        will not

She play'd the loon or she was married,    fool, before
She play'd the loon or she was married,
She play'd the loon or she was married,
    She'll do it again or she die.

She sell'd her coat and she drank it,
She sell'd her coat and she drank it,
She row'd hersell in a blanket,        rolled
    She winna be guided for me.

She mind't na when I forbade her,
She mind't na when I forbade her,
I took a rung and I claw'd her,        cudgel
    And a braw gude bairn was she.        child

## LASSIE LIE NEAR ME

Probably based on a traditional ballad, although no earlier version has been traced.

CHORUS

*Near me, near me,*
*Lassie lie near me;*
*Lang hast thou lien thy lane,*       alone
*Lassie lie near me.*

Lang hae we parted been,
 Lassie my dearie;
Now we are met again,
 Lassie lie near me.

A' that I hae endur'd,
 Lassie, my dearie,
Here in thy arms is cur'd,
 Lassie lie near me.

## THE GARD'NER WI HIS PAIDLE

TUNE: *The Gardener's March*

In his annotated copy of SMM Burns wrote 'the title of the song only is old, the rest is mine.'

When rosy May comes in wi flowers,
To deck her gay, green-spreading bowers,
Then busy, busy are his hours,
 The gard'ner wi his paidle.     spade

The crystal waters gently fa',
The merry birds are lovers a',
The scented breezes round him blaw –
 The gard'ner wi his paidle.

When purple morning starts the hare
To steal upon her early fare,
Then thro the dew he maun repair –    must
 The gard'ner wi his paidle.

When Day, expiring in the west,
The curtain draws o Nature's rest,
He flies to her arms, he lo'es best,
 The gard'ner wi his paidle.

## ON A BANK OF FLOWERS

*TUNE: The Bashful Lover*

This song is based on a poem of the same name by Theobald in *The Tea-Table Miscellany.*
The situation is a familiar one in Restoration and eighteenth century pastoral.

On a bank of flowers in a summer day,
    For summer lightly drest,
The youthful, blooming Nelly lay,
    With love and sleep opprest;
When Willie, wand'ring thro the wood,
Who for her favour oft had sued –
    He gaz'd, he wish'd,
    He fear'd, he blush'd,
And trembled where he stood.

Her closèd eyes, like weapons sheath'd,
    Were seal'd in soft repose;
Her lips, still as she fragrant breath'd,
    It richer dyed the rose;
The springing lilies, sweetly prest,
Wild-wanton kiss'd her rival breast:
    He gaz'd, he wish'd,
    He fear'd, he blush'd,
His bosom ill at rest.

Her robes, light-waving in the breeze,
    Her tender limbs embrace;
Her lovely form, her native ease,
    All harmony and grace.
Tumultuous tides his pulses roll,
A faltering, ardent kiss he stole;
    He gaz'd, he wish'd,
    He fear'd, he blush'd,
And sigh'd his very soul.

As flies the partridge from the brake
    On fear-inspired wings,
So Nelly starting, half-awake,
    Away affrighted springs.
But Willie follow'd – as he should,
He overtook her in the wood;
    He vow'd, he pray'd,
    He found the maid
Forgiving all, and good.

13

## MY LOVE, SHE'S BUT A LASSIE YET

*TUNE: Miss Farquharson's Reel*

Burns took the title from a snatch of old song and added the rest from his own composition.

My love, she's but a lassie yet,
My love, she's but a lassie yet,
We'll let her stand a year or twa,
　She'll no be half sae saucy yet!
I rue the day I sought her, O!
I rue the day I sought her, O!
Wha gets her need na say he's woo'd,
　But he may say he has bought her, O.

Come draw a drap o the best o't yet,　　　　　　　　　　drop
Come draw a drap o the best o't yet,
Gae seek for pleasure whare ye will,　　　　　　　　　　Go
　But here I never miss'd it yet,
We're a' dry wi drinkin o't,
We're a' dry wi drinkin o't!
The minister kiss't the fiddler's wife –
　He could na preach for thinkin o't!

## CAULD FROSTY MORNING

That Burns had a hand in this, there can be no doubt but it is well below his usual standard. Kinsley considers that Burns attempted here to produce a Scottish version of the well-known song by Colley Cibber 'Twas past twelve o'clock on a fine summer morning.'

'Twas past ane o'clock in a cauld frosty morning,
　When cankert November blaws over the plain,
I heard the kirk-bell repeat the loud warning,
　As, restless, I sought for sweet slumber in vain:
Then up I arose, the silver moon shining bright;
　Mountains and valleys appearing all hoary white;
Forth I would go, amid the pale, silent night,
　And visit the Fair One, the cause of my pain. –

Sae gently I staw to my lovely Maid's chamber,
　And rapp'd at her window, low down on my knee;
Begging that she would awauk from sweet slumber,
　Awauk from sweet slumber and pity me:
For, that a stranger to a' pleasure, peace and rest,
　Love into madness had fired my tortur'd breast;
And that I should be of a' men the maist unblest,
　Unless she would pity my sad miserie!

My True-love arose and whispered to me,
(The moon looked in, and envy'd my Love's charms;)
'An innocent Maiden, ah, would you undo me!'
I made no reply, but leapt into her arms:
Bright Phoebus peep'd over the hills and found me there;
As he has done, now, seven lang years and mair:
A faithfuller, constanter, kinder, more loving Pair,
His sweet-chearing beam nor enlightens nor warms.

## JAMIE, COME TRY ME

'Mr. Burns's old words' in Law MS, No. 34. It is thought that this song is modelled on the air of this name, published in Oswald's *Curious Scots Tunes* (1742), although no original words have been traced.

### CHORUS

*Jamie, come try me,*
*Jamie, come try me!*
*If thou would win my love,*
*Jamie, come try me!*

If thou should ask my love,
Could I deny thee?
If thou would win my love,
Jamie, come try me!

If thou should kiss me, love,
Wha could espy thee?
If thou wad be my love,
Jamie, come try me!

## THE CAPTAIN'S LADY

The old broadside *The Liggar Lady*, or some variant of it was probably the basis of this song.

### CHORUS

*O, mount and go, mount and make ye ready!*
*O, mount and go, and be the Captain's Lady!*

When the drums do beat,
And the cannons rattle,
Thou shalt sit in state,
And see thy love in battle.

When the vanquish'd foe
Sues for peace and quiet,
To the shades we'll go,
And in love enjoy it:

## JOHNIE COPE

One of several extant versions of an old Jacobite ballad. Burns reworked it for SMM. It deals with the Battle of Prestonpans (1745) when the army of Bonnie Prince Charlie defeated the Hanoverian troops of General Sir John Cope.

### CHORUS

*Hey Johnie Cope are ye wauking yet,*
*Or are ye sleeping I would wit:*
*O haste ye get up for the drums do beat,*
*O fye Cope rise in the morning.*

Sir John Cope trode the north right far,
Yet ne'er a rebel he cam naur,      near
Until he landed at Dunbar
Right early in a morning.

He wrote a challenge for Dunbar,
Come fight me Charlie an ye daur;     if you dare
If it be not by the chance of war
I'll give you a merry morning.

When Charlie look'd the letter upon
He drew his sword and scabbard from –
'So Heaven restore to me my own,
I'll meet you, Cope, in the morning.'

Cope swore with many a bloody word
That he would fight them gun and sword,
But he fled frae his nest like an ill scar'd bird,
And Johnie he took wing in the morning.

It was upon an afternoon,
Sir Johnie march'd to Preston town;
He says, my lads come lean you down,
And we'll fight the boys in the morning.

But when he saw the Highland lads
Wi tartan trews and white cokauds,
Wi swords and guns and rungs and gauds,  cudgels, goads
O Johnie he took wing in the morning.

On the morrow when he did rise,
He look'd between him and the skies;
He saw them wi their naked thighs,
Which fear'd him in the morning.

O then he flew into Dunbar,
Crying for a man of war;
He thought to have pass'd for a rustic tar,
And gotten awa in the morning.

Sir Johnie into Berwick rade,
Just as the devil had been his guide;
Gien him the warld he would na stay'd
To foughten the boys in the morning.

Says the Berwickers unto Sir John,
O what's become of all your men,
In faith, says he, I dinna ken,
I left them a' this morning.

Says Lord Mark Car, ye are na blate,                        bashful
To bring us the news o your ain defeat;
I think you deserve the back o the gate,
Get out o my sight this morning.

## O DEAR MINNY

This variant of 'O dear mother, what shall I do' in Herd's MSS was reworked by Burns.

CHORUS

*O dear minny, what shall I do?*
*O dear minny, what shall I do?*
*O dear minny, what shall I do?*
*Daft thing, doylt thing, do as I do.*

If I be black, I canna be lo'ed;
If I be fair, I canna be gude;
If I be lordly, the lads will look by me:
O dear minny, what shall I do?

## CARL, AN THE KING COME

It is uncertain how much of this song was original and how much was traditional. Several versions of it were published in the eighteenth century. 'Carl' is Bonnie Prince Charlie.

CHORUS

Carl, an the King come,                              if
Carl, an the King come,
Thou shalt dance and I will sing,
Carl, an the King come!

An somebodie were come again,
Then somebodie maun cross the main,          must
And every man shall hae his ain,               own
Carl, an the King come!

I trow we swapped for the worse:          believe
We gae the boot and better horse,
An that we'll tell them at the Cross,
Carl, an the King come!

Coggie, an the King come,                    Beaker
Coggie, an the King come,
I'll be fou, an thou'se be toom,        drunk, empty
Coggie, an the King come!

## THERE'S A YOUTH IN THIS CITY

*The first half-stanza of the song is old; the rest is mine. This air is claimed by Niel Gow who calls it his lament for his brother' wrote Burns in his Notes for SMM.*

There's a youth in this city, it were a great pity
   That he from our lasses should wander awa;
For he's bonie and braw, weel-favor'd witha',        handsome
   An his hair has a natural buckle an a'.           curl

His coat is the hue o his bonnet sae blue,
   His fecket is white as the new-driven snaw,     waistcoat
His hose they are blae, and his shoon like the slae,   blue, sloe
   And his clear siller buckles, they dazzle us a'.     silver

For beauty and fortune the laddie's been courtin:
   Weel-featur'd, weel-tocher'd, weel-mounted, an braw,   well-endowed
But chiefly the siller that gars him gang till her –    money, makes
   The penny's the jewel that beautifies a'!

There's Meg wi the mailen, that fain wad a haen him,   farm, gladly
   And Susie, wha's daddie was laird o the Ha',     would have
There's lang-tocher'd Nancy maist fetters his fancy,    almost
   But the laddie's dear sel', he loes dearest of a'.     self


## MY HEART'S IN THE HIGHLANDS

*TUNE: Failte na miosg*

The refrain is traditional, the rest Burns's own composition.

### CHORUS

*My heart's in the Highlands, my heart is not here*
*My heart's in the Highlands, a-chasing the deer,*
*A-chasing the wild deer, and following the roe –*
*My heart's in the Highlands, wherever I go!*

Farewell to the Highlands, farewell to the North,
The birthplace of valour, the country of worth!
Wherever I wander, wherever I rove,
The hills of the Highlands for ever I love.

Farewell to the mountains, high-cover'd with snow,
Farewell to the straths and green valleys below,
Farewell to the forests and wild-hanging woods,
Farewell to the torrents and loud-pouring floods!

## JOHN ANDERSON, MY JO

This is a sanitised version of an old bawdy ballad. One of the traditional variants was included in the *Merry Muses*.

| | |
|---|---|
| John Anderson my jo, John, | darling |
| When we were first acquent, | acquainted |
| Your locks were like the raven, | |
| Your bonie brow was brent; | smooth |
| But now your brow is beld, John, | bald |
| Your locks are like the snaw, | |
| But blessings on your frosty pow, | pate |
| John Anderson, my jo! | |

| | |
|---|---|
| John Anderson my jo, John, | |
| We clamb the hill thegither, | climbed, together |
| And monie a cantie day, John, | happy |
| We've had wi ane anither; | |
| Now we maun totter down, John, | must |
| And hand in hand we'll go, | |
| And sleep thegither at the foot, | |
| John Anderson my jo! | |

## AWA, WHIGS, AWA

Modelled on a fragment in the Herd MSS, this Jacobite song lampoons the Whigs, exponents of the Revolution of 1688 and ancestors of the Liberals.

### CHORUS

| | |
|---|---|
| *Awa, Whigs, awa!* | |
| *Awa, Whigs, awa!* | |
| *Ye're but a pack o traitor louns,* | rogues |
| *Ye'll do nae guid at a'.* | |

| | |
|---|---|
| Our thrissles flourish'd fresh and fair, | thistles |
| And bonie bloom'd our roses; | |
| But Whigs cam like a frost in June, | |
| An wither'd a' our posies. | |

| | |
|---|---|
| Our ancient crown's fa'n in the dust – | |
| Deil blin' them wi the stoure o't, | dust |
| An write their names in his black beuk | book |
| Wha gae the Whigs the power o't! | |

| | |
|---|---|
| Our sad decay in church and state | |
| Surpasses my descriving. | |
| The Whigs cam o'er us for a curse, | |
| An we hae done wi thriving. | |

| | |
|---|---|
| Grim Vengeance lang has taen a nap, | taken |
| But we may see him waukin – | waking |
| Gude help the day when Royal heads | God |
| Are hunted like a maukin! | hare |

## I'LL MAK YOU BE FAIN TO FOLLOW ME

Burns reworked the first twelve lines of an old ballad and completed them with four of his own.

As late by a sodger I chanced to pass,     soldier
I heard him a courtin a bony young lass;
My hinny, my life, my dearest, quo he,     darling
I'll mak you be fain to follow me.
Gin I should follow you, a poor sodger lad,
Ilk ane o my cummers wad think I was mad;    wenches
For battles I never shall lang to see,
I'll never be fain to follow thee.

To follow me, I think ye may be glad,
A part o my supper, a part o my bed,
A part o my bed, wherever it be,
I'll mak you be fain to follow me.
Come try my knapsack on your back,
Alang the king's high-gate we'll pack;
Between Saint Johnston and bony Dundee,    Perth
I'll mak you be fain to follow me.


## KISSIN MY KATIE

*TUNE: The Bob o Dumblane*

Although clearly based on an old song, no traditional version appears to have been preserved.

O, merry hae I been teethin a heckle    heckling-comb
 An merry hae I been shapin a spoon! moulding a horn spoon
O, merry hae I been cloutin a kettle,    patching
 An kissin my Katie when a' was done!
O, a' the lang day I ca' at my hammer,    knock
 An a' the lang day I whistle and sing!
O, a' the lang night I cuddle my kimmer,    mistress
 An a' the lang night as happy's a king!

Bitter in dool, I lickit my winnins    sadness, earnings
 O marrying Bess, to gie her a slave:
Blest be the hour she cool'd in her linens,    shroud
 And blythe be the bird that sings on her grave!
Come to my arms, my Katie, my Katie,
 An come to my arms, and kiss me again!
Drucken or sober, here's to thee, Katie,    Drunken
 An blest be the day I did it again!

## THE WHITE COCKADE

Burns transformed an old song into a specifically Jacobite ballad. The white cockade was the badge of the Jacobite Army.

### CHORUS

*O he's a ranting, roving lad,*
*He is a brisk an a bonny lad,*
*Betide what may, I will be wed,*
*And follow the boy wi the White Cockade.*

My love was born in Aberdeen,
The boniest lad that e'er was seen,
But now he makes our hearts fu sad,
He takes the field wi his White Cockade.

I'll sell my rock, my reel, my tow,      distaff, flax fibre
My gude gray mare and hawkit cow;                spotted
To buy mysel a tartan plaid,
To follow the boy wi the White Cockade.

## EPPIE ADAIR

*TUNE: My Eppie*

Based on a traditional chorus, as the title of the tune implies.

### CHORUS

*An O my Eppie, my jewel, my Eppie!*
*Wha wadna be happy wi Eppie Adair?*

By love and by beauty,
By law and by duty,
I swear to be true to
My Eppie Adair!

A' pleasure exile me,
Dishonour defile me,
If e'er I beguile thee,
My Eppie Adair!

# THE BATTLE OF SHERRAMUIR

*TUNE: The Cameron Rant*

The battle of Sheriffmuir took place on 13th November 1715 between the Jacobites, under the Earl of Mar, and the Hanoverian troops led by the Duke of Argyll. Though the battle was indecisive it brought the rebellion to an end. This song was based on Barclay's 'Dialogue between Will Lick-Ladle and Tom Clean-Cogue, twa shepherds wha were feeding their Flocks on the Ochil Hills on the day the Battle of Sheriff-Muir was fought.'

'O, cam ye here the fight to shun,
    Or herd the sheep wi me, man?
Or were ye at the Sherra-moor,
    Or did the battle see, man?'
'I saw the battle, sair and teugh,            *sore, tough*
And reekin-red ran monie a sheugh;     *bloody, ditch*
My heart, for fear, gae sough for sough,    *gave sigh*
To hear the thuds, and see the cluds      *clouds*
O clans frae woods, in tartan duds,      *clothing*
    Wha glaum'd at kingdoms three, man.   *grasped*
        La, la, la, la, etc.

'The red-coat lads wi black cockauds,   *the Hanoverian badge*
    To meet them were na slaw, man;     *not slow*
They rush'd and push'd, and bluid outgush'd,
    And monie a bouk did fa', man!       *trunk*
The great Argyle led on his files,
I wat they glanc'd for twenty miles;     *wot, shone*
They hough'd the clans like nine-pin kyles,  *mowed, skittles*
They hack'd an hash'd, while braid-swords clash'd,
And thro they dash'd, and hew'd and smash'd,
    Till fey men died awa, man.       *ill-fated*
        La, la, la, la, etc.

'But had ye seen the philibegs,         *kilts*
    And skyrin tartan trews, man;   *flaring, trousers*
When in the teeth they daur'd our Whigs,
    And Covenant trueblues, man!
In lines extended lang and large,
When baig'nets o'erpower'd the targe,  *bayonets, shield*
And thousands hasten'd to the charge,
Wi Highland wrath they frae the sheath
Drew blades o death, till, out o breath
    They fled like frighted dows, man!'   *pigeons*
        La, la, la, la, etc.

'O, how Deil, Tam, can that be true?
    The chase gaed frae the north, man!   *went*
I saw mysel, they did pursue
    The horseman back to Forth, man:
And at Dunblane, in my ain sight,

They took the brig wi a' their might,
And straught to Stirling wing'd their flight;
But, cursed lot! the gates were shut,
And monie a huntit poor red-coat,
　　For fear amaist did swarf, man!'　　　　　　swoon
　　　　La, la, la, la, etc.

My sister Kate came up the gate　　　　　　　　road
　　Wi crowdie unto me, man:　　　　　　　　　gruel
She swoor she saw some rebels run
　　To Perth and to Dundee, man!
Their left-hand general had nae skill;
The Angus lads had nae good will
That day their neebors' bluid to spill;
For fear, by foes, that they should lose
Their cogs o brose; they scar'd at blows,
　　And hameward fast did flee, man.
　　　　La, la, la, la, etc.

'They've lost some gallant gentlemen,
　　Amang the Highland clans, man!
I fear my Lord Panmure is slain,
　　Or in his en'mies' hands, man.
Now wad ye sing this double flight,
Some fell for wrang, and some for right,
But monie bade the world guid-night;
Say, pell and mell, wi muskets' knell
How Tories fell, and Whigs to Hell
　　Flew off in frighted bands, man!'
　　　　La, la, la, la, etc.

## SANDY AND JOCKIE

*TUNE: Jenny's Lamentation*

The opening couplet is traditional, the latter being Burns's contribution.

Twa bonie lads were Sandy and Jockie;
Jockie was lo'ed but Sandy unlucky;
Jockie was laird baith of hills and of valleys,
But Sandy was nought but the king o gude fellows.

Jockie lo'ed Madgie, for Madgie had money,
And Sandy lo'ed Mary, for Mary was bony:
Ane wedded for love, ane wedded for treasure,
So Jockie had siller, and Sandy had pleasure.

## YOUNG JOCKIE WAS THE BLYTHEST LAD

Probably all of this song but the title and the opening lines are Burns's own composition. Another version, entitled 'Willie was a wanton Wag' by William Hamilton was published in *The Tea-Table Miscellany*.

| | |
|---|---|
| Young Jockie was the blythest lad, | |
| In a' our town or here awa: | round about |
| Fu blythe he whistled at the gaud | goad |
| Fu lightly danc'd he in the ha'. | |
| | |
| He roos'd my een sae bonie blue, | praised, eyes |
| He roos'd my waist sae genty sma'; | trimly |
| An ay my heart cam to my mou, | mouth |
| When ne'er a body heard or saw. | |
| | |
| My Jockie toils upon the plain, | |
| Thro wind and weet, thro frost and snaw; | |
| And o'er the lea I leuk fu fain, | look, longingly |
| When Jockie's owsen hameward ca'. | oxen, drive |
| | |
| An ay the night comes round again, | |
| When in his arms he taks me a'; | |
| An ay he vows he'll be my ain, | own |
| As lang's he has a breath to draw. | |

## WAUKRIFE MINNIE

wakeful mother

'I pickt up this old song and tune from a country girl in Nithsdale. I never met with it elsewhere in Scotland,' wrote Burns.

| | |
|---|---|
| 'Whare are you gaun, my bonie lass? | going |
| Whare are you gaun, my hinnie?' | honey |
| She answer'd me right saucilie – | |
| 'An errand for my minnie!' | mother |
| | |
| 'O whare live ye, my bonie lass? | |
| 'O whare live ye, my hinnie? | |
| 'By yon burnside, gin ye maun ken, | brookside |
| In a wee house wi my minnie!' | if must know |
| | |
| But I foor up the glen at e'en, | went, evening |
| To see my bonie lassie; | |
| And lang before the grey morn cam, | |
| She was na hauf sae saucy. | half |
| | |
| O, weary fa' the waukrife cock, | woe befall |
| And the foumart lay his crawin! | polecat |
| He wauken'd the auld wife frae her sleep, | |
| A wee blink or the dawin. | shortly before dawn |

An angry wife I wat she raise,       wot
 And o'er the bed she brought her,
And wi a meikle hazel-rung      big, -rod
 She made her a weel-pay'd dochter. well-thrashed daughter

'O, fare-thee-weel, my bonie lass,
 O, fare-thee-weel, my hinnie!
Thou art a gay and a bonie lass,
 But thou has a waukrife minnie!'

# THO WOMEN'S MINDS

*TUNE: For a' that, an a' that*

This is a variation of the song in 'The Jolly Beggars' (II.208-35)

## CHORUS

*For a' that, an a' that,*
 *And twice as meikle's a' that,*   much as
*The bonie lass that I loe best*    love
 *She'll be my ain for a' that!*

Tho women's minds like winter winds
 May shift and turn, an a' that,
The noblest breast adores them maist – most
 A consequence, I draw that.

Great love I bear to a' the fair,
 Their humble slave, an a' that;
But lordly will, I hold it still   contradict
 A mortal sin to thraw that.

In rapture sweet this hour we meet,
 Wi mutual love an a' that,
But for how lang the flie may stang,  fly, sting
 Let inclination law that!

Their tricks an craft hae put me daft,  mad
 They've taen me in an a' that,
But clear your decks, and here's – 'The Sex!'
 I like the jads for a' that!    jades

# KILLIECRANKIE

*TUNE: An ye had been whare I hae been*

This is the reworking of an old Jacobite song about the battle fought on 27th July 1689 between the Highlanders led by James Graham of Claverhouse, Viscount Dundee and the Anglo-Dutch troops commanded by General Hugh Mackay of Scourie. The speaker is one of Mackay's men saved only by the deaths, in pursuit, of Haliburton of Pitcur and Claverhouse himself.

## CHORUS

| | |
|---|---|
| An ye had been whare I hae been, | If |
| Ye wad na been sae cantie, O! | |
| An ye had seen what I hae seen, | cheerful |
| On the braes o Killiecrankie O! | |

| | |
|---|---|
| 'Whare hae ye been sae braw, lad? | fine |
| Whare hae ye been sae brankie, O? | spruce |
| Whare hae ye been sae braw, lad? | |
| Cam ye by Killiecrankie, O? | |

'I faught at land, I faught at sea,
    At hame I faught my auntie, O;
But I met the Devil an Dundee,
    On the braes o Killiecrankie, O.

| | |
|---|---|
| 'The bauld Pitcur fell in a furr, | ditch |
| An Clavers gat a clankie, O, | knock |
| Or I had fed an Athole gled, | Else, hawk |
| On the braes o Killiecrankie, O!' | |

# THE CAMPBELLS ARE COMIN

The melody and first line of the chorus came from a Jacobite song of the 1715 Rebellion, but the verses by Burns allude to the imprisonment of Mary, Queen of Scots in Lochleven Castle in 1567. 'Great Argyle' was the 5th Earl of Argyll who came to her rescue.

## CHORUS

*The Campbells are comin, Oho! Oho!*
    *The Campbells are comin, Oho! Oho!*
*The Campbells are comin to bonie Lochleven,*
    *The Campbells are comin Oho! Oho!*

Upon the Lomonds I lay, I lay,
Upon the Lomonds I lay, I lay,
I looked down to bonie Lochleven,
    And saw three bonie perches play

Great Argyle he goes before,
He maks his cannons and guns roar,
Wi sound o trumpet, pipe and drum
    The Campbells are comin Oho, Oho!

The Campbells they are a' in arms
Their loyal faith and truth to show,
Wi banners rattling in the wind
    The Campbells are comin Oho, Oho!

## SCOTS PROLOGUE FOR MRS. SUTHERLAND

### ON HER BENEFIT NIGHT AT THE THEATRE, DUMFRIES

In a letter to Mrs. Dunlop in March 1790 Burns refers to George Sutherland 'Manager of a company of Comedians at present in Dumfries. The following is a Prologue I made for his wife, Mrs. Sutherland's benefit night. You are to understand that he is getting a new Theatre built here, by subscription.' Burns was closely involved with the theatre at this time, and was clearly (ll.5-6, 13-16) contemplating play-writing though nothing ever came of it. It was at Dumfries, on 4th February 1306, that Robert Bruce slew the Red Comyn and began the War of Independence (l.17). No Scottish playwright had repeated the success of John Home (1722-1808) whose *Douglas*, premiered at Covent Garden in 1757, was widely acclaimed in both England and Scotland.

What needs this din about the town o Lon'on,
How this new play an that new sang is comin?                  song
Why is outlandish stuff sae meikle courted?                  much
Does nonsense mend, like brandy – when imported?
Is there nae poet, burning keen for fame,
Will bauldly try to gie us plays at hame?
For Comedy abroad he need na toil:
A knave and fool are plants of every soil.
Nor need he hunt as far as Rome or Greece
To gather matter for a serious piece:
There's themes enow in Caledonian story
Would show the tragic Muse in a' her glory.

Is there no daring Bard will rise and tell
How glorious Wallace stood, how hapless fell?
Where are the Muses fled that could produce
A drama worthy o the name o Bruce?
How here, even here, he first unsheath'd the sword
'Gainst mighty England and her guilty lord
And after monie a bloody, deathless doing,
Wrench'd his dear country from the jaws of Ruin!
O, for a Shakespeare, or an Otway scene                  Thomas Otway
To paint the lovely, hapless Scottish Queen!                  (1652-85)

Vain all th' omnipotence of female charms
'Gainst headlong, ruthless, mad Rebellion's arms!
She fell, but fell with spirit truly Roman,
To glut the vengeance of a rival woman:                  Queen Elizabeth
A woman (tho the phrase may seem uncivil),
As able – and as cruel – as the Devil!

One Douglas lives in Home's immortal page,    Sir James Douglas
But Douglasses were heroes every age:    (1286-1330)
And tho your fathers, prodigal of life,
A Douglas followed to the martial strife,
Perhaps, if bowls row right, and Right succeeds,
Ye yet may follow where a Douglas leads!

As ye hae generous done, if a' the land
Would take the Muses' servants by the hand;
Not only hear, but patronise, befriend them,
And where ye justly can commend, commend them;
And aiblins, when they winna stand the test,
Wink hard, and say: 'The folks hae done their best!'
Would a' the land do this, then I'll be caition,    surety
Ye'll soon hae Poets o the Scottish nation
Will gar Fame blaw until her trumpet crack,    make
And warsle Time, an lay him on his back!    beat

For us and for our stage, should onie spier: –    ask
'Whase aught thae chiels maks a' this bustle here?'    Whose, those
My best leg foremost, I'll set up my brow: –    chaps
'We have the honour to belong to you!'
We're your ain bairns, e'en guide us as ye like,    own children
But like good mithers, shore before ye strike;    warn
And gratefu still, I trust ye'll ever find us,
For gen'rous patronage, and meikle kindness
We've got frae a' professions, setts an ranks:
God help us! we're but poor – ye'se get but thanks!    you'll

## LAMENT OF MARY QUEEN OF SCOTS

### ON THE APPROACH OF SPRING

Sent on 6th June 1790 to Mrs. Dunlop who shared the poet's sympathies for the great tragic heroine of Scottish history.

Now Nature hangs her mantle green
    On every blooming tree,
And spreads her sheets o daisies white
    Out o'er the grassy lea;
Now Phoebus cheers the crystal streams,
    And glads the azure skies:
But nought can glad the weary wight
    That fast in durance lies.

Now laverocks wake the merry morn,    larks
    Aloft on dewy wing;
The merle, in his noontide bow'r,    hawk
    Makes woodland echoes ring;

The mavis wild wi monie a note,
 Sings drowsy day to rest:
In love and freedom they rejoice,
 Wi care nor thrall opprest.

Now blooms the lily by the bank,
 The primrose down the brae,
The hawthorn's budding in the glen,
 And milk-white is the slae:
The meanest hind in fair Scotland
 May rove their sweets amang;
But I, the Queen of a' Scotland,
 Maun lie in prison strang.       *must*

I was the Queen o bonie France,
 Where happy I hae been;
Fu lightly rase I in the morn,        *rose*
 As blythe lay down at e'en:
And I'm the sov'reign of Scotland,
 And monie a traitor there;
Yet here I lie in foreign bands
 And never-ending care.

But as for thee, thou false woman,   *Elizabeth of England*
 My sister and my fae,          *foe*
Grim vengeance yet shall whet a sword
 That thro thy soul shall gae!
The weeping blood in woman's breast
 Was never known to thee;
Nor th' balm that drops on wounds of woe
 Frae woman's pitying e'e.

My son! my son! may kinder stars   *King James VI and I*
 Upon thy fortune shine;
And may those pleasures gild thy reign,
 That ne'er wad blink on mine!      *would*
God keep thee frae thy mother's faes,
 Or turn their hearts to thee;
And where thou meet'st thy mother's friend,
 Remember him for me!

O! soon, to me, may summer suns
 Nae mair light up the morn!
Nae mair to me the autumn winds
 Wave o'er the yellow corn!
And, in the narrow house of death,
 Let winter round me rave;
And the next flow'rs that deck the spring,
 Bloom on my peaceful grave.

# ON SENSIBILITY

Included in a letter to Mrs Dunlop written on 9th July 1790, offering the poet's condolences on the death of her son-in-law, James Henri, were some stanzas of this poem on which he was then working. The complete poem followed with a letter of 30th July. Nevertheless, he sent a copy to Clarinda a year later, telling her that it was 'just composed.'

Sensibility how charming,
 Thou, my friend, canst truly tell!
But Distress with horrors arming
 Thou alas! hast known too well!

Fairest flower, behold the lily
 Blooming in the sunny ray:
Let the blast sweep o'er the valley,
 See it prostrate in the clay.

Hear the woodlark charm the forest,
 Telling o'er his little joys;
But alas! a prey the surest
 To each pirate of the skies!

Dearly bought the hidden treasure
 Finer feelings can bestow:
Chords that vibrate sweetest pleasure
 Thrill the deepest notes of woe.

# ELECTION BALLAD

## AT CLOSE OF THE CONTEST FOR
## REPRESENTING THE DUMFRIES BURGHS 1790

### Addressed to R. Graham Esq., of Fintry

The general election was held on 12th July 1790 and this ballad was composed soon afterwards.

Fintry, my stay in worldly strife,
Friend o my Muse, friend of my life,
 Are ye as idle's I am?
Come, then! Wi uncouth kintra fleg!     *country fling*
O'er Pegasus I'll fling my leg,
 And ye shall see me try him!

But where shall I gae rin or ride,      *go run*
That I may splatter nane beside?      *splash*
 I wad na be uncivil:        *would not*
In manhood's various paths and ways
There's ay some doytin body strays,   *doddering creature*
 And I ride like a devil.

Thus I break aff wi a' my birr,                  *force*
An down yon dark, deep alley spur,
  Where Theologics dander:            *saunter*
Alas! curst wi eternal fogs,
And damn'd in everlasting bogs,
  As sure's the Creed I'll blunder!

I'll stain a band, or jaup a gown,          *splash*
Or rin my reckless, guilty crown
  Against the haly door!             *holy*
Sair do I rue my luckless fate,          *sore*
When, as the Muse an Deil wad hae't,
  I rade that road before!           *rode*

Suppose I take a spurt, and mix
Amang the wilds o Politics –
  Electors and elected –
Where dogs at Court (sad sons o bitches!)   *Elections had to be held*
Septennially a madness touches,       *at least every seven years*
  Till all the land's infected?

All hail, Drumlanrig's haughty Grace,   *William Douglas, 4th Duke*
Discarded remnant of a race         *of Queensberry (1724-1810)*
  Once godlike – great in story!
Thy fathers' virtues all contrasted,
The very name of Douglas blasted,
  Thine that inverted glory!

Hate, envy, oft the Douglas bore;
But thou hast superadded more,
  And sunk them in contempt!
Follies and crimes have stain'd the name;
But, Queensberry, thine the virgin claim,
  From aught that's good exempt!

I'll sing the zeal Drumlanrig bears,
Who left the all-important cares
  Of fiddlers, whores, and hunters,
And, bent on buying Borough Towns,
Came shaking hands wi wabster-loons,     *weaver rascals*
  And kissing barefit bunters.         *harlots*

Combustion thro our boroughs rode,
Whistling his roaring pack abroad
  Of mad unmuzzled lions,
As Queensberry buff and blue unfurl'd,    *the Whig colours*
And Westerha' and Hopeton hurl'd,   *Sir James Johnstone of*
  To every Whig defiance.    *Westerhall, Earl of Hopetoun,*
                                 *his patron*

But cautious Queensberry left the war
(Th' unmanner'd dust might soil his star;
   Besides, he hated bleeding).
But left behind him heroes bright,
Heroes in Caesarean fight
   Or Ciceronian pleading.

O, for a throat like huge Mons-Meg,        *the famous cannon of*
To muster o'er each ardent Whig           *Edinburgh Castle*
   Beneath Drumlanrig's banner!
Heroes and heroines commix,
All in the field of politics,
   To win immortal honor!

M'Murdo and his lovely spouse           *John McMurdo*
(Th' enamour'd laurels kiss her brows!)      *Jane Blair*
   Led on the Loves and Graces:
She won each gaping burgess' heart,
While he, sub rosa, played his part        *in secret (Latin)*
   Among their wives and lasses.

Craigdarroch led a light-arm'd core:      *Alexander Fergusson*
Tropes, metaphors, and figures pour,
   Like Hecla streaming thunder.       *the Icelandic volcano*
Glenriddel, skill'd in rusty coins,        *Robert Riddell*
Blew up each Tory's dark designs,
   And bared the treason under.

In either wing two champions fought:    *David Staig (1740-1824)*
Redoubted Staig, who set at nought      *provost of Dumfries*
   The wildest savage Tory;            *John Welsh,*
And Welsh, who ne'er yet flinch'd his ground,   *Sheriff Substitute of*
High-wav'd his magnum-bonum round       *Dumfriesshire*
   With Cyclopeian fury.            *double-quart bottle*

Miller brought up th' artillery ranks,      *Captain Miller*
The many-pounders of the Banks,
   Resistless desolation!
While Maxwelton, that baron bold,       *Sir Robert Lawrie*
'Mid Lawson's port entrench'd his hold,     *John Lawson*
   And threaten'd worse damnation.      *(1769-1809)*

To these what Tory hosts oppos'd,
With these what Tory warriors clos'd,
   Surpasses my descriving:
Squadrons, extended long and large,
With furious speed rush to the charge,
   Like furious devils driving.

What verse can sing, what prose narrate
The butcher deeds of bloody Fate
   Amid this mighty tulyie?                                *struggle*
Grim Horror girn'd, pale Terror roar'd,            *snarled*
As Murther at his thrapple shor'd,      *windpipe, menaced*
And Hell mix'd in the brulyie.                 *brawl*

As Highland craigs by thunder cleft,           *crags*
When lightnings fire the stormy lift,           *sky*
   Hurl down with crashing rattle,
As flames among a hundred woods –
As headlong foam a hundred floods,
   Such is the rage of Battle!

The stubborn Tories dare to die:
As soon the rooted oaks would fly
   Before th' approaching fellers!
The Whigs come on like Ocean's roar,
When all his wintry billows pour
   Against the Buchan Bullers.       *a landmark near Peterhead*

Lo, from the shades of Death's deep night,
Departed Whigs enjoy the fight,
   And think on former daring!
The muffled murtherer of Charles          *Oliver Cromwell*
The Magna Charta flag unfurls,           *Magna Carta*
   All deadly gules its bearing.

Nor wanting ghosts of Tory fame:     *John Scrimgeour, Viscount*
Bold Scrimgeour follows gallant Graham,   *Dudhope (d. 1668)*
   Auld Covenanters shiver –    *Graham of Claverhouse (d. 1689)*
Forgive! forgive! much-wrong'd Montrose!   *Marquis of Montrose*
Now Death and Hell engulph thy foes,        *(1612-50)*
   Thou liv'st on high for ever!

Still o'er the field the combat burns;
The Tories, Whigs, give way by turns;
   But Fate the word has spoken;
For woman's wit and strength o man,
Alas! can do but what they can;
   The Tory ranks are broken.

O, that my een were flowing burns!         *eyes, brooks*
My voice, a lioness that mourns
   Her darling cubs' undoing!
That I might greet, that I might cry,         *weep*
While Tories fall, while Tories fly,
   And furious Whigs pursuing!

What Whig but melts for good Sir James,
Dear to his country, by the names,
    Friend, Patron, Benefactor?
Not Pulteney's wealth can Pulteney save;
And Hopeton falls! – the generous, brave –
    And Stewart bold as Hector.

> Sir James Johnstone
> (1726-94)
> Sir James's son William
> married the daughter of
> William Pulteney, one of
> the country's richest men

Thou, Pitt, shalt rue this overthrow,
And Thurlow growl this curse of woe,
    And Melville melt in wailing!
Now Fox and Sheridan rejoice,
And Burke shall Sing: – 'O Prince, arise!
    Thy power is all prevailing!'

> William Pitt
> Edward, Baron Thurlow
> Henry Dundas
> Richard Sheridan
> Edmund Burke

For your poor friend, the Bard, afar
He sees and hears the distant war,
    A cool spectator purely:
So, when the storm the forest rends,
The robin in the hedge descends,
    And, patient chirps securely.

Now for my friends' and brethren's sakes,
And for my dear-lov'd Land o Cakes,
    I pray with holy fire: –
Lord, send a rough-shod troop o Hell
O'er a' wad Scotland buy or sell,
    To grind them in the mire!

> Scotland
>
> would

# ON THE BIRTH OF A POSTHUMOUS CHILD

## BORN IN PECULIAR CIRCUMSTANCES OF FAMILY DISTRESS

James Henri, husband of Susan Dunlop, died on 22nd June 1790 and his son was born posthumously on 15th November. On hearing this news 'out skipt I among the broomy banks of Nith to muse over my joy by retail... I extempore almost poured out to him... the following' as he wrote to Mrs Dunlop senior.

Sweet flow'ret pledge o meikle love,
    And ward o monie a prayer,
What heart o stane wad thou na move,
    Sae helpless, sweet, and fair!

> much

November hirples o'er the lea,
    Chill, on thy lovely form:
And gane, alas! the shelt'ring tree,
    Should shield thee frae the storm.

> limps

May He who gives the rain to pour,
And wings the blast to blaw,
Protect thee frae the driving show'r,
The bitter frost and snaw!

May He, the friend of Woe and Want,
Who heals life's various stounds,
Protect and guard the mother plant,
And heal her cruel wounds!

But late she flourish'd, rooted fast,
Fair on the summer morn,
Now feebly bends she in the blast,
Unshelter'd and forlorn.

Blest be thy bloom, thou lovely gem,
Unscath'd by ruffian hand!
And from thee many a parent stem
Arise to deck our land!

## YESTREEN I HAD A PINT O WINE

### TUNE: *Banks of Banna*

This song was probably written in 1790 when Burns was having an affair with Ann Park (1770-c1799), second cousin of William Hyslop who kept the Globe Inn in Dumfries. Ann gave birth to a daughter at Leith on 31st March 1791. Nine days later Jean Armour presented Burns with a son, christened after William Nicol. With remarkable forbearance Jean eventually raised the little girl Elizabeth as one of her own family. Contrary to popular belief, Ann did not die giving birth to this child; she subsequently married John Greenshields in November 1794. No record of her death has been traced, but as he remarried in September 1799 she must have been dead by that time, and the fable about death in childbirth may relate to her marriage to Greenshields.

Yestreen I had a pint o wine,            Last night
    A place where body saw na;
Yestreen lay on this breast o mine
    The gowden locks of Anna.            golden

The hungry Jew in wilderness
    Rejoicing o'er his manna
Was naething to my hiney bliss            honey
    Upon the lips of Anna.

Ye Monarchs take the East and West
    Frae Indus to Savannah:
Gie me within my straining grasp
    The melting form of Anna!

There I'll despise Imperial charms,
    An Empress or Sultana,
While dying raptures in her arms,            orgasmic
    I give and take wi Anna!

Awa, thou flaunting God of Day!
   Awa, thou pale Diana!
Ilk Star, gae hide thy twinkling ray,           Each, go
   When I'm to meet my Anna!

Come, in thy raven plumage, Night
   (Sun, Moon, and Stars, withdrawn a',)
And bring an Angel-pen to write
   My transports with my Anna!

POSTSCRIPT

The Kirk an State may join, an tell
   To do sic things I maunna:           such, must not
The Kirk an State may gae to Hell,
   And I'll gae to my Anna.

She is the sunshine o my e'e,               eye
   To live but her I canna:          without, cannot
Had I on earth but wishes three,
   The first should be my Anna.


# BURNS GRACE AT KIRKCUDBRIGHT

Traditionally ascribed to Burns, from the collection of James Grierson of Dalgoner, and alternatively known as the Selkirk Grace, from the Earl of Selkirk in whose presence Burns is said to have delivered it extempore in Standard English. The Lallans version usually given at Burns Suppers, however, is very much older and known as the Galloway Grace, or the Covenanters' Grace, and probably dates from the 17th centruy.

Some have meat and cannot eat.
   Some cannot eat that want it:
But we have meat and we can eat,
   Sae let the Lord be thankit.


# GRACE AFTER MEAT

This grace, like the variant which follows, was composed in the Globe Inn, Dumfries 'for these many years... my Howff (to Thomson, 1796). William Hyslop and his wife Jean were the hosts, and Ann Park, mother of Elizabeth Burns was their second cousin. In 1795 their son John married Margaret (Meg) Geddes and they took over the running of the inn.

Lord, we thank, and Thee alone,
   For temporal gifts we little merit!
At present we will ask no more –
   Let William Hislop bring the spirit.

## GRACE BEFORE AND AFTER MEAT

An apocryphal tale goes that Burns once forgot to order dinner for Nicol, Masterton and himself. Meg Hyslop produced a sheep's head which she and Jock intended for themselves. Nicol 'fined' Burns for his neglect by ordering him to compose a grace. When they had eaten he was commanded to compose thanks. These stanzas were allegedly the result.

O Lord, when hunger pinches sore,
    Do Thou stand us in stead,
And send us, from Thy bounteous store,
    A tup or wether head!

O Lord, since we have feasted thus,
    Which we so little merit,
Let Meg now take away the flesh,
    And Jock bring in the spirit!

## GODLY GIRZIE

TUNE: *Wat ye wha I met yestreen*

Burns annotated this as 'A new Song - from an old story' and sent it to William Stewart. The 'Cragie hills' (1.8) lie in Craigie parish between Kilmarnock and Tarbolton.

| | |
|---|---|
| The night it was a haly night, | holy |
|     The day had been a haly day; | |
| Kilmarnock gleam'd wi candle light, | |
|     As Girzie hameward took her way. | |
| A man o sin, ill may he thrive! | |
|     And never haly-meeting see! | |
| Wi godly Girzie met belyve, | by and by |
|     Amang the Cragie hills sae hie. | high |
| | |
| The chiel was wight, the chiel was stark, | fellow, strong |
|     He wad na wait to chap nor ca', | knock |
| And she was faint wi haly wark, | work |
|     She had na pith to say him na. | strength |
| But ay she glowr'd up to the moon, | stared |
|     And ay she sigh'd most piouslie; | |
| 'I trust my heart's in heaven aboon, | above |
|     'Whare'er your sinfu pintle be.' | penis |

# TAM O SHANTER

## A TALE

Of Brownyis and of Bogillis full is this Buke.– GAWIN DOUGLAS

Composed for Francis Grose to accompany an engraving of Alloway Kirk, and published in the second volume of *Antiquities of Scotland* in April 1791. It was written in fulfilment of a promise to Grose in 1789 but not carried out before the winter of 1790. In November that year Burns sent the first fragment to Mrs Dunlop. Grose received the complete poem at the beginning of December. Like 'Halloween' it draws heavily on the lore of witchcraft which Burns imbibed from Betty Davidson. The story is loosely based on Douglas Graham of Shanter (1739-1811), whose wife Helen was a superstitious shrew. He was prone to drunkenness on market-day and on one such occasion the wags of Ayr clipped his horse's tail – a fact he explained away by this story of witches which mollufied his credulous wife.

| | |
|---|---|
| When chapman billies leave the street, | pedlars |
| And drouthy neebors, neebors meet; | thirsty neighbours |
| As market-days are wearing late, | |
| An folk begin to tak the gate; | road |
| While we sit bousing at the nappy, | ale |
| An getting fou and unco happy, | drunk, mighty |
| We think na on the lang Scots miles, | |
| The mosses, waters, slaps, and styles, | bogs, pools, openings |
| That lie between us and our hame, | |
| Whare sits our sulky, sullen dame, | |
| Gathering her brows like gathering storm, | |
| Nursing her wrath to keep it warm. | |
| | |
| This truth fand honest Tam o Shanter, | found |
| As he frae Ayr ae night did canter: | one |
| (Auld Ayr, wham ne'er a town surpasses, | |
| For honest men and bonie lasses). | |
| | |
| O Tam had'st thou but been sae wise, | |
| As taen thy ain wife Kate's advice! | to have taken |
| She tauld thee weel thou was a skellum, | good-for-nothing |
| A blethering, blustering, drunken blellum; | chattering, babbler |
| That frae November till October, | |
| Ae market-day thou was nae sober; | every meal-grinding |
| That ilka melder wi the miller, | Hugh Broun of Ardlochan |
| Thou sat as lang as thou had siller; | money |
| That ev'ry naig was ca'd a shoe on, | nag |
| The smith and thee gat roarin fou on; | John Niven of Carrick |
| That at the Lord's house, even on Sunday, | |
| Thou drank wi Kirkton Jean till Monday. | Jean Kennedy, who kept |
| She prophesied that, late or soon, | a pub in Kirkoswald |
| Thou would be found, deep drown'd in Doon, | |
| Or catch'd wi warlocks in the mirk, | wizards, dark |
| By Alloway's auld, haunted kirk. | in decay since 1690, when |
| | Alloway parish was joined to Ayr |

Ah, gentle dames, it gars me greet,          *makes, weep*
To think how monie counsels sweet,
How monie lengthen'd, sage advices
The husband frae the wife despises!

But to our tale: – Ae market-night,
Tam had got planted unco right,
Fast by an ingle, bleezing finely,
Wi reaming swats, that drank divinely;       *foaming ale*
And at his elbow, Souter Johnie,     *John Davidson (1786-1806)*
His ancient, trusty, drouthy cronie:       *a cobbler*
Tam lo'ed him like a very brither;
They had been fou for weeks thegither.
The night drave on wi sangs and clatter;
And ay the ale was growing better:
The landlady and Tam grew gracious,
Wi secret favours, sweet and precious:
The Souter tauld his queerest stories;       *told*
The landlord's laugh was ready chorus:
The storm without might rair and rustle,     *roar*
Tam did na mind the storm a whistle.

Care, mad to see a man sae happy,
E'en drown'd himsel amang the nappy.
As bees flee hame wi lades o treasure,      *loads*
The minutes wing'd their way wi pleasure:
Kings may be blest but Tam was glorious,
O'er a' the ills o life victorious!

But pleasures are like poppies spread:
You seize the flow'r, its bloom is shed;
Or like the snow falls in the river,
A moment white – then melts for ever;
Or like the borealis race,     *Aurora or Northern Lights*
That flit ere you can point their place;
Or like the rainbow's lovely form
Evanishing amid the storm.
Nae man can tether time or tide,
The hour approaches Tam maun ride:      *must*
That hour o night's black arch the key-stane,
That dreary hour Tam mounts his beast in:
And sic a night he taks the road in,      *such*
As ne'er poor sinner was abroad in.

The wind blew as 'twad blawn its last;    *would have blown*
The rattling showers rose on the blast;
The speedy gleams the darkness swallow'd;
Loud, deep, and lang the thunder bellow'd;
That night, a child might understand,
The Deil had business on his hand.

Weel mounted on his gray mare Meg,
A better never lifted leg,
Tam skelpit on thro dub and mire,                    *spanked, puddle*
Despising wind, and rain, and fire;
Whiles holding fast his guid blue bonnet,            *Now*
Whiles crooning o'er an auld Scots sonnet,
Whiles glow'ring round wi prudent cares,             *staring*
Lest bogles catch him unawares:                      *bogies*
Kirk-Alloway was drawing nigh,
Whare ghaists and houlets nightly cry.               *ghosts, owls*

By this time he was cross the ford,                  *Slaphouse Burn*
Whare in the snaw the chapman smoor'd;               *smothered*
And past the birks and meikle stane,                 *birches, big*
Whare drunken Charlie brak's neck-bane;
And thro the whins, and by the cairn,                *Cambusdoon*
Whare hunters fand the murder'd bairn;
And near the thorn, aboon the well,
Whare Mungo's mither hang'd hersel.                  *St Mungo's Well*
Before him Doon pours all his floods;
The doubling storm roars thro the woods;
The lightnings flash from pole to pole,
Near and more near the thunders roll:
When, glimmering thro the groaning trees,
Kirk-Alloway seem'd in a bleeze,
Thro ilka bore the beams were glancing,              *every chink*
And loud resounded mirth and dancing.

Inspiring bold John Barleycorn,
What dangers thou canst make us scorn!
Wi tippenny, we fear nae evil;                       *twopenny beer*
Wi usquabae, we'll face the Devil!                   *whisky*
The swats sae ream'd in Tammie's noddle,             *brain*
Fair play, he car'd na deils a boddle.               *farthing*
But Maggie stood, right sair astonish'd,
Till, by the heel and hand admonish'd,
She ventur'd forward on the light;
And, vow! Tam saw an unco sight!                     *wondrous*

Warlocks and witches in a dance:
Nae cotillion, brent new frae France,                *brand*
But hornpipes, jigs, strathspeys, and reels,
Put life and mettle in their heels.
A winnock-bunker in the east,                        *window seat*
There sat Auld Nick, in shape o beast;
A touzie tyke, black, grim and large,                *shaggy dog*
To gie them music was his charge:
He screw'd the pipes and gart them skirl,            *made, squeal*
Till roof and rafters a' did dirl.                   *ring*

Coffins stood round, like open presses,         *cupboards*
That shaw'd the dead in their last dresses;
And, by some devilish cantraip sleight,         *magic device*
Each in its cauld hand held a light:
By which heroic Tam was able
To note upon the haly table,
A murderer's banes, in gibbet-airns;         *-irons*
Twa span-lang, wee, unchristen'd bairns;         *babies*
A thief new-cutted frae a rape –         *rope*
Wi his last gasp his gab did gape;         *mouth*
Five tomahawks, wi bluid red-rusted.
Five scymitars, wi murder crusted;
A garter which a babe had strangled;
A knife a father's throat had mangled –
Whom his ain son o life bereft –
The grey-hairs yet stack to the heft;
Wi mair of horrible and awefu,
Which even to name wad be unlawfu.

As Tammie glowr'd, amaz'd and curious,         *stared*
The mirth and fun grew fast and furious;
The piper loud and louder blew,
The dancers quick and quicker flew,
They reel'd, they set, they cross'd, they cleekit,         *took hold*
Till ilka carlin swat and reekit,         *beldam, sweated, steamed*
And coost her duddies to the wark,         *stripped off clothes*
And linket at it in her sark!         *tripped, chemise*

Now Tam, O Tam! had thae been queans,         *these, girls*
A' plump and strapping in their teens!
Their sarks, instead o creeshie flannen,         *greasy flannel*
Been snaw-white seventeen hunder linen! –         *fine (1700 thread gauge)*
Thir breeks o mine, my only pair,         *These breeches*
That ance were plush, o guid blue hair,         *once*
I wad hae gien them off my hurdies,         *buttocks*
For ae blink o the bonie burdies!         *one, glimpse, maidens*
But wither'd beldams, auld and droll,
Rigwoodie hags wad spean a foal,         *Withered, abort*
Louping and flinging on a crummock,         *Leaping, cudgel*
I wonder did na turn thy stomach!

But Tam kend what was what fu brawlie:         *knew, well*
There was ae winsome wench and wawlie,         *comely, choice*
That night enlisted in the core,         *crew*
Lang after kend on Carrick shore
(For monie a beast to dead she shot,         *death*
An perish'd monie a bonie boat,
And shook baith meikle corn and bear,         *barley*
And kept the country-side in fear).

Her cutty sark, o Paisley harn,    *short shift, coarse cloth*
That while a lassie she had worn,
In longitude tho sorely scanty,
It was her best, and she was vauntie...    *proud*
Ah! little kend thy reverend grannie,
That sark she coft for her wee Nannie,    *bought*
Wi twa pund Scots ('twas a' her riches),    *3s4d sterling*
Wad ever grac'd a dance of witches!

But here my Muse her wing maun cour,    *must curb*
Sic flights are far beyond her power:
To sing how Nannie lap and flang
(A souple jade she was and strang),
And how Tam stood like ane bewitch'd,
And thought his very een enrich'd;
Even Satan glowr'd, and fidg'd fu fain,    *fidgeted, fondly*
And hotch'd and blew wi might and main:    *jerked*
Till first ae caper, syne anither,    *then*
Tam tint his reason a' thegither,    *lost*
And roars out, 'Weel done, Cutty-sark!'
And in an instant all was dark:
And scarcely had he Maggie rallied,
When out the hellish legion sallied.

As bees bizz out wi angry fyke,    *fret*
When plundering herds assail their byke;    *hive*
As open pussie's mortal foes,    *hare's*
When, pop! she starts before their nose;
As eager runs the market-crowd,
When 'Catch the thief!' resounds aloud:
So Maggie runs, the witches follow,
Wi monie an eldritch skriech and hollow.    *unearthly*

Ah, Tam! Ah, Tam! thou'll get thy fairin!    *reward*
In hell they'll roast thee like a herrin!
In vain thy Kate awaits thy comin!
Kate soon will be a woefu woman!
Now, do thy speedy utmost, Meg,
And win the key-stane of the brig;    *bridge*
There, at them thou thy tail may toss,
A running stream they dare na cross!
But ere the key-stane she could make,
The fient a tail she had to shake;    *not*
For Nannie, far before the rest,
Hard upon noble Maggie prest,
And flew at Tam wi furious ettle;    *aim*
But little wist she Maggie's mettle!
Ae spring brought off her master hale,    *whole*
But left behind her ain grey tail:
The carlin claught her by the rump,    *clawed*
An left poor Maggie scarce a stump.

Now, wha this tale o truth shall read,
Ilk man, and mother's son, take heed:
Whene'er to drink you are inclin'd,
Or cutty sarks rin in your mind,
Think! ye may buy the joys o'er dear:
Remember Tam o Shanter's mare.

## ON CAPTAIN GROSE

### WRITTEN ON AN ENVELOPE, ENCLOSING A LETTER TO HIM

Addressed 'extempore and anonymous' to Adam de Cardonnel Lawson, a numismatist and antiquary who assisted Grose. The basis of these lines is an oysterdredging song from the Firth of Forth with a dog-Latin chorus.

Ken ye ought o Captain Grose? *Igo and ago,*
If he's among his friends or foes? *Iram, coram, dago.*

Is he south or is he north? *Igo and ago,*
Or drownèd in the river Forth? *Iram, coram, dago.*

Is he slain by Hielan bodies? *Igo and ago,*
And eaten like a wether haggis? *Iram, coram, dago.*     sheep

Is he to Abra'm's bosom gane? *Igo and ago,*
Or haudin Sarah by the wame? *Iram, coram, dago.*     holding, belly

Where'er he be, the Lord be near him! *Igo and ago,*
As for the Deil, he daur na steer him, *Iram, coram, dago.*     dare not

But please transmit th' enclosed letter, *Igo and ago,*
Which will oblige your humble debtor, *Iram, coram, dago.*

So may ye hae auld stanes in store, *Igo and ago,*
The very stanes that Adam bore, *Iram, coram, dago.*

So may ye get in glad possession, *Igo and ago,*
The coins o Satan's coronation! *Iram, coram, dago.*

## EPIGRAM ON
## FRANCIS GROSE THE ANTIQUARY

Captain Grose was in Ireland in 1790-1 gathering material for a projected work on the antiquities of that country, when he died at Dublin in May 1791.

The Devil got notice that Grose was a-dying,
So whip! at the summons, old Satan came flying;
But when he approach'd where poor Francis lay moaning,
And saw each bed-post with its burthen a-groaning,
Astonish'd, confounded, cries Satan – 'By God,
I'll want him ere I take such a damnable load!'

# ELEGY ON THE LATE
# MISS BURNET OF MONBODDO

Elizabeth Burnett, referred to in the 'Address to Edinburgh' died of TB on 17th June 1790. Burns laboured for several months to produce a satisfactory elegy which he sent to Alexander Cunningham on 23rd January 1791. A more polished copy was sent to Mrs Dunlop on 7th February.

Life ne'er exulted in so rich a prize
As Burnet, lovely from her native skies;
Nor envious Death so triumph'd in a blow,
As that which laid th' accomplish'd Burnet low.

Thy form and mind, sweet maid, can I forget?
In richest ore the brightest jewel set!
In thee, high Heaven above was truest shown,
For by His noblest work the Godhead best is known.

In vain ye flaunt in summer's pride, ye groves!
Thou crystal streamlet with thy flowery shore,
Ye woodland choir that chaunt your idle loves,
Ye cease to charm: Eliza is no more.

Ye heathy wastes immix'd with reedy fens,
Ye mossy streams with sedge and rushes stor'd,
Ye rugged cliffs o'erhanging dreary glens,
To you I fly: ye with my soul accord.

Princes whose cumb'rous pride was all their worth,
Shall venal lays their pompous exit hail,
And thou, sweet Excellence! forsake our earth,
And not a Muse with honest grief bewail?

We saw thee shine in youth and beauty's pride,
And Virtue's light, that beams beyond the spheres;
But, like the sun eclips'd at morning tide,
Thou left us darkling in a world of tears.

The parent's heart that nestled fond in thee,
That heart how sunk, a prey to grief and care!
So deckt the woodbine sweet yon aged tree,
So, rudely ravish'd, left it bleak and bare.

# EPISTLE TO JOHN MAXWELL, ESQ., OF TERRAUGHTIE

## ON HIS SEVENTY-FIRST BIRTHDAY

John Maxwell (1720-1814) was a joiner of Dumfries who prospered, enabling him to buy back Terraughty, the family estate west of Dumfries which had been sold because of financial problems. Later he acquired Portrack, north of Dumfries and, by his second marriage, Munches near Dalbeattie. By the 1790s he was one of the leading gentlemen of Dumfriesshire and the Stewartry. His 71st birthday occurred on 7th February 1791.

Health to the Maxwells' vet'ran Chief!
Health ay unsour'd by care or grief!
Inspir'd, I turn'd Fate's sibyl leaf
    This natal morn;
I see thy life is stuff o prief,                   *proof*
    Scarce quite half-worn.

This day thou metes threescore eleven,
And I can tell that bounteous Heaven
(The second-sight, ye ken, is given       *know*
    To ilka Poet)                    *every*
On thee a tack o seven times seven   *lease*
    Will yet bestow it.

If envious buckies view wi sorrow     *youngsters*
Thy lengthen'd days on thy blest morrow,
May Desolation's lang-teeth'd harrow,
    Nine miles an hour,
Rake them, like Sodom and Gomorrah,
    In brunstane stoure!         *brimstone dust*

But for thy friends, and they are monie,
Baith honest men and lasses bonie,
May couthie Fortune, kind and cannie   *loving, careful*
    In social glee,
Wi mornings blythe, and e'enings funny,
    Bless them and thee!

Fareweel, auld birkie! Lord be near ye,   *fellow*
And then the Deil, he daurna steer ye!   *date not*
Your friends ay love, your foes ay fear ye!
    For me, shame fa' me,
If neist my heart I dinna wear ye,     *next, do not*
    While Burns they ca' me!

14

## TO THE MEMORY OF THE
## UNFORTUNATE MISS BURNS 1791

Margaret Burns, the celebrated Edinburgh prostitute, died at Roslin within three years of her banishment from the city. Burns deplored this harshly puritanical treatment of his namesake. This 'epitaph on a certain frail sister' was composed a year before her death.

Like to a fading flower in May,
    Which Gardner cannot save,
So Beauty must, sometime, decay
    And drop into the grave.

Fair Burns, for long the talk and toast
    Of many a gaudy Beau,
That Beauty has forever lost
    That made each bosom glow.

Think, fellow sisters, on her fate!
    Think, think how short her days!
Oh! think, and, e'er it be too late,
    Turn from your evil ways.

Beneath this cold, green sod lies dead
    That once bewitching dame
That fired Edina's lustful sons,
    And quench'd their glowing flame.

## THERE'LL NEVER BE PEACE TILL
## JAMIE COMES HAME

A development of an old Jacobite song: 'Jamie' is, of course, King James VIII and III, the Old Pretender.

By yon castle wa' at the close of the day,
I heard a man sing, tho his head it was grey,
And as he was singing, the tears doon came, –
'There'll never be peace till Jamie comes hame!'

'The Church is in ruins, the State is in jars,
Delusion, oppressions, and murderous wars,
We dare na weel say't, but we ken wha's to blame –
There'll never be peace till Jamie comes hame!

'My seven braw sons for Jamie drew sword,
But now I greet round their green beds in the yerd;   weep, kirkyard
It brak the sweet heart o my faithfu auld dame –
There'll never be peace till Jamie comes hame!

'Now life is a burden that bows me down,
Sin I tint my bairns, and he tint his crown;          lost, children
But till my last moments my words are the same –
There'll never be peace till Jamie comes hame!'

## OUT OVER THE FORTH

Perhaps based on a fragment in the Herd MSS and mentioned in a letter to Alexander Cunningham on 11th March 1791.

Out over the Forth, I took to the north –
    But what is the north, and its Highlands to me?
The south nor the east gie ease to my breast,
    The far foreign land, or the wide rolling sea!

But I look to the west, when I gae to rest,
    That happy my dreams and my slumbers may be;
For far in the west lives he I loe best,
    The man that is dear to my babie and me.

## YE FLOWERY BANKS

In his letter of 11th March 1791 to Cunningham, Burns wrote: 'I have this evening sketched out a Song...intended to sing to a Strathspey reel.'

Ye flowery banks o bonie Doon,
    How can ye blume sae fair?                 bloom
How can ye chant, ye little birds,
    And I sae fu o care?

Thou'll break my heart, thou bonie bird,
    That sings upon the bough:
Thou minds me o the happy days
    When my fause Luve was true!           false

Thou'll break my heart, thou bonie bird,
    That sings beside thy mate:
For sae I sat, and sae I sang,            knew not
    And wist na o my fate!

Aft hae I rov'd by bonie Doon,          Often
    To see the woodbine twine,
And ilka bird sang o its luve,
    And sae did I o mine.

Wi lightsome heart I pu'd a rose
    Frae aff its thorny tree,
And my fause luver staw my rose,      stole
    But left the thorn wi me.

## THE BANKS O DOON

An extensive revision of the previous song, which Burns sent to Johnson for publication in SMM.

Ye banks and braes o bonie Doon,      slopes
    How can ye bloom sae fresh and fair?
How can ye chant, ye little birds,
    And I sae weary fu o care!

Thou'll break my heart, thou warbling bird,
    That wantons thro the flowering thorn!
Thou minds me o departed joys,
    Departed never to return.

Aft hae I rov'd by bonie Doon
    To see the rose and woodbine twine,
And ilka bird sang o its luve,                        *every*
    And fondly sae did I o mine.
Wi lightsome heart I pu'd a rose,
    Fu sweet upon its thorny tree!
And my fause luver staw my rose –
    But ah! he left the thorn wi me.

## EPIGRAM ON MR. JAMES GRACIE

James Gracie (1756-1814), manager of the Dumfries Commercial Bank and Dean of Guild, was captain in the Dumfries Volunteers. A week before he died, Burns wrote to Gracie thanking him for the offer of an outing in his carriage.

Gracie, thou art a man of worth,
    O, be thou Dean for ever!
May he be damn'd to Hell henceforth,
    Who fauts thy weight or measure!

## THE SONG OF DEATH

*TUNE: Oran an Aoig*

Writing to Mrs Dunlop in May 1791, Burns mentions this song 'which to a lady the descendant of Wallace...and herself the mother of several soldiers, needs neither preface nor apology.'

Farewell, thou fair day, thou green earth and ye skies,
    Now gay with the broad setting sun!
Farewell, loves and friendships, ye dear tender ties –
    Our race of existence is run!
Thou grim King of Terrors! thou Life's gloomy foe!
    Go, frighten the coward and slave!
Go, teach them to tremble, fell tyrant, but know,
    No terrors hast thou to the brave!

Thou strik'st the dull peasant – he sinks in the dark,
    Nor saves e'en the wreck of a name!
Thou strik'st the young hero – a glorious mark,
    He falls in the blaze of his fame!
In the field of proud honour, our swords in our hands,
    Our king and our country to save,
While victory shines on Life's last ebbing sands,
    O, who would not die with the brave?

# ADDRESS TO THE SHADE
# OF THOMSON

### ON CROWNING HIS BUST AT EDNAM,
### ROXBURGHSHIRE, WITH A WREATH OF BAYS

James Thomson (1700-48) the poet and precursor of Romanticism, was born at Ednam. Renowned in his lifetime for *The Seasons*, he is now best remembered for his song 'Rule Britannia', composed for the musical *Alfred*, from which also come the lines 'What makes the hero truly great, is never, never, to despair' – Burns's favourite quotation. In 1791 David Erskine, 11th Earl of Buchan proposed to commemorate Thomson, by erecting a bust of him on Ednam Hill and decorating it with a laurel wreath. Lord Buchan wrote to Burns inviting him to attend the crowning ceremony on 22nd September and soliciting an ode for the occasion. As the harvest season was in full swing by that time Burns tactfully declined the prospect of an arduous 75-mile journey overland. In the event, the ceremony was a fiasco, the bust having got broken in a midnight frolic during Race Week, and Lord Buchan had to substitute a copy of Thomson's poem *The Seasons*.'

While virgin Spring by Eden's flood
    Unfolds her tender mantle green,
Or pranks the sod in frolic mood,
    Or tunes Eolian strains between.

While Summer, with a matron grace,
    Retreats to Dryburgh's cooling shade,
Yet oft, delighted, stops to trace
    The progress of the spikey blade:

While Autumn, benefactor kind,
    By Tweed erects his aged head,
And sees, with self-approving mind,
    Each creature on his bounty fed.

While maniac Winter rages o'er
    The hills whence classic Yarrow flows,
Rousing the turbid torrent's roar,
    Or sweeping, wild, a waste of snows.

So long, sweet Poet of the year!
    Shall bloom that wreath thou well has won;
While Scotia, with exulting tear,
    Proclaims that Thomson is her son.

# ON SOME COMMEMORATIONS
# OF THOMSON

Composed in the autumn of 1791 in the aftermath of the farcical ceremony at Ednam.

Dost thou not rise, indignant Shade,
    And smile wi spurning scorn,
When they wha wad hae starved thy life
    Thy senseless turf adorn?

They wha about thee mak sic fuss                such
  Now thou art but a name,
Wad seen thee damn'd ere they had spar'd
  Ae plack to fill thy wame.          One farthing, belly

Helpless, alane, thou clamb the brae      climbed, slope
  Wi meikle honest toil,                 much
And claucht th' unfading garland there,    grasped
  Thy sair-won, rightful spoil.

And wear it there! and call aloud
  This axiom undoubted: –
Would thou hae Nobles' patronage?
  First learn to live without it!

'To whom hae much, more shall be given.'
  Is every great man's faith;
But he, the helpless, needful wretch,
  Shall lose the mite he hath.


# LONELY DAVIES

Deborah Duff Davies was the daughter of Dr Daniel Davies of Tenby, Pembrokeshire and a relation of the Riddell family. Burns met her at Friars' Carse and corresponded with her thereafter. The petite Miss Davies was also the inspiration of 'Bonie Wee Thing'. She died of consumption at an early age.

O, how shall I, unskilfu, try
  The Poet's occupation?
The tunefu Powers, in happy hours
  That whisper inspiration,
Even they maun dare an effort mair      must, more
  Than aught they ever gave us,
Ere they rehearse in equal verse
  The charms o lovely Davies.

Each eye, it cheers, when she appears,
  Like Phoebus in the morning,
When past the shower, and every flower
  The garden is adorning!
As the wretch looks o'er Siberia's shore,
  When winter-bound the wave is,
Sae droops our heart, when we maun part
  Frae charming, lovely Davies.

Her smile's a gift frae 'boon the lift,          *above, horizon*
   That makes us mair than princes.
A sceptred hand, a king's command,
   Is in her darting glances.
The man in arms 'gainst female charms,
   Even he her willing slave is:
He hugs his chain, and owns the reign
   Of conquering lovely Davies.

My Muse to dream of such a theme
   Her feeble powers surrenders;
The eagle's gaze alone surveys
   The sun's meridian splendours.
I wad in vain essay the strain –
   The deed too daring brave is!
I'll drap the lyre, and, mute, admire
   The charms o lovely Davies.

## LAMENT FOR JAMES, EARL OF GLENCAIRN

James Cunningham, 14th Earl of Glencairn (1749-91) was the second son of the 13th Earl, but his brother having predeceased him he succeeded to the title on the death of his father in 1775. From 1780 to 1784 he was one of the Scottish representative peers in the House of Lords. He was greatly impressed by the Kilmarnock Edition and gave Burns a warm welcome when he arrived in Edinburgh, armed with an introduction from Dalrymple of Orangefield. The Earl introduced Burns into Edinburgh society and gave him the patronage necessary for success. It was due to his influence that the members of the Caledonian Hunt subscribed 'universally, one and all' to the first Edinburgh Edition. The Earl went to Portugal in the autumn of 1790 for his health's sake, but returned to England where he died at Falmouth soon after landing, on 30th January 1791. Burns named his third surviving son (b. 1794) in memory of his early patron.

The wind blew hollow frae the hills;
   By fits the sun's departing beam
Look'd on the fading yellow woods,
   That wav'd o'er Lugar's winding stream.
Beneath a craigy steep, a Bard,          *craggy precipice*
   Laden with years and meikle pain,          *much*
In loud lament bewail'd his lord,
   Whom Death had all untimely ta'en.

He lean'd him to an ancient aik,          *oak*
  Whose trunk was mould'ring down with years;
His locks were bleached white with time,
  His hoary cheek was wet wi tears;
And as he touch'd his trembling harp.
And as he tun'd his doleful sang,
The winds, lamenting thro their caves,
  To echo bore the notes alang: –

'Ye scatter'd birds that faintly sing,
  That reliques o the vernal quire!         *choir*
Ye woods that shed on a' the winds
  The honours o the aged year!
A few short months, and, glad and gay,
  Again ye'll charm the ear and e'e;         *eye*
But nocht in all revolving time
  Can gladness bring again to me.

'I am a bending agèd tree,
  That long has stood the wind and rain;
But now has come a cruel blast,
  And my last hold of earth is gane;
Nae leaf o mine shall greet the spring,
  Nae simmer sun exalt my bloom;
But I maun lie before the storm,         *must*
  And ithers plant them in my room.

'I've seen sae monie changefu years,
  On earth I am a stranger grown:
I wander in the ways of men,
  Alike unknowing and unknown:
Unheard, unpitied, unreliev'd,
  I bear alane my lade o care;         *alone, load*
For silent, low, on beds of dust,
  Lie a' that would my sorrows share.

'And last (the sum of a' my griefs!)
  My noble master lies in clay;
The flow'r amang our barons bold,
  His country's pride, his country's stay:
In weary being now I pine,
  For a' the life of life is dead,
And hope has left my agèd ken,
  On forward wing for ever fled.

'Awake thy last sad voice, my harp!
  The voice of woe and wild despair!
Awake, resound thy latest lay,
  Then sleep in silence evermair!

And thou, my last, best, only friend,
    That fillest an untimely tomb,
Accept this tribute from the Bard
    Thou brought from Fortune's mirkest gloom.        darkest

'In Poverty's low barren vale,
    Thick mists obscure involv'd me round;
Though oft I turn'd the wistful eye,
    Nae ray of fame was to be found;
Thou found'st me, like the morning sun
    That melts the fogs in limpid air:
The friendless Bard and rustic song
    Became alike thy fostering care.

'O, why has Worth so short a date,
    While villains ripen grey with time!
Must thou, the noble, gen'rous, great,
    Fall in bold manhood's hardy prime?
Why did I live to see that day,
    A day to me so full of woe?
O, had I met the mortal shaft
    Which laid my benefactor low!

'The bridegroom may forget the bride
    Was made his wedded wife yestreen;        last night
The monarch may forget the crown
    That on his head an hour has been;
The mother may forget the child
    That smiles sae sweetly on her knee;
And I'll remember thee, Glencairn,
    And a' that thou hast done for me!'

## LINES TO SIR JOHN WHITEFOORD, BART.

### SENT WITH THE FOREGOING POEM

Sir John Whiteford (1734-1803), a friend of Glencairn and a patron of Burns (see 'The Vision') wrote to the poet on 16th October acknowledging these lines with the view that 'temporal misfortunes shall receive an eternal recompense. Let us cherish this hope for our departed friend, and moderate our grief…knowing that he cannot come to us, but we may go to him.'

Thou, who thy honour as thy God rever'st,
Who, save thy mind's reproach, nought earthly fear'st,
To thee this votive off'ring I impart,
The tearful tribute of a broken heart.
The Friend thou valued'st, I, the Patron lov'd;
His worth, his honour, all the world approved:
We'll mourn till we too go as he has gone,
And tread the shadowy path to that dark world unknown.

# ON GLENRIDDELL'S FOX BREAKING HIS CHAIN

## A FRAGMENT, 1791

Captain Robert Riddell of Glenriddell kept a pet fox in a dog-kennel – something which Burns with his libertarian principles abhorred. When the fox escaped Burns seized the opportunity to compose these lines on his favourite theme of Liberty. Though undated, this poem was probably written at Ellisland.

Thou, Liberty, thou art my theme:
Not such as idle poets dream,
Who trick thee up a heathen goddess
That a fantastic cap and rod has!
Such stale conceits are poor and silly:
I paint thee out a Highland filly,
A sturdy, stubborn, handsome dapple,
As sleek's a mouse, as round's an apple,
That, when thou pleasest can do wonders,
But when thy luckless rider blunders,
Or if thy fancy should demur there,
Wilt break thy neck ere thou go further.

These things premis'd, I sing a Fox –
Was caught among his native rocks,
And to a dirty kennel chained –
How he has liberty regained.

Glenriddell! a Whig without a stain,
A Whig in principle and grain,
Could'st thou enslave a free-born creature,
A native denizen of Nature?
How could'st thou, with a heart so good
(A better ne'er was sluiced with blood),
Nail a poor devil to a tree,
That ne'er did harm to thine or thee?

The staunchest Whig Glenriddell was,
Quite frantic in his country's cause;
And oft was Reynard's prison passing,  poetic name for a fox
And with his brother-Whigs canvassing
The rights of men, the powers of women,
With all the dignity of Freemen.

Sir Reynard daily heard debates
Of princes', kings', and nations' fates,
With many rueful, bloody stories
Of tyrants, Jacobites, and Tories:
From liberty how angels fell,
That now are galley-slaves in Hell;
How Nimrod first the trade began  Genesis x. 8-10
Of binding Slavery's chains on man;
How fell Semiramis - God damn her! –  Queen of Assyria who
Did first, with sacrilegious hammer  killed her husband

(All ills till then were trivial matters),
For Man dethron'd forge hen-peck fetters;
How Xerxes, that abandoned Tory,
Thought cutting throats was reaping glory,
Until the stubborn Whigs of Sparta
Taught him great Nature's Magna Charta;
How mighty Rome her fiat hurl'd
Resistless o'er a bowing world,
And, kinder than they did desire,
Polish'd mankind with sword and fire:
With much too tedious to relate
Of ancient and of modern date,
But ending still, how Billy Pitt      William Pitt who devised
(Unlucky boy!) with wicked wit           new fiscal measures
Has gagg'd old Britain, drain'd her coffer,   including income tax
As butchers bind and bleed a heifer.          at 3d in the £

   Thus wily Reynard, by degrees,
In kennel listening at his ease,
Suck'd in a mighty stock of knowledge,
As much as some folks at a college;
Knew Britain's rights and constitution,
Her aggrandisement, diminution;
How Fortune wrought us good from evil:
Let no man, then, despise the Devil,
As who should say: 'I ne'er can need him,'
Since we to scoundrels owe our Freedom.


# LINES TO CAPTAIN RIDDELL

## ON RETURNING A NEWSPAPER

Though undated, these lines belong to 1791 and are a charming relic of the friendship between Burns and Riddell, who also founded the communal library known as the Monkland Friendly Society. Riddell gave a great many of his old books and Burns bought most of the others from his friend Peter Hill, bookseller in Edinburgh. At Riddell's instigation Burns contributed an article about the society to Sir John Sinclair's *Statistical Account*.

   Your News and Review, Sir,
   I've read through and through, Sir,
With little admiring or blaming:
    The Papers are barren
    Of home-news or foreign –
No murders or rapes worth the naming.

Our friends, the Reviewers,
Those chippers and hewers,
Are judges of mortar and stone, Sir;
But of meet or unmeet,
In a fabric complete,
I'll boldly pronounce they are none, Sir.

My goose-quill too rude is
To tell all your goodness
Bestow'd on your servant, the Poet;
Would to God I had one
Like a beam of the sun,
And then all the world, Sir, should know it!

*ELLISLAND, Monday morning*

# REPLY TO A NOTE FROM
# CAPTAIN RIDDELL

[Dear Bard
    To ride this day is vain
For it will be a steeping rain
    So come and sit with me
Wee'l twa or three leaves fill up with scraps
And whiles fill up the time with Crack
    And spend the day with glee.

R.R.]

Dear Sir, at onie time or tide
I'd rather sit wi you than ride,
    Tho 'twere wi royal Geordie:
And trowth! your kindness, soon and late
Aft gars me to myself look blate –                    makes, backward
    The Lord in Heaven reward ye!

*ELLISLAND*          R. BURNS

# GRIM GRIZZEL

Burns wrote this parody about 1791. The origin of this burlesque is mentioned in a note: 'Passing lately through Dunblane, while I stopped to refresh my horse, the following ludicrous epitaph, which I pickt up from an old tombstone among the ruins of the ancient Abbey, struck me particularly, being myself a native of Dumfriesshire.' The tombstone apostrophized: 'Here lyes with Dethe auld Grizzel Grimme, Lincluden's ugly witche. O Dethe, an what a taste hast thou Cann lye with siche a bitche!'

Grim Grizzel was a mighty Dame
  Weel kend on Cluden-side:
Grim Grizzel was a mighty Dame
  O meikle fame and pride.

When gentles met in gentle bowers
  And nobles in the ha',
Grim Grizzel was a mighty Dame,
  The loudest o them a'.

Where lawless Riot rag'd the night
  And Beauty durst na gang,
Grim Grizzel was a mighty Dame
  Wham nae man e'er wad wrang.

Nor had Grim Grizzel skill alane
  What bower and ha' require;
But she had skill, and meikle skill,                                    much
  In barn and eke in byre.                                   also, cow-shed

Ae day Grim Grizzel walked forth,
  As she was wont to do,
Alang the banks o Cluden fair
  Her cattle for to view.

The cattle shat o'er hill and dale
  As cattle will incline,
And sair it grieved Grim Grizzel's heart                               sore
  Sae muckle muck to tine.                                            lose

And she has ca'd on John o Clods,
  Of her herdsmen the chief,
And she has ca'd on John o Clods,
  And tell'd him a' her grief: –

'Now wae betide thee, John o Clods!
  I gie thee meal and fee,
And yet sae meikle muck ye tine
  Might a' be gear to me!                                          wealth

'Ye claut my byre, ye sweep my byre,                               scrape
  The like was never seen;
The very chamber I lie in
  Was never half sae clean.

'Ye ca' my kye adown the loan           *cattle, pasture*
   And there they a' discharge:
My Tammy's hat, wig, head and a'
   Was never half sae large!

'But mind my words now, John o Clods,
   And tent me what I say:             *heed*
My kye shall shit ere they gae out,     *before*
   That shall they ilka day.          *every*

'And mind my words now, John o Clods,
   And tent now wha ye serve;
Or back ye'se to the Colonel gang,      *go*
   Either to steal or starve.'

Then John o Clods he lookèd up,
   And syne he lookèd down;          *then*
He looked east, he lookèd west,
   He lookèd roun and roun.

His bonnet and his rowantree club
   Frae either hand did fa';
Wi lifted een and open mouth         *eyes*
   He naething said at a'.

At length he found his trembling tongue,
   Within his mouth was fauld:      *folded*
'Ae silly word frae me, madam,        *One*
   Gin I daur be sae bauld.     *dare, so bold*

'Your kye will at nae bidding shite,
   Let me do what I can;
Your kye will at nae bidding shite
   Of onie earthly man.

'Tho ye are great Lady Glaur-hole,     *Mud-*
   For a' your power and art
Tho ye are great Lady Glaur-hole,
   They winna let a fart.'

'Now wae betide thee, John o Clods!
   An ill death may ye die!
My kye shall at my bidding shite,
   And that ye soon shall see.'

Then she's ta'en Hawkie by the tail,
   And wrung wi might and main,
Till Hawkie rowted through the woods    *routed*
   Wi agonising pain.

'Shite, shite, ye bitch,' Grim Grizzel roar'd,
   Till hill and valley rang;
'And shite, ye bitch,' the echoes roar'd
   Lincluden wa's amang.

## TO ROBERT GRAHAM, ESQ., OF FINTRY

Robert Graham, 12th laird of Fintry in Angus (1749-1815) was a distant kinsman of James Graham of Claverhouse. Burns first met him at Blair Atholl on 31st Agusut 1787 during his Highland tour. In that year Graham was appointed a Commissioner of the Scottish Board of Excise and through his 'warmest exertions' he secured for Burns an Excise appointment in 1788.

Late crippl'd of an arm, and now a leg;
About to beg a pass for leave to beg;
Dull, listless, teas'd, dejected, and deprest
(Nature is adverse to a cripple's rest);
Will generous Graham list to his Poet's wail
(It soothes poor Misery, hearkening to her tale),
And hear him curse the light he first survey'd,
And doubly curse the luckless rhyming trade?

Thou, Nature! partial nature! I arraign;
Of thy caprice maternal I complain:
The lion and the bull thy care have found,
One shakes the forests, and one spurns the ground;
Thou giv'st the ass his hide, the snail his shell;
Th' envenom'd wasp, victorious, guards his cell;
Thy minions kings defend, control, devour,
In all th' omnipotence of rule and power.
Foxes and statesmen subtile wiles ensure;
The cit and polecat stink, and are secure;                    *city-dweller*
Toads with their poison, doctors with their drug,
The priest and hedgehog in their robes, are snug;
Ev'n silly woman has her warlike arts,
Her tongue and eyes – her dreaded spear and darts.

But O thou bitter step-mother and hard,
To thy poor, fenceless, naked child – the Bard!
A thing unteachable in world's skill,
And half an idiot too, more helpless still:
No heels to bear him from the op'ning dun,
No claws to dig, his hated sight to shun;
No horns, but those by luckless Hymen worn,          *god of marriage*
And those, alas! not, Amalthea's horn;              *daughter of Melissus*
No nerves olfact'ry, Mammon's trusty cur,                      *of Crete*
Clad in rich Dulness' comfortable fur;
In naked feeling, and in aching pride,
He bears th' unbroken blast from ev'ry side:
Vampyre booksellers drain him to the heart,                 *an insulting*
And scorpion critics cureless venom dart.            *reference to Creech*
                                                    *Alexander Monroe*
Critics - appall'd, I venture on the name;              *(1696-1767), son*
Those cut-throat bandits in the paths of fame;          *(1733-1817) and*
Bloody dissectors, worse than ten Monroes: `      *grandson (1773-1859)*
He hacks to teach, they mangle to expose.             *professors of*
                                                    *anatomy, Edinburgh*

His heart by causeless wanton malice wrung,
By blockheads' daring into madness stung;
His well-won bays, than life itself more dear,
By miscreants torn, who ne'er one sprig must wear;
Foil'd, bleeding, tortur'd in th' unequal strife,
The hapless Poet flounders on thro life:
Till, fled each hope that once his bosom fir'd,
And fled each Muse that glorious once inspir'd,
Low sunk in squalid, unprotected age,
Dead even resentment for his injur'd page,
He heeds or feels no more the ruthless critic's rage!
So, by some hedge, the gen'rous steed deceas'd,
For half-starv'd snarling curs a dainty feast,
By toil and famine wore to skin and bone,
Lies, senseless of each tugging bitch's son.

O Dulness! portion of the truly blest!
Calm shelter'd haven of eternal rest!
Thy sons ne'er madden in the fierce extremes
Of Fortune's polar frost, or torrid beams.
If mantling high she fills the golden cup,
With sober, selfish ease they sip it up:
Conscious the bounteous meed they well deserve,
They only wonder 'some folks' do not starve
The grave, sage hern thus easy picks his frog,
And thinks the mallard a sad, worthless dog.
When Disappointment snaps the clue of hope,
And thro disastrous night they darkling grope,
With deaf endurance sluggishly they bear,
And just conclude 'that fools are fortune's care.'
So, heavy, passive to the tempest's shocks,
Strong on the sign-post stands the stupid ox.

Not so the idle Muses' mad-cap train;
Not such the workings of their moon-struck brain:
In equanimity they never dwell;
By turns in soaring heav'n, or vaulted hell.

I dread thee, Fate, relentless and severe,
With all a poet's, husband's, father's fear!
Already one strong hold of hope is lost:
Glencairn, the truly noble, lies in dust
(Fled, like the sun eclips'd as noon appears,
And left us darkling in a world of tears).
O! hear my ardent, grateful, selfish pray'r!
Fintry, my other stay, long bless and spare!
Thro a long life his hopes and wishes crown,
And bright in cloudless skies his sun go down!
May bliss domestic smooth his private path;
Give energy to life; and soothe his latest breath,
With many a filial tear circling the bed of death!

## WILLIAM SMELLIE - A SKETCH

William Smellie (1740-95) was Burns's printer and a founder of the Crochallan Fencibles. The son of a Duddingston stone-mason, he was an antiquary, natural historian, and prolific writer, best remembered as first Editor of the Enclyclopaedia Britannica. 'Many letters from Burns to Smellie...being totally unfit for publication...have been burnt,' wrote Kerr.

Crochallan came:
The old cock'd hat, the brown surtout the same, overcoat
His grisly beard just bristling in its might
('Twas four long nights and days to shaving-night):
His uncomb'd, hoary locks, wild-staring, thatch'd
A head for thought profound and clear unmatch'd;
Yet, tho his caustic wit was biting rude,
His heart was warm, benevolent, and good.

## THOU GLOOMY DECEMBER

This and the following song were written for Clarinda on the eve of her departure for Jamaica. Burns had been in Edinburgh early in December and sent these songs to her on 27th of that month. 'Nancy' is, of course, Agnes McLehose herself.

Ance mair I hail thee, thou gloomy December!
    Ance mair I hail thee wi sorrow and care!
Sad was the parting thou makes me remember:
    Parting wi Nancy, O, ne'er to meet mair!

Fond lovers' parting is sweet, painful pleasure,
    Hope beaming mild on the soft parting hour;
But the dire feeling, O farewell for ever!
    Anguish unmingled and agony pure!

Wild as the winter now tearing the forest,
    Till the last leaf o the summer is flown –
Such is the tempest has shaken my bosom,
    Till my last hope and last comfort is gone!

Still as I hail thee, thou gloomy December,
    Still shall I hail thee wi sorrow and care;
For sad was the parting thou makes me remember;
    Parting wi Nancy, O, ne'er to meet mair!

## SAE FAR AWA

*TUNE: Dalkeith Maiden Bridge*

Traditionally associated song with the parting of Burns and Nancy McLehose when she was leaving for Jamaica in 1791.

O, sad and heavy should I part
    But for her sake sae far awa,
Unknowing what my way may thwart –
    My native land sae far awa.

Thou that of a' things Maker art,
   That formed this Fair sae far awa,
Gie body strength, then I'll ne'er start
   At this my way sae far awa!

How true is love to pure desert!
   So mine in her sae far awa,
And nocht shall heal my bosom's smart,
   While, O, she is sae far awa!

Nane other love, nane other dart
   I feel, but hers sae far awa;
But fairer never touch'd a heart
   Than hers, the Fair sae far awa.

# AE FOND KISS

*TUNE: Rory Dall's Port*

As Maurice Lindsay has said, 'a song so genuine in its resigned passion that it relegates the other nine songs he had written for her, full of "sensibility" and drawing-room manners, to the realms of the insignificant.' In January 1792 Nancy sailed from Greenock aboard the *Roselle* - ironically the ship that should have carried Burns himself to Jamaica five years earlier.

Ae fond kiss, and then we sever!
Ae farewell, and then forever!
Deep in heart-wrung tears I'll pledge thee,
Warring sighs and groans I'll wage thee.
Who shall say that Fortune grieves him,
While the star of hope she leaves him?
Me, nae cheerfu twinkle lights me,
Dark despair around benights me.

I'll ne'er blame my partial fancy:
Naething could resist my Nancy!
But to see her was to love her
Love but her, and love for ever.
Had we never lov'd sae kindly,
Had we never lov'd sae blindly,
Never met – or never parted –
We had ne'er been broken-hearted.

Fare-thee-weel, thou first and fairest!
Fare-thee-weel, thou best and dearest!        every
Thine be ilka joy and treasure,
Peace, Enjoyment, Love and Pleasure!
Ae fond kiss, and then we sever!
Ae farewell, alas, for ever!
Deep in heart-wrung tears I'll pledge thee,
Warring sighs and groans I'll wage thee.

## THERE WAS TWA WIVES

*TUNE: Take Your Old Cloak About You*

Burns's revision of a popular ballad, which he sent to Robert Cleghorn about January 1792, describing it as 'a new Edition of an old Cloaciniad song, a species of composition which I have heard you admire.'

| | |
|---|---|
| There was twa wives, and twa witty wives, | |
| As e'er play'd houghmagandie, | fornication |
| And they coost oot, upon a time, | cast |
| Out o'er a drink o brandy; | |
| Up Maggy rose, and forth she goes, | |
| And she leaves auld Mary flytin, | scolding |
| And she farted by the byre-en' | |
| For she was gaun a shiten. | |

| | |
|---|---|
| She farted by the byre-en', | |
| She farted by the stable; | |
| And thick and nimble were her steps | rapid |
| As fast as she was able: | |
| Till at yon dyke-back the hurly brak, | diarrhoea |
| But raxin for some dockins, | reaching, dock-leaves |
| The beans and pease cam down her thighs, | |
| And she cackit a' her stockins. | fouled |

## SAW YE BONIE LESLEY

*TUNE: The Collier's 'Bony Dochter'*

Lesley Baillie (d. 1843) was the daughter of Robert Baillie of Mayfield, Ayrshire. In a letter of 22nd August 1792 Burns wrote to Mrs Dunlop that Mr Baillie and his two daughters on their way to England, had visited him a few days earlier - 'on which I took my horse... and convoyed them fourteen or fifteen miles and dined and spent the day with them. 'Twas about nine, I think, when I left them; and riding home I composed the following ballad.' It was modelled on the old ballad 'My bonie Lizie Bailie.'

O, saw ye bonie Lesley,
    As she gaed o'er the Border?
She's gane, like Alexander,
    To spread her conquests farther!

To see her is to love her,
    And love but her for ever;
For Nature made her what she is,
    And never made anither!

Thou art a queen, fair Lesley –
    Thy subjects, we before thee!
Thou art divine, fair Lesley –
    The hearts o men adore thee.

The Deil he could na skaith thee,        *not harm*
   Or aught that wad belang thee;
He'd look into thy bonie face,
   And say: – 'I canna wrang thee!'

The Powers aboon will tent thee,
   Misfortune sha'na steer thee:
Thou'rt like themsel sae lovely,
   That ill they'll ne'er let near thee.

Return again, fair Lesley,
   Return to Caledonie!
That we may brag we hae a lass
   There's nane again sae bonie.

# CRAIGIEBURN WOOD

This was Burns's first contribution to SMM vol.iv. The subject was Jean Lorimer (1775-1831), daughter of William Lorimer of Kemmishall on the Nith two miles south of Ellisland. She was courted by a fellow-exciseman, John Gillespie, for whom Burns composed several poems. Unmoved by these effusions Jean eloped to Gretna Green with a young spendthrift, Andrew Whelpdale (1774-1816) who, after three weeks of marriage, abandoned his bride to escape his creditors. She returned to her father's home. She later became Burns's Chloris, for whom he wrote at least two dozen songs including some of his very best. Craigieburn was Jean's birthplace, near Moffat. James Hogg, the Ettrick Shepherd, alleged that Burns himself had an ongoing affair with Jean, and stayed with her every time his business took him to Moffat.

## CHORUS

*Beyond thee, dearie, beyond thee, dearie,*
   *And O, to be lying beyond thee!*
*O, sweetly, soundly, weel may he sleep*
   *That's laid in the bed beyond thee!*

Sweet closes the ev'ning on Craigieburn Wood
   And blythely awaukens the morrow,
But the pride o the spring on the Craigieburn Wood
   Can yield me naught but sorrow.

I see the spreading leaves and flowers,
   I hear the wild birds singing;
But pleasure they hae nane for me,
   While care my heart is wringing.

I can na tell, I maun na tell,        *must*
   I daur na for your anger;        *dare not*
But secret love will break my heart,
   If I conceal it langer.

I see thee gracefu, straight, and tall,
   I see thee sweet and bonie;
But O, what will my torment be,
   If thou refuse thy Johnie!

To see thee in another's arms
   In love to lie and languish,
'Twad be my dead, that will be seen –
   My heart wad burst wi anguish!

But, Jeanie, say thou wilt be mine,
   Say thou lo'es nane before me,
And a' my days o life to come
   I'll gratefully adore thee.

# FRAE THE FRIENDS AND LAND
# I LOVE

Burns alleged that this was a traditional ballad to which he merely added the last four lines, though no original has ever been traced. Dewar considered this a subterfuge whereby Burns might distance himself from authorship of such an avowedly Jacobite song, but the only overtly Jacobite lines are the last - those very lines which he claimed as his own.

Frae the friends and land I love        *From*
   Driv'n by Fortune's felly spite,        *deadly*
Frae my best belov'd I rove,
   Never mair to taste delight!
Never mair maun hope to find
   Ease frae toil, relief frae care.
When remembrance wracks the mind,
   Pleasures but unveil despair.

Brightest climes shall mirk appear,
   Desert ilka blooming shore,        *each*
Till the Fates, nae mair severe,
   Friendship, love, and peace restore;
Till Revenge, wi laurell'd head,
   Bring our banish'd hame again,
And ilk loyal, bonie lad
   Cross the seas, and win his ain!        *own*

# HUGHIE GRAHAM

*TUNE: Druimionn dubh*

Many versions exist of this old ballad; this one, according to Burns, 'was from oral tradition in Ayrshire, where, when I was a boy, it was a popular song.' Burns extensively revised it, compressed the opening, and added eight lines of his own. Though set in Stirling a local touch was added by the inclusion of the Whitefoords, a prominent Ayrshire family in Burns's day.

Our lords are to the mountains gane,
    A hunting o the fallow deer;
And they hae gripet Hughie Graham          arrested
    For stealing o the bishop's mare.

And they hae tied him hand and foot,
    And led him up thro Stirling town;
The lads and lasses met him there,
    Cried, Hughie Graham thou art a loun.      fool

O lowse my right hand free, he says,      release
    And put my braid sword in the same;
He's no in Stirling town this day,
    Daur tell the tale to Hughie Graham.      Dare

Up then bespake the brave Whitefoord,
    As he sat by the bishop's knee;
Five hundred white stots I'll gie you,      young bullocks
    If ye'll let Hughie Graham gae free.

O haud your tongue, the bishop says,
    And wi your pleading let me be;
For tho ten Grahams were in his coat,
    Hughie Graham this day shall die.

Up then bespake the fair Whitefoord,
    As she sat by the bishop's knee;
Five hundred white pence I'll gie you,
    If ye'll gie Hughie Graham to me.

O haud your tongue now lady fair,
    And wi your pleading let me be;
Altho ten Grahams were in his coat,
    It's for my honor he maun die.

They've taen him to the gallows knowe,      hillock
    He looked to the gallows tree,
Yet never color left his cheek,
    Nor ever did he blin' his e'e.

At length he looked round about,
    To see whatever he could spy;
And there he saw his auld father,
    And he was weeping bitterly.

O haud your tongue, my father dear,        hold
  And wi your weeping let it be;
Thy weeping's sairer on my heart,        sorer
  Than a' that they can do to me.

And ye may gie my brother John
  My sword that's bent in the middle clear,
And let him come at twelve o'clock
  And see me pay the bishop's mare.

And ye may gie my brother James
  My sword that's bent in the middle brown;
And bid him come at four o'clock,
  And see his brother Hugh cut down.

Remember me to Maggy my wife,
  The niest time ye gang o'er the moor;   next, go
Tell her, she staw the bishop's mare,     stole
  Tell her, she was the bishop's whore.

And ye may tell my kith and kin,
  I never did disgrace their blood;
And when they meet the bishop's cloak,
  To mak it shorter by the hood.

## JOHN COME KISS ME NOW

This widely popular song has been traced back to late medieval times and numerous versions have been recorded before Burns revised it and added a stanza, for SMM.

### CHORUS

*O John, come kiss me now, now, now;*
  *O John, my luve, come kiss me now;*
*O John, come kiss me by and by,*
  *For weel ye ken the way to woo.*       know

O some will court and compliment,
  And ither some will kiss and daut;     caress
But I will mak o my gudeman,
  My ain gudeman, it is nae faute.      fault

O some will court and compliment,
  And ither some will prie their mou,  prise, mouth
And some will hause in ithers arms,   embrace
  And that's the way I like to do.

## COCK UP YOUR BEAVER

This is a revision of an old fragment in the Herd MSS (II.205).

When first my brave Johnie lad came to this town,
He had a blue bonnet that wanted the crown,
But now he has gotten a hat and a feather –
Hey, brave Johnie lad, cock up your beaver!       beaver-hat

Cock up your beaver, and cock it fu sprush!       spruce
We'll over the border and gie them a brush:
There's somebody there we'll teach better behaviour
Hey, brave Johnie lad, cock up your beaver!

## MY TOCHER'S THE JEWEL

The last four lines, annotated 'Stanza of an old song, tune bonie Dundee' were included in a collection of poetic scraps sent by Burns to Tytler of Woodhouselee, probably in August 1787 as 'a sample of the old pieces that are still to be found among our Peasantry in the West.'

O, meikle thinks my luve o my beauty,
   And meikle thinks my luve o my kin;
But little thinks my luve I ken brawlie       finely
   My tocher's the jewel has charms for him.       dowry
It's a' for the apple he'll nourish the tree,
   It's a' for the hiney he'll cherish the bee!       honey
My laddie's sae meikle in luve wi the siller,       much, money
   He canna hae luve to spare for me!

Your proffer o luve's an airle-penny,       bargain penny
   My tocher's the bargain ye wad buy;
But an ye be crafty, I am cunnin,       if
   Sae ye wi anither your fortune may try.
Ye're like to the timmer o yon rotten wood,       timber
   Ye're like to the bark o yon rotten tree:
Ye'll slip frae me like a knotless thread,
   An ye'll crack ye're credit wi mair nor me!

## GUIDWIFE, COUNT THE LAWIN

According to Burns, the chorus of this song was part of an old ballad, but the verses were his own work.

### CHORUS

| | |
|---|---|
| *Then, guidwife, count the lawin,* | mistress, reckoning |
| *The lawin, the lawin!* | |
| *Then, guidwife, count the lawin,* | |
|   *And bring a coggie mair!* | another jug |

| | |
|---|---|
| Gane is the day, and mirk's the night, | dark's |
| But we'll ne'er stray for faut o light, | lack |
| For ale and brandy's stars and moon, | |
| And blude-red wine's the risin sun. | |

| | |
|---|---|
| There's wealth and ease for gentlemen, | |
| And semple folk maun fecht and fen'; | simple, must fight |
| But here we're a' in ae accord, | one |
| For ilka man that's drunk's a lord. | each |

| | |
|---|---|
| My coggie is a haly pool | holy |
| That heals the wounds o care and dool, | woe |
| And Pleasure is a wanton trout: | |
| An ye drink it a', ye'll find him out! | If |

## WHAT CAN A YOUNG LASSIE DO WI
## AN AULD MAN

Listed in the Gray MS as 'Mr B-'s words,' and signed in SMM as his work.

| | |
|---|---|
| What can a young lassie, what shall a young lassie, | |
|   What can a young lassie do wi an auld man? | |
| Bad luck on the penny that tempted my minnie | mother |
|   To sell her puir Jenny for siller an lan'! | money |

| | |
|---|---|
| He's always compleenin frae morning to eenin; | |
|   He hoasts and he hirples the weary day lang; | coughs, limps |
| He's doylt and he's dozin, his blude it is frozen – | senile |
|   O, dreary's the night wi a crazy auld man! | |

| | |
|---|---|
| He hums and he hankers, he frets and he cankers, | crabs |
|   I never can please him do a' that I can. | |
| He's peevish an jealous o a' the young fellows – | |
|   O, dool on the day I met wi an auld man! | woe |

| | |
|---|---|
| My auld auntie Katie upon me taks pity, | |
|   I'll do my endeavour to follow her plan; | |
| I'll cross him an wrack him, until I heartbreak him, | |
|   And then his auld brass will buy me a new pan. | |

## THE BONIE LAD THAT'S FAR AWA

Burns modelled this song on the seventeenth century ballad 'The Unconstant Shepherd
or the Forsaken Lass's Lamentation.'

O how can I be blythe and glad,
 Or how can I gang brisk and braw,         go, fine
When the bonie lad that I lo'e best
 Is o'er the hills and far awa?

It's no the frosty winter wind,
 It's no the driving drift and snaw;
But ay the tear comes in my e'e,
 To think on him that's far awa.

My father pat me frae his door,          put, from
 My friends they hae disown'd me a'!:
But I hae ane will tak my part –
 The bonie lad that's far awa.

A pair o glooves he bought to me,
 And silken snoods he gae me twa,       bandeaux, gave
And I will wear them for his sake,
 The bonie lad that's far awa.

O, weary Winter soon will pass,
 And Spring will cleed the birken shaw,    clothe, birch wood
And my sweet babie will be born,
 And he'll be hame that's far awa!

## I DO CONFESS THOU ART SAE FAIR

In his annotated copy of SMM Burns wrote: 'This song is altered from a poem by Sir
Robert Ayton, private Secretary to Mary and Anne, queens of Scotland... I think I have
improved the simplicity of the sentiments, by giving them a Scots dress.'

I do confess thou art sae fair,
 I wad been o'er the lugs in luve,      head over heels
Had I na found the slightest prayer
 That lips could speak thy heart could muve.

I do confess thee sweet, but find
 Thou art so thriftless o thy sweets,
Thy favours are the silly wind
 That kisses ilka thing it meets.        every

See yonder rosebud rich in dew,
 Amang its native briers sae coy,
How sune it tines its scent and hue,       loses
 When pu'd and worn a common toy!

Sic fate ere lang shall thee betide,
 Tho thou may gaily bloom awhile,
And sune thou shalt be thrown aside,
 Like onie common weed, an vile.

## GALLOWAY TAM

Burns's hand in this traditional ballad is uncertain, despite the note in the Law MS
(annotations for SMM) 'Mr. Burns's old words.'

O Galloway Tam came here to woo,
 I'd rather we'd gin him the brawnit cow;    given, brindled
For our lass Bess may curse and ban
 The wanton wit o Galloway Tam.

O Galloway Tam came here to shear,     clip fleeces
 I'd rather we'd gin him the gude gray mare;
He kist the gudewife and strack the gudeman,  wife, struck,
 And that 's the tricks o Galloway Tam.    husband


## AS I CAM DOWN BY YON CASTLE WA'

Communicated by Burns to Johnson as 'a very popular Ayrshire song'. Kinsley admits
this to the canon although there is no evidence that Burns corrected the words in any
way, and it retains the rough vigour of the original.

As I cam down by yon castle wa',
 And in by yon garden green,
O there I spied a bony bony lass,
 But the flower-borders were us between.

A bony bony lassie she was,
 As ever mine eyes did see:
O five hundred pounds would I give,
 For to have such a pretty bride as thee.

To have such a pretty bride as me,
 Young man ye are sairly mista'en;
Tho ye were king o fair Scotland,
 I wad disdain to be your queen.

Talk not so very high, bony lass,
 O talk not so very, very high:
The man at the fair that wad sell,
 He maun learn at the man that wad buy.

I trust to climb a far higher tree,
 And herry a far richer nest:
Tak this advice o me, bony lass,
 Humility wad set thee best.

## LORD RONALD MY SON

Sent by Burns to Johnson, this is a fragment of the widespread old ballad 'Lord Randal'. Much longer versions were in print before Burns's time and it seems that he reduced these two stanzas to make a song.

O where hae ye been, Lord Ronald, my son?
O where hae ye been, Lord Ronald, my son?
I hae been wi my sweetheart, mother, make my bed soon;
For I'm weary wi the hunting, and fain wad lie down.

What got ye frae your sweetheart, Lord Ronald, my son?
What got ye frae your sweetheart, Lord Ronald, my son?
I hae got deadly poison, mother, make my bed soon;
For life is a burden that soon I'll lay down. –

## I HAE BEEN AT CROOKIEDEN

There were several traditional ballads by the name of 'Highland Laddie.' Burns believed this to be the oldest of them and revised it extensively. Nevertheless, the reference to 'Willie' (1.3) - the Duke of Cumberland and victor of Culloden - puts this version no earlier than 1746.

I hae been at Crookieden
    My bonie laddie, Highland laddie!
Viewing Willie and his men –
    My bonie laddie, Highland laddie!
There our foes that burnt and slew –
    My bonie laddie, Highland laddie –
There at last they gat their due –
    My bonie laddie, Highland laddie!

Satan sits in his black neuk –              *corner*
    My bonie laddie, Highland laddie!
Breaking sticks to roast the Duke –
    My bonie laddie, Highland laddie!
The bloody monster gae a yell –          *gave*
    My bonie laddie, Highland laddie!
And loud the laugh gaed round a' Hell.    *went*
    My bonie laddie, Highland laddie!

## IT IS NA, JEAN, THY BONIE FACE

*TUNE: The Maid's Complaint*

Burns took some old English verses and 'gave them their Scots dress.' This poem was written for Jean Armour.

It is na, Jean, thy bonie face
    Nor shape that I admire,
Altho thy beauty and thy grace
    Might weel awauk desire.          *awaken*

Something in ilka part o thee        *each*
  To praise, to love, I find;
But, dear as is thy form to me,
  Still dearer is thy mind.

Nae mair ungen'rous wish I hae,
  Nor stronger in my breast,
Than, if I canna mak thee sae,
  At least to see thee blest.

Content am I, if Heaven shall give
  But happiness to thee,
And, as wi thee I wish to live,
  For thee I'd bear to dee.       *die*

## MY EPPIE MACNAB

'The old song with this title has more wit than decency' says Burns in his SMM notes. The bawdy version first appeared in print about 1806 in the *Giblet Pye*.

O, saw ye my dearie, my Eppie Macnab?
O, saw ye my dearie, my Eppie Macnab?
  She's down in the yard, she's kissin the laird,
She winna come hame to her ain Jock Rab!'    *will not, own*

O, come thy ways to me, my Eppie Macnab!
O, come thy ways to me, my Eppie Macnab!
  Whate'er thou hast done, be it late, be it soon,
Thou's welcome again to thy ain Jock Rab.

What says she, my dearie, my Eppie Macnab?
What says she, my dearie, my Eppie Macnab?
  'She lets thee to wit that she has thee forgot,
And forever disowns thee, her ain Jock Rab.'

O, had I ne'er seen thee, my Eppie Macnab!
O, had I ne'er seen thee, my Eppie Macnab!
  As light as the air, and as fause as thou's fair,    *false*
Thou's broken the heart o thy ain Jock Rab!

## 'INDEED WILL I,' QUO FINDLAY

*TUNE: Lass, an I come near thee*

Although the immedite model for this nocturnal dialogue was a broadside 'Wha's that at my chamber door?' the theme behind it can be traced back through medieval ballads to the Song of Solomon itself.

'Wha, is that at my bower-door?'
'O, wha is it but Findlay!'
'Then gae your gate, ye'se nae be here.'      go your way,
'Indeed maun I!' quo Findlay.      you shall not
     must, said

'What mak ye, sae like a thief?'
'O come and see!' quo Findlay.
'Before the morn ye'll work mischief?'
'Indeed will I,' quo Findlay.

'Gif I rise and let you in' –      If
'Let me in!' quo Findlay –
'Ye'll keep me waukin wi your din?'      awake
'Indeed will I!' quo Findlay.

'In my bower if you should stay' –
'Let me stay!' quo Findlay –
'I fear ye'll bide till break o day?'      stay
'Indeed will I!' quo Findlay.

'Here this night if ye remain' –
'I'll remain!' quo Findlay –
'I dread ye'll learn the gate again?'
'Indeed will I!' quo Findlay.

'What may pass within this bower' –
('Let it pass!' quo Findlay)
'Ye maun conceal till your last hour' –
'Indeed will I!' quo Findlay.

## BONIE WEE THING

Dedicated to that petite beauty Deborah Duff Davies, to whom he sent this song with one of his more turgid epistles on 6th April 1793. In another letter to her, about two month later, he wrote: 'I am a good deal luckier than most poets. When I sing of Miss Davies or Miss Lesley Baillie, I have only to feign the passion - the charms are real.'

CHORUS

*Bonie wee thing, cannie wee thing,*
*Lovely wee thing, wert thou mine,*
*I wad wear thee in my bosom*
*Lest my jewel it should tine.*      lose

Wishfully I look and languish
   In that bonie face o thine,
And my heart it stounds wi anguish,
   Lest my wee thing be na mine.

Wit and Grace and Love and Beauty
   In ae constellation shine!
To adore thee is my duty,
   Goddess o this soul o mine!

## GEORDIE - AN OLD BALLAD

Numerous versions of this song have survived. Burns appears to have collected it during his Highland tour and probably revised it before sending it to Johnson. Geordie has been identified as George Gordon, 4th Earl of Huntly, imprisoned in Edinburgh Castle (1554) for failing to catch a Highland reiver, but Kinsley thought the 6th Earl more likely. He rebelled against James VI (1589), was imprisoned as a traitor, but amnestied during the Kings's wedding celebrations. The identity of Sir Charles Hay has never been traced.

There was a battle in the north,
   And nobles there was many,
And they hae kill'd Sir Charlie Hay,
   And they laid the wyte on Geordie.      blame

O he has written a lang letter,
   He sent it to his lady;
Ye maun cum up to Enbrugh town      must
   To see what words o Geordie.

When first she look'd the letter on,
   She was baith red and rosy;
But she had na read a word but twa,
   Till she wallow't like a lily.      paled

Gar get to me my gude grey steed,      Make ready
   My menzie a' gae wi me;      retinue
For I shall neither eat nor drink,
   Till Enbrugh town shall see me.

And she has mountit her gude grey steed,
   Her menzie a' gaed wi her;
And she did neither eat nor drink
   Till Enbrugh town did see her.

And first appear'd the fatal block,
   And syne the aix to head him;      axe, behead
And Geordie cumin down the stair,
   And bands o airn upon him.      iron

But tho he was chain'd in fetters strang,
   O airn and steel sae heavy,
There was na ane in a' the court,
   Sae braw a man as Geordie.                   *fine*

O she's down on her bended knee,
   I wat she's pale and weary,               *wot*
O pardon, pardon, noble king,
   And gie me back my Dearie!

I hae born seven sons to my Geordie dear,
   The seventh ne'er saw his daddie:
O pardon, pardon, noble king,
   Pity a waefu lady!

Gar bid the headin-man mak haste!         *headsman*
   Our king reply'd fu lordly:
O noble king, tak a' that's mine,
   But gie me back my Geordie.

The Gordons cam and the Gordons ran,
   And they were stark and steady;        *strong*
And ay the word amang them a'
   Was, Gordons keep you ready.

An aged lord at the king's right hand
   Says, noble king, but hear me:
Gar her tell down five thousand pound     *Make*
   And gie her back her Dearie.

Some gae her marks, some gae her crowns,
   Some gae her dollars many;
And she's tell'd down five thousand pound,
   And she's gotten again her Dearie.

She blinkit blythe in her Geordie's face,    *glanced*
   Says, dear I've bought thee, Geordie:
But there sud been bluidy bouks on the green,  *should have,*
   Or I had tint my laddie.          *trunks, Ere, lost*

He claspit her by the middle sma',
   And he kist her lips sae rosy:
The fairest flower o woman-kind
   Is my sweet, bonie Lady!

# THE PLOUGHMAN'S LIFE

*TUNE: Rinn m'eudail mo mhealladh*

Several versions of this old ballad exist. Burns rejected the third and fourth stanzas in the Herd MSS, in which the girl's mood changes dramatically, and he changed the remaining lines extensively to suit the rhythm of the old Gaelic air.

As I was a-wand'ring ae morning in spring,        one
I heard a young ploughman sae sweetly to sing;
And as he was singin, thir words he did say, –
There's nae life like the ploughman's in the month o sweet May.

The lav'rock in the morning she'll rise frae her nest,     lark
And mount i' the air wi the dew on her breast,
And wi the merry ploughman she'll whistle and sing,
And at night she'll return to her nest back again.

# THE WEARY PUND O TOW

Burns took a rather artless ballad, published in *The Charmer* (1782) and transformed it into a neat and witty domestic comedy. Tow is the flax fibre for spinning by breaking, beating and heckling (dressing).

## CHORUS

*The weary pund, the weary pund,*     dressed flax fibre
   *The weary pund o tow!*
*I think my wife will end her life*
   *Before she spin her tow.*

I bought my wife a stane o lint     stone (14 pounds)
   As guid as e'er did grow,
And a' that she has made o that
   Is ae puir pund o tow.     one

There sat a bottle in a bole     hole
   Beyont the ingle low;
And ay she took the tither souk     suck
   To drouk the stourie tow.     drench, dusty

Quoth I: – 'For shame, ye dirty dame,
   Gae spin your tap o tow!'
She took the rock, and wi a knock     distaff
   She brake it o'er my pow.     pate

At last her feet – I sang to see't! –
   Gaed foremost o'er the knowe,     Went, knoll
And or I wad anither jad,     ere, wed, jade
   I'll wallop in a tow.

# I HAE A WIFE O MY AIN

Traditionally this ballad has been assigned to 1788, soon after Burns finally settled
down to married life, but Kinsley doubts this, and places it in 1792 along with other
adaptations and revisions of old ballads.

I hae a wife o my ain,
    I'll partake wi naebody;
I'll take cuckold frae nane,
    I'll gie cuckold to naebody.

I hae a penny to spend,
    There – thanks to naebody.
I hae naething to lend,
    I'll borrow frae naebody.

I am naebody's lord,
    I'll be a slave to naebody.
I'll hae a guid braid sword,
    I'll tak dunts frae naebody.         blows

I'll be merry and free,
    I'll be sad for naebody.
Naebody cares for me,
    I care for naebody.

# WHEN SHE CAM BEN, SHE BOBBED

A revision of an old ballad in Herd MSS (II.206-7). Traditionally the laird of this song
was a close friend of King Charles II. Cockpen, Midlothian belonged in Burns's day to
the factor of Lord Cockburn and later to the Earl of Dalhousie.

O, when she cam ben, she bobbed fu law,
O, when she cam ban, she bobbed fu law,
And when she cam ben, she kiss'd Cockpen,
    And syne she deny'd she did it at a'!     then

And was na Cockpen right saucy witha'?
And was na Cockpen right saucy witha'?
In leaving the dochter o a lord     daughter
    And kissin a collier lassie an a'!

O, never look down, my lassie, at a'
O, never look down, my lassie, at a'
Thy lips are as sweet, and thy figure complete,
    As the finest dame in castle or ha'.

Tho thou hast nae silk, and holland sae sma',
Tho thou hast nae silk, and holland sae sma',
Thy coat and thy sark are thy ain handywark,     shirt
    And lady Jean was never sae braw.     handsome

## O, FOR ANE-AND-TWENTY, TAM

In a letter to George Thomson on 19th October 1794 Burns claimed this song as his own.

### CHORUS

*An O, for ane-and-twenty, Tam!*
*And hey, sweet ane-and-twenty, Tam!*
*I'll learn my kin a rattlin sang,*
*An I saw ane-and-twenty, Tam.*                    If

They snool me sair, and haud me down,          snub, sorely, hold
   And gar me look like bluntie, Tam;              make, fool
But three short years will soon wheel roun –
   And then comes ane-and-twenty, Tam!

A gleib o lan, a claut o gear                       portion, handful
   Was left me by my auntie, Tam.
At kith or kin I needna spier,                          enquire
   An I saw ane-and-twenty, Tam.

They'll hae me wed a wealthy coof,                       fool
   Tho I mysel hae plenty, Tam;
But hear'st thou, laddie – there's my loof:             palm
   I'm thine at ane-and-twenty, Tam.

## O, KENMURE'S ON AND AWA, WILLIE

Believed to be based on a Galloway ballad, although no authentic version earlier than 1810 is known in published form, Burns re-wrote it for SMM in 1792. William Gordon, 6th Viscount Kenmure raised the Jacobite standard at Lochmaben in 1715 and commanded the rebels in southern Scotland. He was beheaded at the Tower and his title attainted. Burns stayed with his grandson the 7th Viscount at Kenmure Castle on 27th July 1793 when he and John Syme made their tour through Galloway.

O, Kenmure's on and awa, Willie,
   O, Kenmure's on and awa!
An Kenmure's lord's the bravest lord
   That ever Galloway saw!
Success to Kenmure's band, Willie,
   Success to Kenmure's band!
There's no a heart that fears a Whig
   That rides by Kenmure's hand.

Here's Kenmure's health in wine, Willie,
   Here's Kenmure's health in wine!
There's ne'er a coward o Kenmure's blude,
   Nor yet o Gordon's line.
O, Kenmure's lads are men, Willie,
   O, Kenmure's lads are men!
Their hearts and swords are metal true,
   And that their faes shall ken.                          foes

They'll live or die wi fame, Willie,
  They'll live or die wi fame!
But soon wi sounding Victorie
  May Kenmure's lord come hame!
Here's him that's far awa, Willie,
  Here's him that's far awa!
And here's the flower that I lo'e best,
  The rose that's like the snaw!        the Jacobite rose

## BESSY AND HER SPINNIN-WHEEL

*TUNE: Sweet's the lass that loves me*

Henderson linked this, one of Burns's most charming pastorals, to 'The Loving Lass and
Spinning-wheel' in *The Tea-Table Miscellany* but Kinsley dismissed this relationship.
The heroine was Elizabeth Burgess of Watcarrick, Eskdalemuir, portions of whose
spinet are preserved at Ellisland.

| | |
|---|---|
| O, leeze me on my spinnin-wheel! | Blessings |
| And leeze me on my rock and reel, | distaff |
| Frae tap to tae that cleeds me bien, | clothes, snugly |
| And haps me fiel and warm at e'en! | covers, well |
| I'll set me down, and sing and spin, | sit |
| While laigh descends the summer sun, | low |
| Blest wi content, and milk and meal – | |
| O, leeze me on my spinnin-wheel! | |
| | |
| On ilka hand the burnies trot, | either, brooks |
| And meet below my theekit cot. | thatched cottage |
| The scented birk and hawthorn white | birch |
| Across the pool their arms unite, | |
| Alike to screen the birdie's nest | |
| And little fishes' caller rest. | cool |
| The sun blinks kindly in the biel, | glances, shelter |
| Where blythe I turn my spinnin-wheel. | |
| | |
| On lofty aiks the cushats wail, | oaks, pigeons |
| And Echo cons the doolfu tale. | woeful |
| The lintwhites in the hazel braes, | linnets, slopes |
| Delighted, rival ither's lays. | |
| The craik amang the claver hay, | corncrake, clover |
| The paitrick whirrin o'er the ley, | partridge, meadow |
| The swallow jinkin round my shiel, | darting, shieling |
| Amuse me at my spinnin-wheel. | |
| | |
| Wi sma' to sell and less to buy, | |
| Aboon distress, below envy, | Above |
| O, wha wad leave this humble state | |
| For a' the pride of a' the great? | |
| Amid their flaring, idle toys, | |
| Amid their cumbrous, dinsome joys, | |
| Can they the peace and pleasure feel | |
| Of Bessy at her spinnin-wheel? | |

# MY COLLIER LADDIE

Though Stenhouse claimed that this song was largely Burns's it is likely to have been traditional with revisions and additions. Coalmining was already a major Ayrshire industry in Burns's day, particularly in the vicinity of Kilmarnock. It was thought that the girl herself was a mineworker but Kinsley has pointed out that 5d (1.17) was a farm labourer's daily wage, whereas miners (including girls) got 4d per 30cwt of coal raised from the coal-face – a good daily average.

'O, whare live ye, my bonie lass,
    And tell me how they ca' ye?'
'My name,' she says, 'is Mistress Jean,
    And I follow the collier laddie.'

'O, see you not yon hills and dales
    The sun shines on sae brawlie?                           finely
They a' are mine, and they shall be thine,
    Gin ye'll leave your collier laddie!

'An ye shall gang in gay attire,
    Weel buskit up sae gaudy,                              dressed
And ane to wait on every hand,
    Gin ye'll leave your collier laddie!

'Tho ye had a' the sun shines on,
    And the earth conceals sae lowly,
I wad turn my back on you and it a',
    And embrace my collier laddie.

'I can win my five pennies in a day,
    An spend it at night fu brawlie,
And make my bed in the collier's neuk,           corner
    And lie down wi my collier laddie.

'Loove for loove is the bargain for me,
    Tho the wee cot-house should haud me,        keep
And the warld before me to win my bread –
    And fair fa' my collier laddie!'

# THE SHEPHERD'S WIFE

Burns's emendation of an old ballad in the Herd MSS, with minor changes and refinements.

The Shepherd's wife cries o'er the knowe,         knoll
    Will ye come hame, will ye come hame;
The Shepherd's wife cries o'er the knowe,
    Will ye come hame again e'en, jo?           darling

What will I get to my supper,
    Gin I come hame, gin I come hame?            If
What will I get to my supper,
    Gin I come hame again e'en, jo?

Ye'se get a panfu o plumpin parridge,         porridge
   And butter in them, and butter in them,
Ye'se get a panfu o plumpin parridge,
   Gin ye'll come hame again e'en, jo.

Ha, ha how! that 's naething that dow,         can
   I winna come hame, I canna come hame;  will not, cannot
Ha, ha how! that 's naething that dow,
   I winna come hame gin e'en, jo.

The Shepherd's wife &c.
What will I get &c.

A reekin fat hen, weel fryth'd i' the pan,     steaming
   Gin ye'll come hame, gin ye'll come hame,
A reekin fat hen weel fryth'd i' the pan,
   Gin ye'll come hame again e'en jo.

Ha, ha, how! &c.
The Shepherd's wife &c.
What will I get &c.

A weel made bed and a pair o clean sheets,
   Gin ye'll come hame, gin ye'll come hame,
A weel made bed and a pair o clean sheets,
   Gin ye'll come hame again e'en, jo. –

Ha, ha, how! &c.
The Shepherd's wife &c.
What will I get &c.

A luving wife in lily-white linens,
   Gin ye'll come hame, gin ye'll come hame,
A luving wife in lily-white linens,
   Gin ye'll come hame again e'en jo.

Ha, ha, how! that 's something that dow,
   I will come hame, I will come hame;
Ha, ha, how! that 's something that dow,
   I will come hame again e'en, jo.

## JOHNIE BLUNT

Johnson's note in the index to SMM suggests that the hero of this ballad 'lived
somewhere in Crawford Muirs,' but the name is proverbial for any dull-witted person.
Burns reworked a traditional version of this familiar song.

There liv'd a man in yonder glen,
   And John Blunt was his name, O;
He maks gude maut, and he brews gude ale,   malt
   And he bears a wondrous fame, O.

The wind blew in the hallan ae night,                    porch
   Fu snell out o'er the moor, O;                    bitter
'Rise up, rise up, auld Luckie,' he says,
   'Rise up and bar the door, O.'

They made a paction tween them twa,
   They made it firm and sure, O,
Whae'er sud speak the foremost word,                    should
   Should rise and bar the door, O.

Three travellers that had tint their gate,                    lost way
   As thro the hills they foor, O,                    travelled
They airted by the line o light                    were guided
   Fu straught to Johnie Blunt's door, O.                    straight

They haurl'd auld Luckie out o her bed,                    hauled
   And laid her on the floor, O;
But never a word auld Luckie wad say,
   For barrin o the door, O.

'Ye've eaten my bread, ye hae druken my ale,                    drunk
   'And ye'll mak my auld wife a whore, O – '
Aha, Johnie Blunt! he hae spoke the first word.
   Get up and bar the door, O.

## THE COUNTRY LASS

Acknowledged by Burns to Thomson in a letter of 19th October 1794. This song, says
Cunningham 'has the air and tone of the ancient lyrics of Caledonia. It hovers between
the dramatic and the sentimental, and partakes of the character of both.'

In simmer, when the hay was mawn                    mown
   And corn wav'd green in ilka field,                    every
While claver blooms white o'er the ley                    clover, meadow
   And roses blaw in ilka bield                    shelter
Blythe Bessie in the milking shiel                    shieling
   Says:- 'I'll be wed, come o't what will!'
Out spake a dame in wrinkled eild: –                    age
   'O guid advisement comes nae ill.

'It's ye hae wooers monie ane,                    many a one
   And lassie, ye're but young, ye ken!                    know
Then wait a wee, and cannie wale                    bit, prudently choose
   A routhie butt, a routhie ben.                    well-stocked kitchen,
There's Johnie o the Buskie-Glen,                    parlour
   Fu is his barn, fu is his byre.                    cow-shed
Tak this frae me, my bonie hen:
   It's plenty beets the luver's fire!'                    fans

'For Johnie o the Buskie-Glen
    I dinna care a single flie:
He lo'es sae weel his craps and kye,           crops, cattle
    He has nae love to spare for me.
But blythe's the blink o Robie's e'e,
    And weel I wat he lo'es me dear:
Ae blink o him I wad na gie                 one glimpse
    For Buskie-Glen and a' his gear.'

'O thoughtless lassie, life's a faught!          fight
    The canniest gate, the strife is sair.    quietest way, sore
But ay fu-han't is fechtin best:      full-handed, fighting
    A hungry care's an unco care.
But some will spend and some will spare,
    An wilfu folk maun hae their will.          must
Syne as ye brew, my maiden fair,
    Keep mind that ye maun drink the yill!'    ale

'O, gear will buy me rigs o land,
    And gear will buy me sheep and kye!
But the tender heart o leesome loove         lawful
    The gowd and siller canna buy!       gold, silver
We may be poor, Robie and I;
    Light is the burden luve lays on;
Content and loove brings peace and joy:
    What mair hae Queens upon a throne?'

# FAIR ELIZA

Writing to Johnson in July 1788 Burns asked: 'Have you never a fair goddess that leads
you a wild-goose-chase of amorous devotion? Let me know a few of her qualities...and
chuse your air, and I shall task my Muse to celebrate her.' In the original version (Hastie
MSS) the girl's name was Rabina (!), mercifully changed to Eliza before publication in
SMM.

Turn again, thou fair Eliza!
    Ae kind blink before we part!         One glance
Rew on thy despairing lover –
    Canst thou break his faithfu heart?
Turn again, thou fair Eliza!
    If to love thy heart denies,
For pity hide the cruel sentence
    Under friendship's kind disguise!

Thee, dear maid, hae I offended?
  The offence is loving thee.
Canst thou wreck his peace for ever,
  Wha for thine wad gladly die?
While the life beats in my bosom,
  Thou shalt mix in ilka throe,               every
Turn again, thou lovely maiden,
  Ae sweet smile on me bestow!

Not the bee upon the blossom
  In the pride o sinny noon,
Not the little sporting fairy,
  All beneath the simmer moon,
Not the Poet, in the moment
  Fancy lightens in his e'e,
Kens the pleasure, feels the rapture,       Knows
  That thy presence gies to me.


# YE JACOBITES BY NAME

An old Jacobite song. Burns's hand in it seems uncertain.

Ye Jacobites by name, give an ear, give an ear!
Ye Jacobites by name, give an ear,
  Ye Jacobites by name,
  Your fautes I will proclaim,           faults
Your doctrines I maun blame - you shall hear!   must

What is Right, and what is Wrang, by the law, by the law?
What is Right, and what is Wrang, by the law?
  What is Right, and what is Wrang?
  A short sword and a lang,
A weak arm and a strang, for to draw!

What makes heroic strife, famed afar, famed afar?
What makes heroic strife famed afar?
  What makes heroic strife?
  To whet th' assassin's knife,
Or hunt a Parent's life, wi bluidy war!

Then let your schemes alone, in the State, in the State!
Then let your schemes alone, in the State!
  Then let your schemes alone,
  Adore the rising sun,
And leave a man undone, to his fate!

## THE POSIE

In a letter of 19th October 1794 to Thomson, Burns wrote: 'My composition, the air was taken down from Mrs. Burns's voice. It is well known in the West Country, but the old words are trash.'

O, luve will venture in where it daur na weel be seen!    <small>dare not</small>
O, luve will venture in, where wisdom ance hath been!
But I will doun yon river rove amang the wood sae green,
    And a' to pu a posie to my ain dear May!    <small>pluck, own</small>

The primrose I will pu, the firstling o the year,
And I will pu the pink, the emblem o my dear,
For she's the pink o womankind, and blooms without a peer –
    And a' to be a posie to my ain dear May!

I'll pu the budding rose, when Phoebus peeps in view,
For it's like a baumy kiss o her sweet, bonie mou.    <small>balmy, mouth</small>
The hyacinth's for constancy wi its unchanging blue
    And a' to be a posie to my ain dear May!

The lily it is pure, and the lily it is fair,
And in her lovely bosom I'll place the lily there.
The daisy's for simplicity and unaffected air –
    And a' to be a posie to my ain dear May!

The hawthorn I will pu, wi its locks o siller gray,
Where, like an aged man, it stands at break o day;
But the songster's nest within the bush I winna tak away –    <small>will not</small>
    And a' to be a posie to my ain dear May!

The woodbine I will pu, when the e'ening star is near,
And the diamond draps o dew shall be her een sae clear!
The violet's for modesty, which weel she fa's to wear –
    And a' to be a posie to my ain dear May!

I'll tie the posie round wi the silken band o luve,
And I'll place it in her breast, and I'll swear by a' above
That to my latest draught o life the band shall ne'er remove
    And this will be a posie to my ain dear May!

## WILLIE WASTLE

This song has elements of the traditional children's game 'I'm the King of the Castle' and the seventeenth century verses 'I William of the Wastle', said to have been inspired by the Parliamentary siege of Hume Castle, Roxburghshire in 1651. 'Wastle' is probably the cake-shaped roundel of heraldry. Linkumdoddie was a cottage on the modern A702 road 5 miles north of Broughton, where the Logan Water joins the Tweed. It was inhabited in Burns's day by a weaver named Gideon Thomson.

Willie Wastle dwalt on Tweed,
    The spot they ca'd it Linkumdoddie.
Willie was a wabster guid             *weaver*
    Could stown a clue wi onie body.     *have stolen*
He had a wife was dour and din,     *stubborn, saturnine*
    O, Tinkler Maidgie was her mither!
Sic a wife as Willie had,
    I wad na gie a button for her.

She has an e'e (she has but ane),     *eye*
    The cat has twa the very colour,
Five rusty teeth, forbye a stump,     *as well as*
    A clapper-tongue wad deave a miller;     *deafen*
A whiskin beard about her mou,     *mouth*
    Her nose and chin they threaten ither:     *each other*
Sic a wife as Willie had,
    I wad na gie a button for her.

She's bow-hough'd, she's hem-shin'd,     *bandy-legged, shins like haims*
    Ae limpin leg a hand-breed shorter;     *hand's-breadth*
She's twisted right, she's twisted left,
    To balance fair in ilka quarter;     *each*
She has a hump upon her breast,
    The twin o that upon her shouther:     *shoulder*
Sic a wife as Willie had,
    I wad na gie a button for her.

Auld baudrans by the ingle sits,     *Old cat*
    An wi her loof her face a-washin;     *paw*
But Willie's wife is nae sae trig,     *trim*
    She dights her grunzie wi a hushion;     *wipes, snout, footless stocking*
Her walie nieves like midden-creels,     *ample fists*
    Her face wad fyle the Logan Water:     *foul*
Sic a wife as Willie had,
    I wad na gie a button for her.

## LADY MARY ANN

Several editors have based this song on the true story of John Urquhart of Craigston (d. 1634) who, as a boy, was married off on Elizabeth Innes, the plain daughter of his guardian who had designs on his estates. Kinsley, however, casts doubt on this, in view of the names mentioned in the text, though they have not been identified with any real persons.

O, Lady Mary Ann looks o'er the Castle wa',
She saw three bonie boys playing at the ba',
The youngest he was the flower amang them a'
    My bonie laddie's young, but he's growin yet!

'O father, O father, an ye think it fit,            if
We'll send him a year to the college yet;
We'll sew a green ribbon round about his hat,
    And that will let them ken he's to marry yet!'    know

Lady Mary Ann was a flower in the dew,
Sweet was its smell and bonie was its hue,
And the longer it blossom'd the sweeter it grew,
    For the lily in the bud will be bonier yet.

Young Charlie Cochran was the sprout of an aik,    oak
Bonie and bloomin and straucht was its make;    straight
The sun took delight to shine for its sake,
    And it will be the brag o the forest yet.

The simmer is gane when the leaves they were green,
And the days are awa that we hae seen;
But far better days I trust will come again,
    For my bonie laddie's young, but he's growin yet.

## SUCH A PARCEL OF ROGUES
## IN A NATION

Feelings ran high (and continue to do so) over the Act of Union, 1707 which suppressed Scotland's Parliament and her existence as an independent political entity. The 'parcel of rogues' were the 31 Scottish commissioners who sold out to England, and were well rewarded with land and money for their treachery. The Sark and the Tweed are the rivers marking the western and eastern borders with England.

Fareweel to a' our Scottish fame,
    Fareweel our ancient glory!
Fareweel ev'n to the Scottish name,
    Sae famed in martial story!
Now Sark rins over Solway sands,        runs
    An Tweed rins to the ocean,
To mark where England's province stands –
    Such a parcel of rogues in a nation!

What force or guile could not subdue
   Thro many warlike ages
Is wrought now by a coward few
   For hireling traitor's wages.
The English steel we could disdain,
   Secure in valour's station;
But English gold has been our bane –
   Such a parcel of rogues in a nation!

O, would, or I had seen the day
   That Treason thus could sell us,
My auld grey head had lien in clay,
   Wi Bruce and loyal Wallace!
But pith and power, till my last hour,
   I'll mak this declaration: –
'We're bought and sold for English gold' –
   Such a parcel of rogues in a nation!

# KELLYBURN BRAES

An allegedly traditional ballad similar to this appears in Cromek's *Remains of Nithsdale and Galloway Song* (1810), in which case 'Kellyburn' may refer to Kello Water which rises in the Cumnock Hills and runs into the Nith near Sanquhar. The theme of the nagging wife whom even the Devil could not control is ancient and widespread in folklore.

There lived a carl in Kellyburn Braes            old man
   (Hey, and the rue grows bonie wi thyme!)
And he had a wife was the plague o his days
   (And the thyme it is wither'd, and rue is in prime!).

Ae day as the carl gaed up the lang glen            one
   (Hey, and the rue grows bonie wi thyme!),
He met wi the Devil, says:- 'How do you fen?'
   (And the thyme it is wither'd, and rue is in prime!).

'I've got a bad wife, sir, that's a' my complaint
   (Hey, and the rue grows bonie wi thyme),
For, saving your presence, to her ye're a saint'
   (And the thyme it is wither'd, and rue is in prime!).

'It's neither your stot nor your staig I shall crave     bullock, colt
   (Hey, and the rue grows bonie wi thyme!),
'But gie me your wife, man, for her I must have'
   (And the thyme it is wither'd, and rue is in prime!).

'O welcome most kindly!' the blythe carl said
    (Hey, and the rue grows bonie wi thyme),
'But if ye can match her ye're waur than ye're ca'd,'    worse
    (And the thyme it is wither'd, and rue is in prime!).

The Devil has got the auld wife on his back
    (Hey, and the rue grows bonie wi thyme),
And like a poor pedlar he's carried his pack
    (And the thyme it is wither'd, and rue is in prime!).

He's carried her hame to his ain hallan-door    porch
    (Hey, and the rue grows bonie wi thyme),
Syne bade her gae in for a bitch and a whore    go
    (And the thyme it is wither'd, and rue is in prime!).

Then straight he makes fifty, the pick o his band
    (Hey, and the rue grows bonie wi thyme),
Turn out on her guard in the clap o a hand
    (And the thyme it is wither'd, and rue is in prime!).

The carlin gaed thro them like onie wud bear,    beldam
    (Hey, and the rue grows bonie wi thyme),
Whae'er she gat hands on cam ne'er her nae mair
    (And the thyme it is wither'd, and rue is in prime!).

A reekit wee devil looks over the wa'    smoking
    (Hey, and the rue grows bonie wi thyme),
'O help, maister, help, or she'll ruin us a'!'
    (And the thyme it is wither'd, and rue is in prime!).

The Devil he swore by the edge o his knife
    (Hey, and the rue grows bonie wi thyme!),
He pitied the man that was tied to a wife
    (And the thyme it is wither'd, and rue is in prime!).

The Devil he swore by the kirk and the bell
    (Hey, and the rue grows bonie wi thyme!),
He was not in wedlock, thank Heav'n, but in Hell,
    (And the thyme it is wither'd, and rue is in prime!).

Then Satan has travell'd again wi his pack
    (Hey, and the rue grows bonie wi thyme!),
And to her auld husband he's carried her back
    (And the thyme it is wither'd, and rue is in prime!).

'I hae been a Devil the feck o my life    most
    (Hey, and the rue grows bonie wi thyme!),
But ne'er was in Hell till I met wi a wife'
    (And the thyme it is wither'd, and rue is in prime!).

## LOVE FOR LOVE

A stanza composed by Burns to accompany an old ballad in *The Tea-Table Miscellany* (i.187-8).

Let loove sparkle in her e'e,
Let her lo'e nae man but me:
That's the tocher guid I prize,                  dowry
There the luver's treasure lies.

## THE SLAVE'S LAMENT

There is absolutely no truth in the canard that this song was based on an original African melody. Kinsley has traced its origins to a seventeenth century broadside in the *Roxburghe Ballads*.

It was in sweet Senegal that my foes did me enthral
    For the lands of Virginia, -ginia, O!
Torn from that lovely shore, and must never see it more,
    And alas! I am weary, weary, O!

All on that charming coast is no bitter snow and frost
    Like the lands of Virginia, -ginia, O!
There streams for ever flow, and flowers for ever blow
    And alas! I am weary, weary, O!

The burden I must bear, while the cruel scourge I fear,
    In the lands of Virginia, -ginia, O!
And I think on friends most dear with the bitter, bitter tear,
    And alas! I am weary, weary, O!

## MY BONIE BELL

Signed in SMM as Burns's work.

The smiling Spring comes in rejoicing,
    And surly Winter grimly flies.
Now crystal clear are the falling waters,
    And bonie blue are the sunny skies.
Fresh o'er the mountains breaks forth the morning,
    The ev'ning gilds the ocean's swell:
All creatures joy in the sun's returning,
    And I rejoice in my bonie Bell.

The flowery Spring leads sunny Summer,
    The yellow Autumn presses near;
Then in his turn comes gloomy Winter,
    Till smiling Spring again appear.
Thus seasons dancing, life advancing,
    Old Time and Nature their changes tell;
But never ranging, still unchanging,
    I adore my bonie Bell.

## THE GALLANT WEAVER

Another reworking of a traditional ballad. The river Cart runs through Paisley, centre
of Scotland's textile industry in the eighteenth century.

Where Cart rins rowin to the sea             runs
  By monie a flower and spreading tree,
There lives a lad, the lad for me –
    He is a gallant weaver!
O, I had wooers aught or nine,           eight
  They gied me rings and ribbons fine,
And I was fear'd my heart wad tine,      would be lost
    And I gied it to the weaver.

My daddie sign'd my tocher-band      marriage settlement
  To gie the lad that has the land,
But to my heart I'll add my hand,
    And give it to the weaver.
While birds rejoice in leafy bowers,
While bees delight in opening flowers,
While corn grows green in summer showers,
    I love my gallant weaver.

## HEY, CA' THRO

Possibly collected by Burns while jouneying in Fife at the close of the Highland tour in
1787. Dysart, Buckhaven, Largo and Leven were, in Burns's day, fishing villages on the
south coast of Fife, on the Firth of Forth. The chorus was allegedly sung as the fishing-
boats were hauled up on the beach.

### CHORUS

*Hey, ca' thro, ca' thro,*
  *For we hae mickle ado!*           much
*Hey, ca' thro, ca' thro,*
  *For we hae mickle ado!*

Up wi the carls o Dysart           old men
  And the lads o Buckhaven,
And the kimmers o Largo,          wenches
  And the lasses o Leven!

We hae tales to tell,
  An we hae sangs to sing;
We hae pennies to spend,
  An we hae pints to bring.

We'll live a' our days,
  And them that comes behin',
Let them do the like,
  And spend the gear they win!      wealth

## O, CAN YE LABOUR LEA

A bawdy version collected in Nithsdale appears in the *Merry Muses*. Burns cleaned up the original and grafted on 'an auld sang o my Mither's' to produce this ballad.

### CHORUS

*O, can ye labour lea, young man,*
*O, can ye labour lea?*
*Gae back the gate ye came again*      Go, way
*Ye'se never scorn me!*

I fee'd a man at Michaelmas
    Wi airle-pennies three;      coins exchanged on
But a' the faut I had to him      making a bargain
    He couldna labour lea.

O, clappin's guid in Febarwar,      caressing
    An kissin's sweet in May;
But what signifies a young man's love,
    An't dinna last for ay?      ever

O, kissin is the key o love
    And clappin is the lock;
An makin of's the best thing,
    That e'er a young thing got!

## THE DEUK'S DANG O'ER MY DADDIE

The theme of the wife's nagging arising out of frustratation at her husband's impotence is an old one in folk tales. Burns probably took some lines from an old ballad, but this song is substantially his own. 'Paidlin' here has a double meaning, both pottering about and sexual foreplay.

The bairns gat out wi an unco shout: –      mighty
    'The deuk's dang o'er my daddie, O!'      duck, beaten
'The fien-ma-care', quo the feirrie auld wife,      devil-may-care, lusty
    'He was but a paidlin body, O!      wading
He paidles out, and he paidles in,
    An he paidles late and early, O!
This seven lang years I hae lien by his side,
    An he is but a fusionless carlie, O!'      useless old fellow

'O, haud your tongue, my feirrie auld wife,      hold
    O, haud your tongue, now Nansie, O!
I've seen the day, and sae hae ye,
    Ye wad na been sae donsie, O.      testy
I've seen the day ye butter'd my brose,      enjoyed coitus
    And cuddl'd me late and early, O;
But downa-do's come o'er me now.      'can't-do' has
    And och, I find it sairly, O!'

## AS I WENT OUT AE MAY MORNING

A pastourelle dialogue collected by Burns for Johnson in 1792, with minor improvements.

As I went out ae May morning,                                    one
  A May morning it chanc'd to be;
There I was aware of a weelfar'd Maid                     beautiful
  Cam linkin o'er the lea to me.                              dancing

O but she was a weelfar'd maid,
  The boniest lass that's under the sun;
I spier'd gin she could fancy me,                            asked if
  But her answer was, I am too young.

To be your bride I am too young,
  To be your loun wad shame my kin,                        fool
So therefore pray young man begone,
  For you never, never shall my favor win.

But amang yon birks and hawthorns green,           birches
  Where roses blaw and woodbines hing,            bloom, hang
O there I learn'd my bonie lass
  That she was not a single hour too young.

The lassie blush'd, the lassie sigh'd,
  And the tear stood twinklin in her e'e;
O kind Sir, since ye hae done me this wrang,
  It's pray when will ye marry me.

It's of that day tak ye nae heed,
  For that's ae day ye ne'er shall see;
For ought that pass'd between us twa,
  Ye had your share as weel as me.

She wrang her hands, she tore her hair,
  She cried out most bitterlie,
O what will I say to my mammie,
  When I gae hame wi my big bellie!

O as ye maut, so maun ye brew,                        malt, must
  And as ye brew, so maun ye tun;                           barrel
But come to my arms, my ae bonie lass,
  For ye never shall rue what ye now hae done!

# SHE'S FAIR AND FAUSE

TUNE: *The Lads of Leith*

Traditionally regarded as written about Anne Stewart, the inconstant mistress of Alexander Cunningham (see 'Anna, thy Charms'), but Kinsley dismisses this, suggesting that Burns may have Scotticized an English lyric.

| | |
|---|---|
| She's fair and fause that causes my smart; | false |
|     I lo'ed her meikle and lang; | |
| She's broken her vow, she's broken my heart; | |
|     And I may e'en gae hang. | |

| | |
|---|---|
| A coof cam in wi routh o gear, | fool, plenty, money |
| And I hae tint my dearest dear; | lost |
| But Woman is but warld's gear, | |
|     Sae let the bonie lass gang! | go |

| | |
|---|---|
| Whae'er ye be that Woman love, | |
|     To this be never blind: | |
| Nae ferlie 'tis, tho fickle she prove, | marvel |
|     A woman has't by kind. | nature |

| | |
|---|---|
| O Woman lovely, Woman fair, | |
| An angel form's faun to thy share, | fallen |
| 'Twad been o'er meikle to gien thee mair! | have given |
|     I mean an angel mind. | |

# THE DEIL'S AWA WI TH' EXCISEMAN

TUNE: *The Hemp-dresser*

Lockhart claims that Burns composed these verses extempore while waiting for his colleague John Lewars to bring up reinforcements before seizing the brig *Rosamond* at Sarkfoot on the Solway on 28th February 1792. Burns more probably composed it after the event, and sang it at an Excise dinner in Dumfries the following month.

CHORUS
*The Deil's awa, the Deil's awa,*
    *The Deil's awa wi th' Exciseman!*
*He's danc'd awa, he's danc'd awa,*
    *He's danc'd awa wi th' Exciseman!*

| | |
|---|---|
| The Deil cam fiddlin thro the town, | |
|     And danc'd awa wi th' Exciseman, | |
| And ilka wife cries: – 'Auld Mahoun, | every |
|     I wish you luck o the prize man!' | |

| | |
|---|---|
| 'We'll mak our maut, and we'll brew our drink, | malt |
|     We'll laugh, sing, and rejoice, man, | |
| And monie braw thanks to the meikle black Deil, | fine, great |
|     That danc'd awa wi th' Exciseman. | |

There's threesome reels, there's foursome reels,
   There's hornpipes and strathspeys, man,
But the ae best dance e'er cam to the land
   Was *The Deil's awa wi th' Exciseman.*

## THE HUE AND CRY OF JOHN LEWARS

A poor man ruined and undone by Robbery and Murder. Being an
aweful WARNING to the young men of this age, how they look well
to themselves in this dangerous, terrible WORLD.

Despite the above annotation, this poem was probably written on the love affair of John
Lewars, the poet's Excise colleague, with Agnes Wood (b. 1771) who assisted at Miss
McMurdo's boarding school for girls in Dumfries.

A thief, and a murderer! stop her who can!
   Look well to your lives and your goods!
Good people, ye know not the hazard you run,
   'Tis the far-famed and much-noted Woods.

While I looked at her eye, for the devil is in it,
   In a trice she whipt off my poor heart:
Her brow, cheek and lip – in another sad minute,
   My peace felt her murderous dart.

Her features, I'll tell you them over – but hold!
   She deals with your wizards and books;
And to peep in her face, if but once you're so bold
   There's witchery kills in her looks.

But softly – I have it – her haunts are well known,
   At midnight so slily I'll watch her;
And sleeping, undrest, in the dark, all alone
   Good lord! the dear Thief how I'll catch her!

## WILL YE GO TO THE INDIES,
## MY MARY

*TUNE: Ewe-Bughts, Marion*

Burns took the old ballad 'Will ye go to the Ewe-Bughts, Marion?' and set his own words
to it, sending these verses to Thomson on 27th October 1792 as a 'farewell of a dear girl...
when I was thinking of going to the West Indies... all my earlier love-songs were the
breathings of ardent Passion... Their uncouth simplicity was, as they say of wines, their
RACE.' The heroine was Margaret Campbell. By substituting 'my Mary' for Marion to
fit the cadence of the original song, Burns may have accidentally stumbled on a name
whereby he could subconsciously distance himself from the reality of the girl who died
so tragically in 1786. Thus the myth of 'Highland Mary' was initiated by the poet himself.

Will ye go to the Indies, my Mary,
   And leave auld Scotia's shore?
Will ye go to the Indies, my Mary,
   Across th' Atlantic's roar?

O, sweet grows the lime and the orange,
 And the apple on the pine;
But a' the charms o the Indies
 Can never equal thine.

I hae sworn by the Heavens to my Mary,
 I hae sworn by the Heavens to be true,
And sae may the Heavens forget me,
 When I forget my vow!

O, plight me your faith, my Mary,
 And plight me your lily-white hand!
O, plight me your faith, my Mary,
 Before I leave Scotia's strand!

We hae plighted our troth, my Mary,
 In mutual affection to join;
And curst be the cause that shall part us!
 The hour and the moment o time!

# MY WIFE'S A WINSOME WEE THING

### AIR: *My Wife's a Wanton Wee Thing*

A later version of the song 'My Wife's a Wanton Wee Thing', sung to the same tune. Burns sent these verses to Thomson on 8th November 1792. Thomson was dissatisfied with them and not only tinkered with the lines but added a stanza of his own. Burns acquiesced as part of a bargain that Thomson would not meddle with 'Bonie Lesley.' Later editors, however, have ignored Thomson and printed this song in Burns's original form.

## CHORUS

*She is a winsome wee thing,*
*She is a handsome wee thing,*
*She is a lo'esome wee thing,*
 *This sweet wee wife o mine!*

I never saw a fairer,
I never lo'ed a dearer,
And neist my heart I'll wear her,        next
 For fear my jewel tine.

The warld's wrack we share o't;        wreckage
The warstle and the care o't,         struggle
Wi her I'll blythely bear it,
And think my lot divine.

## HIGHLAND MARY

*TUNE: Katherine Ogie*

In his letter of 14th November 1792 to Thomson, Burns wrote 'I agree with you that the song K. Ogie, is very poor stuff, and unworthy, altogether unworthy, of so beautiful an air.' He tried to mend the original but gave it up and substituted verses of his own. In writing 'The Subject of the song is one of the most interesting passages of my youthful days' Burns was uncharacteristically economical with the truth, recalling an incident which had taken place only six years earlier, when he was 27 years old.

Ye banks and braes and streams around            *slopes*
   The castle o Montgomery,
Green be your woods, and fair your flowers,
   Your waters never drumlie!                        *muddly*
There Summer first unfald her robes,
   And there the longest tarry!
For there I took the last fareweel
   O my sweet Highland Mary!

How sweetly bloom'd the gay, green birk,           *birch*
   How rich the hawthorn's blossom,
As underneath their fragrant shade
   I clasp'd her to my bosom!
The golden hours on angel wings
   Flew o'er me and my dearie:
For dear to me as light and life
   Was my sweet Highland Mary.

Wi monie a vow and lock'd embrace
   Our parting was fu tender;
And, pledging aft to meet again,
   We tore oursels asunder.
But O! fell Death's untimely frost,
   That nipt my flower sae early!
Now green's the sod, and cauld's the clay,
   That wraps my Highland Mary!

O, pale, pale now, those rosy lips
   I aft hae kiss'd sae fondly;
And clos'd for ay, the sparkling glance
   That dwalt on me sae kindly;
And mouldering now in silent dust
   That heart that lo'ed me dearly!
But still within my bosom's core
   Shall live my Highland Mary.

# AT THE GLOBE TAVERN,
# DUMFRIES

*TUNE: Killiecrankie*

The first stanza was inscribed on a window-pane at the Globe Inn, probably as a comment on the French Revolutionary War, 1792-3. Socrates drank hemlock in execution of his sentence of death; Leonidas, hero of Thermopylae, preferred to die for Sparta than rule over it; and Cato, strengthened by Plato's treatise on immortality, committed suicide rather than flee or surrender to Caesar.

I murder hate by field or flood,
    Tho Glory's name may screen us;
In wars at hame I'll spend my blood –
    Life-giving wars of Venus.
The deities that I adore
    Are Social Peace and Plenty:
I'm better pleas'd to make one more,
    Than be the death of twenty.

I would not die like Socrates,
    For all the fuss of Plato;
Nor would I with Leonidas,
    Nor yet would I with Cato:
The zealots of the Church and State
    Shall ne'er my mortal foes be;
But let me have bold Zimri's fate,
    Within the arms of Cozbi.


# THE RIGHTS OF WOMAN

AN OCCASIONAL ADDRESS
SPOKEN BY MISS FONTENELLE ON HER
BENEFIT NIGHT, NOVEMBER 26, 1792

Louisa Fontenelle (1773-99) was a London actress who came to the Theatre Royal, Edinburgh in 1789 and joined George Sutherland's touring company, which played in Dumfries in the winters of 1792 and 1793. She married John Brown Williamson, manager of the Dumfries Theatre in 1796 and emigrated with him to the United States. She died of yellow fever at Charleston, S.C. on 30th October 1799. These lines, mirrored on fellow exciseman Tom Paine's *Rights of Man* (1791-2), place Burns in the forefront of the feminist movement.

While Europe's eye is fix'd on mighty things,
The fate of empires and the fall of kings;
While quacks of State must each produce his plan,
And even children lisp the Rights of Man;
Amid this mighty fuss just let me mention,
The Rights of Woman merit some attention.

First, in the sexes' intermix'd connexion,
One sacred Right of Woman is Protection:
The tender flower that lifts its head elate,
Helpless must fall before the blasts of fate,
Sunk on the earth, defac'd its lovely form,
Unless your shelter ward th' impending storm.

Our second Right – but needless here is caution –
To keep that right inviolate's the fashion:
Each man of sense has it so full before him,
He'd die before he'd wrong it – 'tis Decorum!

There was, indeed, in far less polish'd days,
A time, when rough rude Man had naughty ways:
Would swagger, swear, get drunk, kick up a riot,
Nay, even thus invade a lady's quiet!
Now, thank our stars! these Gothic times are fled;
Now, well-bred men – and you are all well-bred –
Most justly think (and we are much the gainers)
Such conduct neither spirit, wit, nor manners.
For Right the third, our last, our best, our dearest:
That right to fluttering female hearts the nearest,
Which even the Rights of Kings, in low prostration,
Most humbly own – 'tis dear, dear Admiration!
In that blest sphere alone we live and move;
There taste that life of life – Immortal Love.
Smiles, glances, sighs, tears, fits, flirtations, airs –
'Gainst such an host what flinty savage dares?
When awful Beauty joins with all her charms,
Who is so rash as rise in rebel arms?
But truce with kings, and truce with constitutions,
With bloody armaments and revolutions;
Let Majesty your first attention summon,
Ah! ça ira! THE MAJESTY OF WOMAN!                    French Revolutionary
                                                     slogan

# HERE'S A HEALTH TO THEM THAT'S AWA

Based on an old Jacobite song, Burns published this song in the *Edinburgh Gazeteer* in 1792, up-dating its political flavour to the period at the outbreak of the French Revolutionary Wars. The personalities mentioned in this poem were outspoken radicals who, like Burns, sympathized with the Revolution – at least in its early stages.

Here's a health to them that's awa,
   Here's a health to them that's awa!
And wha winna wish guid luck to our cause,
   May never guid luck be their fa'!
It's guid to be merry and wise,
   It's guid to be honest and true,
It's guid to support Caledonia's cause,
   And bide by the buff and the blue.       the Whig colours

Here's a health to them that's awa,
   Here's a health to them that's awa!
Here's a health to Charlie, the chief o the clan,      Charles James Fox
   Altho that his band be sma'!
May Liberty meet wi success,
   May Prudence protect her frae evil!
May tyrants and Tyranny tine i' the mist      be lost
   And wander their way to the Devil!

Here's a health to them that's awa,
   Here's a health to them that's awa;
Here's a health to Tammie, the Norlan' laddie,      Thomas Erskine
   That lives at the lug o the Law!      (1750-1823) defence
Here's freedom to them that wad read,      lawyer of Tom Paine
   Here's freedom to them that would write!
There's nane ever fear'd that the truth should be heard,
   But they whom the truth would indite!

Here's a health to them that's awa,
   An here's to them that's awa!
Here's to Maitland and Wycombe! let wha does na like 'em      James
   Be built in a hole in the wa'!      Maitland, 8th Earl of
Here's timmer that's red at the heart,      Lauderdale
   Here's fruit that is sound at the core,      (1759-1839)
And may he that wad turn the buff and blue coat      John Petty,
   Be turn'd to the back o the door!      Earl of Wycombe
      (1765-1809)

Here's a health to them that's awa,
   Here's a health to them, that's awa,
Here's Chieftain M'Leod, a chieftain worth gowd,      Col. Norman
   Tho bred amang mountains o snaw!      McLeod of McLeod
Here's friends on baith sides o the Forth,      (1754-1801)
   And friends on baith sides o the Tweed,
And wha wad betray old Albion's right,
   May they never eat of her bread!

## THE LEA-RIG

*TUNE: My ain kind dearie, O.*

Burns re-fashioned the traditional ballad of this name, and sent the result to Thomson on 26th October 1792. Thomson complained of its brevity, and Burns sent this expanded version on 1st December.

When o'er the hill the eastern star
    Tells bughtin time is near, my jo,            folding, darling
And owsen frae the furrow'd field                   oxen
    Return sae dowf and weary, O,                 dull
Down by the burn, where scented birks         birches
    Wi dew are hangin clear, my jo,
I'll meet thee on the lea-rig,
    My ain kind dearie, O!                        own

At midnight hour in mirkest glen,           darkest
    I'd rove, and ne'er be eerie, O,        frightened
If thro that glen I gaed to thee,             went
    My ain kind dearie, O!
Altho, the night were ne'er sae wild,
    And I were ne'er sae weary, O,
I'll meet thee on the lea-rig,
    My ain kind dearie, O!

The hunter lo'es the morning sun,
    To rouse the mountain deer, my jo,
At noon the fisher takes the glen
    Adown the burn to steer, my jo:
Gie me the hour o gloamin grey –
    It maks my heart sae cheery, O,
To meet thee on the lea-rig,
    My ain kind dearie, O!

## AULD ROB MORRIS

Modelled on a traditional dialogue song, between a mother and daughter, originally published in *The Tea-Table Miscellany*, Burns adapted the situation to illustrate the theme of love versus wealth.

There's Auld Rob Morris that wons in yon glen,      dwells
He's the king o guid fellows and wale o auld men:   pick
He has gowd in his coffers, he has owsen and kine,  gold, oxen,
And ae bonie lassie, his dautie and mine.    cattle, one, darling

She's fresh as the morning, the fairest in May,
She's sweet as the ev'ning amang the new hay,
As blythe and as artless as the lambs on the lea,
And dear to my heart as the light to my e'e.

But O, she's an heiress, auld Robin's a laird,
And my daddie has nocht but a cot-house and yard!     cottage
A wooer like me maunna hope to come speed:     must not
The wounds I must hide that will soon be my dead.

The day comes to me, but delight brings me nane;
The night comes to me, but my rest it is gane;
I wander my lane like a night-troubled ghaist,     alone, ghost
And I sigh as my heart it wad burst in my breast.

O, had she but been of a lower degree,
I then might hae hop'd she wad smil'd upon me!
O, how past descriving had then been my bliss,
As now my distraction no words can express!

## DUNCAN GRAY

Like the earlier version 'Weary Fa' You' this song was based on an old ballad in the Herd collection, and was sent to Thomson on 4th December 1792.

Duncan Gray cam here to woo
    (Ha, ha, the wooing o't!)
On blythe Yule-night when we were fou     drunk
    (Ha, ha, the wooing o't!).
Maggie coost her head fu high,     tossed
Look'd asklent and unco skeigh,     disdainfully, very skittish
Gart poor Duncan stand abiegh,     Made, off
    Ha, ha, the wooing o't!

Duncan fleech'd, and Duncan pray'd:     wheedled
    (Ha, ha, the wooing o't!)
Meg was deaf as Ailsa Craig,
    (Ha, ha, the wooing o't!),
Duncan sigh'd baith out and in,     both
Grat his een baith blear't an blin',     Wept, blurred
Spak o lowpin o'er a linn –     leaping, waterfall
    Ha, ha, the wooing o't!

Time and Chance are but a tide
    (Ha, ha, the wooing o't!):
Slighted love is sair to bide
    (Ha, ha, the wooing o't!).
'Shall I like a fool,' quoth he,
'For a haughty hizzie die?     hussy
She may gae to – France for me!'
    Ha, ha, the wooing o't!

How it comes, let doctors tell,
  (Ha, ha, the wooing o't!):
Meg grew sick, as he grew hale,                healthy
  (Ha, ha, the wooing o't!),
Something in her bosom wrings,
For relief a sigh she brings,
And O! her een they spak sic things! –      eyes
  Ha, ha, the wooing o't!

Duncan was a lad o grace
  (Ha, ha, the wooing o't!),
Maggie's was a piteous case,
  (Ha, ha, the wooing o't!):
Duncan could na be her death,
Swelling pity smoor'd his wrath;         smothered
Now they're crouse and canty baith –   proud, jolly
  Ha, ha, the wooing o't!

## WHY SHOULD NA POOR FOLK MOWE

*TUNE: The Campbells are comin*

Sent to Robert Cleghorn on 12th December 1792 as 'a song, just finished this moment.'
A copy was sent to Thomson in July 1794. This song celebrates the levelling power of
copulation, reducing the high and mighty to the same basic human level. The Duke of
Brunswick (1735-1806), brother-in-law of King George III, led the Austrians and
Prussians against France in 1792, but was defeated by 'the cannonade of Valmy'. The
second last stanza refers to the second Partition of Poland which took place in 1792.
Catherine II was notorious for her immorality and frequently satirised in Britain in
terms far coarser than Burns used here. She made her lover Stanislaus Poniatowski
puppet ruler of the rump of Poland, before absorbing it in 1793.

### CHORUS

*And why shouldna poor folk mowe, mowe, mowe,*   copulate
  *And why shouldna poor folk mowe:*
*The great folk hae siller, and houses and lands,*   money
  *Poor bodies hae naething but mowe.*

When Princes and Prelates and het-headed zealots   hot-
  All Europe hae set in a lowe,               rage
The poor man lies down, nor envies a crown,
  And comforts himsel with a mowe.

When Brunswick's great Prince cam a cruising to France
  Republican billies to cowe,
Bauld Brunswick's great Prince wad hae shawn better sense,
  At hame with his Princess to mowe.

Out over the Rhine proud Prussia wad shine,
   To spend his best blood he did vow;        Frederick William
But Frederic had better ne'er forded the water,      II (1744-97)
   But spent as he docht in a mowe.            should have

By sea by shore! the Emperor swore,      Leopold II (1747-92)
   In Paris he'd kick up a row;
But Paris sae ready just leugh at the laddie        laughed
   And bade him gae tak him a mowe.

Auld Kate laid her claws on poor Stanislaus,   Empress Catherine
   And Poland has bent like a bow:      of Russia (1729-96)
May the deil in her ass ram a huge prick o brass!
   And damn her in hell with a mowe!

But truce with commotions and new-fangled notions,
   A bumper I trust you'll allow:
Here's George our gude king and Charlotte his queen,    toast
   And lang may they tak a gude mowe!


# WHILE PROSE-WORK AND RHYMES

*TUNE: The Campbells are comin*

Although this glorification of copulation was not published till the Barke-Goodsir Smith edition of *The Merry Muses* in 1959, it has all the hallmarks of Burns about it. Its opening stanza refers to the charge made against Burns in 1792-3 of sympathising with the French Revolution. It was clearly intended as a companion to the foregoing song.

While Prose-work and rhymes
   Are hunted for crimes,
And things are – the devil knows how;
   Aware o my rhymes,
   In these kittle times,              ticklish
The subject I chuse is a mowe.       copulation

Some cry, Constitution!
   Some cry, Revolution!
And Politicks kick up a rowe;
   But Prince and Republic,
   Agree on the Subject,
No treason is in a good mowe.

Th' Episcopal lawn,
   And Presbyter band,
Hae lang been to ither a cowe;          terror
   But still the proud Prelate,
   And Presbyter zealot
Agree in an orthodox mowe.

Poor Justice, 'tis hinted –
  Ill natur'dly squinted,
The Process – but mum – we'll allow
  Poor Justice has ever
  For Cunt had a favour,
While Justice could tak a gude mowe.

Now fill to the brim –
  To her, and to him,
Wha willingly do what they dow;                    can
  And ne'er a poor wench
  Want a friend at a pinch,
Whase failing is only a mowe.                      Whose

# THE TREE OF LIBERTY

Controversy continues to rage over this revolutionary song, and Kinsley urged caution
in attribution. On the other hand, it was first published by Chambers from a holograph,
apparently now lost, and accords with Burns's Jacobin sympathies in 1792-3.

Heard ye o the tree o France,
  I watna what 's the name o't;                     don't know
Around it a' the patriots dance,
  Weel Europe kens the fame o't.                     knows
It stands where ance the Bastile stood,             once
  A prison built by kings, man,
When Superstition's hellish brood
  Kept France in leading strings, man.

Upo' this tree there grows sic fruit,
  Its virtues a' can tell, man;
It raises man aboon the brute,                       above
  It maks him ken himsel, man.
Gif ance the peasant taste a bit,                    If
  He's greater than a lord, man,
An wi the beggar shares a mite
  O a' he can afford, man.

The fruit is worth a' Afric's wealth,
  To comfort us 'twas sent, man:
To gie the sweetest blush o health,                  give
  An mak us a' content, man.
It clears the een, it cheers the heart,              eyes
  Maks high and low gude friends, man;
And he wha acts the traitor's part
  It to perdition sends, man.

My blessings aye attend the chiel
    Wha pitied Gallia's slaves, man,            France
And staw a branch, spite o the deil,            stole
    Frae yont the western waves, man.     America
Fair Virtue water'd it wi care,
    And now she sees wi pride, man,
How weel it buds and blossoms there,
    Its branches spreading wide, man.

But vicious folks aye hate to see
    The works o Virtue thrive, man;
The courtly vermin 's banned the tree,     cursed
    And grat to see it thrive, man;          wept
King Loui' thought to cut it down.
    When it was unco sma', man;     quite small
For this the watchman cracked his crown,
    Cut aff his head an a', man.

A wicked crew syne, on a time,          then
    Did tak a solemn aith, man,         oath
It ne'er should flourish to its prime,
    I wat they pledged their faith, man.     wot
Awa they gaed wi mock parade,         went
    Like beagles hunting game, man,
But soon grew weary o the trade
    And wished they'd been at hame, man.

For Freedom, standing by the tree,
    Her sons did loudly ca', man:
She sang a sang o liberty,
    Which pleased them ane and a', man.
By her inspired, the new-born race
    Soon drew the avenging steel, man;
The hirelings ran – her foes gied chase,
    And banged the despot weel, man.

Let Britain boast her hardy oak,
    Her poplar and her pine, man,
Auld Britain ance could crack her joke,     once
    And o'er her neighbours shine, man.
But seek the forest round and round,
    And soon 'twill be agreed, man,
That sic a tree can not be found,
    'Twixt London and the Tweed, man.

Without this tree, alake this life
    Is but a vale o woe, man;
A scene o sorrow mixed wi strife,
    Nae real joys we know, man.

We labour soon, we labour late,
　To feed the titled knave, man;
And a' the comfort we're to get
　Is that ayont the grave, man.　　　　　　　　　　beyond

Wi plenty o sic trees, I trow,　　　　　　　　　such, believe
　The warld would live in peace, man;
The sword would help to mak a plough,
　The din o war wad cease, man.
Like brethren in a common cause,
　We'd on each other smile, man;
And equal rights and equal laws
　Wad gladden every isle, man.

Wae worth the loon wha wadna eat　　　　woe, betide, fool
　Sic halesome dainty cheer, man;　　　　　　wholesome
I'd gie my shoon frae aff my feet,　　　　　　　　shoes
　To taste sic fruit, I swear, man.
Syne let us pray, auld England may
　Sure plant this far-famed tree, man;
And blythe we'll sing, and hail the day
　That gave us liberty, man.

# WANDERING WILLIE

A remodelling of an old song in the Herd collection, published in SMM (1787). The earliest version by Burns was written in an undated letter to John McMurdo (c.1792), and a revised version was sent to Thomson on 27th March 1793.

Here awa, there awa, wandering Willie,
　Here awa, there awa, haud awa hame!
Come to my bosom, my ae only dearie,　　　　　　　one
　And tell me thou bring'st me my Willie the same.
Loud tho the Winter blew cauld at our parting,
　'Twas na the blast brought the tear to my e'e,
Welcome now Simmer, and welcome my Willie,
　The Simmer to Nature, my Willie to me!

Rest, ye wild storms in the cave of your slumber –
　How your wild howling a lover alarms!
Wauken, ye breezes, row gently, ye billows,
　And waft my dear laddie ance mair to my arms.
But O, if he's faithless, and minds na his Nannie,
　Flow still between us, thou wide-roaring main!
May I never see it, may I never trow it,
　But, dying, believe that my Willie's my ain!

## BRAW LADS O GALLA WATER

Based on 'Braw, braw lads of Galla Water' in Herd MSS (ii.202) and in SMM, 1788, this version was sent to Thomson in January 1793.

Braw, braw lads on Yarrow braes,
   They rove amang the blooming heather;
But Yarrow braes nor Ettrick shaws           slopes, woods
   Can match the lads o Galla Water.

But there is ane, a secret ane,                one
   Aboon them a' I loe him better;    Above
And I'll be his, and he'll be mine,
   The bonie lad o Galla Water.

Altho his daddie was nae laird,
   And tho I hae nae meikle tocher,      not much dowry
Yet, rich in kindest, truest love,
   We'll tent our flocks by Galla Water.       tend

It ne'er was wealth, it ne'er was wealth,
   That coft contentment, peace, and pleasure:    bought
The bands and bliss o mutual love,
   O, that's the chiefest warld's treasure!

## POORTITH CAULD

*TUNE: Cauld Kail in Aberdeen*

Sent to Thomson early in January 1793 along with the foregoing. It is likely that this song was written for Jean Lorimer (see 'Craigieburn Wood').

### CHORUS

*O, why should Fate sic pleasure have,*       such
   *Life's dearest bands untwining?*
*Or why sae sweet a flower as love*
   *Depend on Fortune's shining?*

O poortith cauld and restless Love,        poverty
   Ye wrack my peace between ye!
Yet poortith a' I could forgive,
   An 'twere na for my Jeanie.

The warld's wealth when I think on,
   Its pride and a' the lave o't –          rest
My curse on silly coward man,
   That he should be the slave o't!

Her een sae bonie blue betray
  How she repays my passion;
But prudence is her o'erword ay:                                by-word always
  She talks o rank and fashion.

O, wha can prudence think upon,
  And sic a lassie by him?
O, wha can prudence think upon,
  And sae in love as I am?

How blest the wild-wood Indian's fate!
  He woos his artless dearie -
The silly bogles, Wealth and State,                            demons
  Can never make him eerie.                                    frightened


# LORD GREGORY

Burns wrote these verses as a much more preferable alternative to the traditional ballad
'The Lass of Lochryan' and the poem of the same name by John Wolcot under the *nom
de plume* of Peter Pindar.

O, mirk, mirk is this midnight hour,                           dark
  And loud the tempest's roar!
A waefu wanderer seeks thy tower –                             doleful
  Lord Gregory, ope thy door.
An exile frae her father's ha',
  And a' for the sake o thee,
At least some pity on me shaw,
  If love it may na be.

Lord Gregory mind'st thou not the grove
  By bonie Irwine side,
Where first I own'd that virgin love
  I lang, lang had denied?
How aften didst thou pledge and vow,
  Thou wad for ay be mine!
And my fond heart, itsel sae true,
  It ne'er mistrusted thine.

Hard is thy heart, Lord Gregory,
  And flinty is thy breast:
Thou bolt of Heaven that flashest by,
  O, wilt thou bring me rest!
Ye mustering thunders from above,
  Your willing victim see,
But spare and pardon my fause love,
  His wrangs to Heaven and me!

## ON HEARING A THRUSH SING IN
## HIS MORNING WALK

Composed in January 1793 and sent to Alexander Cunningham on 20th February. This was one of Burns's first essays in the sonnet 14-line form.

Sing on, sweet thrush, upon the leafless bough,
Sing on, sweet bird, I listen to thy strain:
See aged Winter, 'mid his surly reign,
At thy blythe carol, clears his furrowed brow,
So in lone Poverty's dominion drear
Sits meek Content with light, unanxious heart,
Welcomes the rapid moments, bids them part,
Nor asks if they bring ought to hope or fear.
I thank thee, Author of this opening day,
Thou whose bright sun now gilds yon orient skies!
Riches denied, Thy boon was purer joys:
What wealth could never give nor take away!
Yet come, thou child of Poverty and Care,
The mite high Heav'n bestow'd, that mite with thee I'll share.

## EPITAPH FOR
## MR. GABRIEL RICHARDSON

Reproduced by Alexander Cunningham from the lines engraved by Burns on a crystal goblet owned by Gabriel Richardson (1759-1820). Richardson complained to Burns that he had to pay more tax on his brewery than brewers outside the burgh of Dumfries. Burns took up the case with Provost Staig in January 1793. That tax was consequently adjusted and Burns celebrated with this mock-epitaph. Richardson became Provost himself in 1801.

Here Brewer Gabriel's fire's extinct,
    And empty all his barrels:
He's blest – if as he brew'd, he drink –
    In upright, honest morals.

## ON COMMISSARY GOLDIE'S BRAINS

Colonel Thomas Goldie of Goldielea - 'Colonel Tam' of Burns's second Heron election ballad - was president of the Loyal Natives, the right-wing political club in Dumfries and commissary of the sheriff-court, an official dealing with adultery, divorce and the confirmation of testaments.

Lord, to account who does Thee call,
    Or e'er dispute Thy pleasure?
Else why within so thick a wall,
    Enclose so poor a treasure?

## ON GENERAL DUMOURIER'S DESERTION

### FROM THE FRENCH REPUBLICAN ARMY

Charles François Dumouriez (1739-1823) was a career officer in the French Army who joined the revolutionaries and won the battle of Valmy which repelled the Austro-German invasion of 1792. Having won the battle of Jemappes and conquered Belgium, he was defeated by the Austrians at Neerwinden on 18th March 1793. Denounced as a traitor and recalled to Paris he chose instead to go over to the Royalist side, and eventually settled in England. Burns misspelled his surname.

You're welcome to Despots, Dumourier!
You're welcome to Despots, Dumourier!                   Dumouriez's
  How does Dampiere do?                        second-in-command
  Ay, and Bournonville too?                    emissary of the
Why did they not come along with you, Dumourier?        Convention

I will fight France with you, Dumourier,
I will fight France with you, Dumourier,
  I will fight France with you,
  I will take my chance with you,
By my soul, I'll dance with you, Dumourier!

Then let us fight about, Dumourier!
Then let us fight about, Dumourier!
  Then let us fight about
  Till Freedom's spark be out,
Then we'll be damn'd, no doubt, Dumourier.

## ON THE COMMEMORATION OF RODNEY'S VICTORY

Admiral George Brydges Rodney (1718-92) confronted the French navy off Dominica in the West Indies on 12th April 1792 and destroyed several warships. This decisive victory restored British control of the Atlantic and was enthusiastically celebrated at the time. These lines were probably composed extempore at a celebration in the King's Arms, Dumfries but not published in the *Advertiser* till the following year.

Instead of a song, boys, I'll give you a toast:
Here's to the mem'ry of those on the Twelfth that we lost! –
That we lost, did I say? – no, by Heav'n, that we found!
For their fame it shall live while the world goes round.
The next in succession I'll give you: The King!
And who would betray him, on high may he swing!
And here's the grand fabric, the Free Constitution,
As built on the base of our great Revolution!
And, longer with Politics not to be cramm'd,
Be Anarchy curs'd, and be Tyranny damn'd!
And who would to Liberty e'er prove disloyal,
May his son be a hangman – and himself his first trial!

## THANKSGIVING FOR A NATIONAL VICTORY

This quotation appears in all major editions except Kinsley (1968) - usually linked to the preceding poem. Though the national victory is unspecified it is thought to refer to one of the naval victories in the early stages of the French Revolutionary War. Kinsley rejected it on account of its similarity to lines beginning 'Ye bloody Whigs' which were nailed to the door of a Manchester church on the day of thanksgiving after Culloden in 1746.

Ye hypocrites! are these your pranks?
To murder men, and give God thanks?
Desist, for shame! Proceed no further:
God won't accept your thanks for Murther!

## OPEN THE DOOR TO ME OH

*TUNE: Open the door softly*

Sent to Thomson in April 1793 and published in SC as 'altered by Robert Burns.'

Oh, open the door, some pity to shew,
    If love it may na be, Oh;
Tho thou hast been false, I'll ever prove true,
    Oh, open the door to me, Oh.

Cauld is the blast upon my pale cheek,
    But caulder thy love for me, Oh:
The frost that freezes the life at my heart,
    Is nought to my pains frae thee, Oh.

The wan moon sets behind the white wave,
    And time is setting with me, Oh:
False friends, false love, farewell! for mair
    I'll ne'er trouble them, nor thee, Oh.

She has open'd the door, she has open'd it wide,
    She sees his pale corse on the plain, Oh:
My true love! she cried, and sank down by his side,
    Never to rise again, Oh.

## YOUNG JESSIE

TUNE: *Open the door softly*

Sent to Thomson in April 1793 and published in his *Select Collection of Original Scottish Airs*, along with the preceding song. The subject was Jessie Staig (1775-1801), daughter of Provost David Staig of Dumfries.

True hearted was he, the sad swain o the Yarrow,
    And fair are the maids on the banks of the Ayr;
But by the sweet side o the Nith's winding river
    Are lovers as faithful, and maidens as fair:
To equal young Jessie seek Scotia all over –
    To equal young Jessie you seek it in vain!
Grace, beauty, and elegance fetter her lover,
    And maidenly modesty fixes the chain.

Fresh is the rose in the gay, dewy morning,
    And sweet is the lily at evening close;
But in the fair presence o lovely young Jessie,
    Unseen is the lily, unheeded the rose.
Love sits in her smile, a wizard ensnaring;
    Enthron'd in her een he delivers his law;
And still to her charms she alone is a stranger;
    Her modest demeanour's the jewel of a'.

## FAREWELL, THOU STREAM

TUNE: *Nansie's to the greenwood gane*

Burns wrote these words for the air that accompanied Allan Ramsay's song 'the last time I came o'er the moor.' He then sent a copy to Maria Riddell, with her name in the second line (April 1793), but in December he sent a revised version to Mrs Dunlop with 'Eliza' substituted, after the bitter quarrel with the Riddell family.

Farewell, thou stream that winding flows
    Around Eliza's dwelling!
O Mem'ry, spare the cruel throes
    Within my bosom swelling:
Condemn'd to drag a hopeless chain
    And yet in secret languish,
To feel a fire in every vein,
    Nor dare disclose my anguish!

Love's veriest wretch, unseen, unknown,
    I fain my griefs would cover:
The bursting sigh, th' unweeting groan
    Betray the hapless lover.

I know thou doom'st me to despair,
　　Nor wilt, nor canst relieve me;
But, O Eliza, hear one prayer –
　　For pity's sake forgive me!

The music of thy voice I heard,
　　Nor wist while it enslav'd me!
I saw thine eyes, yet nothing fear'd,
　　Till fears no more had sav'd me!
Th' unwary sailor thus, aghast
　　The wheeling torrent viewing,
'Mid circling horrors sinks at last
　　In overwhelming ruin.


# THE SOLDIER'S RETURN

*TUNE: The Mill, Mill, O*

An ancient piece of bawdry had been refined by Ramsay as 'Beneath a green Shade'
(1733) and this was Burns's exercise in the same process of refinement.

When wild War's deadly blast was blawn,
　　And gentle Peace returning,
Wi monie a sweet babe fatherless
　　And monie a widow mourning
I left the lines and tented field,
　　Where lang I'd been a lodger,
My humble knapsack a' my wealth,
　　A poor and honest sodger.　　　　　　　　　　　soldier

A leal, light heart was in my breast,　　　　　　　true
　　My hand unstain'd wi plunder,
And for fair Scotia, hame again,
　　I cheery on did wander:
I thought upon the banks o Coil,
　　I thought upon my Nancy,
And ay I mind't the witching smile
　　That caught my youthful fancy.

At length I reach'd the bonie glen,
　　Where early life I sported,
I pass'd the mill and trysting thorn,
　　Where Nancy aft I courted.
Wha spied I but my ain dear maid,
　　Down by her mother's dwelling,
And turn'd me round to hide the flood
　　That in my een was swelling!

Wi alter'd voice, quoth I: – 'Sweet lass,
    Sweet as yon hawthorn's blossom,
O, happy, happy may he be,
    That's dearest to thy bosom!
My purse is light, I've far to gang,
    And fain would be thy lodger;
I've served my king and country lang –
    Take pity on a sodger.'

Sae wistfully she gaz'd on me,
    And lovelier was than ever.
Quo she - 'A sodger ance I lo'ed,
    Forget him shall I never:
Our humble cot, and hamely fare,
    Ye freely shall partake it;
That gallant badge – the dear cockade –
    Ye're welcome for the sake o't!'

She gaz'd, she redden'd like a rose,
    Syne, pale like onie lily,                                    Then
She sank within my arms, and cried: –
    'Art thou my ain dear Willie?'
'By Him who made yon sun and sky,
    By whom true love's regarded,
I am the man! And thus may still
    True lovers be rewarded!

'The wars are o'er, and I'm come hame,
    And find thee still true-hearted.
Tho poor in gear, we're rich in love,                            wealth
    And mair, we'se ne'er be parted.'
Quo she: – 'My grandsire left me gowd,                           gold
    A mailen plenish'd fairly!                        farm, well-stocked
And come, my faithfu sodger lad,
    Thou'rt welcome to it dearly!'

For gold the merchant ploughs the main,
    The farmer ploughs the manor;
But glory is the sodger's prize,
    The sodger's wealth is honour!
The brave poor sodger ne'er despise,
    Nor count him as a stranger;
Remember he's his country's stay
    In day and hour of danger.

## MEG O THE MILL

*TUNE: O bonie lass, will ye lie in a barrack?*

This was indubitably Burns's own composition, which he sent to Thomson in April 1793: '..my song "O ken ye what Meg o' the mill has gotten" pleases myself so much, that I cannot without disgust try my hand at another song to the air; so I shall not attempt it.' Thomson commented 'he does not generally praise his own songs so much.'

O ken ye what Meg o the mill has gotten?
An ken ye what Meg o the mill has gotten?
She's gotten a coof wi a claute o siller,    dolt, hoard,
And broken the heart o the barley miller!    money

The miller was strappin, the miller was ruddy,
A heart like a lord, and a hue like a lady.
The laird was a widdifu, bleerit knurl! –   gallows-worthy,
She's left the guid fellow, and taen the churl!   dwarf

The miller, he hecht her a heart leal and loving;  offered, loyal
The laird did address her wi matter mair moving:
A fine pacing-horse wi a clear, chained bridle,
A whip by her side, and a bonie side-saddle!

O, wae on the siller – it is sae prevailing!    woe
And wae on the love that is fixed on a mailen!   farm
A tocher's nae word in a true lover's parl,   dowry, speech
But gie me my love, and a fig for the warl!

## MEG O THE MILL

*TUNE: O ken ye what, Meg, etc*

'Written for this work by Robert Burns' (SMM). Nevertheless it seems probable that it was merely a revision of a traditional ballad, before Burns composed the preceding version.

O, ken ye what Meg o the Mill has gotten?    know
An ken ye what Meg o the Mill has gotten?
A braw new naig wi the tail o a rottan,    nag, rat
And that's what Meg o the Mill has gotten!

O, ken ye what Meg o the Mill lo'es dearly?
An ken ye what Meg o the Mill lo'es dearly?
A dram o guid strunt in a morning early,    liquor
And that's what Meg o the Mill lo'es dearly!

O, ken ye how Meg o the Mill was married?
An ken ye how Meg o the Mill was married?
The priest he was oxter'd, the clark he was carried, held up by
And that's how Meg o the Mill was married!   the armpits

O, ken ye how Meg o the Mill was bedded?
An ken ye how Meg o the Mill was bedded?
The groom gat sae fu he fell awald beside it,   drunk,
And that's how Meg o the Mill was bedded!   backwards

## BLYTHE HAE I BEEN ON YON HILL

*TUNE: Merrily dance the Quaker*

The subject of this song is Lesley Baillie, in whose honour Burns had previously written 'Saw ye Bonie Lesley,' and he sent her a copy in May 1793. By September of that year he was describing it as 'one of the finest songs I ever made in my life; and, besides, is composed on a young lady, positively the most beautiful, lovely woman in the world.'

Blythe hae I been on yon hill
    As the lambs before me,
Careless ilka thought, and free,                      every
    As the breeze flew o'er me.
Now nae langer sport and play,
    Mirth or sang can please me:
Lesley is sae fair and coy,
    Care and anguish seize me.

Heavy, heavy is the task,
    Hopeless love declaring!
Trembling, I dow nocht but glow'r,
    Sighing, dumb despairing!
If she winna ease the thraws              will not, throes
    In my bosom swelling,
Underneath the grass-green sod,
    Soon maun be my dwelling.                must

## LOGAN BRAES

*TUNE: Logan Water*

'Composed in three-quarters of an hour's lucubrations in my elbow-chair' - Burns to Thomson (25th June 1793). The Logan Water rises in the hills on the Ayrshire-Lanarkshire border and flows eastwards to join the river Nethan in Lesmahagow parish.

O Logan, sweetly didst thou glide
That day I was my Willie's bride,
And years sin syne hae o'er us run        since then
Like Logan to the simmer sun.
But now thy flowery banks appear
Like drumlie winter, dark and drear,      muddy
While my dear lad maun face his faes    must, foes
Far, far frae me and Logan braes.        hillsides

Again the merry month of May
Has made our hills and vallies gay;
The birds rejoice in leafy bowers,
The bees hum round the breathing flowers;
Blythe Morning lifts his rosy eye,
And Evening's tears are tears o joy:
My soul delightless a' surveys,
While Willie's far frae Logan braes.

490

Within yon milk-white hawthorn bush,
Amang her nestlings sits the thrush:
Her faithfu mate will share her toil,
Or wi his song her cares beguile.
But I wi my sweet nurslings here,
Nae mate to help, nae mate to cheer,
Pass widow'd nights and joyless days,
While Willie's far frae Logan braes.

O, wae upon you, Men o State,     woe
That brethren rouse in deadly hate!
As ye make monie a fond heart mourn,
Sae may it on your heads return!
Ye mind na 'mid your cruel joys
The widow's tears, the orphan's cries
But soon may peace bring happy days,
And Willie hame to Logan braes!

## EPIGRAM ON MISS DAVIES

Composed about Deborah Davies, previously the subject of 'Bonie Wee Thing,' and again commenting flatteringly on her smallness of stature. The lines were inscribed on a window-pane of the Black Bull Inn at Moffat.

Ask why God made the gem so small,
And why so huge the granite?
Because God meant mankind should set
  That higher value on it.

## EPIGRAM ON A COUNTRY LAIRD

### NOT QUITE SO WISE AS SOLOMON

The subject of this and the following was David Maxwell of Cardoness (d. 1825) 'a stupid, money-loving dunderpate of a Galloway laird,' as Burns commented to Mrs Dunlop when sending her these lines in June 1793.

Bless Jesus Christ, O Cardoness,
  With grateful lifted eyes,
Who taught that not the soul alone
  But body too shall rise!

For had He said 'The soul alone
  From death I will deliver,'
Alas, alas! O Cardoness,
  Then hadst thou lain for ever.

## ON BEING SHOWN A BEAUTIFUL
## COUNTRY SEAT

### BELONGING TO THE SAME LAIRD

This epigram on Maxwell of Cardoness was composed during Burns's tour of Galloway
with John Syme in July-August 1793.

We grant they're thine, those beauties all,
    So lovely in our eye:
Keep them, thou eunuch, Cardoness,
    For others to enjoy.

## LINES INSCRIBED IN A LADY'S
## POCKET ALMANAC

Written, in fact, in John Syme's copy of the *Della Cruscan British Album* which Burns
had borrowed in June 1793.

Grant me, indulgent Heaven, that I may live,
To see the miscreants feel the pains they give!
Deal Freedom's sacred treasures free as air,
Till Slave and Despot be but things that were!

## O, WERE MY LOVE

### TUNE: *Hughie Green*

The second stanza comes from a fragment in the Herd MSS. Writing to Thomson in June
1793 Burns said,c 'It is too short... I have often tried to eke a stanza to it, but in vain.
After balancing myself for a musing five minutes, in the hind-legs of my elbow-chair,
I produced [the first lines], far inferior to the foregoing, I frankly confess.'

O, were my love yon lilac fair
    Wi purple blossoms to the spring,
And I a bird to shelter there,
    When wearied on my little wing.
How I wad mourn when it was torn
    By Autumn wild and Winter rude!
But I wad sing on wanton wing,
    When youthfu May its bloom renew'd.

O, gin my love were yon red rose,
    That grows upon the castle wa',
And I mysel a drap o dew
    Into her bonie breast to fa',
O, there, beyond expression blest,
    I'd feast on beauty a' the night,
Seal'd on her silk-saft faulds to rest,
    Till fley'd awa by Phoebus' light!

## BONIE JEAN

In a letter of April 1793 to Thomson, Burns mentioned some Scots airs which he had picked up from country lasses. 'They please me vastly; but your learned lugs would perhaps be displeased with the very feature for which I like them - I call them Simple; you would pronounce them Silly.' He enclosed a 'beautiful little air' and some lines set to it. The subject was Jean McMurdo, daughter of the chamberlain of Drumlanrig.

There was a lass, and she was fair!
   At kirk and market to be seen
When a' our fairest maids were met,
   The fairest maid was bonie Jean.

And ay she wrought her country wark,
   And ay she sang sae merrilie:
The blythest bird upon the bush
   Had ne'er a lighter heart than she!

But hawks will rob the tender joys,
   That bless the little lintwhite's nest,      *linnet*
And frost will blight the fairest flowers,
   And love will break the soundest rest.

Young Robie was the brawest lad,      *finest*
   The flower and pride of a' the glen,
And he had owsen, sheep, and kye,      *oxen, cattle*
   And wanton naigies nine or ten.      *horses*

He gaed wi Jeanie to the tryste,      *cattle-fair*
   He danc'd wi Jeanie on the down,
And, lang ere witless Jeanie wist,      *realised*
   Her heart was tint, her peace was stown!      *lost, stolen*

As in the bosom of the stream,
   The moonbeam dwells at dewy e'en.
So, trembling pure, was tender love
   Within the breast of bonie Jean.

And now she works her country's wark,
   And ay she sighs wi care and pain,
Yet wist na what her ail might be,      *ailment*
   Or what wad make her weel again.      *would*

But did na Jeanie's heart loup light,      *leap*
   And didna joy blink in her e'e;      *glance*
As Robie tauld a tale of love
   Ae e'enin on the lily lea?

While monie a bird sang sweet o love,
   And monie a flower blooms o'er the dale,
His cheek to hers he aft did lay,
   And whisper'd thus his tender tale.

'O Jeanie fair, I lo'e thee dear.
  O canst thou think to fancy me?
Or wilt thou leave thy mammie's cot,            cottage
  And learn to tent the farms wi me?

'At barn or byre thou shalt na drudge,      cow-shed
  Or naething else to trouble thee,
But stray amang the heather-bells,
  And tent the waving corn wi me.'

Now what could artless Jeanie do?
  She had nae will to say him na!
At length she blush'd a sweet consent,
  And love was ay between them twa.

# EPIGRAMS AGAINST THE
# EARL OF GALLOWAY

John Stewart, 7th Earl of Galloway (1736-1806), was a Scottish representative peer from 1774 to 1790. Burns heartily detested him, both personally and for his High Tory political viewpoint. The Earl was savagely lampooned in Burns's third Election Ballad, 'John Bushby's Lamentation,' as well as in these epigrams. This impression is oddly at variance with all other published references to the Earl who was noted for his great piety and generosity to his servants. The Earl was later quoted as saying 'it would not become him, when his good old master the King despised and disregarded the paltry attacks of a Peter Pindar, to feel himself hurt by those of a licentious, rhyming ploughman.'

What dost thou in that mansion fair?
  Flit, Galloway, and find              Move away
Some narrow, dirty, dungeon cave,
  The picture of thy mind.

No Stewart art thou, Galloway:
  The Stewarts all were brave.
Besides, the Stewarts were but fools,
  Not one of them a knave.

Bright ran thy line, O Galloway,
  Thro many a far-famed sire!
So ran the far-famed Roman way,
  And ended in a mire.

Spare me thy vengeance, Galloway!
  In quiet let me live:
I ask no kindness at thy hand,
  For thou has none to give.

## EPITAPH ON A LAPDOG

While Burns was staying with Gordon of Kenmure late in July 1793, Mrs Gordon's lap-dog Echo died. She asked Burns to write an epitaph for him, and though he disliked the subject he tried to please the lady.

In wood and wild, ye warbling throng,
    Your heavy loss deplore:
Now half extinct your powers of song –
    Sweet Echo is no more.

Ye jarring, screeching things around,
    Scream your discordant joys:
Now half your din of tuneless sound
    With Echo silent lies.

## EPIGRAM ON THE LAIRD OF LAGGAN

Syme records Burns's bouts of ill-humour during their Galloway tour. While these displays of bad temper are inexplicable they resulted in some savage epigrams. John Morine of Laggan bought Ellisland when Burns moved to Dumfries. Morine disagreed with Burns over the value of some manure and insisted on the fences being repaired. On removals day Burns sent Adam Armour back to Ellisland to smash every pane of glass there on which he had inscribed verses in diamond-point, paying his brother-in-law six shillings for carrying out his orders.

When Morine, deceas'd, to the Devil went down,
Twas nothing would serve him but Satan's own crown.
'Thy fool's head,' quoth Satan, 'that crown shall wear never:
I grant thou'rt as wicked, but not quite so clever.'

## PHILLIS THE FAIR

Phillis of the title was the younger daughter of John McMurdo of Drumlanrig and, like the following, this song was set to Robin Adair, 'a crinkum-crankum' Gaelic tune which Burns got from a 'musical Highlander in Breadalbane's Fencibles,' quartered at Dumfries in 1793.

While larks, with little wing, fann'd the pure air,
Viewing the breathing Spring, forth I did fare.
    Gay, the sun's golden eye
    Peep'd o'er the mountains high;
'Such thy bloom,' did I cry, 'Phillis the fair.'

In each bird's careless song, glad, I did share;
While yon wild flowers among, chance led me there.
    Sweet to the opening day,
    Rosebuds bent the dewy spray;
'Such thy bloom,' did I say – 'Phillis the fair!'

Down in the shady walk, doves cooing were;
I mark'd the cruel hawk caught in a snare.
    So kind may Fortune be!
    Such make his destiny,
He who would injure thee, Phillis the fair!

# HAD I A CAVE

*TUNE: Robin Adair*

Burns wrote to Thomson in August 1793: 'I succeeded so ill in my last attempt [supra] that I have ventured, in this morning's walk, one essay more...'

Had I a cave on some wild distant shore,
Where the winds howl to the wave's dashing roar,
   There would I weep my woes,
   There seek my lost repose,
   Till grief my eyes should close,
     Ne'er to wake more!

Falsest of womankind, can'st thou declare
All thy fond, plighted vows fleeting as air?
   To thy new lover hie,
   Laugh o'er thy perjury,
   Then in thy bosom try
     What peace is there!

# WHISTLE AN I'LL COME TO YOU, MY LAD

Derived from an old fragment in the Herd collection, this song was sent to Thomson in August 1793. He showed these verses to Pietro Urbani (1749-1816), the Milanese composer who was in Galloway at the time of Burns's tour in that district, who begged a copy which the poet declined to supply. 'I understand he looks with rather an evil eye on your work...'

## CHORUS

*O, whistle an I'll come to ye, my lad!*
*O, whistle an I'll come to ye, my lad!*
*Tho father an mother an a' should gae mad,*
*O, whistle an I'll come to ye, my lad!*

| | |
|---|---|
| But warily tent when ye come to court me, | take care |
| And come nae unless the back-yett be a-jee; | -gate, ajar |
| Syne up the back-style, and let naebody see, | Then, -stile |
| And come as ye were na comin to me, | |
| And come as ye were na comin to me! | |

| | |
|---|---|
| At kirk, or at market, whene'er ye meet me, | |
| Gang by me as tho that ye car'd na a flie; | Go |
| But steal me a blink o your bonie black e'e, | |
| Yet look as ye were na lookin to me, | |
| Yet look as ye were na lookin to me! | |

| | |
|---|---|
| Ay vow and protest that ye care na for me, | |
| And whyles ye may lightly my beauty a-wee; | sometimes, a little |
| But court na anither tho jokin ye be, | |
| For fear that she wyle your fancy frae me, | lure |
| For fear that she wyle your fancy frae me! | |

## ADOWN WINDING NITH

TUNE: *The Muckin o Geordie's Byre*

The subject of this song is, again, Phillis McMurdo. A pretty footpath along the east bank of the Nith north of Dumfries is known as Burns Walk to this day.

CHORUS

*Awa wi your belles and your beauties –*
  *They never wi her can compare!*
*Whaever has met wi my Phillis,*
  *Has met wi the Queen o the Fair.*

Adown winding Nith I did wander,
  To mark the sweet flowers as they spring.
Adown winding Nith I did wander,
  Of Phillis to muse and to sing.

The Daisy amus'd my fond fancy,
  So artless, so simple, so wild:
'Thou emblem,' said I, 'o my Phillis' –
  For she is Simplicity's child.

The rosebud's the blush o my charmer,
  Her sweet balmy lip when 'tis prest.
How fair and how pure is the lily!
  But fairer and purer her breast.

Yon knot of gay flowers in the arbour,
  They ne'er wi my Phillis can vie:
Her breath is the breath of the woodbine,
  Its dew-drop o diamond her eye.

Her voice is the song o the morning,
  That wakes thro the green-spreading grove,
When Phoebus peeps over the mountains
  On music, and pleasure, and love.

But Beauty, how frail and how fleeting!
  The bloom of a fine summer's day!
While Worth in the mind o my Phillis
  Will flourish without a decay.

# BY ALLAN STREAM

*TUNE: Allan Water*

'I walked out yesterday evening with a volume of the Museum in my hand, when turning up "Allan Water"...It appeared to me rather unworthy of so fine an air; and recollecting that it is on your list, I sat, and raved, under the shade of an old thorn, till I wrote one to suit the measure. I may be wrong; but I think it not in my worst syle.' - letter to Thomson, 19th August 1793. Allan Water winds through Strathallan, Perthshire; Ben Ledi (2873 ft) towers over the Trossachs to the west.

By Allan stream I chanc'd to rove,
    While Phoebus sank beyond Benledi;
The winds were whispering thro the grove,
    The yellow corn was waving ready;
I listen'd to a lover's sang,
    An thought on youthfu pleasures monie,         many
And ay the wild-wood echoes rang: –
    'O, my love Annie's very bonie!'

'O, happy be the woodbine bower,
    Nae nightly bogle make it eerie!         demon, frightful
Nor ever sorrow stain the hour,
    The place and time I met my dearie!
Her head upon my throbbing breast,
    She, sinking, said: – 'I'm thine for ever!'
While monie a kiss the seal imprest –
    The sacred vow we ne'er should sever.'

The haunt o Spring's the primrose-brae.         -slope
    The Summer joys the flocks to follow.
How cheery thro her short'ning day
    Is Autumn in her weeds o yellow!
But can they melt the glowing heart,
    Or chain the soul in speechless pleasure,
Or thro each nerve the rapture dart,
    Like meeting her, our bosom's treasure?

# COME, LET ME TAKE THEE

*TUNE: Cauld Kail*

'That tune, Cauld Kail in Aberdeen is such a favourite of yours,' wrote Burns to Thomson on 28th August 1793, 'that I once more roved out yesterevening for a gloamin-shot at the Muses; when the Muse that presides o'er the shores of Nith...whispered me the following.' Jean Lorimer is thought to have been the subject.

Come, let me take thee to my breast,
    And pledge we ne'er shall sunder,
And I shall spurn as vilest dust
    The world's wealth and grandeur!
And do I hear my Jeanie own
    That equal transports move her?
I ask for dearest life alone,
    That I may live to love her.

Thus in my arms, wi a' her charms,
    I clasp my countless treasure,
I'll seek nae mair o Heav'n to share
    Than sic a moment's pleasure!
And by thy een sae bonie blue
    I swear I'm thine for ever,
And on thy lips I seal my vow,
    And break it shall I never!

# DAINTY DAVIE

Thomson and Burns disagreed violently on the musical setting of this song. '...nothing, since a Highland wench in the Cowgate once bore me three bastards at a birth, has surprised me so much as your opinion on this subject.'Thomson's dogmatism hardened against Burns's self-assurance and he was unmoved by the poet's colourful (and wholly fictitious) comparison.

## CHORUS

*Meet me on the Warlock Knowe,*    wizard knoll
    *Dainty Davie, Dainty Davie!*
*There I'll spend the day wi you,*
    *My ain dear Dainty Davie.*    own

Now rosy May comes in wi flowers
To deck her gay, green-spreading bowers;
And now comes in the happy hours
    To wander wi my Davie.

The crystal waters round us fa'
The merry birds are lovers a',
The scented breezes round us blaw
    A wandering wi my Davie.

When purple morning starts the hare
To steal upon her early fare,
Then thro the dews I will repair
    To meet my faithfu Davie.

When day, expiring in the west,
The curtain draws o Nature's rest,
I flee to his arms I loe the best:
    And that's my ain dear Davie!

## SCOTS WHA HAE

### TUNE: *Hey Tutti Taitie*

Burns visited the field of Bannockburn, near Stirling on 26th August 1787. 'I said a fervent prayer for Old Caledonia over the hole in a blue whinstone, where Robert de Bruce fixed his royal standard...' Burns introduced the tune, popularly believed to have been Bruce's march at the battle. 'Urbani begged me to make soft verses for it; but I had no idea of giving myself any trouble on the subject, till the accidental recollection of that glorious struggle for Freedom...roused my rhyming Mania.' The theme of Liberty was uppermost in Burns's mind, as the French Republic was then just a year old (August 1793).

| | |
|---|---|
| Scots, wha hae wi Wallace bled, | Sir William Wallace (d.1305) |
| Scots, wham Bruce has aften led, | King Robert I (1306-28) |
| Welcome to your gory bed | |
|     Or to victorie! | |
| Now's the day, and now's the hour: | |
| See the front o battle lour, | look menacingly |
| See approach proud Edward's power – | Edward II (1307-27) |
|     Chains and slaverie! | |

Wha will be a traitor knave?
Wha can fill a coward's grave?
Wha sae base as be a slave? –
    Let him turn, and flee!
Wha for Scotland's King and Law
Freedom's sword will strongly draw,
Freeman stand, or Freeman fa',
    Let him follow me!

By Oppression's woes and pains,
By your sons in servile chains,
We will drain our dearest veins,
    But they shall be free!
Lay the proud usurpers low!
Tyrants fall in every foe!
Liberty's in every blow! –
    Let us do, or die!

## ON MARIA RIDDELL

Maria Banks Woodley Riddell (1772-1808) was the youngest daughter of William Woodley, Governor of the Leeward Islands. She married Walter Riddell in 1790 and settled at Goldielea (renamed Woodley Park) near Dumfries in 1792. Burns probably met her at Friars' Carse, home of her brother-in-law, and gave her an introduction to Smellie who published her *Voyages to the Madeira and Leeward and Caribee Islands.* By April 1793 Maria had become 'thou first of Friends, and most accomplished of Women.' These lines are believed to date from August 1793.

'Praise Woman still,' his lordship roars,
   'Deserv'd or not, no matter!'
But thee whom all my soul adores,
   There Flattery cannot flatter!
Maria, all my thought and dream,
   Inspires my vocal shell:
The more I praise my lovely theme,
   The more the truth I tell.

## AS DOWN THE BURN

*TUNE: Down the Burn Davie*

This was the 'single elegant stanza' which Thomson commissioned from Burns in August 1793 as a substitute for the concluding 'objectionable verses' of the traditional ballad, 'so that this most exquisite song may no longer be excluded from good company.'

As down the burn they took their way,        brook
   And thro the flowery dale;
His cheek to hers he aft did lay,
   And love was ay the tale,
With: – 'Mary, when shall we return,
   Sic pleasure to renew?'
Quoth Mary: – 'Love, I like the burn,
   And ay shall follow you.'

## PASSION'S CRY

*I cannot but remember such things were,*
*And were most dear to me–*

Burns began composing this poem in 1788 during his affair with Clarinda. He revised it in 1789 and completed it in 1793. It represents one of Burns's essays in Augustan composition, not really his metier.

In vain would Prudence, with decorous sneer,
Point out a cens'ring world, and bid me fear:
Above that world on wings of love I rise:
I know its worst and can that worst despise.
'Wronged, injured, shunned, unpitied, unredrest;
'The mocked quotation of the scorner's jest'
Let Prudence' direst bodements on me fall,
Clarinda, rich reward! o'erpays them all.

As low-borne mists before the sun remove,
So shines, so reigns, unrivalled mighty Love.
In vain the laws their feeble force oppose;
Chained at his feet, they groan Love's vanquished foes;
In vain Religion meets my shrinking eye;
I dare not combat, but I turn and fly:
Conscience in vain upbraids th' unhallowed fire;
Love grasps his scorpions, stifled they expire:
Reason drops headlong from his sacred throne,
Thy dear idea reigns, and reigns alone;
Each thought intoxicated homage yields,
And riots wanton in forbidden fields.

By all on High, adoring mortals know!
By all the conscious villain fears below!
By, what, Alas! much more my soul alarms,
My doubtful hopes once more to fill thy arms!
E'en shouldst thou, false, forswear each guilty tie
Thine, and thine only, I must live and die!!!!

# THE PRIMROSE

*TUNE: Todlin Hame*

The English original was written by Robert Herrick in the mid-17th century. Burns's
revision of the first six lines is, however, minimal.

Dost ask me, why I send thee here,
This firstling of the infant year?
Dost ask me, what this primrose shews,
Bepearled thus with morning dews? –

    I must whisper to thy ears,
    The sweets of love are wash'd with tears.

This lovely native of the dale
Thou seest, how languid, pensive, pale:
Thou seest this bending stalk so weak,
That each way yielding doth not break?

    I must tell thee, these reveal,
    The doubts and fears that lovers feel.

## THOU HAS LEFT ME EVER, JAMIE

*TUNE: Fee him, father, fee him*

Sent to Thomson in September 1793 with the note 'I composed them [two stanzas] at the time in which Patie Allan's mither died - that was, "About the back o' midnight" - and by the leaside of a bowl of punch...'

Thou has left me ever, Jamie,
　Thou has left me ever!
Thou hast me forsaken, Jamie,
　Thou hast left me ever!
Aften hast thou vow'd that Death
　Only should us sever;
Now thou'st left thy lass for ay –
　I maun see thee never, Jamie,
　I'll see thee never!

Thou hast me forsaken, Jamie,
　Thou hast me forsaken!
Thou hast me forsaken, Jamie,
　Thou hast me forsaken!
Thou canst love another jo,
　While my heart is breaking;
Soon my weary een I'll close,
　Never mair to waken, Jamie,
　Never mair to waken!

## BEHOLD THE HOUR, THE BOAT, ARRIVE

*TUNE: Oran gaoil*

The first version of this song was sent to Clarinda on 27th December 1791 when her departure for the West Indies was imminent. It is a Scotticized version of an English song 'Behold the fatal hour arrive' (1774).

Behold the hour, the boat, arrive!
　My dearest Nancy, O, fareweel!
Severed frae thee, can I survive,
　Frae thee whom I hae lov'd sae weel?　　　　from

Endless and deep shall be my grief,
　Nae ray of comfort shall I see,
But his most precious, dear belief,
　That thou wilt still remember me.

Along the solitary shore,
　Where flitting sea-fowl round me cry,
Across the rolling, dashing roar,
　I'll westward turn my wistful eye.

'Happy thou Indian grove,' I'll say,
　'Where now my Nancy's path shall be!
While thro your sweets she holds her way,
　O, tell me, does she muse on me?'

## BEHOLD THE HOUR, THE BOAT ARRIVE

*(Second Version)*

The second version, from which 'dearest Nancy' and the Scotticisms were removed, was sent to Thomson in September 1793.

Behold the hour, the boat arrive!
    Thou goest, the darling of my heart!
Sever'd from thee, can I survive?
    But fate has will'd and we must part.
I'll often greet the surging swell,
    Yon distant Isle will often hail:-
'E'en here I took the last farewell;
    There, latest mark'd her vanish'd sail.'

Along the solitary shore,
    While flitting sea-fowl round me cry,
Across the rolling, dashing roar,
    I'll westward turn my wistful eye:-
'Happy, thou Indian grove,' I'll say,
    'Where now my Nancy's path may be!
While thro thy sweets she loves to stray,
    O, tell me, does she muse on me?'

## WHERE ARE THE JOYS?

*TUNE: Saw ye my father*

Probably the song sent to Janet Miller of Dalswinton, eldest daughter of Burns's former landlord, on 9th September 1793. In an accompanying letter Burns wrote: 'I have taken the liberty to make you the Heroine... I have formed a little love-story for you...' Miss Miller married the 28th Earl of Mar in 1795.

Where are the joys I hae met in the morning,
    That danc'd to the lark's early sang?
Where is the peace that awaited my wand'ring
    At e'ening the wild-woods amang?

Nae mair a-winding the course o yon river
    And marking sweet flowerets sae fair,
Nae mair I trace the light footsteps o Pleasure,
    But Sorrow and sad-sighing Care.

Is it that Summer's forsaken our vallies,
    And grim, surly Winter is near?
No, no, the bees humming round the gay roses
    Proclaim it the pride o the year.

Fain wad I hide what I fear to discover,
    Yet lang, lang, too well hae I known:
A' that has caused the wreck in my bosom,
    Is Jenny, fair Jenny alone!

Time cannot aid me, my griefs are immortal,
    Not Hope dare a comfort bestow,
Come then, enamour'd and fond of my anguish,
    Enjoyment I'll seek in my woe!


## EPITAPH ON A NOTED COXCOMB

### CAPTAIN WM. RODDICK, OF CORBIETON

Sent to Maria Riddell in October 1793 and later inscribed with other epigrams in the
Glenriddell MS, parodying lines from Henry Mackenzie's *The Man of Feeling* (1771).
Corbieton is an estate south of Urr Water, a mile west of Haugh of Urr.

Light lay the earth on Billy's breast,
    His chicken heart's so tender;
But build a castle on his head -
    His scull will prop it under.


## THINE AM I, MY FAITHFUL FAIR

### TUNE: *The Quaker's Wife*

Originally sent to Maria Riddell in 1793. 'Nancy' refers, of course, to Clarinda. In
September 1794 he instructed Thomson to delete 'Nancy' and substitute 'Chloris', as
his interest had switched to Jean Lorimer by that time.

Thine am I, my faithful Fair,
    Thine my lovely Nancy!
Ev'ry pulse along my veins,
    Ev'ry roving fancy!

To thy bosom lay my heart,
    There to throb and languish.
Tho despair had wrung its core,
    That would heal its anguish.

Take away those rosy lips
    Rich with balmy treasure!
Turn away thine eyes of love,
    Lest I die with pleasure!
What is life when wanting love?
    Night without a morning!
Love the cloudless summer's sun,
    Nature gay adorning.

# BONIE MARY

*TUNE: Minnie's ay glowerin o'er me*

Sent to Cleghorn, with the following ballad, on 25th October 1793: 'Mair for taiken of my violent propensity to Baudry...'Kinsley comments that bawdry on the theme of pubic hair is common in Scottish folk literature.

### CHORUS
*Come cowe me, minnie, come cowe me;*
*Come cowe me, minnie, come cowe me;*
*The hair o my arse is grown into my cunt,*
*And they canna win to, to mowe me.*                    copulate with

When Mary cam over the Border,
When Mary cam over the Border;
As eith 'twas approachin the Cunt of a hurchin,         hedgehog
Her arse was in sic a disorder.

But wanton Wattie cam west on 't,
But wanton Wattie cam west on 't,
He did it sae tickle, he left nae as meikle             much
'S a spider wad bigget a nest on 't.                    build

And was nae Wattie a Clinker,                           lively rascal
He mow'd frae the queen to the tinkler,
Then sat down, in grief, like the Macedon chief         Alexander the Great
For want o mae warlds to conquer.                       more

And O, what a jewel was Mary!
And O, what a jewel was Mary!
Her face it was fine, and her bosom divine,
And her cunt it was theekit wi glory.                   thatched

# ACT SEDERUNT OF THE SESSION –
# A SCOTS BALLAD

*TUNE: O'er the muir amang the heather*

'The Law is good for something, since we can make a Baudy-song out of it', wrote Burns to Cleghorn. Thus Burns neatly combined his delight in bawdry with his penchant for fine legal phraseology. An Act Sederunt is an ordinance for regulating the forms of procedure before the Court of Session, used here loosely as synonymous with the judgment of a law-court.

In Edinburgh town they've made a law,
    In Edinburgh at the Court o Session,
That standing pricks are fauteors a',                   defaulters
    And guilty of a high transgression.

### CHORUS
*Act sederunt o the Session,*
*Decreet o the Court o Session,*
*That standing pricks are fauteors a',*
*And guilty of a high transgression.*

And they've provided dungeons deep,
    Ilk lass has ane in her possession;          Each
Untill the wretches wail and weep,
    They there shall lie for their transgression. –

CHORUS

*Act Sederunt o the Session,*
*Decreet o the Court o Session,*
*The rogues in pouring tears shall weep,*
*By act Sederunt o the Session.* –

# TO CAPTAIN GORDON, ON BEING ASKED WHY I WAS NOT TO BE OF THE PARTY WITH HIM AND HIS BROTHER KENMURE AT SYME'S

Adam Gordon of the 81st Regiment was third son of John Gordon of Kenmure. His elder brother John was M P for Kirkcudbright in 1784-6. The title of Viscount Kenmure, attainted since 1716, was restored to him in 1824. Burn met 'noble Kenmure' in 1793, during his Galloway tour with Syme. Tiresias (1.16) was blinded by Juno for saying that women got greater sexual enjoyment than men did.

Dost ask, dear Captain, why from Syme
    I have no invitation,
When well he knows he has with him
    My first friends in the nation?

Is it because I love to toast,
    And round the bottle hurl?
No! there conjecture wild is lost,
    For *Syme* by God's no churl!

Is 't lest with bawdy jests I bore,
    As oft the matter of fact is?
No! *Syme* the theory can't abhor
    Who loves so well the practice.

Is it a fear I should avow
    Some heresy seditious?
No! *Syme* (but this entre nous)
    Is quite an old Tiresias.

In vain Conjecture thus would flit
    Thro mental clime and season:
In short, dear Captain, Syme 's a Wit
    Who asks of Wits a reason?

Yet must I still the sort deplore
    That to my griefs adds one more,
In balking me the social hour
    With you and noble Kenmure.

## ON MRS. RIDDELL'S BIRTHDAY

### NOVEMBER 4, 1793

Written when the friendship with Maria Riddell was at its height. A month later, however, it was violently disrupted as a result of the poet's disorderly conduct during a drunken party, at Friars' Carse - the 'Rape of the Sabines' incident. See also the 'Monody.'

Old Winter, with his frosty beard,
Thus once to Jove his prayer preferred: –
'What have I done of all the year,
To bear this hated doom severe?
My cheerless suns no pleasure know;
Night's horrid car drags dreary slow;
My dismal months no joys are crowning,
But spleeny, English hanging, drowning.

'Now Jove, for once be mighty civil:
To counterbalance all this evil
Give me, and I've no more to say,
Give me Maria's natal day!
That brilliant gift shall so enrich me,
Spring, Summer, Autumn, cannot match me.'
''Tis done!' says Jove; so ends my story,
And Winter once rejoiced in glory.

## ADDRESS

### SPOKEN BY MISS FONTENELLE ON HER BENEFIT NIGHT, DECEMBER 4, 1793, AT THE THEATRE, DUMFRIES

Burns sent these lines to Louisa Fontenelle on 1st December: 'May it be a prologue to an overflowing House! If all the Town put together, have half the ardour for your success and welfare, of my individual wishes, my prayer will most certainly be granted.'

Still anxious to secure your partial favor,
And not less anxious, sure this night than ever,
A Prologue, Epilogue, or some such matter,
'Twould vamp my bill, said I, if nothing better:
So sought a Poet roosted near the skies;
Told him I came to feast my curious eyes;
Said, nothing like his works was ever printed;
And last, my prologue-business slily hinted.
'Ma'am, let me tell you,' quoth my man of rhymes,
'I know your bent – these are no laughing times:
Can you – but, Miss, I own I have my fears –
Dissolve in pause, and sentimental tears?
With laden sighs, and solemn-rounded sentence,
Rouse from his sluggish slumbers, fell Repentance?
Paint Vengeance as he takes his horrid stand,
Waving on high the desolating brand,
Calling the storms to bear him o'er a guilty land?'

I could no more! Askance the creature eyeing:-
'D'ye think,' said I, 'this face was made for crying?
I'll laugh, that's poz - nay more, the world shall know it;    possible
And so, your servant! gloomy Master Poet!'
   Firm as my creed, Sirs, 'tis my fix'd belief
That Misery's another word for Grief.
I also think (so may I be a bride!)
That so much laughter, so much life enjoy'd.

Thou man of crazy care and ceaseles sigh,
Still under bleak Misfortune's blasting eye;
Doom'd to that sorest task of man alive -
To make three guineas do the work of five;
Laugh in Misfortune's face - the beldam witch -
Say, you'll be merry tho you can't be rich!

Thou other man of care, the wretch in love!
Who long with jiltish arts and airs hast strove;
Who, as the boughs all temptingly project,
Measur'st in desperate thought - a rope - thy neck -
Or, where the beetling cliff o'erhangs the deep,
Peerest to meditate the healing leap:
Would'st thou be cur'd, thou silly, moping elf?
Laugh at her follies - laugh e'en at thyself;
Learn to despise those frowns now so terrific,
And love a kinder: that's your grand specific.

To sum up all: be merry, I advise;
And as we're merry, may we still be wise!

## ON SEEING MISS FONTENELLE IN A
## FAVOURITE CHARACTER

Possibly sent to Miss Fontenelle along with the 'Address' in December 1793.

Sweet näiveté of feature,
   Simple, wild, enchanting elf,
Not to thee, but thanks to Nature
   Thou art acting but thyself.

Wert thou awkward, stiff, affected,
   Spurning Nature, torturing art,
Loves and Graces all rejected
   Then indeed thou'dst act a part.

# HUSBAND, HUSBAND, CEASE YOUR STRIFE

*TUNE: My Jo Janet*

This was an Anglicization of the traditional ballad 'My Jo Janet' sent to Thomson in December 1793. Though this is one of Burns's better English songs it lacks the naturalism of the original.

'Husband, husband, cease your strife,
   Nor longer idly rave, sir!
Tho I am your wedded wife,
   Yet I am not your slave, sir.'
'One of two must still obey,
   Nancy, Nancy!
Is it Man or Woman, say,
   My spouse Nancy?'

'If 'tis still the lordly word,
   Service and obedience,
I'll desert my sov'reign lord,
   And so, good-bye, allegiance!'
'Sad will I be, so bereft,
   Nancy, Nancy!
Yet I'll try to make a shift,
   My spouse Nancy!'

'My poor heart, then break it must,
   My last hour I am near it:
When you lay me in the dust,
   Think, how you will bear it?'
'I will hope and trust in Heaven,
   Nancy, Nancy!
Strength to bear it will be given,
   My spouse Nancy.'

'Well, sir, from the silent dead,
   Still I'll try to daunt you:
Ever round your midnight bed
   Horrid sprites shall haunt you!'
'I'll wed another like my dear
   Nancy, Nancy!
Then all Hell will fly for fear,
   My spouse Nancy!'

## TO MISS GRAHAM OF FINTRY

Anne Graham (d.1852) was the eldest daughter of Robert Graham of Fintry, the poet's patron in the Excise. These lines accompanied a copy of *A Select Collection of Scottish Airs* which Burns sent to her on 31st January 1794.

Here, where the Scottish Muse immortal lives,
   In sacred strains and tuneful numbers join'd,
Accept the gift! Though humble he who gives,
   Rich is the tribute of the grateful mind.

So may no ruffian feeling in thy breast,
   Discordant, jar thy bosom-chords among!
But Peace attune thy gentle soul to rest,
   Or love ecstatic wake his seraph song!

Or Pity's notes in luxury of tears,
   As modest Want the tale of woe reveals;
While conscious Virtue all the strain endears,
   And heaven-born Piety her sanction seals!

## MONODY

### ON A LADY FAMED FOR HER CAPRICE

Maria Riddell rebuked Burns for his outrageous behaviour at Friars' Carse in December 1793 and the rift between them was confirmed by her letter to him on 12th January 1794, as a result of which Burns composed this tasteless libel. In a letter to Clarinda in June 1794 he described the subject of this poem as 'a woman of fashion in this country, with whom, at one period, I was well acquainted. By some scandalous conduct to me...she steered so far to the north of my good opinion, that I have made her the theme of several ill natured things.' The 'scandalous conduct' was her temerity in rebuking Burns!

How cold is that bosom which Folly once fired!
   How pale is that cheek where the rouge lately glisten'd!
How silent that tongue which the echoes oft tired!
   How dull is that ear which to flatt'ry so listen'd!

If sorrow and anguish their exit await,
   From friendship and dearest affection remov'd,
How doubly severer, Maria, thy fate!
   Thou diedst unwept, as thou livedst unlov'd.

Loves, Graces, and Virtues, I call not on you:
   So shy, grave, and distant, ye shed not a tear.
But come, all ye offspring of Folly so true,
   And flowers let us cull for Maria's cold bier!

We'll search through the garden for each silly flower,
   We'll roam thro' the forest for each idle weed,
But chiefly the nettle, so typical, shower,
   For none e'er approach'd her but rued the rash deed.

We'll sculpture the marble, we'll measure the lay:
    Here Vanity strums on her idiot lyre!
There keen Indignation shall dart on his prey,
    Which spurning Contempt shall redeem from his ire!

### THE EPITAPH

Here lies, now a prey to insulting neglect,
    What once was a butterfly, gay in life's beam:
Want only of wisdom denied her respect,
    Want only of goodness denied her esteem.

# WILT THOU BE MY DEARIE?

*TUNE: The Sutor's Dochter*

First published in the *Morning Chronicle* on 10th May 1794, though written earlier.
Patrick Miller Jr. of Dalswinton had offered Burns a position with this newspaper in
April 1794. He declined, but contributed occasional verses to it.

Wilt thou be my dearie?
When Sorrow wrings thy gentle heart,
O, wilt thou let me cheer thee?
By the treasure of my soul –
    That's the love I bear thee –
I swear and vow that only thou
    Shall ever be my dearie!
Only thou, I swear and vow,
    Shall ever be my dearie!

    Lassie, say thou lo'es me,
Or, if thou wilt na be my ain,
    Say na thou'lt refuse me!
If it winna, canna be,
    Thou for thine may choose me,
Let me, lassie, quickly die,
    Trusting that thou lo'es me!
Lassie, let me quickly die,
    Trusting that thou lo'es me!

## SONNET ON THE DEATH OF
## ROBERT RIDDELL

### OF GLENRIDDELL AND FRIARS' CARSE

Although estranged from the Riddell family after the 'Sabine Women' incident, Burns was moved by the sudden death of Robert Riddell, on 20th April 1794, to write this sonnet - 'a small heart-felt tribute to the memory of the man I loved.'

No more, ye warblers of the wood, no more,
    Nor pour your descant grating on my soul!
    Thou young-eyed Spring, gay in thy verdant stole,
More welcome were to me grim Winter's wildest roar!

How can ye charm, ye flowers, with all your dyes?
    Ye blow upon the sod that wraps my friend.
    How can I to the tuneful strain attend?
That strain flows round the untimely tomb where Riddell lies.

Yes, pour, ye warblers, pour the notes of woe,
    And sooth the Virtues weeping o'er his bier!
    The man of worth - and 'hath not left his peer'! –
Is in his 'narrow house', for ever darkly low.

Thee, Spring, again with joy shall other greet;
Me, memory of my loss will only meet.

## INSCRIPTION AT FRIARS' CARSE HERMITAGE

### TO THE MEMORY OF ROBERT RIDDELL

Alleged to have been inscribed on the window of the Hermitage on Burns's first visit there after the death of Robert Riddell.

To Riddell, much lamented man,
    This ivied cot was dear:
Wand'rer, dost value matchless worth?
    This ivied cot revere.

## HERE IS THE GLEN

Sent to Thomson about May 1794 with a letter describing how Burns 'got an air, pretty enough composed by Lady Elizabeth Heron of Heron...Cree is a beautiful romantic stream; and as her Ladyship is a particular friend of mine, I have written the following song to it.' Lady Elizabeth (1745-1811) was a daughter of the Earl of Dundonald and married Patrick Heron. The Cree forms the western boundary of Kirkcudbrightshire.

Here is the glen, and here the bower
    All underneath the birchen shade,
The village-bell has toll'd the hour –
    O, what can stay my lovely maid?

'Tis not Maria's whispering call –
   'Tis but the balmy-breathing gale,
Mixed with some warbler's dying fall
   The dewy star of eve to hail!

Is it Maria's voice I hear –
   So calls the woodlark in the grove
His little faithful mate to cheer:
   At once 'tis music and 'tis love!

And art thou come? And art thou true?
   O, welcome, dear, to love and me,
And let us all our vows renew
   Along the flowery banks of Cree!

## PINNED TO MRS. WALTER RIDDELL'S CARRIAGE

Offered to Patrick Miller as a contribution to the *Morning Chronicle*. Burns subsequently inserted these scurrilous lines in the Glenriddell MS after Elizabeth Riddell had returned the collection at Burns's request.

If you rattle along like your mistress's tongue,
   Your speed will out-rival the dart;
But, a fly for your load, you'll break down on the road,
   If your stuff be as rotten's her heart.

## ON HEARING IT ASSERTED FALSEHOOD

### IS EXPRESSED IN THE REV. DR. BABINGTON'S VERY LOOKS

William Babington (1746-1818), a native of Ireland, became priest of the Episcopal Congregation of Dumfries in 1772 and a D.D. of Trinity College, Dublin in 1781. Burns had a twinkle in his eye when he composed this epigram as Dr Babington was a much-loved member of the community and Chairman of Dumfries and Galloway Infirmary for 28 years. Syme, Bushby, McMurdo and De Peyster were close friends and members of his congregation.

That there is a falsehood in his looks
   I must and will deny:
They tell their Master is a knave,
   And sure they do not lie.

## YE TRUE LOYAL NATIVES

A conservative political club formed on 18th January 1793 for 'Supporting the Laws and Constitution of the Country.' Some verses attacking Burns and his friends John Syme, Dr James Maxwell and James Mundell were composed by a club member and circulated in Dumfries. This was Burns's riposte.

Ye true 'Loyal Natives' attend to my song:
In uproar and riot rejoice the night long!
From Envy and Hatred your core is exempt,
But where is your shield from the darts of Contempt?

## ODE FOR GENERAL WASHINGTON'S BIRTHDAY

George Washington was born in Virginia on 22nd February 1732, but the first draft of this ode was composed about 25th June 1794 and sent to Mrs Dunlop from Castle Douglas during Burns's visit to Galloway. Washington, recently entered on his second term as president of the United States, was merely the pretext for this ode whose subject was Liberty-'...how dear the theme is to me.'

No Spartan tube, no Attic shell,
   No lyre Aeolian I awake.
'Tis Liberty's bold note I swell:
   Thy harp, Columbia, let me take!       i.e. America
See gathering thousands, while I sing,
A broken chain, exulting, bring
   And dash it in a tyrant's face,
And dare him to his very beard,
And tell him he no more is fear'd,
   No more the despot of Columbia's race!
A tyrant's proudest insults brav'd,
They shout a People freed! They hail an Empire sav'd!

Where is man's godlike form?
   Where is that brow erect and bold,
   That eye that can unmov'd behold
The wildest rage, the loudest storm
That e'er created Fury dared to raise?
Avaunt! thou caitiff, servile, base,
That tremblest at a despot's nod,
Yet, crouching under the iron rod,
Canst laud the arm that struck th' insulting blow!
Art thou of man's Imperial line?
Dost boast that countenance divine?
   Each skulking feature answers: No!
But come, ye sons of Liberty,
Columbia's offspring, brave as free,
In danger's hour still flaming in the van,
Ye know, and dare maintain the Royalty of Man!

Alfred, on thy starry throne
  Surrounded by the tuneful choir,
  The Bards that erst have struck the patriot lyre,
  And rous'd the freeborn Briton's soul of fire,
No more thy England own!
Dare injured nations form the great design
  To make detested tyrants bleed?
  Thy England execrates the glorious deed!
  Beneath her hostile banners waving,
  Every pang of honour braving,
England in thunder calls: 'the Tyrant's cause is mine!'

  That hour accurst how did the fiends rejoice,
  And Hell thro all her confines raise the exulting voice!
  That hour which saw the generous English name
Link't with such damned deeds of everlasting shame!

Thee, Caledonia, thy wild heaths among,
Fam'd for the martial deed, the heaven-taught song,
  To thee I turn with swimming eyes!
Where is that soul of Freedom fled?
Immingled with the mighty dead
  Beneath that hallow'd turf where Wallace lies!
Hear it not, Wallace, in thy bed of death!
  Ye babbling winds, in silence weep!
  Disturb not ye the hero's sleep,
Nor give the coward secret breath!
Is this the ancient Caledonian form,
Firm as the rock, resistless as her storm?
Show me that eye which shot immortal hate,
  Blasting the Despot's proudest bearing!
Show me that arm which, nerv'd with thundering fate,
  Crush'd Usurpation's boldest daring!
Dark-quench'd as yonder sinking star,
No more that glance lightens afar,
That palsied arm no more whirls on the waste of war.

# EPITAPH FOR MR. WALTER RIDDELL

Walter Riddell (1764-1802), younger brother of Robert Riddell, inherited estates in Antigua from his first wife Ann Doig (d. 1788) and married Maria Woodley in 1790. Burns always had a poor opinion of Maria's husband, who incurred some of his spleen when Maria sided with the Riddells over the 'Sabine Rape' incident.

So vile was poor Wat, such a miscreant slave,
That the worms ev'n damn'd him when laid in his grave
'In his scull there's a famine' a starved reptile cries,
'And his heart it is poison!' another replies.

## MY LUVE IS LIKE A RED, RED ROSE

This is an amalgam of several old ballads and illustrates Burns's genius for reworking folk material and producing a poetic gem of the first rank. It was first published by Pietro Urbani in April 1794.

O, my luve is like a red, red rose,
    That's newly sprung in June.
O, my luve is like the melodie,
    That's sweetly play'd in tune.

As fair art thou, my bonie lass,
    So deep in luve am I,
And I will luve thee still, my dear,
    Till a' the seas gang dry.

Till a' the seas gang dry, my dear,
    And the rocks melt wi the sun!
And I will luve thee still, my dear,
    While the sands o life shall run.

And fare thee weel, my only luve!
    And fare thee weel, a while!
And I will come again, my luve,
    Tho it were ten thousand mile!

## ON THE SEAS AND FAR AWAY

*TUNE: O'er the hills and far away*

The quality of this song is uneven and Thomson was very critical of it. Burns later withdrew it with the comment 'Making a poem is like begetting a son; you cannot know whether you have a wise man or a fool, untill you produce him to the world and try him.'

### CHORUS

*On the seas and far away,*
*On stormy seas and far away –*
*Nightly dreams and thoughts by day,*
*Are ay with him that's far away.*

How can my poor heart be glad
When absent from my sailor lad?
How can I the thought forego –
He's on the seas to meet the foe?
Let me wander, let me rove,
Still my heart is with my love.
Nightly dreams, and thoughts by day,
Are with him that's far away.

When in summer noon I faint,
As weary flocks around me pant,
Haply in this scorching sun
My sailor's thund'ring at his gun.
Bullets, spare my only joy!
Bullets, spare my darling boy!
Fate, do with me what you may,
Spare but him that's far away!
   On the seas and far away,
   On stormy seas and far away –
   Fate, do with me what you may,
   Spare but him that's far away!

At the starless, midnight hour
When Winter rules with boundless power,
As the storms the forests tear,
And thunders rend the howling air,
Listening to the doubling roar
Surging on the rocky shore,
All I can – I weep and pray
For his weal that's far away.
   On the seas and far away,
   On stormy seas and far away,
   All I can – I weep and pray
   For his weal that's far away.

Peace, thy olive wand extend
And bid wild War his ravage end;
Man with brother man to meet,
And as a brother kindly greet!
Then may Heav'n with prosperous gales
Fill my sailor's welcome sails,
To my arms their charge convey,
My dear lad that's far away!
   On the seas and far away!
   On stormy seas and far away,
   To my arms their charge convey,
   My dear lad that's far away!

# TO DR. MAXWELL

## ON MISS JESSIE STAIG'S RECOVERY

Jessie Staig, daughter of the provost of Dumfries, was gravely ill and her own doctor gave her only hours to live. Dr Maxwell was then called in 'and his prescriptions in a few hours altered her situation, and have now cured her.' (Burns to Mrs Dunlop, September, 1794). Unhappily the 'Angel' died in 1801 in her 26th year. William Maxwell (1760-1834), son of James Maxwell of Kirkconnell, was educated by the Jesuits at Dinant and studied medicine in Paris, serving in the National Guard at the execution of Louis XVI. He returned to Scotland and settled in Dumfries in 1794. His 'Jacobinism' endeared him to Burns and they became close friends. He attended the poet during his final illness.

Maxwell, if merit here you crave,
    That merit I deny:
You save fair Jessie from the grave! –
    An Angel could not die!

# CA' THE YOWES TO THE KNOWES

## (Second Version)

The first version had been sent to SMM but Burns was not satisfied with it. Writing to Thomson in September 1794 Burns said 'In a solitary stroll which I took today, I tried my hand on a few pastoral lines...Here it is, with all its crudities and imperfections on its head.' The 'Clouden' is a tributary of the Nith and the 'silent towers' are the ruins of Lincluden Abbey.

### CHORUS

*Ca' the yowes to the knowes,*        ewes, knolls
*Ca' them where the heather grows,*
*Ca' them where the burnie rowes,*        streamlet
    *My bonie dearie.*

Hark, the mavis e'ening sang        thrush
Sounding Clouden's woods amang
Then a-faulding let us gang,        folding sheep
    My bonie dearie.

We'll gae down by Clouden side,        go
Thro the hazels, spreading wide
O'er the waves that sweetly glide
    To the moon sae clearly.

Yonder Clouden's silent towers
Where, at moonshine's midnight hours,
O'er the dewy bending flowers
    Fairies dance sae cheery.

Ghaist nor bogle shalt thou fear –        Ghost, demon
Thou'rt to Love and Heav'n sae dear
Nocht of ill may come thee near,
    My bonie dearie.

## SAE FLAXEN WERE HER RINGLETS

*TUNE: Oonagh's Waterfall*

The 'blackguard Irish song' which 'Our friend Cunningham sings delightfully' was a urolagniac piece of bawdry in the *Merry Muses*. 'The air is charming, and I have often regretted the want of decent verses to it,' wrote Burns to Thomson in September 1794, submitting these lines dedicated to Chloris.

Sae flaxen were her ringlets,
   Her eyebrows of a darker hue,
Bewitchingly o'er-arching
   Twa laughing een o bonie blue.
Her smiling, sae wyling,
   Wad make a wretch forget his woe!
What pleasure, what treasure,
   Unto those rosy lips to grow!
Such was my Chloris' bonie face,
   When first that bonie face I saw,
And ay my Chloris' dearest charm –
   She says she lo'es me best of a'!

Like harmony her motion,
   Her pretty ankle is a spy
Betraying fair proportion
   Wad make a saint forget the sky!
Sae warming, sae charming,
   Her faultless form and gracefu air,
Ilk feature – auld Nature
   Declar'd that she could dae nae mair!        do no more
Hers are the willing chains o love
   By conquering beauty's sovereign law,
And ay my Chloris' dearest charm –
   She says she lo'es me best of a'.

Let others love the city,
   And gaudy show at sunny noon!
Gie me the lonely valley,
   The dewy eve, and rising moon,
Fair beaming, and streaming
   Her silver light the boughs amang,
While falling, recalling,
   The amorous thrush concludes his sang!

Then, dearest Chloris, wilt thou rove
   By wimpling burn and leafy shaw,
And hear my vows o truth and love,
   And say thou lo'es me best of a'?

## ON A SWEARING COXCOMB

Here cursing, swearing Burton lies,
A buck, a beau, or 'Dem my eyes!'
Who in his life did little good,
And his last words were, 'Dem my blood!'

## ON A SUICIDE

Alexander Cunningham says that the subject of these lines was 'a melancholy person of the name of Glendinning', buried near Dumfries. Dr Copland Hutchison claimed to have seen Burns write this epitaph and push the paper into the earth over the grave. John Glendoning or Glendonwyn (b. 1744) killed himself in a room at the George Inn, where his daughter, overcome with grief, died soon afterwards.

Here lies in earth a root of Hell,
Set by the Deil's ain dibble;                        planting-stick
This worthless body damned himsel,
To save the Lord the trouble.

## ON AN INNKEEPER NICKNAMED 'THE MARQUIS'

According to Cunningham, 'This personage was landlord of a respectable public-house in Dumfries...and the little court or alley where his change-house stood is still called "The Marquis's Close".'

Here lies a mock Marquis, whose titles were shamm'd,
If ever he rise, it will be to be damn'd.

## ON JOHN BUSHBY, ESQ., TINWALD DOWNS

Legend has it that Burns and Bushby were good friends but fell out when Burns was scalded by a very hot pudding which Bushby jokingly claimed was cold. Thereafter Burns satirised him and his friends in 'John Bushby's Lamentation' and this mock-epitaph.

Here lies John Bushby – honest man,
Cheat him, Devil – if you can!

## ON CAPTAIN LASCELLES

Edward Lascelles (1740-1820) was M P for Northallerton (1761-74) but on losing his seat entered the Army and eventually rose to the rank of colonel. He regained his seat in 1790 and became 1st Earl of Harewood in 1812.

When Lascelles thought fit from this world to depart
Some friends warmly thought of embalming his heart.
A bystander whispers – 'Pray don't make so much o't –
The subject is poison, no reptile will touch it.'

## ON WM. GRAHAM, ESQ., OF MOSSKNOWE

William Graham (1756-1832) married Grace Gordon, grand-daughter of the Earl of Aboyne and was laird of Mossknowe, between Annan and Ecclefechan.

'Stop, thief!' Dame Nature call'd to Death,
As Willie drew his latest breath:
'How shall I make a fool again?
My choicest model thou hast ta'en.'

## EPIGRAM AT BROWNHILL INN

In 1782 William Stewart's sister Catherine married John Bacon, the landlord of the inn at Brownhill about five miles north of Ellisland, hence this punning epigram which was preserved by an English commercial traveller named Ladyman who dined with Burns at this inn.

At Brownhill we always get dainty good cheer
And plenty of bacon each day in the year;
We've a' thing that's nice, and mostly in season,
But why always bacon – come, tell me the reason?

## YOU'RE WELCOME, WILLIE STEWART

William Stewart (1749-1812) was the son of the publican at Closeburn, Dumfriesshire and father of 'lovely Polly Stewart'. Burns often visited him on Excise duties and engraved these lines on a crystal tumbler. 'The landlady [Stewart's mother] being very wroth at what she considered the disfigurement of her glass, a gentleman present appeased her by paying down a shilling, and carried off the relic.' This engraved glass was eventually acquired by Sir Walter Scott and is now on display at Abbotsford.

### CHORUS

*You're welcome, Willie Stewart!*
*You're welcome, Willie Stewart!*
*There's ne'er a flower that blooms in May,*
*That's half sae welcome's thou art!*

Come, bumpers high! express your joy!
The bowl we maun renew it –                                        must
The tappet hen, gae bring her ben,            6-pint pewter vessel
To welcome Willie Stewart!

May foes be strong, and friends be slack!
Ilk action, may he rue it!                                            Each
May woman on him turn her back,
That wrangs thee, Willie Stewart!

## LOVELY POLLY STEWART

*TUNE: Ye're welcome, Charlie Stewart*

Polly Stewart (1775-1847) was daughter of William Stewart, factor of Closeburn Estate, Dumfriesshire. She had an erratic life, first marrying her cousin, by whom she had three sons. When he absconded she contracted a 'quasimatrimonial alliance' with a farmer George Welsh (great uncle of Jane Welsh Carlyle). She left him in 1806, went off with a Swiss soldier called Fleitz and wandered all over Europe, before dying in Florence.

CHORUS

O lovely Polly Stewart,
   O charming Polly Stewart,
There's ne'er a flower that blooms in May,
   That's half so fair as thou art!

The flower it blaws, it fades, it fa's,
   And art can ne'er renew it;
But Worth and Truth, eternal youth
   Will gie to Polly Stewart!

May he whase arms shall fauld thy charms
   Possess a leal and true heart!
To him be given to ken the heaven
   He grasps in Polly Stewart!

## O, SAW YOU MY DEAR, MY PHILLY

*TUNE: When she cam ben she bobbet*

Composed as a variant of 'My Eppie McNab', and submitted to Thomson in the autumn of 1794.

O, saw ye my Dear, my Philly?
O, saw ye my Dear, my Philly?
She's down i' the grove, she's wi a new love,
   She winna come hame to her Willy.

What says she my Dear, my Philly?
What says she my Dear, my Philly?
She lets thee to wit she has thee forgot,
   And for ever disowns thee, her Willy.

O, had I ne'er seen thee, my Philly!
O, had I ne'er seen thee, my Philly!
As light as the air, and fause as thou's fair,          false
   Thou's broken the heart o thy Willy.

## HOW LANG AND DREARY IS THE NIGHT

*TUNE: Cauld Kail*

'I met with some such words in a Collection of songs somewhere, which I altered and enlarged, and to please you and to suit your favourite air...I have taken a stride or two across my room, and have arranged it anew...' (to Thomson, 19th October 1794).

CHORUS
*For O, her lanely nights are lang,*
*And O, her dreams are eerie,*
*And O, her widow'd heart is sair,*
*That's absent frae her dearie!*

How lang and dreary is the night,
    When I am frae my dearie!
I restless lie frae e'en to morn,             from, evening
    Tho I were ne'er sae weary:

When I think on the lightsome days
    I spent wi thee, my dearie,
And now what seas between us roar,
    How can I be but eerie?             fearful

How slow ye move, ye heavy hours,
    The joyless day how dreary!
It was na sae ye glinted by,             glanced
    When I was with my dearie!

## HOW LONG AND DREARY IS THE NIGHT

Second Version
How long and dreary is the night,
    When I am frae my dearie!
I sleepless lie frae e'en to morn,
    Tho I were ne'er sae weary:
I sleepless lie frae e'en to morn,
    Tho I were ne'er sae weary!

When I think on the happy days
    I spent wi you, my dearie:
And now what lands between us lie,
    How can I be but eerie?
And now what lands between us lie,
    How can I be but eerie?

How slow ye move, ye heavy hours,
    As ye were wae and weary!
It was na sae – ye glinted by,
    When I was wi my dearie!
It was na sae – ye glinted by,
    When I was wi my dearie!

## LET NOT WOMEN E'ER COMPLAIN

*TUNE: Duncan Gray*

Sent to Thomson on 19th October 1794 in response to the demand for 'English songs' to old Scottish airs. 'These English songs gravel me to death. I have not that command of the language that I have of my native tongue,' wrote Burns, self-deprecatingly.

Let not women e'er complain
　　Of inconstancy in love!
Let not women e'er complain
　　Fickle man is apt to rove!
Look abroad thro Nature's range,
Nature's mighty law is change:
Ladies, would it not seem strange
　　Man should then a monster prove?

Mark the winds, and mark the skies,
　　Ocean's ebb and ocean's flow.
Sun and moon but set to rise,
　　Round and round the seasons go.
Why then ask of silly man
To oppose great Nature's plan?
We'll be constant, while we can –
　　You can be no more, you know!

## THE WINTER OF LIFE

Sent to Thomson on 19th October as verses to 'a Musical curiosity - an East Indian air, which you would swear was a Scottish one.'

But lately seen in gladsome green,
　　The woods rejoiced the day;
Thro gentle showers, the laughing flowers
　　In double pride were gay;
But now our joys are fled
　　On winter blasts awa,
Yet maiden May in rich array,
　　Again shall bring them a'.

But my white pow – nae kindly thowe　　　　　　　pate
　　Shall melt the snaws of Age!
My trunk of eild, but buss and bield,　　　　age, bush, shelter
　　Sinks in Time's wintry rage.
O, Age has weary days
　　And nights o sleepless pain!
Thou golden time o youthfu prime,
　　Why comes thou not again?

# SLEEP'ST THOU

*TUNE: Deil tak the wars*

'I have been out in the country, taking dinner with a friend where I met with [Chloris]...As usual, I got into song; and returning home, I composed the following...' (Burns to Thomson, 19th October 1794).

Sleep'st thou, or wauk'st thou, fairest creature?        wakest
   Rosy Morn now lifts his eye,
Numbering ilka bud, which Nature        each
   Waters wi the tears o joy.
   Now to the streaming fountain
   Or up the heathy mountain
The hart, hind, and roe, freely, wildly-wanton stray;
   In twining hazel bowers,
   His lay the linnet pours,
   The laverock to the sky        lark
   Ascends, wi sangs o joy.
While the sun and thou arise to bless the day!

Phoebus, gilding the brow of morning,
   Banishes ilk darksome shade,
Nature, gladdening and adorning:
   Such to me my lovely maid!
   When frae my Chloris parted,
   Sad, cheerless, broken-hearted,
The night's gloomy shades, cloudy, dark, o'ercast my sky;
   But when she charms my sight
   In pride of Beauty's light,
   When thro my very heart
   Her beaming glories dart,
'Tis then – 'tis then I wake to life and joy!

# ON SEEING MRS. KEMBLE IN YARICO

George Colman's drama *Yarico*, first performed in 1787, centred on the love affair of an English merchant, Inkle, and a beautiful savage, here played by Mrs Stephen Kemble (1763-1841) at Dumfries in October 1794. The allusion in the last line is to Moses striking the rock of Horeb to give water to the Israelites.

Kemble, thou cur'st my unbelief
   Of Moses and his rod:
At Yarico's sweet notes of grief
   The rock with tears had flow'd.

## TO THE HONORABLE MR. R. MAULE OF PANMURE, ON HIS HIGH PHAETON

This epigram was sent to Mrs Dunlop on 29th October 1794 and was provoked by the activities of the Caledonian Hunt in Dumfries, in particular the spectacle of William Ramsay Maule (1771-1852), Earl of Panmure, 'driving away in his fine and elegant Phaeton on the Race Ground at Tinwald Downs October '94.' Despite this epigram Lord Panmure settled an annuity of £60 on Jean Armour in 1817.

Thou fool, in thy Phaeton towering,
　　Art proud when that Phaeton's praised?
This the pride of a Thief's exhibition
　　When higher his pillory's rais'd.


## THE CHARMING MONTH OF MAY

*TUNE: Daintie Davie*

A reworking, in English, of an old Scottish ballad in *The Tea-Table Miscellany*, sent to Thomson in November 1794.

### CHORUS

*Lovely was she by the dawn,*
　　*Youthful Chloe, charming Chloe,*
*Tripping o'er the pearly lawn,*
　　*The youthful, charming Chloe!*

It was the charming month of May,
When all the flow'rs were fresh and gay,
One morning, by the break of day,
　　The youthful, charming Chloe,
From peaceful slumber she arose,
Girt on her mantle and her hose,
And o'er the flow'ry mead she goes –
　　The youthful, charming Chloe!

The feather'd people you might see
Perch'd all around on every tree!
In notes of sweetest melody
　　They hail the charming Chloe,
Till, painting gay the eastern skies,
The glorious sun began to rise,
Outrival'd by the radiant eyes
　　Of youthful, charming Chloe.

## LASSIE WI THE LINT-WHITE LOCKS
### TUNE: *Rothiemurchie's Rant*

Sent to Thomson in November 1794, who commented that he would 'scarcely conceive a woman to be a beauty, on reading that she had lint-white locks!' Despite the mention of Cynthia (1.17) this song was written for Jean Lorimer.

### CHORUS
*Lassie wi the lint-white locks,*
  *Bonie lassie, artless lassie,*
*Wilt thou wi me tent the flocks –*                     tend
  *Wilt thou be my dearie, O?*

Now Nature cleeds the flowery lea,              clothes, meadow
And a' is young and sweet like thee,
O, wilt thou share its joys wi me,
  And say thou'lt be my dearie, O?

The primrose bank, the wimpling burn,           meandering brook
The cuckoo on the milk-white thorn,
The wanton lambs at early morn
  Shall welcome thee, my dearie, O.

And when the welcome simmer shower
Has cheer'd ilk drooping little flower,                  each
We'll to the breathing woodbine-bower
  At sultry noon, my dearie, O.

When Cynthia lights wi silver ray                    the moon
The weary shearer's hameward way,
Thro yellow waving fields we'll stray,
  And talk o love, my dearie, O.

And when the howling wintry blast
Disturbs my lassie's midnight rest,
Enclasped to my faithfu breast,
  I'll comfort thee, my dearie, O.

## AH, CHLORIS
### TUNE: *Major Graham*

Burns took the opening line of Sedley's song 'Ah, Chloris, cou'd I now but sit' and provided new words for Jean Lorimer. This song was sent to Alexander Findlater in September 1794 with the confession 'I am in the clouds elsewhere'.

Ah, Chloris, since it may not be
  That thou of love wilt hear,
If from the lover thou maun flee,
  Yet let the friend be dear!

Altho I love my Chloris mair
  Than ever tongue could tell,
My passion I will ne'er declare –
  I'll say I wish thee well.

Tho a' my daily care thou art,
    And a' my nightly dream,
I'll hide the struggle in my heart,
    And say it is esteem.


# PHILLY AND WILLY

*TUNE: The Sow's tail to Geordie*

These verses were meant 'to be in the alternate way of a lover and his Mistress chanting together.' He had intended to use Thomson's name, but dropped the idea as 'Geordie' was already associated with the bawdy ballad whose tune he borrowed. Thomson thought his wife's name Katherine was unpoetical anyway - so Willy and Philly were substituted.

## CHORUS

*For a' the joys that gowd can gie,*           HE AND SHE
*I dinna care a single flie!*
*The lad/lass I love's the lad/lass for me,*
    *And that's my ain dear Willy/Philly*

O Philly, happy be that day,                HE
When roving thro the gather'd hay,
My youthfu heart was stown away,
    And by thy charms, my Philly!
O Willy, ay I bless the grove            SHE
When first I own'd my maiden love
Whilst thou did pledge the Powers above,
    To be my ain dear Willy.

As songsters of the early year          HE
Are ilka day mair sweet to hear,        every
So ilka day to me mair dear
    And charming is my Philly.
As on the brier the budding rose        SHE
Still richer breathes and fairer blows,
So in my tender bosom grows
    The love I bear my Willy.

The milder sun and bluer sky,           HE
That crown my harvest cares wi joy,
Were ne'er sae welcome to my eye
    As is a sight o Philly.

| | |
|---|---|
| The little swallow's wanton wing, | SHE |
| Tho wafting o'er the flowery spring, | |
| Did ne'er to me sic tidings bring | such |
|     As meeting o my Willy. | |

| | |
|---|---|
| The bee that thro the sunny hour | HE |
| Sips nectar in the op'ning flower, | |
| Compar'd wi my delight is poor | |
|     Upon the lips o Philly | |
| The woodbine in the dewy weet, | SHE |
| When ev'ning shades in silence meet | |
| Is nocht sae fragrant or sae sweet | |
|     As is a kiss o Willy. | |

| | |
|---|---|
| Let Fortune's wheel at random rin, | HE |
| And fools may tyne, and knaves may win, | lose |
| My thoughts are a' bound up on ane, | |
|     And that's my ain dear Philly. | |
| What's a' the joys that gowd can gie? | SHE |
| I dinna care a single flie! | gold |
| The lad I love's the lad for me, | |
|     And that's my ain dear Willy. | |

## CANST THOU LEAVE ME THUS,
## MY KATIE?

*TUNE: Roy's Wife*

This song, composed during the night of 19th-20th November 1794 and sent to
Thomson the following morning, may have been intended as a compliment to Thomson's
wife, though in one version 'Betty' was substituted, leading some editors improbably to
link the song with Elizabeth Riddell.

### CHORUS

*Canst thou leave me thus, my Katie!*
    *Canst thou leave me thus, my Katie!*
*Well thou know'st my aching heart,*
    *And canst thou leave me thus, for pity?*

Is this thy plighted, fond regard:
    Thus cruelly to part, my Katie?
Is this thy faithful swain's reward:
    An aching broken heart, my Katie?

Farewell! And ne'er such sorrows tear
    That fickle heart of thine, my Katie!
Thou may'st find those will love thee dear,
    But not a love like mine, my Katie.

## BEHOLD, MY LOVE, HOW GREEN
## THE GROVES

*TUNE: My lodging is on the cold ground*

Sent to Thomson in November 1794 and allegedly written for Chloris.

Behold, my love, how green the groves,
    The primrose banks how fair;
The balmy gales awake the flowers,
    And wave thy flowing hair.

The lav'rock shuns the palace gay,              lark
    And o'er the cottage sings:
For Nature smiles as sweet, I ween,
    To Shepherds as to Kings.

Let minstrels sweep the skilfu strings,
    In lordly lighted ha':
The Shepherd stops his simple reed,
    Blythe in the birken shaw.              birch wood

The Princely revel may survey
    Our rustic dance wi scorn;
But are their hearts as light as ours,
    Beneath the milk-white thorn?

The shepherd, in the flowery glen;
    In shepherd's phrase, will woo:
The courtier tells a finer tale,
    But is his heart as true?

These wild-wood flowers I've pu'd, to deck
    That spotless breast o thine:
The courtier's gems may witness love,
    But, 'tis na love like mine.

## CONTENTED WI LITTLE AND
## CANTIE WI MAIR

*TUNE: Lumps o Puddins*

Composed on 18th November 1794, this song was regarded by Burns as a self-portrait
and when he sat to Alexander Reid the following summer for his portrait miniature, he
had some idea of linking it to this song 'in order that the portrait of my face and the
picture of my mind may go down the stream of Time together.'

Contented wi little, and cantie wi mair,        joyful
Whene'er I forgather wi Sorrow and Care,
I gie them a skelp, as they're creepin alang,    smack
Wi a cog o guid swats and an auld Scottish sang.    cup, ale

I whyles claw the elbow o troublesome Thought;       *sometimes clasp*
But Man is a soger, and Life is a faught.       *soldier, fight*
My mirth and guid humour are coin in my pouch,
And my Freedom's my lairdship nae monarch daur touch.    *dare*

A towmond o trouble, should that be my fa',    *twelvemonth, fate*
A night o guid fellowship sowthers it a':    *shoulders*
When at the blythe end o our journey at last,
Wha the Deil ever thinks o the road he has past?

Blind Chance, let her snapper and stoyte on her way;   *stumble, stagger*
Be't to me, be't frae me, e'en let the jade gae!   *go*
Come Ease, or come Travail, come Pleasure or Pain,
My warst word is: – 'Welcome, and welcome again!'

## MY NANIE'S AWA

*TUNE: There'll never be peace till Jamie comes hame*

Sent to Thomson on 9th December 1794.

Now in her green mantle blythe Nature arrays,
And listens the lambkins that bleat o'er the braes,   *hillsides*
While birds warble welcome in ilka green shaw,   *every, wood*
But to me it's delightless – my Nanie's awa.

The snawdrap and primrose our woodlands adorn,
And violets bathe in the weet o the morn,
They pain my sad bosom, sae sweetly they blaw;
They mind me o Nanie – and Nanie's awa!

Thou lav'rock that springs frae the dews of the lawn   *lark*
The shepherd to warn o the grey-breaking dawn,
And thou mellow mavis, that hails the night-fa',   *thrush*
Give over for pity – my Nanie's awa.

Come Autumn, sae pensive in yellow and grey,
And soothe me wi tidings o Nature's decay!
The dark, dreary Winter, and wild-driving snaw
Alane can delight me – now Nanie's awa.

## DUMFRIES EPIGRAMS

This group of epigrams, dating from 1794-5, survives only in the transcript of John Syme of Ryedale.

*The subject of this is not known but could be William Copland of Collieston, mentioned in the Second Election Ballad.*

C—d faithful likeness, friend Painter, would'st seize?
Keep out Worth, Wit and Wisdom: Put in what you please.

The only lady who fits this description was Elizabeth, second daughter of the Rev. William Inglis, minister of the Loreburn Street congregation, whose sermons Burns enjoyed above all others.

### Extempore on Miss E. I —, a Lady of a figure indicating amazonian strength.

Should he escape the slaughter of thine Eyes,
Within thy strong Embrace he struggling dies.

The Loyal Natives were formed in January 1793 from among the more reactionary citizens of Dumfries. Their scurrilous verses lampooning Burns and other radicals provoked this response.

### To a Club in Dumfries who styled themselves the Dumfries Loyal Natives and exhibited violent party work and intemperate Loyalty... 10th June 1794.

Pray, who are these Natives the Rabble so ven'rate?
They're our true ancient Natives, and they breed undegen'rate
The ignorant savage that weather's the storm,
When the man and the Brute differed but in the form.

The identity of 'Billy' has mercifully passed into oblivion! Possibly the subject was Captain William Roddick whom Burns satirised in 'Epitaph on a Noted Coxcomb' or William Graham of Mossknowe.

### On an old acquaintance who seemed to pass the Bard without notice.

Dost hang thy head, Billy, asham'd that thou knowest me?
'Tis paying in kind a just debt that thou owest me.

Dost blush, my dear Billy, asham'd of thyself,
A Fool and a Cuckold together?
The fault is not thine, insignificant elf,
Thou was not consulted in either.

Commissary Goldie was President of the Loyal Natives and thus raised a special animosity in the poet.

### Immediate extempore on being told by W. L. of the Customs Dublin that Comm. Goldie did not seem disposed to push the bottle.

Friend Commissar, since we're met and are happy,
Pray why should we part without having more nappy!        ale
Bring in t'other bottle, for faith I am dry –
Thy drink thou can't part with and neither can I.

The subject of this quatrain was Edmund Burke (1729-97) the celebrated Irish orator and politician. Warren Hastings' trial for maladminstration in India ended with his acquittal in April 1795.

### *On Mr. Burke by an opponent and a friend to Mr. Hastings*

Oft I have wonder'd that on Irish ground
No poisonous Reptile ever has been found:
Revealed the secret stands of great Nature's work:
She preserved her poison to create a Burke!

James Swan (b. 1751), elected a bailie of Dumfries in 1794, was re-elected in 1795 but ceased to be a magistrate in October 1796 and was voted off the Council a year later, so Burns's prophecy came true.

### *At the election of Magistrates for Dumfries, 1794, John McMurdo Esqr., was chosen Provost and a Mr. Swan one of the Baillies; and at the Entertainment usually given on the occasion Burns, seeing the Provost's Supporters on the Bench, took his pencil and wrote the following.*

Baillie Swan, Baillie Swan,
Let you do what you can,
God ha' mercy on honest Dumfries:
But e'er the year's done,
Good Lord! Provost John
Will find that his Swans are but Geese.

## ON CHLORIS

### REQUESTING ME TO GIVE HER A SPRIG OF BLOSSOMED THORN

At one time these lines were attributed to Charles Dibdin, but the truth is that Dibdin borrowed Burns's lines and added a stanza of his own. 'Chloris' was, of course, Jean Lorimer.

From the white-blossom'd sloe my dear Chloris requested
    A sprig, her fair breast to adorn:
No, by Heaven! I exclaim'd, 'let me perish for ever
    Ere I plant in that bosom a thorn!'

# ODE TO SPRING

*TUNE: The tither morn*

This mock pastoral was sent to Thomson in January 1795 - allegedly composed some years earlier 'when I was younger, and by no means the saint I am now', as a wager with a friend that he could compose an Ode to Spring on an original plan.

| | |
|---|---|
| When maukin bucks, at early fucks, | buck-hares |
| In dewy glens are seen, Sir; | |
| And birds, on boughs, take off their mows, | complete, copulation |
| Amang the leaves sae green, Sir; | |
| Latona's sun looks liquorish on | |
| Dame Nature's grand impetus, | |
| Till his pego rise, then westward flies | |
| To roger Madam Thetis. | |

| | |
|---|---|
| Yon wandering rill that marks the hill, | |
| And glances o'er the brae, Sir, | hillside |
| Slides by a bower where many a flower | |
| Sheds fragrance on the day, Sir; | |
| There Damon lay, with Sylvia gay, | |
| To love they thought no crime, Sir; | |
| The wild-birds sang, the echoes rang, | |
| While Damon's arse beat time, Sir. | |

| | |
|---|---|
| First wi the thrush, his thrust and push | |
| Had compass large and long, Sir; | |
| The blackbird next, his tuneful text, | |
| Was bolder, clear and strong, Sir: | |
| The linnet's lay came then in play, | |
| And the lark that soar'd aboon, Sir; | above |
| Till Damon, fierce, mistim'd his arse, | |
| And fuck'd quite out o tune, Sir. | |

# A MAN'S A MAN FOR A' THAT

*TUNE: For a' that*

Sent to Thomson in January 1795. The intense contempt of rank has made this a revolutionary song with a central place in the psalmody of radicalism.

| | |
|---|---|
| Is there for honest poverty | |
| That hings his head, an a' that? | hangs |
| The coward slave, we pass him by – | |
| We dare be poor for a' that! | |
| For a' that, an a' that, | |
| Our toils obscure, an a' that, | |
| The rank is but the guinea's stamp, | |
| The man's the gowd for a' that. | gold |

535

What though on hamely fare we dine,
   Wear hoddin grey, an a' that?            coarse woollen cloth
Gie fools their silks, and knaves their wine –
   A man's a man for a' that.
For a' that, an a' that,
   Their tinsel show, an a' that,
The honest man, tho e'er sae poor,
   Is king o men for a' that.

Ye see yon birkie ca'd 'a lord,'                 fellow
   Wha struts, an stares, an a' that?
Tho hundreds worship at his word,
   He's but a cuif for a' that.                 fool
For a' that, an a' that,
   His ribband, star, an a' that,
The man o independent mind,
   He looks an laughs at a' that.

A prince can mak a belted knight,
   A marquis, duke, an a' that!
But an honest man's aboon his might –       above
   Guid faith, he mauna fa' that!         must not
For a' that, an a' that,
   Their dignities, an a' that,
The pith o sense an pride o worth,
   Are higher rank than a' that.

Then let us pray that come it may
   (As come it will for a' that),
That Sense and Worth o'er a' the earth,
   Shall bear the gree an a' that.       have priority
For a' that, an a' that,
   It's comin yet for a' that,
That man to man, the world, o'er
   Shall brithers be for a' that.

## CRAIGIEBURN WOOD

(Second Version)

This version was composed in the winter of 1794-5 and sent to Thomson on 15th
January 1795.

Sweet fa's the eve on Craigieburn,
   And blythe awakes the morrow
But a' the pride o Spring's return
   Can yield me nocht but sorrow.

I see the flowers and spreading trees,
   I hear the wild birds singing;
But what a weary wight can please,
   And Care his bosom is wringing?

Fain, fain would I my griefs impart,
    Yet dare na for your anger;
But secret love will break my heart,
    If I conceal it langer.

If thou refuse to pity me,
    If thou shalt love another,
When yon green leaves fade frae the tree,
    Around my grave they'll wither.

## DOES HAUGHTY GAUL INVASION THREAT?

*TUNE: Push about the Jorum*

At the end of January 1795 the Volunteer movement to raise forces for home defence got under way. Burns played a prominent part in the formation of the Dumfries Volunteers. It is probable that Burns wrote this song in March and it was published in various newspapers in May. The occasion of the song was the rumoured invasion of Britain by Napoleon's forces. Corsincon and Criffel are hills, on the Ayrshire border and the Stewarty side of the Nith estuary respectively.

| | |
|---|---|
| Does haughty Gaul invasion threat? | |
|     Then let the loons beware, Sir! | fools |
| There's wooden walls upon our seas | |
|     And volunteers on shore, Sir! | |
| The Nith shall run to Corsincon, | |
|     And Criffel sink in Solway, | |
| Ere we permit a foreign foe | |
|     On British ground to rally! | |
| | |
| O, let us not, like snarling tykes, | dogs |
|     In wrangling be divided, | |
| Till, slap! come in an unco loon, | uncommon |
|     And wi a rung decide it! | cudgel |
| Be Britain still to Britain true, | |
|     Amang ourselves united! | |
| For never but by British hands | |
|     Maun British wrangs be righted! | Must |
| | |
| The kettle o the Kirk and State, | |
|     Perhaps a clout may fail in't; | patch |
| But Deil a foreign tinkler loon | |
|     Shall ever ca' a nail in't! | drive |
| Our fathers' blude the kettle bought, | |
|     And wha wad dare to spoil it, | |
| By Heav'ns! the sacrilegious dog | |
|     Shall fuel be to boil it! | |

The wretch that would a tyrant own,
   And the wretch, his true-sworn brother,
Who would set the mob above the throne,
   May they be damn'd together!
Who will not sing God Save the King
   Shall hang as high's the steeple;
But while we sing God Save the King,
   We'll ne'er forget the people!

## O, LET ME IN THIS AE NIGHT

Thomson rejected the first draft of this song in August 1793. Burns began again in
September 1794 and completed it early in Febraury 1795.

### CHORUS

*O, let me in this ae night,*                             one
*This ae, ae, ae night!*
*O, let me in this ae night,*
*And rise, and let me in!*

O lassie, are ye sleepin yet,
Or are you waukin, I wad wit?                          awake
For Love has bound me hand an fit,               foot
   And I would fain be in, jo.                 darling

Thou hear'st the winter wind an weet:
Nae star blinks thro the driving sleet!          shines
Tak pity on my weary feet,
   And shield me frae the rain, jo.

The bitter blast that round me blaws,
Unheeded howls, unheeded fa's:
The cauldness o thy heart's the cause
   Of a' my care and pine, jo.

### HER ANSWER

### CHORUS

*I tell you now this ae night,*
*This ae, ae, ae night,*
*And ance for a' this ae night,*
*I winna let ye in, jo.*

O, tell na me o wind an rain,
Upbraid na me wi cauld disdain,
Gae back the gate ye cam again,            go way
   I winna let ye in, jo!

The snellest blast at mirkest hours,      bitterest, darkest
That round the pathless wand'rer pours
Is nocht to what poor she endures,
   That's trusted faithless man, jo.

The sweetest flower that deck'd the mead,
Now trodden like the vilest weed –
Let simple maid the lesson read!
   The weird may be her ain, jo.                     fate, own

The bird that charm'd his summer day,
And now the cruel fowler's prey,
Let that to witless woman say: –
   'The gratefu heart of man,' jo.

# FROM ESOPUS TO MARIA

Esopus (an actor in Imperial Rome) conceals the identity of James Williamson (d. 1802) manager of a theatrical company which played occasionally behind the George Inn, Dumfries. When the company was playing at Whitehaven, the 'bad Earl of Lonsdale' imprisoned the entire troupe as vagrants. Burns used this incident to hit back at Maria Riddell and Lord Lonsdale. Williamson had, like Burns, been admitted to the Riddell social circle.

From those drear solitudes and frowsy cells,
Where infamy with sad Repentance dwells;
Where turnkeys make the jealous portal fast,
And deal from iron hands the spare repast;
Where truant 'prentices, yet young in sin,
Blush at the curious stranger peeping in;
Where strumpets, relics of the drunken roar,
Resolve to drink, nay half – to whore – no more;
Where tiny thieves, not destin'd yet to swing,
Beat hemp for others, riper for the string:
From these dire scenes my wretched lines I date,
To tell Maria her Esopus' fate.

'Alas! I feel I am no actor here!'
'Tis real hangmen real scourges bear!
Prepare, Maria, for a horrid tale
Will turn thy very rouge to deadly pale;
Will make thy hair, tho erst from gipsy poll'd,
By barber woven and by barber sold
Though twisted smooth with Harry's nicest care,
Like hoary bristles to erect and stare!

The hero of the mimic scene, no more
I start in Hamlet, in Othello roar;
Or, haughty Chieftain, 'mid the din of arms,
In Highland bonnet woo Malvina's charms:

539

While sans-culottes stoop up the mountain high,    nickname of the
And steal me from Maria's prying eye.    French revolutionaries,
Blest Highland bonnet! once my proudest dress,    but here signifying
Now, prouder still, Maria's temples press!    kilted Highlanders
I see her wave thy towering plumes afar,
And call each coxcomb to the wordy war!

I see her face the first of Ireland's sons,
And even out-Irish his Hibernian bronze!    Captain Gillespie
The crafty Colonel leaves the tartan'd lines    Col. McDougal of Logan,
For other wars, where he a hero shines;    'a noted Lothario'
The hopeful youth, in Scottish senate bred,
Who owns a Bushby's heart without the head,    Maitland Bushby
Comes 'mid a string of coxcombs to display    (b. 1767) Sheriff of
That Veni, vidi, vici, is his way;    Wigtownshire
The shrinking Bard adown the alley skulks,
And dreads a meeting worse than Woolwich hulks,    prison ships
Though there, his heresies in Church and State
Might well award him Muir and Palmer's fate:    Thomas Muir (1765-98)
Still she, undaunted, reels and rattles on,    Thomas Palmer
And dares the public like a noontide sun.    tried for sedition (1793)
   and transported to Australia
What scandal called Maria's jaunty stagger
The ricket reeling of a crooked swagger?
Whose spleen (e'en worse than Burns's venom, when
He dips in gall unmix'd his eager pen
And pours his vengeance in the burning line),
Who christen'd thus Maria's lyre-divine,
The idiot strum of Vanity bemus'd,
And even th' abuse of Poesy abus'd?
Who called her verse a Parish Workhouse, made    a slighting reference
For motley foundling Fancies, stolen or strayed?    to Maria's own poems

A Workhouse! Ah, that sound awakes my woes,
And pillows on the thorn my rack'd repose!
In durance vile here must I wake and weep,
And all my frowsy couch in sorrow steep:
That straw where many a rogue has lain of yore,
And vermin'd gipsies litter'd heretofore.

Why Lonsdale, thus thy wrath on vagrants pour?    James Lowther, Earl
Must earth no rascal save thyself endure?    of Lonsdale (1736-1802)
Must thou alone in guilt immortal swell,
And make a vast monopoly of Hell?
Thou know'st the Virtues cannot hate thee worse:
The Vices also, must they club their curse?
Or must no tiny sin to others fall,
Because thy guilt's supreme enough for all?

Maria, send me too thy griefs and cares,
In all of thee sure thy Esopus shares:
As thou at all mankind the flag unfurls,
Who on my fair one Satire's vengeance hurls!
Who calls thee, pert, affected, vain coquette,
A wit in folly, and a fool in wit!
Who says that fool alone is not thy due,
And quotes thy treacheries to prove it true!

Our force united on thy foes we'll turn,
And dare the war with all of woman born:
For who can write and speak as thou and I?
My periods that decyphering defy,
And thy still matchless tongue that conquers all reply!

## EPIGRAM ON MISS JEAN SCOTT

According to local tradition Jeanie was the daughter of John Scott, postmaster of
Ecclefechan, whom Burns met while detained by a snowstorm in February 1795. He
is said to have inscribed these lines on a window-pane. Jean was then just past her
sixteenth birthday.

O had each Scot of ancient times
   Been, Jeanie Scott, as thou art,
The bravest heart on English ground
   Had yielded like a coward.

## O, WAT YE WHA'S IN YON TOWN?

*TUNE: I'll gang nae mair to yon town*

Burns was trapped at Ecclefechan by a snowstorm on 7th February 1795 while on
Excise duties and whiled away the time working on this song. 'Jean' in this context could
be Jean Armour, Jean Lorimer or Jean Scott (see the foregoing), though later he claimed
that the subject of this song was Lucy Johnston, wife of Richard Oswald of Auchencruive.

### CHORUS

*I wat ye wha's in yon town*                          wot
   *Ye see the e'enin sun upon?*
*The dearest maid's in yon town,*
   *That e'enin sun is shining on!*

Now haply down yon gay green shaw             that, wood
   She wanders by yon spreading tree.
How blest ye flowers that round her blaw!
   Ye catch the glances o her e'e.

How blest ye birds that round her sing,
   And welcome in the blooming year!
And doubly welcome be the Spring,
   The season to my Jeanie dear!

The sun blinks blythe in yon town,
  Among the broomy braes sae green;              slopes
But my delight in yon town,
  And dearest pleasure is, my Jean.

Without my Love, not a' the charms
  O Paradise could yield my joy;
But gie me Jeanie in my arms,
  And welcome Lapland's dreary sky!

My cave wad be a lover's bower,
  Tho raging winter rent the air,
And she a lovely little flower,
  That I wad tent and shelter there.

O, sweet is she in yon town
  The sinking sun's gane down upon!
A fairer than's in yon town
  His setting beam ne'er shone upon.

If angry Fate be sworn my foe,
  And suff'ring I am doom'd to bear,
I'd careless quit aught else below,
  But spare, O spare me Jeanie dear!

For, while life's dearest blood is warm,
  Ae thought frae her shall ne'er depart,
And she, as fairest is her form,
  She has the truest, kindest heart.

## ON CHLORIS BEING ILL

*TUNE: Ay wauken, O*

Burns and Maria Riddell were reconciled in the spring of 1795 and he sent this song
to her in March, and to Thomson a month later, although the subject was Jean Lorimer.

### CHORUS

Long, long the night,
  Heavy comes the morrow,
While my soul's delight
  Is on her bed of sorrow.

Can I cease to care,
  Can I cease to languish,
While my darling fair
  Is on the couch of anguish!

Ev'ry hope is fled,
  Ev'ry fear is terror;
Slumber ev'n I dread,
  Ev'ry dream is horror.

Hear me, Powers Divine:
  O, in pity, hear me!
Take aught else of mine,
  But my Chloris spare me!


## EPITAPH FOR MR. W. CRUIKSHANK

William Cruikshank (d. 1795), a native of Duns, graduated M A Edinburgh University and became Rector of the High School in the Canongate and, in 1772, Latin master at Edinburgh High School. Burns first met him in 1786-7, through William Nicol, and stayed with the Cruikshank family at the end of his Highland tour. It was for Cruikshank's daughter Jean that Burns wrote 'The Rosebud'.

| | |
|---|---|
| Now honest William's gaen to Heaven | gone |
| I wat na gin't can mend him; | if it |
| The fauts he had in Latin lay, | faults |
| For nane in English kent them. | knew |


## BALLADS ON MR. HERON'S
## ELECTION, 1795

*TUNE: For a' that*

Patrick Heron (1736-1803) was a partner in Douglas, Heron & Co, the Ayr bank which failed so disastrously in 1773. Twenty years later Heron bounced back as Whig candidate in the Election of 1795. Burns met him at Kerroughtree, Heron's estate near Creetown, in June 1794 and helped his election campaign by writing four satirical political ballads.

Wham will we send to London town,
  To Parliament and a' that?
Or wha in a' the country round
  The best deserves to fa' that?
    For a' that, and a' that,
    Thro Galloway and a' that,
  Where is the Laird or belted Knight
    That best deserves to fa' that?

Wha sees Kerroughtree's open yett –         *gate*
  And wha is't never saw that? –
Wha ever wi Kerroughtree met,
  And has a doubt of a' that?
    For a' that, and a' that,
    Here's Heron yet for a' that!
  The independent patriot,
    The honest man, and a' that!

Tho wit and worth, in either sex,     *Selkirk mansion*
  Saint Mary's Isle can shaw that,     *near Kirkcudbright*
Wi Lords and Dukes let Selkirk mix,     *Dunbar Douglas, 4th Earl*
  And weel does Selkirk fa' that.     *of Selkirk (1722-99)*
    For a' that, and a' that,
    Here's Heron yet for a' that!
  The independent commoner
    Shall be the man for a' that.

But why should we to Nobles jeuk,     *bow*
  And it against the law, that,
And even a Lord may be a gowk,     *cuckoo*
  Wi ribban, star, and a' that?
    For a' that, and a' that,
    Here's Heron yet for a' that!
  A Lord may be a lousy loon,     *fool*
    Wi ribban, star, and a' that.

A beardless boy comes o'er the hills     *Thomas Gordon of*
  Wi's uncle's purse and a' that;     *Balmaghie (d. 1806), James*
But we'll hae ane frae 'mang oursels,     *Murray of Broughton (1727-99)*
  A man we ken, and a' that.     *know*
    For a' that, and a' that,
    Here's Heron yet for a' that!
  We are na to be bought and sold,
    Like nowte, and naigs, and a' that.     *cattle, horses*

Then let us drink: – 'The Stewartry,     *Kirkcudbrightshire*
  Kerroughtree's laird, and a' that,
Our representative to be':
  For weel he's worthy a' that!
    For a' that, and a' that!
    Here's Heron yet for a' that!
  A House of Commons such as he,
    They wad be blest that saw that.

## BALLAD SECOND

### THE ELECTION

*TUNE: Fy, Let Us A' to The Bridal*

Fy, let us a' to Kirkcudbright,
   For there will be bickerin there;
For Murray's light horse are to muster
   An O, how the heroes will swear!
And there will be Murray commander,
   An Gordon the battle to win:
Like brothers, they'll stan' by each other,
   Sae knit in alliance and kin.

> Murray of Broughton
> uncle of the Tory candidate
>
> Gordon of Balmaghie

An there'll be black-nebbit Johnie,
   The tongue o the trump to them a':
Gin he get na Hell for his haddin,
   The Deil gets nae justice ava!
And there'll be Kempleton's birkie,
   A boy no sae black at the bane;
But as to his fine nabob fortune –
   We'll e'en let the subject alane!

> John Bushby (d. 1802)
> sheriff-clerk of Dumfries
> If, inheritance
> at all
> William Bushby, brother of John
>
> veiled reference to his wealth
> acquired in India in
> questionable circumstances

An there'll be Wigton's new sheriff –
   Dame Justice fu brawly has sped:
She's gotten the heart of a Bushby,
   But Lord! what's become o the head?
An there'll be Cardoness, Esquire,
   Sae mighty in Cardoness' eyes:
A wight that will weather damnation,
   For the Devil the prey would despise.

> Maitland Bushby (b. 1767),
> son of John
>
> David Maxwell of Cardoness

An there'll be Douglasses doughty,
   New christening towns far and near:
Abjuring their democrat doings
   An kissing the arse of a peer!
An there'll be Kenmure sae generous,
   Wha's honor is proof to the storm:
To save them from stark reprobation
   He lent them his name to the firm!

> Sir William Douglas and his
> brother James; Carlinwark
> (now Castle Douglas); Newton
> Stewart (briefly Newton Douglas)
> John Gordon, Viscount
> Kenmure (1750-1840)

But we winna mention Redcastle,
   The body – e'en let him escape!
He'd venture the gallows for siller,
   An 'twere na the cost o the rape!
An whare is our King's Lord Lieutenant,
   Sae famed for his gratefu return?
The billie is getting his Questions
   To say at St. Stephen's the morn!

> Walter Lawrie of Redcastle
>
> money
> If, rope
> George Stewart, Lord Garlies
>
> fellow
> House of Commons

An there'll be lads of the gospel:     *Rev. James Muirhead*
    Muirhead, wha's as guid as he's true;     *(1742-1805)*
An there'll be Buittle's Apostle,     *Rev. George Maxwell (1762-1807)*
    Wha's mair o the black than the blue;
An there'll be folk frae St. Mary's,     *the family of the Earl of Selkirk*
    A house o great merit and note:
The Deil ane but honors them highly,     *not one of*
    The Deil ane will gie them his vote!

An there'll be wealthy young Richard,     *Oswald of Auchencruive*
    Dame Fortune should hang by the neck:     *(1771-1841)*
But for prodigal thriftless bestowing,
    His merit had won him respect,
An there'll be rich brither nabobs;     *D & J Anderson of St. Germains*
    Tho nabobs, yet men o the first!
An there'll be Collieston's whiskers,     *William Copland of Collieston*
    An Quinton - o lads no the warst!     *Quinton McAdam of*
    *Craigengillan*

An there'll be Stamp-Office Johnie:     *John Syme of Ryedale*
    Tak tent how ye purchase a dram!     *(1755-1831)*
An there'll be gay Cassencarry,     *Col. Mackenzie of Cassencarry*
    An there'll be Colonel Tam;     *Thomas Goldie of Goldielea*
An there'll be trusty Kerroughtree,     *Patrick Heron*
    Wha's honour was ever his law:
If the virtues were pack't in a parcel,
    His worth might be sample for a'!

An can we forget the auld Major,     *Major Basil Heron, Patrick's*
    Wha'll ne'er be forgot in the Greys?     *brother*
Our flatt'ry we'll keep for some other:
    Him only it's justice to praise!
An there'll be maiden Kilkerran,     *Sir Adam Fergusson of Kilkerran*
    An also Barskimming's guid Knight.     *Sir William Miller of Barskimming*
An there'll be roaring Birtwhistle –     *Alexander Birtwhistle, provost*
    Yet luckily roars in the right!     *of Kirkcudbright*

An there frae the Niddlesdale border
    Will mingle the Maxwells in droves:     *Maxwells of Terraughty,*
Teuch Johnie, Staunch Geordie, and Wattie     *Carruchan and the Grove*
    That girns for the fishes an loaves!
An there'll be Logan's McDoual –     *Andrew McDoual of Logan*
    Sculdudd'ry an he will be there!
An also the wild Scot o Galloway,
    Sogering, gunpowther Blair!     *Major Blair of Dunskey*

Then hey the chaste interest of Broughton,
    An hey for the blessings 'twill bring!
It may send Balmaghie to the Commons –
    In Sodom 'twould mak him a King!
An hey for the sanctified Murray     *Murray of Broughton*
    Our land wha wi chapels has stor'd;
He founder'd his horse among harlots,
    But gie'd the auld naig to the Lord!

# BALLAD THIRD

## JOHN BUSHBY'S LAMENTATION

### TUNE: *Babes in the Wood*

John Bushby was a Dumfries lawyer and sheriff-clerk, formerly a partner of Douglas, Heron & Co. and manager of the Dumfries branch of this ill-fated bank. His brother William, 'the gamesome billie', is alleged to have absconded with some of the bank's funds and used it to build a fortune in India. Bushby was not bothered by these lampoons, though he observed 'that he could not conceive why the poor devil [Burns] had thought proper to run a muck against all those who could best do him a service, and none of whom, as far as he knew, held him at ill will.' The 'lanentation' was for Gordon of Balmaghie who lost the Election.

'Twas in the Seventeen Hunder year
    O grace, and Ninety-Five,
That year I was the wae'est man           *saddest*
    Of onie man alive.                   *any*

In March the three-an-twentieth morn,
    The sun raise clear an bright;
But O, I was a waefu man,            *woeful*
    Ere to-fa' o the night!        *beginning*

Yerl Galloway lang did rule this land    *Earl*
    Wi equal right and fame,
Fast knit in chaste and holy bands,    *Lady Euphemia Stewart, the*
    With Broughton's noble name.    *Earl 's daughter, married Alexander*
                           *Murray of Broughton*

Yerl Galloway's man o men was I,
    And chief o Broughton's host:
So twa blind beggars, on a string,
    The faithfu tyke will trust!        *dog*

But now Yerl Galloway's sceptre's broke,
    And Broughton's wi the slain,
And I my ancient craft may try,     *legal profession*
    Sin' honesty is gane.

'Twas by the banks o bonie Dee,
    Beside Kirkcudbright's towers,
The Stewart and the Murray there
    Did muster a' their powers.

Then Murray on the auld grey yaud,    *mare*
    Wi winged spurs did ride,
That auld grey yaud a' Nidsdale rade,
    He staw upon Nidside.        *stole*

An there had na been the Yerl himsel,    *If*
    O, there had been nae play!
But Garlies was to London gane,    *the Earl's eldest son*
    And say the kye might stray.    *cattle*

And there was Balmaghie, I ween –
    In front rank he wad shine;
But Balmaghie had better been
    Drinkin Madeira wine.

*Gordon of Balmaghie*

And frae Glenkens cam to our aid
A chief o doughty deed!
In case that worth should wanted be,
    O Kenmure we had need.

*Viscount Kenmure*

And by our banners march'd Muirhead,
    And Buittle was na slack,
Whase haly priesthood nane could stain,
    For wha could dye the black?

*Rev. James Muirhead*
*Rev. George Maxwell*

And there was grave squire Cardoness,
    Look'd on till a' was done:
Sae in the tower o Cardoness
    A howlet sits at noon.

*David Maxwell*

And there led I the Bushby clan:
    My gamesome billie, Will,
And my son Maitland, wise as brave,
    My footsteps follow'd still.

*comrade*

The Douglas and the Heron's name,
    We set nought to their score;
The Douglas and the Heron's name
    Had felt our weight before.

*a side-swipe at the*
*failed bank of 1773*

But Douglasses o weight had we,
    The pair o lusty lairds,
For building cot-houses sae fam'd,
    And christenin kail-yards.

*James and Sir*
*William Douglas*

*cabbage patches*

And then Redcastle drew his sword
    That ne'er was stain'd wi gore,
Save on a wand'rer lame and blind,
    To drive him frae his door.

*Walter Sloan Lawrie*

And last cam creepin Collieston,
    Was mair in fear than wrath;
Ae knave was constant in his mind –
    To keep that knave frae scaith.

*William Copland*

# HERON ELECTION: BALLAD FOURTH

### THE TROGGER                                    Pedlar

Written in May-June 1796 when Patrick Heron was up for re-election, following the dissolution of Parliament. On this occasion his Tory opponent was Montgomery Stewart, (d. 1833), younger son of the Earl of Galloway.

### CHORUS

### TUNE: *Buy Broom Besoms*

*Buy braw troggin frae the banks o Dee!*                    fine wares
*Wha wants troggin let him come to me!*

Wha will buy my troggin, fine election ware,               James Murray of
Broken trade o Broughton, a' in high repair?                    Broughton

There's a noble Earl's fame and high renown,                    Galloway
For an auld sang – it's thought the guids were stown.             stolen

Here's the worth o Broughton in needle's e'e;
Here's a reputation tint by Balmaghie.              Gordon of Balmaghie, lost

Here's its stuff and lining, Cardoness's head –      Maxwell of Cardoness
Fine for a soger, a' the wale o lead.                              pick

Here's a little wadset, Buittle's scrap o truth,               mortgage
Pawn'd in a gin-shop, quenching holy drouth.                     thirst

Here's an honest conscience might a prince adorn,  John Bushby's estate,
Frae the downs o Tinwald, so was never worn!               Tinwald Downs

Here's armorial bearings frae the manse o Urr:          a reference to Rev.
The crest, a sour crab-apple rotten at the core.          Dr James Muirhead

Here is Satan's picture, like a bizzard gled                buzzard hawk
Pouncing poor Redcastle, sprawlin like a taed.       Walter Sloan Lawrie,
                                                                    toad

Here's the font where Douglas stane and mortar names,      Cally House,
Lately used at Caily christening Murray's crimes.       Gatehouse of Fleet

Here's the worth and wisdom Collieston can boast:        William Copland
By a thievish midge they had been nearly lost.            of Collieston

Here is Murray's fragments o the Ten Commands,
Gifted by Black Jock to get them aff his hands.               John Bushby

Saw ye e'er sic troggin? – if to buy ye're slack,
Hornie's turnin chapman: he'll buy a' the pack!               the Devil

## TO THE WOODLARK

*TUNE: Loch Erroch Side*

Supposedly written by Burns at the request of Mrs John McMurdo of Drumlanrig and
sent to Thomson in April 1795.

O, stay, sweet warbling wood-lark, stay,
Nor quit for me the trembling spray!
A hapless lover courts thy lay,
    Thy soothing, fond complaining.
Again, again that tender part,
That I may catch thy melting art!
For surely that wad touch her heart,             would
    Wha kills me wi disdaining.

Say, was thy little mate unkind,
And heard thee as the careless wind?
O, nocht but love and sorrow join'd          naught
    Sic notes o woe could wauken!           such
Thou tells o never-ending care,
O speechless grief and dark despair –
For pity's sake, sweet bird, nae mair,        no more
    Or my poor heart is broken!

## THEIR GROVES O SWEET MYRTLE

*TUNE: Humours of Glen*

A tribute to Jean Armour, sent to Thomson in April 1795.

Their groves o sweet myrtle let foreign lands reckon,
    Where bright-beaming summers exalt the perfume!
Far dearer to me yon lone glen o green breckan,     bracken
    Wi the burn stealing under the lang, yellow broom;     brook
Far dearer to me are yon humble broom bowers,
    Where the blue-bell and gowan lurk lowly, unseen;
For there, lightly tripping among the wild flowers,
    A-list'ning the linnet, aft wanders my Jean.

Tho rich is the breeze in their gay, sunny vallies,
    And cauld Caledonia's blast on the wave,
Their sweet-scented woodlands that skirt the proud palace,
    What are they? – The haunt of the tyrant and slave!
The slave's spicy forests and gold-bubbling fountains
    The brave Caledonian views wi disdain:
He wanders as free as the winds of his mountains,
    Save Love's willing fetters – the chains o his Jean.

## 'TWAS NA HER BONIE BLUE E'E

*TUNE: Laddie, lie near me*

These verses, addressed to Chloris, were requested by Thomson who wanted some decent lines to the traditional tune.

'Twas na her bonie blue e'e was my ruin:
Fair tho she be, that was ne'er my undoin.
'Twas the dear smile when naebody did mind us,
'Twas the bewitching, sweet, stoun glance o kindness!     stolen

Sair do I fear that to hope is denied me,     Sore
Sair do I fear that despair maun abide me;     must
But tho fell Fortune should fate us to sever,
Queen shall she be in my bosom for ever.

Chloris, I'm thine wi a passion sincerest,
And thou hast plighted me love o the dearest,
And thou'rt the angel that never can alter –
Sooner the sun in his motion would falter!

## HOW CRUEL ARE THE PARENTS

*TUNE: John Anderson, my jo*

Burns rewrote this song, which had appeared in several eighteenth century miscellanies.

How cruel are the parents
   Who riches only prize,
And to the wealthy booby
   Poor Woman sacrifice!
Meanwhile the hapless daughter
   Has but a choice of strife:
To shun a tyrant father's hate
   Become a wretched wife!

The ravening hawk pursuing,
   The trembling dove thus flies:
To shun impelling ruin
   Awhile her pinions tries,
Till, of escape despairing,
   No shelter or retreat,
She trusts the ruthless falconer,
   And drops beneath his feet.

## MARK YONDER POMP
*TUNE: Deil tak the wars*

Sent to Thomson in May 1795; yet another song to Chloris.

Mark yonder pomp of costly fashion
    Round the wealthy, titled bride!
But, when compar'd with real passion,
    Poor is all that princely pride.
What are the showy treasures?
What are the noisy pleasures?
The gay, gaudy glare of vanity and art!
    The polish'd jewel's blaze
    May draw the wond'ring gaze,
    And courtly grandeur bright
    The fancy may delight,
But never, never can come near the heart!

But did you see my dearest Chloris
    In simplicity's array,
Lovely as yonder sweet opening flower is,
    Shrinking from the gaze of day?

    O, then, the heart alarming
    And all resistless charming,
In love's delightful fetters she chains the willing soul!
    Ambition would disown
    The world's imperial crown!
    Ev'n Avarice would deny
    His worshipp'd deity,
And feel thro every being love's raptures roll!

## O, LAY THY LOOF IN MINE, LASS
*TUNE: The Shoemaker's March*

Traditionally believed to be a tribute to Jessie Lewars who nursed Burns during his last illness, although Johnson actually had it some time before May 1795.

### CHORUS

| | |
|---|---|
| O, lay thy loof in mine, lass, | palm |
| In mine, lass, in mine, lass, | |
| And swear on thy white hand, lass, | |
|     That thou wilt be my ain! | |

| | |
|---|---|
| A slave to Love's unbounded sway, | |
| He aft has wrought me meikle wae; | much grief |
| But now he is my deadly fae, | |
|     Unless thou be my ain. | own |

| | |
|---|---|
| There's monie a lass has broke my rest, | many |
| That for a blink I hae lo'ed best; | glimpse |
| But thou art queen within my breast, | |
|     For ever to remain. | |

## ADDRESS TO THE TOOTHACHE

First published in the *Belfast News Letter* of 11th September 1797. It has been argued that this Address was written in 1786-7 but Kinsley has argued plausibly for May-June 1795, when Burns was enduring 'the delightful sensations of an omnipotent Toothache, while fifty troops of infernal spirits are riding past from ear to ear along my jawbones.'

My curse upon your venom'd stang,          sting
That shoots my tortur'd gums alang,
An thro my lug gies monie a twang      ear, twinge
     Wi gnawing vengeance,
Tearing my nerves wi bitter pang,
     Like racking engines!

A' down my beard the slavers trickle,       saliva
I throw the wee stools o'er the mickle,
While round the fire the giglets keckle,      cackle
     To see me loup,                        dance
An raving mad, I wish a heckle      heckling-comb
     Were i' their doup!                backside

When fevers burn, or ague freezes,
Rheumatics gnaw, or colic squeezes,
Our neebors sympathise to ease us,      neighbours
     Wi pitying moan;
But thee! – thou hell o a' diseases –
     They mock our groan!

Of a' the numerous human dools –        woes
Ill-hairsts, daft bargains, cutty-stools,   harvests, mad
Or worthy frien's laid i' the mools,    crumbling earth
     Sad sight to see!
The tricks o knaves, or fash o fools –     annoyance
     Thou bear'st the gree!       takest the prize

Whare'er that place be priests ca' Hell,
Whare a' the tones o misery yell,
An ranked plagues their numbers tell,
     In dreadfu raw,                      row
Thou, Toothache, surely bear'st the bell,
     Amang them a'!

O thou grim, mischief-making chiel,      fellow
That gars the notes o discord squeel,      makes
Till human kind aft dance a reel
     In gore, a shoe-thick,
Gie a' the faes o Scotland's weal      Give, foes
     A towmond's toothache!     twelve month's

# FORLORN MY LOVE, NO COMFORT NEAR

*AIR: Let me in this ae night*

The first draft was sent to Thomson in June 1795 - 'I have written it within this hour; so much for the speed of my Pegasus; but what say you to his bottom?' A revised version was sent on 3rd August.

## CHORUS

*O wert thou, love, but near me,*
*But near, near, near me,*
*How kindly thou would cheer me,*
    *And mingle sighs with mine, love!*

Forlorn my love, no comfort near,
Far, far from thee I wander here;
Far, far from thee, the fate severe,
    At which I most repine, love.

Around me scowls a wintry sky,
Blasting each bud of hope and joy,
And shelter, shade, nor home have I
    Save in these arms of thine, love.

Cold, alter'd friendship's cruel part,
To poison fortune's ruthless dart!
Let me not break thy faithful heart,
    And say that fate is mine, love!

But, dreary tho the moments fleet,
O, let me think we yet shall meet!
That only ray of solace sweet
    Can on thy Chloris shine, love!

# NOW SPRING HAS CLAD THE GROVE IN GREEN

*TUNE: Auld lang syne*

Some detached stanzas were sent to Maria Riddell in the summer of 1795 which 'I intend to interweave in some disastrous tale of a Shepherd despairing beside a clear stream.' The song was completed by 3rd August.

Now spring has clad the grove in green,
    And strew'd the lea wi flowers;
The furrow'd, waving corn is seen
    Rejoice in fostering showers;
While ilka thing in nature join                     every
    Their sorrows to forego,
O, why thus all alone are mine
    The weary steps o woe!

The trout within yon wimpling burn       *meandering brook*
   Glides swift, a silver dart,
And, safe beneath the shady thorn,
   Defies the angler's art:
My life was ance that careless stream
   That wanton trout was I,
But Love wi unrelenting beam
   Has scorch'd my fountains dry.

The little floweret's peaceful lot,
   In yonder cliff that grows,
Which, save the linnet's flight, I wot,
   Nae ruder visit knows,
Was mine, till Love has o'er me past,
   And blighted a' my bloom;
And now beneath the withering blast
   My youth and joy consume.

The waken'd lav'rock warbling springs,      *lark*
   And climbs the early sky,
Winnowing blythe his dewy wings
   In Morning's rosy eye:
As little reck't I Sorrow's power,
   Until the flowery snare
O witching Love, in luckless hour,
   Made me the thrall o care!

O, had my fate been Greenland snows
   Or Afric's burning zone,
Wi Man and Nature leagu'd my foes,
   So Peggy ne'er I'd known!

The wretch, whose doom is 'hope nae mair,'
   What tongue his woes can tell,
Within whose bosom, save Despair,
   Nae kinder spirits dwell!

## THE BRAW WOOER

*TUNE: The Lothian Lassie*

Sent to Thomson on 3rd July 1795, it is one of Burns's best genre song, expressing 'the inter-play of character, motife and mask....with ruthless economy.'

Last May a braw wooer cam down the lang glen,    *fine*
   And sair wi his love he did deave me.    *sore, deafen*
I said there was naething I hated like men:
   The deuce gae wi'm to believe me, believe me –    *go*
   The deuce gae wi'm to believe me!

He spak o the darts in my bonie black een,        *eyes*
  And vow'd for my love he was diein.
I said, he might die when he liket for Jean:
  The Lord forgie me for liein, for liein –
  The Lord forgie me for liein!

A weel-stocket mailen, himself for the laird,    *well-stocked farm*
  And marriage aff-hand were his proffers:
I never loot on that I kenn'd it, or car'd,    *let, know*
  But thought I might hae waur offers, waur offers –    *worse*
  But thought I might hae waur offers.

But what wad ye think? In a fortnight or less
  (The Deil tak his taste to gae near her!)    *a pass through the*
He up the Gate-Slack to my black cousin, Bess!    *Lowther Hills*
  Guess ye how, the jad! I could bear her, could bear her –
  Guess ye how, the jad! I could bear her.    *jade*

But a' the niest week, as I petted wi care,    *next*
  I gaed to the tryste o Dalgarnock,    *in upper Nithsdale*
And wha but my fine fickle lover was there?
  I glowr'd as I'd seen a warlock, a warlock –    *stared, wizard*
  I glowr'd as I'd seen a warlock.

But owre my left shouther I gae him a blink,    *glance*
  Lest neebours might say I was saucy.
My wooer he caper'd as he'd been in drink,
  And vow'd I was his dear lassie, dear lassie –
  And vow'd I was his dear lassie!

I spier'd for my cousin fu couthy and sweet:    *enquired, loving*
  Gin she had recover'd her hearin?    *If*
And how her new shoon fit her auld, schachl'd feet?    *shoes, shapeless*
  But heavens! how he fell a swearin, a swearin –
  But heavens! how he fell a swearin!

He begged, for gudesake, I wad be his wife,
  Or else I wad kill him wi sorrow;
So e'en to preserve the poor body in life,
  I think I maun wed him to-morrow, to-morrow –    *must*
  I think I maun wed him to-morrow!

## WHY, WHY TELL THY LOVER
*TUNE: Caledonian Hunt's delight*

Sent to Thomson on 3rd July 1795.

Why, why tell thy lover
  Bliss he never must enjoy?
Why, why undeceive him,
  And give all his hopes the lie?
O, why, while Fancy, raptur'd, slumbers,
  'Chloris, Chloris,' all the theme,
Why, why wouldst thou, cruel,
  Wake thy lover from his dream?

## INSCRIPTION FOR AN ALTAR OF INDEPENDENCE
### AT KERROUGHTREE, THE SEAT OF MR HERON

Lines addressed to Patrick Heron, about July 1795.

Thou of an independent mind,
With soul resolv'd, with soul resign'd,
Prepar'd Power's proudest frown to brave,
Who wilt not be, nor have a slave,
Virtue alone who dost revere,
Thy own reproach alone dost fear:
Approach this shrine, and worship here.

## INSCRIPTION

WRITTEN ON THE BLANK LEAF OF A COPY OF THE LAST
EDITION OF MY POEMS, PRESENTED TO THE LADY WHOM, IN
SO MANY FICTITIOUS REVERIES OF PASSION, BUT WITH THE
MOST ARDENT SENTIMENTS OF REAL FRIENDSHIP, I HAVE SO
OFTEN SUNG UNDER THE NAME OF 'CHLORIS'

Sent to Alexander Cunningham on 3rd August, 1795.

'Tis Friendship's pledge, my young, fair Friend,
    Nor thou the gift refuse;
Nor with unwilling ear attend
    The moralising Muse.

Since thou in all thy youth and charms
    Must bid the world adieu
(A world 'gainst peace in constant arms),
    To join the friendly few;

Since, thy gay morn of life o'ercast,
    Chill came the tempest's lour
(And ne'er Misfortune's eastern blast
    Did nip a fairer flower);

Since life's gay scenes must charm no more
    Still much is left behind,
Still nobler wealth hast thou in store –
    The comforts of the mind!

Thine is the self-approving glow
    Of conscious honor's part;
And (dearest gift of Heaven below)
    Thine Friendship's truest heart!

The joys refin'd of sense and taste,
    With every Muse to rove:
And doubly were the Poet blest,
    These joys could he improve.                R.B.

## O, THIS IS NO MY AIN LASSIE

*TUNE: This is no my ain house*

'This is a great favourite of mine,' Burns told Thomson in September 1793, 'and if you will send me your set of it, I shall task my Muse to her highest effort.' Nevertheless two years elapsed before he produced these verses.

O, this is no my ain lassie,
    Fair tho the lassie be:
Weel ken I my ain lassie –
    Kind love is in her e'e.

I see a form, I see a face,
    Ye weel may wi the fairest place:
It wants to me the witching grace,
    The kind of love that's in her e'e.

She's bonie, blooming, straight, and tall,
    And lang has had my heart in thrall;
And ay it charms my very saul,
    The kind love that's in her e'e.

A thief sae pawkie is my Jean,          sly
    To steal a blink by a' unseen!       glance
But gleg as light are lover's een,       bright
    When kind love is in the e'e.

It may escape the courtly sparks,
It may escape the learned clerks;
But well the watching lover marks
    The kind love that's in her e'e.

## O, BONIE WAS YON ROSY BRIER

*TUNE: I wish my love was in a mire*

Copies of this song were sent to Alexander Cunningham and Maria Riddell early in August 1795.

O, bonie was yon rosy brier
    That blooms sae far frae haunt o man,
And bonie she – and ah, how dear! –
    It shaded frae the e'enin sun!

Yon rosebuds in the morning dew,
    How pure among the leaves sae green!
But purer was the lover's vow
    They witness'd in their shade yestreen.     last night

All in its rude and prickly bower,
    That crimson rose how sweet and fair!
But love is far a sweeter flower
    Amid life's thorny path o care.

The pathless wild and wimpling burn,
  Wi Chloris in my arms, be mine,
And I the warld nor wish nor scorn –
  Its joy and griefs alike resign!


# O, THAT'S THE LASSIE O
# MY HEART

*TUNE: Morag*

Burns's poetic activities suffered a series of severe setbacks: recurring toothache and
a prolonged bout of rheumatic fever over the last three months of 1795. In addition his
three year-old daughter, Elizabeth Riddell Burns, died in September. This song was
probably written about August 1795 but a copy not sent to Robert Cleghorn till January
1796 - 'since I saw you, I have been much the child of disaster.'

## CHORUS

*O, that's the lassie o my heart,*
  *My lassie ever dearer!*
*O, that's the queen o womankind,*
  *And ne'er a ane to peer her!*                                one

O, wat ye wha that lo'es me,                                    wot
  And has my heart a keeping?
O, sweet is she that lo'es me
  As dews o summer weeping,
  In tears the rosebuds steeping!

If thou shalt meet a lassie
  In grace and beauty charming,
That e'en thy chosen lassie,
  Erewhile thy breast sae warming,
  Had ne'er sic powers alarming: –                             such

If thou hadst heard her talking
  (And thy attention's plighted),
That ilka body talking                                         every
  But her by thee is slighted,
  And thou art all-delighted: –

If thou hast met this fair one,
  When frae her thou has parted,
If every other fair one
  But her thou hast deserted,
  And thou art broken-hearted.

559

# TO JOHN SYME OF RYEDALE

## WITH A PRESENT OF A DOZEN OF PORTER

John Syme (1755-1831), Army officer and later Writer to the Signet, suffered from the collapse of the Ayr bank, but obtained the sinecure of Distributor of Stamps for Dumfries and Galloway. His office was on the ground floor of the house in Bank Street where Burns lived in 1791-3.

> O had the malt thy strength of mind,
>   Or hops the flavour of thy wit,
> 'Twere drink for the first of human kind –
>   A gift that ev'n for Syme were fit.

JERUSALEM TAVERN, DUMFRIES

# APOLOGY FOR DECLINING AN INVITATION TO DINE

On refusing to dine with him, after having been promised the first of company, and the first of Cookery, 17th December, 1795.

> No more of your guests, be they titled or not,
>   And cookery the first in the nation:
> Who is proof to thy personal converse and wit,
>   Is proof to all other temptation.

# ON MR PITT'S HAIR-POWDER TAX

The tax on hair-powder was one of the imposts levied in 1795 to meet the cost of the French Revolutionary War. 'Guinea' here is a play on words, that being the amount of the tax levied in each instance.

> Pray Billy Pitt explain thy rigs,
>   This new poll-tax of thine!
> 'I mean to mark the Guinea pigs
>   'From other common swine.'

# THE SOLEMN LEAGUE AND COVENANT

Burns inscribed these lines in the volume of the *Statistical Account* (1794) describing the martyred Covenanters of Balmaghie, the two David Hallidays, who were shot in 1685.

> The Solemn League and Covenant
>   Now brings a smile, now brings a tear.
> But sacred Freedom, too, was theirs:
>   If thou'rt a slave, indulge thy sneer.

# THE BOB O DUMBLANE

Sent by Burns to Johnson late in 1795 for the fifth volume of SMM but omitted on grounds of indelicacy. The original song was by Ramsay and Burns claimed to have heard it from the hostess of the principal inn in Dunblane in 1787.

| | |
|---|---|
| Lassie, lend me your braw hemp-heckle, | flax comb |
| And I'll lend you my thripplin kame: | separating comb |
| My heckle is broken, it canna be gotten, | |
| And we'll gae dance the Bob o Dumblane. | go |
| | |
| Twa gaed to the wood, to the wood, to the wood, | went |
| Twa gaed to the wood, three cam hame: | |
| An 't be na weel bobbit, weel bobbit, weel bobbit, | If |
| An 't be na weel bobbit, we'll bob it again. | |

# TO COLLECTOR MITCHELL

John Mitchell (1731-1806), studied for the Ministry but entered the Excise instead and was appointed Collector at Dumfries in 1788. Burns met him in May 1789 when he called on him with Graham of Fintry's introduction. Thereafter Mitchell took an active interest in the poet's career.

| | |
|---|---|
| Friend of the Poet tried and leal, | true |
| Wha wanting thee might beg or steal; | |
| Alake, alake, the meikle Deil | great |
| Wi a' his witches | |
| Are at it, skelpin jig and reel | spanking |
| In my poor pouches! | pockets |
| | |
| I modestly fu fain wad hint it, | would |
| That One-pound-one, I sairly want it; | a guinea |
| If wi the hizzie down ye sent it, | maid |
| It would be kind; | |
| And while my heart wi life-blood dunted, | throbbed |
| I'd bear't in mind! | |
| | |
| So may the Auld Year gang out moanin | |
| To see the New come laden, groanin, | |
| Wi doubly plenty o'er the loanin | down the lane |
| To thee and thine: | |
| Domestic peace and comfort crownin | |
| To hale design! | whole |

## POSTSCRIPT

| | |
|---|---|
| Ye've heard this while how I've been licket, | a reference to his |
| And by fell Death was nearly nicket: | grave illness of |
| Grim loon! He got me by the fecket, | December, 1795, waistcoat |
| And sair me sheuk; | sore |
| But by guid luck I lap a wicket, | leaped, fence |
| And turn'd a neuk. | corner |

561

But by that health, I've got a share o't,
And by that life, I'm promis'd mair o't,
My hale and weel, I'll take a care o't,        health, welfare
    A tentier way;                             more careful
Then farewell folly, hide and hair o't.
    For ance and ay!                          once and all

# THE DEAN OF THE FACULTY

## A NEW BALLAD

*TUNE: The Dragon of Wantley*

Composed some time after 12th January 1796, when Robert Dundas was elected Dean
of the Faculty of Advocates. His defeated rival was Burns's friend Henry Erskine. 'Old
Harlaw' was the battle fought in 1411 between the Lord of the Isles and the Earl of Mar
(an ancestor of Erskine). Mary Queen of Scots was defeated at Langside in 1568.

Dire was the hate at Old Harlaw,
    That Scot to Scot did carry;
And dire the discord Langside saw
    For beauteous, hapless Mary.
But Scot to Scot ne'er met so hot,
    Or were more in fury seen, Sir,
That 'twixt Hal and Bob for the famous job,
    Who should be the Faculty's Dean, sir.

This Hal for genius, wit, and lore
    Among the first was number'd;
But pious Bob, 'mid learning's store
    Commandment the tenth remember'd:
Yet simple Bob the victory got,
    And won his heart's desire:
Which shows that Heaven can boil the pot,
    Tho the Deil piss in the fire.

Squire Hal, besides, had in this case
    Pretensions rather brassy;
For talents, to deserve a place,
    Are qualifications saucy.
So their worships of the Faculty,
    Quite sick of Merit's rudeness,
Chose one who should owe it all, d'ye see,
    To their gratis grace and goodness.

As once on Pisgah purg'd was the sight      Deuteronomy iii. 27
    Of a son of Circumcision,
So, may be, on this Pisgah height,
    Bob's purblind mental vision.
Nay, Bobby's mouth may be open'd yet,
    Till for eloquence you hail him,
And swear that he has the Angel met      Numbers xxii. 22
    That met the Ass of Balaam.

In your heretic sins may you live and die,
    Ye heretic Eight-and-Thirty!      Dundas's opponents
But accept, ye sublime majority,
    My congratulations hearty!
With your honors, as with a certain King,
    In your servants this is striking,
The more incapacity they bring
    The more they're to your liking.

# A LASS WI A TOCHER

*TUNE: Ballinamona Ora*

Thomson planned to publish a volume of Irish airs. Writing in February 1796 Burns promised 'I shall cheerfully undertake the task of finding verses for them.... the other day I strung up a kind of rhapsody to another Hibernian melody which I admire much.'

### CHORUS

*Then hey for a lass wi a tocher,*      dowry
*Then hey for a lass wi a tocher,*
*Then hey for a lass wi a tocher,*
    *The nice yellow guineas for me!*

Awa wi your witchcraft o Beauty's alarms,
The slender bit beauty you grasp in your arms!
O, gie me the lass that has acres o charms!      give
O, gie me the lass wi the weel-stockit farms.

Your Beauty's a flower in the morning that blows,
And withers the faster the faster it grows;
But the rapturous charm o the bonie green knowes,      hillocks
Ilk spring they're new deckit wi bonie white yowes!      Each, ewes

And e'en when this Beauty your bosom has blest,
The brightest o Beauty may cloy when possess'd;
But the sweet, yellow darlings wi Geordie impress'd      guineas
The langer ye hae them, the mair they're carest!

## EPISTLE TO COLONEL DE PEYSTER

Colonel Arentz Schuyler de Peyster was born in New York in 1736 and served in the British Army from 1755 till April 1794. He married Rebecca Blair, John McMurdo's sister-in-law, and settled at Mavis Grove near Dumfries, where he became Major-Commandant of the Volunteers. This verse-epistle was written in answer to an enquiry about the poet's health. De Peyster published his own poems *Miscellanies of an Officer* in 1813. He died in 1822.

My honor'd Colonel, deep I feel
Your interest in the Poet's weal:  welfare
Ah! now sma' heart hae I to speel  climb
   The steep Parnassus,
Surrounded thus by bolus pill
   And potion glasses.

O, what a canty warld were it,  jolly
Would pain and care and sickness spare it,
And Fortune favor worth and merit
   As they deserve,
And ay rowth – roast-beef and claret! –  plenty
   Syne, wha wad starve?  Then, would

Dame Life, tho fiction out may trick her,
And in paste gems and frippery deck her,
Oh! flickering, feeble, and unsicker  unsure
   I've found her still:
Ay, wavering, like the willow-wicker,
   'Tween good and ill!

Then that curst carmagnole Auld Satan,  nickname for a French
Watches, like baudrons by a ratton,  revolutionary, hence a rascal
Our sinfu saul to get a claut on  in general; cats, rat; grasp
   Wi felon ire;
Syne, whip! his tail ye'll ne'er cast saut on –  salt
   He's aff like fire.

Ah Nick! Ah Nick! it is na fair,
First showing us the tempting ware,
Bright wines and bonie lasses rare,
   To put us daft;  send us mad
Syne weave, unseen, thy spider snare
   O Hell's damn'd waft!  web

Poor Man, the flie, aft bizzes by,
And aft as chance he comes thee nigh,
Thy auld damn'd elbow yeuks wi joy  itches
   And hellish pleasure.
Already in thy fancy's eye
   Thy sicker treasure!  sure

Soon, heels o'er gowdie, in he gangs,  *topsy-turvy, goes*
And, like a sheep-head on a tangs,  *singeing-tongs*
Thy girning laugh enjoys his pangs  *snarling*
 And murdering wrestle,
As, dangling in the wind, he hangs
 A gibbet's tassle.

But lest you think I am uncivil
To plague you with this draunting drivel,  *droning*
Abjuring a' intentions evil,
 I quat my pen:  *leave*
The Lord preserve us frae the Devil!
 Amen! Amen!

## HERE'S A HEALTH TO ANE I LOE DEAR

Sent to Thomson in April 1796. A copy went to Alexander Cunningham on 12th July 'as the last I made or probably will make for some time.' He died just nine days later. The subject of this song was Jessie Lewars (1778-1855), younger daughter of John Lewars, Supervisor of Excise at Dumfries.

### CHORUS

*Here's a health to ane I loe dear!*  *one, love*
 *Here's a health to ane I loe dear!*
*Thou art sweet as the smile when fond lovers meet,*
 *And soft as their parting tear, Jessie –*
 *And soft as their parting tear!*

Altho thou maun never be mine,  *must*
 Altho even hope is denied,
'Tis sweeter for thee despairing
 Than ought in the world beside, Jessie –
 Than ought in the world beside!

I mourn thro the gay, gaudy day,
 As hopeless I muse on thy charms;
But welcome the dream o sweet slumber!
 For then I am lockt in thine arms, Jessie –
 For then I am lockt in thine arms!

# VERSICLES TO JESSIE LEWARS

Jessie Lewars, last of the poet's heroines, lived with her brother John Lewars, Jr. who, like his father, was an Excise colleague of Burns. Their house was in Mill Vennel (now Burns Street) opposite the poet's residence. Jessie helped to nurse Burns during his last illness.

### THE TOAST

Fill me with the rosy wine;
Call a toast, a toast divine:
Give the Poet's darling flame,
Lovely Jessie be her name:
Then thou mayest freely boast
Thou hast given a peerless toast.

### THE MENAGERIE

Talk not to me of savages
    From Afric's burning sun!
No savage e'er can rend my heart
    As, Jessie, thou hast done.

But Jessie's lovely hand in mine,
    A mutual faith to plight –
Not even to view the heavenly choir
    Would be so blest a sight.

### JESSIE'S ILLNESS

Say, sages, what's the charm on earth
    Can turn Death's dart aside?
It is not purity and worth,
    Else Jessie had not died!

### ON HER RECOVERY

But rarely seen since Nature's birth
    The natives of the sky!
Yet still one seraph's left on earth,
    For Jessie did not die.

# INSCRIPTION
## TO MISS JESSIE LEWARS

Burns asked Johnson for a set of volumes of the *Scots Musical Museum* which he
presented to Jessie, placing this inscription on the back of the title-page of the first
volume. Jessie took charge of the poet's four sons for some time after Burns died.

Thine be the volumes, Jessie fair,
And with them take the Poet's prayer:
That Fate may in her fairest page,
With ev'ry kindliest, best presage
Of future bliss enrol thy name;
With native worth, and spotless fame,
And wakeful caution, still aware
Of ill – but chief, Man's felon snare!
All blameless joys on earth we find,
And all the treasures of the mind –
These be thy guardian and reward!
So prays thy faithful friend, the Bard.

DUMFRIES, June 26, 1796        ROBERT BURNS


# O, WERT THOU IN THE CAULD
# BLAST

*TUNE: Lenox love to Blantyre*

Written for Jessie Lewars, by way of thanking her for nursing the poet during his final
illness, and surely some of the most poignant lines ever penned.

O, wert thou in the cauld blast
    On yonder lea, on yonder lea,
My plaidie to the angry airt,                               quarter
    I'd shelter thee, I'd shelter thee.
Or did Misfortune's bitter storms
    Around thee blaw, around thee blaw,
Thy bield should be my bosom,                              shelter
    To share it a', to share it a'.

Or were I in the wildest waste,
    Sae black and bare, sae black and bare,
The desert were a Paradise,
    If thou wert there, if thou wert there.
Or were I monarch o the globe,
    Wi thee to reign, wi thee to reign,
The brightest jewel in my crown
    Wad be my queen, wad be my queen,                      Would

## FAIREST MAID ON DEVON BANKS

*TUNE: Rothiemurchie*

This song accompanied a letter to Thomson on 12th July 1796, written from the Brow: 'After all my boasted independence, curst necessity compels me to implore you for five pounds - A cruel scoundrel of a Haberdasher to whom I owe an account, taking it into his head that I am dying, has commenced a process, and will infallibly put me into jail - Do, for God's sake, send me that sum, and that by return of post...upon returning health, I hereby promise and engage to furnish you with five pounds' worth of the neatest song-genius you have seen...' To his credit, Thomson responded promptly. The 'Crystal Devon' is the Clackmannanshire river.

CHORUS

*Fairest maid on Devon banks,*
*Crystal Devon, winding Devon,*
*Wilt thou lay that frown aside,*
*And smile as thou wert wont to do?*

Full well thou know'st I love thee dear –
Couldst thou to malice lend an ear!
O, did not Love exclaim: – 'Forbear,
Nor use a faithful lover so!'

Then come, thou fairest of the fair,
Those wonted smiles, O, let me share,
And by thy beauteous self I swear
No love but thine my heart shall know!

## REMORSEFUL APOLOGY

Early editors assumed that these lines were addressed to Maria Riddell after the quarrel of 1793-4 but Kinsley has tentatively identified the recipient as Simon McKenzie, who attended the inaugural meeting of the Dumfries Volunteers on 31st January 1796.

The friend whom, wild from Wisdom's way,
The fumes of wine infuriate send
(Not moony madness more astray),
Who but deplores that hapless friend?

Mine was th' insensate frenzied part –
Ah! why should I such scenes outlive?
Scenes so abhorrent to my heart!
'Tis thine to pity and forgive.

## LINES WRITTEN ON WINDOWS OF THE GLOBE TAVERN, DUMFRIES

These three short pieces were probably written extempore at the Globe, the Poet's 'favourite howff.'

The greybeard, old wisdom, may boast of his treasures,
Give me with gay folly to live;
I grant him his calm-blooded, time-settled pleasures,
But folly has raptures to give.

My bottle is a holy pool,
That heals the wounds o care an dool;     woe
And pleasure is a wanton trout,
An ye drink it, ye'll find him out.      If

In politics if thou would'st mix,
 And mean thy fortunes be;
Bear this in mind, be deaf and blind,
 Let great folks hear and see.

## THE TOADEATER

Burns produced several variants of this epigram, of which the most notable are given
here. James McClure claimed that Burns delivered these lines during a dinner-party
at Terraughty. Syme annotated his copy: 'Extempore on a young fellow W.I. who had
made about £10,000 by a lucky speculation and who vaunted of keeping the highest
company, &c. N.B. he was of low extraction.'

Of Lordly acquaintance you boast,
 And the Dukes that you dined with yestreen;
Yet an insect's an insect at most,
 Tho it crawl on the curl of a Queen!

### ALTERNATIVE VERSION

No more of your titled acquaintances boast,
 Nor of the gay groups you have seen;
A crab louse is but a crab louse at last,
 Tho stack to the —— of a Queen.    stuck

## THE LOVELY LASS O INVERNESS

This and the following fifty songs were published posthumously in the SMM of 1796 and
1803 and are believed to date from the last three years of the poet's life. This ballad was
based on a Jacobite original; 'Drumossie' alludes to the battle of Culloden, near
Inverness, in 1746.

The lovely lass of Inverness,
 Nae joy nor pleasure can she see;
For e'en to morn she cries 'Alas!'
 And ay the saut tear blin's her e'e: –   salt, eye

'Drumossie moor, Drumossie day –
 A waefu day it was to me!      sad
For there I lost my father dear,
 My father dear and brethren three.

'Their winding-sheet the bluidy clay,
 Their graves are growin green to see,
And by them lies the dearest lad
 That ever blest a woman's e'e.

'Now wae to thee, thou cruel lord,   Duke of Cumberland
 A bluidy man I trow thou be,
For monie a heart thou hast made sair
 That ne'er did wrang to thine or thee!'

## AS I STOOD BY YON ROOFLESS TOWER

*TUNE: Cumnock Psalms*

Burns sent to Thomson in September 1794 a copy of 'a droll Scots song, more famous for its humor than delicacy, called The grey goose and the gled.' Later he composed these lines to the same tune. The 'roofless tower' was Lincluden Abbey, north of Dumfries on the banks of the Nith.

### CHORUS

*A lassie all alone, was making her moan*
   *Lamenting our lads beyond the sea: –*
*'In the bluidy wars they fa', and our honor's gane an a',*
   *And broken-hearted we maun die.'*       must

As I stood by yon roofless tower,
   Where the wa'flow'r scents the dewy air,
Where the houlet mourns in her ivy bower,     owl
   And tells the midnight moon her care:

The winds were laid, the air was still,
   The stars they shot along the sky,
The tod was howling on the hill,       fox
   And the distant-echoing glens reply.

The burn, adown its hazelly path,       brook
   Was rushing by the ruin'd wa',
Hasting to join the sweeping Nith,
   Whase roaring seemed to rise and fa'.     Whose

The cauld blae North was streaming forth
   Her lights, wi hissing, eerie din:
Athort the lift they start and shift,     Athwart, horizon
   Like Fortune's favors, tint as win.       lost

Now, looking over firth and fauld,       fold
   Her horn the pale-faced Cynthia rear'd,    the moon
When lo! in form of minstrel auld
   A stern and stalwart ghaist appear'd.     ghost

And frae his harp sic strains did flow,     such
   Might rous'd the slumbering Dead to hear,
But O, it was a tale of woe
   As ever met a Briton's ear!

He sang wi joy his former day,
   He, weeping, wail'd his latter times:
But what he said – it was nae play!
   I winna ventur't in my rhymes.

## THE LASS O ECCLEFECHAN

*TUNE: Jack o Latin*

Says Cunningham: '...during the Poet's first visit to Annandale, an old song, called "The Lass of Ecclefechan," was sung to him, with which he was so amused that he wrote it down, and, at a leisure moment, rendered the language more delicate, and the sentiments less warm' for SMM. A less delicate version was preserved in the *Merry Muses*.

| | |
|---|---|
| 'Gat ye me, O, gat ye me, | |
| Gat ye me wi naething? | |
| Rock and reel, an spinning wheel, | Distaff |
| A mickle quarter basin: | big |
| Bye attour, my gutcher has | Moreover, goodsir |
| A heich house and a laich ane, | high, low |
| A' forbye my bonie sel, | All besides |
| The toss o Ecclefechan!' | toast |
| | |
| 'O, haud your tongue now, Lucky Lang, | hold |
| O, haud your tongue and jauner! | jabber |
| I held the gate till you I met, | kept to the straight path |
| Syne I began to wander: | Then |
| I tint my whistle and my sang, | lost |
| I tint my peace and pleasure; | |
| But your green graff, now Lucky Lang, | grave |
| Wad airt me to my treasure.' | Would direct |

## THE WREN'S NEST

Burns took down this song from his own wife's lips and, after revision, sent this fragment to Johnson for SMM.

| | |
|---|---|
| The Robin cam to the wren's nest | |
| And keekit in and keekit in, | peeped |
| O weel's me on your auld pow, | pate |
| Wad ye be in, wad ye be in. | Would |
| Ye'se ne'er get leave to lie without, | |
| And I within, and I within, | |
| As lang's I hae an auld clout | cloth |
| To row you in, to row you in. | roll |

## O AN YE WERE DEAD GUDEMAN

A revision of a traditional ballad in Herd MS, rejecting part of the original and developing the theme of the cuckold's horns.

### CHORUS

| | |
|---|---|
| *O an ye were dead gudeman,* | if |
| *A green turf on your head, gudeman,* | |
| *I wad bestow my widowhood* | would |
| *Upon a rantin Highlandman.* | rollicking |

There's sax eggs in the pan, gudeman,
There's sax eggs in the pan, gudeman;
There's ane to you, and twa to me,
And three to our John Highlandman.

A sheep-head's in the pot, gudeman,
A sheep-head's in the pot, gudeman;
The flesh to him the broo to me,                                broth
An the horns become your brow, gudeman.

### CHORUS TO THE LAST VERSE

*Sing round about the fire wi a rung she ran,*           cudgel
*An round about the fire wi a rung she ran:*
*Your horns shall tie you to the staw,*                 stall
*And I shall bang your hide, gudeman.*

# TAM LIN

Several versions of this ancient ballad are known from the 16th century, but these lines communicated by Burns to SMM are the most complete version extant. An unpolished, original version was also taken down by Robert Riddell, possibly from the same source. Carterhaugh is a plain near Selkirk, where the Ettrick and Yarrow meet.

O I forbid you, maidens a'
    That wear gowd on your hair,                        gold
To come, or gae by Carterhaugh,                   go
    For young Tom-lin is there.

There's nane that gaes by Carterhaugh
    But they leave him a wad;
Either their rings, or green mantles,
    Or else their maidenhead.

Janet has kilted her green kirtle,                petticoat
    A little aboon her knee;                     above
And she has broded her yellow hair           braided
    A little aboon her bree;                     brow
And she's awa to Carterhaugh
    As fast as she can hie.

When she cam to Carterhaugh
    Tom-lin was at the well,
And there she fand his steed standing       found
    But away was himsel.

She had na pu'd a double rose,               plucked
    A rose but only tway,                     two
Till up then started young Tom-lin,
    Says, Lady, thou's pu nae mae.        no more

Why pu's thou the rose, Janet,
    And why breaks thou the wand?
Or why comes thou to Carterhaugh
    Withoutten my command?

Carterhaugh it is my ain,                         own
    Ma daddie gave it me;
I'll come and gang by Carterhaugh
    And ask nae leave at thee.

Janet has kilted her green kirtle
    A little aboon her knee,
And she has snooded her yellow hair,           banded
    A little aboon her bree,
And she is to her father's ha,
    As fast as she can hie.

Four and twenty ladies fair
    Were playing at the ba,
And out then cam the fair Janet,
    Ance the flower amang them a'.

Four and twenty ladies fair
    Were playing at the chess,
And out then cam the fair Janet,
    As green as onie glass.

Out then spak an auld grey knight,
    Lay o'er the castle-wa,
And says, Alas, fair Janet for thee
    But we'll be blamed a'.

Haud your tongue ye auld-fac'd knight,
    Some ill death may ye die,
Father my bairn on whom I will,                child
    I'll father nane on thee.

Out then spak her father dear,
    And he spak meek and mild,
And ever alas, sweet Janet, he says,
    I think thou gaes wi child.

If that I gae wi child, father,
    Mysel I maun bear the blame;            must
There's ne'er a laird about your ha,
    Shall get the bairn's name.

If my Love were an earthly knight,
    As he's an elfin grey;
I wad na gie my ain true-love
    For nae lord that ye hae.

The steed that my true-love rides on,
    Is lighter than the wind;
Wi siller he is shod before,                    silver
    Wi burning gowd behind.               gold

Janet has kilted her green kirtle
    A little aboon her knee;
And she has snooded her yellow hair
    A little aboon her brie;
And she's awa to Carterhaugh
    As fast as she can hie.

When she cam to Carterhaugh,
    Tom-lin was at the well;
And there she fand his steed standing,
    But away was himsel.

She had na pu'd a double rose,
    A rose but only tway,
Till up then started young Tom-lin,
    Says, Lady thou pu's nae mae.

Why pu's thou the rose Janet,
    Amang the groves sae green,
And a' to kill the bonie babe
    That we gat us between.

O tell me, Tom-lin she says,
    For's sake that died on tree,
If e'er ye was in holy chapel,
    Or Christendom did see.

Roxburgh he was my grandfather,
    Took me with him to bide,
And ance it fell upon a day               once
    That wae did me betide.             woe

Ance it fell upon a day,
    A cauld day and a snell,            bitter
When we were frae the hunting come
    That frae my horse I fell.

The queen o Fairies she caught me,
    In yon green hill to dwell,         that
And pleasant is the fairy-land;
    But, an eerie tale to tell!       strange

Ay at the end of seven years
    We pay a tiend to hell;          tithe
I am sae fair and fu of flesh
    I'm fear'd it be mysel.

But the night is Halloween, lady,
  The morn is Hallowday;
Then win me, win me, an ye will,
  For weel I wat ye may.

Just at the mirk and midnight hour                    dark
  The fairy folk will ride;
And they that wad their truelove win,
  At Milescross they maun bide.

But how shall I thee ken, Tom-lin,
  O how my truelove know,
Amang sae mony unco knights                           mighty
  The like I never saw.

O first let pass the black, Lady,
  And syne let pass the brown;                        then
But quickly run to the milk-white steed,
  Pu ye his rider down:

For I'll ride on the milk-white steed,
  And ay nearest the town;
Because I was an earthly knight
  They gie me that renown.

My right hand will be glov'd lady,
  My left hand will be bare;
Cockt up shall my bonnet be,
  And kaim'd down shall my hair;                      combed
And thae's the tokens I gie thee,                     those are
  Nae doubt I will be there.

They'll turn me in your arms, lady,
  Into an ask and adder,                              viper
But hald me fast and fear me not,
  I am your bairn's father.

They'll turn me to a bear sae grim,
  And then a lion bold;
But hold me fast and fear me not,
  As ye shall love your child.

Again they'll turn me in your arms
  To a red het gaud of airn;                          hot goad iron
But hold me fast and fear me not,
  I'll do you nae harm.

And last they'll turn me, in your arms,
  Into the burning lead;
Then throw me into well-water,
  O throw me in wi speed!

And then I'll be your ain truelove,
   I'll turn a naked knight:
Then cover me wi your green mantle,
   And cover me out o sight.

Gloomy, gloomy was the night,
   And eerie was the way,
As fair Jenny in her green mantle
   To Milescross she did gae.

About the middle o the night
   She heard the bridles ring;
This lady was as glad at that
   As any earthly thing.

First she let the black pass by,
   And syne she let the brown;
But quickly she ran to the milk-white steed,
   And pu'd the rider down.

Sae weel she minded what he did say
   And young Tom-lin did win;
Syne cover'd him wi her green mantle
   As blythe's a bird in spring.

Out then spak the queen o Fairies,
   Out of a bush o broom;
Them that has gotten young Tom-lin,
   Has gotten a stately groom.

Out then spak the queen o Fairies,
   And an angry queen was she;
Shame betide her ill-fard face,
   And an ill death may she die,
For she's ta'en awa the boniest knight
   In a' my companie.

But had I kend, Tom-lin, she says,          known
   What now this night I see,
I wad hae taen out thy twa grey een,       eyes
   And put in twa een o tree.           wood

# HAD I THE WYTE?

*TUNE: Come kiss with me*

Based on a traditional fragment in the Herd collection and a bawdy version in the *Merry Muses*, which Burns had a hand in, even if he did not wholly compose it as well.

Had I the wyte? had I the wyte?     *Was I to blame?*
    Had I the wyte? she bade me!
She watch'd me by the hie-gate side,     *high road*
    And up the loan she shaw'd me;     *lane, showed*
And when I wadna venture in,     *would not*
    A coward loon she ca'd me!     *fool*
Had Kirk and State been in the gate,     *way*
    I'd lighted when she bade me.

Sae craftilie she took me ben     *inside*
    And bade me mak nae clatter: –     *no noise*
'For our ramgunshoch, glum guidman     *surly*
    Is o'er ayont the water.'     *away beyond*
Whae'er shall say I wanted grace
    When I did kiss and dawte her,     *fondle*
Let him be planted in my place,
    Syne say I was the fauter!     *Then, trangressor*

Could I for shame, could I for shame,
    Could I for shame refus'd her?
And wadna manhood been to blame     *would not have been*
    Had I unkindly used her?
He claw'd her wi the ripplin'-kame,     *wool-comb*
    And blae and bluidy bruis'd her –     *blue*
When sic a husband was frae hame.
    What wife but wad excus'd her!

I dighted ay her een sae blue,     *wiped, eyes*
    An bann'd the cruel randy,     *cursed, scoundrel*
And, weel I wat, her willin mou     *wot, mouth*
    Was sweet as sugarcandie.
At gloamin-shot, it was, I wot,     *sunset*
    I lighted – on the Monday;
But I cam thro the Tyseday's dew,     *Tuesday's*
    To wanton Willie's brandy.

# COMIN THRO THE RYE
*TUNE: Miller's Wedding*

This was a version and expansion of an old song in the collection of Thomas Mansfield formed in 1770-80. Various bawdy versions were current in the eighteenth century, and there was even an English pantomime song 'If a body meet a body' entered at Stationers' Hall on 6th June 1796.

CHORUS

*O, Jenny's a' weet, poor body,*
*Jenny's seldom dry:*
*She draigl't a' her petticoatie,*
*Comin thro the rye!*

Comin thro the rye, poor body,
Comin thro the rye,
She draigl't a' her petticoatie,
Comin thro the rye!

Gin a body meet a body,                                                    If
Comin thro the rye,
Gin a body kiss a body,
Need a body cry?

Gin a body meet a body
Comin thro the glen,
Gin a body kiss a body,
Need the warld ken?                                                        know

# THE ROWIN 'T IN HER APRON

A ballad collected by Burns in the vicinity of Dumfries, dealing with the story of the aftermath of the 1715 Rebellion. 'Young Terreagles' (1.25) was John, Lord Maxwell who died in 1776.

Our young lady's a huntin gane,
Sheets nor blankets has she ta'en,
But she's born her auld son or she cam hame,                    before
And she's row'd him in her apron.                                  rolled

Her apron was o the hollan fine,
Laid about wi laces nine;
She thought it a pity her babie should tyne,                      perish
And she's row'd him in her apron.

Her apron was o the hollan sma,
Laid about wi laces a',
She thought it a pity her babe to let fa,
And she row'd him in her apron.

Her father says within the ha,
Amang the knights and nobles a',
I think I hear a babie ca,
In the chamber amang our young ladies.

O father dear it is a bairn,
I hope it will do you nae harm,
For the daddie I lo'ed, and he'll lo'e me again,
    For the rowin 't in my apron.

O he is a gentleman, or is he a clown,
That has brought thy fair body down,
I would not for a' this town
    The rowin 't in thy apron.

Young Terreagles he's nae clown,
He is the toss of Edinborrow town,          *toast*
And he'll buy me a braw new gown          *fine*
    For the rowin 't in thy apron.

It's I hae castles, I hae towers,
I hae barns, I hae bowers,
A' that is mine it shall be thine,
    For the rowin 't in thy apron.

# CHARLIE, HE'S MY DARLING

The original was a street-ballad of about 1775, which Burns reduced in length and greatly refined. The 'Young Chevalier' was Prince Charles Edward Stuart, the Young Pretender.

## CHORUS

*An Charlie he's my darling,*
   *My darling, my darling,*
*Charlie he's my darling –*
   *The Young Chevalier!*

'Twas on a Monday morning
   Right early in the year,
That Charlie came to our town –
   The Young Chevalier!

As he was walking up the street
   The city for to view,
O, there he spied a bonie lass
   The window looking thro!

Sae light's he jimped up the stair,          *jumped*
   And tirl'd at the pin;      *rattled on the latch*
And wha sae ready as hersel
   To let the laddie in!

He set his Jenny on his knee,
    All in his Highland dress;
For brawlie weel he kend the way                   *finely, knew*
    To please a bonie lass.

It's up yon heathery mountain
And down the scroggy glen,                         *scrubby*
We daurna gang a-milking                *dare not go*
    For Charlie and his men!

# THE COOPER O CUDDY

*TUNE: Bab at the bowster*

Ascribed to Burns on the basis of the Hastie MS and in his characteristic comic style.
The terminology of the barrelmaker's trade is used here very humorously with sexual
overtones, though less explicit than 'Cuddy the Cooper' in the *Merry Muses*.

## CHORUS

*We'll hide the cooper behint the door,*
*Behint the door, behint the door,*
*We'll hide the cooper behint the door,*
    *And cover him under a mawn, O.*            *basket*

The Cooper o Cuddy came here awa,        *here about*
He ca'd the girrs out o'er us a',       *knocked hoops*
An our guidwife has gotten a ca',
    That's anger'd the silly guidman, O.

He sought them out, he sought them in,
Wi 'Deil hae her!' an' 'Deil hae him!'
But the body he was sae doited and blin',     *senile, blind*
    He wist na where he was gaun, O.     *knew not, going*

They cooper'd at e'en, they cooper'd at morn,
Till our guidman has gotten the scorn:
On ilka brow she's planted a horn,      *each, cuckold's horn*
    And swears that there they sall stan', O!      *shall*

## LEEZIE LINDSAY

This fragment, collected by Burns, was sent to Johnson for SMM. The complete ballad was not published till 1806 and has since become a popular song.

Will ye go to the Highlands, Leezie Lindsay,
    Will ye go to the Highlands wi me;
Will ye go to the Highlands, Leezie Lindsay,
    My pride and my darling to be.

## FOR THE SAKE O SOMEBODY

Based on Allan Ramsay's lovers' dialogue in *The Tea-Table Miscellany* and composed by Burns for SMM. 'Somebody' was a synonym for Bonnie Prince Charlie.

My heart is sair – I dare na tell –          sore
    My heart is sair for Somebody:
I could wake a winter night
    For the sake o Somebody.
        O-hon! for Somebody!
        O-hey! for Somebody!
I could range the world around
    For the sake o Somebody.

Ye Powers that smile on virtuous love,
    O, sweetly smile on Somebody!
Frae ilka danger keep him free,          each
    And send me safe my Somebody!
        O-hon! for Somebody!
        O-hey! for Somebody!
I wad do – what wad I not? –
    For the sake o Somebody!

## THE CARDIN O'T, THE SPINNIN O'T

*TUNE: Queensberry's Scots Measure*

Allegedly based on a traditional ballad no longer extant.

The cardin o't, the spinnin o't,
    The warpin o't, the winnin o't!
When ilka ell cost me a groat,      each yard, fourpence
    The tailor staw the lynin o't.         stole

I coft a stane o haslock woo,    bought the soft wool from
    To mak a wab to Johnie o't,    the lamb's neck, web
For Johnie is my only jo –          darling
    I lo'e him best of onie yet!

For tho his locks be lyart gray,       withered
    And tho his brow be beld aboon,    bald above
Yet I hae seen him on a day
    The pride o a' the parishen.      whole parish

# SUTORS O SELKIRK

This old ballad was allegedly composed for a group of Selkirk cobblers who enlisted in the army of James IV, decimated at Flodden in 1513. The blame for this disaster was popularly, though unjustly, laid on the Earl of Home. The Forest and the Merse allude to Ettrick Forest and Berwickshire respectively.

| | |
|---|---|
| Its up wi the Sutors o Selkirk, | Cobblers |
| And down wi the Earl o Hume; | |
| And here is to a' the braw laddies | fine |
| That wear the single sol'd shoon: | |
| Its up wi the Sutors o Selkirk, | |
| For they are baith trusty and leal; | true |
| And up wi the lads o the Forest, | |
| And down wi the Merse to the deil. | |

# TIBBIE FOWLER

Herd's MSS contain two unrelated fragments of this song. Burns collected it in its entirety and corrected it, with some stanzas of his own.

## CHORUS

| | |
|---|---|
| *Wooin at her, pu'in at her,* | pulling |
| *Courtin at her, canna get her:* | cannot |
| *Filthy elf, it's for her pelf,* | money |
| *That a' the lads are wooin at her.* | |

Tibbie Fowler o the glen,
  There's o'er mony wooin at her,
Tibbie Fowler o the glen,
  There's o'er mony wooin at her.

| | |
|---|---|
| Ten cam east and ten cam west, | |
| Ten cam rowin o'er the water; | |
| Twa came down the lang dyke side, | fence |
| There's twa and thirty wooin at her. | |

| | |
|---|---|
| There's seven but, and seven ben, | out front, inside |
| Seven in her pantry wi her, | |
| Twenty head about the door, | |
| There's ane and forty wooin at her. | |

| | |
|---|---|
| She's got pendles in her lugs, | pendants, ears |
| Cockle-shells wad set her better; | |
| High-heel'd shoon and siller tags, | silver |
| And a' the lads are wooin at her. | |

| | |
|---|---|
| Be a lassie e'er sae black, | |
| An she hae the name o siller, | If, money |
| Set her upo' Tintock-tap, | Tinto Hill, Lanarkshire |
| The wind will blaw a man till her. | |

Be a lassie e'er sae fair,
    An she want the pennie siller;
A flie may fell her in the air,                    kill
    Before a man be even till her.

## THERE'S THREE TRUE GUDE FELLOWS

*TUNE: Three guid fellows ayont the glen*

The three of this title were Alexander Cunningham, Robert Cleghorn and William Dunbar, whom Burns regarded as 'Dear [to me] as the ruddy drops that warm my heart... I have a good mind to make verse on you all.'

There's three true gude fellows,
There's three true gude fellows,
There's three true gude fellows
    Down ayont the glen.                  beyond

Its now the day is dawin,           dawning
But or night do fa' in,       before nightfall
Whase cock's best at crawin,        Whose
Willie thou sall ken.         shall know

## THE LASS THAT MADE THE BED TO ME

Derived from a version of the Restoration ballad 'The Cumberland Lass.'

When Januar wind was blawin cauld,
    As to the North I took my way,
The mirksome night did me enfauld,    dark, enfold
    I knew na where to lodge till day.
But by guid luck a maid I met
    Just in the middle o my care,
And kindly she did me invite
    To walk into a chamber fair.

I bow'd fu low unto this maid,
    And thank'd her for her courtesie;
I bow'd fu low unto this maid,
    An bade her make a bed to me.
She made the bed baith large and wide,    both
    Wi twa white hands she spread it down,
She put the cup to her rosy lips,
    And drank: – 'Young man, now sleep ye soun.'

She snatch'd the candle in her hand,
   And frae my chamber went wi speed,
But I call'd her quickly back again
   To lay some mair below my head:          *more*
A cod she laid below my head,              *pillow*
   And served me with due respeck,
And, to salute her wi a kiss,
   I put my arms about her neck.

'Haud aff your hands, young man!' she said,
   'And dinna sae uncivil be;         *do not*
Gif ye hae onie luve for me,              *If*
   O, wrang na my virginitie!'
Her hair was like the links o gowd,      *gold*
   Her teeth were like the ivorie,
Her cheeks like lilies dipt in wine,
   The lass that made the bed to me!

Her bosom was the driven snaw,
   Twa drifted heaps sae fair to see;
Her limbs the polish'd marble stane,
   The lass that made the bed to me!
I kiss'd her o'er and o'er again,
   And ay she wist na what to say.
I laid her 'tween me and the wa' –
   That lassie thocht na lang till day.   *thought it not long*

Upon the morrow, when we raise,      *arose*
   I thank'd her for her courtesie;
But ay she blush'd and ay she sigh'd,
   And said: – 'Alas, ye've ruined me!'
I clasp'd her waist, and kiss'd her syne,   *then*
   While the tear stood twinkling in her e'e,   *eye*
I said: – 'My lassie, dinna cry,
   For ye ay shall mak the bed to me.'

She took her mither's holland sheets,
   An made them a' in sarks to me,      *shirts*
Blythe and merry may she be,
   The lass that made the bed to me!
The bonie lass made the bed to me,
   The braw lass made the bed to me!
I'll ne'er forget till the day I die,
   The lass that made the bed to me.

## THE REEL O STUMPIE

A traditional piece of bawdry which Burns refashioned to fit the well-known air of the title.

| | |
|---|---|
| Wap and rowe, wap and row, | wrap, roll |
| Wap and row the feetie o't, | feet |
| I thought I was a maiden fair, | |
| Till I heard the greetie o't. | crying |

| | |
|---|---|
| My daddie was a Fiddler fine, | |
| My minnie she made mantie O; | mother, gown |
| And I mysel a thumpin quine, | strapping wench |
| And danc'd the reel o Stumpie O. | |

## I'LL AY CA' IN BY YON TOWN

*TUNE: I'll gang nae mair to yon town*

Ascribed to Burns on the basis of the Hastie MS.

### CHORUS

*I'll ay ca' in by yon town*
*And by yon garden green again!*
*I'll ay ca' in by yon town,*
*And see my bonie Jean again.*

| | |
|---|---|
| There's nane shall ken, there's nane can guess | know |
| What brings me back the gate again, | way |
| But she, my fairest faithfu lass, | |
| And stow'nlins we sall meet again. | stealthily |

| | |
|---|---|
| She'll wander by the aiken tree, | oaken |
| When trystin time draws near again; | meeting |
| And when her lovely form I see, | |
| O haith! she's doubly dear again. | |

## THE RANTIN LADDIE

The earliest published version of an old ballad known generally as 'Lord Aboyne', possibly collected by Burns on his tour of the northeast in 1787.

| | |
|---|---|
| Aften hae I play'd at the cards and the dice, | |
| For the love of a bonie rantin laddie; | rollicking |
| But now I maun sit in my father's kitchen neuk, | must, corner |
| And balou a bastart babie. | sing a lullaby |

| | |
|---|---|
| For my father he will not me own, | |
| And my mother she neglects me, | |
| And a' my friends hae lightlyed me, | slandered |
| And their servants they do slight me. | |

| | |
|---|---|
| But had I a servant at my command, | |
| As aft-times I've had many, | |
| That wad rin wi a letter to bonie Glenswood, | |
| Wi a letter to my rantin laddie. | |

Oh, is he either a laird, or a lord,
  Or is he but a cadie,                           lackey
That ye do him ca' sae aften by name,
  Your bonie, bonie rantin laddie.

Indeed he is baith a laird and a lord,
  And he never was a cadie;
But he is the Earl o bonie Aboyne,
  And he is my rantin laddie.

O ye'se get a servant at your command,
  As aft-times ye've had many,
That sall rin wi a letter to bonie Glenswood,       shall run
  A letter to your rantin laddie.

When lord Aboyne did the letter get,
  O but he blinket bonie;
But or he had read three lines of it,
  I think his heart was sorry.

O wha is he daur be sae bauld,           dare, bold
  Sae cruelly to use my lassie?
   * * * * * * * * * * * *
     * * * * * * * * * *

For her father he will not her know,
  And her mother she does slight her,
And a' her friends hae lightlied her,
  And their servants they neglect her.

Go raise to me my five hundred men,
  Make haste and make them ready;
With a milkwhite steed under every ane,
  For to bring hame my lady.

As they cam in thro Buchan shire,
  They were a company bonie,
With a gude claymore in every hand,
  And O, but they shin'd bonie.

## O MAY, THY MORN

### TUNE: *The Rashes*

A blend of love and convivality in Burns's finest lyric style.

O May, thy morn was ne'er sae sweet
  As the mirk night o December!          murky
For sparkling was the rosy wine,
  And private was the chamber,
And dear was she I dare na name,
  But I will ay remember:

And here's to them that, like oursel,
   Can push about the jorum!
And here's to them that wish us weel –
   May a' that's guid watch o'er 'em!
And here's to them, we dare na tell,
   The dearest o the quorum!

## AS I CAM O'ER THE CAIRNEY MOUNT

Burns took an original but bawdy ballad and expurgated it to produce this beautiful song.

### CHORUS

*O my bonie Highland lad,*
   *My winsome, weelfar'd Highland laddie;*         handsome
*Wha wad mind the wind and rain,*
   *Sae weel row'd in his tartan plaidie.*         well wrapped

As I cam o'er the Cairney mount,
   And down amang the blooming heather,
Kindly stood the milkin-shiel         -shed
   To shelter frae the stormy weather.

Now Phebus blinkit on the bent,         bent-grass
   And o'er the knowes the lambs were bleating:    knolls
But he wan my heart's consent,         won
   To be his ain at the neist meeting.         next

## HIGHLAND LADDIE

One of a number of songs bearing this title, this version dates from 1745. Burns added opening lines of his own.

### She

The bonniest lad that e'er I saw,
   Bonie laddie, highland laddie,
Wore a plaid and was fu braw,         handsome
   Bonie Highland laddie.

On his head a bonnet blue,
   Bonie &c.
His royal heart was firm and true,
   Bonie &c.

He

Trumpets sound and cannons roar,
Bonie lassie, Lawland lassie,
And a' the hills wi echoes roar,
Bonie Lawland lassie.

Glory, Honor now invite
Bonie &c.
For freedom and my King to fight
Bonie &c.

She

The sun a backward course shall take,
Bonie laddie &c.
Ere ought thy manly courage shake;
Bonie laddie &c.

Go, for yourself procure renown,
Bonie &c.
And for your lawful King his crown,
Bonie Highland laddie.

## THE HIGHLAND BALOU

A versification by Burns of an old Gaelic nursery song 'Cagaran Gaolach.'

| | |
|---|---|
| Hee balou, my sweet wee Donald, | lullaby |
| Picture o the great Clanronald! | |
| Brawlie kens our wanton Chief | Finely knows |
| Wha gat my young Highland thief. | |
| | |
| Leeze me on thy bonie craigie! | Blessings, throat |
| An thou live, thou'll steal a naigie, | If, horse |
| Travel the country thro and thro, | |
| And bring hame a Carlisle cow! | |
| | |
| Thro the Lawlands, o'er the Border, | |
| Weel, my babie, may thou furder, | further |
| Herry the louns o the laigh Countrie, | Harry, fools, low |
| Syne to the Highlands hame to me! | Then |

## BANNOCKS O BEAR MEAL

Ascribed to Burns, on the basis of the Hastie MS, but probably as taken down by him without revision.

CHORUS

*Bannocks o bear meal,*                                                   barley
  *Bannocks o barley,*
*Here's to the Highlandman's*
  *Bannocks o barley!*

Wha in a brulyie will                                                     brawl
  First cry 'A parley?'
Never the lads wi the
  Bannocks o barley!

Wha, in his wae days,                                                        sad
  Were loyal to Charlie?                                          Prince Charles
Wha but the lads wi the                                            Edward Stuart
  Bannocks o barley!


## WAE IS MY HEART

Another old ballad, more or less as taken down, with some slight revision.

Wae is my heart, and the tear's in my e'e;                             Sad, eye
Lang, lang Joy's been a stranger to me:
Forsaken and friendless my burden I bear,
And the sweet voice o pity ne'er sounds in my ear.

Love thou has pleasures – and deep hae I lov'd!
Love thou has sorrows and sair hae I prov'd!
But this bruised heart that now bleeds in my breast,
I can feel by its throbbings, will soon be at rest.

O, if I were where happy I hae been,
Down by yon stream and yon bonie castle green!
For there he is wand'ring and musing on me,
Wha wad soon dry the tear frae his Phillis' e'e!

# HERE'S HIS HEALTH IN WATER

*TUNE: The Job of Journey-work*

A song of illicit love with Jacobite overtones, it refers to the toast to the 'King o'er the water' (i.e. the English Channel) - hence the custom of raising glasses over a bowl of water, or drinking the toast in water.

| | |
|---|---|
| Altho my back be at the wa', | |
| And tho he be the fautor, | transgressor |
| Altho my back be at the wa', | |
| Yet, here's his health in water! | |
| O, wae gae by his wanton sides, | sadly go |
| Sae brawly's he could flatter! | finely |
| Till for his sake I'm slighted sair, | sore |
| And dree the kintra clatter! | suffer, country gossip |
| But, tho my back be at the wa', | |
| Yet, here's his health in water! | |
| | |
| He follow'd me baith out and in, | both |
| Thro a' the nooks o Killie; | corners, Kilmarnock |
| He follow'd me baith out an in, | |
| Wi a stiff stanin pillie. | erect penis |
| But when he gat atween my legs, | |
| We made an unco splatter; | splash |
| An haith, I trow, I soupled it, | oath, believe, softened |
| Tho bauldly he did blatter; | boldly, work vigorously |
| But now my back is at the wa', | |
| Yet here's his health in water. | |

# GUDE WALLACE

This popular ballad was derived from an episode in Blind Harry's 'Schir Willyame Wallace.' Burns reworked it and added seven stanzas of his own, particularly the Lochmaben episode which he probably collected locally.

| | |
|---|---|
| O for my ain king, quo gude Wallace, | own |
| The rightfu king o fair Scotland; | |
| Between me and my Sovereign Blude | |
| I think I see some ill seed sawn. | sown |
| | |
| Wallace out over yon river he lap, | that, leaped |
| And he has lighted low down on yon plain, | |
| And he was aware of a gay ladie, | |
| As she was at the well washing. | |
| | |
| What tydins, what tydins, fair lady, he says, | tidings |
| What tydins hast thou to tell unto me; | |
| What tydins, what tydins, fair lady, he says, | |
| What tydins hae ye in the South Countrie. | |

Low down in yon wee Ostler house,
　　There is fyfteen Englishmen,
And they are seeking for gude Wallace,
　　It's him to take and him to hang.

There's nocht in my purse, quo gude Wallace.
　　There's nocht, not even a bare pennie;
But I will down to yon wee Ostler house
　　Thir fyfteen Englishmen to see.　　　　　　　　Those

And when he cam to yon wee Ostler house,
　　He bad benedicite be there;　　　　　　　　good fortune
.............................
.............................

Where was ye born, auld crookit Carl,　　　　　old man
　　Where was ye born, in what countrie;
I am a true Scot born and bred,
　　And an auld, crookit carl just sic as ye see.　　such

I wad gie fyfteen shilling to onie crookit carl,
　　To onie crookit carl just sic as ye,
If ye will get me gude Wallace,
　　For he is the man I wad very fain see.

He hit the proud Captain alang the chafft-blade,　jawbone
　　That never a bit o meat he ate mair;
And he sticket the rest at the table where they sat　stabbed
　　And he left them a' lyin sprawlin there.

Get up, get up, gudewife, he says,
　　And get to me some dinner in haste;
For it will soon be three lang days
　　Sin I a bit o meat did taste.

The dinner was na weel readie,
　　Nor was it on the table set,
Till other fyfteen Englishmen
　　Were a' lighted about the yett.　　　　　　　　gate

Come out, come out now, gude Wallace,
　　This is the day that thou maun die;　　　　　must
I lippen nae sae little to God, he says,　　　　　depend
　　Altho I be but ill wordie.　　　　　　　　　unworthy

The gudewife had an auld gudeman,　　　　　husband
　　By gude Wallace he stiffly stood,
Till ten o the fyfteen Englishmen
　　Before the door lay in their blude.

The other five to the greenwood ran,
　　And he hang'd these five upon a grain:　　　　bough
And on the morn wi his merry men a'
　　He sat at dine in Lochmaben town.

## THE AULD MAN'S MARE'S DEAD

This song by Peter Birnie, an itinerant fiddler in Fife c.1710, was revised by Burns for SMM in 1795. The poor old horse seems to have been a veritable catalogue of veterinary ailments.

CHORUS

*The auld man's mare's dead,*
*The poor man's mare's dead,*
*The auld man's mare's dead,*
    *A mile aboon Dundee.*                    above

She was cut-luggit, painch-lippit,          -ered, pinch-lipped
Steel-waimit, staincher-fittit,          -bellied, stanchion-footed
Chanler-chaftit, lang-neckit,          lantern-jawed, long-necked
    Yet the brute did die.

Her lunzie-banes were knaggs and neuks,    haunch-bone, knots, corners
She had the cleeks, the cauld, the crooks,    cramps, wryneck
The jawpish and the wanton yeuks,          urethritis, itch
    And the howks aboon her e'e.          eye disease of animals

My Master rade me to the town,                    rode
He ty'd me to a staincher round,              hitching-rail
He took a chappin till himsel,          chopin (Scots measure)
    But fient a drap gae me.              not drop gave

## THE TAYLOR

Burns reworked an old ballad 'The Taylor of Hogerglen's Wedding' and added a final chorus of his own.

The Taylor he cam here to sew,
    And weel he kend the way to woo,              well knew
For ay he pree'd the lassie's mou              pried, mouth
    As he gaed but and ben O.              went in and out
CHORUS
*For weel he kend the way O*
*The way O, the way O,*
*For weel he kend the way O*
*The lassie's heart to win O.*

The Taylor rase and sheuk his duds,        rose, shook, clothes
    The flaes they flew awa in cluds,              fleas, clouds
And them that stay'd gat fearfu thuds,              blows
    The Taylor prov'd a man O.
CHORUS
*For now it was the gloamin,*                    twilight
*The gloamin, the gloamin,*
*For now it was the gloamin*
*When a' the rest are gaun O.*              gone

592

## THERE GROWS A BONIE BRIER-BUSH

No original of this ballad has been traced, but it has all the hallmarks of Burns's revision of a folk-song he had collected.

There grows a bonie brier-bush in our kail-yard,        *vegetable-*
There grows a bonie brier-bush in our kail-yard;        *patch*
And below the bonie brier-bush there's a lassie and a lad,
And they're busy, busy courtin in our kail-yard.

We'll court nae mair below the buss in our kail-yard,        *bush*
We'll court nae mair below the buss in our kail-yard;
We'll awa to Athole's green, and there we'll no be seen,
Whare the trees and the branches will be our safe-guard.

Will ye go to the dancin in Carlyle's ha',
Will ye go to the dancin in Carlyle's ha';
Whare Sandy and Nancy I'm sure will ding them a'?        *beat*
I winna gang to the dance in Carlyle-ha'.        *will not go*

What will I do for a lad, when Sandy gangs awa?
What will I do for a lad, when Sandy gangs awa?
I will awa to Edinburgh and win a pennie fee,
And see an onie bonie lad will fancy me.        *if any bonny*

He's comin frae the North that's to fancy me,
He's comin frae the North that's to fancy me;
A feather in his bonnet and a ribbon at his knee,
He's a bonie, bonie laddie and yon be he.

## HERE'S TO THY HEALTH
### TUNE: *Laggan Burn*

The manuscript of this song (now at Alloway) bears Burns's annotation '...as far as I can recollect, the compilation of an illiterate Millwright, about thirty or forty years ago, somewhere in Ayrshire.'

Here's to thy health, my bonie lass!
    Guid night and joy be wi thee!
I'll come nae mair to thy bower-door        *no more*
    To tell thee that I lo'e thee.
O, dinna think, my pretty pink,
    But I can live without thee:
I vow and swear I dinna care        *do not*
    How lang ye look about ye!

Thou'rt ay sae free informing me
    Thou hast nae mind to marry,        *desire*
I'll be as free informing thee
    Nae time hae I to tarry:
I ken thy freens try ilka means        *friends, every*
    Frae wedlock to delay thee
(Depending on some higher chance),
    But fortune may betray thee.

I ken they scorn my low estate,
   But that does never grieve me,
For I'm as free as any he –
   Sma' siller will relieve me!           *a little money*
I'll count my health my greatest wealth
   Sae lang as I'll enjoy it.
I'll fear nae scant, I'll bode nae want
   As lang's I get employment.

But far off fowls hae feathers fair,
   And, ay until ye try them,
Tho they seem fair, still have a care –
   They may prove as bad as I am!
But at twel at night, when the moon shines bright,    *twelve*
My dear, I'll come and see thee,
For the man that loves his mistress weel,
   Nae travel makes him weary.

# IT WAS A' FOR OUR RIGHTFU KING

Burns rewrote the chap-book ballad 'Mally Stewart' (c. 1746) which deals with an
episode in the Williamite War of 1689-90 in Ireland. The 'rightfu king' was King James
VII and II.

It was a' for our rightfu King
   We left fair Scotland's strand;
It was a' for our rightfu King
   We e'er saw Irish land, my dear –
   We e'er saw Irish land.

Now a' is done that men can do,
   And a' is done in vain,
My Love and Native Land fareweel,
   For I maun cross the main, my dear –        *must*
   For I maun cross the main.

He turn'd him right and round about
   Upon the Irish shore,
And gae his bridle reins a shake,         *gave*
   With adieu for evermore, my dear –
   And adieu for evermore!

The soger frae the war returns,
   The sailor frae the main,
But I hae parted frae my love,
   Never to meet again, my dear –
   Never to meet again.

When day is gane, and night is come,
And a' folk bound to sleep,
I think on him that's far awa
  The lee-lang night, and weep, my dear –
  The lee-lang night and weep.

## THE HIGHLAND WIDOW'S LAMENT

Attributed to Burns (on the basis of the Hastie MS). Not surprisingly, he seldom
admitted authorship of Jacobite songs at a time when expression of such sentiments
could still be dangerous.

O, I am come to the low countrie –
  Ochon, ochon, ochrie! –                    alas, alack
Without a penny in my purse
  To buy a meal to me.

It was na sae in the Highland hills –
  Ochon, ochon, ochrie! –
Nae woman in the country wide
  Sae happy was as me.

For then I had a score o kye –               cattle
  Ochon, ochon, ochrie! –
Feeding on yon hill sae high
  And giving milk to me.

And there I had three score o yowes –        ewes
  Ochon, ochon, ochrie! –
Skipping on yon bonie knowes                 knolls
  And casting woo to me.                     wool

I was the happiest of a' the clan –
  Sair, sair may I repine! –
For Donald was the brawest man,
  And Donald he was mine.

Till Charlie Stewart cam at last    Prince Charles Edward Stuart
  Sae far to set us free:
My Donald's arm was wanted then
  For Scotland and for me.

Their waefu fate what need I tell?           sad
  Right to the wrang did yield;
My Donald and his country fell
  Upon Culloden field.

Ochon! O Donald, O!
  Ochon, ochon, ochrie!
Nae woman in the warld wide,
  Sae wretched now as me!

## O, STEER HER UP AN HAUD HER GAUN

Apparently a reconstruction of a traditional fragment in *The Tea-Table Miscellany*.

| | |
|---|---|
| O, steer her up, an haud her gaun – | guide, hold, going |
| Her mither's at the mill, jo, | dear |
| An gin she winna tak a man | if, will not |
| E'en let her tak her will, jo. | |
| First shore her wi a gentle kiss, | offer |
| And ca' anither gill, jo, | order, drink |
| An gin she tak the thing amiss, | |
| E'en let her flyte her fill, jo. | scold |

| | |
|---|---|
| O, steer her up, an be na blate, | bashful |
| An gin she tak it ill, jo, | |
| Then leave the lassie till her fate, | |
| And time nae langer spill, jo! | |
| Ne'er break your heart for ae rebute, | |
| But think upon it still, jo, | |
| That gin the lassie winna do't, | |
| Ye'll find anither will, jo. | |

## WEE WILLIE GRAY

A nursery jingle (other versions are 'Wee Totum Fogg' and the English 'Tommy Tacket'). revised by Burns according to James Johnson.

| | |
|---|---|
| Wee Willie Gray an his leather wallet, | |
| Peel a willow-wand to be him boots and jacket! | |
| The rose upon the brier will be him trouse an doublet – | trousers |
| The rose upon the brier will be him trouse an doublet! | |

| | |
|---|---|
| Wee Willie Gray an his leather wallet, | |
| Twice a lily-flower will be him sark and gravat! | shirt, neck-tie |
| Feathers of a flie wad feather up his bonnet – | |
| Feathers of a flie wad feather up his bonnet! | |

## GUDEEN TO YOU KIMMER

Burns appears to have taken the fragments of two traditional ballads and welded them together, with extensive revision to produce this song for SMM. Part of this was preserved in the Herd MSS, which Burns probably examined during his stay in Edinburgh.

### CHORUS

*We're a' noddin, nid nid noddin,*
*We're a' noddin at our house at hame,*
*We're a' noddin, nid nid noddin,*
*We're a' noddin at our house at hame.*

| | |
|---|---|
| Gudeen to you kimmer | Good evening, wench |
| And how do ye do? | |
| Hiccup, quo kimmer, | |
| The better than I'm fou, | drunk |

Kate sits i' the neuk,            corner
   Suppin hen-broo;        -brew
Deil tak Kate
   An she be na noddin too!

How's a' wi you, kimmer,
   And how do ye fare?
A pint o the best o't,
   And twa pints mair.          more

How's a' wi you, kimmer,
   And how do ye thrive;
How mony bairns hae ye?    children
   Quo kimmer, I hae five.

Are they a' Johny's?
   Eh! atweel no:
Twa o them were gotten    conceived
   When Johny was awa.

Cats like milk
   And dogs like broo;
Lads like lasses weel,
   And lasses lads too.

## O, AY MY WIFE SHE DANG ME

Based on a traditional piece of bawdry, revised for SMM.

### CHORUS

*O, ay my wife she dang me,*    struck
   *An aft my wife she bang'd me!*
*If ye gie a woman a' her will,*
   *Guid faith! she'll soon o'er-gang ye.*  dominate

On peace an rest my mind was bent,
   And, fool I was! I married;
But never honest man's intent
   Sae cursedly miscarried.

Some sairie comfort at the last,   sorry
   When a' thir days are done, man:  their
My 'pains o hell' on earth is past,
   I'm sure o bliss aboon, man.   above

## SCROGGAM

David Murison suggests that the title comes from 'scrag 'em', one of the cries of the London street-mob, and may have been derived from a traditional English lynching ballad. Ruffum ('rough 'em') has the same source but Kinsley thought it may have also had sexual connotations.

There was a wife wonn'd in Cockpen,                                    dwelt
    Scroggam!
She brew'd guid ale for gentlemen:
    Sing Auld Cowl, lay you down by me –            a Catholic priest
    Scroggam, my dearie, ruffum!                            or monk

The guidwife's dochter fell in a fever,                         daughter
    Scroggam!
The priest o the parish fell in anither:
    Sing Auld Cowl, lay you down by me –
    Scroggam, my dearie, ruffum!

They laid the twa i' the bed thegither,
    Scroggam!
That the heat o the tane might cool the tither;     the one, the other
    Sing Auld Cowl, lay you down by me –
    Scroggam, my dearie, ruffum!


## O, GUID ALE COMES

Stenhouse claimed this as wholly Burns's work, but Johnson's annotation 'Corrected by R. Burns' is probably more accurate.

### CHORUS

*O, guid ale comes, and guid ale goes,*
*Guid ale gars me sell my hose,*                                makes
*Sell my hose, and pawn my shoon –*                    shoes
*Guid ale keeps my heart aboon!*                           above

I had sax owsen in a pleugh,                                       oxen
And they drew a' weel eneugh:
I sell'd them a' just ane by ane –
Guid ale keeps the heart aboon!

Guid ale hauds me bare and busy,                          keeps
Gars me moop wi the servant hizzie,         copulate, wench
Stand i' the stool when I hae dune –      stool of repentance
Guid ale keeps the heart aboon!

## MY LORD A-HUNTING HE IS GANE

TUNE: *My lady's gown, there's gairs upon't*

Burns wrote to Johnson in May 1795 saying he hoped to procure the air, for which he subsequently wrote these words, published in SMM, 1803. The tune was composed by the Ayrshire musician James Gregg. The Kennedy family, Earls of Cassilis, were the chief family in Carrick.

CHORUS

| | |
|---|---|
| My lady's gown, there's gairs upon't, | stripes |
| And gowden flowers sae rare upon't; | |
| But Jenny's jimps and jirkinet, | skirts, bodice |
| My lord thinks meikle mair upon't! | much more |

My lord a-hunting he is gane,
But hounds or hawks wi him are nane;
By Colin's cottage lies his game,
If Colin's Jenny be at hame.

| | |
|---|---|
| My lady's white, my lady's red, | |
| And kith and kin o Cassillis' blude; | |
| But her ten-pund lands o tocher guid | dowry |
| Were a' the charms his lordship lo'ed. | |

| | |
|---|---|
| Out o'er yon muir, out o'er yon moss, | bog |
| Whare gor-cocks thro the heather pass, | red grouse |
| There wons auld Colin's bonie lass, | dwells |
| A lily in a wilderness. | |

Sae sweetly move her genty limbs,
Like music notes o lovers' hymns!
The diamond-dew in her een sae blue,
Where laughing love sae wanton swims!

| | |
|---|---|
| My lady's dink, my lady's drest, | trim |
| The flower and fancy o the west; | |
| But the lassie that a man lo'es best, | |
| O, that's the lass to mak him blest! | |

## SWEETEST MAY

TUNE: *Kinloch of Kinloch*

This is a revision of 'There's my Thumb I'll ne'er beguile thee', published by Ramsay in *The Tea-Table Miscellany*.

Sweetest May let love inspire thee;
Take a heart which he designs thee;
As thy constant slave regard it;
For its faith and truth reward it.

Proof o shot to Birth or Money,
Not the wealthy, but the bonie;
Not high-born, but noble-minded,
In Love's silken band can bind it.

## JOCKIE'S TA'EN THE PARTING KISS

TUNE: *Bonie lass tak a man*

A Scottish version of an English song published as a 'Scotch' ballad in 1776.

Jockie's ta'en the parting kiss,
  O'er the mountains he is gane,
And with him is a' my bliss –
  Nought but griefs with me remain.
Spare my luve, ye winds that blaw,
  Plashy sleets and beating rain!
Spare my luve, thou feathery snaw,
  Drifting o'er the frozen plain!

When the shades of evening creep
  O'er the day's fair, gladsome e'e,
Sound and safely may he sleep,
  Sweetly blythe his waukening be!
He will think on her he loves,
  Fondly he'll repeat her name;
For where'er he distant roves,
  Jockie's heart is still at hame.

## BONIE PEG-A-RAMSAY

Peg-a-Ramsay or Peggy Ramsay is a well-known figure in Anglo-Saxon bawdry from medieval times onward. Burns here conceals the lady's legendary sexual prowess until the punch-line – the milling metaphor was a familiar euphemism in his day for sexual activity.

Cauld is the e'enin blast
  O Boreas o'er the pool                          the north wind
An dawin, it is dreary,                                  dawn
  When birks are bare at Yule.                birches, Christmas

O, cauld blaws the e'enin blast,
  When bitter bites the frost,
And in the mirk and dreary drift                      dark
  The hills and glens are lost!

Ne'er sae murky blew the night
  That drifted o'er the hill,
But bonie Peg-a-Ramsay
  Gat grist to her mill.

## OVER SEA, OVER SHORE

'A cento of old catchwords' (Henley and Henderson).

There was a bonie lass, and a bonie, bonie lass,
  And she lo'ed her bonie laddie dear,
Till War's loud alarms tore her laddie frae her arms
  Wi monie a sigh, and a tear.

Over sea, over shore, where the cannons loudly roar,
    He still was a stranger to fear,
And nocht could him quail, or his bosom assail,
    But the bonie lass he loed sae dear.

## THERE'S NEWS, LASSES, NEWS

*TUNE: Captain Mackenzie's Reel*

A blend of nursery rhyme chorus, old fragments from the Herd collection and original lines.

### CHORUS

| | |
|---|---|
| *The wean wants a cradle,* | baby |
| *  And the cradle wants a cod,* | pillow |
| *I'll no gang to my bed,* | go |
| *  Until I get a nod.* | |

There's news, lasses, news,
  Guid news I've to tell!
There's a boatfu o lads
  Come to our town to sell!

'Father,' quo she, 'Mither,' quo she,
  'Do what you can:
I'll no gang to my bed
  Until I get a man!'

| | |
|---|---|
| I hae as guid a craft rig | croft-ridge |
|   As made o yird and stane; | earth, stone |
| And waly fa' the ley-crap | woe befall, meadow crop |
|   For I maun till'd again. | must plough it |

## O, THAT I HAD NE'ER BEEN MARRIED

The first eight lines are 'an old Scots ballad' which Burns quoted to Mrs Dunlop, and added the final stanza to complete an eloquently simple expression of fear and want. The air dates from the seventeenth century.

### CHORUS

| | |
|---|---|
| *Ance crowdie, twice crowdie,* | gruel |
| *  Three times crowdie in a day!* | |
| *Gin ye crowdie onie mair,* | If, any more |
| *  Ye'll crowdie a' my meal away.* | |

| | |
|---|---|
| O, that I had ne'er been married, | |
|   I wad never had nae care! | |
| Now I've gotten wife an bairns, | children |
|   An they cry 'Crowdie' ever mair. | |

| | |
|---|---|
| Waefu Want and Hunger fley me, | Woeful, thrash |
|   Glowrin by the hallan en'; | Staring, porch-end |
| Sair I fecht them at the door, | Sore, fight |
|   But ay I'm eerie they come ben. | afraid, inside |

## THE GERMAN LAIRDIE

Burns's abridged version of a lengthy political ballad, current in the period following the accession of George Louis, Elector of Hanover as King of Great Britain in 1714. The Whigs were the ascendant party at the time. The Revolution referred to in 1.9 was the overthrow of the old Stuart dynasty in 1688.

CHORUS

*Sing heedle liltie, teedle liltie,*
*Andum tandum tandie;*
*Sing fal de dal, de dal lal lal,*
*Sing howdle liltie dandie.*

What merriment has taen the whigs,
   I think they be gaen mad, Sir,
Wi playing up their whiggish jigs,
   Their dancin may be sad, Sir.

The Revolution principles
   Has put their heads in bees, Sir;       a spin
They're a' fa'n out amang themsels,
   Deil tak the first that grees, Sir.       wins

## EPITAPH FOR HUGH LOGAN OF LOGAN

Hugh Logan (1739-1802), laird of Logan near Cumnock, enjoyed quite a reputation as a man who delighted in wine, women and song - a man very much after Burns's own heart.

Here lyes Squire Hugh – Ye harlot crew,
   Come mak your water on him,
I'm sure that he well pleas'd would be
   To think ye pish'd upon him.

## MUIRLAND MEG

*TUNE: Saw Ye My Eppie McNab*

Muirland Meg, alias Meg Hog or Monkery Meg, kept a brothel at Dumfries Whitesands and died c. 1811.

Amang our young lassies there's Muirland Meg,
She'll beg or she work, and she'll play or she beg,   before
At thretten her maidenhead flew to the gate,   thirteen
And the door o her cage stands open yet.

Her kittle black een they wad thirl you thro,   skittish eyes, thrill
Her rose-bud lips cry, kiss me now;
The curls and links o her bonie black hair,   locks
Wad put you in mind that the lassie has mair.

An armfu o love is her bosom sae plump,
A span o delight is her middle sae jimp;   neat
A taper, white leg, and a thumpin thie,   thigh
And a fiddle near by, an ye play a wee!   a little

Love's her delight, and kissin's her treasure,
She'll stick at nae price, and ye gie her gude measure.          if
As lang's a sheep-fit, and as girt's a goose-egg,    sheep-foot, broad
And that's the measure o Muirland Meg.

# THE PATRIARCH

*TUNE: The auld cripple Dow*

A curious safety-valve for the extreme puritanism of Scottish Calvinism has been the abundance of comic - not to say coarse - verse with biblical themes. This composition by Burns belongs to an old and well-established genre.

As honest Jacob on a night,
    Wi his beloved beauty,
Was duly laid on wedlock's bed,
    And noddin at his duty:
        Tal de dal, &c.

'How lang' she says, 'ye fumblin wretch,
    Will ye be fuckin at it?
My eldest wean might die of age,
    Before that ye could get it.

'Ye pegh, and grane, and groazle there,                pant, groan,
                                                    breathe heavily
    And mak an unco splutter,                             mighty
And I maun ly and thole you here,                  must, endure
    And fient a hair the better.'                             not

Then he, in wrath, put up his graith,                       tool
    'The deevil's in the hizzie!                           hussy
I mow as I mow the lave,                          copulate, rest
    And night and day I'm bisy.                             busy

'I've bairn'd the servant gypsies baith,       impregnated, both
    Forbye your titty Leah;                                sister
Ye barren jad, ye put me mad,                                jade
    What mair can I do wi you.

'There's ne'er a mow I've gi'en the lave,                   rest
    But ye ha'e got a dizzen;                             dozen
And dam a ane ye'se get again,
    Altho your cunt should gizzen.                        shrivel

Then Rachel calm, as ony lamb,                              any
    She claps him on the waulies,                       genitals
Quo she, 'ne'er fash a woman's clash,              heed, tongue
    In trowth, ye mow me braulies.                     splendidly

603

'My dear 'tis true, for mony a mow,
　I'm your ungratefu debtor;
But ance again, I dinna ken,　　　　　　　　　　　don't know
　We'll aiblens happen better.'　　　　　　　　　　perhaps

Then honest man! wi little wark,
　He soon forgat his ire;
The patriarch, he coost the sark,　　　　　　　　cast off, shirt
　And up and till 't like fire!!!


# THE TROGGER

*TUNE: Gillicrankie*

Probably traditional to some extent, it was largely inspired by John Lewars who wagered
that Burns 'could not get a word to clink with' Ecclefechan, which they were visiting at
the time. Burns uses 'troggin' (trucking) as a metaphor for coitus.

As I cam down by Annan side,
　Intending for the border,
Amang the scroggie banks and braes,　　　　　　scrubby
　Wha met I but a trogger.　　　　　　　　　　　pedlar
He laid me down upon my back,
　I thought he was but jokin,
Till he was in me to the hilts,
　O the deevil tak sic troggin!　　　　　　　　　pack-ware

What could I say, what could I do,
　I bann'd and sair misca'd him,　　　　　　　　cursed, sore
But whiltie-whaltie gae'd his arse　　　　　　　up and down
　The mair that I forbade him:
He stell'd his foot against a stane,　　　　　　braced, stone
　And doubl'd ilka stroke in,　　　　　　　　　every
Till I gaed daft amang his hands,　　　　　　　went crazy
　O the deevil tak sic troggin!

Then up we raise, and took the road,
　And in by Ecclefechan,
Where brandy-stoup we gart it clink,　　　　　　made
　And the strang-beer ream the quech in.　froth, cup (quaich)
Bedown the bents o Bonshaw braes,　　below, bent-grass, slopes
　We took the partin yokin;
But I've claw'd a sairy cunt synsine,　　scratched, sorry, since then
　O the deevil tak sic troggin!

## THE JOLLY GAUGER

*TUNE: We'll gang nae mair a rovin*

A fellow-exciseman is said to have composed the original, but it incorporates an anecdote picked up by Burns, concerning a beggar woman in the Merse, and may have been reworked by him.

There was a jolly gauger, a gauging he did ride,
And he has met a beggar down by yon river side.
An we'll gang nae mair a rovin wi ladies to the wine,
When a beggar wi her meal-pocks can fidge her tail sae fine. -bags. shake

Amang the broom he laid her, amang the broom sae green,
And he 's fa'n to the beggar, as she had been a queen.
An we'll gang, &c.

My blessings on thee, laddie, thou 's done my turn sae weel,
Wilt thou accept, dear laddie, my pock and and pickle meal?    little
An we'll, &c.

Sae blyth the beggar took the bent, like ony bird in spring,
Sae blyth the beggar took the bent, and merrily did sing.
An we'll, &c.

My blessings on the gauger, o gaugers he 's the chief.
Sic kail ne'er crost my kettle, nor sic a joint o beef.    cabbage
An we'll, &c.

## WHA'LL MOW ME NOW?

*TUNE: Comin thro the rye*

Attributed to Burns by Scott Douglas and DeLancey Ferguson on stylistic grounds. In this case military terms (bandoliers, pistol) are used as sexual metaphors.

O wha'll mow me now, my jo,    darling
An wha'll mow me now:
A sodger wi his bandileers    bandoliers (testicles)
Has bang'd my belly fu.

O, I hae tint my rosy cheek,    lost
Likewise my waste sae sma',    waist
O wae gae by the sodger lown,    woe befall, fool
The sodger did it a'.
An wha'll, &c.

Now I maun thole the scornfu sneer    must, tolerate
O mony a saucy quine;    girl
When, curse upon her godly face!
Her cunt 's as merry 's mine.
An wha'll, &c.

Our dame hauds up her wanton tail,          holds, vulva
    As due as she gaes lie;
An yet misca's a young thing,              miscalls
    The trade if she but try.
        An wha'll, &c.

Our dame can lae her ain gudeman,      leave own husband
    An mow for glutton greed;
An yet misca's a poor thing
    That 's mowin for its bread.
        An wha'll, &c.

Alake! sae sweet a tree as love,
    Sic bitter fruit should bear!
Alake, that e'er a merry arse,
    Should draw a sa'tty tear.              salty
        An wha'll, &c.

But deevil damn the lousy loun,
    Denies the bairn he got!              brat
Or lea's the merry arse he lo'ed           leaves
    To wear a ragged coat!
        An wha'll, &c.

# O SAW YE MY MAGGIE

Burns's burlesque parody of 'Saw ye nae my Peggy' was probably based on a bawdy original. The Abbotsford MS has a mock-testament from Burns bequeathing these verses to his friend Alexander Findlater.

Saw ye my Maggie?
    Saw ye my Maggie?
Saw ye my Maggie?
    Comin oer the lea?

What mark has your Maggie,
What mark has your Maggie,
What mark has your Maggie,
    That ane may ken her be?           one, know

My Maggie has a mark,
Ye'll find it in the dark,
It 's in below her sark,               chemise
    A little aboon her knee.

What wealth has your Maggie,
What wealth has your Maggie,
What wealth has your Maggie,
    In tocher, gear, or fee?        dowry, possessions

My Maggie has a treasure,
A hidden mine o pleasure,
I'll howk it at my leisure,                                    dig
    It 's alane for me.

How loe ye your Maggy,
How loe ye your Maggy,
How loe ye your Maggy,
    An loe nane but she?

Ein that tell our wishes,
Eager glowing kisses,
Then diviner blisses,
    In holy ecstacy!

How meet you your Maggie,
How meet you your Maggie,
How meet you your Maggie,
    When nane 's to hear or see?

Heavenly joys before me,
Rapture trembling o'er me,
Maggie I adore thee,
    On my bended knee!!!

## GIE THE LASS HER FAIRIN

*TUNE: Cauld kail in Aberdeen*

This song was set to one of the poet's favourite melodies. A fairing was a present from
a fairground, a favour given as a love-token, and hence used as a metaphor for sexual
favours.

O gie the lass her fairin, lad,
    O gie the lass her fairin,
An something else she'll gie to you,
    That 's waly worth the wearin;                            choice
Syne coup her o'er amang the creels,                 then knock her
    When ye hae taen your brandy,                       over baskets
The mair she bangs the less she squeels,
    An hey for houghmagandie.                               fornication

Then gie the lass a fairin, lad,
    O gie the lass her fairin,
An she'll gie you a hairy thing,
    An of it be na sparin;
But coup her o'er amang the creels,
    An bar the door wi baith your heels,
The mair she gets the less she squeels;
    An hey for houghmagandie.

## THE BOOK-WORMS

Said by Cunningham to have been inscribed in a volume of Shakespeare in a nobleman's library. A variant copied by John Syme was written in a Bible which a friend offered Burns for his inscription.

Through and through th' inspir'd leaves,
    Ye maggots, make your windings;
But O, respect his lordship's taste,
    And spare the golden bindings!

## ON MARRIAGE

Published in the Henley-Henderson edition (1896), from an undated holograph.

The hackney'd judge of human life,         King Solomon
    The Preacher and the King,
Observes: 'The man that gets a wife
    He gets a noble thing.'

But how capricious are mankind,
    Now loathing, now desirous!
We married men, how oft we find
    The best of things will tire us!

## HERE'S A BOTTLE

*'There's nane that's blest of human kind,*
*But the cheerful and the gay, man.'*

In this drinking toast Burns combines two of the things in life he valued: good wine and good companionship.

Here's a bottle and an honest friend!
    What wad ye wish for mair, man?       would, more
Wha kens, before his life may end,       knows
    What his share may be o care, man?

Then catch the moments as they fly,
    And use them as ye ought, man!
Believe me, Happiness is shy,
    And comes not ay when sought, man!

## HER FLOWING LOCKS

An undated fragment which Burns no doubt intended to set to some popular tune.

Her flowing locks, the raven's wing,
    Adown her neck and bosom hing.
How sweet unto that breast to cling,
    And round that neck entwine her!

Her lips are roses wat wi dew –                                    wet
  O, what a feast, her bonie mou!                               mouth
Her cheeks a mair celestial hue,
  A crimson still diviner!

# A TALE

The origin of this poem has long been disputed, in spite of the existence of a revised holograph. Dewar suggested that Burns may have copied out a poem sent to him and corrected it for the author, but Kinsley quite rightly points out that it would not have been necessary to make a fair copy before making a few minor corrections.

'Twas where the birch and sounding thong are plyed,
The noisy domicile of Pedant-pride;
Where Ignorance her darkening vapour throws,
And cruelty directs the thickening blows;
Upon a time, Sir Abece the great,                            Alphabet
In all his pedagogic powers elate,
His awful Chair of state resolves to mount,
And call the trembling Vowels to account.

    First enter'd A; a grave, broad, solemn Wight,
But ah! deform'd, dishonest to the sight!
His twisted head look'd backward on his way,
And flagrant from the scourge he grunted, AI!

Reluctant, E stalk'd in; with piteous race
The jostling tears ran down his honest face!
That name, that well-worn name, and all his own,
Pale he surrenders at the tyrant's throne!
The Pedant stifles keen the Roman sound
Not all his mongrel diphthongs can compound;
And next the title following close behind,
He to the nameless, ghastly wretch assign'd.

    The cob-webb'd, Gothic dome resounded, Y!
In sullen vengeance, I, disdain'd reply;
The Pedant swung his felon cudgel round,
And knock'd the groaning Vowel to the ground!

In rueful apprehension enter'd O,
The wailing minstrel of despairing woe;
Th' Inquisitor of Spain the most expert
Might there have learnt new mysteries of his art:
So grim, deform'd, with horrors, entering U,
His dearest friend and brother scarcely knew!

As trembling U stood staring all aghast,
The Pedant in his left hand clutch'd him fast;
In helpless infant's tears he dipp'd his right,
Baptiz'd him EU, and kick'd him from his sight.

609

20

## THE HENPECKED HUSBAND

Burns's robust commentary on nagging wives and the way to cure them of the habit.

Curs'd be the man, the poorest wretch in life,
The crouching vassal to the tyrant wife!
Who has no will but by her high permission;
Who has not sixpence but in her possession;
Who must to her his dear friend's secret tell,
Who dreads a curtain lecture worse than hell!
Were such the wife had fallen to my part,
I'd break her spirit, or I'd break her heart.
I'd charm her with the magic of a switch,
I'd kiss her maids, and kick the perverse bitch.

## ON A DOG OF LORD EGLINTON'S

One of a number of short pieces and fragments collected by James Grierson of Dalgoner, an early collector of Burnsiana (c.1805)

I never barked when out of season,
    I never bit without a reason;
I ne'er insulted weaker brother,
    Nor wronged by force or fraud another.
We brutes are placed a rank below;
    Happy for man could he say so.

## EPITAPH

A stark little couplet, collected by James Grierson.

Lo worms enjoy the seat of bliss
Where Lords and Lairds afore did kiss.

## BROOM BESOMS

These traditional couplets are redolent of phallic symbolism: 'buying brooms' was a popular Scottish euphemism for female sexual adventures.

CHORUS
*Buy broom besoms! wha will buy them now;*
*Fine heather ringers, better never grew.*

I maun hae a wife, whatsoe'er she be;
An she be a woman, that 's eneugh for me.

If that she be bony, I shall think her right:
If that she be ugly, where's the odds at night?

O, an she be young, how happy shall I be!
If that she be auld, the sooner she will die.

If that she be fruitfu, O! what joy is there!
If she should be barren, less will be my care.

If she like a drappie, she and I'll agree;         drink
If she dinna like it, there's the mair for me.   does not, more

Be she green or gray; be she black or fair;
Let her be a woman, I shall seek nae mair.       no more

Alternative Verses

Young and souple was I, when I lap the dyke;   pliant, leaped fence
Now I'm auld and frail, I douna step a syke.    cannot, stream

Young and souple was I, when at Lautherslack,
Now I'm auld and frail, and lie at Nansie's back.

Had she gien me butter, when she gae me bread,
I wad looked baulder, wi my beld head.       bolder, bald

# NOW HEALTH FORSAKES THAT ANGEL FACE

Burns's authorship has been questioned, despite the existence of a holograph in the
Alloway MS.

Now health forsakes that angel face,
    Nae mair my Dearie smiles;         no more
Pale sickness withers ilka grace,           every
    And a' my hopes beguiles:
The cruel Powers reject the prayer
    I hourly mak for thee;
Ye heavens how great is my despair,
    How can I see him die!

# PRETTY PEG

Burns's revision of a song which may have been traditional, first published from his
holograph in 1808.

As I gaed up by yon gate-end,
    When day was waxin weary,
Wha did I meet come down the street,
    But pretty Peg, my dearie?

Her air sae sweet, an shape complete,
    Wi nae proportion wanting
The Queen of Love did never move
    Wi motion mair enchanting!

Wi linked hands we took the sands
    Down by yon winding river;
And O! that hour and shady bower,
    Can I forget it? Never!

# WHEN FIRST I SAW

TUNE: *Maggie Lauder*

Published in all major editions except Kinsley who rejected it as spurious. Perhaps the references to 'fair Jeanie' were too obvious. Henry Dundas (1742-1811), Treasurer of the Navy (1782), Home Secretary (1791), created Viscount Melville (1802) was the most powerful man in Scotland in his time. The 4th Earl of Hopetoun was one of Scotland's wealthiest landowners in the 1790s.

CHORUS
She's aye, aye sae blythe, sae gay,
    She's aye sae blythe and cheerie,
She's aye sae bonie, blythe and gay,
    O, gin I were her dearie!         *if*

When first I saw fair Jeanie's face,
    I couldna tell what ail'd me:
My heart went fluttering pit-a-pat,
    My een they almost fail'd me.         *eyes*
She's aye sae neat, sae trim, sae tight,
    All grace does round her hover!
Ae look deprived me o my heart,
    And I became her lover.

Had I Dundas's whole estate,
    Or Hopetoun's wealth to shine in;
Did warlike laurels crown my brow,
    Or humbler bays entwining;
I'd lay them a' at Jeanie's feet,
    Could I but hope to move her,
And, prouder than a belted knight
    I'd be my Jeanie's lover.

But sair I fear some happier swain
    Has gained my Jeanie's favour.
If so, may every bliss be hers,
    Though I maun never have her!         *must*
But gang she east, or gang she west,         *go*
    'Twixt Forth and Tweed all over,
While men have eyes, or ears, or taste,
    She'll always find a lover.

# SWEET ARE THE BANKS

TUNE: *Cambdelmore*

Sweet are the banks – the banks o Doon,
    The spreading flowers are fair,
And everything is blythe and glad,
    But I am fu o care.
Thou'll break my heart, thou bonie bird,
    That sings upon the bough!

Thou minds me o the happy days
   When my fause Luve was true.
Thou'll break my heart, thou bonie bird,
   That sings beside thy mate;
For sae I sat, and sae I sang,
   And wist na o my fate!

Aft hae I rov'd by bonie Doon,
   To see the woodbine twine,
And ilka bird sang o its luve,
   And sae did I o mine.
Wi lightsome heart I pu'd a rose,
   Upon its thorny tree,
But my fause luver staw my rose,
   And left the thorn wi me.
Wi lightsome heart I pu'd a rose,
   Upon a morn in June,
And sae I flourished on the morn,
   And sae was pu'd or noon.             before

# OPEN THE DOOR TO ME

*TUNE: Open the door softly*

Included in all major editions except Kinsley.

O, open the door some pity to shew,
   If love it may na be, O!
Tho thou hast been false, I'll ever prove true –
   O, open the door to me, O!

Cauld is the blast upon my pale cheek,
   But caulder thy love for me, O:
The frost, that freezes the life at my heart,
   Is nought to my pains frae thee, O!

The wan moon sets behind the white wave,
   And Time is setting with me, O:
False friends, false love, farewell! for mair
   I'll ne'er trouble them nor thee, O!

She has open'd the door, she has open'd it wide,
   She sees the pale corse on the plain, O,       corpse
'My true love!' she cried, and sank down by his side
   Never to rise again, O!

## ALTHO HE HAS LEFT ME

Published in many editions up to 1959, but omitted by Barke (1955) and Kinsley (1968) as spurious.

Altho he has left me for greed o the siller,
   I dinna envy him the gains he can win:
I rather wad bear a' the lade o my sorrow
   Than ever hae acted sae faithless to him.

## NO COLD APPROACH

*TUNE: Ianthy the lovely*

No cold approach, no alter'd mien,
   Just what would make suspicion start,
No pause the dire extremes between:
   He made me blest – and broke my heart.

## DELUDED SWAIN, THE PLEASURE

*TUNE: The Collier's Dochter*

Deluded swain, the pleasure
   The fickle Fair can give thee,
Is but a fairy treasure –
   Thy hopes will soon deceive thee:
The billows on the ocean,
   The breezes idly roaming,
The cloud's uncertain motion,
   They are but types of Woman.

O, art thou not ashamed
   To doat upon a feature?
If Man thou wouldst be named
   Despise the silly creature!
Go, find an honest fellow,
   Good claret set before thee,
Hold on till thou are mellow,
   And then to bed in glory!

## YOUNG JAMIE, PRIDE OF A' THE PLAIN

*TUNE: The carlin o the glen*

Young Jamie, pride of a' the plain,
Sae gallant and sae gay a swain,
Thro a' our lasses he did rove,
And reign'd resistless King of Love.

But now, wi sighs and starting tears,
He strays amang the woods and breers;
Or in the glens and rocky caves
His sad complaining dowie raves: –                    gloomy

'I, wha sae late did range and rove,
And chang'd with every moon my love –
I little thought the time was near,
Repentance I should buy sae dear.

'The slighted maids my torments see,
And laugh at a' the pangs I dree;                    endure
While she, my cruel, scornful Fair,
Forbids me e'er to see her mair.'

## THE WITCH OF DUNDRUM

This fragment, probably collected by Burns from a traditional ballad, is known in holograph, complete with the poet's signature, and was sold for £675 at an auction in London in 1982.

Hae ye heard o the Witch o Dundrum
When she tae Scotland did come,
   'Twas Ireland's lament
   And Scotland's content
Hurrah for the Witch o Dundrum.

Ye ken what she's done for us a'
What enchantments she's used and a'
How she's simply lo'ed us and a'
   God bless the Witch o Dundrum.
And her at the tale o the Year
Well of this let us have little fear
All of us can truthfully cheer
   Hurroo! for the Witch o Dundrum.

# APPENDIX
## SPURIOUS, DUBIOUS OR
## UNPUBLISHED WORKS

Appendix B of *Burns A-Z, The Complete Word Finder* (1990) gives the text of 111 songs and poems which have, at one time or another, been credited to Burns but which are regarded as dubious or spurious. Even in the poet's lifetime works were being published falsely under his name. 'I myself have lately seen a couple of Ballads sung through the streets of Dumfries, with my name at the head of them as the Author, though it was the first time ever I had seen them' he complained to George Thomson (CL 664) in November 1794. James Kinsley's monumental three-volume edition (1968) attempted to define the canon for all time, listing 632 poems and songs which were incontrovertibly the work of Burns, as well as giving the titles and first lines of some 53 doubtful or spurious works which had been admitted to the canon at various times but which he rejected on a number of grounds; either it was demonstrated that they had been published elsewhere before the time of Burns, or were clearly derived from another source, or, on stylistic evidence, or the use of later words and phrases, were unlikely to have been composed by Burns.

My own researches in the late 1980s uncovered a further 58 pieces which had appeared in print at various times down to 1988, and since then a further two have been brought to my attention.

# ROBERT BURNS'S CREED

Ross Roy has kindly sent me a copy of an undated broadsheet (but probably belonging to the early nineteenth century). According to the sheet 'The following poem was printed in first volume (sic) of his poems in Kilmarnock and never printed again'. Clearly the perpetrator had never seen the Kilmarnock Poems. Apart from 'wholly' (holy), WE (Wi'), 'dam' (damned) and Hoard (Hard), which may only have been printer's errors, the defective metre and grammar point to another hand than Burns's. From marked similarities to 'Look Up and See' (Barke, 1955) it may have been the work of William Stewart Ross who published poems of this sort in the *Agnostic Journal* under the pen-name of Saladin.

To quell the mob and keep them under,
The ancients told this tale of wonder;
A pious fraud, a wholly blunder,
　　A rainbow sign;
An earthquake or a blast of thunder,
　　Were held divine.

By those who've faith to swallow doses,
A wondrous story nothing loses;
The dextrous feats ascribed to Moses,
　　Are proof as plain;
O sleight of hand as Norman Bougas,
　　Legerdemain.

Beware the stories of tradition,
Lest wise give way to superstition;
The royal mager competition,
　　O sacred fountain;
Which can a midge by faith volation,
　　Swell to a mountain.

A "God of Mercy", just and good,
Held forth as in an angry mood;
Drowned the world in a flood,
　　To punish hyman;
And turning waters into blood,
　　Just like a demon.

He murdered thousands in a trice,
Made Egypt swarm with frogs and lice;
Had he sent sheep and cows and rice,
　　His hungry hordes;
Might ilka ane have got a slice,
　　And praised the Lord.

With hocus, pocus rod in hand,
Like Mother Goose's magic wand;
They could the elements command.
　　As legends ran;
Divide the sea, burn up the land.
　　Or stop the sun.

Their prodigious bombast surpasses,
Like dikes the ocean stood in masses;
They had flying prophets speaking asses,
    Beside a salt wife;
Their amorous ghosts o'er ran the lasses,
    Who lived that life.

There Samson's strength lay in his hair,
There generous waters sterling were;
And showers of fire came through the air,
    Like brimstone danders;
Saints lived in fire by virtue rare,
    Like salamanders.

The apostle Paul by fancy's whim,
Stared up to heaven in a dream;
But Satan brought him back, 'twould seem,
    So says himsel';
But how could Nick to heaven climb,
    Chained fast to hell.

This d-- old wily serpent Nick,
Who promised long a mighty kick;
He turned chase and played a trick,
    WE, God's first born;
He got him scourged, nailed to a stick,
    And crowned with thorns.

Just search the subject through the piece,
'Tis brought we, blunders such as these;
That reverend priests their flocks may please,
    WE weakly conscience;
Teach humble beings by degrees,
    To swallow nonsense.

The sovereign leader of each faction,
Join hand in hand in close compaction;
To set God's Kingdom up at auction,
    A tempting bargain;
Drive silly mortals to distraction,
    With their dam jargon.

Yet moral truth shall gain the day,
Alarmed by nature's glorious ray;
Anathemas shall fly away,
We priests and diels;
Sound reason shall the scepter sway,
Hoard at their heels.

# TO THE OWL

Attributed to Burns by Laurence Cotterell in *100 Favourite Animal Poems* (Piatkus, 1992), pp80-1. The provenance of this poem is not known, but stylistically Donald Low suggests the second half of the nineteenth century as the date of composition.

Sad bird of night, what sorrows call thee forth,
To vent thy plaints thus in the midnight hour?
Is it some blast that gathers in the north,
Threatening to nip the verdure of thy bower?

Is it, sad owl, that Autumn strips the shade,
And leaves thee here, unsheltered and forlorn?
Or fear that Winter will thy nest invade?
Or friendless melancholy bids thee mourn?

Shut out, lone bird, from all the feathered train,
To tell thy sorrows to the unheeding gloom;
No friend to pity when thou dost complain,
Grief all thy thought, and solitude thy home.

Sing on, sad mourner! I will bless thy strain,
And pleased in sorrow listen to thy song;
Sing on, sad mourner! to the night complain,
While the lone echo wafts thy notes along.

Is beauty less when down the glowing cheek
Sad, piteous tears in native sorrows fall?
Less kind the heart when anguish bids it break?
Less happy he who lists to pity's call?

Ah no, sad owl! nor is thy voice less sweet
That sadness tunes it, and that grief is there;
That Spring's gay notes, unskilled, thou canst repeat;
That sorrow bids thee to the gloom repair.

Nor that the treble songsters of the day
Are quite estranged, sad bird of night, from thee;
Nor that the thrush deserts the evening spray
When darkness calls thee from thy reverie –

From some old tower, thy melancholy dome,
While the gray walls and desert solitudes
Return each note, responsive to the gloom
Of ivied coverts and surrounding woods.

There hooting, I will list more pleased to thee
Than ever lover to the nightingale;
Or drooping wretch, oppressed with misery,
Lending his ear to some condoling tale.

# EXTRACTS FROM THE GRIERSON MSS

The notebooks of Thomas B. Grierson of Thornhill were deposited, along with his antiquarian collections, in the Dumfries Museum. In 1993 James Williams of Dumfries and Galloway Antiquarian and Natural History Society made extracts from the Grierson MSS relative to Burns and these are now published for the first time.

## JOHN ANDERSON MY JO

Grierson MSS, vol. 10, p142. A hitherto unpublished stanza of this song (391) which Grierson recovered orally from William Ewart of Dumfries on 14th January 1865. Grierson suspected that it came from the original ballad, but these words do not appear in the bawdy version published in the *Merry Muses*.

John Anderson my Jo, John,
When nature first began
To try her canny hand, John,
Her master work was man.
And you amang them a', John,
Sae trig from top to toe,
Aspired to be my journey wark,
John Anderson, my jo.

## LINES WRITTEN IN
## GAVIN HAMILTON'S PRIVY

Grierson MSS, vol. 10, p22. The following lines were wrote by Burns in a privy belonging to Mr. Hamilton, Mauchlan. Burns wrote the lines in a letter addressed to Mr. Morton of Mauchlan. The letter was preserved at the hands of Mr. Miller, Schoolmaster Ballantrae. I had this from Mr. Alexander Hewison.'

That man hath perfect blessedness,
Who comes here once a day
And does it neither thick nor thin,
But in a middling way.

# WHEN BEAUTY RIDES
## ON SKIN AND BANE

Grierson MSS, vol. 8, p5. 'Mr. Taylor of Glasgow gave me the following. Burns being on his tour along the Tweed was at an inn named the Beild Inn. He saw a young girl mounted on an old worn out horse, a Miss Tweedie. He wrote on a pane of glass in the inn the following lines. The pane of glass was long preserved.' The visit to the Beild, then a coaching-inn of considerable importance, was not recorded by Burns in his journal of the Border tour, but the description of Miss Tweedie and her mount bears an uncanny resemblance to that of Nancy Sherriff and her 'old cart-horse' Jolly who insisted on riding with Burns to Dunbar and who provoked a very ungallant description in a letter to Ainslie (CL 327).

> When beauty rides on skin and bane,
>     The moral then is plain;
> Therefore, my dearest girl, be not
>     Of fading beauty vain.
> For shoulders though come to skin and bane,
>     Thy fate it still may be:
> Worse than the beast thou ridest on,
>     For nane will ride on thee.


# ON COMMISSARY GOLDIE'S BRAINS

Grierson MSS, vol. 8 p5 gives an alternate version of the epigram on Commissary Goldie (483), with the following note: 'A person of the name of Gaudy or Guldy, understood to be the Depute Town Clerk in Dumfries, died. He was not of the kind of people that Burns liked. Burns coming out of the Old Church one day observed a new tombstone erected over his grave. Burns went forward to it and wrote these lines.'

> O Lord we question not thy sovereign will and pleasure,
> But why so strong a wall to guard so poor a treasure?


# MY NAME IS ROBERT BURNS

Grierson MSS, vol. 8 p5, concludes these unpublished versions with an unlikely quatrain. 'Burns one morning, having wandered to the Pier of Leith after a night's debauch, was leaning against a post vomiting. A man in charge came up to him and asked him who he was. His reply was – '

> My name is Robert Burns,
> I am on the Pier of Leith;
> And because my arse is stopped up
> I am shiting through my teeth.

# WANTON WILLIE

Legman. *The Horn Book*. 1964, p136, from Cunningham's transcript of the Gracie MS, bound in a copy of the *Merry Muses* (1827[1872]). Possibly collected by Burns, but bearing no evidence of his reworking.

O wanton Willie yir wame rins out,
O wanton Willie, etc.
But ye'll get a needle an I'll get a clout
To clap on the hole that yir wame rins out.

O wanton Willie, etc. [*bis*]
I'll haud up my pitcher to kep the spout
That naething be tint when yir wame rins out.

O wanton Willie, etc. [*bis*]
Just gie me a hotch an I'll turn about
An cannily kep whan yir wame rins out.


# ON TOM PAIN'S DEATH

Kinsley, 1968. Cowie MSS, attributed to Burns. Kinsley considered that it might have been Burns's work 'but he usually managed to be wittier on this theme'.

All Pale and Ghastly Tammy Pain
    Gaed down ae night to Hell, –
The Devil shook him by the Hand
    Saying, 'Tammy – I hope ye're well' –
He shut him up in Dungeon Hot
    And on him clapp'd the Door, –
Lord! How the Devil Lap and Leuch
    To hear the Bastart roar!


# AS I WALK'D BY MYSEL

Kinsley, 1968. Holograph owned by Professor G. Ross Roy; probably traditional.

As I walk'd by mysel, I said to mysel,
    And mysel said again to me;
Look weel to thysel, or not to thysel,
    There's nobody cares for thee.

Then I answer'd mysel and I said to mysel;
    Whatever be my degree,
I'll look to mysel, and I'll think o mysel,
    And I care for nobodie.

# WAT YE WHAT MY MINNIE DID

Legman. *The Horn Book*, 1964, p137, from Cunningham's transcript. It also appears in Burns's holograph in Laing III, 586, Edinburgh University MSS, and was reproduced in BC, 1922, p7.

Wat ye what my minnie did,
My minnie did, my minnie did,
An wat ye what my minnie did,
   My minnie did to me, jo?

She put me in a dark room,
A dark room, a dark room,
She put me in a dark room,
   A styme I could na see, jo.

And there came in a lang man,
A meikle man, a strang man,
And there came in a lang man,
   He might hae worried me! jo

For he pou'd out a lang thing,
A meikle thing, a strang thing,
For he pou'd out a lang thing
   Just like a stannin tree, jo.

An I had but a wee thing,
A little thing, a wee thing,
An I had but a wee thing,
   Just like a needle e'e, jo.

But an I had wanted that,
Had wanted that, had wanted that,
But an I had wanted that,
   He might hae sticket me, jo.

For he shot in his lang thing,
His meikle thing, his strang thing,
For he shot in his lang thing,
   Into my needle e'e, jo.

But had it no come out again,
Come out again, come out again,
But had it no come out again,
   It might hae stay't for me, jo.

# MR AULD AND ELDER BLAIR

Mackay, *Burns-Lore of Dumfries and Galloway*, 1988, p82. An apocryphal tale concerning Burns in Dumfries is preserved in the family of Jock Brodie (1777-1875) who ran errands for Robert and Jean Burns. The story goes that the Rev. Mr Auld and Elder Blair passed Burns in the street one day and shouted 'Baa!' at him. Burns is alleged to have responded with the following quatrain. It should be noted that no minister named Auld was ever in Dumfries and the only Blairs were the family of Mrs John McMurdo, close friends of the poet.

> Mr Auld and Elder Blair
> Oh guid manners you are bare.
> Like twa sheep among folk's kye
> Juist ca' 'Baa' as folk gae by.


# TO EDWARD CAIRNS

Mackay, *Burns-Lore of Dumfries and Galloway*, 1988, p154. Scott Douglas (1876) alleges that Burns sent Edward Cairns of Torr a copy of 'The Whistle' (CW p368), written on Excise paper, accompanied by a short verse epistle. Neither this copy of 'The Whistle' nor the quatrain, appear to be extant.

> But one sorry quill, and that worne to the core,
>     No paper – but such as I shew it;
> But such as it is, will the good Laird of Torr
>     Accept, and excuse the poor Poet?


# EPITAPH FOR JOHNSTON
# OF ELSHIESHIELDS

William Graham, *Eventide Meditations* (1887), a volume of reminiscences about the Lochmaben and Lockerbie area, contains the following satirical epitaph attributed by the author to Burns but not apparently printed anywhere else.

> Here lies the Laird of Elshieshields
> Wha's left Lochmaben's bonnie fields
> An a' her lochs an a' her eels
> An gaun to dwell amang the deils.
> But whaur he's gaun an how he fares
> There's few that ken
> An nane that cares.

# YE CALVINISTS O AUCHINLECK

Mackay, *Burns-Lore of Dumfries and Galloway*, 1988, p157. According to Robert Malcolmson, these lines were sent by Burns to John Kennedy, factor to the Earl of Dumfries at Cumnock. Kennedy gave a copy to the Rev. Yates, Unitarian minister at Liverpool, who favoured John Heughan of Dumfries, an erstwhile crony of Burns, with a sight of them. Malcolmson transcribed the lines from Heughan's recitation about 1830. The poem satirises the Rev. John Dun, minister of Auchinleck, who fell from his horse and got a soaking in the White Esk at Watcarrick.

Ye Calvinists o Auchinleck,
In mourning weeds yourselves bedeck,
An shew how much ye did respect
    Your great divine,
Wha fell, poor saul, and broke his neck,
    On Esk langsyne.

Had he been deaf, blind, dumb or lame,
Like mony a priest that I could name,
Wha's merits nae encomiums claim,
    You might indeed
Let dark oblivion blast his fame
    Since now he's dead.

But sure am I ye a' can say
He took good tent for mony a day,
That nane 'mang Whigs might doit astray
    To yon hill head;
He was a nonesuch in his way,
    But oh! he's dead.

His hame-spun zeal and catechizin,
An lecturin! an sermonizin!
Set mony an auld wife's heart a bleezin;
    But now I dread
In spite o fate they'll fa' a' freezin,
    Since now he's dead.

When frae his horse his carcase fell,
His saul went – but I darena tell –
Ye cannot fail to guess yoursel;
    For fifty head
Can swear his Reverence wrote frae H-ll,
    Since he was dead.

A, he, she, it
A, have
A', all
ABACK, away, aloof, in the rear
ABEIGH, aside, at a distance
ABOON, ABUNE, above, overhead
ABOUT, here and there
ABREAD, ABREED, in breadth, abroad
ACQUENT, acquainted
ADLE, slurry
ADO, to do
ADVICES, counsel
ADVISEMENT, thought, deliberation
AE, one
AFF, off
AFF-HAN', on the spur of the moment
AFF-LOOF, extempore, off the cuff
A-FIEL, outside, in the field
AFORE, before
AFT, AFTEN, often
AGLEY, askew
AHINT, behind
AIBLINS, perhaps
AIK, AIKEN, oak, oaken
AIN, own
AIR, early
AIRLE-PENNY, contract money
AIRN, iron
AIRT, quarter, direction
AITH, oath
AITS, oats
AIVER, old horse
AIX, axe
AIZLE, ember, cinder
A-JEE, ajar
ALAKE, alas
ALANE, alone
AMAIST, almost
AMANG, among
AN, if, and
ANATHEM, curse
ANCE, once
ANE, one
ANEUCH, enough
ANITHER, another
AQUA-FONTIS, spring water
AQUA VITAE, spirits (whisky)
ARCH, rise in a curve
ASE, ashes
ASK, lizard
ASKLENT, slanting, askance
ASPAR, legs apart
ASTEER, stirring
ATHORT, across
ATWEEL, indeed
AUGHT, eight, anything
AUGHT, possessed of
AULD, old
AULD-FAC'D, ancient looking
AULDFARRAN, old fashioned
AUMOUS, alms dish
AVA, at all
AWAUK, awake
AWE, owe
AWEE, for a moment
AWNIE, bearded
AYONT, beyond
BA', ball
BABIE-CLOUTS, baby linen, nappies
BACKLINS, backwards
BACK-STYLE, fence gate at rear of house
BAGGIE, belly
BAIGINETS, bayonets
BAIR, uncover
BAIRN, child
BAIRNTIME, offspring
BAITH, both
BAKES, biscuits

BAN, curse
BANDILEERS, bandoliers, testicles
BANE, bone
BANG, thrash, thump, copulate vigorously
BANIE, big-boned, stout
BANNOCK, round flat cake of oats or barley
BARDIE, minor poet
BAREFIT, barefoot
BARLEY-BREE, whisky
BARMIE, fermenting with ideas
BASTART, bastard
BATCH, crew, gang
BATTS, colic
BAUCKIE-BIRD, bat
BAUDRONS, cat
BAUK, cross-beam
BAULD, bold
BAUMY, balmy
BAWBEE, billon coin worth 6d Scots (½d sterling)
BAWK, strip of unploughed land
BAWS'NT, white-faced
BAWTIE, pet name for a dog
BEAR, barley
BEARERS, legs
BEASTIE, animal
BEAVER, kind of hat
BECK, curtsey
BEDEEN, early, quickly
BEESE, vermin
BEET, mend, kindle, stoke a fire
BEFA', befall
BELANG, belong to
BELD, bald
BELLUM, onslaught, force
BELLYS, bellows
BELYVE, by and by
BEN, inside, indoors, inner room of house
BENMOST, innermost
BENORTH, to the north of
BENT, bent-grass, hillock thus covered
BESOUTH, to the south of
BESTEAD, placed
BEUK, book
BICKER, rush, scurry
BICKER, wooden drinking vessel
BID, ask
BIDE, remain, stay
BIELD, shelter
BIEN, cosy, snug
BIG, build
BIGGIN, building
BIKE, BYKE, hive, swarm, crowd
BILL, bull
BILLIE, friend, comrade, fellow
BIRDIE, BURDIE, diminutive of bird
BIRDY, chicken
BIRK, birch tree
BIRKIE, lively lad
BIRRIN, noise of partridges in flight
BIRSE, bristle, hair
BIRTH, berth
BIT, nick of time
BITCH-FOU, beastly drunk
BIZZ, buzz
BIZZARD, buzzard
BLACKGUARDING, roistering
BLACK-NEBBIT, radical
BLAE, blue
BLAST, cursed, withered, blight
BLATE, bashful
BLATHER, bladder
BLATTER, work noisily
BLAUD, piece, example
BLAUD, slap, beat
BLAW, blow
BLAZE, brilliance
BLEAR, BLEERIT, bleary

BLEEZE, blaze
BLELLUM, babbler, blusterer
BLETHER, babble, talk nonsense
BLIN', blind
BLINK, glance, glimpse, an instant
BLINKERS, girls (contemptuous)
BLITTER, snipe
BLOOSTER, bluster
BLUDE,BLUID, blood
BLUE-BORAM, syphilis
BLUE-CLUE, blue yarn used in
  divining
BLUE-GOWN, beggar
BLUNTIE, fool
BLYPE, shred
BOB, move up and down
BOCK, vomit, belch
BOD(D)LE,'copper twopenny piece
  (one sixth of a penny sterling)
BODE, look for
BODIE, BODY, person, fellow
BOGGIE, marsh
BOGLE, demon, goblin
BOLE, wall recess, hole
BOLUS, large pill
BON TON, good breeding
BONE, BONY, fair, pretty, fine
BOON, see aboon
BOORD-EN', table-end
BOORTREE, shrub elder
BOOST, must, ought
BORE, crack, crevice
BOTCH, angry tumour
BOTHER, fuss
BOUK, body, carcase
BOW, bend, subdue
BOW'T, crooked, bent
BOW-HOUGH'D, bandy-legged
BOW-KAIL, cabbage
BOWSE, booze
BRA', fine
BRACHEN, BRECKAN, ferns,
  bracken
BRAE, slope, hills
BRAID, broad
BRAID MONEY, gold coins
BRAID-CLAITH, broad-cloth
BRAIK, harrow
BRAINGE, plunge
BRAK, broke
BRANKIE, finely dressed
BRANKS, halter, bridle
BRASH, sudden illness
BRAT, child
BRATS, rags
BRATTLE, clatter, rush, noise
BRAULIES, finely, admirably
BRAW, fine, handsome
BRAWDS, ruffians
BRAWNIT, brindled
BRAXIES, diseased sheep carcasses
BREASTIT, pulled forward
BREASTIE, breast
BRECHAN, horse-collar lined with
  straw
BREE, brew
BREE, BRIE, brow
BREEKS, breeches
BREER, briar
BRENT, smooth
BRENT, branded, brand new
BRIEF, literary skill
BRIG, bridge
BRISKET, breast
BRITHER, brother
BROCK, badger
BRODED, braided
BROGUE, trick, hoax
BROO, water, soup
BROOSE, wedding race
BROSE, gruel
BROWST, brew, mischief

BROWSTER, brewer
BRUGH, borough
BRULZIE, brawl, affray
BRUNSTANE, brimstone
BRUNT, burnt
BRUSH, onset, attack
BUCKIE, buck
BUCKLE, curliness
BUCKSKIN, American
BUDGET, leather wallet
BUFF, thrash
BUGHT, fold sheep
BUIRDLY, stalwart
BULLER, loud roar, whirlpool
BUM, hum
BUM-CLOCK, cockchafer, humming-
  beetle
BUMMLE, idle bungler
BUNTER, drab, whore
BURDIE, girl
BURE, won, carried
BURN, BURNIE, brook, stream
BURNEWIN, blacksmith
BUSK, dress, prepare
BUSS, bush
BUSSLE, bustle, fuss
BUT, without
BUTT OUT, outer room
BUTT AND BEN, two-roomed
  cottage
BUTCHING, butchering
BUTTOCK-HIRE, church penalty for
  fornication
BYE ATTOUR, in addition
BY-JOB, fornication
BYKE, BIKE, hive, swarm, crowd
BYRE, cowshed
BYRE-EN', gable-end of cowshed
CA', call, drive
CA' THE CRACK, gossip
CA' THRO, work away
CACKIT, soiled with excrement
CAD(D)IE, lackey, vassal, servant,
  rascal
CADGER, pedlar
CAFF, chaff
CAIRD, tinker, itinerant blacksmith
CAITION, surety
CALCES, chalk powder
CALF-WARD, enclosure for calves
CALLAN(T), stripling, youth
CALLER, cool, fresh
CALLET, wench, trollop
CAM, came
CANKER, become peevish
CANKERT, ill-natured
CANKRIE, peevish
CANNA, cannot
CAN(N)IE, careful, cautious, shrewd,
  frugal
CANT, chant, song, tale
CANTAN, whining
CANTIE,CANTY, cheerful, jolly,
  lively
CANTRAIP, magic
CAPE-STONE, coping stone
CAR, primitive wheelless cart
CARD, chart
CARE, sweetheart
CAREERIN, running this way and
  that
CARELESS, untroubled
CARITCH, catechism
CARL, CARLIE, old man
CARL-HEMP, seed-bearing hemp
CARLIN, old woman, beldam
CARMAGNOLE, rascal
CARTES, playing cards
CASE, enclose
CAST OUT, quarrel
CATCH-THE-PLACK, money-
  grubbing

627

CATTLE, horses, beasts
CAUDRON, cauldron
CAUF, calf
CAUF-LEATHER, calfskin
CAUK AND KEEL, (literally 'chalk and pencil') - drawing
CAULD, cold
CAUP, wooden bowl
CAUSE, legal case
CAUSEY-CLEANER, street sweeper
CAVIE, hencoop
CESS, land-tax
CHAFFT-BLADE, jaw-bone
CHAINET, fitted with chains
CHAMER, bedroom, chamber
CHANGE-HOUSE, ale-house
CHANLER-CHAFFIT, lantern-jawed
CHANTER, bagpipe
CHAP, blow, knock
CHAPPIN, CHOPIN, half a Scots pint
CHAPMAN, pedlar
CHEEK, side-piece
CHEEK FOR CHOW, cheek by jowl
CHIEL, CHIELD, lad, fellow
CHIMLA, CHIMLIE, fireplace, hearth
CHITTERING, shivering, trembling
CHOW, chew
CHUCK(IE), mother hen, sweetheart
CHUFFIE, fat-faced
CIT, city-dweller
CLACHAN, hamlet
CLAES, CLAISE, CLAITHING, clothes, dress
CLAG, burden on property
CLAMB, climbed
CLANKIE, knock, blow
CLAP, caress, fondle
CLARK, scholar
CLARKET, written up
CLARTY, dirty, sticky
CLASH, chatter, gossip
CLATTER, uproar, gossip
CLAUGHT, clutched
CLAUT(E) grip, handful
CLAVER, clover
CLAVERS, chatter, babble
CLAW, scratch, beat
CLAYMORE, Highland broadsword
CLEAN, comely, empty, quite
CLEAR, quite free
CLEARIN, beating
CLECKIN, brood
CLEED, clothe
CLEEK, clutch, pilfer, link arms in a dance
CLEEKS, cramps in horses
CLEG, horse-fly
CLEW, scratched
CLINK, cash, jingle, rhyme
CLINKER, roguish fellow
CLIPS, clippers, shears
CLISHMACLAVERS, tittle-tattle
CLOCKIN-TIME, hatching time, childbirth
CLOOT, cloven hoof
CLOOTS, CLOOTIE, the Devil
CLOSE, constant
CLOUR, bruise, swelling
CLOUT, cloth, patch
CLUD, cloud
CLUNK, gurgle
COATIE, petticoat
COAXIN, wheedling
COCK, good fellow
COCKIE, crony
COD, pillow
COFF, buy
COFT, bought
COG(GIE), staved wooden vessel, womb
COLLIESHANGIE, dispute, quarrel, brawl

COMMAND, commandment
COMMERCE-CHAUMER, chamber of commerce
COMPLEENIN, complaining
COOD, cud
COOF, CUIF, dolt, fool, lout
COOKET, appeared and disappeared by fits
COOR, cover, protect
COOSER, stallion, lecher
COOST, cast, thrown off, discarded
COOTIE, basin, tub
COOTIE, with feathered legs
CORBIE, raven
CORE, crew, crowd, band
CORN-MOU, corn stack
CORSS, cross
COT (-HOUSE), cottage
COTILLION, French dance
COTTER, cottager
COULDNA, could not
COUNTRA, countrified, rustic
COUP, COWP, capsize, upset
COUP THE CRAN, somersault, become ruined
COUPER, cooper
COUR, lower, fold crouch
COURT-DAY, rent day
COUTHIE, loving, kindly
COW(E), crop, trim, scold
COWE, demon, goblin, terror
COWT(E), colt
COZIE, snug, comfortable
CRABBET, crabbed, ill-natured
CRACK, chat, gossip
CRAFT, croft
CRAIG, crag
CRAIGIE, neck, windpipe, throat, gullet
CRAIK, corncake
CRAMBO-CLINK, doggerel verse
CRAN, crane, tripod for cooking pot
CRANKOUS, fretful
CRANK, harsh, grating
CRANREUCH, hoar-frost
CRAP, trim, crop
CRAW, crow
CREEL, wicker basket
CREEPIE-CHAIR, stool of repentance
CREESHIE, filthy, greasy
CRIB, barred manger
CROCK, old ewe
CROOD, coo
CROOKIT, crooked, deformed
CROOKS, disease of sheep resulting in neck curvature
CROON, moan, whine, bellow
CROOSE, CROUSE, cocksure
CROUCHIE, hunchbacked
CROWDIE, gruel, porridge
CROWDIE-TIME, breakfast
CROWLAN, crawling
CRUMMIE, crooked-horned cow
CRUMMOCK, crook, stick with curved head
CRUNT, blow from a cudgel
CRY, call, summon, protest
CUMMER, wench, hussy
CUMMOCK, short staff with crooked head
CURCH, kerchief
CURCHIE, curtsey
CURMURRING, slight, rumbling noise, flatulence
CURPAN, crupper, rump
CURPLE, buttocks
CURRY, dressing, beating
CUSHANT, wood-pigeon
CUSTOCK, cabbage stalk
CUTE, ankle
CUT-LUGGIT, crop-eared
CUTTY, short, brief
CUTTY-STOOL, stool of repentance

628

DADIE, father
DAEZ'T, dazed, stupefied
DAFFIN, fooling about, frolic, flirting
DAFT, mad, silly, foolish, wild
DAIL, dale
DAIL, deal, pinewood
DAIMEN-ICKER, occasional ear of corn
DAINTY, treat, worthy, pleasant, agreeable
DANDER, saunter, stroll
DANG, pushed, overcome
DARKLINS, in the dark
DASHING, cast down
DATE, season, time of life
DAUD, thrash, abuse, pelt
DAUNTON, subdue, discourage, put down
DAUR, dare
DAURK, day's labour
DAUT, DAWT, fondle, caress
DAWTIE, pet, darling
DAW, DAWIN, dawn
DAWD, hunk, piece
DEAD, death
DEAD—SWEER, quite disinclined
DEAL ABOUT, distribute, share out
DEARTHFU, costly
DEAVE, deafen
DECREET, judgement in a court of law
DEEP-LAIRING, sinking into snowdrifts
DEEVIL, DEIL, devil
DEIL A, not a
DEIL NA, DEIL NOR, strong negative
DEIL-MAK-MATTER, no matter
DEIL-HAET, devil take it
DELEERIT, delirious
DELVER, gardener
DELVIN, digging
DEN, dean, dingle
DERN, hide
DETACH, disengage
DEU(C)K, duck
DEVEL, violent blow
DIBBLE, pointed stick for planting seedlings, penis
DID(D)LE, jig, move jerkily
DIGHT, wipe, clean, prepare
DIN, dun, dark, dingy
DINE, dinnertime
DING, overcome, beat, vanquish, be worn out
DINK, trim, neat, finely dressed
DINNA, do not
DINSOME, noisy
DINT, chance, occasion, pierce with an arrow
DIRL, shake, rattle, reel off
DISCOVER, reveal pregnancy
DITTY, ground of indictment, reproof
DIZZEN, dozen
DO, put up with
DOCHT, DOGHT, dared
DOCHTER, daughter
DOCK(IE), backside
DOCKIN, dock-leaf
DOIT, to be crazed, enfeebled
DOITED, senile, stupefied, bemused
DONSIE, hapless, unlucky, ill-tempered
DOOL, misery, woe, sorrow
DOOLFU, doleful
DORY, haughty, arrogant
DOUBT, fear, think, suspect
DOUCE, douse, sedate, sober, prudent
DOUDLE, dandle

DOUK, dip duck
DOUNA, DOWNA, cannot
DOUP, buttocks
DOUP-SKELPER, lecher
DOUR, stubborn, harsh, severe
DOW, dove, pigeon
DOW, be able, dare
DOWF, listless, dull
DOWIE, gloomy, sad
DOWNA, cannot
DOWN-BRAE, downhill
DOWR, see DOUR
DOXY, beggar's wench
DOYLT, DAZED, muddled
DOYTAN, stumbling, blundering
DOZEN, DOZIN, impotent
DRAIGLE, bedraggle
DRANT, DRUNT, sulks
DRAP(PIE) drop, liquor
DRAUNT, drone, whine
DRAVE ON, passed
DREE, put up with
DREEPING, dripping
DREICH, DREIGH, tedious, dreary
DRESS YOUR DRODDUM, thrash your backside
DRID(D)LE, dawdle
DRIFT, flock, herd, windblown snow
DRODDUM, bottom
DRONE, supplementary pipe of bagpipe, monotonous humming
DROOP-RUMPL'T, with drooping haunches
DROOK, DROUK, soak, drench
DROUKIT, drenched
DROUTH, thirst
DROUTHY, thirsty
DRU(C)KEN, drunken
DRUMLIE, muddy
DRUMMOCK, oatmeal and water
DRY, thirsty
DRY-BOB, masturbation
DUAN, canto
DUB, puddle, stagnant pool
DUDDIE, ragged
DUD(D)IES, DUDS, clothes
DUNT, dull knock, thud
DURK, dirk
DUSHT, butted by a ram
DWALL, dwell
DYKE, low dry-stone fence
DYVOR, bankrupt

EASTLIN, easterly
E'E, eye
E'EN, eyes, evening, even, simply
EERIE, apprehensive, fearful, gloomy
EFTER, afterwards
EILD, ELD, old age
EITH, easy
ELBUCK, elbow
ELDRITCH, uncanny, unearthly, supernatural
ELECKIT, elected, chosen
ELL, unit of length (37.059 inches)
ELLER, church elder
ENEUCH, ENEUGH, enough
ENOW, sufficient
ERSE, Irish, Gaelic
ETHER-STANE, adder stone (used as a talisman)
ETTLE, aim, purpose
EVEN TILL, mathced with
EV'N DOWN, downright, sheer
EXPECKIT, expected
EYDENT, alert, diligent

FA', fall, befall, come by, win
FA', fortune, turn of events
FADDOM, fathon
FAE, foe

629

FAEM, foam, froth
FAIKIT, excused
FAIN, glad, content
FAIN O' ITHER, fond of each other
FAIR, easy
FAIR FA', good luck to
FAIRIN, present from a fair, reward
FAIRY, dwarfish
FAITH YE, damn you
FALLOW, fellow
FAMOUS, grand, fine
FAND, found
FANK, entangle
FARINA, flour, meal
FARL, quarter bannock
FASH, bother, trouble
FASHIOUS, tricky, awkward
FATT'RELS, ribbon ends
FAUGHT, fought
FAULD, enfold, enclose, gather
  (sheep) in a pen
FAULDING SLAP, fold gate
FAUSE, false
FAUSONT, FAWSONT, decent,
  seemly
FAUT(E), fault, transgression
FAUTEOR, defaulter, wrong-doer
FEAR, frighten, scare
FEAR'D, afraid
FEAT, trim, spruce, neat
FECHT, fight
FECHTIN, FECHTAN, fighting
FECKET, waistcoat
FEE, hire, wages
FEETIE, feet
FEG, fig
FEGS, indeed
FEIDE, enmity
FEIRRIE, sturdy
FELL, quick (cuticle)
FELL, pungent, harsh, dread
FELLY, bitter
FEND, support, effort
FERLIE, marvel, wonder
FETCH, gasp, pant
FEY, doomed
FIDGE, fidget, twitch, shrug
FIDGE FU' FAIN, twitch with
  excitement
FIDGIN FAIN, excited, eager
FIEL, softly, cosily
FIENT A, strong negative
FIER, hearty, sound
FIERE, comrade, friend
FIN', find
FISCAL, procurator fiscal, attorney
FISSLE, bustle
FIT, foot, foothold
FIT, poem, melody
FITTIE-LAN', rear left-hand horse in
  plough team
FLAE, flea
FLAFF, flap, flutter
FLANNEN, flannel
FLAIRING, gaudy, extravagant
FLEE, fly
FLEECH, wheedle, coax
FLEESH, fleece
FLEET-WING, fly swiftly
FLEG, blow, kick
FLETH'RAN, wheedling, flattering
FLEWIT, slap
FLEY, terrify
FLICHTER, flutter
FLIE, fly, something worthless
FLINDERS, fragments
FLINGIN-TREE, flail-swingle
FLISK, fret at the yoke
FLIT, move, shift, change abode
FLITTERING, fluttering
FLYTE, scold, rail
FOCK, folk

FODGEL, plump, good-humoured
FOGGAGE, coarse grass
FOOR, fared, went, travelled
FORBYE, besides, as well as
FORFAIRN, undone, worn out
FORGATHER, assemble
FORGIE, forgive
FORJESKET, vitiated, worn out
FORRIT, forward
FOTHER, fodder
FOU, FU, full, drunk, very
FOUGHTEN, harassed
FOUMART, pole-cat
FOUTH, abundance
FOW, firlot, full measure
FRAE, from
FRAETH, foam, froth
FRANK, lavish
FREAK, fancy, notion
FREE, leap over
FREMIT, strange, cold
FRIEN, FREEN, friend
FRIG, masturbation
FRIGHT, freak
FRYTHE, fry
FU, full, drunk
FU-HAN'T, having enough
FUD, backside, tail, scut
FUFF, puff of smoke
FUN', found
FURDER, progress
FURM, form, bench
FURR, furrow, ditch
FURR AHIN, right-hand rear horse
  in plough team
FUSION, melting
FUSHIONLESS, weak, feeble, useless
FYKE, fidget, fuss
FYLE, foul, defile

GAB, noisy chatter, eloquence,
  mouth
GAE, go, walk
GAE, gave
GAETS, habits
GAILIES, well enough
GAIR, strip of cloth, gusset
GAIT, goat
GAMESOME, merry, sportive
GANG, go, depart
GAR, make, cause, compel
GARTEN, garter
GASH, prattle, smart, shrewd, witty
GAT, got
GATE, way, road, fashion
GAUD, goad
GAUDSMAN, boy who goads the
  team
GAUGER, exciseman
GAUN, going
GAUNT, gasp, gape
GAUSIE, GAWSY, jovial, plump,
  ample
GAWKIE, fool, booby
GAWKY, stupid, empty-headed
GEAR, wealth, possessions, money
GECK, scoff at
GED, pike (fish)
GENTLES, gentry
GENTY, dainty, graceful, genteel
GET, offspring
GHAIST, ghost
GIE, give
GIEN, have given
GIF, if
GIFTIE, talent, power
GIGA, jig, gigue
GILPEY, young girl
GIMMER, pet lamb
GIN, if, whether
GIRD, iron hoop
GIRDIN, girthing, copulation

630

GIRDLE, iron plate for baking, griddle
GIRN, snarl
GIRR, hoop of a barrel
GIRT, great
GIZ(Z), wig
GIZZEN, wither, shrivel
GLAIKIT, giddy, careless, stupid, irresponsible
GLAIVE, sword
GLAZIE, glittering, glassy
GLAUM, grab, snatch
GLAUR, mud
GLED, kite
GLEEDE, live coal
GLEESOME, cheerful
GLEG, smart
GLEIB, glebe, portion of land
GLIB-GABBET, smooth-tongued
GLIMPSE, take a look at
GLINT, go quickly
GLOAMIN, twilight
GLOWR, stare, gaze, scowl
GLUNCH, frown, scowl
GOAVE, stare vacantly at
GOOM, gum
GOR-COCK, grouse
GOS, goshawk
GOSSIP, neighbour woman
GOWAN, daisy, dandelion
GOWD, gold
GOWDSPINK, goldfinch
GOWFF, golf, hit with open palm
GOWK, cuckoo, dolt, fool
GOWLING, howling, yelling
GRACE-PROOD, sanctimonious
GRACIOUS, amiable
GRAFF, grave
GRAIN, bough of a tree
GRAIP, pitchfork
GRAITH, equipment, tools, dress
GRAITHING, vestments
GRAIZLE, scrape, grind
GRANE, groan
GRAPE, grope
GRAT, wept
GRAY-NECK, gambler
GREAT, intimate, friendly
GREE, social degree
GREE, CARRY THE, come off best
GREE, agree
GREEN, yearn for
GREET, weep
GREIVE, farm-manager
GRIP, grasp
GRIPET, apprehended, gripes
GRISSLE, gristle, stump of quill pen
GROAT, small silver coin
GROAZLE, grunt, breathe heavily
GROZET, gooseberry
GRUMPHIE, grumbler, sow
GRUN', ground
GRUNSTANE, grindstone
GRUNTLE, snout, nose, grunt
GRUNZIE, snout
GRUSHIE, lusty, strong
GRUTTEN, cried, wept
GUDE, GUID, good
GUIDEEN, good evening
GUID-FATHER, father-in-law
GUDEMAN, husband, head of household
GUDEWIFE, mistress of household
GUDE-WILLY, generous
GUDE-WILLIE-WAUGHT, cup of kindness
GULLIE, GULLY, large knife, dig, cut
GULRAVAGE, romp, roister, horseplay
GUMLIE, muddy
GUMPTION, commonsense

GUST, taste, relish, flavour
GUSTY, appetising
GUTCHER, grandfather
GUTSCRAPER, fiddler
GUTTY, pot-bellied
GYVEL, gable, vulva

HA', hall
HA' FOLK, servants
HA', have
HAE, have
HAERSE, hoarse
HAE'T, have it
HAFF, half
HAFFET, temple, sideburn
HAFFLINS, partly, half-measure
HAG(G), scar in moorland
HAGGIS, economic pudding boiled in a sheep's stomach
HAIL, small shot, pellets
HAIN, save, spare
HAINCH, haunch, hip
HAIR, whit, trifle
HAIRST, harvest
HAITH, a petty oath
HAIVERS, nonsense
HALD, hold, dwelling
HALE, whole, sound, healthy
HALF-LANG, half-length
HALLAN, porch, partition between house and byre
HALLION, idler, rascal
HALLOWEEN, All Hallows Eve
HALY, holy
HAME, home
HAMELY, homely, familiar
HAMEWARD, homewards
HAMMERS, clumsy fellows
HAN', HAUN, hand
HAN' DAURK, manual labour
HAN'-BREAD, hand's breadth
HAN' WALED, hand-picked
HANGIT, hung
HANGIE, hangman, the Devil
HANKER, hang about, loiter
HANSEL, new-year or good-luck gift
HANSEL IN, be a first gift of the new year
HAP, cover, protect
HAP, hop, drop in quick succession
HAPPEN, turn out, manage
HAPPER, mill hopper
HAP-STEP-AN-LOUP, hop, step and jump
HARDY, bold, foolhardy
HARK, listen
HARN, coarse linen, sackcloth
HARPY, plundering
HASH, mangle, waste
HASLOCK, wool on sheep's neck
HAUD, hold
HAUD AFF, keep away
HAUD TAE, persist
HAUF, half
HAUF-MUTCHKIN, eighth of a Scots pint
HAUGH, river plain
HAUN, hand
HAURL, drag
HAUSE, embrace
HAUVER, oat
HAUVER-MEAL, oatmeal
HAVINS, behaviour, sense
HAV(E)REL, halfwit, simpleton
HAWKIE, pet cow
HAWKIT, spotted, streaked with white
HEAD, behead
HEADINMAN, executioner, headsman
HEAL, healthy, well
HEALSOME, wholesome

HEAPET, heaped, well-filled
HECH, ejaculation
HECHT, promise, offer, threat
HECKLE, flax comb
HEE-BALOU, hush
HEED, care
HEEZE, lift, elevate
HELD AWA, took way
HELLIM, helm, tiller
HEM-SHIN'D, haim-shinned
HEN, dear
HERD, shepherd, herd-boy
HERE AWA, hereabouts, hither
HERRY, harry, plunder, devastation
HERRYMENT, waste
HET, hot, burning, excited
HEUGH, ravine, steep bank
HEUK, hook, sickle
HICH, HIE, high
HIGH-GATE, highway
HILCH, lurch, limp
HILT AN HAIR, every bit
HILTIE-SKILTIE, helter-skelter, pell-mell
HINDMOST, last, final
HINEY, HINNIE, HINNY honey, sweetheart
HING, hang
HIRPLE, limp
HISSEL, flock of sheep
HISTIE, dry, stony
HIT, manage, achieve
HIZZIE, hussy, wench, silly girl, whore
HOAST, cough
HODDAN, jogging along
HODDEN, coarse grey homespun cloth
HOGGIE, hogget, young sheep
HOG-SCORE, distance-line in curling
HOG-SHOUTHER, shove with the shoulder
HOLLAN(D), fine linen
HOLLOW, halloo
HOODIE (craw), carrion crow
HOODOCK, carrion crow, rapacious person
HOOL, membrane
HOOLIE, gently, slowly
HOORD, hoard, drift
HORN, horn spoon or vessel
HORNIE, the Devil
HOTCH, hitch, jerk
HOUGH, disable by cutting tendons
HOUGHMAGANDIE, fornication
HOULET, owl
HOUPE, hope
HOVE, rise, distend
HOWK, dig up, exhume
HOWDIE, midwife
HOWE, hollow
HOWE-BACKET, sunk in the back
HOWKS, disease affecting animals' eyes
HOYSE, hoist, pull upwards
HOYTE, waddle, lope
HUFF SCOLD, berate
HUM, hoax, humbug
HUM, mumble
HUMPHIE, hunch-back
HUNDER, hundred
HUNG, eloquent
HUNKERS, haunches
HURCHEON, HURCHIN, hedgehog, urchin
HURDIES, buttocks
HURL, drive, trundle, move violently
HURLY, onrush, diarrhoea
HUSHIAN, footless stocking
HYTE, daft, crazy

I', in
IER-OE, great-grandchild

ILK, ILKA, each, every
ILL-TAEN, resented
ILL-THIEF, the Devil
ILL-WILLIE, malignant, ill-disposed
IN FOR 'T, liable to punishment
INDENTIN, pledging
INGINE, talent, genius, wit
INGLE, fire burning on the hearth
INGLE-CHEEK, chimney corner
INGLE-LOWE, firelight
INGLE-NEUK, chimney corner
I'SE, I shall
ITHER, other

JAD, jade, mare, hussy
JAG THE FLAE, tailor
JAUK, daily, trifle with
JAUKIN, delay
JAUNER, idle chatter
JAUNTIE, jaunt, trip
JAUP, splash
JAW, dash, throw, pour
JAWPISH, urethritis
JEE, sideways
JEEG, jig, gigue
JILLET, jilt, silly girl
JIMP, jump
JIMP, gimp, tiny-waisted, slender
JIMPS, skirts
JINGS, mild expletive
JINK, dodge, dart
JINKER, high-spirited beast, a lively girl
JIRKINET, liberty bodice
JIRT, jerk
JO, sweetheart, darling
JOB, intrigue
JOBBIN, fornication
JOCTELEG, clasp-knife
JOG, trudge
JORUM, punch-bowl, drinking vessel
JOUK, dodge, duck
JOW, toll (bell)
JOWLER, heavy-jawed dog
JUNDIE, elbow, jostle, shove aside
JURR, skivvy, servant-maid

KAE, jackdaw, thief
KAIL, greens, broth, semen
KAIL-BLADE, cabbage leaf
KAILYARD, cabbage patch, kitchen garden
KAIM, comb
KALE-RUNT, stalk stripped of leaves
KANE, payment in kind
KEBAR, rafter
KEBBUCK, home-made cheese
KEBBUCK-HEEL, cheese-rind
KECKLE, cackle
KEEK, peer, peep
KEEKIN GLASS, mirror
KELPIE, water demon
KEN, know, be aware of, recognise, identify
KENNIN, trifle
KEP, keep, catch
KET, matted fleece
KETTLE, cauldron, pit, vulva
KIAUGH, anxiety
KILT, hitch up the skirt
KIMMER, CUMMER, gossip, woman, wench
KIN', kind nature, kindly, agreeable
KING'S HOOD, second stomach in a cow, paunch, scrotum
KINTRA, KOONTRIE, country, rustic
KIRK, church
KIRK-HAMMER, church-bell
KIRN, churn
KIRN, harvest home, merrymaking
KIRS'N, christen, dilute with water
KIRTLE, gown, skirts, petticoat

632

KIST, chest, coffer
KITCHEN, season, give relish to
KITH AND KIN, kinsfolk
KITTLE, tickle, excite, tune up, play,
 fickle, ticklish, skittish, tricky,
 dangerous
KITTLEN, kitten
KIUTLE WI, caress, fondle,
KNAG(G), knot, spur, stump
KNAGGIE, knobbly
KNAPPIN HAMMER, stonebreaking
 hammer
KNOIT, knock
KNOWE, knoll, hillock
KNURL, KNURLIN, dwarf
KYE, cows, cattle
KYLES, skittles
KYTCH, toss, jerk
KYTE, belly
KYTHE, discover, tell, inform
KYVEL, thump, bang vigorously

LADE, load
LAE, lay, lie down
LAFT, loft
LAG, laggard, backward
LAGGEN, angle between sides and
 bottom of a dish
LAID UPON, assailed
LAIGH, low
LAIK, LAKE, lack
LAIMPET, limpet
LAIR, grave, bed
LAIRD, squire, landowner
LAITH, loath, unwilling
LAITHRON, lazy, sluggish
LALLAN(D), lowland
LALLANS lowland Scots language
LAMMAS, 1st August
LAN', land, country
LAN' AFORE, front right-hand horse
 in plough team
LAN' AHIN, rear right-hand horse in
 plough team
LANE, alone
LANELY, lonely
LANG, long
LANG-KALE, borecole
LANG SYNE, long ago
LANG-TOCHER'D, well-dowered
LANK, languid
LAP, leapt
LAP, wrapped, enfolded
LAVE, rest, remainder
LAV(E)ROCK, lark
LAW, decree, determine
LAWIN, reckoning, bill
LAWLAND, lowland
LAY, attribute, allay
LAY, LEA, LEE, meadow, pasture
LEA-RIG, ridge of unploughed grass
 between arable fields
LEAD, cart, lead in
LEA'E, leave
LEAL, loyal, true
LEAR, learning, lore
LEARN, teach
LEAST, lest
LEATHER, hide, lining of throat,
 vagina
LEDDY, lady
LEE, leeward
LEE-LANG, live-long
LEFT-HAND, sinister
LEISTER, trident
LEN' give, grant
LET, allow
LET BE, cease
LEUGH, laughed
LEUK, look, watch, appearance
LEEZE . . . ON, blessing
LIBBET, castrated
LICK, measure, little bit, thrashing

LIEN, lain
LIEVE (AS), rather
LIFT, sky, horizon
LIFT, load, amount
LIFT ABOON, boost
LIGHT, alight
LIGHTLY, disparage
LILT, lift up the voice
LIMMER, scoundrel, jade, whore
LIMPAN, limping
LINK, trip, dance, skip
LIN(N), cascade, waterfall
LINNENS, shroud, winding-sheet
LINT, flax
LINTWHITE, flaxen-haired
LINTWHITE, linnet
LIPPEN, trust, depend on
LIST, enlist
LOAN, LOANING, lane, strip of
 grass between fields, used as a
 milking place
LOCKED, closely fastened
LO'E, love
LOGGER, thick, stupid
LOOF, palm, hand-shake
LOON, LOUN, LOWN, rascal, rogue,
 fellow, whore
LOOSOME, lovely, sweet
LOOT, allowed
LOOT ON, revealed, disclosed
LOOVE, love
LOOVES, palms
LOSH, mild expletive
LOUGH, loch, lake
LOUP, leap, jump
LOUPER, dancer
LOUR, look menacingly
LOUSE, LOWSE, loose
LOWE, flame, blaze
LUCKIE, LUCKY, ale-wife
LUG, drag, draw out
LUG, ear
LUGGET CAUP, drinking vessel with
 twin handles
LUGGIE, wooden dish with side
 projections
LUM, chimney
LUNARDI, balloon bonnet named
 after Vincenzo Lunardi
LUNT, smoke (pipe), puff of smoke
LUNZIE-BANES, haunch-bones
LYART, grizzled, withered

MAE, more
MAHOUN, the Devil
MAILEN, MAILIN, small-holding,
 farm
MAINGIE, scabby
MAIR, greater, more
MAIST, most, mostly
MAIST, almost
MAK, make
MAK O, fuss over
MAMIE, mummy, mother
'MANG, among
MANSWEAR, perjure
MANTEELE, mantle, cape
MANTIE, gown
MANTLING, foaming
MARK, two-thirds of a Scots pound
MARLED, marbled, parti-coloured
MASHLUM, mixed meal
MASKIN-PAT, teapot
MASON, Freemason
MAUD, shepherd's grey plaid
MAUKIN, hare
MAUN, must
MAUNA, must not
MAUT(E), malt, barley
MAVIS, thrush
MAW, mow, reap
MAWN, maund, two-handled wicker
 basket

MEARE, MEERE, mare
MEIKLE, MICKLE, MUCKLE, great, large
MELDER, meal ground at a session
MELL, consort with, meddle
MELVIE, soil with meal
MEN', MEND, cure, heal, repair, repent
MENSE, sense, tact, good manners
MENSELESS, boorish, ill-bred
MENZIE, retinue
MERCIES, liquor
MESS, Master of Arts
MESSAN, cur, lap-dog
METE, complete the full measure of
MIDDEN-CREEL, dung basket
MIDDEN-HOLE, dunghill drain
MILKIN-SHIEL, milking shed
MIM, demure, prim
MIM-MOU'D affectedly modest
MIN, mind, recollection
MIND, remind, remember, take care of
MIND'T, minded, disposed, inclined
MINNIE, mummy
MIRK, darkness
MIRKSOME, dark
MISCA', abuse, malign
MISHANTER, mishap
MISGUIDIN, mismanagement
MISLEAR'D, mischievous
MISS, mistress, whore
MIST, missed
MITE-HORN, horn on the harvest-bug
MITHER, mother
MIXTIE—MAXTIE, jumbled, confused
MIZL'D, mystified
MOCK, derision
MONIE, MONY, many
MOOL, earth, clod, grave
MOOP, nibble, copulate
MORN, tomorrow
MOSS, bog
MOTTIE, speckled, spotted, dusty
MOU, mouth
MOUDIEWORT, MOUDIEWARK, mole
MOW(E), copulate
MUCH ABOUT IT, about the same
MUIR, moor
MUSCLE, mussel
MUSLIN-KAIL, thin broth
MUTCHKIN, quarter Scots pint
MUVE, move

NA, NAE, not, no
NAIG, small horse
NAIL, clinch, prove
NANE, none
NAPPY, ale
NATCH, notch
NAUR, near
NEAR-HAND, almost
NEEBOR, neighbour
NEGLECKIT, neglected
NEIST, next
NEUK, corner
NEW-CA'D, newly calved
NICE, neat, fine, dainty
NICK, cut, slit, reap, seize
NICK, the Devil
NIDGE, nudge, push, thrust
NIEST, next
NIEVE, fist
NIFFER, exchange, comparison
NIGHTLY, appearing at night
NIT, nut
NOCHT, nothing, not
NODDLE, head, brain
NOR, than
NORLAND, northern

NOTION, fancy, desire
NOWT(E), cattle
NYVEL, navel

OCH, interjection of surprise
OCHON, alas
O'ER, over
OERGANG, overcome
O'ERLAY, cravat, necktie
OFFER, promise, seem likely to turn out
ONIE, ONY, any
OR, ere, before
ORRA, odd, spare
OSTLER HOUSE, hostelry
O'T, of it
OUGHT, anything
OUGHTLINS, at all
OURIE, poor, dreary
OUTCAST, quarrel
OUTLER QUEY, young cow out all night
OUT OWRE, over across, about, beyond
OUT THRO, right through
OWERWORD, burden, refrain
OWRE, OWER, over, too
OWREHIP, over the hip
OWSEN, oxen
OWTHER, author
OXTER, armpit
OXTER'D, armed

PACK AFF, depart
PACK, intimate, familiar
PAIDLE, wade, paddle
PAIDLE, hoe
PAINCH, paunch, belly
PAINCH-LIPPIT, pouting
PAITRICK, partridge
PALAVER, idle chatter
PANG, cram, stuff
PARLE, speech
PARLIAMENTIN, attending parliament
PARRITCH, porridge
PARTY-MATCH, card contest
PAT, pot
PATTLE, plough-scraper
PAUGHTY, proud, haughty
PAUKY, PAWKIE, cunning, sly, shrewd
PAY, flog, give deserts
PECH, PEGH, pant, gasp
PEEL, palisade, castle, keep
PEER, equal
PEGHAN, stomach
PEGO, penis
PELL MELL, in violent disarray
PENDLE, pendant
PENNY-FEE, cash wages
PENNY-WHEEP, small beer
PERISH, destroy
PET, sulk
PHILIBEG, little kilt
PHIZ, face, countenance, expression
PHRASE, flatter
PHRAISIN, exaggerating
PIBROCH, classical pipe music
PICKLE, small amount
PICTUR'D BEUK, playing card
PIKE, PYKE, pluck, pick at
PILLIE, penis
PIN, skewer, peg, penis
PINE, sorrow, pain
PINTLE, penis
PINT-STOWP, pint tankard
PISH, urinate
PIT, put
PLACAD, placard, proclamation
PLACK, coin worth 4d Scots (about a farthing)

PLAID(E), woollen cloak
PLAISTER, plaster
PLANTED, settled in
PLAY, joy, pleasure
PLEA, legal action
PLEUGH, PLEW, plough
PLISKIE, trick
PLIVER, peewit, plover
PLUMPET, plunged, sank
PLUMPIN, swelling
POACHER-COURT, kirk session
POCK, poke, bag
POIND, distrain
POORTITH, poverty
POOSIE, pussy, female genitalia,
   hence a pejorative name for a
   loose woman
POOSION, posion
POU, POW, PU, pull
POUK, poke, prod
POUSE, push
POUTHER, POWTHER, (gun)powder
POW, pate, head
POWNIE, pony
POWT, poult, chicken
PREE, try, sample, taste
PREEN, pin
PRENT, print
PRESES, president, chairman
PREST, oppressed
PRICK, penis
PRIDE, make proud
PRIDEFU, proud
PRIE, try, taste
PRIE . . . MOU, kiss
PRIEF, proof, quality
PRIGGIN, haggling
PRIMSIE, demure, precise, affected
PROPER, handsome, elegant
PROVES, provost
PU, pull
PUDDOCK-STOOL, toadstool
PUIR, poor
PUN, PUND, pound
PYET, magpie
PYKE, pluck
PYLE, spike, blade, ear of corn

QUARREL, dispute, challenge
QUAT, quit, left abandoned
QUAUKIN, quaking
QUEAN, QUINE, young girl, hussy
QUECH, quaich, shallow drinking
   vessel
QUEER, roguish, odd
QUEIR, choir
QUESTIONS, catechism
QUEY, heifer
QUIETLINSWISE, quietly
QUO, said

RACKED, extortionate, excessive
RADE, rode, copulated with
RAEP, RAPE, rope
RAGGED, unkempt, shaggy
RAGWEED, ragwort
RAIBLE, rabble
RAIR, roar
RASE, rose
RAIZE, provoke, excite, rouse
RAMBLAN, rambling
RAMFEEZL'D, exhausted
RAMGUNSHOCH, ill-tempered
RAM-STAM, headstrong, reckless
RANDOM SPLORE, carousal, frolic
RANDY, rough, rude, riotous,
   roistering
RANT, make merry, spree, tirade
RANTER, roisterer
RAP, knock
RAPE, rope
RAPLOCH, coarse, homely

RARELY, finely
RASH, rush
RASH-BUSS, clump of rushes
RATTAN, RATTON, rat
RATTLIN, loquacious
RAUCLE, rough, coarse, robust
RAUGHT, reached
RAW, row, file
RAX, stretch, elastic
REAM, froth, cream
REAVE, rustle cattle, steal
REBUTE, reproach
RECK, heed, care, regard
REDE, counsel, advise, warn
RED-WAT-SHOD, shod with wet
   blood
RED-WUD, distraught, mad
REEK, smoke
REEKIN-RED, steaming with warm
   blood
REEST, stand restive
REESTET, cured, smoked
REMARKIN, observation
REMEAD, redress, remedy
RESPECKIT, respected
RIBBAN, riband
RICE, branch
RICKLE, pile of sheaves
RIEF, plunder
RIG, arable ridge, vulva
RIGGIN, ridge, roof
RIG-WOODIE, withered, coarse
RIN, run
RINGER, circlet
RIPP, handful of unthreshed corn
RIPPLE, draw flax through a comb,
   heckle
RIPPLIN-KAME, heckling-comb
RISK, grate, rasp
RIVE, break up, tear asunder
ROARING, riotous, noisy
ROCK, distaff
ROOD, quarter-acre
ROGER, penis, copulate with
ROOK, impudent cheat
ROON, circuit, round
ROOSE, stir up, agitate, praise, boast
ROOSTY, rusty
ROTTAN, rat
ROUND, confidently
ROUPET, husky, hoarse
ROUSE, stir up
ROUT, road, route, course
ROUTH, abundance, plenty
ROVE, ramble
ROWAN, mountain ash-tree
ROW(E), roll up, wrap up
ROWTE, bellow, roar
ROZET, resin
RUMMING, drinking
RUN-DEIL, thorough-going devil
RUNG, cudgel
RUNKL'D, wrinkled
RUNT, cabbage stalk, stunted
RUPIT, husky
RUTH, pity
RYKE, reach

SAB, sob
SAE, so
SAFT, soft, silly, lax
SAIR, serve, satisfy sexually
SAIR, sore, very
SAIRIE, SAIRY, sorry, mean
SALD, sold
SALL, shall
SANG, song
SAPPY, succulent
SARK, shirt, chemise
SAUGH, sallow, willow
SAUL, soul
SAUMONT, SAWMONT, salmon

635

SAUNT, saint, godly person
SAUT, salt
SAUT-BUCKET, salt-box
SAW, sow
SAX, six
SCANDAL-POTION, tea
SCAR, cliff, rocky outcrop
SCAUD, scald
SCAUR, see scar
SCAWL, scold
SCHO, she
SCHULIN, schooling
SCLATES, slates
SCONNER, feel sick, revulsion, disgust
SCORE, indentation
SCOW'R, roister
SCOWR'D, ran, ranged
SCRAICHAN, screaming
SCRIEGH, cry shrilly
SCREED, tear, rattle off
SCRIEVE, glide swiftly along
SCRIMP, be sparing
SCRIMPET, stunted
SCROGGIE, scrubby
SEE'D, saw
SEISIN, sasine
SELL'T, sold
SEMPLE-FOLK, common people
SEN', send
SET, start off, suit, become
SHACHL'T, shapeless
SHAIRD, shard, fragment
SHANGAN, cleft stick
SHANK, walk
SHANNA, shall not
SHAUL, shallow
SHAVER, barber, young wag
SHAVIE, trick
SHAW, copse, wood
SHAW, show, reveal
SHEAR, reap with sickle
SHEEPSHANK, person of no importance
SHEERLY, wholly, entirely
SHEUCH, SHEUGH, trench, ditch
SHEUK, shool
SHEIL, sheiling, hut, shanty
SHIFT, change abode
SHILL, shrill
SHOG, jog, shock
SHOOL, shovel
SHOON, shoes
SHORE, threaten, offer
SHOT, movement of weaver's shuttle
SHOUTHER, shoulder
SHURE, reaped
SIB, kin
SIC, such
SICCAN, such-like
SICKER, certain, sure
SIDELINS, sideways
SIE, see
SILLER, money, wealth, silver
SILLY, poor, hopeless
SIMMER, summer
SIN, SEN, since, from that time
SIN, son
SINGET, singed, shrunken
SINN, sun
SINSYNE, since then
SKAITH, harm, damage, hurt
SKEIGH, fierce, proud, disdainful
SKELLUM, rogue, scoundrel
SKELP, thrash, smack, hurry
SKELVY, ledged
SKINKING, watery
SKINKLIN, glittering
SKIRL, shriek, yell
SKLENT, slantin, aslant, squint
SKOUTH, scope, freedom

SKYRE, shine brightly
SKYTE, sudden blow
SLADE, slid, slipped
SLAE, sloe
SLAP, cut, drive down
SLAP, gap in fence
SLAW, slow
SLEE, sly, witty, clever
SLEEKIT, glossy, slick
SLIGHT, skill, dexterity
SLIP, quick-release leash
SLOKEN, slake, satisfy
SLYPE, fall over
SMA', small
SMEDDUM, dust, fine powder
SMEEK, smoke
SMIDDIE, smithy
SMIRKING, smiling
SMIT, smite
SMOOR, smother
SMOUTIE, smutty, obscene
SMYTRIE, numerous collection
SNAP, quick, smart
SNAPPER, stumble
SNASH, abuse
SNAW, snow
SNAW-BROO, slush
SNAW-DRAP, snowdrop
SNED, trim, lop off, prune
SNEESHIN MILL, snuff mull
SNELL, keen, bitter
SNICK, latch
SNICK-DRAWING, crafty
SNIRTLE, snigger
SNOOD, girl's head-band, bandeau
SNOOL, snub, sneak, submit tamely
SNOOVE, go steadily on
SNORE, snort
SNOWCK, snuffle
SNUFF, sniff
SO(D)GER, soldier
SONSIE, SONSY, good-natured, plump, buxom
SORT, meet together
S(O)UGH, deep breath, sigh
SOUK, suck, swig
SOUP(E), SOWP, sup, drink
SOUPLE, soften, soft, pliant
SOUR-MOU'D, peevish, sharp-tongued
SOUSE, beat, strike
S(O)UTER, SOWTER, shoemaker
SOWENS, sour pudding of oats and water
SOWTH, whistle a tune
SOWTHER, solder, patch up
SPAE, foretell
SPAIL, splinter
SPAIR, spare, reticent
SPAIRGE, sprinkle, bespatter
SPAK, spoke
SPAN-LANG, hand-length (22 cm)
SPAVIE, spavin
SPAVET, spavined
SPEAN, wean
SPEAT, spate, flood
SPEEL, climb
SPEET, spit, transfix
SPELL, study, contemplate
SPENCE, parlour, inner room
SPEN'T, spend it
SPENT, ejaculated sexually
SPIER, ask, enquire
SPILL WASTE, destroy
SPIN'LE, spindle, axle
SPLATTER, bespatter, splash
SPLEUCHAN, tobacco-pouch, purse, scrotum, vagina
SPLORE, frolic, carousal
SPORT, gambol
SPORT, sexual adventure
SPORTIN LADY, harlot

SPOTTING, staining
SPOUT, dart, spurt
SPRACHLE, clamber
SPRATTLE, scramble
SPRAWL, struggle
SPRING, lively dance
SPRITTIE, rushy
SPUNK, spirit, spark
SPURTLE, wooden spoon
SPURTLE-BLADE, swordstick
SQUAD, company, party
SQUATTER, flutter in water
SQUATTLE, squat, nestle down
STACHER, stagger, toddle
STACK, stuck
STAIG, young horse
STAINCHER, STANCHEL,
  stanchion, iron bar
STAINCHER-FITTED, iron-footed
STAMMER, stumble
STAN', stand, stop, remain
STAN'IN, erect
STANE, stone, 14 pounds weight
STANG, stake, rail
STANG'D, ridden on a rail
STANG, sting, goad
STANK, pool of stagnant water
STAP, stop
STAPPLE, stopper
STARE, confront, express forcefully
STARK, strong
STARN, star
STARNIES, starlets
STARTLE, stampede, take fright,
  caper
STAUKIN, stalking, walking stealthily
STAUMREL, stammering, silly
STAW, stall, satiate
STAW, stole
STAY, hindrance
STEEK, stitch, shut, enclose
STEEL-WAMIT, steel-bellied
STEER, stir, agitate
STEEVE, firm, strong
STEGH, cram the stomach with food
STELL, (whisky) still
STELL, fix, post
STEN', leap, bound
STENT, turned, reared
STEY, steep
STIBBLE, stubble, pubic hair
STICK, club, cudgel, splinter
STILT, plough handle, prance
STIMPART, quarter peck (grain
  measure)
STIRK, young bullock
STOCK, stem, plant
STOITED, STOITER'D, staggered
STOOK, set of corn sheaves
STOOR, stern, massive, harsh
STOT, young bullock
STOUN(D), thrill of pleasure
STOUP, STOWP(E), tankard,
  measure
STOURE, STOOR, storm, adversity,
  dust
STOURIE, dusty
STOW'D, filled, crammed
STOWNLINS, stealthily
STOYTE, stagger, stumble
STRACK, struck
STRADE, strode
STRAE, straw
STRAE-DEATH, natural death
STRAIK, stroke
STRAK, struck
STRANG, strong, violent
STRAPPAN, sturdy, strapping
STRAUGHT, stretch, straight
STREEK, stretch
STRIDDLE, straddle, stride
STROAN'T, urinated

STRUNT, liquor
STRUNT, move with assurance
STUDE, stood
STUDDIE, anvil
STUFF, store of corn
STUMP, walk clumsily
STUMPIE, worn quill pen
STURT, fret, trouble
STYME, glimmer of light
SUCKER, sugar
SUD, should
SUMPH, simpleton
SUNE, soon
SUTHRON, southern, Englishman
SUTOR, shoemaker
SWAIRD, sward
SWANK, agile
SWANKIE, strapping lad
SWARF, swoon
SWAT, sweated
SWATCH, sample
SWATS, new small beer
SWINGE, flog
SWIRL, knot in wood, whirlpool
  eddy
SWITH, away!, quickly!
SWITHER, flurry
SWOOR, swore
SYBOW, spring onion
SYKE, ditch, brooklet
SYNE, then, now, since

TACK, lease, tenure
TACKET, hobnail
TAE, toe, to
TAED, toad
TA'EN, taken
TAET, taste, tuft, handful, morsel
TAIL, vagina
TAIRGE, constrain
TAK, take, seize
TAK AFF, drink up
TAK THE GATE, take to the road,
  go home
TALD, told
TANE...TITHER, the one... the
  other
TANGLE, seaweed
TANGS, tongs
TAP, top, head
TAPMAIST, topmost
TAPER, slender
TAPETLESS, headless, foolish
TAPPIT-HEN, lidded drinking vessel
TARGE, small shield
TARROW, hestitate, show reluctance
TARROW'T, murmured
TARRY-BREEKS, tarpaulin trousers
  (i.e. a sailor, 'jack tar')
TASSIE, goblet
TAULD, told
TAUTED, TAWTED, matted, shaggy
TAWIE, docile (of a horse)
TAWPIE, silly girl
TEEN, chagrin, vexation
TEETHIN, putting fresh teeth into
TELL, enumerate, count
TELL DOWN, count out, pay
TELL THE TALE TO, defeat, defy
TEMPER-PIN, tuning screw,
  regulator screw
TENT, heed, care, tend
TENTIE, watchful, careful
TESTER, testoon, shilling
TETHER, rope, noose
TEUGH, tough, hardy
THACK, thatch
THAE, those
THAIRM, guts, fiddle strings
THAIRM-INSPIRIN, gifted on the
  fiddle
THANKIT, thanked

THEEK, thatch
THEEKIT, thatched
THEGITHER, together, continuously
THICK, intimate, familiar
THIE, thigh
THIEVELESS, cold, devoid of
warmth
THIG, take, accept, beg
THIR, these
THIRL, pierce, penetrate
THOLE, tolerate, endure, suffer
THOWE, thaw
THOWLESS, spiritless
THRANG, crowd, crowded, busy,
jostle
THRAPPLE, throat
THRAVE, two stooks of corn
THRAW, turn, twist, frustrate
THRAWS, throes, pangs
THREAP, argue, obstinately
THRESH, thrash, flail, copulate
violently
THRETTEN, thirteen
THRETTY, thirty
THRIPPLIN, rippled
THRISSLE, thistle
THRIST, thirst
THRUM, end of warp-thread
THRUM, hum, drone
THRUMMART, polecat
THUMP, strike
THUMPIN, exceptionally large
THYSEL, yourself
TICHED, touched, affected
TICKLE, rouse, amuse
TIEND, tythe, tax, due
TIGHT, neat, shapely, tidy, snug,
capable
TILL, to
TIMMER, timber, trees, wood
TINE, TYNE, lose, get lost
TINT, lost
TINKLER, tinker, itinerant pot-
mender
TIP, young ram
TIPPENCE, twopence
TIPPENNY, small beer sold for 2d
Scots
TIRL, strip, lay bare
TIRL, rattle at door by turning the
latch
TIRLIE-WHIRLIE, vulva
TITTIE, TITTY, sister
TITTLAN, tattling, whispering
TOCHER, dowry
TOCHER BAND, marriage settle-
ment
TOD, fox
TODDLAN, TODLIN, toddling,
hurrying
TON, fashion, mode
TOOFA, falling to, beginning (of
night)
TOOLZIE, quarrel, contest
TOOM, empty
TOOP, TIP, tup, young ram
TOSS, toast, belle
TOUN, TOWN, hamlet, farm
TOUR, turf, sod
TOUT, trumpet blast
TOUZLE, towsle, ruffle
TOWZIE, shaggy, unkempt
TOW, bell-rope, gallows-rope
TOW, flax fibre prepared for spinning
TOWMOND, twelvemonth
TOY, close-fitting cap worn by old
ladies
TRAC'D, fitted in traces, harnessed
TRAM, shaft of cart
TRASHTRIE, trash, rubbish
TREE, timber, wood
TREPAN, ensnare, beguile

TREWS, trousers
TRICK, habit, turn
TRICKIE, crafty, deceitful
TRIG, smart, trim
TRINKLE, trickle, flow
TRIN'LE, wheel of barrow
TROGGER, pedlar
TROGGIN, packware
TROKE, truck, barter
TROT, run
TROW, trust, believe
TROUTH, TROWTH, truly, indeed
TRYSTE, meeting, assembly, cattle-
market
TUG, rawhide
TULZIE, quarrel, contest
TUN, cask
TWA(Y), two
TWA-THREE, two or three
'TWAD, it would
TWAL, twelve
TWALPENNIE, shilling
TWALT, twelfth
TWIN, separate, deprive
TWISSLE, wrench, twist
TYKE, mongrel, cur
TYNE, lose
TYTA, daddy, father

ULZIE, oil
UNCHANCY, dangerous
UNCO, odd, uncommon, very,
mighty
UNCOS, strange tales, news
UNKENN'D, UNKEND, unkown
UNSICKER, uncertain, fickle
UNSKAITH'D, unscathed
UPO', upon
UP WI', here's to
USQUABAE, whisky

VAPOUR, caprice, whim
VAP'RIN, blustering, fuming
VAUNTIE, vain, proud
VEND, sell, advance, utter
VERA, very, real, true
VIEWIN, view, sight
VIRL, ivory or metal band
VITTEL, VITTLE, grain, fodder
VOGIE, vain
WA', wall
WAB, web, woven fabric
WABSTER, weaver
WAD, wed, wager, contract, pledge
WAD, would
WADNA, would not
WADSET, conveyance of land
pledged for a debt
WAE, woe
WAESUCKS, alas
WAFF, WAFT, carry by water,
voyage
WAFT, weft in a web
WAG-WITS, jokers, scandal-mongers
WAIL, bewail
WAIR, spend, bestow
WALE, choice, chose, select
WALIE, WAULIE, handsome, fine
WALIES, genitals
WALLOW, wither, fade, grow pale
WAME, belly, womb
WAMEFOU, meal, bellyful
WAN, won
WANCHANCIE, hazardous,
dangerous, unlucky
WANRESTFU, restless
WAP, wrap
WAPONSCHAW, muster, review of
men at arms
WARE, worn
WARK, work, labour
WARKLUM, tool, penis

638

WARL(D), world
WARLOCK, wizard
WARLOCK-BREEF, charm
WARLY, worldly
WARP, weave
WARRAN, guarantee, warrant
WARSLE, wrestle, struggle
WASTRIE, extravagance, wasteful-
ness
WASTE, waist
WAT, wet
WAT, know, be aware, wot
WATNA, don't know
WATTLE, wand, stick
WAUBLE, swing, wobble
WAUGHT, heavy drink
WAUK, WAUKEN, awake, wake up,
arouse
WAUKRIFE, wakeful, vigilant
WAUKET, calloused, horny
WAUR, worse, get the better of
WAVERING, wandering, fluttering
WEAN, child, infant
WEARING, passing (time)
WEARY FA', a curse upon
WEASON, gullet
WECHT, sieve
WEE, small, a little bit
WEE-THING, infant
WEEL, well, fine, satisfied, welfare,
well-being
WEEL-GAUN, active, good-going
WEEL-HOORDET, closely hoarded
WEEL-KNOOZ'D, well-beaten
WEEL-SWALL'D, fully stretched
WEEL-TOCHER'D, well-dowered
WEEPERS, cuffs
WEET, wet, dew, rain
WENCHING, whoring
WRESTLIN, westering, westerly
WETHER, castrated ram
WHA, who
WHAM, whom
WHASE, whose, who is
WHAIZLE, wheeze
WHALP, whelp
WHAN, when
WHANG, thick slice of cheese
WHANG, beat, flog
WHATFOR NO, why not?
WHATRECK, nevertheless, what
does it matter, fornication
WHATT, whetted
WHAUP, curlew
WHEEP, jig, jerk
WHID, thieving cant, lie
WHID, move nimbly and noiselessly
WHIG, puritan, hypocrite
WHIGGISH, rigid, precise
WHIGMALEERIE, whimsical orna-
ment, trifle
WHILES, WYLES, sometimes, then,
at times
WHIN, gorse, furze
WHINGE, whine, complain
WHIN-ROCK, whinstone
WHIRL, rush
WHIRLYGIGUMS, bizarre orna-
ments
WHIRRY, hurry, drive
WHIST, silence
WHITTER, draught of liquor
WHITTLE, knife
WHUNSTANE, whinstone
WHYLES, sometimes, then
WI, with
WICKER, branch
WIDDEFU, rascally, deserving to be
hanged
WIDDLE, trouble, strife
WIEL, eddy
WIERD, fate, fortune

WIGHT, fellow, chap, creature
WIGHT, strong, stout
WILLIE, willow
WILLYART, shy, awkward
WIMBLE, gimlet, penis
WIMPLE, meander, wind, twist
WIN, reach, get, gain, earn
WIN', wind
WIN'T, wound
WINKERS, eye-lashes, eyes
WINN, winnow
WINNA, will not
WINNOCK, window
WINNOCK-BUNKER, window seat
WINTER-HAP, winter protection
WINTLE, sway, swing from side to
side
WINZE, curse
WISS, wish
WIT, know
WITCHING, fascinating
WITHOUTTEN, without
WON(E), dwell
WONNER, wonder, marvel
WONTED, accustomed
WOO, wool
WOODIE, WOODY, withy, rope,
noose
WOOER-BAB, garter worn by a
suitor
WOOR, worn out
WORDIE, little word
WORM, spiral condensor tube in
whisky still
WORSET, worsted, coarse woollen
fabric
WRACK, wreckage, waste, flotsam
WRACK, rubbish, possessions
WRACK, torment, punish
WRAITH, spirit ghost
WRANG, wrong
WREETH, snowdrift
WUD, angry, enraged
WUMBLE, gimlet, penis
WYLE, lure, beguiled
WYLECOAT, flannel vest
WYTE, blame, reproach

YAD, jade, old mare
YARD, garden
YEALING, co-eval
YEARN, eagle
YELL, barren, dry (of milk)
YERD, yard
YERK, lash, stir up
YE'SE, you shall
YESTREEN, last night
YET(T), gate
YEUK, itch
YILL, ale
YIRD, earth
YIRR, bark
YISK, hiccup, belch
YOKIN, contest, copulation
'YONT, beyond, on far side of
YOUNKERS, youngsters
YOWE, ewe
YOWIE, ewe-lamb
YULE, Christmas

639